Paitarkiutenka

My Legacy to You

Paitarkiutenka
My Legacy to You

Miisaq / Frank Andrew, Sr.

Transcriptions and Translations
by Alice Rearden and Marie Meade
Edited by Ann Fienup-Riordan

University of Washington Press,

Seattle and London, in association with

Calista Elders Council and the Anchorage Museum Association

Design and composition by Michael Travis.
Cover design by Ashley Saleeba.

University of Washington Press
P.O. Box 50096, Seattle, WA 98145-5096
www.washington.edu/uwpress

Library of Congress Cataloging-in-Publication Data

Andrew, Frank.
    Paitarkiutenka = My legacy to you / Frank "Miisaq" Andrew, Sr. ; transcriptions and
translations by Alice Rearden and Marie Meade ; edited by Ann Fienup-Riordan.
        p.   cm.
    Includes bibliographical references and index.
    ISBN 978-0-295-98780-4 (pbk. : alk. paper)
    1. Yupik Eskimos — History. 2. Yupik Eskimos — Folklore. 3. Yupik Eskimos — Social
life and customs. 4. Yupik languages — Texts. I. Fienup-Riordan, Ann. II. Anchorage
Museum of History and Art. III. Calista Elders Council. IV. Title. V. Title: My legacy
to you.
    E99.E7A636 2007
    497'.14 — dc22   2007033423

Contents

Contents

———————

◆

Preface

In 1996, when the Yup'ik mask exhibit *Agayuliyararput (Our Way of Making Prayer)* opened at the Anchorage Museum, it was accompanied by two catalogs — a large, glossy book, written in English and beautifully illustrated with color photographs of Yup'ik masks, and a bilingual volume containing Yup'ik elders' remembrances of masks in their language, with facing page English translations of what they had to say. We quickly realized that elders had shared more than we could include in one book. We suggested, and the University of Washington Press generously agreed, that we turn this potential problem into an opportunity to create a pair of companion volumes — two closely related books on the same subject but aimed at different audiences. As a result, Marie Meade and I worked together to produce *The Living Tradition of Yup'ik Masks* and its bilingual partner *Agayuliyararput: Kegginaqut, Kangiit-llu (Our Way of Making Prayer: Yup'ik Masks and the Stories They Tell).*

In the years that followed, the Calista Elders Council (CEC) built on this successful partnership, and we produced two more "married couples." Following elders' work exploring the collections of Johan Adrian Jacobson at the Berlin Ethnological Museum, Marie Meade carefully translated the elders' words. Based on her fine translations, I was able to write *Yup'ik Elders at the Ethnologisches Museum Berlin: Fieldwork Turned on its Head*, and Marie and I worked together to make *Ciuliamta Akluit (Things of Our Ancestors).*

Beginning in 2000 Alice Rearden, Marie, and I worked together during a number of conventions and gatherings hosted by CEC to document traditional family values. In 2005 we published the results in another paired set — *Wise Words of the Yup'ik People: We Talk to You because We Love You* and its bilingual partner, *Yupiit Qanruyutait (Yup'ik Words of Wisdom).* These two books were even more closely linked than their predecessors. *Wise Words* included hundreds of translated quotations from elders from all over the Yukon-Kuskokwim region, recounting the *qanruyutet* (wise words or instructions) that guided life in the not-so-distant past. *Yupiit Qanruyutait* included selected *qanruyutet* from particularly knowledgeable elders, transcribed in the original Yup'ik with facing page English translations. Each passage was cross referenced with its appearance in more general discussions in *Wise Words*, allowing readers to move easily between the two books. Although written primarily for a non-Native audience, *Wise Words* has helped inform Yup'ik young people not fluent in their language. Conversely, the eloquent translations of *Yupiit Qanruyutait* have attracted English readers who not only seek to learn what the elders had to say, but how they say it.

In 2003 the Calista Elders Council and the Anchorage Museum began planning the exhibition *Yuungnaqpiallerput (The Way We Genuinely Live): Masterworks of Yup'ik Science and Survival.* Beginning in 2002, Alice, Marie, and a number of talented and dedicated Yup'ik speakers transcribed and translated information shared by dozens of elders working in museums describing traditional Yup'ik technology. During 2004 and 2005 these transcripts guided me in writing the text for *Yuungnaqpiallerput (The Way We Genuinely Live).*

Our past success with companion volumes inspired our determination to produce two books to accompany the show. Among the many elders who contributed to *Yuungnaqpiallerput,* Frank Andrew stood out. His concise recollections of the construction techniques, context of use, and care of traditional tools helped us understand the way of life he lived in the Canineq (lower coastal) area at the mouth of the Kuskokwim River. When Frank talked about kayak building, tomcod fishing, or bird hunting, he spoke from a lifetime of personal experience in the area surrounding Kwigillingok, where he spent his life. His immense knowledge, acute recollections, and rich language made him unique among his peers.

This depth and eloquence pervade *Paitarkiutenka (My Legacy to You).* Readers will find details that were shortened in *Yuungnaqpiallerput* to make them more accessible to English readers. They can also enjoy stories and information on seasonal activities in the Canineq area not included in *Yuungnaqpiallerput.*

Paitarkiutenka is not a supplement to *Yuungnaqpiallerput* — it is an equal partner. As in our previous companion volumes, the two books work together in different ways toward a common goal, providing a generation divorced from Yup'ik oral tradition with a deeper understanding of the lifeways of their ancestors. Like *Wise Words, Yuungnaqpiallerput* weaves together hundreds of translated quotations from elders throughout the Yukon-Kuskokwim region to give readers a sense of the complexity and variety of Yup'ik tools and technology. Frank Andrew's contribution, *Paitarkiutenka,* opens the door to appreciation of what a single individual needed to know to live life along the Bering Sea coast.

The book's bilingual format is much more than an academic exercise. Yup'ik is the second most commonly spoken Native language in the United States and the third most common in northern North America after Navajo and Inuktitut. More than twenty thousand people live in southwest Alaska, and more than half speak Yup'ik as their first language. In a quarter of the fifty-six villages in the region, Yup'ik is spoken by everyone from the eldest to the youngest.

When an oral tradition as rich as this takes written form, we lose the elegant figures of speech, the laughter, the love and compassion in the speaker's voice. What we gain is that the knowledge and wisdom these words embody can now be passed on far beyond Frank's children and children's children. He wanted his words written down, and we were honored to help him. Frank Andrew passed away in April 2006, and this book is his legacy to us all.

Acknowledgments

First and foremost, we wish to thank Miisaq (Frank Andrew, Sr.) and his family, especially his son Noah Andrew, Sr. and daughter and son-in-law Mary Ann and Bill Wilkinson, for all their help and support over the last five years. These pages represent a small fraction of the words Frank patiently shared between fall 2000 and fall 2005. Frank was in his eighties at the time, and had Noah been unable to accompany him to Bethel, Anchorage, and Washington D.C., we never would have had the privilege of working with his father. When we visited Kwigillingok to continue these conversations, Noah, Bill, Mary Ann, and many other family and community members made us welcome in their homes and steam baths while we worked with "Pop." As we studied transcripts, maps, and photographs together, hundreds of questions arose, and Noah patiently conferred with his father to help us find the answers. We are forever in their debt.

From the beginning the Calista Elders Council supported our work with Frank, funded by the National Science Foundation's Office of Polar Programs and the Alaska Humanities Forum. The Calista Corporation generously provided us with office space in Anchorage, and Calista's Michelle Pearson lent her map-making expertise, enabling us to reproduce Frank's memory of the Canineq (lower coastal) area. The Anchorage Museum Association supported the final publication in conjunction with the exhibition *Yuungnaqpiallerput (The Way We Genuinely Live): Masterworks of Yup'ik Science and Survival*. Thanks also to Steven Jacobson for providing corrections and additions to the section on Yup'ik transcription and translation, and to Anna Jacobson for her editing of Frank's detailed discussion of kayak construction and use. Judith Meidinger and Janet Klein helped with editing the English texts. Michael Travis ably typeset the manuscript, and the University of Washington Press contributed their considerable expertise to bring our work to completion. Without the support of these organizations and individuals, this book would not exist.

The illustrations we included come from a number of sources. The Moravian Archives in Bethlehem, Pennsylvania, provided copies of photographs taken in the Canineq area by Reverend Ferdinand Drebert during his tenure there in the early decades of the 1900s. Contemporary pictures of the kayak-making process were taken by Bill Wilkinson and his sons Troy and Ethan, and generously provided by the Andrew and Wilkinson families. We also thank Greg Lincoln, editor of the Bethel weekly newspaper, *The Delta Discovery*, for sharing his photographs of Noah and Bill making a kayak frame at the Yupiit Piciryarait Cultural Center and Museum in Bethel in fall 2006. Additional photographs were provided by Sue Gamache, Jim Fitzmaurice, and Michael Whiteneck. Bill Wilkinson and Deborah Reade provided the drawing of a kayak frame. Once again, Matt O'Leary and Patrick Jankanish collaborated on a map of the region.

We are particularly fortunate to be able to include a number of photographs made by Reverend Augustus Martin and his wife Bessie when they lived and taught in Kwigillingok between 1929 and 1935. The best of these photographs were made into stereographs and sold commercially. The Anchorage Museum was able to buy a set at auction in June 2006, which they have shared with community members. The photographs show rare interior views of the Kwigillingok *qasgi* (communal men's house) and surrounding sod homes, as well as candid shots of villagers Frank knew well as he was growing up. Frank passed away before he had a chance to see the Martin photographs, but his contemporaries have helped us identify many of the men and women pictured.

Above all Frank wanted his knowledge and wisdom recorded and shared, not because he was boastful but because of his compassion and love for the younger generation, who have few opportunities today to learn about their history. Alice, Marie, and I were honored to work with this extraordinary man. Our work has helped us live better lives.

NORTON SOUND

ALASKA
Fairbanks
ANCHORAGE
MAP AREA
Juneau

Stebbins · St. Michael
· Pikmiktalik
Kotlik · Pastuliq
· Nunapigluugaq
Cingigmiut · Emmonak
· Alakanuk
Akulurak
Nunam Iqua
Uksuqalleq
Anagciq
Mountain Village
Andreafski
St. Marys
Pitka's Point
Rasboinsky
· Marshall
Cape Romanzof · Scammon Bay
Tallmillermiut
Qissunaq R.
Pilot Station
Sabotnisky
Russian Mission (Ikogmiut)
Crow Village
Askinuk
Hooper Bay · Chevak
Ohagamiut
Kalskag
Qissunaq
Johnson R.
Itercaraaq
Cuukvagtuli
Nanvarnarrlak
Ayikatarmiut
Nunacuaq
Atmauthluak
Tuluksak
Newtok
· Kayalivik
Akiachak Akiak
Cauneq
Elrivak
Nyac
Nerevkartuli
Kasigluk
Nunapitchuk
BETHEL
Toksook Bay (Nunakauyaq)
Baird Inlet
Nunapicuar
Kwethluk
Tununak
Nelson I. (Qaluyaat)
Kangiracuar
Oscarville
Napaskiak
Cape Vancouver
Up'nerkillermiut
Aternermiut
Qalulleq
Muruyaq ·
Qinaq
Napakiak
Mekoryuk · Umkumiut
Qungurmiut
· Nightmute
Jirrayaq R.
Arayakaq
Dall Lake
Tuntutuliak
Akulirarmiut
· Eek
Nunivak Island
Etolin Strait
Cevv'arneq
Cicing
· Chefornak
Keggukar
Qikertaq
Kipnuk
Kangirmaarmiut
Caunermiut
Cape Avinof
Cal'itmiut
· Kongiganak
Pengurpagmiut
· Kwigillingok
Anuurarmiut
· Quinhagak

Kuskokwim Bay

Anvik

Holy Cross
Paimiut

Sleetmute
Kuskokwim River
Aniak
Napamiut
Kolmakovsky

Kilbuck Mountains
Kitaralik R.

Ahklun Mountains
Qissayaarmiut
Cauyarnaq
Angvanermiut
Mequutmiut
Togiak R.
Ingricuaq R.
Tuniakpuk
DILLINGHAM
Goodnews Bay
Togiak
Utngugnarmiut
Tarunguarmiut
Quluqaq
Nushagak
Manokotak
Iquk

Cape Newenham
Cape Peirce
Hagemeister I.
Nunaalukaq Bay
Eqtarmiut
Nushagak Bay
Cape Constantine

MILES
0   30   60
0   50   100
KILOMETERS

· Modern village
⸫ Historic site

BERING SEA

BRISTOL BAY

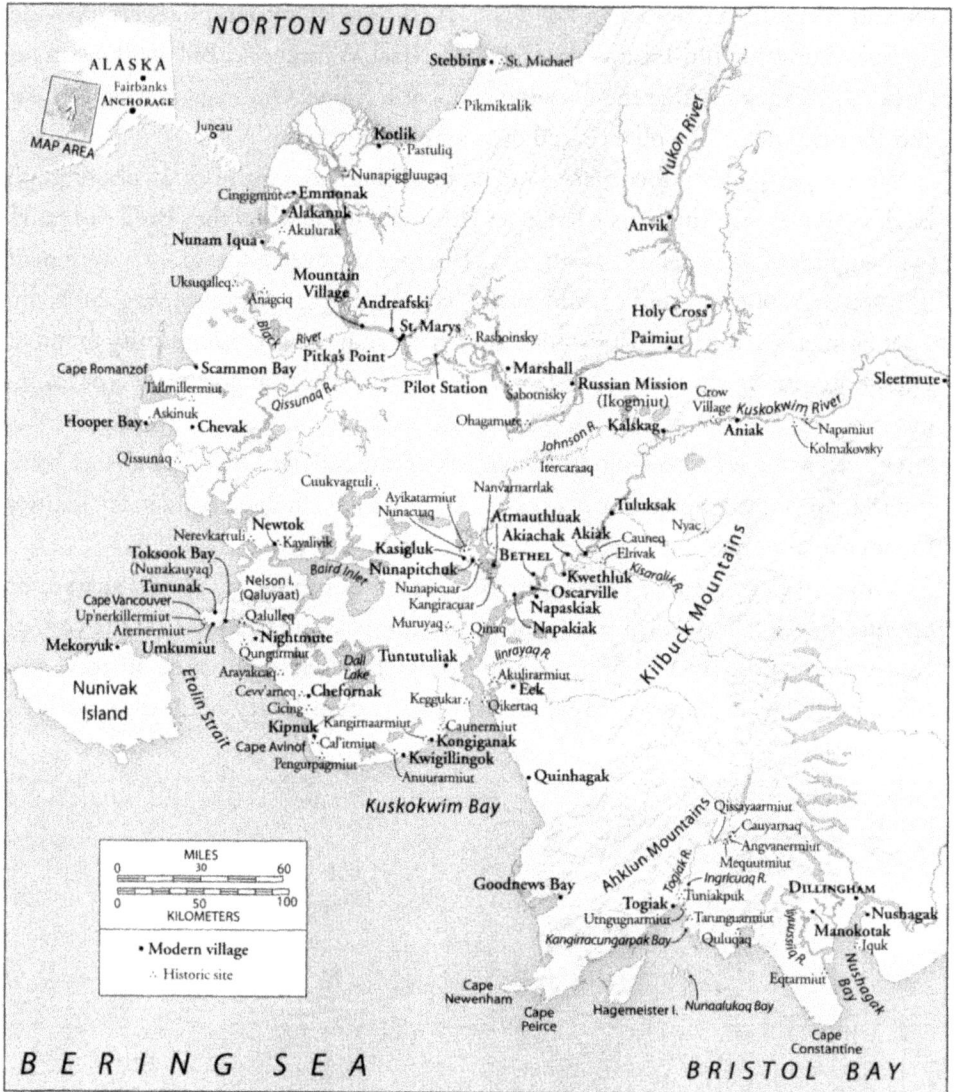

The Yukon-Kuskokwim delta, 2007. Patrick Jankanish and Matt O'Leary

Paitanka elpecenun yuuluaqautekat
My gifts guiding you toward a well-lived life

Miisam ayuqucia man'a tekilluku
Frank Andrew's life up to this time

Miisaq (Frank Andrew, Sr.) was born on February 17, 1917 in the village of Kwigillingok on the flat, windswept tundra of the lower Bering Sea coast. In 2003 he recalled: "Up to this day, I have not moved from that place. I have not stayed in another place, but only in Kwigillingok. My parents did not move and take me to other places to live."

Frank's father, Min'garalria, was born and raised in Qinaq, near present-day Tuntutuliak. He was one of three brothers and six sisters. Min'garalria, whose English name was Andrew, moved to the old village of Kangirnaarmiut when he married Frank's mother, Aamik. Soon after their marriage, Min'garalria moved his family to Kwigillingok. Frank (September 2005:132) reported:

> They say my father, several years after a river formed [at Kwigillingok], told his father-in-law, Canegkaq, that he'd like to move there and build a home because the river might be a good place to harvest fish. His father-in-law encouraged him to go ahead, and [Min'garalria] was among the first to make a home there.
>
> He and his in-laws all moved there. Then their relatives started moving to Kwigillingok. Kungaaq, Cingarturta, Kakianeq, and several others moved there and established homes. Soon more and more people moved there to live. And some families from Cal'itmiut, when they returned home from their fish camps, stayed behind and became residents of Kwigillingok. At first I remember the village had less than fifteen houses. And those living down below hadn't moved up farther [inland] to join those who lived up there.

Kwigillingok (lit., "one with no river") was originally established along a seasonal channel after it became navigable. Today it is a community of more than 350, including its own high school, corporation store, and airstrip located inland from the original site. Frank (February 2003:55) explained:

> They say that they didn't have a river, but there was a slough there that was filled with water when strong south winds came and flooded the coast. Only the high

tide would fill up the slough, and when the tide went out the slough would be all mud. When the channel developed [nearby] the river developed there and didn't dry up when the tide went out.

People who stayed there harvested whitefish in the summer. I've heard that originally there was one house there and that the river was just a stream and not a genuine river. During that time Kangirnaarmiut was a village inhabited by many people. Today, you can see the [abandoned] village of Kangirnaarmiut from Kwigillingok.

Min'garalria and Aamik had six children after moving to their new home. Nuqarrluk (Katie) was eldest, then Frank, then sister Nurataaq, and brothers Qerruircaun, Cagluaq, and Nunurta (John Andrew, Sr. of Kongiganak). Frank (September 2005:135) noted that when he was young they lived in Kwigillingok as a family. In recalling Frank's father's reputation as a *nukalpiaq* (competent hunter and provider), David Martin (May 2004:106) of Kipnuk, Katie's contemporary, noted how people stopped calling him Min'garalria after he began to have children:

It seems that when I first heard of Min'garalria, he was mentioned through his hunting ability. An elder would say that Min'garalria had caught something, since they always spoke of a person who would consistently catch animals. Since they always referred to them by their Yup'ik names, they would say that Min'garalria had caught an animal. And when he had children, they would say that Nuqarrluum Atii [Nuqarrluk's father] had caught an animal.

The point at which children gain consciousness of the world and begin to remember their experiences, usually between the ages of two and four, is marked by the phrase *"Ellangellemni* [When I first became aware]." Frank (February 2003:55) recalled becoming cognizant of his surroundings before he could walk.

I became aware of my surroundings exactly two times when I was little. After it happened the second time I never forgot and always remembered. At that time, I was small and had not started to walk yet.

That's why when I told stories of events that occurred and things I remembered from when I was little, people said that I evidently started to remember things at an early age. They say that some children do become aware at a very early age and have memories of things that took place in their lives.

My earliest memory was seeing those people over there [in Kangirnaarmiut] living at a site below the little river, before they moved to the site they are living at now. I was alone inside a big house with a platform bench on one side as you entered the room. The door was here, and on the floor were three split logs with grass between them. When I suddenly became aware I was crawling on the wooden floor. And as I turned my head and looked up I saw a bench way up above my head. I forgot things after that.

My memory is very brief from that occasion, and I don't remember anything for quite some time after that. The second time I became aware it was summer and I was inside a dug-out space in the ground that I found out later was an old house pit. I was inside the hole and was able to see a house adjacent to it. At the corner inside the hole was a dog tied to a pole. The dog had puppies, and the moment I viewed it, I saw it in human form. After that, I never forgot, and my ability to see and remember never ceased up to this point.

Frank (February 2003:55) remembered his father's father, Pangalgalria, father's mother, Nuqarrluk, mother's father, Canegkaq, but not his mother's mother: "I didn't know my grandmother. But there was a woman who was with my grandfather, and I thought she was my grandmother. Then later I found that she wasn't my real grandmother. She was my grandfather's spouse."

While he was still very young Frank's mother died at their summer fish camp in Keggukar. Frank's father did not immediately remarry, and during the next several years, Frank was cared for by his older sister, Nuqarrluk. Frank (September 2005:132) said that he and his younger siblings were old enough to help out and do chores at that time, and their family continued to live together until his father remarried: "After [my mother] died, my two brothers also died. Then two of my sisters died, too. After that my father finally remarried a woman from Cal'itmiut. That woman had one child. [My stepmother's] name was Imian, and her daughter's name was Naulalria." Frank recalled that as a youngster he sometimes did things against his stepmother's advice and was not always easy to discipline. Yet she never chastised him or threatened punishment: "I was an older boy, but my new stepmother was so kind I immediately liked her and got attached to her. That's when I discovered that one could easily become fond of women who were kind and compassionate. She was like a real mother to me. She died having never scolded me or expressed harsh words toward me."

After Min'garalria's second marriage Frank's older sister, Nuqarrluk, also died, leaving behind an only son, Nurataaq:

He was named after our younger sister who had died. When that child got older he didn't behave like a normal person. He was totally aware of the universe, and he could predict the changes that were about to occur in the natural world.

He died at a young age after he started to use a kayak and hunt seals. Callerkuaq from Iiqaquq used to bring him out with him when he hunted. He was quite amazing and would know the atmospheric changes and forecast weather.

~: *Qasgimi elitnaullra enemi-llu: Education in the qasgi and home* :~

During his young years, before moving to the *qasgi* to live with his father and uncles, Frank lived among women and children in a one-room *ena* (sod house). He not only remembered the life lessons his stepmother and aunts shared, but the manner in which they shared them. For example, he (September 2005:14) recalled his father's sister and how she trained him to work hard.

> I was a boy and aware. In Kwigillingok we always harvest tomcods because we eat them all the time. Arraalek, the wife of Kung'aq, was my late paternal aunt and used to let me sleep at their house. I was little and had no concept of values and wouldn't be shy at all, even though I was naked. Even though I ran around with no pants, I wasn't bashful at all.
>
> When a container of frozen tomcods was brought into the house, my paternal aunt would hand me a tool and say, "Okay! Take this and dig and strip off the fish like I showed you before. Dig real hard and use all your strength so you can grow up fast." I would believe what she said and use the tool and dig and peel off the fish. And as I strained, I would fart loudly if there was gas in my stomach. People in the room would burst out laughing. Sometimes I'd get angry and stop what I was doing and tell them that I wouldn't dig anymore. Then they'd say, "Oh no, don't get angry. When you stop digging and stripping off fish you will get smaller and smaller. If you keep working like this, using all your strength, you will grow up faster and become responsible and learn to work."
>
> I'd instantly change my attitude and keep working on the fish. That was how my late paternal aunt treated me.
>
> After our mother died, my aunts and relatives kept telling us not to play and be rowdy. They said that if we did people would be critical of our behavior and say that we were thoughtless. They'd also mention our mother and say that she wouldn't approve of our behavior.

When still quite young, Frank (September 2005:146) and his male peers were taken to the *qasgi* (communal men's house) where their education continued: "When we were small they'd sometimes take us to the *qasgi*. Once inside we'd sit very still and watch the people in there. While observing, I'd see people looking at others and talking. They were apparently giving instruction to those present. Those talking were huge men and looked very imposing and respectable."

Frank was among the last generation who grew to adulthood in *qasgit*, receiving a traditional education and oral instruction that he continued to view as the moral foundation of a properly lived life. He mourned its loss, convinced that many contemporary social ills could be prevented if young people were taught the things he learned in the *qasgi*. Frank (August 2003:42) noted with regret: "When the *qasgi* disappeared, we no longer heard instructions and were no longer taught how to work. And we no longer learned about our way of life. We live today following our own minds."

When Frank was young, men ate meals in the *qasgi* and slept on woven pads in their designated spots. Very young boys slept on the floor by their male relatives, lying down with their heads on the log headrests toward the middle of the room. Frank (February 2003) recalled:

My two late younger brothers and I started sleeping near my grandfather when we were young. When we slept, he would put his parka over us, and we were warm. When we woke, we would be very cold. Apparently my grandfather would remove our blanket. When we lay down again, he would tell us to go outside, even during winter. When we quickly went out into the cold, our sleepiness would be gone, and we would become fully awake. That was our custom — they didn't let us sleep.

Men not only lived and worked together in the *qasgi*, they also regularly enjoyed fire baths. Frank (February 2003) described how boys determined who would contribute the requisite wood:

They always played darts. There was a piece of wood with a black dot in the middle on each corner post. Each [player] threw [darts] to the piece on the post. When one of the two players won, the player who lost would be obligated to bring wood to the *qasgi*.

When the elders began to yearn to partake in a fire bath, they'd ask us to play the game. When a boy lost the contest, his father would tell him where to find wood to bring to the *qasgi*. Though they weren't asked to do so, others would also go out and fetch wood.

Once wood was gathered, the gut window was removed and the fire lit. The heat was most intense in the back of the room and less so down by the firepit, where men crouched to avoid getting burned. Cooling off was simple. Frank (February 2003) said: "Though it was blowing snow during winter when they were taking fire baths, they would go out of the *qasgi* and roll around in the snow. They would say 'Arrarraarraa' with enthusiasm and go back into the *qasgi*."

Men rose early and retired early as well, listening to each other tell stories. Frank (February 2003) remembered:

> They went to bed early. But at night, in the dark, they would wake us up. Though one had not been asked, he would begin telling a story. When he was done, one of the old men would say, "Oh my, it would be nice if one of you would tell another story." Then from somewhere in the room a person would begin telling another story. That was the way men relaxed and began to fall asleep for the night. We'd listen and enjoy the stories and eventually fall into sleep. Stories were always told at night when everyone retired, stories passed down from generation to generation.

The *qasgi* encompassed all practical aspects of daily life — sleeping, eating, working, visiting, and storytelling. It was also the place where young boys were taught the rules that would guide their lives. When Frank left his mother's home and came to live in the *qasgi* at about age five, he entered a world in which every action was watched and controlled. He (January 2004:104) recalled the quiet atmosphere of the *qasgi*.

> It was very peaceful, and it was very shameful to act improperly inside the *qasgi*. The only noise you might hear was the pounding of wood when work was being carried out. And as soon as an elder began to speak, work would end, and the only noise you would hear would be the speaker's voice. When someone spoke, giving instruction, it wasn't long. Almost every day, those men who were able gave advice on *qanruyutet* [words of wisdom, teachings or oral instructions, from *qaner-*, "to speak"]. Since men and elders who held authority lived in the *qasgi*, it was respected and honored.

Frank (February 2003:740) often emphasized the role that verbal instruction in the *qasgi* played in the moral education of the young: "Everything that young people should learn about proper living and how to work was learned in the *qasgi*. They explained all the instructions. That's why the *qasgi* was honored." Young as they were, boys were expected to carefully attend these teachers. According to Frank (October 2001:22): "When they were giving instruction, we would stay still and our hands would begin to sweat. We would leave only when the person giving instruction left." Boys were admonished to watch the speaker's mouth and not to look away or they would forget what he said. Sometimes a *cigyak* (split strip of wood) was placed across the entryway to discourage them from leaving while someone was giving instruction. Those who left, they were told, would be found with their teeth glistening at the end of a snowdrift — dead in the wilderness because of failure to pay attention to the life lessons that they needed to survive.

They accompanied this constant verbal instruction with observation. Boys were told to watch men work and then, through trial and error, learn to do the same. Frank (June 2001:4) recalled:

> They told us to constantly observe those who were working in the *qasgi*. They always helped one another when they worked, when they built parts for their kayaks or worked on various hunting tools. That is how we were taught, constantly observing them.
>
> And when we were ready, they let us work. They would tell us, "Work on it by remembering what you observed." Then we would work on it, and when our work improved, we would show them. Then they would tell us that it required a little more work, and those elder men who were knowledgeable would have us work on them more. When we were done, they would tell us, "Well then, when you work again, remember what you have learned so you will improve."
>
> That is how we learned. We observed in the beginning, and when we were done observing, they would let us try.

Frank (August 2003:55) explained how important it was that a young man master these technical skills in the *qasgi* before he could begin a family:

> I learned how to do things in the *qasgi*, especially how to work, men's work. That's why the *qasgi* was honored, even though it was mud, and it wasn't a place for merriment. It was where they spoke. It was a place for learning things, a place for men to work on different tools that a person would use trying to survive. That's why a person married only after he had learned to make everything and was no longer going to take his father's implements. They used to get him a wife when he was able to make his own tools.

To reinforce observation and verbal instruction, all of a young boy's actions were strictly controlled within the *qasgi* — sleeping, eating, drinking, and speaking. Boys were woken early and immediately told to tie up their boots and go outside to check the weather. According to Frank (January 2004), "Certain men were assigned to wake us up in the morning, even though they were not our fathers. They would pull us out of bed in the morning when it was time. It would still be dark outside. That routine was done every morning. As soon as we woke up we'd jump up and dash outside."

Frank also recalled being woken up by a loud noise in a room full of smoke — the men in the *qasgi* were testing their ability to reason: "It was known that boys destined to live disorderly lives usually panicked and got disoriented and were unable to find their way out. But those who were thinking clearly would stop and look at the barely visible fire down in the firepit to see which way the air was pushing the flame. Then they knew the direction of the draft hole and the entryway, and they would quickly run out. But those who were not paying attention would get bewildered and run into the wall as they tried to escape."

Once awake, boys were encouraged to take on all manner of chores in the *qasgi*. Before and after the men took a fire bath, it was the task of young boys to remove and replace the floorboards that covered the firepit as well as the gut cover of the skylight. Frank (January 2004:114) recalled the benefits such acts were said to confer: "They said that men who always removed and replaced the boards over the fireplace could easily see *ugtat* [seals sleeping on ice] while seal hunting. And those who removed and replaced the cover for the skylight would easily come across seals that were calling their mates during the mating season. They taught those lessons regarding the floorboards and the skylight."

Boys were also admonished to clear ash and charcoal from the firepit and discard it in the *qanitaq* (refuse pit) and to gather and discard the old grass bedding and replace it with new grass. They were told not to be squeamish about clearing away refuse, even if it was stinky. Frank (June 1995:14) explained: "We boys were taught to handle dirt without any qualms. We were encouraged to handle dirty grass and weeds that were used for matting on floors and to clean dog excrement without reservation. After we discarded debris we were told to brush our hands on our bodies right on the skin. They told us that those things created a barrier against sickness."

Boys competed to accomplish these tasks. Frank (June 2003:25) noted how quickly he and his peers responded to requests: "When they asked someone to do chores, we stood up immediately. If two people stood up, the one who stood first would do the task. That's what we were expected to do. Even though they didn't call our names in the *qasgi* or in the houses, when someone asked that something be done, we would immediately stand. They said not to reply verbally and say that we were going to comply, that by doing that we were wasting time." Frank (February 2003:593) said that as a consequence of such diligence he missed the endings of many stories: "Only when I began to work with wood inside the *qasgi*, I began listening to the complete stories."

One of the most important tasks young men engaged in was cleaning and clearing porches and pathways of ice and snow, acts which were said to remove obstacles from their path while hunting in the future. Frank (January 2004:115) explained:

> While a hunter paddled in his kayak down on the ocean, ice would block his path. Chunks of ice accumulating in an area would prevent him moving forward. The one who diligently took care of those parts of the *qasgi* and around it, even though it appeared impossible for him to go, the ice would begin moving out, forming an opening up ahead so he could continue. Moving through the ice, he would eventually reach open water. His path would always be easy to travel because he had already removed the obstacles and debris.

Frank contrasted the constant wakefulness of hard-working young men with sleep and laziness, both of which he was told would result in illness and poor hunting:

> They said about one who likes to sleep that sleep deprives him of things. A person who willingly does things doesn't have any illness on his body. We didn't sleep during snowstorms, and it wasn't just one person who followed that but many young men. We would run into one another at night in snowstorms as we were holding shovels and ice picks, working to clear the entranceways of houses. When we were finished, we would go to the *qasgi* and stay there trying not to wake the ones who were sleeping, or we would stay in the porch with our eyes closed.

Frank concluded: "Long ago when men worked hard, the area between the shoulder blades on their parkas would rot where they had been constantly sweating."

⌁: *Elitnaullra elitnaurvigmi: Going to school* :⌁

Frank's formal education took the form of his extensive and rigorous training in the *qasgi*. The classroom education he received was informal in comparison. Though he attended the first school built in Kwigillingok, Frank (June 2003:156) chuckled as he recalled, "We went to school when we wanted to, and when we didn't want to we stayed home." Moravian missionary Augustus (Gus) Martin (Anguyagpak or "big government man" in Yup'ik) and his wife, Bessie, were his teachers. Frank continued:

I went to school in the very first schoolhouse, and I quit in third grade when I was able to hunt. I preferred not to speak in English, but I was eager to catch fur animals. I made a mistake, but it's okay.

We attended school there and would return to our houses to eat and then go back up. But during winter, when they began to retrieve their aged fish from up-river, sometimes after we went to eat lunch in our houses, some of our classmates would belch loudly. After a while the school would smell like aged fish. [*laughter*] But our teacher would never say that it stank. It so happened that those who were eating fermented fish would begin to belch loudly. Those two, a husband and wife, never were bothered by the smell.

Frank had other good memories of the Martins, who worked and taught in Kwigillingok from 1929 to 1935, and whose rare photographs of village life during those years illustrate this book. He remembered what Bessie Martin told her pupils on discovering that one of them had head lice: "When the bell rang in the morning, we went inside and sat, and before we began, she told us that when she went out that morning and looked toward the village of Anuurarmiut, a louse was flying toward [our village]. And when it arrived, it went inside one of the houses. She had apparently found lice on one of the school children. She said it had entered that person's home."

School was held all winter in Kwigillingok, closing just before break-up when most families moved to spring camps along the coast. High water and ice conditions prevented even those who remained from attending. Frank continued: "They had them quit coming to school and stopped having them go back and forth when river conditions became bad because they were afraid they might get into an accident."

At first the Martins needed a translator to work with their students, numbering more than twenty in September 1929. Frank noted: "Caaryaraucin, whose English name was Ivan [Petluska of Eek], was the speaker at the school, translating for them. Later when they began to learn, he stopped translating for them." Misunderstandings continued, and Frank remembered a humorous example.

They used to have cod liver oil. The old man they called Canaar wanted to ask for some. Because he had no one to translate for him, he went to Ivan and told him what he wanted. Ivan told him to say, "I need some cod liver oil." He let him practice. When his pronunciation became good, he had him say it continually. He went out saying it constantly, "I need some cod liver oil." He walked with large strides and went up there saying, "I need some cod liver oil." Before he got to the school teacher, he began to change the pronunciation. While those [students] were working he went in and faced that teacher and said, "I need codlibai. I need codlibai." [*laughter*] That school teacher just shook his head. Because he couldn't understand him, he went to retrieve the one who taught him what to say.

Frank (June 2003:156) respected the Martins and compared the discipline they kept in the classroom to the instructions Yup'ik parents used to keep order in their homes: "The first teachers were good because they disciplined the disobedient ones. [Today] the BIA and state schools aren't like that, and no matter what a student does, they won't punish him. Our parents also followed the tradition of disciplining and warning their children, trying to make them feel remorseful. They reprimanded them, and it was a good thing."

~: *Missam qayangeqarraallra: Frank's first kayak* :~

Along with learning in the *qasgi* and school, at an early age Frank began learning to harvest food from the land and sea. His father made him a bow and small, blunt-tipped arrows which he used for hours hunting small birds. A small throwing board allowed him to practice aiming bird spears and lances at larger quarry. A critical skill was learning to use a kayak, the craft that would eventually carry him far out on the ocean as well as inland and upriver in search of food for a growing family.

Toward the end of his life, Frank (September 2005:173) clearly remembered the beginning of his travels: "We used to practice paddling with real kayaks, our fathers' kayaks, to learn, and they let us paddle in the shallow lakes so that we could stand, even though we capsized." Frank's father made him his own kayak when he was old enough to hunt. Frank (February 2003:84) recalled: "I was quite big and had already started to use a kayak and started hunting. The first kayak they made me was not large. It was just big enough for me to use and had an eagle design on it."

Frank (August 2003) lost his first kayak when he was twenty-one, and his father built him a second one: "My first kayak drifted away at night when I went along when they went to gather wood. The one who used it didn't tie it properly, and it untied. This was back when we anchored along the lower Kuskokwim coast to get wood in the fall. We woke and my kayak was gone, and all of its tools and implements were inside. We never found it."

Before Frank married he was allowed to make his own kayak. He (February 2003:84) recalled with feeling:

I made a kayak with the guidance of an expert. They showed me the measurement for each part, and ultimately I learned the measurements and names for all the parts of a kayak.

I've also taught my son [Noah] because we've been constructing kayaks at our home [in Kwigillingok since 1999]. I've taught him the names for every part and what kind of wood to use for the ribs, side stringers, the gunwales, and the cockpit coaming.

When they made kayaks, they looked at the boy who they were making the kayak for and used his body measurements to determine how big it should be. The kayak was sized just like a parka. And when it was done the owner would fit right into it and use it.

When they made a kayak they measured the owner's body parts and completed it, and one who was making a kayak for himself used his own measurements to complete his kayak.

When Frank was young, skilled elders were there to show him how to work:

When you make a kayak for the first time it's difficult, but it doesn't take long to learn. As you make one, an elder looks on and gives you supervision. Men and boys worked together like that. When the younger ones made kayaks or boats, the elders stayed nearby and watched, even though the builder already knew how to make one. They guided the younger ones by watching. That was why some continued to have elders check on their work and then show them where it needed to be adjusted.

Every young man of Frank's generation traveled in kayaks in their youth. Some, like Frank, learned the craft of kayak-making. Frank stands alone in southwest Alaska as one who worked to pass on this skill to his son, Noah Andrew, Sr., and through him generations to follow.

~: *Kassuutellra irniangellra-llu: Marriage and children* :~

Once he became a competent hunter and provider, Frank was allowed to acquire a partner. His parents arranged his marriage to Arnaucuaq, named Constantine in English, from Kwigillingok in 1943. Frank (February 2003) recalled:

I didn't choose my own wife. However, the girl I married died not long after she became my partner, after our three children were born. We had two girls and a boy.

Frank Andrew's father, Andrew Min'garalria (far left), Cimigaq (Adolf Jimmie's father), and Cingarturta (Paul Paul) working in the qasgi in Kwigillingok, 1930s. Ferdinand Drebert, Moravian Archives.

Frank Andrew's older sister, Nuqarrluk (Katie), with her son, Nurataaq.
Martin Family Collection, Anchorage Museum A12.

Frank Andrew's father, Min'garalria, and child. On the left is a log home, made from split driftwood. On the right is a barrel inside a qamigautek qulelgek (kayak sled with upper section). Unlike the sled in the foreground, which was made to be pulled by dogs, kayak sleds with raised backs were made to be pushed when gathering wood or moving things, such as the barrel in the picture. Martin Family Collection, Anchorage Museum B20.

Frank and Nellie Andrew, early 1960s. Andrew Family.

The Andrew family in the 1970s. Nellie and Frank are seated in front, with their children behind them, including (from left to right) Mary Ann, Catherine, Noah, Sophie, and Natalie. Wassilie is seated in front. Andrew Family.

Frank and Nellie Andrew, 1990s. Andrew Family.

*Frank Andrew examining a spear point collected in the Canineq area at the
Smithsonian Museum Support Center, 2003. Ann Fienup-Riordan.*

*Frank Andrew receiving the Traditional Culture Bearer Award
from Calista Corporation, 2000. Sue Gamache.*

Frank and Noah Andrew, Alice Rearden, and Marie Meade during one of many days working together, 2003. Ann Fienup-Riordan.

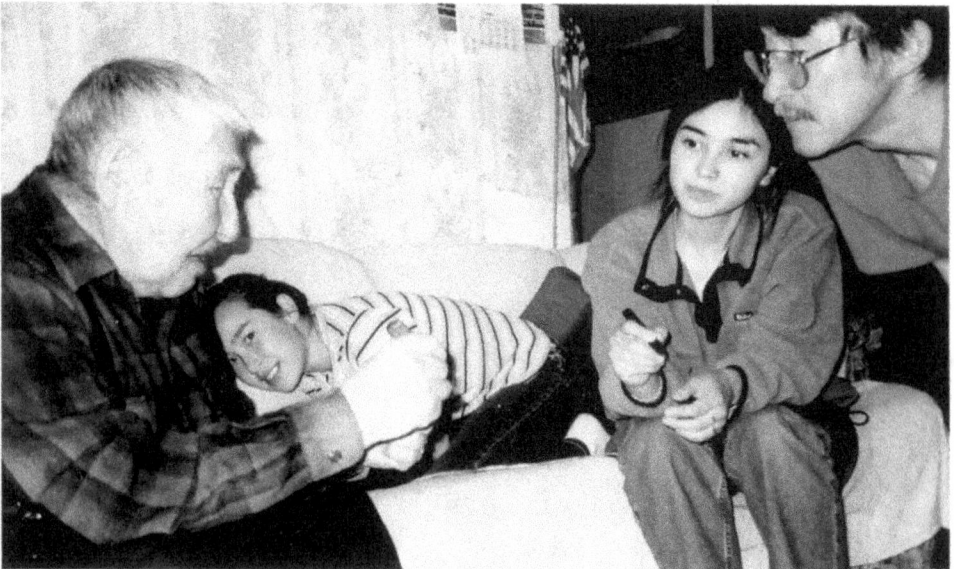

Frank Andrew explaining the use of a carving tool to Alice Rearden and his son, Noah, with granddaughter Kira Wilkinson looking on, Kwigillingok, 2003. Ann Fienup-Riordan.

Then after my wife's death our son died, and his younger sister also died. They were both little when they died. Only one of the three is still alive today. She [Canaar, Catherine Paul] has many children, and her grandchildren are growing in number.

After Arnaucuaq passed away, Frank married Nellie, someone he had known all his life: "After [Arnaucuaq] died they arranged for me to marry the daughter of Tutmaralria, who was the daughter of Cingarturta. After I married her I had more children, who are living here now. We had four children with two boys. One of the two boys [Wassaq, Frank Andrew, Jr.] died not long after he was born. He had an infection in his throat that apparently ruptured, and he died."

Frank and Nellie raised three of their own children to adulthood: Aamik (Sophie John), Aiggailnguq (Noah Andrew, Sr.), and Min'garalria (Mary Ann Wilkinson). They also adopted Arnaucuaq (Natalie Flynn) and Maaraaq (Wassillie Andrew). Mary Ann noted that her father never raised a hand to any of his children, guiding them patiently with love and compassion. She gave an example of his quiet discipline. Once when she and Noah were young they argued over a ball, pulling it back and forth between them and beginning to get noisy. Their father quietly approached them, took the ball, opened the stove door, and placed it carefully inside. He didn't say a word: He didn't need to.

Nellie and Frank lived together until her death in 2002. Frank (February 2003) affectionately recalled the many young people bearing her name today: "I called her Tengmiarsuk. In villages down in my home area there are many children named after her. When [her namesakes] got angry, they'd tease them and say they were fighting over me, their husband."

Frank (September 2005:164) reminisced about his marriages, both Russian Orthodox services held in the upriver village of Napaskiak:

The first time the bishop's name was John Sluben. He was a Russian. The second time it was a Russian bishop named Amverusi. Neither could speak English. [Amverusi] married four couples at once [during the annual summer church conference]. He married my wife and me, Paul Slim and his wife, a couple from Tuntutuliak, and I think a fourth couple from Kwethluk.

Priests rarely visited villages back in those days. There were only two priests — one in the Yukon River area and one in the Kuskokwim River region. Since there were many villages to visit, they'd only come once in a while.

Frank's first marriage ceremony was not without humor:

John Sluben married only my wife and me. The Yup'ik priest Ipcuk [Father Nick Epchook] was mischievous and full of humor. The bishop had come to Napaskiak in the fall just when it was starting to get cold. We went up to Napaskiak by boat when we heard that he was coming.

When the bishop was leaving, they got him ready. We took the bishop across by boat to Oscarville before he was taken to Bethel. We went to a home with two rooms. The rest of us were sitting in the outer room. It was in the morning, and it was cold outside. There was a discussion of finding warm clothes for the bishop. He was wearing thin clothing and didn't even have a warm coat. A woman's parka was hanging on the wall in the house. It was a fancy woman's squirrel parka all covered with tassels. [chuckle]

Ipcuk was moving about in the other room with the bishop while the rest of us were sitting in the outer room. Then we heard Ipcuk talking and saying that the bishop apparently had put on a parka. Then the bishop came out of the back room wearing the woman's fancy squirrel parka.

He had evidently let him put on the woman's parka. Then they let Ipcuk get another parka. This time he got a man's parka, and they let the bishop put it on before bringing him up to Bethel. Ipcuk was impish. He did that naughty thing to his bishop. Though the bishop was renowned, he teased him in that manner. I tell you funny things sometimes.

~: Pingnatullra: Supporting a family :~

Frank was an active hunter and fisherman all his life and supported his growing family with the fish and animals he harvested from the Canineq area. Each spring he moved to the coast for seal hunting. June and July found him and his family at fish camp at Keggukar or Papek at the mouth of the Kuskokwim, where they lived near relatives from Tuntutuliak.

Although Frank worked primarily in and around Kwigillingok as a subsistence hunter, he also did some commercial fishing, first at Togiak and later at Naknek in Bristol Bay. Frank left Kwigillingok in mid-June and returned in late July when fishing ended. He also worked sporadically at canneries and served as deckhand on the Moravian barge hauling freight up the Kuskokwim.

Frank recalled that from late summer to freeze-up in November they were constantly moving and fishing. When the berries ripened in late July, they moved to Nallaukuvik and Ilkivik for berry picking and fall fishing. They moved back to

Kwigillingok for the winter before freeze-up, just in time to harvest tomcod in abundance.

Frank continued hunting and trapping for fox, mink, and otter during winter. Nellie sewed some pelts into parkas for her family, while Frank sold others at the local store to buy tea, flour, cloth, ammunition, and other commercial goods. In what follows, Frank describes all these activities in great detail, providing a unique account of the Canineq area's seasonal round.

~: Kass'alugpiarurtellra: How they became Russian Orthodox :~

By the time Frank was born Russian Orthodox priests had been visiting the lower Kuskokwim for more than seventy years, bringing the rudiments of Christianity to Yup'ik residents from missions at Ikogmiut (Russian Mission) on the Yukon and Kolmakovsky on the Kuskokwim. First one, then two priests served the entire delta, and their annual visits were occasions for marriages, baptisms, and confessions.

The Moravians came later, establishing a mission at Bethel in 1885. During their first two decades on the delta half-a-dozen missionaries and their wives worked to convert and train Yup'ik helpers who, in turn, carried the Word to coastal communities like Kwigillingok. In the beginning, before churches were built, these helpers held services in the qasgi. Looking at a photograph taken in the early 1900s, Frank (June 2005:267) recognized one such helper at work: "That is Allungayagaq, Maqista's [Joshua Phillip's] father, who was the lay pastor in the qasgi, when he was a helper. This photo is inside a qasgi in Qinaq, before they moved to Tuntutuliak. This [qasgi] is called Qasgirpak, and it is my father's qasgi. This is a Bible, and they are having a service in the qasgi, before they got a church."

Frank (September 2005:173) described the shifting balance of power between Christian missionaries and the traditional spiritual leaders, the shamans, they sought to replace:

> When I was small, they used to bring me to church services held in the qasgi. The older folks weren't all converted [to the Moravian Church] when I was little. There were some who were Russian Orthodox members and not Moravians yet.
>
> They were still relying on shamans for guidance and support. Though they relied on them, they were also members of the church and crossed themselves. During that time the old practices slowly stopped. People began to reject the medicine used by shamans, even though they were still using them for healing.

Gradually more turned to Christianity, and soon many of them became Moravians. When they became church members, the older ones were stronger in their faith in God than the younger folks. The elders in the early days of Christianity were easily persuaded to believe in the Word of God.

A Moravian mission house was built at Kwigillingok in 1912. Between 1915 and 1920, Reverend Ferdinand Drebert (Makneq in Yup'ik) lived and taught in the village, visiting many times thereafter. Frank (October 2003:224) recalled with amusement some of his grandfather's brother's memorable interactions with Drebert, who was generally well-liked:

While they were at the *qasgi*, someone came in and said that they were going to have communion at two o'clock. My deceased grandfather's older brother, Alqunalria, said, "I will want more when they let me have communion. I will take communion for a longer time since I usually crave more."

The people in the *qasgi* started laughing. Drebert was the pastor. At two o'clock, when the bell rang, they started going outside. [Drebert] used to let them take communion from an aluminum pitcher, giving them little sips of grape juice. They say that when he gave them communion while they were seated, he would go to each of them but wouldn't let them take [the pitcher].

The ones who heard him talk kept an eye on Alqunalria. They were seated side by side. Alqunalria was in the center, and [Drebert] was getting closer as he let them take communion. When he got to him, he extended his arms, and when he lifted his arms, even though Drebert was holding the pitcher, he put his hands on the sides and took it. When the spout went to him and he put his mouth around it, his Adam's apple started to go up and down. Drebert said to him quietly, "That's enough." Even though he told him to stop, he didn't let go, and his head was gradually moving upward. Drebert said in a louder voice "There won't be any left for the others." [*laughing*] He then let go.

Those first ones were too much, especially that Alqunalria. While they were staying at the *qasgi*, the bell rang on Sunday morning. Since those older men slept in the *qasgi*, they started to get ready. When they were getting ready Alqunalria told them, "Now don't go to church. He doesn't give us anything, even though we ask for things." When he told them not to, they sat down. After a while, Drebert appeared through the doorway of the *qasgi*. When he appeared, the one who had told them not to, since he was by the wall, stretched his neck and said, "Hello Agayulirteyagaq [Little Pastor], we were just on our way."

On a more serious note, Frank (September 2005:173) detailed the unusual events leading up to his conversion to Russian Orthodoxy in 1942 when he was twenty-five years old:

Five of us went inland in the spring after we had become Moravian church members. Otto Friend is still alive in Kwigillingok. The others who were with us have all died. I was hunting at night for muskrats, sitting along the river coming out of Dall Lake, facing east. It was in the early morning, and the sun was about to come up when the muskrats were busy swimming. Then just when daylight was coming my late younger brother and Otto Friend came to where I was sitting. When they said that they wanted to boil some water to make tea, I told them to make a fire right across from where I was on a grassy spot. Behind that spot there was high ground covered with mounds of grass we call *qamiquruat* [tussocks]. I told them that I'd come when the water was ready.

They went across and started making a fire. I think the place was as far as the *qasgi* over there [about fifty yards]. I sat facing them. Dawn was breaking, and the horizon was flashing light from the sun coming up in the east. Then when the corner of my eye detected something moving, I turned and saw a bird in flight visible against the sky.

After I looked away, I turned again to look at it and saw that the bird was more visible. When I looked at it for the third time, I realized that it wasn't a bird. As I looked more closely, it would flash and turn red. It appeared like a bird and moved as if it had wings. The wings would move briefly and fold all the way in. When the object got closer, it was a book. On the book's cover the words "Service Book" were apparently written in Russian. When the book opened the pages moved like they were the wings of a bird, and when it closed it looked as if the wings had folded.

I immediately alerted the two across from me saying, "Look at the book falling from the sky and about to land on the ground!" They quickly looked up, searching for it, but did not see it. To me, it was clearly visible since it was close and about to reach land. As I looked it landed and bounced twice and disappeared, and I couldn't see it anymore.

Then I pointed to the spot where I saw it land and yelled at them, "Okay, go get it! It just landed beyond that mound." They climbed up and started looking back there where I pointed, but they couldn't find it. Then I got up and went across and began looking myself but didn't find the book.

After that incident I went to the Moravian church. In the summer while at fish camp Ipcuk [the Russian Orthodox priest, Father Epchook] came with Ciquyaq [Father Charles Guest] from the tundra area. I had not become Russian Orthodox. Then as I was doing something, they came and got me. They took me inside the tent, and I realized they were getting ready to have service. Evidently my late father had asked someone to go get me. They were getting ready to anoint me to become a Russian Orthodox.

At first I didn't want to convert, but I couldn't say anything. My father said, "I believe you are about to take the book you saw falling from the sky. I believe you are about to begin your work." We were anointed, and we became members of the Russian Orthodox Church.

The following winter Ciquyaq came to our village. When he came, he took out a book that looked exactly like the one I saw fall from the sky. He gave it to me and said that I would use the book during church service. My goodness! I suddenly felt overwhelmed, for I had not received formal education and wasn't smart [in English].

Frank (October 2003:224) said that many in Kwigillingok converted to Russian Orthodoxy at that time. Afterward Father Guest met with the elders of his village and asked them to pick a leader. They chose Frank, who served as a reader for the Russian Orthodox Church for more than fifty years, until he was too old to attend services. To do so, this remarkable man (who did not consider himself smart) taught himself to read the Bible and church service books in both Russian and English. Frank (October 2003:224) recalled:

From that time on, I gradually started to understand English, and I haven't finished up to this day....And I started to understand how to speak Russian. I learned their writing. We [Yupiit] apparently use Russian words for many of our goods — like coffee, sugar, butter, bread, tables, stoves, hammers, milk — because their traders arrived first with their goods. Those were the first things they learned about, using Russian terms for them. When I started reading in Russian, I'd see those terms, and I knew that we said them in Russian.

At the present time I can read English, even sounding out long words, but I don't know what they mean. I understand Russian words better. It's faster and easier to learn Russian. The words resemble Yup'ik words and aren't long.

~: *Yuarutet yuraryarat-llu: Singing and dancing, past and present* :~

Christian activities were replacing many traditional ceremonies by the time Frank was born. Even so, Frank (June 2003:26) was able to recall the past cycle of ceremonies:

> Elriq [the Great Feast for the Dead] was the first and most important, along with Kassiyuq [the Messenger Feast, also known as Kevgiq], the one where they send messengers. Then they had Agayuyaraq [the Masked Dances], Nakaciryaraq [the Bladder Festival], Ingulayaraq [the Berry Festival], Qaaritaaryaraq [house-to-house visiting by village children], Qengarpagyaraq [the Proboscis Festival, from *qengaq*, "nose"], Aaniryaraq [lit., "the process of providing a mother"], Kevgiruaq [pretend Messenger Feast], Tukaaryaraq [from *tukar-*, "to kick with both feet, from a lying position like a baby"]. They practiced ten different festivals.

> This village and others used to have Kevgiq and dance during the winter, inviting guests. And when they were done, they never danced again all winter long, but only had each of those dance festivals once.

When Frank was a young man, the Great Feast for the Dead was no longer practiced:

> I didn't see people participating in Elriq. It was an event that was not held annually, but certain families used to participate after they had prepared. It would take them five years to get ready, gathering *uivutkat* [gifts to present at the ceremony].

> They would compose songs dedicated to their deceased children. The songs were called *qiatet* [lit., "crying songs"]. After five years of preparation, in the summer before the ceremony was held, the other villagers would put aside lots of food to help them during the giveaway. They would also collect foods from other areas to be given to the guests during the event. They said that all kinds of food was available to those who asked for it. Since I never saw people participating in this event, I don't know it.

Recalling the Bladder Festival, Frank (September 2005:146) noted:

> By the time I started remembering things the actual ceremony to honor seal bladders was no longer practiced by our people. I didn't witness men holding ceremonies to honor the seal bladders. But once I saw them do Nakaciruaq [pretend or model Bladder Festival]. Prior to that event, they removed and dried the skins of

the little birds we [young boys] caught and brought home, getting ready for the Nakaciruaq planned for the coming winter. During the celebration they let the young boys take those little bird skins and honor them in a ceremony as if they were the seal bladders.

Frank (September 2005:149) had, however, participated in Ingulayaraq many times and noted that it was commonly held in late summer after the berry harvest:

It didn't take much to take part in Ingulayaraq, and you could do it many times every year. The elders made the announcement to hold it whenever they wanted to eat special foods. Sometimes while we were doing something in the qasgi, one of the elder men would say, "Oh my! It's time to go out and yell 'Aa-aa-aa.'"

And sometimes while we were doing something outside we'd hear someone nearby say, "Listen. They are saying 'Aa-aa-aa.' They apparently are about to hold Ingulayaraq!"

They would tell a young person to go up on top of the qasgi and yell, "Aa-aa-aa. Agayak nangvagtuu-uu-uuq [Agayak is all gone]!" And as soon as the announcement was made, all the women back in their homes would immediately begin preparing food. Then they would bring it to the qasgi and celebrate Ingulayaraq.

During Ingulayaraq, women danced slow, old-style dances. Frank continued: "The dances were different, and dancers didn't use hand and arm movements to illustrate a story. Women would pinch the bottom hem of their garments and slightly bend their knees and dance. The slow songs they sang during that time were from quliraat [ancient sagas]."

Frank also described the intravillage Kevgiruaq (pretend Kevgiq or Messenger Feast) he witnessed twice in Kwigillingok when he was young. During the traditional Messenger Feast, one village hosted another to three days of dancing, feasting, and gift exchanges. Kevgiruaq involved the exchange of gifts between the men and women of a single village: "When village members gathered and celebrated a dance ceremony called Kevgiruaq, one group in the competition would consist of all women while the opposing group consisted of all men."

As a young man Frank (May 2003:69) also witnessed the reception of guests from Napaskiak during a summer festival at Keggukar, where some Kwigillingok people had gone to fish.

When the Kwigillingok people came that summer, the Napaskiak people let them pitch their tents across the river from them. The next day the [people from

Kwigillingok] received them. They used ropes and strips of cloth to tie their boats together side by side.

They let [their Napaskiak guests] come across by boat, and then they danced the *ciuqiq* [first dance]. After that they brought them to the *qasgi* and did *tekiqataar* [the arrival dance].

Soon after that Napaskiak repaid them, inviting the people of Kwigillingok upriver to their village.

To prepare for these events Frank (September 2005:149) learned to drum and sing with his peers:

The older ones were the songwriters and singers. The younger men who had become fathers were chosen and taught how to drum during dance festivals.

At first I didn't join the drummers during the dance festivals. I would attend and listen [when I was young]. I'd learn to sing some songs I heard. I still remember the songs to this day.

I started drumming before I got married. They'd let me assist the other drummers. As the time approached for a dance festival, they would practice almost every night.

Frank (February 2003:88) also composed several songs of his own:

There are two songs I've composed. One talks about showing someone where to pick berries and where to fish with hook and line. The other song talks about singing to my grandchild.

> *Cauyarlua atuagurlii* [*Let me sing while drumming*]
> *Erinamkun nunaniriluku* [*Making it sound joyous and beautiful with my voice*]
> *Yaarraa-raangaa-aa, rriyaaraa-rrangai yiirriya*
> *Yii-ii-rrii-ii*
>
> *Tutgara'urluu atuutnaamken* [*My grandchild, let me sing for you*]
> *Erinamkun nunaniriluku* [*Making it sound joyous and beautiful with my voice*]
> *Yaarraa-raanga-aa, rriyaaraa-rrangai yiirriya*
> *Yii-ii-rrii-ii*
>
> *Cauyarlua atuagurlii* [*Let me sing while drumming*]
> *Erinamkun nunaniriluku* [*Making it sound joyous and beautiful with my voice*]
> *Yaaraa-raangaa-aa, rriyaaraa-rrangai yiirriya*
> *Yii-ii-rrii-ii*

Tutgara'urluu cauyautnaamken [*My grandchild, let me drum for you*]
Qasiaraa nunaniriluku [*Making the drum sound joyous and beautiful*]
Yaaraa-raanga-aa, rriyaaraa-rrangai yiirriya
Yii-ii-rrii-ii

Cauyarlua atuagurlii [*Let me sing while drumming*]
Erinamkun nunaniriluku [*Making it sound joyous and beautiful*]
Yaarraa-raanga-aa, rriyaaraa-rrangai yiirriya
Yii-ii-rrii-ii

Frank concluded: "It's easy to compose a song. First you think about the words and the tune, and the song immediately comes out the way you want it."

Frank's knowledge and love of singing and dancing is not unusual among coastal elders living in Catholic communities on Nelson Island north to the mouth of the Yukon. Moravian communities, however, with their stricter interpretation of acceptable Christian activities, shunned dancing completely. In the 1980s dancing reemerged as a valued activity in some communities. Although the people in Kwigillingok still do not dance, Frank (May 2003:72) wholeheartedly supported this revival:

I haven't forgotten some songs, even though I've gotten this old. Even though it has been a long time, I haven't forgotten the things I heard when I was a young lad. I still sing them, even now!

The dances are so entertaining. Some are not fast; they are so much fun; they are so hilarious! It would be good if we tried doing dances!

It would be good if the Messenger Feast was done, even though not exactly the way it was in the past. Let it be observed by some of these people. Those of you who caught up to it — you must do it!

~: *Cavesratuli: One who knows how to work on everything* :~

Indeed, they refer to one who works from the time he is young as *cavesratuli*. You all know Frank Andrew. He knows how to work on everything. That's what they call a person who is an expert at constructing things with his hands. He is able to construct things without uncertainty. They say he is able to look at something with his eyes and replicate it.

John Phillip, Kongiganak, February 2006

Frank was known locally as a good hunter and provider during the years he and Nellie were raising their family in Kwigillingok. As a young man he was chosen as a church leader. He was an eloquent speaker from an early age, and listeners were impressed not only by what he said but how he said it.

As Frank's generation aged, the depth and precision of his memory became increasingly recognized and valued. The way of life in coastal communities had undergone enormous changes during the first half of the twentieth century. Total reliance on subsistence hunting and fishing had given way to wage employment, deserted seasonal camps, and English-dominated schools. By the 1930s, for example, the sealskin kayaks Min'garalria had used throughout his life and taught his son to construct began to be replaced, first by canvas-covered craft and, beginning in the 1950s, by motor-powered skiffs. By the 1970s traditional kayaks were no longer used, nor the skills to make them. Yet Frank never forgot. His sharp mind retained technical knowledge that past generations had needed to survive but that few of his contemporaries possessed. This keen memory, combined with his desire to teach what he knew, would shape the last twenty years of his life and leave an unparalleled legacy.

As Frank's son and daughters began to raise their own children and send them to the local school, Frank went with them. Whenever he was asked to speak to students and share what he knew, he did so. In 1986, for example, high school teacher Dennis Ronsse invited a number of village elders to work with local students to record the place names in the area around Kwigillingok. Ronsse later described how Frank came with the other elders to the school, where he had spread out a blank map for them to work on. Some spoke, but during the whole day Frank said not a word. He studied the map. The next day the elders returned to the school and, once again, gathered round the map. Frank began to speak and did not stop until more than three hundred place names had been recorded, including names of old village sites, camps, lakes, rivers, sloughs, sandbars, even underwater channels. Students collected stories from Frank and other elders and produced a book titled *Kuigilnguum Nunain Atrit Anguyiit-llu Qanemciit (Place-Name and War Stories of the Kwigillingok Area)* for local distribution. His detailed map remains at the school, and a copy is published here for the first time.

Frank not only worked with students, he also helped to train teachers, traveling to Bethel and Anchorage in the 1990s to speak at workshops for local school district personnel. There he spoke alongside other elders recognized for their knowledge and eloquence, including Paul John and Theresa Moses of Toksook Bay. Paul always deferred to Frank as an elder worthy of respect.

Frank's knowledge of kayak construction and use was the inspiration for the foundation of Qayanek (lit., "of and about kayaks"), a kayak preservation center established in Kwigillingok in 1998 by Frank's daughter and son-in-law, Mary Ann and Bill Wilkinson, and son Noah. Inside the spacious workshop hangs the driftwood frame of Frank's last kayak, as well as arrows, harpoons, throwing boards, and other hunting tools. There Frank showed Noah, Bill, and several grandchildren how to select wood, measure parts, bend ribs with his teeth, cure skins, caulk holes with aged moss and seal oil, and paint the finished frame with red-ocher — essential skills men of his generation needed to live off the land as they had for generations. Elders younger than Frank no longer had this knowledge and sometimes came to watch and learn as well.

In summer 2000 the Alaska Native Heritage Center sponsored Alaska Native boatbuilders from across the state to bring their materials to Anchorage and demonstrate their skills. Bill Wilkinson, who had already built four kayaks with Frank as his advisor, wrote a proposal to the Heritage Center, which chose Qayanek to represent the Yup'ik region. Frank traveled with family members to Anchorage, where they worked together to build a sealskin kayak, which can be seen today in the Heritage Center gallery. Frank directed Noah and Bill, as well as grandsons Troy and Ethan Wilkinson and Noah Andrew, Jr. in how to piece the frame together. Noah then prepared the skins, and Nellie and Mary Ann worked with four other women — Lucy Anver, Margaret S. Beaver, Katherine Paul, and Andrea Beaver — to sew it together and stretch it in place during a marathon thirty-two-hour sitting.

At summer's end, the Heritage Center held a dedication ceremony for all the boats, which Alice Rearden and I attended. We had just started working together that summer with the newly established Calista Elders Council (CEC), a nonprofit organization representing the thirteen hundred Yup'ik elders in the Yukon-Kuskokwim region and dedicated to documenting and sharing traditional knowledge. Neither Alice nor I had ever met Frank, though we had heard a great deal about him. We came to ask Noah and Frank to stay in Anchorage for the week following the dedication ceremony to work with us to begin to document his tremendous knowledge. He agreed, and so began a partnership that would shape all of our lives.

When we began working together in September 2000, Alice was new to interviewing elders, Frank had never before been questioned so intensively, and I had rarely worked with such knowledgeable partners. Initially I asked questions and Alice translated. Noah clearly enjoyed himself, as what we asked sparked Frank to tell stories and recount events Noah had never heard his father talk about before. Alice, who quickly came into her own as an interviewer, continued our initial conversations in Bethel the following spring. In fall 2001 Frank and his family accompanied Nellie to Anchorage for medical treatment, and when time permitted I brought them up to my house where we could all work together.

During the same period, the CEC hosted a series of small gatherings in Bethel, where three to four elders met with a handful of younger Yup'ik men and women for two days at a time to discuss traditional family values. Topics included how parents should treat young children, the proper relations between husband and wife, how to discipline young adults, and the complex system of relational terms people used to refer to family members in the not-so-distant past. Frank was invited to most of these gatherings, where he continued to share his knowledge of traditional *qanruyutet* (words of wisdom) that his parents and elders had taught him when he was young. Yup'ik language expert Marie Meade also attended these gatherings, and she, too, came to value Frank's wise contributions.

Beginning in 2002, the CEC hosted several gatherings on traditional material culture, and Frank was invited to join other elders in examining Yup'ik tools in museum collections. We worked together in the Anchorage Museum, the Yupiit Piciryarait Museum and Cultural Center in Bethel, and finally, in February 2003, the Smithsonian's National Museum of Natural History in Washington, D.C. To narrow our choices of what to examine in the Smithsonian's vast collections we honored Frank's and Noah's strong desire to see objects collected from the Canineq area. Frank was uncomfortable making generalizations about tool types. He was, however, excited to see tools like those used when he was young, and they elicited a stream of stories and comments. Noah carefully photographed the artifacts so that he could replicate them when he returned to Kwigillingok.

Frank, Noah, Marie, Alice, Kwigillingok elder Peter John, Theresa Moses from Toksook Bay, and I made the trip to Washington, D.C. It was supposed to end with a one-day consultation at the new National Museum of the American Indian, whose staff was preparing a Yup'ik exhibit. That evening, however, Frank noted that the snow flakes beginning to fall were *taqailnguut* (ones that don't stop). They didn't, and by the next morning Pennsylvania Avenue was a snowscape with no cars, only the occasional cross-country skier. Government ground to a halt, and so did we.

We were stranded in Washington, D.C. for another three days, during which the elders settled into a comfortable routine of storytelling punctuated by long, comfortable meals in our hotel room. Everyone was used to waiting out bad weather. Food was a potential problem, because no restaurants were open, but Noah and

I went "hunting" each afternoon, returning with whole roasted chickens, tins of smoked oysters, and loaves of bread from small delicatessens. We celebrated Frank's eighty-sixth birthday with a fruit-filled pastry. Throughout, we kept the tape recorder running, capturing another dozen hours of Frank's memories, which we later nicknamed the "blizzard tapes."

Noah had repeatedly encouraged Alice and me to come to Kwigillingok to see Qayanek and talk to his father at home, so in June 2003 we went. What Frank shared during that visit surpassed everything we had previously learned. Seated on his livingroom couch or by a small workbench in Qayanek, Frank spoke most of the words in the following pages. He did so enthusiastically but also patiently, taking time to explain things we did not understand. Especially memorable was his detailed description of how to build a kayak, from choosing the proper pieces of driftwood to launching the finished craft. This he did in one long day, in a seamless fashion as if reading from an inner volume. What Frank shared gave us the core of what would subsequently become the exhibition *Yuungnaqpiallerput (The Way We Genuinely Live)*. Many elders contributed to this project, but Frank led the way.

Our work with Frank continued through fall 2005. During our last meeting together he reaffirmed his commitment to sharing what he knew. He spoke at length about how he was taught and the importance of passing on what he learned to contemporary young people.

> When I was young they continually taught us about life. Because of my upbringing, today my mouth is always open, trying to pass on that knowledge to others over in my village. I talk to young people about values and Yup'ik knowledge when I see them in the store or even when I meet them outside. I mostly teach children over in the school. Whenever I am asked to come to the school, I gladly go and share my knowledge. Depending on their age, I tell them things they need to know about being a person on this land. I give the older children more advanced instructions about values and rules for living.
>
> The school has kept me busy talking to children about values and instructions that will help them grow into healthy human beings. I'm glad I listened carefully and learned the teachings when I was little. The discipline has given me wisdom and an opportunity to pass knowledge on to my people.
>
> I've dragged all of those instructions I learned during my upbringing to this present time. All my life I have tried not to leave them behind. Though I have gotten old and physically weak, they have still asked me to come to the school and teach.

Frank's health began to fail in the fall, and he passed away peacefully at home in Kwigillingok in the early morning of April 2, 2006 after eighty-nine years of living. Friends and relatives gathered from all over the region to celebrate his life. Frank was a humble man and never viewed his experiences as exceptional, yet his clear recollections and the way he passed them on were remarkable. Many mourned the loss of this "living encyclopedia." Thanks to Frank's generosity, his family's support, and the dedication of Alice, Marie, and Noah, his knowledge lives on.

~: *Miisam kalikat: Frank's book* :~

Plans to transform Frank's spoken words into a book began soon after our June 2003 visit to Kwigillingok. By that time we had already recorded more than one hundred hours of interviews and gatherings with Frank, and we continued. Our sessions covered four basic areas, including traditional rules for living, legends and stories, kayak construction and use, and subsistence practices specific to the Canineq area. Frank described each topic in such detail that his words could easily fill many books. Choices had to be made.

The information Frank shared on traditional *qanruyutet* that he learned when young was largely recorded during our early CEC gatherings on family values between 2000 and 2003. Alice, Marie, and I worked to bring these guiding principles together into two, closely related books — *Wise Words of the Yup'ik People: We Talk to You because We Love You* and its bilingual companion volume, *Yupiit Qanruyutait: Yup'ik Words of Wisdom*, both published by University of Nebraska Press in 2005. Frank stands out as the primary contributor in both books. Especially in *Yupiit Qanruyutait*, readers can find transcriptions of Frank's original statements on these important topics, along with careful English translations.

Frank also told many stories over the years, both *quliraat* (legends or tales told by distant ancestors) and *qanemcit* (historical narratives related by known persons). The Iñupiat of northern Alaska also distinguish between *unipkaat* (legends) and *quliaqtuat* (narratives), as do the Siberian Yupik Eskimos of St. Lawrence Island and the Chukchi Peninsula. Frank told a wide variety of legends and stories, including encounters between warriors, shamans, hunters, and animals.

To give readers a sense of the range of stories Frank heard and learned over the years, the book's last section includes half-a-dozen traditional tales that Frank particularly enjoyed telling. Frank's stories are beautiful examples of Yup'ik oratory, often including sequences of events that other contemporary storytellers narrate as separate tales. Stringing them together with artful connections, Frank exemplified traditional Yup'ik storytelling where, it was said, stories went on and on without stopping. Such stories were aimed at a mixed audience going in and out of the *qasgi*, rather than a stationary group of listeners anticipating a narrative of Aristotelian design. Instead of building to a climax and conclusion like Western dramas, the structure of these long narrations resembled pearls on a string. Nineteenth-century naturalist Edward Nelson wrote that long stories were told over successive evenings. He also noted that some important tales were presented by two men sitting facing one another. While one man narrated the tale, the other held a bundle of sticks, placing them on the floor one at a time at certain points in the story, "forming a sort of chapter mark."[1] Until now we had no contemporary Yup'ik examples of such extended storytelling. Frank not only shared particular stories, but provides a window on the shape of traditional Yup'ik narrative more generally. As he noted with characteristic understatement, "Some stories they told were long."

Frank was always careful to explain where he heard particular stories, especially when they were not from the Canineq area. For example, he (October 2003:96) clearly stated how he learned the well-known story *Aanakallii Ner'aqallii* (*I Have Eaten My Mother*) from the Kasigluk shaman, Qerrurpalek:

> When Qerrurpalek from the tundra area was going to tell me the story, he said that that old one from Russian Mission told the story of what he had experienced when he was young. I could tell it through that story.
>
> I listened intently to it, and I didn't forget at all. That's why I told it to you two.
>
> Qerrurpalek said that he heard it elsewhere but that he tells it like that old man did. When Qerrurpalek saw me, and when I slept overnight in his village, he always told me stories all night, and some were long. I try to remember but stop when I forget.

Along with *qanruyutet*, *quliraat*, and *qanemcit*, Frank spent days describing every aspect of the seasonal round of activities that he had followed all his life. These activities began each spring with kayak-building and preparation for seal hunting in coastal waters. Seal hunting was followed each year by bird drives to harvest meat and parka material, summer fish camp at the mouth of the Kuskokwim, fall fishing and trapping at inland camps, and then a return to Kwigillingok to harvest tomcod and ready the village for the coming winter.

To engage in these activities, each hunter had to learn to read ice formations, weather conditions, animal behavior, and landmarks. Each needed knowledge about what to do in an emergency. He must listen closely in the *qasgi* as his companions described their experiences on the land and sea, so that if he got into a difficult situation their words would come to his aid and help him survive.

Frank (February 2003:851) repeatedly stated that his knowledge was based on experience: "A person immediately remembers the things that he has experienced when they are brought up. I do it as well. A person will not forget the things he knows." Like his contemporaries, he did not tell stories that he did not know in detail, nor did he describe past patterns of life, ceremonies, or subsistence pursuits in general. Instead he consistently gave information on the past in the form of detailed first-person narratives. Gifted as he was, Frank (May 2003:107) was humble: "Poor me, I am not smart. I was taught orally about many things, even by my late grandfather. At the present time, I do not know many things. But what I know, I will not forget as long as I live."

What Frank remembered in such detail was the core of what every man needed to know to live life on the lower Kuskokwim coast. Frank was correct — his were not extraordinary experiences. What is extraordinary is the clarity of his memories. Speaking his past, he allows us to capture a sense of the richness and complexity of a way of life slipping away. Frank's gift was his ability to recall and describe, and his book abounds in extraordinary recollections of ordinary times. He (September 2005:128) said of himself, "Things I heard and paid close attention to, I still have not forgotten though they happened a long time ago."

~: *Qaillun ayuqellrat Miisam qanemcikellri: How Frank spoke* :~

Frank did much more than tell stories and describe the way he lived. Whether part of a small gathering of his contemporaries or during interviews with Alice and Marie, Frank's words were always part of ongoing conversations grounded in close personal relations. Early on, Frank identified kinship links between himself, Alice, and Marie. Frank shaped his accounts accordingly, and Alice's and Marie's translations retain direct evidence of the important communicative function of his narrations, including both his explanations and asides. Some of what he said was quite serious, but he could also be very playful, teasing his young relatives. He spoke to inform us, but he also knew that we enjoyed his deep, steady voice and that we appreciated what he had to say — all components of his skill as an exceptional storyteller.

Beginning in 2000, Alice and Marie carefully transcribed and translated everything we recorded with Frank, sharing transcripts with Noah and other family members. Alice and Marie consistently rendered Frank's accounts according to English word order. They aimed for a fluid English translation that communicates both the literal meaning of his words and the dynamic flow of his original narratives. Although a more convoluted translation might be closer to the Yup'ik original, they strove for natural-sounding translations accessible to contemporary English readers, including many Yupiit. Other characteristics of the Yup'ik originals, however, have been carefully retained. For example, redundancies and repetitions have been commonly edited out of translated texts in the past, but Alice and Marie have kept them as integral to both the structure and meaning of Frank's accounts.

In fact, Frank included frequent repetitions in his oratory, giving his texts a denser texture than typical English phrasings. He also often framed a statement with repeated phrases to mark its beginning and ending and to set it apart. Structured repetitions and framing are characteristic of Yup'ik oratory and vital to its integrity. Repetition in oral literature generally enhances memory and adds emphasis and depth. This was important as, until recently, the minds of elders were the stories' sole repositories.

Though Yup'ik oral tradition values close attention to detail and consistent retellings, as Elsie Mather noted, "The most respected conveyers of Yup'ik knowledge are those who express things that listeners already know in artful or different ways, offering new expressions of the same."[2] Central Alaska Yup'ik is a complex language in which the same noun and verb bases can be ordered differently or combined with different postbases to produce varying rhetorical effects, depending on the narrator's audience and the context of their storytelling. Although a gifted orator like Frank does not have the freedom to change the sequence of events, he can embellish this sequence with considerable effect, as in his continuous interaction with his audience. Yup'ik narrative is far from rigid repetition, and no two tellings of the same story, even by Frank, were ever exactly alike.

∾: *Miisam Qanellri: What Frank said* :∾

Frank's dedication to documenting a lifetime of experiences was grounded in his profound respect for his ancestors' ways. When he spoke at gatherings and during private conversations, this respect was always abundantly clear. When he described how to make a kayak, Frank was sharing technical skills that left no doubt about the ingenuity and depth of knowledge of the generations of Yup'ik men and women who lived before him. The legends he chose to tell communicated his own artistry as well as that of his ancestors. The qanruyutet he so often shared embodied rules for living that he believed were still valuable life lessons.

Frank embraced Christianity, came to live within four walls, drove a four-wheeler, and traveled by small plane and jet to Bethel, Anchorage, and Washington, D.C. Yet he remained a Yup'ik man who lived by Yup'ik principles which he honored throughout his life. He spoke primarily to communicate that view, both to Yup'ik young people fast losing touch with their heritage and non-Native readers who, through his words, he hoped would gain a measure of understanding and compassion for his people.

A mechanical genius, Frank's understanding of the world reached far beyond practical knowledge. Like other elders of his generation, he viewed the world as responsive to human action and intention. When describing the continued relevance of traditional qanruyutet, Frank rarely failed to mention a special class of rules known collectively as eyagyarat — the traditional abstinence practices following birth, death, illness, and first menstruation. Diverse eyagyarat practiced in a variety of situations were tied together by a common purpose — restraining and guiding behavior during life's transformations to avoid annoying or frightening human and nonhuman companions in a sentient universe. Frank viewed these abstinence practices as connected and interrelated, allowing men and women in a vulnerable condition to safely coexist with their fellow humans and animals in a knowing and responsive world.

Eyagyarat codified the restraint and special care people must exercise during critical phases of their lives. As in the rules for living generally, people were enjoined to follow the rules rather than their own minds and desires. Frank (September 2000:32) described the centrality of eyagyarat in a well-lived life:

> Everything we do must be practiced by following eyagyarat. When we take care of something such as a piece of clothing, it tells us not to wash it in hot water, and there are directions on how to use the machine. Trying not to break the inerquun [prohibition], a person can take good care of that belonging and use it for a long time. That is how our body is and why we should not let it experience bad things. Not following our desires but doing what is expected of us and being respectful of everything can lead us toward good fortune.

Frank (October 2001:106) later compared eyagyarat to the laws of physics, the principles underlying the admonishments of daily life.

Eyagyarat are an abiding expression of the personhood not only of humans and animals, but also of the land and sea. As Frank (September 2000:32) said, the ocean has eyes and the world knows. This understanding of the world as a knowing and responsive place, possessing both agency and will, finds expression in myriad ways throughout his descriptions.

Contemporary elders do not agree on the continued relevance of *eyagyarat*. Some evangelical Christians dismiss such abstinence practices as empty superstition. Others acknowledge their critical importance as guides for action in a sentient universe. Frank (October 2001:106) set great store by *eyagyarat* as the founding principles of human action in the world. At the same time he dismissed as "untrue" many specific practices associated with shamanism.

Frank (October 2001:42) felt strongly that *eyagyarat*, like Yup'ik oral traditions generally, are no longer valued because they are not written down: "All the things we do on this earth have admonitions, but those who do not know this say that *eyagyarat* are not true. They live by *kass'aq* [non-Native] instructions because white people have written them down. We know our ways and are still living by them today, but our younger generation do not know them because we do not have them written down. Many people do not value them anymore." Frank's tireless work documenting his way of life is grounded in this strong belief in the continuing value of the past and the urgent need to share it in written form with a generation of young people increasingly ignorant of their history.

It is useful to compare Frank's work with that of Paul John, another eminent Yup'ik elder who has worked to share Yup'ik traditions in written form. CEC's first major publication was *Qulirat Qanemcit-llu Kinguvarcimalriit (Stories for Future Generations): The Oratory of Yup'ik Eskimo Elder Paul John*. Translated by Sophie Shield, this bilingual book contains more than seven hundred pages of legends and narratives Paul originally shared with students at the Nelson Island High School during a two-week period in 1977. Paul complimented his stories with advice and instruction. Throughout, he was not only sharing Yup'ik history, he was continuing the process of creating a moral universe for future generations through stories about the special knowledge and, ultimately, special rights of Yup'ik people.

Paul John is a well known and respected leader in southwest Alaska today. He is an accomplished orator who continues to "speak his past"— not to recite dead facts but to provide tools for understanding the present. His narratives not only seek to explain contemporary events with reference to Yup'ik traditions, but to claim legitimacy for these explanations as alternatives to Western ones. Beyond informing young people about their heritage, Paul seeks to make a political statement that compares the advantages of the old ways to the problems engendered by increased contact with the non-Native world. His orations on change during his life are influenced by both traditional Yup'ik oratory and Biblical precedent, yet they are used to reflect contemporary Yup'ik concerns.

Frank shared Paul's goal of informing, and thereby empowering, future generations. Yet he did so in very different ways. First, Frank never aspired to political leadership. From the time he was born, Kwigillingok had an active Moravian mission and growing congregation, and the majority of residents were Moravian. The two churches coexisted without conflict, but Russian Orthodox members were in the minority and political power in the community was primarily in Moravian hands.

While not a man who sat on many boards or attended meetings, Frank was early recognized as a spiritual leader and moral force. His appointment as church reader when still a young man is noteworthy. In 2000, following his work at the Alaska Native Heritage Center, Frank received both the Alaska Federation of Native's Culture Bearer Award and the Traditional Culture Bearer Award from Calista Corporation for his contribution to revitalizing the art of kayak making.

At home in Kwigillingok Frank lived the ideal Yup'ik life he described, guided by compassion and restraint. People respected his wisdom as well as his knowledge, and they sought him out for advice and direction. Frank, of all people, would never presume to say that he was better than his peers, that his way of living life was superior. What he did was eloquently describe the events of his life and the activities that made it meaningful, leaving it to listeners to draw their own conclusions.

Yugtun Igautellrit Kass'atun-llu Mumigtellrit
Yup'ik Transcription and Translation

The Central Alaskan Yup'ik language is spoken on the Bering Sea coast from Norton Sound to the Alaska Peninsula as well as along the lower Yukon, Kuskokwim, and Nushagak rivers. Central Yup'ik is closely related to the Inuit/Iñupiaq language of the Arctic coast of Alaska, northern Canada, and Greenland, although they are not mutually intelligible. Central Yup'ik is one of four Yupik Eskimo languages. The other three are Pacific Yupik (Alutiiq or Sugpiaq), which is spoken around Prince William Sound, the tip of the Kenai Peninsula, Kodiak Island, and part of the Alaska Peninsula; Naukan of East Cape Siberia; and Siberian Yupik, spoken on St. Lawrence Island in Alaska and across the Bering Strait in Siberia. Together, Inuit/Iñupiaq and Yupik constitute the Eskimo branch of the Eskimo-Aleut family of languages.[3]

There are four dialects of Central Yup'ik: Norton Sound, Hooper Bay/Chevak, Nunivak, and General Central Yup'ik. All are mutually intelligible with some phonological and vocabulary differences.[4] Frank Andrew from Kwigillingok, Alice Rearden from Napakiak, Marie Meade from Nunapitchuk, and Anna Jacobson from Kwethluk are all speakers of General Central Yup'ik.

The Central Yup'ik language remained unwritten until the end of the nineteenth century, when Russian Orthodox, Moravian, and Jesuit Catholic missionaries, working independently of one another but in consultation with Native converts, developed a variety of orthographies. The orthography used consistently throughout this book is the standard one developed in 1967–1972 at the University of Alaska Fairbanks and detailed in works published by the Alaska Native Language Center and others.[5]

The standard orthography for Central Yup'ik represents the language with letters and letter combinations, each corresponding to a distinct sound as follows:

Vowels	front		back
high	i		u
mid		e	
low		a	

liv

Consonants	labials	apicals		front velars	back velars
stops	p	t	c	k	q
voiced fricatives	v	l	s/y	g (ûg̑)	r (ûȓ)
voiceless fricatives	vv	ll	ss	gg (w)	rr (ûȓr)
voiced nasals	m		n	ng	
voiceless nasals	m̓		ń	ńg	

Symbols in parentheses represent the sounds made with the lips rounded.

Apostrophe represents consonant gemination, or doubling (and serves several other less important functions). There are also conventions for undoubling the letters for voiceless fricatives under certain circumstances.[6] This standard orthography accurately represents the Yup'ik language in that a given word can be written in only one way, and a given spelling can be pronounced in only one way. Note that certain predictable features of pronunciation, specifically automatic gemination and rhythmic length, are not explicitly shown in the spelling.

Like all Eskimo languages, Central Yup'ik is a "suffixing language" in which words can be formed by adding postbases (like English suffixes but much more powerful) and an ending (indicting number, case, person, position, etc.) to word bases. For example, the word *Yupiit* is derived from the noun *yuk* "person" to which the postbase *-pik* "real" or "authentic" and the plural ending *-t* have been added, producing literally, "real people" (in the sense of "our kind").

Because suffixes in Yup'ik often serve the same function as separate words do in English, the two languages sometimes appear as mirror images of each other. For example, the English phrase "my little boat" corresponds to *angyacuarqa*, which consists of *angya-* "boat," plus *-cuar-* "little," plus *-qa* "my," so that the order of the parts within the Yup'ik word is "boat, little, my." Thus translation involves a continuous process of reordering.

~: Translation :~

"Much of great importance is lost and added in translation," A. L. Becker reminds us.[7] The truth of his words captures both this book's weaknesses and strengths. Each translated text is at once less than the original telling — devoid of the shapes and sounds of the speaker's voice — and more. Through the double process of translation from Yup'ik to English and from oral to written form, readers gain access to the observations and experiences of a man renowned for his knowledge and wisdom.

Linguist Gregory Shreve aptly describes the paradox of translation. Languages themselves can never be translated, only the "sociocultural containers of social meaning and communicative value" called texts. He concludes:

> One could claim that all of translation is patently impossible, but because we so much desire to read, in our own language, what others have written in theirs, about their experiences,…we do it anyway. We must accept translation's inherent faults, or rather faulting…in the geological sense. The translation…slips away from the source along the fault line of sociocultural difference.…The translation is like the Phoenix, it rises from the ashes of the old text, its parent, but it is a new being, alive in its own right, alive in its own writing.[8]

In their roles as translators, Alice Rearden and Marie Meade offer distinctive strategies for bridging differences between Yup'ik and English without erasing them. Their goal throughout has been a "natural sounding," free translation, as opposed to either literal translation (at one extreme) or paraphrasing (at the other). Paraphrasing may communicate some of the sense of the original, but such interpretive translations modify the original to the point where the speaker's voice is alternately erased or transformed. Literal, word-for-word translation is also inadequate. At best it is awkward, and at worst it makes no sense. Alice's and Marie's translations employ a free style in which Frank's choice of words is respected, while word order and sentence structure are modified where necessary to communicate his original meaning.

Several grammatical features pose potential problems in the translation of Frank's statements. First, relatively free word order characterizes the Yup'ik language. For example, the meaning of the English sentence "The man lost the dog" can only be conveyed by placing the words "man," "lost," and "dog" in this order. A Yup'ik speaker, however, can arrange the three words *angutem* (man), *tamallrua* (s/he lost it), and *qimugta* (dog) in any of six possible word orders with no significant change in meaning. Nevertheless, it is not totally irrelevant to interpreting Yup'ik sentences. Word order may be the only key to appropriate interpretation where the ending alone is insufficient. For example, the sentence *Arnam atra nallua* (lit., "woman – his/her name – s/he not knowing it") can mean either "The woman does not know his name" or "He does not know the woman's name." The same three words in a different word order, however, are less ambiguous. *Arnam nallua atra* is commonly taken to mean "The woman does not know his name." Contrasted with languages that have a freer word order, the relative position of postbases inside a Yup'ik word is very rigid. Consequently a word may comprise syntactic problems that occur only in sentences in other languages.

Translation is further complicated by the fact that the Yup'ik language does not specify gender in third-person endings. The listener is left to deduce gender from the context of the account. When Frank describes women's tasks, we have translated the pronominal ending as "she," as that is the way an English speaker can best understand his intent. Conversely, pronominal endings are translated as "he" when Frank is describing a hunter's activities. In general discussions we have used either "it" or "he," depending on the context. Readers should also know that Frank, like Yup'ik orators generally, sometimes mixes singular and plural endings in a single oral "sentence," and we have retained these grammatical variations to reflect the complexity of the Yup'ik original.

Yup'ik verb tenses also differ from English. Although some postbases place an action clearly in the future and others place action definitely in the past, a verb without one of these time-specific postbases may refer to an action which is happening either in the past or present.[9] Accounts of events or customs that are no longer practiced in southwest Alaska have been translated in the past tense. Readers should also note that tense may vary within a paragraph, especially in discussions of *qanruyutet* marked by the enclitic *-gguq*, which can be translated "they said," "they say," or "it is said" depending on the context. Traditional activities that Frank indicates still take place are translated using the present tense.

As if translation from one language to another were not challenging enough, this book involves the movement from oral to written language. Our starting point has been Frank's verbal artistry, but critical to understanding his words is the transformation of his voice onto the page. Through the 1970s little attention was given to reflecting the dynamics and dramatic techniques of the performance, including the speakers' shifts in tone and rhythm. The oral origins of texts were all but hidden from view. Texts were routinely transcribed in paragraph form, as if the paragraph were the "natural" form of all speech.

Beginning in the 1980s, when so many basic tenets of anthropology were being scrutinized, the ubiquitous paragraph came under attack, especially in the work of Dell Hymes and fellow linguist Dennis Tedlock. Together Tedlock and Hymes inspired a generation of linguists and anthropologists who have since adopted and adapted their insights in a variety of ethnopoetic transcription styles, igniting a veritable "renaissance" in the translation of Native American literature.[10] Although

Alice and Marie have not chosen to employ the "short line" verse format favored by many translators, they use the prose format with a new sensitivity. In their work paragraphs are no longer arbitrary groupings disconnected from the speaker's original oral performance, but are distinguished by prominent line-initial particles like *tua-i-llu* ("so then"), by cohesion between contiguous lines, and by pauses between units.

As we ponder both the limitations and power of translation to communicate meaning across cultural and linguistic boundaries, it is useful to turn to Becker's recognition that translation is not the endpoint of understanding, but the beginning.[11] Similarly the reader is invited to engage Alice and Marie's translations and use them as starting points for understanding and respecting the differences between literary traditions which, in turn, make it possible for us to better understand ourselves.

Good translation is much more than a technical process — it is a moral act involving responsibility and respect. A Malay friend once told Becker that he hoped he would not translate a Malay classic into English, because then no one would read the original. All indigenous people face the same dilemma. Alice's and Marie's efforts to understand and provide access to Frank Andrew's words are not neutral acts but are "necessarily full of politics and semi-intended errors." Becker concludes: "Translation fidelity itself demands reciprocity, a sorting out of exuberances and deficiencies, a confession of failures and sleights of hand. It is the only way I know of by which to make restitution to those who, in old Malay, 'wrought the words and in that sense own them.'"[12]

Notes

1. Nelson 1899:451.

2. Mather 1995:32.

3. No apostrophe is used when speaking of the Yupik family of languages, but an apostrophe is used for Central Alaskan Yup'ik (called simply Yup'ik here), including dialects of this language such as Cup'ig and General Central Yup'ik.

4. Jacobson 1984:28–37; Woodbury 1984:49–63.

5. Reed, Miyaoka, Jacobson, Afcan, and Krauss 1977; Miyaoka and Mather 1979; Jacobson 1995.

6. Jacobson 1995:6–7.

7. Becker 2000:90.

8. Shreve 2002:7.

9. Jacobson 1984:22.

10. Swann 1994:xxviii.

11. Becker 2000:18.

12. Becker 2000:19.

Nerangnaqsaraq

Ways of Seeking Sustenance in the Past

Nerangnaqsaraq

~: Up'ngetullrat up'nerkami pissullerkaatnun :~

Atam uksumi, tua-i December-aam maani kinguani, February-mi, January-m maani nangyartullranek ayagluku qayarkanek-llu up'ngetullrulriit. Arnat-llu cali imarnitnek, taq'laagngailnguut ciukluki; imarnitnek, ivrucirkaitnek ayagningtull-rulriit, arillugkaitnek-llu.

Cali-ll' augkunek neqnek kevirautarkiurturluteng tamatum nalliini tangvalall-renka. Allakarilluki, makunek-llu iqalluut kemgitnek, kangitneret, taryaqviit-llu kemgitnek allakarilluki. Tamakut iqertagnek caquluki kevirautnek pitukait nunam-teni. Neqnek imirturluki ingqiurluki. Ayagastemeng tamakut neqkaitnek taquar-kaitnek allakarilluki. Tamaa-i tamatum nalliini tekicugnaunaku kevirauciluteng, tua-i ilangarrngaunaki. Taquarkiurluki. Umciggluki tua-i. Muiraqata, neggluki tua-i imirluki, ingqiurluki, anutaqluki ellivignun. Ilangartessngaunaki tua-i maku-nun irniameggnun-llu.

Piciatun tua-i nerkengameggnek, piciatun unani, uqumelngurnek, piirrallugnek tuaten, kumlanernek-llu ceturrnanek, wall' Akulmiutarnek pikangqerraqameng, Akulmiutarnek ilaluki.

Tamakunek tamaa-i allakariqurluki pitukait pingnaqestekateng. Tua-i aturkait-nek-gguq upengluteng, up'ngulluki. Angutait-wa call' tua-i pissurcuutekameggnek cimirnariaqata, qayateng-llu cimirkiurluki, aminqiggluki tuaten. Akluteng-llu assiv-lalriit cimirkiurluki tua-i piqainaurrluki tekipailgan. Qasgi tua-i tamatum nalliini, February-m-llu iluani tua-i calilriaruaqluni. Muragnimek tepengluni qasgi tua-i. Acia tua-i maqarpak canillernek. Tamalkurmeng yagingaluteng tua-i, ikayuulluteng-llu pituameng pinrilngermeng.

Taumek caliarit qayat-llu cukamek tuvtaqaceteng apeqmeggnek unugpailgan taq-tullrulriit, quyurulluki waten pitullruameng qasgimi. Caliaqellratni tua-i ikayualuki, cuqtaarillratni taugaam ikayuyuunaki. Taum taugaam caliaqestiin cuqnemikun cuq-taarluki, allamun cuqcecuunaki, cuqneteng angtatkenrilata. Tuaten pitullruit. Tua-i

2

Ways of Seeking Sustenance in the Past

~: *Getting ready for spring hunting* :~

Now during winter, sometime after December, starting in February, at the end of January, they started preparing kayak parts. And women started making seal-gut parkas, first making things that took time to complete; they made gut raingear, waterproof boots, and fish-skin mittens they would wear.

And the people I saw back then started making containers during that time. They prepared and set aside food for [their men who hunted], including dried chum, dried silver, and dried king salmon. They stored those in fish-skin containers they called *kevirautet* in my hometown. They filled [the containers] with fish after cutting them into pieces. They set aside provisions for those who hunted for them. They prepared *kevirautet* long before the time came to use them, and they wouldn't eat any of the contents. They prepared provisions [for the hunters]. They filled the bags with fish cut into pieces, and they would pack down the fish until the bag was full. The bags were brought out to the food cache. They wouldn't let anyone open them and eat their contents, including their children.

They'd [fill the bags] with all sorts of food from the coast, including dried tomcod that was processed in seal oil, dried tomcod, and frozen tomcod, or when they had food from the tundra area, they included it.

They always set those aside for their hunters. They prepared things they would use. And their men worked on hunting tools that needed to be replaced. They also made replacement parts for their kayaks, and even changed their skin coverings. And they replaced the implements that were in poor condition and got them ready before the time came to use them. The *qasgi* during that time, and in the month of February, was a place of work. The *qasgi* would start to smell of wood. And the area underneath [them] would be filled with leftover shavings. Everyone was busy because they helped one another, even though they didn't ask for assistance.

That's why they finished things they worked on, including kayaks, before night, when they gathered together, working as a group to complete a task. They helped others during the construction, but they didn't help them when they measured the parts. Only the person who was constructing it would measure using his body

cuqnarqelria cuqtaarcetaqluku taumun pikestekaatnun. Cuqceqaarluku nutaan ikayurluku caliaqaqluki.

Tua-i-ll' aklukai qaqitqapiaraata tua-i apamak-llu qaqicagnek nutaan palurcan
quyurulluku tua-i nutaan tumarrluku. Unugpailgan taq'errnauraat qayaq. Wall'u
malrugnek qayagnek taqutnaurtut unugpailgan.

Atu'urkait upluki tua-i pivailgata-ll' tua-i qaqilluki, piqainaurrluki tua-i. Upesku-
neng tua-i piqainaurrluki. Qaqilluki tua-i aklukait.

Nutaan qaqicamegteki, ukut-am ikamrartekat, arnat ivrucirkaitnek cali caliluteng nutaranek. Yum'eggnek tuamtell' piilnguut pisteteng cali kevgiurteteng cali
pikirluki pituluki. Angayuqaqenrilengermegteki yuut avegvilget up'nerkami pis-
tailnguut kevgiutuit angayuqaqelriatun. Tamakut-llu kevgiuqengaita atu'urkiutu-
lliniluki pimeggnek ellaita, kevgiurtekateng tamakut, aqvalgirtekat, ikamrartekat,
pitaitnek aqvauquriarkat.

Nutaan qavaq peggluku pituut up'nerkami pissungaqameng imarpigmiut.

Elitnauyuitellermeggni avani tua-i tamarmeng *family*-t ayagatuut.

Spring-ami-w' tua-i up'nerkami *camp*-allret makut amllertut maani, ikna-ll' ika-i
Nukcaq, Anuuraaq, ingna-ll' Penguq, Kuigglucugguq, Centuli, Urutuq, Kuiggluk,
Pengurpak, Enpakaq. Maa-i makut atrit, up'nerkami *camp*-at, up'nerkiyarallrit avani,
elitnaurvigtavngvailgan. Maa-i elitnaurvingameng ayagasciigaliut.

Kiugkut aterpagtalallrit Esrimiut, Aqumgallermiut, Cevv'arnermiut camatiitni
uitalriit, up'nerkiyarallrit tamakut tamaa-i. Yungqerrnanrirluteng cali. Qipnermiut
ketiitni Enpakarmiut Pengurpagmiut, Kuigglugmiut, Centulirmiut. Taukut Qipnermiut, Cal'itmiut, up'nerkiyarallrit. Ukurmiut-wa, Pengurmiut, Cevv'artellermiut,
Anuurarmiut. Mat'um-llu painga call' ugna, Kukcaarmiut-llu. Ingkut Kangirnaam
painga Caunermiut-llu, Cingigmiut-llu, Mimernarugarmiut-llu, Nunapigmiut, Pa-
pegmiut-wa. Tamaa-i up'nerkiyarallrit, Qinarmiut Tuntutuliarmiungurpailgata ilakluki.

measurements, and he didn't have another person measure it because their measurements weren't the same. That's what they did. When a part needed measuring, after having the owner measure it, they helped him construct it.

Then when all the [kayak] parts were finished and when the gunwales were constructed, when they turned it over, a group gathered around him, and they put the frame together. They finished the kayak quickly before dark. Or they would finish the assembly of two kayaks before dark.

They completed all the things they would use long before they [hunted]. They got them ready to use. They would be ready when they prepared to leave. They finished all their implements.

When they completed [the kayak parts and implements], the women sewed new waterproof boots for the ones who would be going back and forth with the sleds [to retrieve their catch]. And they sewed for their helpers who didn't have a family member to sew for them. The ones without anyone to sew clothing for them would help those who weren't their parents with their tasks in the spring, like parents. And those who had extras would sew clothing for the ones who helped them with tasks, using their own materials for the ones who would retrieve the animals they caught, the ones who would use the sleds.

The people of the ocean gave up sleep during the spring when they started hunting.

Back when they didn't have formal schooling, the whole family went [to spring camp together].

There were many old spring camping sites around here, including Nukcaaq across here, Anuuraaq and Penguq over there, Kuigglucugguq, Centuli, Urutuq, Kuiggluk, Pengurpak, and Enpakaq. These are the names of the old spring camps people used to go to before schools were built. Now that they have schools, they no longer go to spring camps.

[The spring camps] back there that they mentioned in the past that were located below Chefornak, their spring camp sites were places like Esrimiut and Aqumgallermiut. People no longer stay [in those spring camps] either. Down below Kipnuk were Enpakarmiut, Pengurpagmiut, Kuigglugmiut, and Centulirmiut. Those were the spring camps where people from Kipnuk and Cal'itmiut used to stay. And the spring camps for people from this village were Pengurmiut, Cevv'artellermiut, and Anuurarmiut. And at the mouth of this river was Kukcaarmiut, also down there. And at the mouth of the Kangirnaaq River were Caunermiut, Cingigmiut, Mimernarugarmiut, Nunapigmiut, and Papegmiut. Those were the spring camps people used to stay in. They stayed in those camps with people from Qinaq before they moved to Tuntutuliak.

March-aam-wa nuniini qaniiqurangetulriit, *ready*-rluki tua-i tumairupailgan. Aturyugngalriit *camp*-ameggnun ciumek ayauqurluki tamaavet *camp*-ameggnun, tumairpailgan ikamratgun. Tua-i-ll' nutaan pinarian *camp*-ameggnun upagluteng nunamek.

Yuirucuilnguut-wa Kuigilngurmiut ketseng pissuryaraqngamegteggu. Ilait tua-i nugtara'arrluteng pissutuut. Kangit augkut kuiguyuut amllertut avani ketemteni pissuryarat. Cetamanek Kuigilngurmiut ketiit pissuryarartangqertuq kan'a ketvut, kuiguyunek aterluteng. Kangirpak, Kangiqutaller, Kangicuar, Nayirtuli, Kangirnaq; tallimaulliniut kuiget taukut unani imarpigmi ketemteni pissuryaraput. Augkunek atengqertut ava-i.

Kuiguluteng tua-i, *bar*-anek akulerluteng, qaugyanek pengunek akulerluteng. Kuiguluteng kelutmun tua-i akulait. Tamakut tamaa-i kuiguyunek pilaraput. Ukuk waniwa ketemteni yaani Kangirnaq, Kangirpak-llu *clam*-anek imangqertuk amllepianek. Taumek asevret tekitaqameng ayagarcuilnguut taukugnek kuignek. Amllepiaraqluteng asevret tamakunek neqengqerrameng.

Qagataitut. Augkut avani mermi uitalriit qagatengqessuitut. Elatmun tua-i yaavet tuaten ayuqut tuaten ketvut, kuiguyunek kuigtarluni elatmun, avavet elalirnemtenun qakmavet qagataunateng. Taumek asevret piaqamteki tua-i ilait aqsaqurrit tua-i muirumaqapiaralalriit *clam*-anek. Aling tua-lli-w' cailkamun kuvlaqput assigtairutaqata assilriit neqet *clam*-at. Tua-i kemegnek tua-i arcaqayulaamta asevret-llu qeciitnek canek nerait tua-i tamakut ilakuiluki tua-i piaqluki, kuvyuumiilengramteki unitaqluki. Qassarrlainarluki cali nertuluki.

Piciryararluteng-am augkut ciulirnerput asvernek wall'u waten qavalrianek pugtaluteng tangrraqameng. Quyurrluteng cikumun mayutulriit. Mayuameng taugken qantateng piluk' nerqerluteng, quyurmeng cikum qaingani asvercuqataameng. Ner'irluki-gguq tua-i pitarkateng augkunek *clam*-anek ulunek, tamakunek ner'angqesqumaluki. Piciryaraqluku-am, nerqerluteng tua-i neqnek nerellgutekluteng. Nerqerraarluteng-llu tua-i nutaan ullagluki qavalriit pissurluki. Tuaten-am piciryararluteng augkut ciuqliput.

During March they would start to go back and forth to take supplies out with sleds, getting [their camps] ready before their trail was no longer suitable for travel. First they brought things they would need out to their camp with sleds before their trail was no good for travel. Then when it was time, they moved from the village to their camps.

The village of Kwigillingok isn't completely deserted because the shore below them is their hunting area. Some move and hunt. There are many bays out there, many ocean channels down below our shore where they hunt. There are four hunting areas down below Kwigillingok on our shore down there, called *kuiguyut* [channels]. Kangirpak, Kangiqutaller, Kangicuar, Nayirtuli, Kangirnaq; there are actually five channels down on the ocean below the land where we hunt, and those were their names.

They are rivers with sandbars between them. Between [the sandbars] are channels that go up toward the shore. We call those *kuiguyuut*. The two [channels] right below our shore out there, Kangirnaq and Kangirpak, are filled with many, many clams. That's why the walrus don't leave for a long time from those two rivers when they arrive. There are many walrus because they have that type of food to eat there.

Those [channels] don't have a source. [Channels] down on the water don't have sources. Down below our shore, the river channels that extend out there are lined up to the area outside ours and have no sources. That's why when we catch walrus, some of their stomachs are completely filled with clams. We spill some tasty clams onto the ground when we no longer have containers for them. Because we place more value on the meat and skin, we leave their stomach contents behind although we are reluctant to spill them out. We always ate them raw, too.

Our ancestors had a custom when they saw walrus sleeping and floating. [The hunters] went on top of the ice as a group. When they went up, they took their bowls and ate a small amount as a group on top of the ice when they were about to hunt walrus. They say they fill the animals they are hunting with clams, wanting their stomachs to be filled with those. That was their tradition, eating a small meal together. After eating a small meal, they went to the sleeping [walrus] and hunted them. The ones who came before us followed that custom.

Paitarkiutenka

My Legacy to You

~: *At spring camps* :~

They hunted at spring camps. And the women processed the animals they caught and placed *pasvaagutet* [pieces of stiff sealskin sewn around the hole at the head opening of a sealskin poke, used as both a funnel and a fastening device] separately on the seal-oil containers while the skins were soft and raw in the place where they had removed the seal's face. They widened the skin like this. They sewed [the *pasvaagutet*] onto their chins here where [the seal's] head had been removed, onto the [sealskin pokes] that they would fill with seal oil, walrus meat, and cooked seal lungs and livers mixed with seal oil. They knew which ones were going to be filled with what. And they cut off the tips of the claws of the seal pokes they were preparing.

Also, back in those times when they caught belugas, they placed the beluga meat inside their stomachs. They call their stomachs *imanarviit* [beluga stomach containers] down in my village. They also prepared those when they worked on beluga whales among other things.

Then they also took care of the seal blubber that they removed from the skin. When they were about to render oil, they split them into strips. They also knew which ones they had caught first. The fresher ones that they caught later didn't render as quickly. Starting with the ones that had been caught first, the women placed them inside seal pokes. They cut them into strips and placed them inside seal pokes.

[They stored separately] ones that would be marked as being *tangviarrluut* [strips of seal blubber from which oil was rendered]. They stored the ringed-seal oil separately, and the spotted-seal oil, and added the two-year-old spotted-seal oil to the ringed-seal oil. And they stored the oil of *maklagaat* [bearded seals in their first year] separately and the oil of *makliit* [adult bearded seals] separately as well. The oil of *makliit* is reddish in color because their blubber is reddish. But the oil of *maklagaat* is clearer. The ringed-seal oil and the spotted-seal oil are very delicious. Ringed seals and spotted seals have very good oil as well as the bearded seals in their first year. But adult bearded-seal oil is reddish because [the blubber] is reddish. But they don't prepare and eat the walrus oil and beluga oil. Some do, but they cook the beluga oil, cooking the oil, what they call *ullauluki*. But they don't consume walrus oil.

They used to cook the adult bearded-seal blubber during spring as well by cutting them into strips. They called them *uullat*. They cooked them and placed them in seal pokes. The ones that are cooked don't render. That's what they did with a lot

tamaani tuatnarpallutullruit, qimugtenun-llu atutullruamegteki makliit uquit, uullat keniumalriit.

Tua-i taugken tamakut tua-i uqut nangengata kinercirluki, cali qeciit caquit murilkelluki tua-i, mumigtaqluki uqunek imalget, nallunailkucirluki-ll' asvernek qecignek imalget, putukuanek-llu imalget, cuakaayagnek-llu imalget, nayilinrarnek-llu imalget, issurilinrarnek-llu imalget maklaginrarnek-llu imalget, maklinrarnek-llu imalget. Tamakutgun pasvaagutait canek mingqarulluki ellivikaqluki, nallunailkucirturluki, katagngailkaitnun.

Kenirluki cuakayituut, uqunek avuluki, caqutnun ekluki. Tamaa-i tamakut cuakaayagnek aterpaggluki. Tenguitnek avuluki cali, kenirluki cali. Ingqiluki. Tua-i uqunek avuurluki tua-i tamakulituut, uqunek nayilinrarnek wall'u maklinrarnek-llu avuluki. Tua-i-am tamakunek pinanrilriit cuakaayagnek. Piiyuirulluki tua-i tayima.

Quunaqluteng. Imkut *bacon*-aat it'gait kass'artaat. Tuaten ayuqut, tukniluteng quunarqellrat tamakut cuakayiit tuaten ayuqluteng caqutni uitalriit. Assikluki taugaam tua-i neqekngamegteki, quunarqengraata tuaten.

Tua-i-ll' nutaan pinariata uquucillernun nunamun ekluki. Nutaan tua-i ekumariaqamegteki kiagpak-llu uqurturkateng ekevkenaki allakarluki, ilaluki imkut anrutanek-llu uqunek imirluki ilaluki caqutet. Tuatnatuit kiagpak uqurturkateng. Cali-ll' tamakunek uqunek pikalget tuneniarrarkameggnek ilaqerluki cali neqliyaucetuluki.

~: *Neqlilleq* :~

Tua-i caarkairutaqameng nutaan neqliyarluteng. Nunameggnek up'nerkiyallret tamakut angyateng aqvauqurluki cali caarkairtaqameng. Nutaan tua-i neqliyatuut tuaten piaqameng, caarkairutaqameng. Kiagpak-llu tua-i neqlillerni uitaluteng. Tua-i-ll' neqet makut qemagcamegteki uterqaqengluteng, qakiiyiarkat taugaam unkarluteng, qakiiyarnek piarkat. Neqtateng taugaam qaniigaqluki uksillernun ut'rulluki kinrumarilriit caqumarilriit. Qakiiyil̥uteng taugken tua-i qemagcamegteki-ll' tua-i qemagqaarluki nutaan uterrluteng. Uksillmeggnun taugken piarkat engellicuunateng.

of adult bearded-seal blubber, cook them, preparing them into *uullat*. They mostly prepared them that way back when they had dogs, since they used to let dogs eat cooked bearded-seal blubber.

When there was no longer any oil and blubber to process, they dried [the skins], and they also kept a close eye on their seal pokes, turning over the pokes filled with seal oil, and marking the ones that were filled with walrus meat, and the ones filled with seal hands and feet, and the ones filled with *cuakayiit* [cooked seal lungs and livers mixed with seal oil], and the ones filled with ringed-seal oil, spotted-seal oil, and the ones filled with the oils of bearded seals in their first year and adult bearded seals. They would sew something onto their *pasvaagutet*, marking them with something that wouldn't come off.

They prepare *cuakayiit* by cooking [seal lungs and livers], adding seal oil to them, and placing them in seal pokes. They called those *cuakayiit*. And they added livers to them, and cooked them as well. They cut them into small pieces. They add seal oil when they make those, either ringed-seal oil or bearded-seal oil. Presently, they no longer prepare those *cuakayiit*. They no longer prepare them.

They are sour. You know the pigs' feet prepared in the Western way. The sour taste of *cuakayiit* in seal pokes is strong like them. But they enjoyed eating them because it was their food, even though they were sour.

Then when it was time, they placed them inside *uquucillret* [underground seal-oil caches]. When they put them inside, they didn't include the seal oil they would eat all summer, but set them aside with the stomach containers filled with oil. They do that with the seal oil that they would eat all summer. And those who had enough seal oil would set aside some seal oil for trading and bring them to their summer fish camps.

~: Summer fish camp :~

When they had no work left, they went to cut and dry fish at their summer fish camps. When they no longer had work to do, the ones who moved from their villages to the spring camps retrieved their boats. Then they went to their fish camps when they no longer had work to do. Then they stayed in their fish camps all summer. After storing their fish, they started returning home, but the ones who would fish for silver salmon would stay behind. But they would take the fish that they harvested, dried, and placed in storage containers home to their winter camps. They then fished for silver salmon. After storing them away, they returned home. But the ones who were moving to their fall camps wouldn't return home.

~: *Uksuilleq* :~

Wangkuta-w'imkut wii angliviinka Kuigilngurmun tekilluteng [pillrunritut], Ilkivigmun arulaitullruut, Ilkiviim pakmani avvenrani kangrani uksuitullruamta. Tuavet
piarkat neqet asguulluki tuavet uksuillernun. Muragnek-llu tua-i asguuquriluteng
tuavet, nutaan-llu uqut ukut tangerrluki uksillmeggnun amavet Kuigilngurmun agluteng uqut iliitnek tegulluteng uksuillermeggnun call' piarkameng, ukut uitavkarluki tamaani nunam akuliini.

Cali-am neqsurluteng tuani ceturrnanek Ilkivigmi. Arnat taugaam nallmegteggun neqsurluteng, imkunek qalurpagnek uksuarmi [aturluteng]. Tua-i ceturrnanek kinernernek amllernek unangluteng. Tua-i tuatnaaqameng nutaan uqumel-
nguucituut.

Cali-am caqutnek pikameggnek upcimalrianek up'nerkami taqutellruameng
tua-i, tamakunun tamaa-i ekluki. Nutaan uqumek egnermek kuvluki miiraqluki
caqutem iluanun. Uqumelnguucituteng. Tua-i-llu muirata, qavcinek-llu cetamanek-
llu *poke*-anek waten piirrallugnek uqumelnguuciaqameng, ilait ukut uksillernun
agulluki nutaan ellivignun tua-i nutaan piaqluki taliyucirluki, uugnarnun-llu pingairutelluki. Tuatnatuluki, naternautet-llu cali agulluki cali.

Nutaan-llu tua-i cikuviqungarcan, nutaan uksuillemtenun tuavet asgurluta, catai-
rulluku tua-i tauna. Tua-i uksuarpak tuani uksuillerni uitaluta, can'giirnek tua-i neqsurluteng cali, melqulegnek tuaten. Uksuillerni kanaqlagnek atkugkanek, imarmiutarnek atkugkanek naarqiluteng. Cuignilngurtaqluteng. Paluqtaat piiyuitellruut
avani un'gaani nunamteni.

Imarmiutarnek tua-i atkungqetuut uksuillernek utertaqameng arnat caliaqaqamegteki. Arnat atkukellruit imarmiutaat cuignilnguut-llu. Nutaranek tamakunek
atkuliqutullruut.

Cam-wa nalliini, December-aam-wa iluani maani ayagnillrani taugaam kacete-
tullrulriit uksillernun. Cali uksuillerni ellivililuteng waten ayuqelrianek nunam
qaingani nunapigmi. Naparyak ukuk kapullukek, aglirlukek, pagna, qalirluku-ll'
tua-i waten ayuqelriamek, qupuumanrilngurnek muragnek; ciqunek taugaam, ciqunek pirpalluulartut. Nunamek-llu tua-i nutaan maaken angluki, kiitaarpallraat,
amirluki tamakut elliviit, *camp*-ani pavani. Nutaan can'giirnek imirluk kumlanek,
kumlaskainek, muirluki tua-i kaceteqatarqameng uksillmeggnun, tamaaken *camp*-
ameggnek upakata'arqameng. Can'giirutnek amllernek call' tua-i. Tua-i taugken aqvauqurluki tua-i can'giirutailnguut makut cikiraqluki cali avegvilegnek unangaqa-
meng, tuatnatuluteng.

~: *Fall camp* :~

The people who I grew up with didn't return home to Kwigillingok, but they stopped at the Ilkivik River because we used to go fall camping on a tributary of the upper part of the Ilkivik River. We would go upriver to bring the fish to the fall camp. And then they took logs upriver to that place, and they would check on their supply of seal oil and travel to Kwigillingok to their winter village to take some of their seal oil supply to their fall camps, leaving the other seal-oil containers underground.

They fished again for tomcod in the Ilkivik River. Only the women fished, using those *qalurpiit* [large dip nets without frames or handles] during falltime. They harvested a lot of dried tomcod. When they did that, they prepared [dried tomcod] in seal oil.

Since they had already prepared sealskin pokes during spring, they placed [the dried tomcod] inside them. Then they poured rendered seal oil inside the seal pokes. They prepared dried tomcod in seal oil. Then when they were filled, when they had filled a number of them, or even four pokes filled with dried tomcod soaked in seal oil, they brought some to their winter village, and they placed them in caches and covered them and secured them so that mice wouldn't get to them. That's what they did, and they also brought over containers filled with prepared, dried flounders.

Then when it started to freeze [and all the fish had been put away], we'd finally go upriver to our fall camp. We stayed in our fall camp all winter, and harvested blackfish and hunted and trapped fur animals. They would hunt muskrat and mink and get enough to make parkas. They caught otters. There weren't any beavers in our area on the coast at that time.

They had mink parkas when they returned home from fall camps when women sewed them. Women used mink and otter skins for parkas. They used to make new parkas out of those skins.

They gathered in their winter villages, probably during the beginning of December from the fall camps. In their fall camps, they also built storage caches like this on the tundra. They would stake two posts up and place a beam up there, and they would put on roof boards that looked like this out of unsplit cottonwood driftwood logs; they mostly used cottonwood driftwood. Then they got those large chunks of pried sod from the ground to cover those storage caches out in those inland camps. They then filled them with frozen blackfish, filling them full when they were about to move from their fall camps and gather in their winter villages. They also harvested a lot of blackfish. Then they would go back and forth and get them and give to those who had no blackfish when they had caught enough to share.

Cali tua-i aqvauqulteng nangkata nutaan, *camp*-ateng tamakut kitugtaqluki assircarluki, camun pingairutell'uki, itqetaayunairutell'uki, tamaantarkat taugaam. Taluyat-llu nutaan iluvauqurluki; anguterrlainaululuteng ullagluki qavartaraluteng. *Camp*-ami atutukteng ut'ruqaqluki ellivigmun tuavet itertaqluki, enem-llu iluanun piaqluki piyunarqelriit. Umegluku-ll' tua-i nutaan unilluku.

~: Uksillernun uterrluteng pilallrat :~

Nantellret tua-i uksuillret uterqaqaqluteng. Piciryarangqellruut taugaam waten uksillernun utertaqameng uksuarmi. Tamarmirtaqameng nunameggni, nanelngurtairutaqan, kalukaqutuut-am kalukaqutullruut. Tua-i tamana pitekluku tua-i quyungqatuut, uksuillernek-llu uterqaqluteng tua-i tuavet. Tua-i nanelnguirucameng nutaan tamana aturluku, tua-i Alussistuatullinilriit tamatumek. Tamatuuluni tua-i. Imkut unangkengateng, up'nerkamek ayagluku unangkengateng ilangarqurluki, uksullran tuavet engeliinun. Can'giirtateng nangneqluki pissutuameng allrakum iluani augkut murilkellemni. Tamakut ilangarqurluki unangkengateng. *Family*-t tua-i tamalkurmeng tua-i neqnek qasgimun nerevkariluteng. Tua-i piciryaraqluku tuaten. Pinricuunateng.

Makut-llu imkut cali neqlilluki-gguq apqiitnek. Waten makut, nulirqelriik-llu ukuk irniarak yuunrilleq, yuum allam irniaran ateqluku, tauna tua-i irniamek piunrillrem atqestii, angutem uum neqlitarkauluku. Neqkiurtelluk' assilrianek tua-i neqkegtaarnek, aklunek-llu tapirluku ilukegcitkainek, quyatekainek. Tua-i-llu itrucamiu, angayuqaagken akuliignun aqumevkarluku, mermek-llu cikiqertelluni. Tua-i-ll' qantaq tauna piaku, aviukarqevkarluku tuavet, taukut qantam imaitnek aviukaqluni mermek-llu taumek. Nutaan-llu qaqicata mertelluku. Tua-i-gguq neqlilluku. Amlleret tua-i tuaten pituluteng cali arnaungermeng-llu tua-i tuatnatuluteng. Tamaa-i tamana call' piciryarallrat, piciryaraqluku tua-i tamana.

Natermun piiyuitait, tutmallrunrilngurmun taugaam. Elakaulluki nunamun pituit, piciatun pivkenateng. Enem-wa iluani tuani, maani marayaullilria nateq.

Ukut curut-llu engelaitnun unavet, nuna tungaiqerluku, pakikarluku, aviukarqetuut. Yuilqurrungraan-llu tua-i alerquutekluku yuilqumi piciryaraqluku-am cali. Nunam yui qalarulluki cali aviukarqetuluteng. Tauna iqvallerkarteng-llu pisqumaluku, maniitesqelluteng-llu piaqluteng piyukengameggnek. Qanengssagluteng aviukaqtuut tuaten. Iqvalrianun-llu maligut'langama tua-i niicugniaqluki tuatnaaqata.

When all the food had been retrieved, they secured their fall camps and closed up the dwellings so that nothing would get into them, only leaving things that would be kept there. After that, they began bringing the fish traps to their winter village; only men would go and [gather their traps], spending a night out on the land. They would bring home all the implements they used at fall camp and store them inside the cache, and they stored some inside the home. Then they'd close it up and leave.

~: Return to the winter village :~

People who had stayed in various fall camps returned home. They had a tradition though, when they returned home to their winter villages in the fall. When everyone had returned to their village, they held a community feast. That was why people gathered and returned to their villages. When everyone was present in the village, they held [the feast], just like Christmas. That's what it was. They used food they had harvested since spring up until winter. When I watched them, the last thing they got each year was blackfish. They'd take a little from each of the foods they had harvested. All of the families would bring food to the *qasgi* to share with everyone. That was their tradition. They always did that.

And they also practiced a ceremony they called *neqlilluki* [offering food and water to the spirits of the deceased]. For instance, if a couple had lost a child, and another couple named their child after the child who died, the [father of the deceased] would do a ceremony [to honor the namesake]. [His wife] prepared delicious foods along with articles of clothing the child would appreciate. Then when [the man] brought [the child] inside, he would let the child sit between his parents and ask for a little bit of water. And when the bowl of food was delivered, he then let [the child] give an offering. He gave an offering from the food and water. When he was done, he let the child drink the water, *neqlilluku*, as they call it. Many people practiced that ceremony, including women. It was another custom they followed in the past.

They didn't put [the offerings] on the floor but only where it wouldn't be stepped on. They dug a small hole in the ground and placed the offerings inside, and not just anywhere. It was placed in the ground inside the house.

They also placed an offering along the edge of the bedding, exposing the ground and prying it open a little. That was a custom that was practiced, even out on the land. They spoke to the spirits of the land, *nunam yui*, and gave an offering. They asked that they be presented with berries or things they wanted. They speak in that way when they give offerings. And when I began accompanying berry pickers, I listened to them when they [gave offerings and asked for things].

Tuamtellu wangkuta unavet imarpigmun atraqarraaraqamta tamana atunricuunaku, aviukaqsaraq. Qalarulluki cali imarpigmiutaat, piyukengamtenek cikiumasqelluta. Tuaten tua-i piciryaraqellruat tamana. Tuaten tua-i atutuluku.

Tua-i-ll' nutaan aug'um tuatnallermeng kinguani yuraryaraq nutaan yagulluku, nerevkarillermeng kinguani ayagnirluku. Quyurrluteng-am cali *meeting*-aarluteng qasgimi anguterrlainaat, *elder*-aat ilakluki tamakut. Tua-i picirkaq-llu taqngan yuugnek nutaan malrugnek nunanun nutaan ayagceciluteng. Tua-i-ll' taukut piyugluteng piata yurararkaurrluteng. Tua-i taukut nuniitnun tailuteng.

Tua-i-llu cali tamana ut'raruciyaraq aturyukunegteggu taukut kelkengaita piiyuutekluku cali ukunun kelegtemeggnun. Nunameggni yurarraarluteng, ellait nuniitni nunameggnun agluki cali yuraasqumaluki. Tamaa-i ut'raruciyaraq-gguq tamaa-i. Amkut piiyuutektuluku caaqameng ukunun kelegtemeggnun. Tua-i tuatnatuluteng iliini. Atunrilatgu taugken nunameggni tamarkenka yuraryaraq aturluku. Allanret yurarluteng nunalget-llu yurarluteng cali.

Ut'rarulluteng taugken piiyuiceteng ukut kelegtellrit yurarpek'nateng, allanrit nallmegteggun yurarluteng. Utercata-llu ukut nuniitnun agluteng nunalget kelegtellrit yuraryarturluteng. Ut'rarulluki-gguq tua-i. Tamana piciryaraqluku cali.

~: Cilkiayaraq :~

Natret-llu cali carriraqluki unkut, nateq carangllugnek qalliliqerluk'. Tua-i tangerrluku carriraqluku. Wangkuta-w' pilallrukput tamaani. Kiimeteksaitelalrianga-ll' alerquutekngamteggu. Unugmi tua-i kangaraqluta. Pirciraqan-llu amiiget nunat qanikcamek imircetengnaqenriqu'urluki unugpak, ercan-llu tua-i nutaan qavarluta.

Cilkialuteng-gguq.

Piciryarallerput-wa. Tumyarani-llu waten camek tekiskuni, egmian cali calligarterrlainaasqelluku. Kesianek amiiget-llu carrirturluki, cat piurluki. Pinauraitkut imarpigmi kanani anguarinanemteni cikum quugaruciiqaakut aipaagni. Piiyuilkumta-gguq tuaten, qes'arucunqegciqaakut mermi imarpigmi ayagviircetaqluta.

And again, when we were about to go down to the ocean for the first time, we always gave an offering of food and water. We also spoke to the spirits of the ocean and asked that we be given what we wanted. That was a custom that was practiced. That's how they practiced it.

Then after that initial feasting, they started getting ready for dance festivals and ceremonies. All men gathered in the *qasgi* to have a meeting, along with the elders. When the discussion was over and the decision was made, they sent two men out to a village [to invite them to a festival]. Then when [that village] accepted the invitation, they were set to have the dance festival. The [invited village] would come [to the host village for the festival].

And if the two villages agreed, the guests would invite the hosts to come to their village for a festival. They would ask the host village to come to their village and dance after having the festival in their village. They call that *ut'raruciyaraq* [from *ut'rarute-*, "to pay back, to reciprocate"]. Sometimes that's what the invited guests requested from their hosts. That's what [the two villages] did sometimes. And when they didn't do that, both villages would dance and distribute gifts at the same time [in the host village]. The guests would dance [one night], and the host village would dance [the next day].

But if the guests wanted the hosts to come to their village to dance, only the invited guests would dance and not the hosts. And when [the guests] returned home, the host village would travel to their village to dance. They called it *ut'rarulluki*. That was also their custom.

~: *Rigorous training to become a good hunter* :~

And [in the *qasgit* and homes] they cleaned the floors down below and put down a little layer of new grass. They would clean and replace [the grass] when they saw the need. We boys did that work back then. I wasn't the only one who worked because we were all instructed to help like that. We would walk around at night, [working and helping]. And when there was a blizzard, we tried not to let the snow fill up the passages into houses and worked all night long, finally going to sleep at daybreak.

They called it *cilkialuteng* [going through rigorous training to become good hunters].

That was what we always did. And when one came upon something along the pathways people used, he was told to always set it aside immediately. And they always cleaned the passages into dwellings, always taking care of things that needed to be done. They told us that if we were down on the ocean in a kayak, ice might

Taugken-gguq carrirturatukumteggu man'a tumyarat-llu tuatnamaangaunata imarpigmi. Cali-llu tangerqayuluta-gguq pitarkanek. Tua-i-gguq tamana pisqutiit caliaqngamteggu, carrirturluku man' tumkarput, atu'urkaq.

Qasgi alerquutekluku cali. Egalengqetullruut qasgit pikaggun irnerrlugnek teggalqunek nanerterluteng. Tamakut tamaa-i egalirturatulit-gguq qalricuut. Tamakuculuteng. Tuamtell' nacitait qasgit, kenilleq kan' maqirraartelluki, aruvairucanllu, egalirraarluku itrameng, nacicirluku, elliluki nacitai. Tuatnauratulit-gguq-am cikum qaingani maklagnek qavalrianek nalleksuluteng. Ugtarcuyuluteng-gguq nacicirturatulit. Tuaten qaneryarartangqerraqluni. Tua-i tamakunek piiyuumiuterluni yuk cilkiatuluni, tamakutaqluni yuuyugyaaqluni; qalriculuni wall' ugtarcuyuluni.

~: *Angun imarpigmi qayailleq* :~

Pulengtaq qanemciknauraat tauna angun imarpigmi qayailleq, cikumi pugtalriami qayaa tenglluku. Atreskiin tua-i qaingani uitaluni, negcigmek taugaam tegumiarluni. Tamatum-gguq ciungani qasgim-llu kangiplui carrirturatukai net-llu natrita curuluit can'get uqlangraata tegularluki tua-i pituluki. Neryuniuruterluni-llu-gguq tua-i qaillun tamakut atuugarkauciit nalluamiki, canun atuugarkauciat pitekluku alerquatngulauciitnek.

Caqerluni pilliniuq qagaani Qaluyaat elatiitni, tuaq paugna nunamun tekisngalria navguumanrilnguq alaillinilria, negetmun-gguq ayaulluku carvanrem. Mallguirucani tua-i pugtalrianun cikunun, piyunarqelriakun qeckarluni angenra-llu imna tauna atreskii qaingakun ayalliniluni. Iqua tekicartullinia, aivkangqaluni ciku, akiqlini augna canimenaku.

Tekitellinia, aqvaqurluni-llu qeckang'ermi nuruciiqellinilria, allataunani-llu una avatii. Tungiinun-llu quungiinarpek'nani. Utqetaarluni-am piinanermini piqalliniuq mer'em akuliini tungulria. Ullagluki pilliniuq, qaillun tua-i aciqsigtaluni, qaillun-gguq iqtutaluni. Cauciinaku, tagumaluni-llu uavet cikumun agaavet tekisnganganani. Negciminek-llu tua-i tugauryaaqellinikii asvaitqapiarluni. Cuqyutlinia-

move in and block our way. They said if we didn't [continually clean and clear pathways and passages], ice would tend to impede us and prevent us from going forward. But if we always cleared the surrounding pathways, that wouldn't happen to us out on the ocean. And they said that it would be easy for us to spot animals because we had followed their instruction, continually clearing the pathways we used.

We were also instructed to do work in the *qasgi*. The window coverings for the skylights in the *qasgit* were made out of seal gut, with stones on the sides to weigh them down. They say those who always replaced the coverings on the skylight [after fire baths] are good at catching bearded seals that are mating. They are good at catching those. And after a fire bath, when the smoke dissipated, after replacing the window covering, they would put the floor planks back over the fire pit. They say those who always did that were good at finding bearded seals asleep on the ice. Ones who always put the floor planks down were good at catching seals lying on the ice. Instructions like that were mentioned. A person would go through rigorous training, hoping to become good at catching bearded seals giving their mating calls or bearded seals lying on the ice.

~: *A man who lost his kayak down on the ocean* :~

Many times they told about a man who lost his kayak down on the ocean; his kayak was blown when it was on floating ice. He was on an ice floe with just his gaff. It is said that before that time he had always cleaned out the charcoal in the *qasgi* and the grass matting in the houses with his bare hands, even though they were dirty. It is said that he anticipated finding out the reason behind those instructions, since he did not know their purpose, and that he was eager to know the consequence of following those instructions.

One day, up north outside of Nelson Island, he saw what appeared to be unbroken shore ice that reached the land, and the floe he was on was being moved in a northerly direction by the current. When the current brought him close to the floating ice, he jumped from floe to floe where he could, and walked on top of a large floe. Approaching the edge, he saw that the ice was cracked, and it was close to the ice on the other side.

When he reached the edge of the ice, he estimated that even if he ran and jumped he wouldn't be able to make it across the gap, but he saw that there were no other places to cross nearby. And the gap between the two pieces of ice wasn't closing either. While walking back and forth, he saw something dark in the water. He went to it and saw that it was at a certain depth, and was a certain width. He was not

am maatekaaryugngallinilria ekekuni. Tamatumek tua-i pirraarluni atralliniluni qainganun. Cauciinaku tua-i tamana tungulria tua-i tamana ayaruminek piurluku qeralliniluni. Aterrluni-gguq taugken aterrluni, un'a-llu maligulluni tungulria. Ciku-mun-am tekicami ciisqumiggluni qainganun mayulliniluni. Nangerteqanrakun-am llerr'allalliniluni kingunra. Kingyaartelliniuq kangipluut makut pugleqralriit. Ka-ngipluullinilriit tamakut imarpigmi unani, imkut carrilallri, ciqitelallri!

Tangvakarraarluki taugaam ayalliniluni-am tua-i, paug'um uitalriim tungiinun cikut aturluki. Tua-i piyunarqelriamun qeckarluni cikumun piaqluni. Cikumun-am mat'umun pirraarluni aturluki iqua nanglliniuq-am. Aqvaqurluni-am ping'ermi nu-rucugngaluni, tuamun paug'umun nunamun tekisngaluni cikusngakiinun, pektenril-ngurmun. Caq'iqtaarluni-am piinanermini pilliniuq cat-am augkut mer'em akuliini, augkutun ayuqevkenateng, qatqetaarluteng-gguq cat augkut. Ullagluki-am pillinii, cat-am unkut unani mer'em akuliini. Negciminek-am piluku tugauryaaqellinii, as-vaitqapiarluteng. Nugcamiu cuqtellinia, aciqsinruurallinilriit tamakuni.

Tua-i-am qalucugnganrilagnek ivrucigni, nengkanirraarlukek-am ayaruni pi-luku ekliniluni qaingatnun. Aug'utun-am tugaurturluki tua-i tag'uralliniluni tua-mun pavavet. Atertengraani-am tua-i, uitangraan, unkut atuqengai maligulluteng, paugna-llu unisngiinaqsaunaku tuaq. Tuamun-am tekicami piyugngariami tua-i ayapqerluni ciisqumikun mayurtelliniluni. Mayurteqanrakun-am llerr'allallinilu-teng pamkut. Kingyaartellinii caranglluut!

Tua-i elitaqa'artelliniluki natrem pii imkut carrilallri. Nutaan umyuarteqliniuq, "Makunun cunawa aturarkaulliniata alerquatek'lallrukait!"

Taum-gguq tua-i arcaqerluni qalarutkelallrui qalarucimaaqata tamakunek piciun-ricukluki umyuarteqeksaunaki niicugnilaasqelluki. Tua-i kingunilluni tamaavet, ta-makutgun tamakut aturluki, qeraraqluni tuani. Caranglluut-gguq tua-i tamakut aciqsinrulliniut, kangipluut-llu quyinruluteng. Tamakunek-am tua-i qalaruqaar-luta qanemcitullruitkut taumek. Avani cat irr'inarqellriit amllellruyugnarqut ayuq-luteng tuaten.

sure what it was, and he noticed that it was at the ice edge down there and that it appeared to reach to the ice across there. He jabbed it with his gaff to test it, and it was very stable. He estimated how far down it was, and it seemed that if he got on it, it would reach up to here on his legs, and so he got on it after ascertaining its safety. He did not know what the black substance was, but he crossed on it, jabbing it to check its stability as he crossed. But he saw that it was drifting, that the dark part was drifting. When he reached the ice on the other side, he kneeled on its rim and climbed up on the ledge. Just as he stood up, there was a blast of sound of churning water behind him. When he glanced back he saw a lot of charcoal coming to the surface. Lo and behold there was charcoal down there on the ocean, the charcoal that he had cleaned out in the past, the very ones he had dumped in the past!

After watching them for a while he continued going toward the shorefast ice, jumping the distance that he was able to from ice floe to ice floe. When he went onto a particular sheet of ice, he followed it and reached the end of it. Upon estimating the distance across to the shorefast ice, he realized that he would not be able to jump that far, even with a running start. As he walked back and forth searching for a place to cross, he saw an indeterminate object in the water, but it was mixed with some light colored matter. When he went to it he jabbed at it with his gaff, and he found that it was very solid. When he pulled his gaff out of the water, he measured its depth in the water and saw it was deeper than where [the charcoal] had been.

Seeing that his waterproof boots would not get water in them, he pulled them up, and then using his gaff he went into the water on top of that thing. As he had done previously he went toward the shorefast ice, checking his path as he walked along. Although he was drifting along with that thing, it wasn't getting farther away from the shorefast ice. When he got to the shorefast ice and was able to do it, he lifted himself up with his arms and pulled himself up using his knees. Just as he got up, that thing made a loud churning sound. He looked back and saw that it was old grass debris!

He recognized them as the old grass debris that he cleaned from the floors. He finally understood and thought, "So that's why they gave us that precept since they can be useful in such circumstances!"

When these maxims were conveyed to the young, it is said that one had stressed the importance of heeding that precept about cleaning debris without questioning it. He made it home using the charcoal and old grass debris that he had cleaned out to get across the gaps. They said that grass debris was at a lower level and charcoal was at a higher level. After they gave that precept, they used to tell us that story. There were probably many astonishing things in the past, such as this one.

Imarpigmiutaat

~: Makliit :~

Makliit makut amllertut. Qaralingqertut ayuqenrilngurnek aterluteng-llu ayu-qevkenateng. Amlleq taugaam tangrruuyuituq maani; nurnartut ilait. Imkut-llu ungalget takqupagnek, pegtaqameng qungagartaqluteng waten. Pug'aqameng tuar keggmiangqelalriit, ungait *curl*-aumaluteng. Nengugtellriani tak'aqluteng waten. Peg'artellriani qungagarrluteng waten. Waten tua-i ayuqluteng. Keggempalalriit tuar' pug'aqameng, ungait angqatun ayuqluteng waten. Nurnarluteng taugaam. Ungagciiret-ggut tamaa-i, maklauluteng taugken.

Augkut-wa cali amllellriit, mermek nugtellriani, tua-i-ll' meq qaingatni ellnga-nga'arcan, ukatmun melqurrit pet'ngartarluteng waten, qaralirluteng waten akul-tutauralrianek qaingit kepelmun. Meriucartuan qaingat pet'ngartaqluteng tamakut. Tua-i-ll' qainganun kinran uunguciirulluteng tayima. Nemercauget-gguq tamaa-i. Ii-i, nemercauget, maklauluteng taugken.

Tuamtell' augkut yaalirtaat tungupiat makliit angtuat nutaan, tulukarugtun qai-ngit ayuqluteng. Aqsait-llu qat'rissagluteng. Angluteng, angenruluteng tamakut maklaullgutmeggni. Yaalirtaat-gguq. Qevleq qaingit tua-i kinrumaaqata, qevlerpak. Tulukaruut tua-i qaingit tunguluteng. Yaalirtaat-gguq tamaa-i.

Ayugesviit tuamtell' augkut ukuit engellekluki, talliquteng man'a engelekluku ka-vircetqapiarluni qamiqurra tua-i, kavirlimek tuar' nacartulalriit pug'aqameng.

Ayugesvignek. Atellgutkenritut. Cali angluteng tamakut taugaam tamakuni yaa-lirtani mikellruurluteng. Augkut tua-i nemercauget pitacqegtut. Amllertut maani tamakut.

Augkut-wa cali waken ayagluni tunguqapiarluteng tua-i aqsait makut uatmun. Tulignat-gguq. Makliit qaralirluteng tua-i waken ayagluni tunguqapiarmek makut aqsait, qaingit taugken tua-i *gray*-aaruluteng paugkut. Tulignat-gguq.

Tuamtell' augkut kuimatulit nevermeng. Makliit nevermeng kuimaraqluteng waten elliurluteng. Cikumun-llu tekicameng palurrluteng mayurluteng, pangaleg-luteng, qerarluku mermun-llu piameng atrarluteng. Pugngameng-llu neverrluteng.

22

Sea Mammals

~: *Bearded seals* :~

There are many bearded seals. They have different patterns on their fur, and they all have different names. We don't see many of them here though; some are rare. And there are those that have long whiskers that curl up when released. When they came out of the water, they appeared as though they had something big hanging out of their mouths with their whiskers all curled up. When you pull [their whiskers], they are very long like this. When you let go, they curl back up. That's how they looked. They looked like they had large things in their mouths when they came up in water, with their rolled-up whiskers looking like balls. But they are rarely seen. They called them *ungagciiret*, but they are actually bearded seals.

And there are many of those others that when pulled out of the water, when the surface water on their bodies begins to flow down, their fur springs up in this direction, and they have lengthwise designs on their bodies, about so far apart. As the water slid down and began to disappear, their fur would spring up. And when their body dried the fur would return to normal. They call those *nemercauget*. Yes, *nemercauget*, but they are bearded seals.

And the *yaalirtaat* are very large, dark bearded seals that look like ravens. And their bellies are a little whitish. They are larger than the other bearded seals. They call them *yaalirtaat*. Their fur shines when it's dry, very shiny and dark like raven feathers. They call those *yaalirtaat*.

Then there are those *ayugesviit*, where this part of their bodies, their heads down to their front flippers, is very red, and they appear as though they are wearing red hats when they surface from the water.

They are called *ayugesviit*. [Bearded seals] have different names. Those are also large but a little smaller than the *yaalirtaat*. Those *nemercauget* are just right in size. There are many of those here.

And then there are those that have very dark bellies toward the bottom of their bodies. They call those bearded seals *tulignat*. They are bearded seals that are very dark on their bellies, but they are gray on top. They call them *tulignat*.

Then there are those that swim on their backs. Bearded seals that swim on their backs, making this motion. And when they get to the ice, they turn over on their bellies and climb up and gallop across, and then when they get to the water, they

Qavarningelriit-gguq tua-i tuaten pituut tamakucit. Allakat-am cali, papangluat-gguq. Papangluanek aterluteng. Tamakucimek-gguq tua-i tangerqumta pitsaqev-kenak' maligqurrararkaugarput. Atam-gguq tua-i ayainanermini cikumun mayur-piirluni arulairluni qavarniartuq. Nutaan pissuusqaat tuatnakan. Papangluat-gguq tamakut.

Tumatellu-gguq ilait makliit qaillun ayuqsaaqelriit, qavarnaurtut tua-i-ll' uica-meng, paivciqataameng, paivciameng, avatseng kiarteqataamegteggu, qalemluteng waten wavet taugaam inglumeggnun tusngaurluteng. Qalemluteng, it'gait wanllu-teng qamiqurit-llu. Uivluteng-gguq taugken tua-i waten ayuqluteng, pamatmun, pamatmun waten qinerrluteng, kiarrluk' un'a avatseng. Uivluteng waten. Tuaten ayuqluteng. Kassuameng-llu-gguq tua-i nutaan saggluk' inarrluteng qavarluteng. Ipuuyulit-gguq tamaa-i. Ipuuyulit.

Imkut paivciuratuut tua-i, pugtat-llu tamakut. Tua-i uigarrluteng avatseng kiar-quaqaqluku. Pamna arcaqerluku tunuseng alikenruat. Taumek tunuitgun ullaas-qessuilkait, tangvaurtelluteng taugaam. Tangvaurtelluta tua-i ullagaqluki. Aliken-ruat-gguq tunuseng pamna. Tangvaurluku-gguq taugken alikenrillruluku. Tuaten alerquutengqertut.

Augkut tuamtell' uuggun un'um aciakun kep'alget iqtulriamek tungulriamek. Cauciitellrukvuk tang. Aiparma tua-i cauciilkii, maklauyaaqniluku taugken qaner-luni. Cauciinaku taugaam tua-i. Camek atengqerruciinaku.

Cali taugaam aug'umek tangellruunga, maklacugmek-gguq. Maklacuk. Mik'nani tua-i naninani. Maklassuugartun angtaluni. Amtall' qamiqurluni maklinrarmek, te-mircinrarmek. Unaterluni-ll' temircinrarnek it'garluni-ll' qiluluni-ll' uqua-w' call' ka-virpak. Temircinraq maklinraq, amta-ll' mik'nani. Maklacuut-gguq tamaa-i. Tama-kucimek tangellruunga cali. Mik'nani tua-i naninani. Amtall' qingarluni. Ing'um Kangirnarmium, Frank Mute-am pitaanek. Tuaten tua-i amllertangatut ukut mak-liit, aterpagtelallrit.

Qununillernek cali pitangqelliniuq. Ing'um Angutekaraam Atii qununillermek maklagtellruuq maani. Yuut-gguq keggasgitnek keggasengqertut. Yuugut-gguq ta-makut qununit.

Ukinengqertut-gguq imkut keggasgit. Tamakucimek-gguq tamaa-i maklagtell-ruuq Tanqiulria makumiu, qununillermek.

go underwater again. When they surface, they go on their backs again. They say that the ones that get sleepy do that. They are also different, and they call them *papangluat*. They said if we happened to see one like that, we should follow it. They said that it will climb on top of the ice after awhile and stop and sleep. They say to hunt it when it does that. They called those *papangluat*.

Then there is another kind of bearded seal that would sleep, and when they woke, when they were about to look at their surroundings, they curled up [on their stomachs], leaning on one side of their bodies, curling their bodies with their head and hind flippers touching. Then they turned all the way around, looking behind them, scanning their surroundings. They turned around in a circle in that position. That's what they did. And after they turned all the way around, they lay down to sleep. They call those *ipuuyulit* [from *ipug-*, "to move with one's front high in the air"].

Those mentioned earlier always search their surroundings, and those just mentioned also do that while floating in the water. They wake from sleep and quickly check the area around them from time to time. They are particularly wary of the area behind them. That's why they say not to approach them from behind, only from the front with our eyes on them constantly. We would approach them with them watching us. They say they are more afraid of the area behind them. But they are less afraid when we approach from the front, facing them. That was the instruction given to us [for hunting them].

Then there are those that have a wide, dark, lengthwise design under this part down there. We didn't know what it was. The person with me also didn't know what it was, but he said that it was actually a bearded seal. But he didn't know what it was. He didn't know what it was called.

But there is also another kind I saw that they called *maklacuk*. It was small and short. It was as big as a two-year-old bearded seal. But its head was as big as an adult bearded seal. And its hands and feet and intestines were the same size as an adult bearded seal, and its blubber was also very red. It was an adult, but it was small. They call those *maklacuut*. I've seen one of those as well. It was small and short. And yet it was pregnant. I saw one that Frank Mute from Kongiganak caught. I think that is how many bearded seals there are, the ones that they identified.

Evidently there are also those *qununillret* [ones that had been *qununit* (bearded seals that are humans)]. Angutekaraam Atii [Roland Phillip's father] caught a bearded seal that was referred to as a *qununilleq*. It is said they have shoulder blades that are exactly like a human's. They say those *qununit* are people.

They say their shoulder blades have holes in them. They say Tanqiulria from this village caught one of those bearded seals, a *qununilleq*.

Nepaitnek taugaam niirqelallruukut wani. Nutem-gguq wani tuatnatuut. Nep-
liratuut-gguq caaqameng, uurallrit (niitnaqluteng). Qastulriamek-gguq niiskumta
qununimek canimecukluku umyuarteqsaqunata. Yaaqsigaqameng-gguq qastutuut
nepait. Canimelameng-gguq taugken qaskitkacagarluteng. Ircenrraungameng-gguq
irranarqut tamakut. Pitaqesteteng-gguq uitacuitait. Tuqutaqluki pitaqesteteng qununillret tamakut, qununit. Inerquutaqkait taumek, tamakucimek pingramta pisqevkenaku.

Yuuluteng-gguq ilait pituut, imarnitnek, ivrucinek aturluteng, arillugturluteng-
llu. Ugingaluteng-gguq pilrianek ilait tangtullruut maklagnek, cururluteng maklagnek cikum qaingani. Elqiamek-llu aturluteng muragmek imumek. Imarnitegnek-
llu aturluteng, arillugluteng-llu, ivrucirluteng-llu. Akuat-gguq taugken cagingaluni
waten maavet. Uurata-gguq taugken ak'a waten elliuksuarturluni tamana mengliit,
patgumallra. Ciuggluteng-gguq uutuut paivciaqameng. Yuuluteng-gguq taugken
tua-i.

Tua-i-llu-gguq narulkaqataamegteki, imarnitet imkut mingqellrita taqellratgun,
akuatgun kanaggun, mingqenrirluki tua-i taqellratgun, tuaggun tua-i cavegmek
narulkarluki, temiikun pivkenaku. Tua-i narulkaqani-gguq curuni tauna, curuan
taum qes'arrluku mermun qecngarkauluni.

Angalkut-gguq taugaam pitaqsugngait. Yuunginaat-gguq piyunaitait. Alingnar-
qelliniut-am tamakut. Cat-gguq ayuqenritellruut avani ciuqvani. Imkut-llu qungut,
qungunek unani cikum qaingani ugtarciaqluteng avani ciuqvani, tauna ugtarciyaa-
qelleq alingengami tua-i elitaqngamikek qunguulliniagnek arulairluni. Uitaqanran-
gguq patuagnek mengliignek unatet pugluteng nuluralliniluku. Nutaan tua-i alinga-
llavsiarami unitellinia.

Tuamtell' tauna maklagmek ugtarculria. Tekilluku waniw' narulkaqatarluku piinanermini, ukatiikun ingelran mengliikun una talliq mayulliniluni, unatet tungiinun
caumaluteng, unatet. Qukaa ukinerluni unatain una. Ingna maklak capumaluku
unatminek waten ukinerkun taugaam yaaggun alaitelluku. Ukua narulkayunarqe-
llerkaa alaitelluku tuaggun. Tua-i piqataamiu, taq'ivkenani narulkalliniluku tauna
ukineq nall'arrluku. Asaaqurra maklagmun tut'elliniluni.
Niirarautni tauna qirussiutuuq, qaraliutuut. Unatnguat ukut ukatiini, qayaruaq-
wa, una asaaqumek taprualuum nuvumaluku, ingna ugtaruaq asaaqumek kapus-
nganguarluni. Tauna tua-i. Imkuni niirarautni qaraliutuuq maani.

We only heard their noises here. They say they have always made noise like that here. They say their sound could be heard sometimes. They say that if we hear a loud *qununiq* sound, we should not think that it is close by. They say their noise is loud though they are far away. But when they're close, the sound they make is very faint. Because they are *ircenrraat* [extraordinary persons who can appear in human or animal form], they are amazing. They say they seek retaliation from those who catch them. *Qununit* kill the person who caught them. That is why we were warned not to go after them when we saw one.

They say some [*qununit*] appear as humans, wearing seal-gut rain garments, waterproof boots, and fish-skin mittens. They say some [hunters] used to see ones that were sitting on bearded-seal skins on ice. And they would be wearing bent-wood hats. They would be wearing seal-gut rain garments and fish-skin mittens and waterproof boots. But they said the bottom of their garments would be spread out on the ice all around them. And when they made their sounds, the bottom of their garments lying on the ice would vibrate. They say they tilt their heads up when making their sound, revealing themselves as human.

And when they were going to harpoon them, at the place where the stitches ended on the seal-gut garment, down at the bottom of the garment where the last piece of gut was sewn, right at that spot, a hunter would aim and hit it with his spear point and not hit its body. That person on the ice would then grab the skin he was sitting on and jump in the water.

They say only shamans were able to catch them. Regular people were warned not to go after them. They are apparently dangerous. Back in the early days, it is said there were more amazing events reveled to people, and [hunters] would come upon coffins sitting on the ice long ago. There was a hunter who thought he had come to a seal on ice, but he realized that it was a coffin. He got scared and stopped, and soon a human hand appeared on the side of the cover and motioned him to come. [The hunter] became even more petrified and left.

Then once there was a hunter going after a bearded seal on ice. Just as he reached it and was about to harpoon it, on this side of it, along the edge it was lying on, an arm came up, with the palm of a hand facing toward him. There was a hole in the palm's center. The hand was covering the bearded seal, but the animal was visible through the hole. The part that the spear could easily hit was visible. So, without hesitation, he thrust his spear right at that hole and hit the animal and caught it.

[The story about that hunter] is usually carved on dancing sticks. On the dance stick there is a hand [with a hole] and behind that there is a model of a kayak and a spear with a skin line attachment thrust [through the hole] and the spear point

Tuamtell'-am iliit caqerluni ugtarculliniuq, eluciiinani. Tekicartullinia imna neq-nugulleq, kumlanrutleq naparcilluk caranglluk palurmi uitaluni cikum qaingani. Tu-pillranek nangnerin qulliqluku, quliulutek. Yuuluni-gguq qayani mayurqaarluku ullagluku pia can'giirutellrullinilria, *black-fish*-anek imangqellrullinilria. Qaill' tua-i picirkailami neq'aamiu tamana, qununinek-llu piaqata nangellritgun, taqellritgun pilauciat, asaaqumi cingilga kaputelliniluku tuavet, piirriluni kanan' taqellranun. Tapqaarluku-ll' tua-i mermun piluku asaaqumek negtaarluku camavet, cinguur-luku cikum acianun. Piuraqertelluni nek'venga'artelliniluni taprualua. Iqua tua-i te-guluku akgenqegcarluni qelluqican nuqingallinikii. Tua-i nuqingaluku piuraqerluni qac'uqerteqerluni puggliniuq maklak asaaquanun kapusngaluni, narulkaumaluni. Tua-i pitaqelliniluku, qaill' pivkenani. Kalngauluku taugaam tangerrluku cikum qaingani.

Avani-gguq ciuqvani tamakut tamaa-i pitullruut yaaqvani avani ciuqvani, tama-kut alingnarqelriit ilait.

Piciuluteng-gguq tua-i piciunritevkenateng. Piciungameng tua-i qanemciulu-teng. Yung'elraarutet-gguq tamakut mallegtellermeggni tuaten ayuqellruut, ellam yung'eqarraarutai. Irranaqluteng ilait.

~: Qalrit :~

Makliit imkut angtuat maklagpallraat mermi camani nulirtengaqameng up'nerka-mi — tuntuviit-llu arnacaluteng qalrialuteng pitukait. Tamakut tua-i tuatnatuut qal-rirluteng, angllurluteng nep'ngaqluteng camani, leryiyagaat taugken tua-i pugluteng. Leryiyagaat, camna-w' camaani (qalrilria), "*Uuuuuuuuuuuu-uuuu.*" Arulairtaqluni. Allamek piaqluni, "*Uuuuuuu.*" Leryiyagaat an'ngartaqluteng, uivaarturluteng waten. Kiarrluteng-gguq tua-i arnacalumeggnek neplituut. Qalrirluteng-gguq. Tua-i taug-ken iquani qerrsiqerrluteng, "*Uuuuuuu.*" Ulevlarpallraat-llu anqerrluteng. Tua-i-ll' piuraqerluni yaatiitgun anqerrluni maklak, egmianun-llu-gguq cikemlun' pull'uni, qamiquni akurrluku, una taugaam alaitelluku qavarluni.

stuck to a model seal sitting on ice. [The carving on the dance stick] is about that. Here in this area those designs were on dance sticks.

And again, once [a hunter] approached what he thought was a seal sitting on ice, but it was oddly shaped. As he came near it, he saw that it was an old grass storage basket for frozen fish sitting upside down on the ice. The strands of grass that were twined last were up on top. He got out on the ice and after pulling up his kayak, he went to it and saw that it was an old grass basket used to store blackfish. He didn't know what to do, but since he remembered the place to hit *qununit* was on the last strand [of the garment's bottom edge], he pierced the point of his toggling harpoon there at the very tip where a weaver finished [closing the basket's bottom]. Then after folding [the basket], he put it in the water and began pushing it down with the toggling harpoon, pushing it down under the ice. After awhile, the skin line attached to the harpoon began to unravel and go underwater. When the line ended, he held it tightly, bracing himself. He held the line, and immediately after the line suddenly slackened, a seal surfaced with the harpoon point in its body, having been struck. He caught it and nothing happened to him. But he saw it as a grass container on top of the ice.

They say those things happened long ago in the old days way in the past, things that were astonishing.

They were true, and they were not lies. They were told because they were actually facts. They say it was like that back when the *yung'elraarutet* were close, the first humans that inhabited the world. Some were astonishing.

⌁: Male bearded seals giving their mating call :⌁

When the large, male bearded seals begin to mate underwater during spring — moose call their females, too. Those [bearded seals] also dive underwater to make their mating calls, and they get noisy underwater, but only little bubbles come to the surface. Little bubbles appear along the surface while the animal down below is calling, "*Uuuuuuuuuuuu-uuuu.*" It would suddenly stop calling, and soon it would call again, "*Uuuuuu.*" Small bubbles would appear going around in a circle like this. It is said when they make noise like that, they are searching for a female [to mate with], *qalrirluteng* as they called it. And at the end of that call, the sound would suddenly get low "*Uuuuuu,*" and large bubbles would surface. Then after a short time, from the side where [the big bubbles] surfaced, a bearded seal would suddenly pop out of

Tua-i piuraqerluni nutaan makluni paivciluni nutaan kiarqaarluni, egmian ang-llurluni tayima. Tua-i taugken muluuraqerluni tell'icamiu camna, imarpiim natra-nun tekicami, nutaan ayagnirluni aug'utun, "*Uuuuuu-uu.*" Leryiyagaat taugken mik-cuayagaat anuranga'arrluteng uivurluteng. Tua-i piciryaraqluk' tuaten.

Anguarngaunata-ll' cama'anlluku. Anguarun tua-i waten piyaaqekumteggu eg-mianun elpenga'artarkauluni. Elpekarkauluta kiartelalliniameng tuaten piaqameng. Tuaten taugaam pugluteng qavaraqata, nutaan anguarluta ullakaniraqluki.

Tua-i ilaita tekitqapiarluki asaaqunek narulkatullrulliniit. Anglluumaluku taug-ken cali anguayunaunani. Taum milqagtarkauluku tua-i egtarkauluni elpengares-kuni tua-i, egqaqluni neqtun, aarnaqluni. Acini-ll' qerratarrluk' ag'aqluni. Alingnaq-luni tua-i nutaan kitngutnayukluni.

Piuraqerluni pinriqerrluni tayima, pugeksaunani wanirpak. Nuvingalluku tua-i nutaan nutegmek. Taqluni tua-i aug'utun pugpiarluni pugqata'arqami tuaten pituuq. Nutyunaqluni tua-i nutaan. Maaggun pikan nutyunaunani, uuggun taugaam ciu-qakun nutyunaqluni. Tuaten-am tamakut pituut makliit nulirtaqameng arnacalu-meggnek. Qalrirluteng-gguq.

~: *Asevret* :~

Asevret-gguq cali makut assirtut yuut. Ikayurtartut-gguq asevret, *walrus*-aat yuut.

Atertellria tauna asevret yuurulluku tegullrulliniat. Asevrullinilriit-gguq. Ar-namek-gguq ilaluteng. Qayat tekicarturai uqruta'arluteng unani nani atertauluni. Cunawa asevret, asevrullunilriit. Yuuluki taugaam tangerrluki, arnamek-gguq ila-luteng. Teguamegteggu tang tuani imkunek naunranek, *salmonberries*, tamakurrlai-narnek neqirluku, tan'gerpagnek piiyuunaku. Cunawa tamakut tan'gerpiit teggalqu-rrullinilriit, teggalquyagaat nerlallrit taukut ilain. Taukut-gguq tamakut naunraat *clam*-aulliniluteng. Tua-i ellaicetun tangvagluki ellaicecicetun elliin.

the water and immediately close its eyes, bowing its head and dipping it in the water, and it would fall asleep with this part of its body visible, floating in the water.

Then after a while, it would lift its head up and look around and immediately dive under water and disappear. After disappearing for a while, when reaching the bottom down there, when reaching the bottom of the ocean, it would start calling again, "*Uuuuuu-uu.*" Small bubbles would begin to show on the water's surface going around in circles. That's what they do.

And we would not paddle while they were [calling] underwater. If we dipped the paddle in the water, it would immediately sense our presence. They would sense us because they apparently look around when they do that. But when they came out of the water and fell asleep, we would then paddle and move closer to them.

Evidently some hunters would get right up to them and harpoon them with toggling spears. But one should not paddle when they are underwater. When it sensed [the person], it would stop its mating call and throw itself out of the water and continue to thrash around dangerously like a fish. And it would completely come out of the water and fly forward. The man in the kayak would get concerned about getting tipped over.

After a while, it would suddenly stop [making its call] and wouldn't come up for a while. Then [the hunter] aimed his gun and got ready to shoot it. That's what it does when it stops calling and gets ready to surface like normal. It was easy to shoot at that time. If it came up over here it would be difficult to hit, but if it came up right here in front, it would be easy to shoot. That is what bearded seals do when they mate with their females. They call it *qalrirluteng.*

~: *Walrus* :~

It is said that walrus are very good people. They say that walrus are helpful, the walrus people.

Walrus apparently transformed themselves into humans and rescued a hunter who was lost and drifting on the ocean. They were actually walrus. They had a woman with them. [A hunter] while adrift down on the ocean arrived at kayakers sheltered with windbreaks on the ice. They were actually walrus. But he saw them as human, and there was a woman with them. When they took him in, they only gave him salmonberries to eat and never served him blackberries. The blackberries that those he was with were eating were apparently pebbles. And those salmonberries were actually clams. The hunter saw [the walrus as human].

Ayautellinikiit tua-i tamaani. Caqerluteng tua-i cikumun aug'umun tekicameng mayulliniluteng, pamyuteng uyangqaurtelluki mer'em mengliinun. Atakutarraarluteng inartelliniluteng. Arvinelguluteng-gguq taukut. Tauna arvinlekluku ellii atertelleq. Cunawa tauna nayagaqlinikiit, arnaq tauna. Taukut-wa angutet cetaman. Qayarluni-gguq taugken tua-i ellaicetun. Mengkugluteng-gguq taugaam tamarmeng tua-i. Tuluit-gguq cunaw'. Qavallerminek tupakaami makcaaqelliniuq ilai imkut tayima. Piqalliniuq, ak'aki camani. Nunivaam camalirnerani-gguq, penam qaingani pikani mayuumaluni, pamyua-gguq uyangqaurluni. Ilai-gguq taugken imkut tayima cataunateng. Tua-i tuaggun tut'elliniluni maavet nunamun, Nunivaam camalirnerakun. Ilain tua-i unitelliniluku tuavet asevret.

Tuamtell' imna Isaac-aaq Qiatuaq, Atertayagaq, qanemcillermini cali tua-i asevret taukut yuuluki tangvagluki ullagyaaqelliniluki. Uluqanrilkuniki tautun piyarniluni qanellruuq. Caumaqarraarluki tekiteqatarluki-gguq iliit tagluni camek qaltarrarmek-gguq negcimek tegumiarluni. Qanikcamek-llu-gguq tua-i tauna imirraarluku atrarluni tuavet ilaminun qayanun. Canimelliluteng-gguq waniw'. Cameg-am piluni uluqerraarluk' piluni tangllinii asevret ukut ugingalriit. Quyayaaqluni-gguq yugnek taukunek. Anirtima-gguq ikayurtarniluki pilarait. Taum tua-i asevrem cali unitnaciallrullinia unani atertaullrani. Tua-i maligqurluku ayallra tamalkuan. Wavet nugtartaqan nugtartaqluni tauna. Asveyagaq-gguq temirtenguvkenani.

ALICE: Mengkungqetulit-qaa tamana neq'erluku asevret pingqelallrat mengkungqelartut?

FRANK: Naamell'. Pitullrullilriit-wa. Nunivaarmiut-wa imkut arcaqerluteng mengkungqetullrulriit. Mengkugnek piaqluki. Ilait-llu nerqata'arqameng qaill' piqerluteng aug'aqernaurait. Nernermek-llu taqngameng elliluki.

Pingakellruit-gguq Nunivaarmiut asevret. Tekitaqata-llu-gguq aqvalgirceteng nulirrit antullruut imarnitnek aturluteng, asvertellriit Nunivaarmiut. Asevrem-gguq taugken tua-i qilua, ikamragni pillragni, nangercan taum uingan asvertellrem, asevrem qiluinek uyamilirluku waten, ukua nuliami imarnitegnek aturluni. Uyamilirluku waten asevrem qiluanek, tamalkuan tua-i iquklican-llu agavkarluku itrulluku.

They took him and they traveled at that time. One day, when they got to ice somewhere along the way, they climbed up on it with the ends of their kayaks hanging over the edge, over the water. Then they went to sleep after having dinner. It is said there were six of them. He, the one who drifted away, was the sixth person in that group. The woman with them apparently was their younger sister. There were four men. But she had a kayak like the others. They all had labrets [on their chins], which were evidently their tusks. When [the hunter] woke from his sleep and got up, his companions were gone. Then he checked his surroundings and saw that they were way down there. He was on the other side, the south side of Nunivak Island, on top of a cliff with the tail of his kayak hanging over the edge. But the others were gone. That was how he got to land, to the south side of Nunivak Island. The ones he was with, the walrus, had left him there.

And when Isaac Qiatuaq, Atertayagaq, told the story about [the time he drifted on the ocean], he said that he had seen walrus as people and had gone to them. He said that if he hadn't looked away while approaching them, he would have been [taken by the walrus people] like the one just mentioned. He said he was looking at them and approaching them, and when he was just about to reach them, one of them went up behind them, holding a small bucket and a gaff. Then after he filled the bucket with snow, he went down to the others and their kayaks. He was getting close to them. And for some reason he looked away briefly, and when he looked at them again he saw walrus lying on the ice. He had been so happy to see people when he first saw them. He said it is no wonder they say walrus are helpful. And he said that there was one particular walrus that stayed with him and didn't leave right away when he was adrift. [The walrus] followed him wherever he went. When he moved to another place, [the walrus] would move, too. He said it was a small walrus that wasn't an adult.

ALICE: Do those who wear labrets do so remembering the tusks on walrus?

FRANK: I don't know. They probably did so. The [men] from Nunivak Island especially wore labrets. They called them *mengkuut*. When some were going to eat, they would remove them somehow. And they would place them back in when they finished eating.

They say that people on Nunivak Island revere [walrus]. It is said that on Nunivak when the hunters returned with their catches, their wives, wearing their seal-gut parkas, went down to the shore to get the walrus. When a wife stood up while still in the sled wearing her seal-gut parka, her husband would put the walrus intestines around her neck. He wound the entire walrus intestine very loosely around

Tuatnatuut-gguq. Angkait-gguq Nunivaarmiut asevret; pingakait. Pirpakluki. Nu-kalpiarita-gguq tua-i pingakait asveret. Angekluki pitautulini.

Nunivaarmi angtuamek asverpagtellrulliniut ak'a ciuqvaarni, angtuamek asver-mek, asverpagmek. Camalirnermi taugaam nunat taukut iliit, asverpagtellrulli-niuq.

Cevv'arnermi taugaam ukaqvani Kayirayuam qetunraan iliit asvercaaqelliniuq ce-tamanek tululegmek atliqelriignek, akagarrluni kit'elliniuq. Tuqucaaqluku. Maani-llu cali ak'a ciuqvani cali asvercaaqellrulliniut cetamanek cali tululegmek, cali te-guvkenaku cali akagarrluni cali kill'uni. Cevv'arnermi-am Kayirayuam ukaqvani pillruanga, kit'enrilkan qamiqurra asveq cetamanek tululek tangerrsarniluku tekitel-lemni camavet Cevv'arnermun. Yuan iliit asvercaaqellrulliniuq tuaten cetamanek tululegmek.

Tauna-llu tua-i maani piyaaqellrat, Qumaqnim pinguaqengallra angalkuum, tuunrangayiim. Asveruallruuq-gguq maani Qumaqniq tauna angalkuq, taqngami-llu qanrulluki cetamanek asvermek tululegmek tangerciqniluki uksuqu, tuquteng-naqesqelluku. Aug'um-llu tua-i Robert Strauss-am pilliniluku piarkaqngamiu, ta-makucimek niicuitniluni ak'a avaken ciulianek cetamanek asvermek tululegmek niicuitniluni. Qumaqniim pillinia niicuilengraan tangerqatgu piluaqangnaqluku pisqelluku. Cunawa-gguq taum pistekaan asgurakellinikii Kakianrem. Up'nerkaan elliin tanglliniluku tauna asveq, ugtaluni qavalria asevret ilaluki. Ullallermeggni tua-i tuani canimellian maktellrani iliita tangrramiu qanrutlinia, ingna-gguq tang asveq cetamanek tulungqellinilria. Tua-i Kakianrem tangrramiu pilliniuq, Qumaq-nimi-llu-gguq ilumuullinivaa.

Tegunritliniluku.

~: Issurit nayiit-llu :~

ALICE: Kuigilngurmi iciw' augkut qanrutkellruketen makliit ayuqenritniluki. Una paqnayugtuq, issurit-llu-gguq-qaa ayuqenritut qaraliit?

FRANK: Ayuqenritut. Qasrulget, yaalirtaat, issurit, avani nunamteni pitulit. Aug-kut-wa issurirpiit angtuat cali, taugaam nurnarluteng. Issuritun ayuqsaaqelriameng, augkut taugaam qaraliit takaayiurluteng, waten ayuqurluteng. Ukatmun qaraling-

her neck, and once that was done she went back with the intestine loosely dangling around her neck. It is said that they did that. They say the people of Nunivak Island consider the walrus to be most important; they revere them greatly. They say their great hunters revered the walrus. They considered them the most important catch.

They evidently caught a large walrus on Nunivak Island long ago, a very large walrus. A person from a village on the south side of Nunivak Island caught a huge walrus.

But recently, in Chefornak, one of Hilary Kairaiuak's sons caught a walrus with four tusks, one tusk above the other. Evidently it rolled off and sank. He had killed it. And long ago someone here in Kwigillingok also caught a walrus with four tusks. He also lost it. It rolled off and sank, too. When I went to Chefornak recently Kairaiuak told me that I would have seen a walrus head with four tusks there at Chefornak. One of his sons had caught a walrus with four tusks.

And one was caught here but not retrieved, the one that the shaman Qumaqniq conjured up with his helping spirits. They say that here in this village the shaman Qumaqniq conjured up a walrus. Upon completing his conjuring Qumaqniq told the people that they would see a walrus with four tusks that winter and that they must kill it. Kakianeq, Robert Strauss, told him, since he was his teasing cousin, that he had never heard, even going back to the times of their ancestors, of a walrus with four tusks. Qumaqniq told him that, even though he had never heard of one, if they saw it he must try to kill it. Apparently Kakianeq, who would be the one to kill it, was skeptical. During that spring he saw that walrus sleeping on the ice along with the other walrus. When they stalked the walrus and got closer to them, one of them saw it when it raised its head and told Kakianeq that there was a walrus with four tusks. When Kakianeq saw it, he said that indeed Qumaqniq was a genuine shaman.

They didn't retrieve it.

~: Spotted seals and ringed seals :~

ALICE: You know how you talked about the different kinds of bearded seals in Kwigillingok. [Ann] is wondering if the designs on spotted seals are also different.
FRANK: There are different kinds. *Qasrulget* [ribbon seals], *yaalirtaat* [dark seals], and *issurit* [spotted seals] are the different types in our area. Then there are the very large spotted seals, but they're rare. They look like spotted seals, but their designs

qetuut-gguq tamakut. Maklagtun angtaluteng. Makliit tayima *seven feet* taktalar-
tut makliit wall'u *eight feet*. Tuaten angtaluteng issurirpiit tamakut. Asevret-llu call'
angnerluteng.

Issurit makut ayuqut kukupait, kukupacuarait. Nayiit taugaam iluqlirrarluteng
laqliqelrianek, waten iluqlirrarluteng. Angluteng. Imkut qaill' angtauralriit, peq'urrit
qaralirrarluteng nayiit. Issurit taugaam qaralirluteng kukupagnek. Angucaluit-llu
tungunruluteng issurit. Taugken tamakut issurirpiit takaayiurluteng allayuggauluteng qaraliit angtuat. Cali tamakunek tangeqsaitua, taugaam augna George Canegkaq tamakucaaqellrulliniuq issurirpagmek, sevqerrulluni kitellrulliniuq.

Tua-i-llu augkut yaalirtaat. Nayiit-llu yaalirtangqertut, nayiit. Tamarmeng. Makliit yaalirtangqelliniut. Issurit-llu nayiit-llu yaalirtarluteng.

Tungupagluteng. Tungulrianek ilaluteng. Issurit-llu kukupangqerruciinateng, tunguluteng peq'urrit tua-i paugkut, aqsait taugaam nallunaiterrlugluteng. Yaalirtaat,
tunguluteng. Uksuarmi taugken avani nunamteni qasrulget pituluteng. Issuriuyaa-
qelriameng, imkut qaralirluteng maaggun waten, pamna-ll' tunuat, *vest*-anek tuar-
tang atulalriit. Tamaa-i tamakut qasrulget, taugaam kukupaunateng, tamakunek
tamaa-i qaralirluteng, issuriuyaaqluteng taugken. Taugaam qeciit makut qayaqsuunaki, asvaitenrilata. Elnguitut qeciit. Caksuunaki tua-i amiit makut, melquqeg-
cingraata, qaraliqegcingraata tamakut qasrulget. Uksuarmi tua-i avani nunamteni
pituut; qenuqataarqan tangruuqatuut.

Tua-llu nayiit makut cali, nayiit, nayissuat-wa. Angnengqerrluteng nayissuanek.
Nayiit maklaartun angtaluteng tua-i. Qaill' angtatuat. Taugaam pilalriani tua-i waten ayuqaqluteng uivenqeggluteng nayiit, nayirpakayiit angtuat, nayissuanek piaqluki nunamteni un'gaani. Nurnartut, taugaam nurnangraata wii tamatumek pitell-
ruunga, cauciinaku-ll' wii. Maklagauyukluku-ll' piiyaaqekeka allayuuluni qamiqurra.
Kukupai-ll' tamakut nayinrartun ayuqluteng. Nutaan ciulirnema tangrramegteggu
tamakuuniluku nayirpauniluku, nayissuanek pituniluki tamakut tamaa-i.

Yaqulengvailegmi cikuyugturatuuq imarpik. Atakuyarturaqami cikullaq pinga'ar-
taqluni. Pagaanlluni tua-i [akerta] teviryugnaunaku cikuyungluku mer'em qainga.
Tua-i-ll' yaqulget nacaullget pinga'arteqertelluki cikuyuk pinrirluni, ellma taugaam
tua-i piuraqa'aqluni, cikuyunrirluni tua-i. Uksumi taugken tua-i February-mi-ll'
issurit-llu it'gait kumlanaki, cetengqilluki amtall' kuimarluteng. Cikumaluteng tua-i

Homes covered with snowdrifts by the strong coastal winds. Frank Andrew recalled: "In winter no houses were visible, only the sleds and the huge dip nets posted in the snow. The houses would be inside the snow." Martin Family Collection A2.

The following photographs were taken by Augustus Martin in Kwigillingok in the early 1930s and are part of the Martin Family Collection, Anchorage Museum at Rasmuson Center

Kuskokwim River

Dall Lake
Anuqluq

Kongiganak

Kwigillingok

Frank Andrew's map of the Canineq (lower coastal) area.

Dennis Ronsse, Alice Rearden,
Noah Andrew Sr., and Michelle Pearson

- Village or Camp
- Mud Flat
- Sand Bar
- Ocean Channel
- Water Body
- Stream or River

Projection: UTM Zone 3N, NAD 1983

N

0   5   10 Miles

Children wearing reindeer-skin parkas, with patterns indicating they may be from the tundra region. Martin noted that the pups they hold would be trained to pull sleds. Martin Family Collection A3.

Young woman, possibly related to the Temples of Napakiak, wearing a squirrel-skin parka. Martin Family Collection A4.

Man wearing a bird-skin parka, standing near a house entrance, with dogs on the roof.
Martin noted that dogs rested on roof tops because they were warm and that they
often fell through the seal-gut skylight on top. Martin Family Collection A5.

Woman twining an issran (grass carrying bag). Martin wrote that she did not
use the gasoline lamp hanging to her left very often, as gas was both scarce
and expensive: "Most of the time this woman uses a seal-oil lamp
with a moss wick." Martin Family Collection A6.

Young woman standing at the door of a sod house. A kayak sled rests on the porch top. Frank Andrew said, "It doesn't take long to build a sod house. We would help each other. A house would be built in less than two days." Martin Family Collection A7.

Young man — possibly Miisaq (Frank Andrew) — hitching up his dogs for a trip. Wassilie Evan of Akiak noted, "You always heard that a person who had a lot of dogs had three dogs, since they didn't have good nets to acquire dog food. They were grateful for their help." Martin Family Collection A8.

*Paru — possibly Kenneth Peter's father, who moved to Akiachak — coming out of
a home. Martin noted that people made their homes small to conserve heat,
with entrances no larger than necessary. Martin Family Collection A9.*

Young woman — possibly Charlie Lewis's mother's younger sister — wearing a reindeer-skin parka with sealskin boots. The ornaments on her chest consist of two alarm-clock cogwheels with a little bell between them. Martin Family Collection A10.

Boy wearing a uivqurraq *(circular skin cap, lit., "something that encircles [the head]"). Martin Family Collection.*

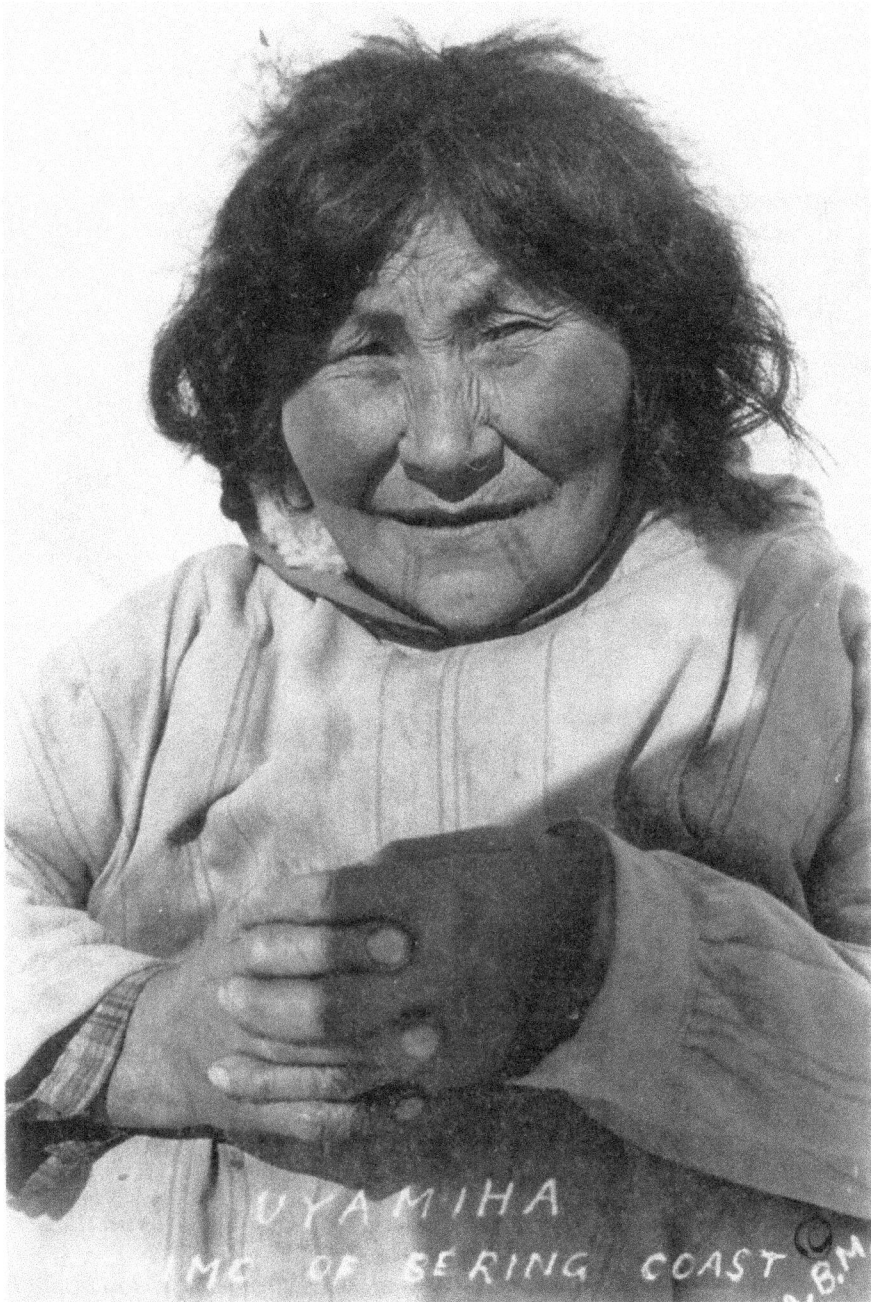

*Coastal woman with chin tatoos like those adorning many
of her generation. Martin Family Collection.*

Interior of a log home. Martin wrote: "The platform you see is made of rails split from driftwood. It serves as a workbench, bed, and dining table. The bird skins hanging from the wall will be used for clothing. The fish net is important equipment for the family. Under this platform is storage space." Martin Family Collection A14.

An elderly woman eats needlefish from a wooden bowl. Kwigillingok elder Roland Phillip recalled that children were always fed the heads but not the bodies of needlefish — so-called because of the long spines along their backs.
Martin Family Collection A15.

Roland Phillip noted, "They would cook like this during summer, using a device to hang their pots." Martin added: "Eskimos are seminomadic; that is, they move from place to place according to the season and where food may be found. When snow is gone, many live in tents or temporary homes. But wherever they go, the country is almost sure to be flat and low, and one will seldom find them far from the water." Martin Family Collection A16.

Kwigillingok children in the early 1930s. Martin wrote: "Eskimo girls play with dolls carved from wood or ivory and dressed in furs. Small boys use bows and arrows during summer. Otherwise they have very few toys. They do not require many things to make them happy. They are usually quiet and respectful of older people." Martin Family Collection A11.

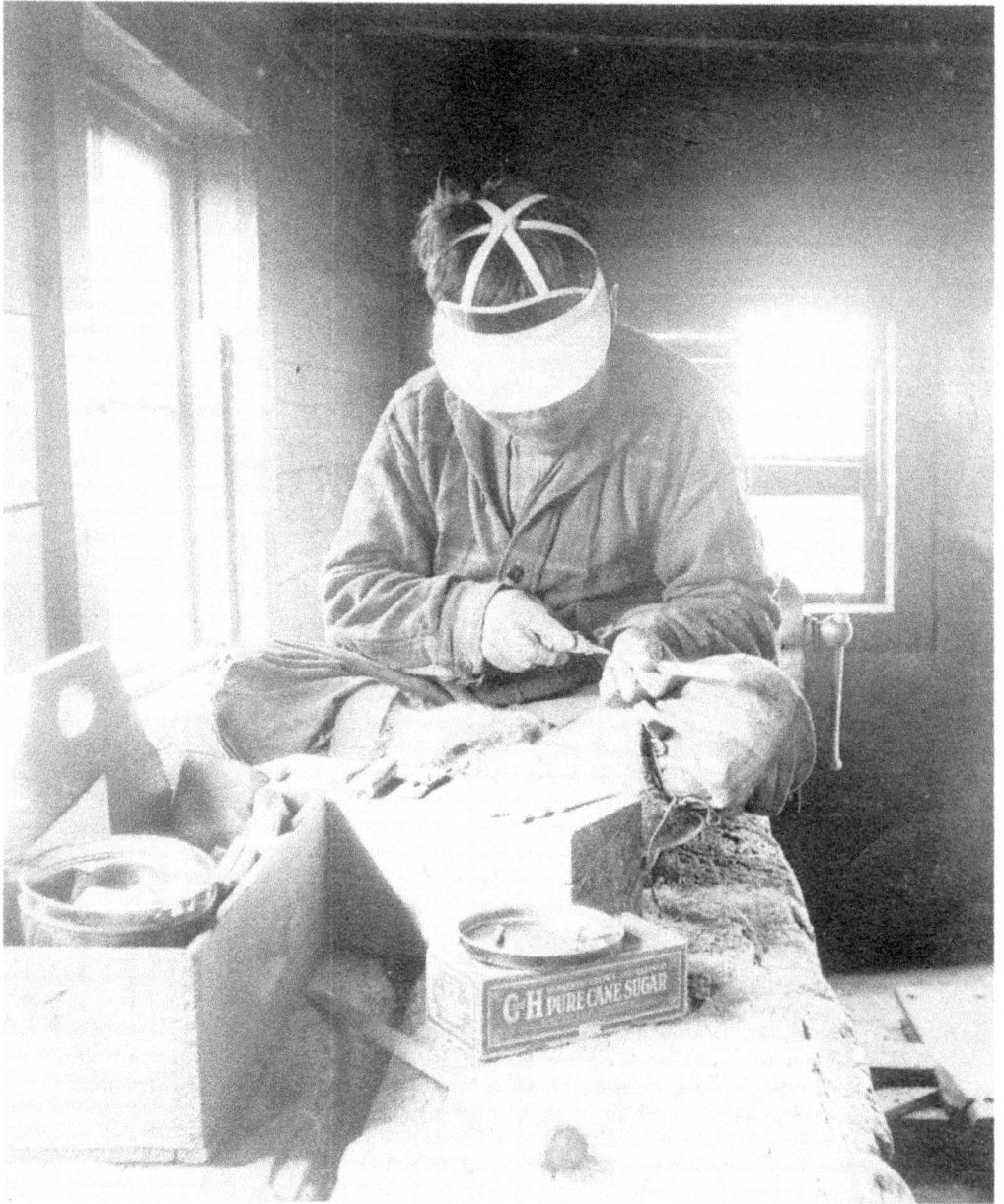

Man carving ivory, possibly in the Kwigillingok school. Martin Family Collection.

Kwigillingok school children. Their teacher, Mrs. Martin, wrote that she had twenty-four students in all, with two missing from this photo. Martin Family Collection.

Coastal graves, including wooden images with ivory eyes and mouths. The foreground image wears a girl's beaded dance hat and necklace and holds a story knife. Her sewing kit is nailed to the wall behind her. Bows and pipes can be seen nailed to the background graveboards. Martin Family Collection.

Above-ground burial and alailutet (belongings of the deceased), including a beaded dance hat and lamp base. Roland Phillip noted that when someone died, all their personal possessions, both new and used, were placed on the grave. Their fellow villagers would never steal these grave goods but might trade for them, putting something in their place. Martin Family Collection.

Smoke rising from the qasgi, indicating the men inside are taking a fire bath. The large drums were removed to protect them from the heat. Martin Family Collection.

Martin wrote: "A village of twenty or thirty homes would be considered large. Some consist of only two or three, as you see here.... The man here is stooping to inspect his boots before he goes indoors. If he finds any snow and particles of ice on his footwear, he will remove them. Usually he uses a small stick for this purpose. Most footwear must be kept dry to prevent weakening and rotting." Martin Family Collection B18.

Men outside the qasgi after a fire bath, enjoying the change from hot to cold. Martin wrote: "Sweat bathing is considered great sport for them. Their skin often becomes quite reddened by the heat and smoke inside. That is what makes their bodies look so dark in this view." In the foreground, from left to right, may be Moses Strauss' father, Milton Lewis' father, Charlie Lewis' father, and Katie Albrite's father. The man to the far right in the back may be Frank Andrew's father, recognizable by his distinctive haircut. Martin Family Collection A20.

Jean Cook's father, Unganer, seated by the entrance of the qasgi with a qanermiaq (fire-bath respirator) made of wood shavings in his mouth, having just come out from a sweat bath. Note the slabs of ice used as a windbreak for the entrance. Originally from Kipnuk, Unganer was known as a very fast runner. Roland Phillip told a story of how he once shot a fox, missed, and so ran after it. Although it ran fast, he caught up to it and hit it with his walking stick to kill it. Martin Family Collection B24.

Qasgi entryway. Martin noted: "Different qasgit have different types of entrances. This one is a little different from the one we just looked at [with sweat bathers seated outside]. It is flanked with a lot of hard-packed snow and ice. "Smoke shows that men inside are taking a fire bath. A log placed to one side of the skylight keeps wind from blowing smoke inside. Martin Family Collection A21.

Martin wrote: "This is the qasgi *tunnel which leads from the entrance to the big room inside. It is quite low, and we must stoop or we shall bump our heads. Ahead of us is a door, which leans a little and so stays shut by gravity. "Under the door is an opening what serves as a draft for the fire inside. It is around this fire that the men sit, unclothed, while they indulge in a sweat bath. See how the wood has been neatly piled for the fire." Roland Phillip noted that the doorway above the* cup'urillra *(draft hole) was sometimes covered with cloth and that the hole was closed when not in use. Martin Family Collection* A22.*

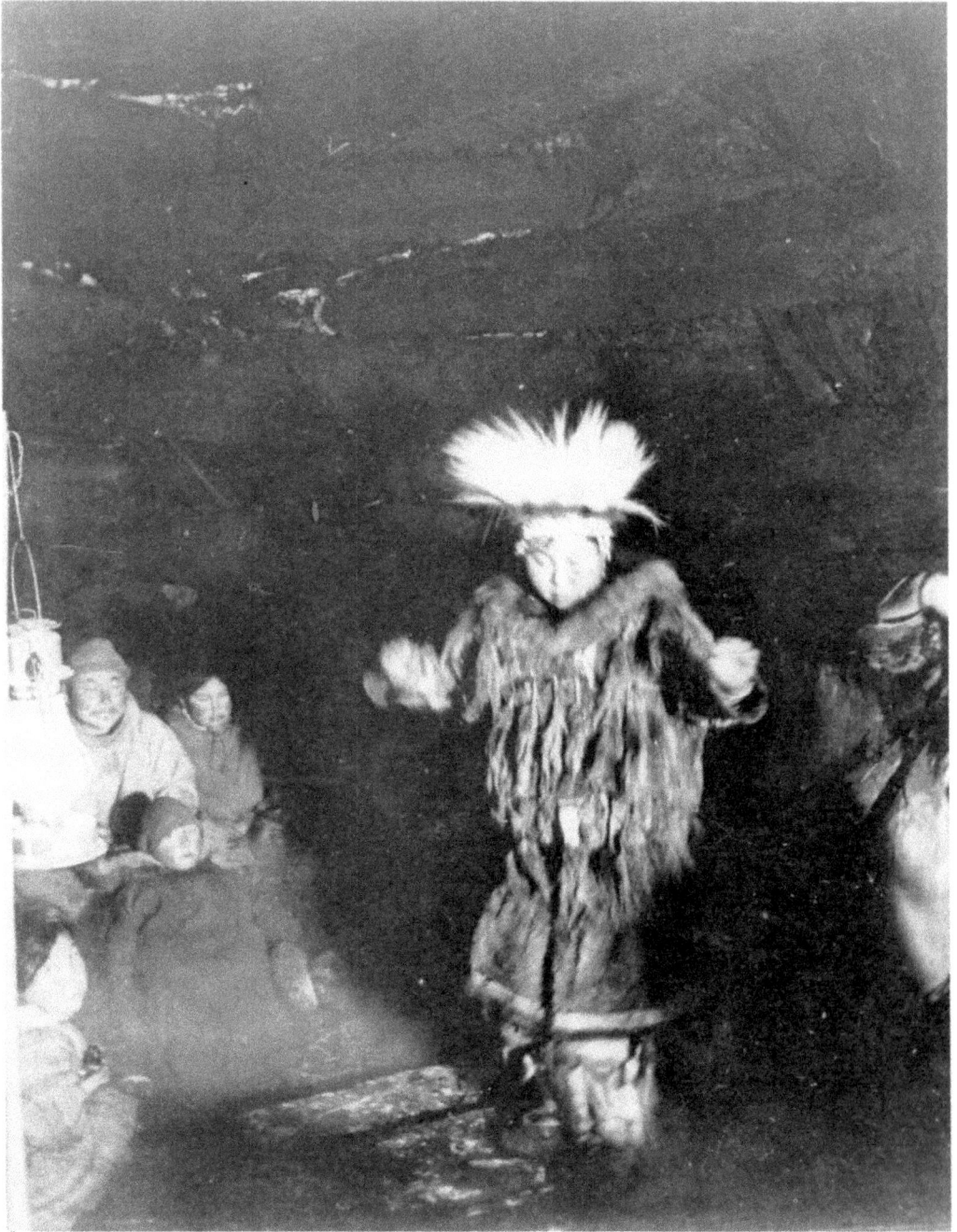

Wearing a dance headdress decorated with caribou throat hair, a woman performs in the Kipnuk qasgi. *Martin Family Collection.*

Martin noted that this dance took place in the Kipnuk qasgi in 1933 and that the decorations were owl feathers. The young girl dancing in the foreground is wearing a beaded nacarrluk *(dance headdress). Roland Phillip added that men made their drum covers with beluga stomachs, fastened down with sealskin line. Martin Family Collection A23.*

At day's end, men and boys gathered in the qasgi *to listen to stories before falling asleep. Roland Phillip vividly remembers listeners encouraging the storyteller by saying "Ii-i (Yes)" emphatically: "Angqaquurluki qulirilriit pitullruit [They would always express agreement to those who were telling stories (to encourage them to continue)]." Martin added: "While he is telling stories, the men and boys listening to him become drowsy and fall asleep. A person is not supposed to stay awake to listen. Instead it is considered improper for the* kulerista *[qulirista, storyteller] to stop telling these stories until the last man has fallen asleep." Martin Family Collection* B25.

Men and boys resting in the qasgi. Note the driftwood plank walls, thick support posts, and heavy log beams. Martin Family Collection.

Martin labeled this photograph "Eskimo bedtime" and wrote: "Sometimes when there are visitors from other places, the qasgi, in its role as hotel, may be pretty well filled, as we see here. They are used to being crowded and will get a good night's rest, sometimes sleeping in a sitting position. "These people have many wonderful qualities, such as patience, loyalty, frankness, honesty, love of peace, and respect for the property of others. They are sensitive and responsive to things that are religious. We who call ourselves civilized could learn much from them." Martin Family Collection A25.

[spots] are longish that look like this. [Their spots] go this way. They are as large as bearded seals. Bearded seals are about seven or eight feet long. Those very large spotted seals are that size. And walrus also have a larger one among them.

The spots on spotted seals are the same, their small spots. But the ringed seals have two layers [of markings], with an outer [ring]. The [spots] are large. The ones that are about so big, the middle part of the backs of the ringed seals that size have designs on them. But the markings on spotted seals are spots. The male spotted seals are darker, too. But the spots on large spotted seals are different. They are oblong. I haven't seen those either, but George Canegkaq apparently caught one of those large spotted seals but it sank.

Then those *yaalirtaat*. There are ringed seals also referred to as *yaalirtaat*. All [seal species] have them. There are apparently bearded seals that are *yaalirtaat*. Spotted seals and ringed seals also have *yaalirtaat*.

They are darker than the rest. There are darker ones among them. And you can't really see the spots on the spotted seal *yaalirtaat* because their backs are dark, but you could see that they are spotted seals by their stomachs. *Yaalirtaat* are dark. But the *qasrulget* [ribbon seals] swim in our area during fall. They are actually spotted seals that have designs here and in back, like they're wearing vests. Those are *qasrulget* with no spots, but they have those designs, but they actually are spotted seals. But they never used their skins on kayaks because they tear easily and are not tough. Their skins are not thick and sturdy. They don't use *qasrulget* skins, even though they have nice fur and nice designs. They are in our area during fall; they are seen for a short while before freeze-up.

Then among these ringed seals, there are *nayiit* and *nayissuat*. Ones they called *nayissuat* are huge. They are ringed seals as large as bearded seals in their first year. Normally, I don't know how big they are. But when butchering them, they are round and very huge, and they call them *nayissuat* in our area. They are rare, but even though they're rare, I caught one, and I didn't know what it was. I thought it was a bearded seal in its first year, but its head was different. And its spots were like those of a ringed seal. Then when my elders saw it, they said it was a ringed seal, and they mentioned that huge ones like that were called *nayissuat*.

The open water on the ocean tends to freeze before the birds arrive. The *cikullaq* [newly frozen ice] starts to form toward the evening. While [the sun] is still up in the sky, long before it goes down, the surface of the water tends to freeze. And right after the birds, the emperor geese start to arrive, ice stops forming, but it forms just a little, and then the ice stops freezing altogether. But during the winter, and in

it'gait. Sagtesciiganateng waten, kuimarluteng taugken. Ellakngamegteggu taugaam qercuayuunaki. Kumlanaki.

Yaa, issuruirucuituq ugna nunavut. Usurpak tua-i pingqetuyaaquq, taugaam mikuunateng. Taugaam February-mi amlleriaqluteng. Kiagmi-ll' qikertat ingkut ketemteni, entaqan tua-i qaingit patuaqluteng issurinek.

Bar-at-llu augkut qikertat atengqertut ketemteni. Yaaken Qukaqliim painganek, keluqlikacagiit Qikertarpagmek pilaraat, Qipnermiut kuigata paingani cakmani. Yaaqlia-wa Kangicuaq. Yaaqlia-w' Kangicualler. Cuirneq-wa, Iretkuk-wa, Qavlunaqvak-wa, Aangaguk-wa, Marasvak-wa. Taukut tua-i atengqertut *sand*-at qikertat. Ketemteni unani uitalriit iquit ingkut Qipnermiut ketliita, aciqsinruluteng taugaam. Ingkut taugken Qukaqliim, Qipnermiut kuigita paiqlii, ula-ll' angeng'ermi qaingiyuunaki. Naruyat-llu irniaqluteng qaingatni. Qikertarpagmi yaani irnitulu-teng, muriit-llu amlleraqluteng tuani qaingiyuilani. Makut taugken ukaqlii ulem angtuam qaingiraqluki. Tua-i-ll' yaaken Iretkugmek qerkelliluteng. Ketemteni ing-kut uitalriit ulem tua-i qaingiqtaarturluki. Aangaguunkut, Qavlunaqvak-llu Ma-rasvak-llu qaingiraurluki. Taugken tauna kellirluni Kuiguyum qukaqliinek, uaqliit-wa Qanermiat, qikertat cali. Kiugna-wa nangenrat Pilot Bar-aq, Kass'atun at'lek, Qaneqliq. Qaneqlirmek aterluni Kusquqviim paingani uitaluni. Kuiguyurpiinkuk Kusquqvak-llu akuliigni. Nangneq tua-i tauna; nangenrunilaraat. Negeqlia-w' Qi-kertaayaaq. Imna-wa Negetmuqrutem uaqlia, kitumek-im' pilaqiit call' marayaq cali, Marasviim kiaqlia. Taum-gguq Qaneqliim uaqlia Teqiyaar taperrnarluni-ll' qainga. Tamaa-i marayat qaugyat atrit.

Cimiyuitut. Taugaam tamakut issurit piiyuunaki. Tauna taugaam Qaneqliq Kusquqviim painganelnguq, issurit cali mayuqetaarvik'laraat. Qikertaayagaam-llu taum uaqlia cali, Ilkiviim ketiinelnguq, Marasviim kiaqlia. Marasviim-llu camna is-qurra cali mayuqetaarviktuluku. Makut tayima et'ulriit engelait camalirnerit isqu-rritnek pituit, waten marayat nengevkenateng waten taugaam ayuqluteng.

Isqurritnek tamaa-i tamakut pituit. Tua-i-ll ingkuk yaani Aangaguunkuk Qav-lunaqvak-llu issurik cali qavarviktulukek. Kelliat Iretkuk, cali issuringqetuluni, amllenrilnguut taugaam piaqluku. Augkut taugaam yaaqlii piiyuunaki; piiyuitellil-

February, the spotted seals' feet are cold and stiff, but they still swim. Their feet are frozen. Their [feet] cannot separate, but here they're swimming. But because they live in the ocean and that's their life, they don't get frostbitten. They're frozen.

The spotted seals don't go away from our area down there. There are actually some around all winter, but not many. But their numbers increase in February. And in the summer the sandbars right below us, when the tide goes out, they'd be covered with spotted seals.

The sandbars down below our village also have names. Below the mouth of Qukaqliq River, the one closest to the mouth is called Qikertarpak, near the mouth of the Qipnermiut River. Then the one beyond it is Kangicuaq. And beyond that is Kangicualler. Then there is Cuirneq, Iretkuk, Qavlunaqvak, Aangaguk, and Marasvak. Those are the names for the sand islands there. Those are the ones at the end of the ones below our place, below Kipnuk, but they are farther down in the ocean. But the ones below the mouth of Qukaqliq River, the river coming out of Kipnuk, even though the tide is very high, [the water] doesn't cover them. And gulls lay their eggs on them. They nest on Qikertarpak, and usually a lot of driftwood is there because the water doesn't cover it. But the high water covers the [islands] on this side of it. Then starting from Iretkuk, [the sand islands] become lower and lower. The tide continually covers the ones over there below us. [The water] covers Aangaguk, Qavlunaqvak, and Marasvak. But the sand islands that are below the mouth of Kuiguyuk and ones below those are also called Qanermiat, sand islands. The last one up there [above us] is called Pilot Bar in English, and we call it Qaneqliq. It's called Qaneqliq. It's at the mouth of the Kuskokwim River. It is located between Kuiguyurpak and the Kuskokwim River. That is the last one; they say it's the last one. Then the one north of it is Qikertaayaaq and down below that is Negetmuqrun. I forgot what else they call that other sand island, the one up behind Marasvak. They say the one down below Qaneqliq, Teqiyaar' has coarse seashore grass on it. Those are the names of the sandbars.

[The sandbars] don't change. But the spotted seals don't go on those islands. But Qaneqliq that is at the mouth of the Kuskokwim River, the spotted seals also go on it. And they also go on the one below Qikertayagaq, the one below Ilkivik River, the one behind Marasvak. And they also go on the side of Marasvak where the water is deep. The side of the sandbars where the water is deep is called *isquq*, the side that is not shallow where the sand extends out far.

They call those their *isqut*. And those [sand islands] over there, Aangaguk and Qavlunaqvak, the spotted seals sleep on them. And Iretkuk below them also had spotted seals on it, but not many. But they don't go on the ones beyond them. They

riit-wa qaill' piat, niiteksaitanka. Tamaa-i tamakut ukaqlii ukut evunengqetuut mik-
cuaraunrilngurnek qikertakayiit augkut. Cikuirupalegmi tua-i tamakut Keggmiqat
issurinek patumatuut yaani Qavlunaqvagmi. Amllepiat issurit, taugaam tepsaqka-
cagarluteng.

Alingnarqut amllerrluteng issurit. Alingengaituq qayamek. Amllerrluki taumek
ullaketayuilkait, atauciuluku [pisqessuunaku]. Nuyurritut cacetuquteklhuteng amllerrluteng piaqameng, alingunateng. Angucalurpalluut tamakut angucaluut tepsarqut angtuat, arnacaluit taugken assirluteng.

∻ Tegiit ∻

Neryunaunateng tua-i tepsaqluteng kemgit-llu angtuat angucalut. Tuamtellu cali
nayiit tamakut angtuanek cali avungqetuluteng kegginait arumaluki, tegagnek-gguq.
Kegginait arumaluteng. Tepsaqpiarluteng tua-i cali nutaan. Tamakut tamaa-i uquit,
gum-at nurnallratni kass'artaat, *bubble gum*-at-llu nurnallratni, tamakut arumalria-
nek kegginalet uquit kenirluki egacirluki, qallarvautelluki ak'anun tua-i. Muraga-
nek tuaten naspaaqaqluki, tua-i uungameng muragaq waten kalevtellria, kenruluni
tua-i, tua-i uuluku tauna. Tua-i-llu qanikcarmun urumanrilngurmun tauna tegu-
llicirluku kuvluku tamalkuan tua-i uquq tamana. *Brown*-aaruluni. *Brown*-aarurr-
luni taugaam. Nenglliani-ll' tua-i yurluku. Tamaa-i tamana *bubble gum*-aq assilria,
tepsaqsugnaunani tua-i. *Bubble gum*-atun-llu qerruraqluku. Elnguriaqan uqumek,
uqupigmek avuluku tamuagaqami assiriaqluni. Tamaa-i taman' angqellruat. Angii-
naq-gguq tamaa-i, angiinamek aterluni. Tamakut tepsarqelriit uquat, tegiit, tegag-
nek piaqluki. Kegginait arumaluteng. Anagutellriit arumalartut kegginait.

Angucaluulalriit-wa. Nayirpakayallraat. Issurit-llu tamaa-i tamakut, tamakut-
llu tepsarqut. Kemgat neryunaunateng, assiinateng, tepsaqluteng cakneq.

∻ Imarpigmiutaat ayuquciit ∻

Cikum qaingani irniaqameng carritulliniit tua-i caunaarirluki, alerpairluki-llu.

Tua-i-ll' aamartelluki. Taqngata-ll' tua-i cugg'emeggnek cinguurluki mermun ig-
telluki. Teguluki-ll' atrarluteng anglluulluki kuimaulluki tua-i tegumiaqluki. Pegta-

probably don't. I don't know, I haven't heard. Those large sand islands below usually have huge piled ice on them. Before the ice is gone, those Keggmiqat are covered with spotted seals over in Qavlunaqvak. It would be covered with spotted seals, but they'd be very stinky.

Spotted seals are dangerous when many are together in one spot. They won't be afraid of a kayaker. That's why they don't go to them when there are lots of them together, and they warn one person [not to go to them]. They aren't afraid when they are numerous and can help one another; they aren't afraid. Mostly the males, the large males have a strong odor, but their females are good.

~: *Ringed seals with rotten faces* :~

The large males are inedible because they smell, along with their meat. And there were large ringed seals whose faces were rotten, and they called them *tegiit*. Their faces were rotten. Those smelled more [than the spotted seals]. When manufactured gum was rare, and when bubble gum was rare, they would cook the blubber of those that had rotten faces in a pot, and they boiled them for a long time. And they would test them with pieces of wood, and when a stick began to burn when put in the pot, it was done cooking. And then they took that oil and spilled it all on the snow, and the snow turned brown. And when it cooled, it hardened. That is good bubble gum and did not smell whatsoever. They would blow bubbles with it like bubble gum. When [the gum] became tough, when adding regular seal oil to it and chewing it again, it would get soft. That was their gum. That was *angiinaq*, called *angiinaq*, from the seal oil of those smelly [ringed seals], the ones they called *tegiit*. Their faces were rotten. The faces of those that were [the worst smelling] were rotten.

They are males. They are very large ringed seals. And those spotted seals stink as well. Their meat is inedible, and they don't taste good; they have a very strong smell.

~: *Sea mammal behavior* :~

When they give birth on the ice, they apparently clean [their pups] very meticulously, removing their *caunaaq* and *al'erpait* [their placentas].

Then they nursed them. Then when they were done, they nudged them with their snouts and let them fall in water. Then they went in the water and took them

qateng kuimaneq nalluluku. Nevermi pugleqertaqluni tua-i, waten elliurluni kuimaneq nalluluku. Issuriyagarnek tanglartua pulengtaq tuaten anenerrayaarnek.
Tuaten-gguq tamarmeng ayuqetuut. Tua-i-llu angliriameng kuimaneq eligarcatgu
aanaita tua-i maligtaquurluki irniateng, etgalngurkun-llu ayagangraata maligtaquurluki. Tuaten ayuqelliniut.

Yugmek-llu alingengaunateng mik'nateng tua-i. Tegulang'ermeng qaill' pingaunateng mik'nateng.
    Kuimaulluki mermi taugaam ayagatetuit, irniateng qimagalluki. Taugken makliit
tamakut cikum qaingani irniani aamaqan, alingengermi yuum pingraani atrarngaunani irniani taqvailgan. Allurrluku atrarciigatuq alingengermi. Taumek alerquuteng-
qellriakut aamalriamek tangerqumata maklagmek cukangnaqluta ullaasqelluku,
irniara taum murilkelluku. Tekiskumteggu-ll' tua-i nutaan nutegluku. Atrayuitut-
gguq [yuk pingraan]. Irniani aamainanrani allurrluku atrarngaunani. Aamani-gguq
taugaam pegeskaku egmian atraqertarkauluni. Tuaten-gguq ayuqut makliit aamar-
cilriit.

Issurit taugaam uirretuut. Alingnarqut angtuat. Irniarit pikegtayuitut. Issuriyagaat usviitut. Yugmek-llu alingengaunateng tua-i tegulangermeng. Wanirpak
eligartetuut issurit. Elisngipiartut issurit irniarit. Wanirpak tua-i eligarrluni,
ung'aqerrluni tua-i egmianun. Ilameggni elisnganruut, elitellra cukauq yugnun.
Amllelaameng avani nallemteni tuaten ayuqelallruut irniarit issuriyagaat. Tua-i
yugmek alingyuunateng tua-i. Angliriqaameng taugaam nutaan alingelangluteng
yugnek issuriyagaat. Maklagaat-llu tua-i makliit irniarit tuaten ayuqluteng. Assipiarluteng qaingit. Nayiit-wa irniarit, nayiyagaat nutaan tua-i mikpiat. Tua-i assiqapiar-
luteng, qamiqucuayagait-wa. Nayiyagaat melqurrit assipiat.

Ut'rucuitait. Unani tua-i qunguturaqerraarluki ilait ayagcetaqluki. Nallunailku-
ciqerluki-ll' ayagcetaqluki. Canek qilqaulluki mer'em pingailkainek. It'gaitgun-wa
pilaqait cagnitevkenaki. Tangrraqluku, una tangrraqluk' uumikuan tamakutgun.
Ayayuitelliniut natmun piyagait. Allam qanrutkaqluku tangerrniluku issuriyagaq.
Mik'nateng alingyuitut yugnek.

ALICE: Ilait-gguq unguiraqluteng.

and dove and swam with them, holding them. When they would let go of them, they wouldn't know how to swim. It would suddenly appear at the surface and float on its back, not knowing how to swim. I have seen many small spotted seals like that, that were just born. They say that's what they all do. And when they get bigger and learn how to swim, their mothers continually follow their offspring, even when they swim through shallow water. That's what they're apparently like.

And they won't be afraid of humans when they're small. When they're small, they won't do anything, even though they're handled.

[When they detect a human] they take their pups and swim away with them. But those bearded seals, if they are nursing their pups on the ice, even though she detected a hunter nearby and is afraid, she won't go into the water before her pup is done [nursing]. She can't suddenly yank [the nipple away from the pup] and dive into the water. That's why we were taught that if we see a bearded seal nursing, we should approach it quickly, keeping an eye on its pup. And to shoot it when we reached it. They say they don't go down in the water [though a hunter is near]. While her pup is nursing, [the mother] won't pull the nipple off abruptly and submerge. She only goes into the water quickly when the pup releases the nipple. They say that's how nursing bearded seals are.

Only spotted seals snarl [at people]. The big ones are dangerous. Their pups don't growl much. Spotted-seal pups are foolish. And they aren't afraid of people, even though they handle them. Spotted seals can be tamed in just a short time. Spotted-seal pups can get adjusted [to people] very quickly. In just a short time they can get accustomed to people and get attached. They learn faster than other seals. Because there were so many of them back when we were young, that's how small spotted seals were. They weren't afraid of people. But when they get a little larger small spotted seals become wary of people. And bearded-seal pups are also like that. Their fur is fine and beautiful. And the ringed-seal pups are very tiny. They look very nice, with tiny heads. The ringed-seal pups' fur is beautiful.

They don't take them home. After [hunters] kept them for pets down on the ocean, some were released. And they even put markers on them before letting them go. They tie things on them that water won't ruin. They tie things on their feet, but not too tight. They would see them and recognize them later by the things they put on them. Their pups apparently don't wander off too far. Someone would say that he had seen the small spotted seal that was let go. They aren't afraid of people when they're small.

ALICE: [Noah] said that some [are still alive inside the womb after their mothers were killed] and come back to life.

NOAH: Qingait.

FRANK: Cegg'araqameng ilait pituut, maklagaat-llu. Tuqurraarluteng piniri-
luteng-llu tua-i. Aqsiit-llu ullirrluki makut amiirinanratni tamakut amirrlainau-
ngermi patkautaqluni tua-i cagnipiarluteng. Tuaten-gguq pituut cegg'araqameng
qamiquteng navguumangraata.

Ancimariluku-llu tuquaqluteng; tuqutaqluki qingait. Taugaam aanameggni aya-
ninruut. Pek'ngetuut pekcimatuut piyagait qamiquteng navgumangraata.

Nalamayuitut atam aanateng nalamangraata. Nalanaciatuut. Ancaceteng-llu pe-
kengluteng kinllerteng maliggluk, pekenqeggiluteng. Tuatnatuut tamarmeng unkut
ungungssit unani cat. Aanateng tuqutengraitki qingait egmian tuquyuitut.

ALICE: Waten-qaa ilait tamakut imarpigmiutaat quyurmeng ayagatuut?

FRANK: Ii-i, amllerrarmeng quyurmeng, issurit-llu piaqameng, wall' makliit-llu
quyungqaluteng qavcin piaqameng. Imkut asevret quyungqarpallutuut, quyungqar-
pallurluteng. Makut taugaam makliit nayiit-llu quyungqarrlainarluteng piiyuunateng. Issurit taugaam cali quyungqayunqegtut, qikertani-ll' quyurmeng kiagmi ui-
tauratuameng issurit, amllepiarluteng nutaan. Amllerraqameng tua-i qavciuluteng
quyungqaaqluteng. Nayiit-llu qavciuluteng quyungqaaqluteng. Nurnaameng taugken tua-i tuatnassiyaayuunateng, quyungqalangermeng.

Ayuqelartut. Arnacaluit taugaam issurit qatertut melqurrit nallunaunateng.
Assirluteng melquqegciluteng arnacalut, qatenruluteng manuit makut. Angutait
taugken tungunruluteng peq'urrit qaingit issurit. Nayiit taugken tua-i ayuqngataq-
luteng angucaluit-llu arnacaluit-llu. Makliit-llu ayuqaqluteng tuacetun; allayugmek
melqerrunateng, ayuqluteng.

ALICE: Imarpigmi-llu-qaa kuimaraqameng wall'u-q' cikum qaingani uitaaqameng ayuqluteng pituut?

FRANK: Qavaraqameng-wa taugaam cikumi; qavarpek'nateng cikum qaingani
uitaurayuitut. Ilait taugken mermi qavatuluteng, putukuarluteng. Pugtauyaartur-
luteng qavarluteng taugaam, pugtarmeng, putukuarluteng. Makliit taugken ilait
naparmeng qavatulliniluteng pugumaluteng. Anglluyuunateng, napangqaluteng
taugaam qavarluteng, qamiqurrit murungqaluteng, suggait taugaam qaimi maani
pugumaurluteng suggait, naparrluteng qavalriit. Ataucimek tangvallruunga ilalua
tamakunek, maklagmek naparmi qavalriamek. Tuaten-gguq tua-i ilait qavatuut,

NOAH: Their fetuses.

FRANK: Some do that when they become fully awake, including bearded-seal pups. After dying, they gain strength. And while they are skinning it, cutting the stomach open, even though the skin was taken off, the carcass of the animal would become very stiff. They say that's what they do when they wake, even though their heads are crushed.

Some would die after they took them out; they killed their fetuses. But they are much stronger than their mothers. They begin to move and move for a long time, even though their heads had been crushed.

They are still alive inside, even though their mothers are dead. It takes a while for them to die. And when they take them out of their [mothers'] bellies, they begin moving as they dry and get lively. That's what all sea mammals do down in the ocean. Even though they've killed their mothers, their fetuses don't die right away.

ALICE: Do some sea mammals travel in groups?

FRANK: Yes, quite a few of them together, like when spotted seals or bearded seals are in a group, there would be quite a few of them together. Walrus mostly stay in groups. But bearded seals and ringed seals do not always stay together in groups. But spotted seals like to stay in groups, because they mostly stay in groups on the islands during summer, and there'd be many of them together on an island at that time. During times when they are numerous, small groups of spotted seals stay together here and there. And ringed seals stay together in groups as well. But if fewer are around in a season, you don't see many in groups.

[Males and females] look the same. But the female spotted seals have white fur and are easy to distinguish from the others. The females have good fur, with whiter bellies. But the backs of male spotted seals are darker. But the male and female ringed seals seem to look the same. And bearded seals are the same; their fur looks the same and doesn't look different.

ALICE: And do they [behave] the same when they are swimming in the ocean and sitting on ice?

FRANK: They only stay on the ice when they sleep, otherwise they never go on ice. But some sleep in the water, *putukuarluteng* [as they call it]. They are floating but are asleep, *putukuarluteng*. But some bearded seals apparently sleep upright with their bodies visible in the water. Those sleeping with their bodies upright stayed like that and slept without diving, with their heads submerged in water, with their snouts poking out on the surface. I and other hunters watched a bearded seal sleeping upright in the water like that once. They say some bearded seals sleep upright

naparmeng makliit. Asevret-llu cali pugtarmeng amlleq qavatuluni, puvyangqerra-meng asevret, anertevkarluteng tuavet puvyameggnun, anglluumangraan.

Anertevkarviit-wa asevret. Imirluku qertunermek pugtaluteng tua-i, pugtautek-luk'. Angluni tua-i ukuatni. Tuavet anertevkarluteng qamiquteng anglluumangraata. Nallunaunateng-llu cauyaqtaatulegnek ilaluteng. Naugg' imkut *guitar*-at kalgaqa-meng, [*teng-teng*-aalalriit]. Tuaten tua-i. Yuum tuar kalelaqai caaqameng. *Teng-teng*-aaraluteng tua-i niitniqpiarluteng. Cauyaqtaalriit-gguq tamaa-i asevret qavaraqa-meng mermi.

Natait-wa neplilartat. Taum-wa iluanek pilallilriit. Qavcirqunek tangvalallruu-kut tamakunek, pugtarmeng qavalrianek. Asevret amllermeng piiyuitut. Tamakut-gguq taugaam cauyaqtaalget tuaten qalriatuluteng, *guitar*-atun erininqigtaarluteng. Qelutait tuar' kalguulaqait. Qerrsineq cuy'aqertaqluni-ll', may'uqertaqluni. Niit-niqluteng tua-i pinaurtut tua-i. Quyurmeng taugaam pugtaluteng waten. Sagtev-kenateng qavalriit pitulliniut mermi asevret, puvyateng qerrurluki. Pugyuunateng tua-i qamiquit, tamakunek taugaam anertevkarluteng taumun, taum iluanek, puv-yameng.

Air-amek-wa tua-i imarluni. Tupiimeng-llu tua-i imairluki. Ellelluki. Qavarninga-qameng-wa tua-i pilallilriit.

Qangqiirtun-gguq ayuqut nakmiin ilu'urqellruameng. *Cousin*-aaqluteng asevret qangqiiret-llu. Taumek-gguq tamakungqellriit tamarmeng qastunarqelriamek. Iciw' imkut qangqiiret may'uqerrluteng imkut elliurluteng pitulriit. Tamakut-am qerrur-luki puvyateng [tuaten pitulliniluteng], neqiviteng-wa imkut qangqiiret.

Qanrutkait-am ciulirneret augkut avani. Qangqiiq-gguq asvertun qalriatullruyaa-quq, asveq-llu qangqiirtun qalriatuluni. Tua-i caqerlutek-gguq asveq qangqiiq-llu piuk, "Usuuq, tang tua-i qalriallren taun' ayuqeksaitelaqen." Aipaan pillinia, "Elpet-llu-w' tua-i ayuqeksaitelaqen qalriallren." Aipaan pillinia, "Elpet-llu-w' tua-i ayuqek-saitelaqen qalriallren. Atag-atak navrutqernaupuk naspaalukek." Tua-i-ll' qangqii-rem qalriacini tunlliniluku asvermun, naspaasqelluku. Qalriarraartelluku pillinia, nutaan-gguq piknganaku pia. Tuarpiaq-gguq pikekii nutem. Angluni-llu-gguq ellii. Tua-i-ll' asevrem qalriacini qangqiirmun tunluku, naspaavkarluku cali. Asevrem-am pillinia, nutaan-gguq atam, engelqaqluku-gguq tua-i. Qalriaciqkii-gguq tuar

like that. And many walrus sleep floating, because walrus have *puvyat* [air pouches] on their backs and can breathe through their air pouches, even though they are underwater.

[*Puvyat*] are the breathing [pouches] of walrus. They fill them with air and float, using it as a float. It is a very large pouch located here. They breathe through them, even though their heads are underwater. And they are noticeable as among them are *cauyaqtaatulit* [those making drumming sounds]. You know those guitars, when they strike the strings, [they make a *teng-teng* sound]. They sounded like that. The sound they made sounded like a person striking guitar strings. They'd make the *teng-teng* sound, and they sounded wonderful. They say it's those walrus making that sound, *cauyaqtaalriit*, while they're sleeping in the water.

I don't know what part of them makes the sound. Maybe it comes from inside [the *puvyat*]. We watched those a number of times, ones that were sleeping afloat. Not many walrus do that. But they say those that have *cauyaqtaat* make those sounds, like the sound of a guitar making different pitches. It sounded as though they were striking their guitar strings. The sound would be low and suddenly go high. They were wonderful to listen to. But they would be floating in a group. Apparently, walrus like to stick together when they sleep in the water by inflating their air pouches. Their heads don't come out of the water, but they'd breathe from inside their air pouches.

It was filled with air. And when they woke up, they'd empty them. They'd let the air out. They probably do that when they get sleepy.

They say they are like ptarmigan because they used to be cross-cousins. The walrus and the ptarmigan were cousins. They say that's why they both have those [air pouches] that allow them to make loud noise. You know how those ptarmigan suddenly lift off and make that particular sound. They say ptarmigan inflate their air pouches, their food cache.

Those elders of the past talked about them. They said the ptarmigan used to sound like a walrus, and the walrus once sounded like a ptarmigan. One day, the walrus and the ptarmigan said, "You there, you don't match the sound you make." The other said, "You don't match the sound you make either. Let's switch them." Then the ptarmigan eventually gave his call to the walrus and asked him to try it out. After the walrus made the call, ptarmigan said that it sounded like his own and had always been his. And the ptarmigan added that [walrus] was a large animal [compared to his small size]. Then the walrus gave his call to the ptarmigan and had him try it. The walrus told him that the sound was just right for him. He told him that

nutem mikelkevkenaku, angkevkenaku-llu. Tua-i-gguq tuaten navrutellruagkek qal-
riacitek. Tuaten-am qanemcitangqertuq.

Asevret atam piyagait imkut qimugcetun qilulriatun ayuqut. Ayuqluteng pituut
mikcuaraat. Angtuat taugken allayuunruluni. "*Uuu-uuu-uu-uu-uu.*" Tuaten elliurluteng piaqluteng.

Temirtengungermeng qalriallagatuut. Asevret makut nutaan kenkuteksaitelartut
quyurmeng qavaraqameng. Ilateng calekcagayugluki qalriallagaluteng, qavamegg-
nek tupagqaqaceteng. Tamaa-i tamakut qalriallagayaraqait. Qenqerrulluteng-wa pilallilriit. Piyagait taugken tuaten qimugtetun qilulriatun neplitululuteng qalriallagaa-
qameng, allayuggauluteng. Temirtait-llu nutaan allakauluteng.

Qavaraqameng-wa tua-i tuaten pitulriit. Call'ugteraqluteng qavameggni.

Arnacaluit ciumek nunamtenun unavet pituut. Kitutuut angucalumek amllermek avuunateng. Kinguqliit-llu tua-i angucalurrlainaat nutaan. Amllepiarluteng
nutaan asevret, asveyagallernek avuluteng. Arnacaluit ciumek pituut piyagamegg-
nek maligluteng.

ALICE: Waten uksumi, uksuarmi, up'nerkami-llu cat wani paivngatuat taukut
nalliitni? Up'nerkami cat ciumek tekitelartat unguvalriit nunavceni?

FRANK: February-mi atam, February pit'aqan issurit amllerituut unani nunamteni. Issurit amlleriluteng. March-aam-llu tua-i maani iluani maklagnek avungluteng nayirnek tuaten avungluteng. Issurit pituut ciumek nunamni kanani Bering
Sea-mi. Avaqliitni maani nalluanka wii, taugaam kanani wii nayuqengamni. Nayu-
qengama nuniinelngurnek qanemcilartua nallunrilkengamnek, avaqliit makut na-
llukenka piksaunaki. Tuaten ayuqut. Tua-i-llu [kinguakun] makliit angucalumegg-
nek avuluteng arnacalut. Tua-i-ll' piuraqerluteng irnialget tekilluteng, irniluteng
tuaten ilait. Imkut *young*-alriit makliit, *young*-alriit ciumek tekilluteng, irniarit-llu.
Maklagaat, qaingit kukupaunateng; tua-i assirluteng qaraliinateng tua-i. Iiliaruka'arluteng, tua-i qimugteni imutun, *husky*-nek iciw' qimugtet pilaqait, tuacetun qaralirluteng maklagaat, iiliaruka'arluteng, kegginait assiq'apiarluteng. Tuaten tua-i ayuqluteng, qaingit-llu assirluteng, makliit-llu *young*-alriit, arnacalut irniarit ayagyualriit.

Tua-i-ll' tamakut piuraqerluki imkut teqiyaaraat yaqulget imkut, tamakut tekicata, nutaan mikurqaat maklagaat tekilluteng, aanameggnek taperluteng. Angtuat
nutaan maklaarpallraat-llu, pequrrit-llu kukupagpagnek qaralirluteng, angtuat maklagaat [tekilluteng]. *Old*-alriit-gguq arnat irniarit makliit arnaita. Temirtengurtell-
riit irniarit nallunaunateng tua-i. Augkucicetun ciuqlirtun ayuqevkenateng irniarit.

he sounded as if he had always made the sound, and it was just right for him. They say that's how they switched their calls. That's a story that has been told.

Walrus pups bark like dogs. The small ones all make the same sound. But the larger ones make a different sound. "*Uuu-uuu-uu-uu-uu.*" That's the noise they make.

They make sudden sounds, even though they're adults. These walrus don't really get along when they're sleeping together in groups. They tend to be aggressive toward others around them and make sudden sounds and hit them when others wake them. That's when they make sudden sounds. They probably get angry at one another. But their pups sound like dogs when they make sounds; they sound strange. But the adults make stranger sounds [than their young].

That's what they do when they're sleeping. They fight in their sleep.

The females are the first to arrive in our area down on the coast. They go by first, accompanied by few males. Then the next group that comes is predominantly male. Many walrus arrive at that time, along with young walrus [that were pups the year before]. The females arrive first with their pups.

ALICE: What are available during the winter, fall, and spring? What sea mammals arrive first during the spring in your village?

FRANK: In February, in the month of February, the number of spotted seals increases down in our area. There would be many spotted seals. And in March, they'd be joined by bearded seals along with ringed seals. Down in my area in the Bering Sea, spotted seals come first. I don't know how it is in surrounding areas, but down where I'm from [that's how it is]. I talk about things I know, things that occur in my area, not mentioning things that I don't know that occur in surrounding areas. That's how they are. Then the female bearded seals [arrived] along with their male counterparts. Then after a while, the bearded seals [that had delivered along the way] arrived with their pups, and some gave birth [after arriving]. Young bearded seals, the young ones arrived first with their pups. Bearded seals in their first year have no spots on their bodies and look very nice. And they would have markings on their faces, *iiliaruka'arluteng* as they called it, and look very nice, the same markings you see on the faces of husky dogs. That's how they looked, and their fur looked nice, the young bearded seals, the young offspring of adult female bearded seals.

And soon after [younger bearded seals with pups] had arrived, when those birds called *teqiyaaraat* [Arctic terns] arrived, then many, many bearded seals in their first year arrived along with their mothers. And also the very large bearded seals with spots on their backs, the large *maklagaat* [bearded seals in their first year] [arrive]. They say they are the offspring of the older female bearded seals. The offspring of

Angenruluteng-llu qaralirluteng-llu peq'urrit. Tuaten-am ayuqut kinguatgun tua-i. Tua-i-ll' tamakut tekiteqerluki asevret tekilluteng nutaan, amllepiat nutaan asevret. Piyagaat nutaan amlleriqerrluteng.

Up'nerkami, tua-i anguarciiganata uitaaqluta, asevret amllessiyaagaqata kuimalriit.

Alingnarqelartut. Ullagaluki-ll' piiyuamegteki, aciiraluki. Taugaam anguarutet waten elliurturluki, agturngaitaa asevrem. Waten elliurturluk' kuimalriit amlleqata avatmini.

Mermun waten elliurluki. Aciirangaunaku asevrem. Amlleraqameng alingnarqut. Taumek anguarayuilngukut tuani amllessiyaagaqata asevret. Ak'anun pilartut, ayagnaciarluteng negetmun asevret. Imkut uani ketemteni kuiget, kuiguyurpallraak augkuk malruk, *clam*-anek amllernek neq'aitnek imangqerrameng, tua-i unitnacialaragket taukuk kuigek malruk, *clam*-anek neqengqerrameng tuani.

Uilunek-llu imkunek kumgayagalegnek. Kumgayagailngurnek-llu imkunek qatellrianek. Augkunek-llu aliruanek, qapilaanek-llu. Tamakunek ner'angqelartut anrutait imangqerraqluteng amllernek. Tua-i nutaraugaqata erurluki tua-i carrirluki nerlaraput qassarluki ungimanrilnguut. Tamakurrlainarnek neqengqelartut. Taugken ilait asevret unguvalrianek ner'angqetuluteng-gguq, taqukaturayulit-gguq tamakut. Issurinek-llu ner'angqerraqluteng allgumaluteng qeciit, asevret ilait. Taqukaturayulit-gguq tamaa-i tamakut.

Carrlugmek tamakurrlugmek avungqerciigatut nerait. Avungqetuut asevret teggalquyagarnek. Tamakunek tamaa-i neqengqertut asevret.

Tua-i-ll' asevret nangyartuqerluki, unguvalriit pellugiinaqerluteng. Tamalkurmeng tua-i ikegliinarluteng, elatmun nutaan ayiimeng. Asvertairulluni-ll' tua-i unguvalriit nurnariluteng, issurit taugaam nayiit-llu ellma kiagpak piqaquuraraqluteng.

Tua-i-ll' naunraam nalliini, August-aam nangyartuqatallrani, makliit alangruungarrluteng nunamni un'gaani, nayirnek avuluteng. Kuignun-llu it'ranglkuteng nayiit. Maklagaat amlleriinarluteng, maklassugnek-llu avungluteng, avungqerraqluteng. Caqapkacaagaraqameng maklagnek avungqerraqluteng. Uksuarmi makliit nurna-

the older females are obvious. Their pups don't look like the first pups of the first ones that arrived. They are bigger and have designs on their backs. The bearded seals that arrived next appeared like that, and soon after they arrived, the walrus arrived; many, many walrus. At that time you see many, many sea-mammal pups.

In spring, we couldn't paddle with our kayaks and stayed when too many walrus were swimming.

They are dangerous because they go right up to [kayakers], swimming under [their kayaks]. But if [the kayaker dipped] the paddle [in and out of water], the walrus won't touch him. [A kayaker] would continually [dip his paddle in and out of water] if many were swimming around him.

They would [dip their paddle in and out] of the water like this. The walrus won't swim under [the kayak]. They are dangerous when they are numerous. They just swim right up to the kayakers and aren't afraid of them. That's why we don't paddle around when there are too many walrus. They stay in our area without continuing northward for a long time. The rivers down below us, those two very large channels, because they are filled with many clams that they eat, they don't leave those two rivers for a while, because they eat clams there.

[They eat] those clams with indented lines on their shells also. And they also eat those with white shells without the little indented lines. And they eat those *aliruat* [razor clams] as well, and *qapilaat* [mussels]. [The walrus] have those inside their stomachs; their stomachs are filled with many [clams]. When they are fresh, we wash them and eat them. We eat them raw, the ones that aren't soft and dissolved. They eat all those kinds of [shellfish]. But they say some walrus have seals in their stomachs, [walrus] they called *taqukaturayulit* [lit., "ones that like to eat seals"]. And some walrus have spotted seals in their stomachs, with their skins all chewed up. They call those *taqukaturayulit*.

The contents of their stomachs cannot have [shells] in them whatsoever. The walrus [stomachs] contain pebbles. That's what walrus eat.

And just as the number of walrus [around our area] decreases, sea mammals gradually diminish. They gradually decrease in number as they travel outside our area. Then walrus are no longer around, just a few sea mammals, but a few spotted seals and ringed seals were seen from time to time all summer.

Then during the time salmonberries are ripe, toward the end of August, the adult bearded seals start to appear down in our area on the coast along with ringed seals. And the ringed seals begin to go up rivers. There are more and more bearded seals in their first year, along with two-year-old bearded seals. Once in a great while, they

qapiaralartut un'gaani nunamteni, up'nerkami amllerraarluteng. Unaggun-gguq utertetuut. Unavet nunamtenun cenavarpek'nateng.

Qasrulget-llu tamakut up'nerkami nurnapiarluteng. Tua-i alangruuyuunateng. Uksuarmi taugaam tua-i, October-aam maani nuniini, October, pivallulartut tama-tum nalliini qasrulget. Utetmun uksuarmi, asvernek avuluteng, maklagaat-llu. Asev-ret makut nenglengqataarqan, nengelqaqataqan alangruutuut nunamteni un'gaani.

Taumek asvernek piqulalriit, piyunarqaqata nunamteni. Asverqaqluteng neng-lengqata'arqan tua-i. Tuaten tua-i ayuqut imarpigmiutaat.

~: Cetuat :~

Avani ciuqvaarni upayuitut cetuat. Kiagpak tua-i alangruugurluteng Kusquqvagmi-ll' maani, kiagpak tua-i kiituan uksurtuq. Tuaten tua-i pitullruut cetuat. Tua-i nu-namteni unani pisciigaliluteng tayima.

Kiagungraan pissutuit piyugaqameng, taugaam amllermek piiyuitut kiagmi. Aveqluki-ll' waten yugnun pituluki cetuat. Ak'allaurtellerkaat-wa tepsarillerkaat pi-tekluki tuatnatuit, egmianun aruqutkaqluki nangluki tua-i. Kemgit iniluki tuaten ilaita. Kinerneruluteng assirtut kemgit cetuat. Maa-i-ll' tua-i piiyuirulluteng.

Cetuat-am makut nallutaitut cali. Pinaqluku piyunaitut, nallutaitut. Tuqungai-tuq inerquutii aturluku pikuniu. Waten piciatun irniani piunrillrukan kassuksau-nani, aanani piunrillrukan kassuksaunani, uingulriim qetunraulriim-llu ayuqlutek, irniari-llu, cegg'atuut. Tua-i kiimenani, caciilngurmek aipirpek'nani, kiimenani qaill' pingaunani, egmian tuquarkauluni. Taugaam pillguterluni tuqungaituq qamiquni navguqapiaraumangraan cetuaq. Tuaten ayagilartut-gguq ilait, cegg'ariluteng.

Taumek ikayuutesqessuilkait, wall'u inerqurluki ilagautesqevkenaki tamakuliul-rianun cetuanek. Taugaam kiimenaku elliit pingraan qaill' pingaitniluku, taugaam

would have adult bearded seals among them. There are very few bearded seals in our area during fall, after there had been many during spring. They say they return home through a route that is farther from land. They don't come up to the shore in the area below us.

And those ribbon seals are very rare during spring. They aren't seen. But during fall, around October, ribbon seals are seen mostly during that time. They return in fall along with walrus and bearded seals in their first year. Walrus are seen right before it gets cold in our area down on the coast.

That's why they bring home walrus when they're available in our area. They would catch walrus just before it gets cold. That's how sea mammals are.

~: Beluga whales :~

Long ago, belugas never migrated [north]. They were seen all summer, and they were on the Kuskokwim River all summer until winter. That's what belugas did. They aren't seen in our area anymore.

They hunted them, even during summer when they wanted to, but not many were caught in summer. They cut belugas into portions and distribute them to people, too. They immediately distribute the whole thing because they might spoil and get smelly. And some people hang the meat. Dried beluga meat is good. They don't prepare them like that anymore these days.

These belugas are also very sensitive and can detect a person [who recently lost an immediate family member]. It's not good to hunt them [when death has just occurred in your family] because they are sensitive and will know that. When one hunts them, breaking the law about hunting belugas, though he tries to kill the animal, it will not die. If the hunter's child had died and the prescribed restriction period had not ended, if a hunter's mother had died and a year hadn't passed, either a husband or son and all their children, when such hunters hunt belugas, [belugas] get fully awake and become energized. If a hunter is alone and not accompanied by a hunter suffering a loss, he can hunt a beluga, and the animal will die right away when hit. But if he is with a person who is bereaved, the beluga will not die, even though its head is completely smashed. That's why some belugas became energized and escaped from some hunters [even after they were hit].

That's why they tell [men whose immediate family members died recently] not to take part in beluga hunts, or they tell them not to join others who are hunting

caskuyaaqaku tuquciqniluku, taugaam ilangqerquni caciilngurmek, tuaten ellmitun pinrilngurmek [tuqungaitniluku]. Tamatumek inerquutengqertut cetuat.

Avani kiagmi qayatgun unani quyurmeng kellutetuit cetuangqellrani. Tua-i-ll' cetuat agiircata qavlunarluteng et'unrilngurmi uitaurluteng, terr'a agtuqeryaaqevkenaku camna. Nallutaitut, ciutekpiartut cetuat. Agtuqayunaunani terr'a, imarpiim unani. Kelumeggnun taugaam elliqata nutaan calekcagarkauluki, imkut paangrutet nutaan anlluki, *double*-aanek paanguarutellget waten. Tamakuliuraqameng atutuit, imkut waten pilget aturpek'naki. Kapuutet-llu augkut cingilgit takluteng enret, akrunateng-llu. Tua-i kapuqaarluteng nagtevkenateng camun amugarcugngaluteng, ipegcenateng taugaam nuugit. Cetuarcuutet, imgutaunateng-llu. Maaggun-llu tua-i aqsaitgun tulimaitgun narulkarluki. Tamakut taugken tua-i mermi elliurluteng, qamna kapusngalria nutaan augmek caliluni iluani. Tua-i qavcinek piuraqerluni, cetuaq egmian illugarrluni tua-i cirlaqerrluni. Allam-llu ullagarrluku, teguteqerluku imgutalegmek. Taum-llu tua-i kapuutem pikestii taigarrluni kapuutni tamana teguluku amugarrluk' egmianun, alla cali maliggluku cetuaq. Taumek patagmek tuqurqilalriit tuaten.

Makut ilait teguteqaarastet imgutalegnek, tamakut-llu tamaa-i kapuutnek caskulget ciuqliuluteng. Tua-i maligtaquluku imgutalegmek pilgem, kapuutmek pilek ciuqliqluku. Tua-i-ll' narulkaqaku kapuutmek kinguqlian taum imgutalgem tegutnek pilgem, egmianun ullagarrluku curukarluku, narulkarluku tamana. Tut'engraan tua-i teguyugngariluku. Tuaten ceciiyuraqameng pituut.

Et'ulriamun ayagceteksaunaki. Unani kellirneratni ilagarpek'naki paangaaluteng utqetaalriit, ketmurtesciigatevkarluki. Tuaten ceciiyutuut. Kapulriit ingkut ullaksaunaki tamakut murilkestaita qayat, paangaaluteng, kipullgutaarluteng waten, ketairumaluki, amllerrluteng. Ketmuqercaaqaqata, ciunrirluki kelutmun kasmaqluki, taukut ullagcetaqluki. Iliini tua-i nangluki piaqluki tuqutaqluki. Ceciiyuraqameng tua-i tuaten pituut. Kapuutnek caskirluteng. Nut'ngeng'ermeng tamakut aturpakayuitellruit, ceciiyuraqameng, kapuutet taugaam.

belugas. A hunter is told that if he wasn't recently bereaved, he can hunt beluga, and the animal would die if hit. But if a hunter is with someone who is bereaved [the beluga will not die]. That's the prohibition concerning belugas.

In summer, back when there were belugas, a group of hunters would go down [to the ocean] in kayaks and watch for them. And when belugas approached with their fins visible at the surface, the hunters assembled in the shallows and waited, trying not to dip their paddles to the ocean bottom. [Belugas] are very sensitive and have good hearing, and one must not touch the bottom of the ocean with his paddle whatsoever. They'd wait, and only after they reached the area behind them [toward the land], the hunters would suddenly create movement and sound with their double-bladed paddles. They use [double-bladed paddles] when they hunt belugas, not using just the [single-bladed paddles]. And they used *kapuutet* [spears] with long, sharp, barbless bone points. After the point pierces something, it could easily come out smoothly because their tips were very straight and sharp. They were spears without line attachments used in beluga hunting. They speared them on their stomachs and ribs. Once the beluga was hit, they would make this motion in the water, and the area inside where the spear point penetrated would start bleeding. After they made that same motion several times, the beluga would suddenly tilt and get weak. Then another person would quickly approach the animal and retrieve it with a *tegun* [large harpoon] with line attachment. Then the owner of the spear would quickly come and pull out his spear and go after another beluga. That's why they kill many belugas in a short time.

The ones using the harpoons with line attachments would be situated right behind the ones who had spears. The hunter using a harpoon would follow the hunter who had a spear. Then when the hunter with a spear hit a beluga, the hunter with a harpoon would immediately go to the animal and retrieve it. He would be able to take the animal, even if it sank to the bottom. That's how they hunt belugas.

[They'd keep the belugas in shallow water] and not let them go to deep water. Right below them, there were men in kayaks paddling back and forth with double-bladed paddles to prevent [belugas] from going down to the deeper water away from shore. That's how they hunted for belugas. Men in many kayaks were guarding, paddling back and forth a distance below the ones who were hitting and spearing the belugas. When the belugas moved toward the ocean, the paddlers down below would block their path and push them back toward the hunters back there. Sometimes they would kill all of them. That's how they hunted belugas. They used *kapuutet* as weapons to strike them. Although they acquired guns they hardly used them when they hunted beluga, only *kapuutet*.

Makut-llu tua-i caviit paivngariata cavignek kapuutengqelangluteng, akrunaki tua-i ingkut cingigluki, naggngairutelluku tua-i amugarcugngavkarluki cali.

Cat-wa piitnek pilartat. Imkut *whale*-at agluqritnek pilaryugnarqut. Tamakung-qelaryugnarqut enernek. Imkunek taugaam uminek teggalqunek ingkulirluki, ak-runaki taugaam. Waten tua-i pimallrit maqarcenateng, camun naggngairutelluki amukata.

Cikulgem nuniini pivakayuitut cetuanek. Kenercetut cikumi. Qaingit piirait-qapiartut. Makut taugken melqulget piiragcenani mayurtellrat; angengermeng pii-ragcenateng. Cetuat taugaam piiraitqapiartut qanikcami. Qaingit assirciqngacaaqlu-teng qanikcami, taugaam piiraitepiartut, qaugyatun ayuqut tua-i. Marayami taugken tua-i assinrurpagluni, piiragcenaki. Uksuragmi pivakalriit akaggluki nugtetuit ciku-mun. Piyunarcarra'arluku ciku, waten ayuqevkarluku unavet, tua-ll' taprualugnek aciirluki, taprarnek, akagtelluki mayurrluki cikumun. Tuaten pituit cetuat uksumi. Qamurluki kenercenateng.

Nunamni taugken avani nunamteni uksuarmi tua-i nutaan amllerrluki pingna-tularait cikuqatarluku. Allamiaqan tua-i tuaterrlainarluteng, cetuat amllepiallruata nunamteni un'gaani.

Piyulriit tua-i tuaten piaqluteng; kapuqengyulriit tua-i kapurilrianun ilautaqlu-teng, teguteqarastet-llu piyugaqameng ilagautetuut. Piyunrilameng-llu paangaal-riani uitaaqluteng.

Cetuat tamakut angelriit ciamcetuit, wall'u asevret uksuarmi. Ukut tua-i nunat *family*-t qaqingnaqluki ayuqluki aruqutkarkauluki, cuqluki tua-i angtaciqeggiluki. Qavciungata-ll' angenruluki tamakut piaqluki cetuat, kinaim' piicetevkenaku nu-nani ukuni, *family*-t. Tuatnatuit ceturraraqameng. Amlleraqata tua-i iliini, cetua-mek-llu ataucitaarturluki aruqaqluki, wall' malrutaarluki. Amllernek piaqameng, tuatnatuut. Asevret-llu call' tuatnatuluki. Up'nerkami tuquciaqameng tua-i amllerr-luteng tuqucitullruut. Nangengnaqluki tua-i kemgitnek qeciitnek-llu qayat uciliraq-luteng amllertatkurluteng, asveq tua-i nangluku. Taugaam temirtet makut angtuat qiluit imkut piiyuitait. Assiitut, imarniteksunaunateng, anrutait taugken tegurrlai-narluki.

And when metal became available, they started making metal points for *kapuutet*, barbless but sharp, so they would not get stuck, so they could pull out smoothly.

I don't know what kind of bone they used [for spear points]. I think they used whale jawbones. I think they made that piece out of bone. But they made the tips out of slate but without barbs. The [point] was smooth and could easily come out when pulled.

They hardly hunt belugas near ice. They are hard to drag on ice. [Their rough skin] makes it difficult [to pull them onto ice]. But sea mammals with fur, even though they're large, can easily be pulled up and slide on ice. But belugas are difficult to move on snow. Even though their bodies look like they could easily be pulled on snow, the texture of their skin is like sand and makes it hard to move them. But it is much easier to drag them on mud. The ones they catch during winter, they mainly pull them out of the water and onto the ice by rolling them and not pulling them head first. After fixing the ice, making it slant toward the water, they placed sealskin line underneath them and rolled them on top of the ice. That's how they move belugas in winter [after killing them]. They have a lot of friction when dragged.

But in my area, they hunted them in great numbers during fall, just before freeze-up. They did that every year because there were many belugas in our area down on the coast.

Those who wanted to took part; those who wanted to would go with those who were striking [the animals], and those who wanted to would join those who were using *tegutet*. And those who didn't want to [strike the animals] would join those guarding with double-bladed paddles.

They cut large belugas or walrus into portions in the fall. Then they try to distribute them to all the families in the village, after determining the number of people, and cutting them in equal portions. And when there were several belugas caught, they'd cut the belugas into larger pieces, and they gave them out to all the families in the village and didn't leave anyone out. That's what they did when they hunted beluga. Sometimes, when they caught lots, they would distribute one beluga [per family] or two when they had caught a lot. That's what they did when they caught lots. And they did that with walrus as well. When they hunted them in the spring many hunters went out in a group and did the killing. The kayaks load up equally, trying to carry away all the meat and skins, taking the entire walrus. But they don't use the intestines of old walrus. They aren't good to make into gut raingear, but they always took their stomachs.

Young-alriit taugaam qiluit taugaam nutaan tegutuluki. Ellalliurcuutekarnirluteng call' tamakut. Cetuat taugken qiluit egcuunaki. Cakuiyuitait cetuat. Tua-i tamaq'apiaraan tua-i cetuaq, enri taugaam nerevkenaki, tamalkuan tua-i nerluku tua-i cetuaq ilakuivkenaku.

Tamana piciatun piyaraunrituq, qaillun ping'ermeng pilatuut tuqumalrianek. Arnat taugaam ilagautaqluteng amllerrameng.

Meqcirluki-am pituit mangtait. Mangtagnek qemagciqatalriit uquituit, mangtait uitavkarluki. Nepingatuameng qeciitni mangtait. Meqvailegmeng navguryugngauq nepingiimi qeciani, augkut cayagait. Melqurrit-gguq tamaa-i mangtiit. Uquirraarluku nutaan meqcirluki. Tua-i teguluteng kiigartelaata, nutaan mangtait aug'arluki. Taugaam qayaqsuunaki qeciit nat'raqsuunaki-llu cetuat. Imkut neqngutnguluki taugaam caqutekaqluki qakiiyarnun caquit tamakut.

Ciqicuitait, nunamun pituit cetuat enrit. Nunamiutaungata-gguq. Keglunruut. Keglunruut ilumun. Keglunrurtetuut. Qakvarniararaqameng-gguq nunamun, qeciraqameng-gguq qaktaqameng kukumyalqitarangtuut. Aneryaaraqami kukumyalqita'arluni piaqluni qakvarniararaqami, keglunrurteqataraqami.

Tuaten-gguq taugken piqatarqameng tuaten qalriangetuut. Alingnaqluni-llu ciunratni uitallerkaq qakvallratni. Nallunaitelliniut tua-i tuatnangaqameng tamakut, keglunrurteqatallrat. Ilait-gguq mangtaitni melqut pugngetuut keglunirnaat, piarkaurtaqata. Nuna-gguq navgurluku, muragat-llu nerluki ciamlluki, ca tamalkuan nerluku qakvaraqameng pituut alingnaqluteng. Tua-i ungungssiungraan yuungraan-llu piyugngaluku. Ciunratni taumek uitasqessuitait.

Enrit-llu tua-i mermun piiyuunaki, nunamun taugaam tua-i piurluki. Keglunruniluki piaqluki, mermun egtesqevkenaki. Imarpigmun taugken unavet anglluqatallrat qaillun qanemciuluku niicuunaku allayuuluku.

Qakvaqatarqameng-gguq taugaam piniararaqameng pituut; kukumyalqitalangengluteng aneryaaraqameng.

They only take the intestines of the young [walrus]. Those are also good to make into gut raingear. But they didn't discard beluga intestines. They don't discard any part of the beluga. They use the whole beluga, but they don't eat the bones, eating the whole beluga and not leaving any leftovers.

There are no restrictions and anyone can butcher [belugas]. Women took part because there were lots of them.

Their *mangtak* [skin with blubber attached] is aged first [before it is processed to be eaten]. The ones who are going to put away *mangtak* removed the blubber first, leaving the *mangtak* on. The *mangtak* adheres to their skin. Before [the skin] comes off, it can be cut up because those little things adhere to the hide. They say *mangtak* is the fur [of the beluga]. After removing the blubber, they'd age [the *mangtak*]. Since you can take them and peel them off, they would then pull the *mangtak* off the skin. But they didn't use beluga skins for kayak coverings and boot soles. But they used them as storage containers for dried silver salmon.

They don't dump them [in their normal refuse pile], but they place beluga bones on land. They say they are mammals that live on land. They're wolves. They are surely wolves. They transform into wolves [on land]. It is said when they are about to come out of the water and onto land, when they spray water through their breathing holes, they begin breaching and making a whistling sound. When they breathe, they begin whistling when they are about to come out of the water and onto land, when they are about to transform into wolves.

They start making that sound when they are going to [go on land and turn into wolves]. It's very dangerous to be in their path just when they go from water onto land. It's easy to know when they were going to transform into wolves. And they say wolf fur starts to come out of their *mangtak* when they were going to transform into wolves. They say when they first come up on land, they destroy the land and chew up driftwood and everything around them. They can attack animals and even humans. That's why people were told not to stay on the land where they came up.

And they don't discard their bones in water, but only on land. It was known that they were wolves, and people were told not to throw their bones in water. But they never talked about what happened when they got ready to go into water [and transform into belugas].

They say when they are about to come out of water onto land, when that time is approaching, they start making a whistling sound when they're breathing.

~: *Arrluut* :~

Imkut *killer whale*-at inerquutnguut. Akngirtesqevkenaki. Ikayurituut.

Wall'u *whale*-amek angtuamek pikata *killer whale*-at, tua-i cucukuni yuk camek cikirraasqumaluni, camek picirraatun aklurraminek mermun ekiarkauguq qanrul-luki, ik'arrarmek pisqumaniluni. Pinricuitait-gguq. Maa-i mat'um-llu nalliini pi-yugngaluki. Ik'anek-gguq tua-i, uluarluteng-gguq tuar pimalalriit. Mermek pugle-qertetuuq cikiutiit tua-i tauna. Makut qayat-llu qaill' pingaunaki tamakut *killer whale*-at. Alingcetaarngaunaki-ll'.

Tangaalallrulrianga-ll' Ilkivigmi-ll' uani tamakunek arrlugnek. Qaraliit atam call' ayuqenritut. *Moon*-aruanek tuaten ukuit qaralingqerraqluteng ilaita ayakutaarait. Qaurraarmiut-wa taukut tuaten qaralingqellrulriit, qaralingqelallrulriit. Kuigmi uani Ilkivigmek aterluni, tangvalartukut pulengtaq tangvalallruukut canimaarmun tua-i asguraqata. Qamani iluqvaarni Qaurraak uitauk, qemirpiik angtuak. Taukuk-gguq tua-i tekitaqamegtekek ketiigni — waten kuik tapingauq qiptellra — ekvik tua-i maan' cauluku qaktetuut, pugevkenateng-llu tayima. Pikani-w' kangragni egal-rat, uum-llu angneqluku. Qaill' angtaa tayima, qemirpiim kangrani pakmani. Kuma-rullugnek nanerterluni waten naumalrianek avatii. Man'a-w' qukaa uruarnganani, tegqapiarluni taugaam. Egalrat-gguq tua-i. Tutmaasqevkenaku-am inerqutuit.

Angluni taugaam. Tamakunek tua-i maa-i, akultutaurluteng qaillun, kumaru-llugpagngalnguut caniqliqluteng. Nanertai-gguq egalrata. Tuunrangayiim-gguq-am taum kelutmun cautellrui. Yuliuryullruut-gguq avani ciuqvaarni Qauraarmiut taukut. Tan'gaurluungraata-ll' itertaqluki nunameggnun ikirulluki. Picirkartullruut-gguq. Tua-i taumek taum angalkuum elpekngamiki kelutmun cautellrullinii. Taqlu-teng-llu-gguq tua-i yuliurnanrirluteng. Luglaarmek aterluni tauna angalkuq. Qetun-rani tauna itercaaqerraartelluku, qetunrani, nasaurlurmek aiparluni.

Nepliraqameng atam nallunaitut. Tem'iqtaarturnaurtuk taukuk Qaurraak. Ka-lliraqami iciw' tem'irtelalria. Tuacetun tua-i niicugnilallrukegka. Tua-i-am cali assir-

~: Killer whales :~

We were admonished about killer whales. They tell us not to hurt them. It was known that they would help people.

Or if killer whales are going after a large whale, if [a person watching them] wants a piece of the killer whales' catch, he would throw any small belonging in the water, asking for a little piece of meat and blubber. They say they always fulfill their request. They can even do that today, too. They say [killer whales] give them a piece of meat and blubber that appears as though it was cut with a knife. The gift given to that person would suddenly pop up in the water. And those killer whales won't do anything to nearby men in kayaks. They'd leave them alone and not try to scare them.

And I used to see killer whales down in the Ilkivik River as well. The designs on their bodies are also different. The sides of some of their faces had designs that look like moons. Qaurraarmiut [those who reside in Qaurraak] had designs like that. We saw them many times at close range when they swam upstream in the river down there called Ilkivik. The two large bluffs called Qaurraak are a good distance upriver. They say when killer whales reach those two bluffs, right below them, right at the bend in the river, they'd face the bluff directly in front of them, breach once, and disappear, and they don't come up again. Their window [into their world] is on top of the bluff, and it's larger than this. I don't know how large it is, on top of the very high bluff. All the way around is a window with wick moss grown as support to keep the window in place. The window looked like regular moss, but it was solid. They say that's the [killer whales'] window. People are warned not to step on it.

But it's large. A strip of wick moss grows all around the window to support the window panel. They say those are the *nanertet* [rocks that weigh down the gut covering] of their window. It is said a shaman turned [their village] around facing inland. They say those Qaurrarmiut used to bother and take people [into their world]. They used to uncover the opening to their world and even bring boys into their village. They say they were mischievous. When that shaman realized what they were doing, he turned [their place] around facing inland. And after that, they stopped taking people. That shaman was named Luglaaq. He did that after they took his son inside their world, along with a girl.

You can hear them when they are making noise. Rumbling noises were heard coming directly from Qaurraak. You know how thunder makes noise. That's how

pek'nani maani avatiigni pisqevkenaki inerquusngaut. Tan'gerpagnek-llu iqvaasqev-
kenaki tamaani. Caciilnguut taugaam.

Tuatnallratni malrurqugnek niicugnilallruaput. Tamakut taugken niitenritlini-
luku, taukut, taum itagnarqelriim. Wangkuta taugaam niiqluku. Qastuluni tua-i
qastuaqluni, tem'iqtaararaqluni.
　　Yuuluki-ll' tangrraqluki yuit tamakut, tamakuuluki-ll' *killer whale*-auluki tangrraqluki, arrluuluki. Avani tan'gaurluulua Ilkivigmi qanemciknaurait tamakut tang-
lliniaqamegteki. Qayarluteng-llu yuuluteng piaqata, ucialarpaa-gguq qayaitni ungu-
valrianek-wa tua-i piciatun.

　　Tayima tua-i pinanrirluteng. Qanruteknanrirluki tamakut avani cetuat tamakut
pinanriata. Maliggluki-am nugtarrnilaryugnarqait. Nugtarrniluki pilarait neqekngamegteki. Kusquqvagmi-ll' piiyuirulluteng cetuat. Tamakut-llu *killer whale*-at pinanrirluteng Kusquqvagmi, tayima tua-i catairulluteng.

　　Tamakunek taugaam *whale*-anek pilallritnek mallungelallruut nunamteni avani,
imkut *rib*-akayait makuit angtuat ayimqumaaqluteng. Equgarluki-gguq pituit.
Imna tua-i qavcirqunek tangvallallrulliniut ikani Kusquqviim paingani, arvermek
callullratni killer *whale*-at. Kanarmi-llu-gguq pugluni, ter'ak pika'anllutek, angtuaq
ungungssirpaller' *whale*-aq imna angtuarpak. Qengmiulluki-gguq tuqutetuit, enrit
makut ayimqelluki mermelngermeng. Qallangelria-gguq avatii uivetmun tamana,
kanarmi alairluni arveq tauna. Nemaaluni-gguq tua-i piyaaqerraarluni, ataam ang-
llurraarluni piaqami pinialikaniraqluni. Kiituan-gguq tua-i tapingaluni alailnguq
cirlaurrluni.

　　Nertulliniit. Ilakuaritnek taugaam pugleraqata yuut pituut kemgitnek. Cetua-
nek-llu pillritnek cali ilakuaritnek piaqluteng. Nuussikun tuar uluarumalalriit, piciatun pimavkenateng. Tua-i waten ayuqluteng tua-i, nuussikun uluarumanganateng.

　　Iliiralria-gguq tuatnakuni, tamakuliullratni qacusngaitaat, cikinrilngaitaat. Pi-
yukengaanek cikiryugngaluku tua-i. Ing'um-llu Peter Jimmie, nunalgutemta atii,
Adolf-aaq cikillrulliniat cali. Qanemcillruuq tungaunani. Nutaan-gguq asgurakenri-
tevsiarluku ilumuucia. Allat taugken tua-i piiyuunateng, ircenrraunilallrit cali allat.
Tamakut taugaam kiimeng tua-i nallunaunateng pilallruut killer *whale*-at.

it sounded when I heard them. But [people who had recently experienced bereavement, miscarriage, or first menstruation] were told not to go near those bluffs, even to pick blackberries. Only those who weren't under such circumstances could do so.

We heard them twice when they did that. But those others didn't hear them, the recently bereaved person didn't hear the sound. But we heard them, and they were making a loud rumbling sound.

They also saw their inhabitants as people, and they saw them as killer whales. When I was a boy when people encountered them in either form, they used to talk about their experience. And if they had seen them in human form traveling in a kayak, they'd comment on the large loads of sea mammals and other things their kayaks carried.

They are no longer around. They stopped talking about them over in my home area when belugas stopped coming around. They've said that they moved to another place because they depend on [belugas] for food. And beluga whales are no longer seen in the Kuskokwim River. And those killer whales are also no longer around in the Kuskokwim River.

But people used to get beached whales that [killer whales] had killed over in our home area, and their enormous ribs would be all broken up. They say [killer whales] catch them. Apparently, several times there were people who witnessed killer whales fighting a whale along the mouth of the Kuskokwim River. They say when it [was injured], that huge whale surfaced upside down with its tail sticking out of the water. It was said that [killer whales] kill whales by breaking their bones, even though they are in water. They said that the water began to churn all the way around in a circle, then shortly afterward, a whale surfaced in the middle of the circle with its head down. When it surfaced again after going down under, it would get weaker. And soon it would start to appear with its body curled up from weakness.

People could apparently eat their meat. But people only take their leftover meat when it pops up in the water. And they take the leftover beluga meat, too, that [killer whales] caught. The portions of meat appear as though they were cut with knives, and not just any old way. That's how they look, like they were cut with knives.

Killer whales will surely give a person any part of the animal he requests. And Peter Jimmie, one who resides in our village over there, his father Adolf was granted a portion of their catch. He talked about his experience and shared it with me [and others]. He said after his personal experience, he believed more about killer whales and what they can do. But other animals don't do that, the others they referred to as *ircenrraat*. But it was a known fact that killer whales could do that.

Keggani-llu-gguq Nelson Island-aami pilallruut tamakut amlleret. Nurnarilu-
teng-llu-gguq tayima. Penakun-gguq, Umkumiut cakmaggun uatiitgun aming-
qertut. Teggalquugut kegkut Qaluyaat. Tekitaqamegteggu-gguq tua-i arrlugugaat
tua-i qaktetuut caumaluku penaq, pugevkenateng-llu-gguq tayim'. Unuakumi-gguq
taugaam caaqameng tanqigiararaqan, kayukitaqan, nepait qayarpallarallrit, uptaqa-
meng-gguq, alaunani tua-i ama-i amaken pinaurtuq. Qaqiucameng-gguq taugken
tua-i nepaiteqertelluki, nutaan ketiitgun arrluut pugluteng, penaq tunusngaluku.
Ketmun-gguq taugken tua-i ayagluteng.

Taumek inerqunqegcaumalallruut pisqevkenaki. Inerquumaluta cakneq, picur-
lagciqniluta pikumteki.

Uani-ll' Qacaruugni cali pitulliniluteng cali. Mamterarmiut qanemcik'lallrukait
cali, nunakngamegteggu tauna uaqliq, arrluut call' tuatnatuniluki. Ingirpallraagnek
ingkugnek Kusquqviim paingani; qertupiartuk penak. Penaulutek kellirnekek Qacaruuk. Aipaani *radar*-aq pika'antuq kangrani. Anguyagtet tua-i kialirnermi Kusquqviim tunglirnerani uitaluni misviat. Unani taugken *south*-alirnerani penaq uitaluni
tua-i, waten uverteqapiarpek'natek, waten ayuqsaaqluni. Keluvut yaaqsilaryaaqell-
ria pikavet tangvagpilaqput pagaavet. Qertupialliniuk.

~: Paivciyaraq :~

Alingniurluten camek pikuvet, alingluten tua-i pikuvet, uitaurarraarluten ak'anun
pivkenak' alikek'ngan kiartelarciqan, pinayukluku nunavni murilkelluku. Tua-i-
gguq paivciluten, kiarrluku man'a. Tua-i camek pinritaqavet inarrluten uitaaqlu-
ten. Tua-i-ll' pituluta, "Kitaki-ata unugpak qavangerpet paivciqaaqluten pikina."
Unani aarnarqelriami qavaraqamta pitullruluta. Tua-i qavamtenek tupakaraqamta,
makluta kiartaqluku [avatvut] niicugniluku-llu. Camek pinritaqamta inartaqluta.
Tamaa-i tuatnauguq, tamatuuguq paivciyaraq. Unguvalriit-llu tua-i makut qavaraqameng tuatnatuluteng. Alikngamegtekut yugni wangkuta, makut-llu nunamiutaat.
Tangrraqamegtekut ayagartaqluteng tua-i. Taumek murilkelluteng tua-i pitulriit,
alikngamegtekut. Yaqulget-llu makut. Taugken pistekenrilkengateng alikesciiga-

And they said there used to be many [killer whales] out on Nelson Island. But they've said that only a few are seen in that area today. They say the opening to their world is below Umkumiut, on the cliff. Qaluuyaat [Nelson Island] is a place that is all rock. They say when many killer whales get to that [cliff], they breach and dive into the water facing the cliff, and they don't resurface. But they say sometimes at dawn, when the weather was calm, people would hear their sounds when they got their kayaks ready to leave from there. And when they were done, after a brief silence, right below the people, killer whales would appear with their backs to the cliff and swim out to the ocean.

That's why people were thoroughly warned not to bother them. If we bothered them at that time we would only bring harm to ourselves later on.

And [killer whales] apparently do that in Qacaruuk [two mountains near Goodnews Bay]. People from Goodnews Bay, because their village is on the lower of two [mountains], have said that killer whales do that below [their mountain]. The two big mountains at the Kuskokwim River mouth, the cliffs there are very steep. It's all cliff there at the base of those two mountains, Qacaruuk. And a radar station is up on top of one of them. The airport for that military station is located above the site toward the Kuskokwim River. But the cliff to the south, a cliff is located on the south side of the station. The cliff side is not straight up and down, but it slopes down like this. Even though we're quite a ways from land, when we are below them, they are actually very steep. We'd look up and down the mountain, and we'd feel like we were right in front of them. They apparently are very steep mountains.

~: Looking around and checking your surroundings :~

If you are afraid of something, if you are wary, after being still for a while, you will look around and search for something you are afraid of, wary that it might come near you. They say *paivciluten* [you are searching your surroundings], looking around. If you don't notice anything, you will lay back down and rest. And they would tell us, "Now even though you're sleeping during the night, get up and check your surroundings from time to time." We did that when we slept down there in a potentially dangerous place. When we woke from our sleep, we would get up and look around and listen. When we didn't encounter anything, we'd go back to sleep. That's what *paivciyaraq* is. That's what sea mammals do when they're sleeping as well. It's because they're afraid of us people, and these land animals as well. When

naki. Elisngaluki pingailaceteng tua-i, piiyuilaceteng ilangciyuunaki ungungssiu-ngermi. Yuk kangangraan alingallauteksuunaku.

Tuaten ilait ayuqut. Tamatuuguq paivciyaraq. Kellelluni tua-i yuk pikuni, tuaten tua-i. Murilkartaqluku tua-i avatni piarkauluku.

Tua-i-wa alerquutii aturluku uum. Tunuakun-llu pingaunaku-gguq. Tangvaurte-lluni taugaam waten qavallrani, uitaqami tangrraqluku. Maaggun tunuakun ullag-ngaunaku; alikenruat-gguq maaken. Pitsaqevkenani tua-i canimellirluku uiskuni, takuyaquni, tangerquniu egmianun mermun qeckararkauluni. Tangvaurluku-gguq taugken pikuniu tuatnangaunani. Tamakunek tamaa-i pissulrianek, asaaqunek cas-kirluteng tangvakallrunritua. Nutegteggun ping'ermeng tua-i tuaten ayuqellruut, ciuqerritgun ullagtura'aqluki, tangvagtelluteng. Paivciaqata tua-i tangvagtelluteng maklagnek tamakunek maklaarnek-llu tuaten.

~: Allanarqellriit unguvalriit :~

Ukut-wa taugaam asevret cali-ll' makliit tamakut pitullrukait. Allanaqluteng pi-kata pissuusqevkenaki. Tua-i-gguq tamakut tamaa-i caskuulartut. Inglukilriim tua-i tuunrangayiim caskukluki, ciknatalriim caskukluki. Pitaqsunarqelriit-gguq tuatnatuut, apqait cucunarqelriit pitarkat. Tuatnatuut-gguq. Caskuktuit tamakut tuunrangayiit. Tua-i pikaku picurlautekarkauvkarluku tauna. Tamaa-i tamakut inerquutaq'larait cali. Allanarqekan pilaucimitun unguvalria pissuusqevkenaku.

Cali-ll' tamakut qanrutkelaqait elpengcangraiceteng-gguq ilait takuyayuunaki tua-i. Canimelngermeng takuyayuunaki pituut cali, pitaqsunarqelriit. Tamaa-i-gguq tamakut tua-i caskuugut. Catailnguum mayuqayunailnguum-llu tungiinun qimagluteng, ayagluteng. Tua-i anagviirutaqan nutaan mallegluku kitngulluku-ll' piunrirtaqluku, cikumun-llu may'uqerviirutaqan. Tuatnatuit-gguq.

they see us, they run away. They were vigilant because they're afraid of us. And these birds are the same way. But they aren't afraid of those who don't hunt them. They seemed to know that they wouldn't do anything to them and would ignore them, even sea mammals or humans. Although a person is walking, they won't get startled.

That's how some [animals] are. That's what *paivciyaraq* is. If a person is vigilant, that's what they do. He would search his surroundings from time to time [when he's out on the land or sea].

One uses this precept in hunting sea mammals. They say one shouldn't approach them from behind. One has to approach it from its front as it sleeps, and when it opens its eyes it would look at one. One never approaches it from its back side, for they say that seals find it extremely frightening to be approached from the back. If the seal happens to wake up and turns its head and sees the approaching hunter closing in on it, it would quickly jump into the water. But if one approaches from the front it would not do that. I never saw anyone hunting using the *asaaquq* [toggling harpoon]. The same procedure still applies in hunting with guns; one still approaches them from the front where the seals can see you. When they search their surroundings, one has to approach bearded seals and bearded seals in their first year face to face where one can be seen.

~: Sea mammals behaving strangely :~

They said that only walrus and bearded seals [behave strangely]. They told us not to hunt them if they behaved strangely. They say those [sea mammals] are weapons [for shamans]. Sea mammals could be used as weapons by shamans who were jealous and were trying to hunt other people. They say that sea mammals acting as if they weren't afraid of you and appearing as easy targets were suspicious and were probably weapons used by shamans. The shamans use those as a weapon to hurt someone. If a hunter pursues it, the hunter would end up in a tragic situation. We were warned about sea mammals that were behaving strangely. They told us not to hunt a sea mammal if it was behaving unusually.

And they say that [sea mammals being used as weapons] don't turn around, even though they try to get their attention. Those that are easy to catch don't turn around to look at them, even though they're close. They say those are weapons [of shamans]. They swim off toward an open area or an area that is not easy to climb on. When [hunters] aren't able to avert danger and save themselves, [the seals] then get

Angalkut-gguq taugaam pivkatuit, tamakut caskukluki, ciknaluteng pilriit angalkut, ciknakluki, umyuarrliqelriit. Inerquutengssiit amllertut. Taumek unani-ll' imarpigmi angalkut nallunrilkengaput pikata, tamakucimek pikumta, pingnaqevkenata
ikayualuku taugaam taumun pivkangnaqluku angalkumun pisqelluta, wangkuta
pingnaqevkenaku. Taugaam-gguq taum pisqekaku wangkutnun nutaan piarkauluku. Ayuqenrilameng tua-i angalkuungermeng. Tamakuyuitut-gguq ilait, cikna-
mek piinateng. Pulengtaq makliit-llu tamakut pit'lallruut yugnek. Takumni-ll' tua-i
maa-i tua-i niitnerunanrirluteng angalkumek pitairucan.

~: Eyagnarqellriit :~

Imkunun-am makunun, eyagnarqelrianun, waten atii wall'u anelgutii, aanii, wall'
tungayii canimelkii yuunriqan, wall'u pania aglenraraukan tamakunun tutmaas-
qessuitait. Qikertanun unavet kemgat tungairluku, tungaunaku qaugyaq tutmaas-
qevkenaku. Apqucingetuut tamakut. Usgunrit assiirulluteng. Unkut marayat unkut alingnarqut; irr'inarqut maa-i call' mat'um nalliini tua-i. Tamatum tamaa-i
ava-i assiirutelluku ipii. Asguraketalriim, piciunritniluku umyualget tuaten ellilar-
tut. Navgungluteng-llu enrit, assiirulluteng, inerquutseng navgualuk' pilriit. Tamakunek tamaa-i pitullruitkut ciulirneret. Tamakut kiagmi waten issurissulrianun-llu
maliguskumta angyamek yuusqevkenata, taugaam pilu'ugturluta, ivrarcuuterluta-
llu yuungramta cangaitnilukek. Kemegput taugaam tungaunak' tutmaasqevkenaki.
Atam issurinek qallingqelalriit qavalrianek. Tua-i tuatnakan issurit-llu elpekarkau-
luku tamakuciq. Taum uitavia qikertam elpengevkarluki.

Tuskan tua-i kemegtuumarmi, eyagnarqelria nallungaunaku. Tuamtellu uksumi
avani ketemteni, pinarqelria, ketemta aug'um nallungaunaku tamakut. Tuara-ll' ke-
purluni, navgurluni. Qairek-llu pinarivailgakek alairlutek, tuaq navgurluku. Maa-i
call' mat'um nalliini call' nallungaunaku tua-i. Amtall' tua-i inerqungermeng tua-i
ayagyuat makut inerciigatut, wangkutni inerciigallruut. Wangkuta navgullrunritar-
put tamana inerquun. Amllertut augkut kinguma yui, ipiit assiirulluteng, ayarurtua-
rangluteng, amtall' wii kinguqlirpakluki. Tuaten ayuqellrata tua-i; ukvekevkenaku.
Ukut piugut tua-i. Ca tamarmi inerquutangqerrami piurcimalria. Taugaam alerqua-

close to them, capsize [their kayaks] and kill them, including in places where there's no way to climb on top of ice. They say that's what they do [to hunters].

They say only shamans allow that to happen, using [sea mammals] as weapons, shamans who are jealous, those deceitful ones who are jealous of others. They have many warnings. That's why when those known shamans were down on the ocean, if we were [hunting] one of those [sea mammals], they told us not to try to catch it ourselves but to help the shaman catch it. But we should only pursue it if that [shaman] asked us to hunt it. Shamans are all different. They say some aren't like that, that they aren't jealous. And those bearded seals killed people many times in the past. You don't hear about that these days now that there are no shamans.

~: *Admonishments for seal hunting* :~

To those who must observe abstinence rules, like if his father or his sibling, his mother, or his cousin or his close relative dies, or if his daughter had her first menstrual period, they tell that person not to step on the sand islands down there with bare feet. Those who [go on those islands with bare feet] develop physical ailments. Their joints get bad. Those sand islands down there are dangerous; they are bewildering even today. [Stepping on sandbars with bare feet] can ruin a person's life. Those who are skeptical, ones who don't believe in [the abstinence rules] end up that way. And those who go against that warning, their bones begin to break; they become brittle. That's what the elders taught us. And when we were going to accompany those who were hunting spotted seals during summer, they told us not to get out of the boats, but only with our boots on. Nothing will happen to us if we get out wearing waterproof skin boots. But they told us not to step on them with our bare skin. There were sleeping spotted seals on top of [sandbars]. If that person [goes on the sandbar with bare skin], the spotted seals will sense him. The island would know his presence and alert [the seals].

They will know if a person who must follow abstinence rules steps on it with bare skin. And during winter down below our shore, our shore will know if those who must follow abstinence rules [go down to the ocean]. The shore ice will break apart. And the two waves will appear before their usual time and break up the shore ice. It will know, even today. Even though these young people are warned, they are disobedient, they are more defiant than we were. We never broke that admonishment. There are many people younger than me whose joints are in bad shape, and they have started to use canes, and here they're much younger than I am. It's because they

tiikun aturluku, elluarrluni aturaqluku, cauli piciatun *snow machine*, *engine*, piciatun tua-i; alerquutiikun taugaam assirluni piyugngaluni. Temvut-llu tuaten ayuquq,
una temvut. Nuna man' allakarmi ellangqertuq, ungungssiit-llu allakarmeng ella-
luteng, nunalgucirciiganaki wangkuta, pillgucirciiganaki. Mer'em-llu akuliini uitalriit ungungssit ciissit-llu yuuyaraatnun ekluta ilagarciiganaki, allakarmeng ellangqe-
rrata. Tamakut tamaa-i inerquutaat tekitapug-am.

~: *Allat pissurviit* :~

Qaluyaat Tununermiut-llu tuangqessuunateng, ateskilngurmek taugaam pitarluni.
Tua-i-llu-gguq ungalangan Tununermiut tuarat ayagluni tamarmi, maaggun nunam engeliikun. Tuqsugmiut-llu pilaryugnarqut.

 Allauluni canimelami man' et'ullra Qaluyaani kegkuni. Aug'utun nunavut etga-
tuq ketvanun, marayat-llu amllerrluteng. Taumek tuara cikua uitatulria.

 Cevv'arnermiut ikegkut ilakluki un'a pissuryararput wangkuta atauciuguq,
tua-i ayuqluni, Cevv'arnermiut ngellekluki ingkut. Tua-i-ll' keggani Tununermi
Tuqsugmi-llu Nunivaami-llu allaurrluteng, allarraurrluni. Taumek qayait-llu ater-
qaqtukait, tuaten tuangqessuitellinian, aarnaqluni tua-i.
 Taugaam ingkut Cevv'arnermiut snuukuuritnek-llu navguilarai imarpiata, ayaulluki, navguuluki-ll' kit'aqluteng snuukuurit maa-i mat'um nalliini, ketiit allayuu-
ngami cali. Nunamteni taugken un'gaani pikegtayuunateng tua-i piqalangermeng.

 Allaugut ugkut Goodnews-armiut Platinum-aarmiut-llu. Kuinerrarmiut taugken ukut aug'utun ayuqluteng nuniit, taugaam taqukaillruaqluni. Angtuat-llu tamakut maklagnek pitulriit alangruukegtayuunateng nuniitni, kangiqutaungami waten. Unaggun ayimqerluteng, nunavuting' tuc'araqaat makliit imkut cat, asevret-llu,
ungungssiit-wa tua-i. Taugken unaggun pilliniata nurnarluteng tua-i; mikurpek'nateng up'nerkat ilaitni. Unagguirnilaqait, piyagait-llu nurnaraqluteng iliini. Unaggui-
rutaqaceteng-gguq. *Short-cut*-arluteng unaggun pinilaqait-am tuaten. Piciuluni-am
call'. Ketvaarni unani paivnganruluteng. Angyalangvailegmeng anguatulit ikgetell-
ruut unani ketvani. Alingtalriit-wa tua-i pillilriit.

were like that; they didn't believe in it. These laws [exist]. It's because everything that exists has an admonishment. It will be used in the right way if they follow its instruction, no matter what it is, a snow machine, engine, anything; it can only be used right if one follows its instructions. That's also how our body is, our body here. The land has a different sense of awareness, and the animals also have their own world and awareness, and we cannot live with them, we cannot stay with them. And we cannot join and live the lives of sea mammals and insects because they have their own existence. We got to talking about those admonishments once again.

~: Other coastal hunting areas :~

Nelson Island and Tununak don't have [much] shore ice, but only a short one. And when the south wind starts blowing, all of the shore ice of Tununak floats away along the edge of the land. And that's probably what happens to the village of Toksook Bay as well.

It's different because the deep area is close out on Nelson Island. In our area, [the ocean] stays shallow for a long ways from shore, and there are many sandbars. That's why the shore ice stays.

Our ways of hunting are the same up to the village of Chefornak. And [their way of hunting] starts to vary out in Tununak, Toksook Bay, and Nunivak Island. That's why their kayaks float away because they evidently don't get shore ice [like we do], and it is dangerous.

But the people in Chefornak, their ocean [ice] breaks and their snow machines drift away and sink when the ice breaks these days, because the ocean below them is also unlike ours. That hardly happens in our village, even though it happens from time to time.

Those down below us down there at Goodnews Bay and Platinum are different. But the area around the village of Quinhagak is the same, but there are fewer seals. And the large ones they call *makliit* [adult bearded seals] aren't seen very often in their area because their place is a bay. The bearded seals, walrus, or animals cut across down there and come to our area. But when they travel farther away from shore, they are scarce here, and sometimes in spring they aren't abundant. They say they go farther from shore, and sometimes there are few pups. They say its because they migrated with them farther from shore. They say they take a shortcut down below [when they migrate]. That's true as well. They are more available farther away from shore. There were few men who paddled farther from shore before they started using boats. Maybe it's those that are more afraid.

∾: *Taitugmi pissulleq* :∾

Tuamtell' unani imarpigmi taitunguskakut, tairvagluni cakneq akerta-ll' cataunaku, cikut-am pugtalriit, piitkut ciulirneret, mengliit tangvaurluk' uivesqelluki, talinrit makut. Uivnginanemteni-gguq imkut qevleqtaayaalriit makut alairciqut mermi, cikum engeliini maani. Tua-i akertem-gguq nallii tunglirnera tuaten qaralingqer-ciquq. Nunam-gguq taugken tunglirnera cataunani. Tamaaggun tamaa-i nallunri-taqluki, cataunani akerta piaqan. Taicingraan tua-i tamakut yuvriqa'aqluki tagnaq-luni. Elisngalriit tamaani taicingraan arulairpek'nateng pissutullruut-gguq, ilateng tagurangraata elisngalriit, pellaayuilnguut.

Angalkuunrilngermeng elisngalriit. Cungagmek at'lek, Kangirnarmiulleq, tauna-gguq pellaasciigatuq. Unuungraan-llu tan'gercetqapiarangraan pellaangaunani imarpigmi. Angalkuuvkenani taugken. Tuaten avungqelartut yuut elisngalrianek. Cuqculriit-gguq tuaten pituut, umyuamegteggun cuqingaluku ca, tuanlucia cuq-taarluteng qaillun pillerkaa. Elisngallermegteggun tua-i nallungaunaku ciunerkar-teng tan'gercelengraan taicingraan-llu cakneq.

Taiciraqami assiituq. Taumek egmianun, nutegnek maa-i caskungamta inerqula-raitkut, taitugmi pugengraakut nutgesqevkenaku ilaput pitekluki nani sagingalriit, saggluteng pilriit. Avani nut'gayuilnguut taiciraqan tua-i. Augna Qipnermiut iliit puulim tucaaqellrullinia, ukuakun taugaam, tamluakun ellma kiliqerluku, tukniali-nermikun. Taugaam tua-i cacini nalluqeryaaqelliniluku, taugaam ellangluni kiime-nani. Yuunrillruuq taugaam tua-i.

Mayuumaluni tuami. Kangiqutami-gguq mayuumaluni, evunret-wa-gguq ukut, una-ll' etgalqitarluni. Amkut-wa-gguq yaatiini cali mayuumalriit, pamatiini. Imku-nek ciuqlirnek nutegnek nutegl006luteng tamakut, imiryaranek. Imiriurallrani-gguq, imiriurallermini nutmi imarkainek qayami iluani, piinanrani taitugmi amaken cing-qullalliniluni yaatii. Tauna tua-i puulia caqirrluni ayallinilria tuavet, amaken yaaq-liitnek. Wavet tut'elliniluni. Ayuqucia-gguq qatngitellria tayima-llu-gguq tua-i. Ella-ngartuq-gguq qayami keluani nangerngaluni, qayami iluani uitallruyaaqluni. Tua-i mer'em tungiinun pikuni ellangyarpek'nani, assitmun taugaam kelutmun ayagar-tellrulliniluni.

⌁ *Seal hunting in foggy conditions* ⌁

And if it became foggy while we were down on the ocean, when heavy fog formed and the sun was gone, the elders told us to go around a sheet of floating ice and watch the edges that are shaded. They said that while we were going around those, particles [of ice dust] that sparkle will appear in the water along the ice edge. They say that the sun's direction will have those small indicators. But there will be nothing [glittering on the side of the ice] in the direction of land. They knew their location through those, when the sun wasn't visible. Even though it was foggy, it was easy to check those [pieces of floating ice] and go back to shore. They say those who were skilled used to hunt, even though it was foggy, and the knowledgeable ones who don't get lost didn't stop, even though their companions went back to shore.

Those who were knowledgeable, even though they weren't shamans [never got lost on the ocean]. They say a person named Cungak from Kongiganak never got lost. And he would not get lost down on the ocean, even though it was dark. But he wasn't a shaman. There are some people who are knowledgeable like that. They say it is those who are good at determining the location of places using their judgement, estimating where something was located and how to get there. They know what is up ahead using their expertise, even though it is dark and extremely foggy.

It's not good when it's foggy. That's why they cautioned us after we began hunting with guns not to shoot at [a sea mammal] in the fog although it came out of the water near us because of our hunting companions who were dispersed out there. They never shot when it was foggy back in those times. Evidentially, a bullet actually hit someone from Kipnuk, it cut him a little when it hit him just as the bullet's impact became weak. He lost awareness but gained consciousness alone. But he has since died.

He was on top of the shore ice. They say he was on a bay, and there was piled ice here, and there were chunks of ice that were on shallow areas. And right beyond him were others who were on top of the shore ice, behind him. They had those first guns, the ones that you had to load. While he was loading his gun inside his kayak in the fog, a shooting sound came from beyond him. The bullet that was shot apparently turned and went in his direction from the area beyond him. It landed here. He felt a jolt and lost consciousness. When he regained consciousness, he was standing right behind his kayak, but he had been inside his kayak at the time it happened. He wouldn't have gained consciousness if he went toward the water, but he apparently went in a good direction, toward the area behind him.

Assiriluni tua-i yuum ullagpailgani. Tauna-gguq taugaam aarnaqngan aunraayaa-
rallini-ll' puulim-gguq tut'ellra, pillra. Qayam iluani kiarrluni pilliniuq, imkut aka-
genqeggluteng waten, *marble*-aat imkut, tuacetun ayuqluni tauna nutgem puulia.

~: *Merr'illuki* :~

Tagutaqatki pilagnarqenrilnguut nayiit, pilaumalriit-llu, akitmun avavet murag-
mun neverqurluki waten inarqurtelluki. Caniqliqluki qavciugaqata unkumiutaat
imarpigmiutaat. Tua-i-ll' qaqicata nutaan, ayunek imkunek makunek — ayut iciw'
imkut akengkupagangqellriit — tamakunek qengait imiqaqluki, ukuit imiqaquur-
luki. Tua-i-ll' qaqicata nutaan qaluurin mermek imirluku, aitara'arrluki mermek
qanritgun kuvqerluki. Iqsulirneritgun-llu unataitgun call' mermek kuvqerluki. Tuaten-am piciryaraqluku unkumiutaat imarpigmiutaat.

Tuamtellu arnam uum qapiaraqamiu, wall'u ullingqalria qamiqurra augaumang-
raan, amia man'a aug'arnauraa, nevetmun-llu ullingqalria. Augaani-ll' tua-i; una tam-
lua cevvingavkenani. Cevtevkenak' pilatuit. Augaamiu, una qamiqurra, uum aciakun,
neverrluk, qamiqurra anlluku, an'arrluku. An'arqaarluku uivevkarluku kassuggluku.
Uivevkarraarluku-ll' nekaanun elliluku nutaan. Una-ll' enertuumalria nayiim pillra
tuaten call' pituluku aug'araqamegteggu. Tautun pivkenaku ullingqalriatun. Aug'araqamegteggu tua-i uivqertelluku, kassuan-llu nutaan elliluku. Tuaten pituluki.

Ayuqluteng tua-i yuut atauciin pivkenateng. Tuaten piciryarangqellruut. Maa-i
taugaam mat'um nalliini tua-i tamana tua-i tamaraat tayima. Yuuyaram; yuut piyarat cagmaraat kinguqlimta makut, wangkuta piqtangramceteng. Atunrirluku tamana tuaten ayuqellrat. Qanrucaaqelriani ilaitni kiugaqluteng, catngunritniluku
tamana. Wangktua tuaten piiyuitellruukut, ciulirneput takaqellruamteki. Arnaung-
raata-ll' qanrutesteput kiumrayuitellruaput.

Tamakut-wa taugaam imarpigmiutaat tuatnatullrukait. Egcuunaki qamiqut ukut
enertuumalriit. Taugaam tamakut amiqainat ayaulluki kuigunrilngurnun, nanvanun piyarameggnun cali, enret-llu unkumiutaat tamakunek tapirluki ektuit tamaavet. Taugken enertuumalriit nayiit qamiqurrit ukut patrit nerenricuitait. Neqliya-

He recovered before anyone went to him. The place where the bullet hit him was bleeding a little because it was dangerous. He searched inside the kayak, and the bullet he found was round like a marble.

∾: *Welcoming seals* :∾

When they brought ringed seals up from the ocean, whole seals and ones that had been cut open in the belly already, they laid them on their backs on a wooden board. They laid sea mammals side by side if there were several of them. Then they'd pinch off the top round part of the Labrador tea plants and put them in their noses. And after their noses were filled, they'd fill a dipper with water and open their mouths and pour a little bit of water in them. And they dropped some water on their left flippers. That was the custom used for sea mammals.

And when a woman skinned a seal with its skin intact, or one that was already cut open with its head already taken off, she'd cut the skin off the body and take the skin off the one that had been cut open. And when she removed the [head]; its chin wasn't cut open. They skinned them without splitting the chin open. And when she removed it, its head here beneath this, laying it on its back, they'd pull out its head, they'd take it out a little. And after they pulled it out a little they'd turn the head all the way around. When they turned it all the way around they'd put it where it would stay. And they also did that to this that is attached to the skeleton when removing it. They didn't do the same thing they did with the head that was removed from the seal that was already split open. When they removed it they'd let it go around, and they'd put it down when the circle was complete. That was what they did to them.

Everyone practiced that custom and not just in one village. That was the practice everyone followed. They have lost that custom today. This present generation doesn't follow those practices anymore, even though we keep telling them about it and encouraging them to practice it. And when you mention it to them, they'd say that it was useless. We never used to talk back at our elders and parents because we respected them. We never even used to argue with women when they talked to us about right living.

That's what they did with sea mammals. They didn't discard their heads. But they would take only the skins, along with sea-mammal bones, and discard them in lakes, not in rivers. But they always ate the ringed seal heads, their marrow. And when people moved to fish camps they always brought the heads they had saved. Then

raqameng-llu unicuunaki qamiquit. Neqlillernun nutaan piyungameng kenirluki qamiqurrit. Qallarvaulluki tua-i ak'anun. Tua-i pinarian nertuluki. Kemgit maani pukugluki, iingit taugaam pivkenaki. Patrit-llu cali aug'arluki patrit nerluki. Tuatnatullruit egtevkenaki.

Unguvaliit tuatnatuit. Angtuat taugaam makut ciamlluki unani pimalriit, qamiqurrit-llu tuatnayuunaki. Makliit taugaam ayagneqluki makliit, issurit, nayiit, qamiqurrit tuatnatuit, tuatnatuluki. Asevret taugken piiyuunaki, qamiqurrit tagutengraitki piiyuunaki.

Unkumiutaat ayunek qengait, mermek-llu; merr'illuki-gguq.

Taugaam merr'itesqaqluki taq'ertaqatki. Waten pituit unkumiut merr'itesqelluki. Ayunek taugken tua-i piqarraarluki, qaluurin mercuun murak mermek imirluki, qanrit kuvqaquurluki, iqsulirneret-llu unatait.

sometime after they got there they'd cook them and eat them. They let the pot boil for a long time when they cooked heads. After cooking them for a long time they'd finally eat them. They ate the meat off the head, but not the eyes. They'd also take out the marrow and eat it. They ate [the heads] and did not throw them away.

That's what they did to sea mammals. But they didn't turn the heads of the big ones they had already butchered on the ocean. But they did the "turning ritual" with the heads of bearded seals, spotted seals, and ringed seals. But they didn't do that with walrus heads, even though they brought them up to shore.

For sea mammals, they'd put tops of Labrador tea in their noses and gave them water; *merr'illuki* was what they called it.

They'd ask them to give them water after they laid them down. They tell them to give the sea mammals some water. After putting tops of Labrador tea in their noses, they filled a wooden dipper with water and poured a little bit in their mouths and on their left flippers.

Imarpigmiutaat Atuullrat

Imarpigmiut atam qeciit atullruit cakneq avani, makut atungvailegmegteki, piitcesciiganateng. Qalluvakluki, iqukelriit imkut melquteng elaqliqluki. Issurit-llu atkukluki nat'raqluki tuaten, ivruciqluki tuaten. Amllertuq nutaan caullrat imarpigmiut.

Atam up'nerkami arcaqerluteng pissulalriit imumi. Tua-i-ll' tekicata unguvalriit, unuaquaqan, tua-i wangkuta pissuryaurpailemta ikamrartenguluta qimugtetgun, unuaquaqan tua-i erniyuunata aqvauquriurturluta. Nallunailkutarluteng-llu pissurtemta aatamta pitait, qaralimeggnek piqa'aqluki. Wangkuta nallusciiganaki tua-i. Ungungssit amllengraata quyungqalriit, qaralimteggun elitaqluki uciliraqluta ikamranun.

~: Qapiaryaraq :~

Tua-i-ll' arnat nunami imkut nayiit qaill' angtauralriit qapiarluki. Makunek maa-i, maa-i tang unkuliurcuutait. Arnat maa-i caskuit. Maa-i tamakunek calissutait. Uuggun kepluki, uuggun qanratgun waten, ciutait ukut keluarrluki. Tua-i-ll' nutaan makunek amiirturluki. Piyunarian-llu tua-i iluit waten piurluki, uivkaniraqluki. Tua-i kiituan tua-i maavet ellirtut, qallaciit taugaam evsiarit-llu kep'arcaaqevkenaki.

Tua-i-ll' nutaan ancamegteki unatait makucinek waten cali-am amiirturluki, unatet. Maa-i-gguq it'gissuutet. It'gait-llu makucinek maa-i caliaqurluki aug'arluki, makunek pivkenaki.

78

How Sea Mammals Were Used

The pelts of sea mammals were extensively used back then, and they couldn't go without them before they began using these [cloth garments]. They were used as pants, the two-piece top and bottom garments made with fur on the outside. And they used the spotted-seal skins as parkas, and as boot soles and waterproof boots. There are many things that can be made from sea mammals.

They mostly hunted in the spring back in those days. Every day when the sea mammals arrived in our area, we [boys], before we began to hunt, went back and forth and delivered them to the village using dog sleds. And our fathers, our hunters' catches had identification marks on them. It was a design belonging to a hunter. We would know which ones belonged to our family. Even though there were many sea mammals grouped together, we recognized them by our family marking and loaded them in the sleds.

~: Skinning seals starting at their heads, :~ leaving their skins intact

And in the village the women would skin the ringed seals that were the right size, qapiarluki [skinning them starting at their heads and pulling the skin over the carcass without cutting the hide]. They used these implements [to skin them]. These were women's tools [used for skinning seals]. They'd make a slit here first, around the mouth right behind the ears. Then they would start skinning [around the seal's head] using this tool. And when [it was skinned far enough inside the head, they'd stick their hand in] and continue cutting, gradually rotating [the body]. By doing that, they'd eventually reach [the midsection], but they were careful not to cut through the hide along their belly buttons and their nipples.

Then after the body was taken out, they would remove the skin from their hands with this tool. They call these it'gissuutet [tools for removing skin from feet]. They skinned their feet using these tools, not with these [qapiarutet, seal-skinning tools].

Tamakut-llu qapiarutet; man'a tua-i waten *skin*-aq nayiim pillra una uyalqurra, una iterrluku, waten taugaam elliurturluku, man'a taugaam manigcetengnaqu'urluku. Waten tua-i kelikarturluku qamna uqua aug'arturluku. Ilait tua-i elisnganrilnguut anqerrucinaurtut, elisnganrilnguut. Elitaqameng taugken tua-i pinrirluteng tuaten.

Makut taugken [it'gissuutet] waten teguqerluki. Waten atutuit, igaqatalriatun. Waten tua-i atutuit. Teguyarangqertut allakarmeng. Imarpigmiutarnek maa-i calissuutet ilait.

~: Qeciit uquiryaraat :~

Tua-i-llu nutaan augaamegteki ullelluki uquit kelikarluki, kemgit ciamqaarluki nang'aqata. Uquit kelikarluki tua-i uquinqegcaarluki. Tua-i-llu pikiurluteng angutet teq'urritnek assigcirluki muriit muragnek angtuanek ilutuluteng qerrullugnek piaqluki. Tamaavet qurrmartelluki angutet. Amllerian tua-i nutaan taqluku. Nutaan augkut qeciit uquirraarluki ekluki tamaavet melqurrit elaqliqluki, ukuit uyait qillerrluki tamatumek teq'umek imirngairutelluki iterngairutelluki.

Melqurrit elaqliqluki. Tua-i taugken erurluki tamatumek teq'umek. Uqua tua-i aug'arluku tamalkuan, uquirluki. Uquirulluku tamana teq'um. Ellami taugaam tua-i uitaluteng. Tepsarilartut ak'anun pikaqameng. Narqallrat tua-i qatlinaqluni. Taumek ellami uitavkarluki pitullrukait. Kuvyuunaki tua-i. Kenriluteng-llu tua-i. Kenriata nutaan ayaulluki kuvluki allamek cimirluku.

Imutun-wa elnguriluni. Elnguriluni tua-i uqurrluk aug'alleq, teq'um aug'allra. Tuaten pirraarluki nutaan *fresh water*, erurluki. Erurraarluki nutaan angilluku tauna. Agarrluki kanarrluki, melqicirluki. Tua-i-ll' kinrata melqurrit ullelluki-am iluit elaqliqsagulluki, melqurrit iluqliqsagulluki. Uyalqurrit ukut uquutekat pasvaagucirluki, mingeqluki augkut iqtulriamek uqumek imirarkateng. Ilait taugken pilu'ugkat melquqegcilriit pivkenaki tuaten. Qillerqaarluki nutaan qertunermek imirluki, qerrurluki, nutaan agarrluki kinercirluki. Tamakut-llu tua-i uquit allakarturluki, kemgirturluki. Qaqicamegteki-ll' kemgit ukliurluki, iniurluki initanun. Angtuat-llu imkut ullirrluteng maaggun pimalriit kemeggluit, uquita kemeggluit aug'arturluki, uquirluki cali. Qeciit nutaan kelikarpek'naki caliaqevkenak, angutet taugaam caliaqetuit tamakut ullingqalriit maklagaat.

And those *qapiarutet*; here is the skin of the ringed seal and the neck opening, and they put this [tool] inside, continually making this motion [with the hand], trying to keep this part smooth. They scrape the inside, removing the blubber [from the skin]. [The tools] of some people who aren't skilled go through the hide. They no longer do that when they become skilled.

But they hold these [*it'gissuutet*] like this [with the thumb, index finger, and middle finger]. They use them like this, like when one is ready to write. That's how they use them. They have a special way to hold them. These are some tools used for processing sea mammals.

~: *Cleaning and processing sealskins* :~

Then after they removed [the feet], they turned [the skin] inside out and scraped the fat off after they were done cutting the meat. They would then thoroughly scrape the fat off the skin. Then they would collect urine from men [to use for cleaning skins] in large wooden containers called *qerrulluut*. They would let the men urinate in them and would stop when there was enough in the container. After removing the fat from the skins, they placed them in there with the fur on the outside, after tieing the neck opening shut so that the urine would not go inside.

The skins were turned, with their fur on the outside. Then they washed them with urine. They would wash them and remove all the oil. The urine cleaned off all the oil. [The urine buckets] were kept outside because the aged urine became very stinky. It stung the nose to smell it even a little. That's why [the buckets] were kept outside. They never spilled them out. The [urine] became very thick. When [the urine] became thick they took [the bucket] away and spilled it out and replaced it.

[The urine in the bucket] became thick. The oil that was washed off would thicken the urine in the bucket. After that, [the skins] were washed in fresh water. Then they untied [the neck openings] after they washed them. Then they hung them upside down to dry the fur. Then when the fur was dry, they turned them inside out with the fur inside. They sewed a *pasvaagun* [thick piece of skin that acted as a funnel to fill the poke and to fasten the opening] onto pokes that they would fill with seal oil. But they didn't do that to some skins with good fur that they would use for making sealskin boots. After tying them, they would fill them with air, inflate them, and then hang and dry them. They would then put the seal blubber aside and remove the meat from each. When they were done, they would cut up their meat and hang them on the drying racks. And they would remove the meaty parts

Augkut tua-i qaill' angtauralriit kameksagkat, uquutekat, ciisqurrilitarkat, issuriyagaat piipiit imkut, qapiarturluki makutgun piaqluki. Tamakut taugken angtuat,
unani tagvailegmeng pitaqestaita ullirrluki pituluki. Tamakut taugken nayiit ullir-
tevkenaki.

Pilugukluki, uquutekluki angtuat, qerruinaqluki. Taukuuluteng.

Pivkaraqluki angtuat. Melqurrit assilrianek pituut, pilu'ugkaqluki tua-i. Piyagait-
llu augkut nayiit tamakut, taqukaayaarnek pitukait melqurrit nutaan assipiat tua-i,
melqurrit. Ungungssiyagaat waten-ll' angtaaqluteng unani kuimayagarluteng. Pinga-
yutellruunga wii tuaten tamakuyagarnek. Amiirameng taugken qerruameng takliri-
luteng. Angpiarluteng amiit *skin*-ait, kemgit taugken naninateng nayiyagaat. Qamiqucuayagait-wa, kuimayagarluteng taugken.

~: Caqutet :~

Tua-i-ll' tamakut nutaan arnat pinariata uqut, imkunun tamakunun uquutekanun,
uquutekat tamakut uyalqurrit tamakut qillerqaarluki mermun akurrluki kenicir-
luki, melqurrit iluqliqluki. Tua-i-ll' assiriata unailiata, nugcamegteki unatait anlluki,
kankut-ll' it'gait, cetuit kepurluki. Kepurraarluki nutaan iterrluki, ukuit-llu kankut
ngelaitgun qillerrluki cagnilluki kankut. Nutaan uqut qaill' iqtutaurluki pinevluki
waten, waten elliurturluki, imarkiurluki uqunek egvailgata. Imirluki taugken tua-i,
qertuniryaaqevkenaki. Melqurrit iluqliqluki. Muirrluki tua-i. Una qesngaurluku,
muiraqata, uqumek teguqaarluni unatni waten piluku kasmaqluku qamavet. Cak-
nengan taugaam tua-i nutaan qillertelluku, qillerrluku.

Qertuniryaaqevkenaku. Nutaan qillerqaarluku, egcillerkaanun, inguqirluku muragnek pela'atekat iluitnun, aciit agtuumavkenaki nunamun. Qerrataruciluku uqut
nutaan tamakut imilteng elliurluki. Ella assiraqan patuirluki, pivkaraqluki. Mecung-
nariqertaqan patuaqluki.

from the blubber of large [seals] that had been cut open down the chest, and all of the blubber from the body would be removed, too. The [women] didn't scrape the skins and didn't work on them, but only the men worked on bearded-seal skins that were cut open down the belly.

The [seals] that were the right size to make into boots, seal pokes, knee pads, those small spotted-seal pups, they used these tools and skinned them starting from the neck area with the skin intact. But the hunters who caught those big ones down there cut them open down the belly before they came up to land. But they didn't cut the ringed seals down the belly.

They made [ringed seals skinned intact] into boots, the larger ones were used as pokes and as floats. That's what they were made into.

The big ones with good fur were made into boots. And the ringed-seal pups called *taqukaayaat*, their fur was the best. They were small animals about this size and would swim down there. I caught three of those cute little ones. But when you skin them and inflate them, they get very long. Their skins stretch, but the bodies of those small ringed seals are short. Their heads were very small, and yet those cute little things could swim around in water.

~: Sealskin pokes :~

And when it was time for the women to fill the pokes with blubber, they would first tie and close the pokes' neck openings and dip them in water to soak, with the fur inside. When they became soft, when they pulled them out of the water, they would pull out the hands and feet and cut off the claws. They would push them back in after cutting [their claws], and they would tie them securely along [the hands] and down on [the feet]. Then they cut the blubber into strips about so wide to be stuffed into seal pokes before they began rendering. Then they filled [the pokes with blubber], trying not to leave air inside. The fur side of the skin was on the inside. They filled them full. While filling the poke they'd be gripping this with one hand, and when the poke was getting full and they placed a strip of blubber in the opening, they'd squeeze that hand and push it down into the poke. They continued filling the poke in that manner until it was completely full and then tied it closed.

They try not to put air in it. After tying it, they placed it inside a tent on top of a wooden base until it rendered. They put all the pokes they had filled with blubber [inside], not letting them sit on the ground. They would remove the covering in good weather. They covered them when it was wet out.

~: *Uquucillret* :~

Tua-i-ll' pinariata nutaan nunam iluanun [elliluki]. Amllepiallruut uani. Qaill' ilu-
tutalallruut waten, uqunun nunami elaumalriit, takluteng-llu. Tamakut-llu *poke*-at
canirqurluki waten, kipulketaarturluki imituluki. Iquklican-llu qallilirluki tuamtell',
muragnek waten ekiirraarluki.

Atam unkut imiqata'arqamegteki qalurraarluki muragnek qupurranek ingu-
qitengqelalriit. Tua-i-ll' nutaan canegnek imirluku, curulirluki. Urunek-llu tua-i
augkunek yuilqumi pitulinek, puyaurtetulinek. Amllepiartut atam maani urut tamakut. Neqnguut. Neqkaput, akutauluteng. Puyaurtaqata neryugngarilaraput. Tamakunek tua-i amllernek tua-i aqvauquriluta yuilqumek maaken keluatni. Uqut
tua-i curulirluki, call' qallilirluki tamakunek urunek mecungengraata. Qaqican-llu
tua-i uqut waten canirqurluki kipullgutaqluki, kipullgutaaruqu'urluki waten piurluki, imirturluku urunek akulait, agtuusngavkarpek'nak'. Urunek ekiirturluki tua-i
akulait-llu tamalkuita, menglait-llu makut urunek piurluki. Qaqican-llu muriignek
cali waten pirraarluki, tuamtell' qallilirluki urunek. Qallirkait tuamtell' elliurluki
tuaten urunek. Arunaitut urut. Arungaituq tua-i urunek caqulek nunam iluani ui-
tang'ermi. Tuaten tua-i pituit. Patuluki-ll' tua-i nunamek. Kiagpak-llu tua-i tamaan-
lluteng nunam iluani uksurluni-llu. Tua-i-ll' kumlaneq mamturiqerpailgan nutaan
ikirrluki, nuggluki nutaan cailkamun kumelqertelluki.

Nutaan ellivignun kumelqaata iterrluki inguqirluki cali. Uugnarnun pillerkaat
murilkelluku. Asevrutnek, asevret *skin*-aitnek, unataitnek-llu it'gaitnek-llu keserr-
lainarnek imirnaurait ilait. Ilait-llu qaingita mat'um amianek *walrus*-aat, asevret,
ingqiurluki keniumaluki taugaam kenirluki, nallunailkucirturluki. Canek nallu-
nailkuciqaqluki, qecignek imalget, putukuanek-llu imalget cali nallunailkuciqaq-
luki. Makut-llu tua-i nayilinrarnek imalget cali nallunailkucirturluki. Amirkat-llu
uquitnek imalget nallunailkucirluki cali. Makliit-llu uquitnek imalget nallunailkucirluki cali. Arnat tua-i nalluvkenaki tamakut caliaqngamegteki, apertuagurluki nug-

~: *Underground storage pits* :~

And when it was time, they put them underground. There were many [underground storage pits] down below the village. Underground storage pits for seal oil were about [four feet] deep, and the holes were long. Then they would fill the hole with pokes sitting side by side, facing in opposite directions. When they got to the end, they put more [pokes] on top after placing a piece of wood [on top of the first layer of pokes].

When they are going to fill [underground storage pits], after scooping the water out, they place split logs at the bottom for a base. Then they put a layer of grass [on the wood] for matting. Then they [add] a layer of moss, the kind of moss they ate as *akutaq* [seal oil or caribou fat mixed with boned fish, berries, greens, or any number of ingredients]. Lots of that moss is around here. They are food. We ate them as *akutaq*. We are able to eat them after they become rancid in seal oil. We would gather lots of that moss from the tundra behind [the storage pits]. We put that moss at the bottom for matting for the pokes, and placed some on top of them, even though they were wet. After [putting down the matting], they placed the pokes down on their sides, side by side, facing opposite directions. They filled the space between with moss to prevent them from touching. Moss was placed on top, and the spaces between each poke and along the edge were stuffed with moss. When that was done, after placing two pieces of wood on the pokes, they'd cover them with more moss. The next layer of pokes was also covered with moss like that. Moss prevents things from rotting. Anything you put underground is covered with moss. That's how they [store pokes underground]. Then they covered them with soil. They stayed in the ground all summer, and they were still there when it became winter. Then before the frozen ground got too thick, they opened them and pulled them out and placed them above ground, and they instantly froze.

Then when they froze they would place them inside caches with matting underneath. They made sure that the mice wouldn't get to them. They would always fill some [seal-oil pokes] with walrus skin, hands, and feet. And some of them would be filled with walrus skin after cutting them into pieces, but only after cooking them, and they marked them for identification. They would mark the ones that were filled with [walrus] skins to identify them, and they marked the ones that were filled with feet. And they marked the ones filled with ringed-seal oil. And they marked the ones filled with young bearded-seal oil. And they marked the ones filled with

taqatki apertuagaqluki. Taukut ilakelrianek imangqerrniluki taukut. Nallunailkutalget ayuqelrianek kal'arluteng.

Lung-aitnek ilait imilarait kenirluki cali, *seal*-at lung-aitnek cuakaayiluteng-gguq. *Liver*-aaritnek tuamtell' kenirluki cali, imirluki tua-i cuakaayagnek-gguq imarluteng. Quunaqluteng cakneq. Kapurnaqluteng nerellrat. Tamakunek nerqerraalleq neqnialliqnaqluni. Eligartellrat assirluteng. Cuakaayiit-gguq. Tua-i tuaten.

Tamakunek tamaa-i imirluki, uqunek, asevrutet, putukuarutet, cuakaayautet, imkut-llu *tomcod*-at kinrumalriit, uqumek egnirluki cali imituit. Imirluki call' tamakut pituit. Tuaten tua-i atutuit.

~: *Nayit atuullrat* :~

Tua-i-llu imairutellret uquutellret pilu'ukluki, ullelluki. Mer'em iterciiganaki, metusciiganateng-llu uqum meciumiiteng. Uqunek imangqellret tua-i ivrucirkautekluki. Ivrangermeng tua-i metungaunateng tamakunek uqunek imangqellernek caqutellernek piaqluki.

Aug'arluki melquit imumek evegtarturluki tungulria imna qaingatni maani aug'arpek'naku. Tuaten-llu tamakut ivruciqluki, ulqucinaqluki tuaten.

Kinrumalriit melqurrit aug'arpek'nateng, melqurrit iluqliqluki pilu'ukluki. Ulqucinat-gguq tamaa-i. Tamaa-i tamakut nayiit angenrilnguut aturtut tuaten. Tuamtell' ilait meqsaqalget nayiit meqcirluki. Meq'ngata-llu pinevkarluki taprualugkiurluki tapriluteng. Tapruariluteng-llu amitqapiarnek tua-i tapruarnek.

Augkut avan' asevret, makliit-llu piksaitanka, issurit-llu maklagaat-llu. Nayirnek taugaam qallatua, atuullratnek. Tua-i tuaten ayuqut. Neqkanun aturluteng nutarameggnun. Augkunun-llu taprarkanun, tapruarkanun-llu, qeciit, tupirkanun aturluteng. Kameksauluteng, uquutnguluteng, piciatun asevrutnguluteng tuaten.

Qayat-llu ilait tamakunek ilangqeqatuut, uquutellernek nayirpallernek, akagtelluki piaqluki. Tamaa-i atuugut, atuullret nayiit issurit-llu angtuarpaunrilnguut.

adult bearded-seal oil. The women knew what they were because they worked on them, and they would identify what kind of oil was in each poke when they pulled them out of the storage pits. They'd identify those that had similar contents in them. They all had the same color and marking on them.

Some were filled with cooked [seal] lungs, and they called them *cuakayiit*. And some were filled with cooked liver, too. They'd say the pokes were filled with *cuakayiit*. They were very sour. Your mouth really stings when you eat them. When eating them for the first time, they taste horrible. But when you get used to them, these are good. They called them *cuakayiit*. That's what they did.

[The pokes] were filled with such things as seal oil, walrus skin, feet, seal lungs and liver, and they also filled them with dried tomcod. They filled the poke with things like that. That's how they use those [seal pokes].

~: Uses of ringed-seal skins :~

Then after the pokes' contents were eaten and they were empty, the skin was made into boots by turning it inside out. The skin was waterproof and not easily soaked because it was saturated with oil. Used seal pokes were kept and made into wading boots. Boots made of skin they called *caqutelleq* don't get soaked, even though you use them to wade in water.

They removed the fur [from the skin] by pulling and cutting it, and they didn't remove the dark layer on the skin's surface. They made them into boots they called *ivrucit* and *ulqucinat*.

[*Ulqucinat* are boots made of] dried sealskin with the fur still on the inside. They were called *ulqucinat*. The small ringed-seal skins were used for things like that. And they would age some of the ringed seals that had bald spots to let the fur come off. And when the fur came off, they cut them into strips and made skin ropes and lines. And some were stripped into very thin twine and thread.

I haven't talked about walrus and adult bearded seals and spotted seals and bearded seals in their first year. I'm only talking about how they used ringed seals. That's how they were used. They were used to store recently caught and processed foods, and the skin was cut and stripped into line and rope. The skins were processed to be used to bind seams in wood working, they were made into boots, seal-oil pokes, and for storing walrus [skins and flippers].

Once in a while some kayaks were covered with old, huge ringed-seal skin pokes, that they just rolled over the frame. Ringed-seal skins and spotted-seal skins that

Tuaten tua-i ayuqut nayiit. Atkungqessuitellruut nayirnek augkut. Atkuuluki tangssuitanka, qerrulliuluki taugaam. Piyagait-llu augkut issurit irniarit melqurrit acetulaameng, qatellriit imkut. Tamakut curungvailgata tuqutaqluki, melqurrit tamakut meqvailgata, katagpailgatki. Ciisqurrilitarkauluki tua-i pituluki. Augkut ava-i nayiit angtaciqellriit, issurit-llu angtaciqellriit, nayirtun angtalriit atuugut augkunun ava-i qanrutkellemnun. Tamalkurmeng tua-i tuaten atuuluteng.

∾: *Imarpigmiutaat atuullrat* :∾

Tua-llu issurit, amirkat, makliit, issurit qayaqetullruit *skin*-ait. Qayanun tua-i atuuluteng. Makliit-llu irniarit cali qayanun cali aturluteng nat'rauluteng tuaten, amirkat. Makliit taugken qayanun ilait atutuluteng mamkellicarluki. Angyanun taugaam aturpallurluki makliit, asvernek aipirluki, mangaggluki. Makliit *skin*-aicetun mamtutariluki mangagtaqluki. Qamkut ilulirnerit aug'arluki, makunek taugaam elalirnernek, amiqegcilrianek pituut, asevret amiitnek. Assiitut imkut waten ayuqellrianek amingqelaameng ak'allaurtaqameng asevret. Pengitagluki-gguq tamaa-i. *Young*-alriit taugken imkut tungulriit assirluteng waten ayuqluteng tua-i, manigcenateng. Tamakunek tamaa-i angyikunaaqameng, piyugluki piaqata pivkatullruit unani. Ullirrluku tua-i kepurpek'naku malruuluku waten amiirluku asveq.

Ullirrluku, kemgan engeliikun uqurtuumaan man'a amia aug'arluku. Tuatnatuit. Makut taugken angyarkaunrilnguut angtaciqeggiluk' waten ceterluki uquit piluki aug'arturluki pilatuluki asevret, kemgit-llu navgurluki. Eksunariluki, teguqayunariluki-ll' angtuarpauvkenaki.

Issurit qayauluteng amirkat-llu call' qayauluteng, nat'rauluteng-llu. Uquutnguaqluteng iliini. Amirkat angtuarpaunrilnguut caqutekiutullruit uquutekauluki. Ullingqallrit makut mingeqluki, nungulluki, melqutuumaita uquirraarluki. Qayilriatun tua-i nungulluku man'a mingeqluku. Uqunek-llu tua-i nutaan imirluki. Qaquarngalngurnek augkunek kankut tukullgit pilirluki teguyarirluki.

Pirrlainayuunateng taugaam. Angenrilnguarnek pitangqerraqata pikiurluteng pitullruut, caqutekaituraqameng. Nuuqitaqameng nayirnek tuaten pitullruut nungutarnek. Tuaten unkut ayuqut imarpigmiutaat.

weren't too big were used like that. That is how ringed seals were used. Those people in the past never had parkas made of ringed seals. I never saw [ringed-seal skin] parkas, but I only saw pants made out of them. And they killed their pups, the pups of spotted seals, the white ones with long fur, before their long fur came off. They made them into knee pads. Ringed seals that are medium length, and medium-sized spotted seals that are the same size as ringed seals, are used in ways that I just mentioned. [All sea mammals] are used.

~: Uses of sea-mammal skins :~

Now the skins of spotted seals, young bearded seals, and adult bearded seals were used as kayak coverings. They used them on kayaks. And they also used bearded-seal pup skins on kayaks, and they were also made into boot soles. But some adult bearded-seal skins were used on kayak covers, too, after thinning them. But adult bearded-seal skins were mostly used on boats along with walrus hides after scraping them and thinning them. They would scrape and thin [walrus skins] until they were the same thickness as adult bearded-seal skins. They would remove the inner layer of the skin. Only the outer layer of the walrus skin is good to use. Those that look [bumpy] like this aren't good because walrus start to look [bumpy] when they get old. They call it *pengitagluki*. But the skins of young ones that are dark are good and smooth. When they were planning to make a boat, they let them use those when they wanted to out on the coast. They'd cut the [walrus] belly down the middle and skin it in two layers instead of cutting up the skin for food.

They cut [the walrus] down the belly and take off the skin along with the fat alongside the meat. That's what they do. But walrus that aren't to be used for boat coverings, they cut up the skin along with the fat in equal pieces and butcher the meat, too. They'd cut up the skin and meat in pieces easy to load in the kayak.

The spotted-seal skins and young bearded-seal skins were used as kayak coverings and also for boot soles. They were used as containers for seal oil sometimes. They fixed up young bearded-seal skins as pokes to store seal oil. The sealskins that had been cut down the belly were sewn to close the opening with their fur still on after removing the blubber. They sewed this part together just like they sew kayak skins together. Then they filled them with seal oil and put a device similar to a paddle grip down on the bottom on their feet for handles.

They didn't always do that, though. They sewed up [bearded-seal skins] like that when they didn't have ringed-seal skin pokes available to store seal oil. That is how sea mammals were used.

Ilaita-gguq qayaqelallruyaaqait, taugaam-gguq-am uquitnek pikaunaki qayaqes-
ciigatait. Allat-gguq uquitnek ping'ermeng mecirngaitaa cetuam qecia. Uquminek
taugaam mingukuni nutaan pulaarkauluku, keniyailkucirluku. Tuaten ayuqut.

Nat'raqesciiganaki-llu uksumi cetuat. Qurrayirnaqpiartut. Tua-i assiinateng
nat'raqlerkaat, qurrayirnaqluteng. Nat'raqsuunaki tua-i. Elliarkautekluki. Qakiiyaat
caqutullruit imumi qecignek. Tamakukluki taugaam pitullruit cetuat qeciit, qakiiyarnek imkunek neqnek uksuarmi. Tamakunek tamaa-i imitullruit, ellianek aterpagtaqluki un'gaani, muirluki tua-i angtuat. Tamakunek tamaa-i caquluki pillruit,
ilait-llu issurinek caquaqluki. Qecignek caquluki pituit tamakut qakiiyaat.

Ellangllugturilaami nalliini qakiiyaam. Taugaam tuatnangraan pituluki, neqsur-
luki qakiiyaat, puyuqluki-ll' tua-i. Tua-i-llu puyuqeqarraarluki ekluki tamakunun.
Uquat cailkarmun pivkarpek'naku, uquqevkarluku tua-i. Umciggluku cakneq, ell-
ngarngairutelluk' caquluki.

Neqkiuraqamegteki-w' tua-i qeciit meqcirluki mangtait, imkut melqurrit makut
cetuat. Meqcirluki-am cali qemagtetuit, ner'aqluki qassaita tua-i, uqumek piurluki
mangtait tamakut cat cetuat. Angtuarpagnek taugaam pituut nunamni un'gaani.

~: Uginat atuullrat :~

Tuamtellu *sea lion*-aat, qiluit augkut tak'ut, unkuni takenruut. Kelikarturluki calia-
qetulliniluki, teq'umun-ll'-am akurrluki, akungqavkarluki. Tua-i-ll' pilnguamegteki
anlluki mermun call' nutaan ekluki, miicirraarluki nutaan iniluki. Tua-i amitqapia-
rangermeng tua-i elngupiat *sea lion*-aat qiluit. Imgutaugaqluteng taprualuuluteng.
Tamakut-llu mikellriit maklagtun angtalriit qiluit tapruaqluki, nemerkautekluki
tua-i canun makunun qayanun, qamigautnun-llu. Tamakut taugken imkut melqur-
palget angtuat *sea lion*-aat qiluit taprualukluki-gguq pituit. Asevrem-llu-gguq anga-
qeng'ermi kevkarrngaitai *sea lion*-aat qiluit. Tua-i tamakunek ilait pingqelallruut.

Caaqameng pituut maani tekiartetuut. Up'nerkami taugaam tangrruuyuitut,
kiagmi taugaam cikuirtaqan iliini tangrrugaqluteng.
Uginat. Kemgit assirtut, angtuat taugaam tepsarqut. Tepsarqelliniut kemgit ner-

They say some used to have [beluga skins] for kayak [skin coverings], but they cannot have them for kayaks when they don't have a supply of their own [beluga] oil. They say that even though [they rub] another animal's oil on them, it won't soak into the beluga skin. But it will soak in only if it's rubbed with its own oil, to prevent it from getting soaked by water. That's how they are.

And they could not use beluga [skins] for boot soles during winter. They are extremely slippery. They are not good as boot soles; they are slippery. They weren't made into boot soles. They use them to store fish, *elliarkautekluki*. They stored dried silver salmon in skin containers. They used beluga skins as containers for dried silver salmon they processed during fall. They filled them with those, and they called them *elliat* down on the coast, filling the large ones full. They stored them in those, and some would use spotted seals for containers. They stored dried silver salmon inside skin containers.

It starts to get wet out during the silver salmon season. But even so, they used to fish for silver salmon and dry and smoke them. After smoking them for a while, they put them in those [containers]. They didn't let their oil drip on the floor [of the smokehouse], but had the oil stay [in the meat]. They stored them [in skin containers] and made it very air tight, so that they wouldn't leak.

When they prepare them into food, they let the fur of these belugas come off the skin first. They let their hair shed and store them away, and eat the *mangtak* of belugas raw with seal oil. But they get very large [belugas] down in my village on the coast.

~: Uses of sea lions :~

Now for sea lions, their intestines are longer than other sea mammals down on the ocean. They apparently prepared them by scraping them first and soaking them in urine. And when they were ready, they took them out after soaking them in water and hung them. Even though they are very thin, sea lion intestines are extremely pliant. They were used as lines on spears. And the intestines of smaller ones, the ones that were the same size as bearded seals, were used as twine in binding wood in kayak and kayak sled construction. But the intestines of large sea lions with large hides were used as rope. And they said that sea-lion intestines won't break, even though a walrus was pulling on it. Some had those [skin lines].

[Sea lions] come here sometimes. We don't see them during spring but only in summer; they are seen sometimes when the ice is gone.

[Sea lions are called] *uginat*. Their meat tastes good, but the meat of the large

yunaunateng. Ikani atam Cape Newenham-ami amllepialartut Uginat, amllepiatu-
lliniut. Uirrelriaruluni tua-i.

Qenngalliniut tua-i cakneq. Yugnek tangvagluteng tua-i uirrelriaruluni, ilateng
tuaten cauvallagaluki. Yugtailan-gguq taugken tuaten pikegtayuunateng tua-i.
Taugaam qayatgun mallguurayunaitelliniut qenngaameng. Augkut ava-i atulriit.

~: Imarpigmiutaat anrutait nakacuit-llu :~

Tua-i-llu cetuat qiluit aturtut cali imumi. Anrutait-llu imanarviit amiitnun tua-i
qeciitnun-llu caquuluteng. Kenirluki makut qeciit, qatellria im' tapeqluku cetuat
amiit kenirluki ceturruciluteng anrutaitnek cetuat. Tamakut tua-i pituluteng.
    Taugken cali asevret anrutait cauyarkiutuluki. Qerrurluki tua-i qerrurraarluki,
kinrata-ll' tua-i imkut waten pillritgun ullirrluk waten, pitacqeggiluk' cauyarkat.
Nutaan murilkestaita teguluki qemaggluki cauyarkautet. Amllepiat, tua-i amllepiat
cauyarkautait qasgit. Qasgim pikluki. Kinerrluki taugaam. Tua-i-ll' cauyanun piqa-
taamegteggu mermun akurrluku, ecirluki tamakut. Yurarluteng-llu aturraarluk' taqngameng aug'arluki qemaggluki.

Kinercirraarluki, tua-ll' kinrata qertunrirraarluki nutaan ullirrluki.

Ukut-llu igyarait qilum-llu uitallra nutaan kepluku augarluku assircarluku elli-
qainaurrluku, nutaan cauyarkauluku. Tua-ll' nutaan kinqan cauyamun elliluku. Elliqata'arqan mecungtaqluku.

Tairit imkut. Qerrurluki qertunermek imirluki makliit-llu cetuat-llu. Qerrurraar-
luki-ll' tua-i makutgun maa-i makutgun nutaan pilagturluki waten mulngaku'urluku. Petengluni-ll' tua-i un'a pian, nutaan cetukun kiigarrluku, tuaten piurluki
aug'arturluki anrutam qainga, taira-gguq.

Asevret-llu tamakut tuaten call' tua-i, qertunermek imirluki tegg'ivkarluki. Ta-
mana-ll' tua-i ullirtelleq anglian, unairucata, tuamtell' qertunermek imiqanirluki.
Aa-a, patagmek piciatun tairiyuunateng. Elitnaurturluki-ll' arnat paniteng, tangvaurluki taircetnaurait. Taumek mikqapiarang'ermeng ilait nasaurlucuayagaat tair-

ones smells. The meat of big ones apparently is stinky and not good to eat. There are many sea lions across at Cape Newenham, there are apparently many of them. They like to snarl at people.

They anger very easily. When they see people, they'd all start growling and turn and attack each other. But they say they don't do that much when people aren't around. But it's not good to go near them in kayaks because they have a temper. Those that I just spoke about, that's how they were used.

~: Sea-mammal stomachs and bladders :~

They used beluga intestines in those days, too. And their stomachs were also used as containers for their skins. They cooked beluga skins, they cooked the skin with the white part and stored them in beluga stomachs. That's how [stomachs] were used.

Walrus stomachs were also processed to be used as drum skins. They inflated the [stomachs], and when they dried, they cut them open along the part of the stomach [that curved], just right to cover the frame. Then those appointed to take care of stomach coverings would put them away. There would be many stomach coverings for the *qasgi* drums. They belonged to the *qasgi*. But they had been dried already. And when they were going to place them on drums, they would immerse them in water. And after they used the drums in a dance, they'd remove the skin covering and put them away.

They dry them first, and when they are dry, they deflate them and cut and flatten them.

They cut off the part where the throat and intestines were attached [to the stomach] and flattened and shaped them ready to put on drum frames. And then they'd put it on the drum frame when it dried. They would wet it before placing it on [the drum frame].

[They carefully removed] the stomach membranes. First they inflated the bearded-seal and beluga [stomachs]. After they inflated them, they carefully cut off [the membrane] with these [skinning tools that are like X-Acto knives]. And when the membrane down below began to spring off, they'd use their fingers to peel off the section they called *taira* [its stomach membrane].

They did that with the walrus [stomach] as well and filled it with air and made it stiff. And if much of the covering had been peeled off and the stomach got softer, they'd put more air into it. They didn't remove the membrane quickly. Mothers taught their daughters how to peel off the coverings and watched their daughters

turnaurtut aanateng ikayualuki. Mik'naki tua-i elitelluki, mingeqsaraq-llu call' arcaqerluku elisngavkarluku tamaa. Tuaten tua-i augkut ava-i aturtut, atutuut.

Aren, augkut-ll' imat'anem asevret nakacuit, nakacuit tairluki cali pitukait. Mer'u-
tekluki taugken tua-i qeciqutaqluki mernek imituluki, paingit-llu piyarirluki muragnek.

Uquutekluki avani. Yuilqumun-llu ayagalriit uqumek imirluki taquaqluki aya-
gaqluteng. Uquukaqluki, taugaam tua-i murilkelluki, qag'ertellerkaat. Up'nerkami-
ll' anguaralallemteni tua-i uquukaqluki, caqumaurluki taugaam tua-i qayam iluani.
Meciarutaqluki-gguq apqiitnek.

Angtatkenritut atam. Maklinraat-llu angenruluteng maklassinraat-llu cali. Ang-
tatkevkenateng anrutait maklinraat, maklassinraat. Issurilinraat piiyuitait nayiit-llu
piit, tamakunek taugaam, maklassuut anrutait.

❧: Imarpigmiutaat qiluit :❧

Irnerrluut-llu *raincoat*-aqluki cetuat. Makliit-llu cali makut irnerrluit, qiluit cali
raincoat-augaqluteng, egalruluki tuaten egalerkiurluki. Tamakunun atuuluteng irnerrluit. Issurit taugken nayiit-llu qiluit piiyuunaki, maklagaat taugaam, makliit,
cetuat-llu, asevret-llu piyagaat, ayagyuat, puyurtat qiluit. Taukut tua-i cetaman atutuit, *raincoat*-auvkaraqluki tuaten. Makut-llu ecuilnguut mikellrit maklaginraat-llu
egalerkiurluku. Egalruaqluteng qasgit enet-llu egaleqluki.

Tanqinruata tamakut. Tamakut tamaa-i cetuat qiluit asvaitut, asevret-llu *young*-
alriit cali qiluit asvaunateng, aarnaunateng *raincoat*-aqellrat. Tuaten tua-i ayuqluteng. Augkut taugken mikcuaraat nayiit issurit-llu piiyuunaki tua-i, taugaam nertuluki imait erurluki.

Makliit makut qiluit waten pituit tekiutaqatki. Imarrluit aug'arluki. Nutaan-llu
augkut, nuussitgun piiyuilamegteki, tairit, anrutatun piiyuilamegteki, cetumeggnek-
am uumek waten elliuqerluki cetumeggnek waten elliurturluki, tairit aug'araqluki,

as they worked. That's why even though some girls were very young, they knew how to remove membranes and helped their mothers. They taught them how to do that at a young age, and they especially taught them the skill of sewing. That's how those [stomachs] were used.

Oh, I forgot to mention that they also removed the outer membrane from walrus bladders. They used them as water containers, as *qeciqutat* [walrus-bladder water containers] and filled them with water and made the openings out of wood.

They filled [these bearded-seal stomachs] with seal oil back then. And the ones who would go out on the land [to hunt] would fill them with seal oil and take them as provisions. It would be their supply of seal oil, but they watched them carefully so that they didn't burst. And they were our seal-oil provision when we paddled during spring, but we kept them covered inside the kayak. We used the seal oil to dip our food in. *Meciarutkat*, as we called it.

[Bearded-seal stomachs] are different sizes. Ones from adult bearded seals are larger and also the two-year-old bearded seals. Adult and two-year-old bearded-seal stomachs come in different sizes. They don't use the spotted-seal and ringed-seal [stomachs], but they use the stomachs of two-year-old bearded seals.

~: Sea-mammal intestines :~

And beluga intestines were made into raincoats. And bearded-seal intestines were also made into raincoats, and they even made them into windows to cover the skylight. That's how their intestines were used. But they didn't use spotted-seal and ringed-seal intestines, but intestines of bearded seals in their first year and adult bearded-seal intestines, beluga intestines, and young walrus intestines. [The intestines] of those four were used and even made into raincoats. And the clear intestines of bearded seals in their first year were made into windows. They were used as skylight coverings in *qasgit* and houses.

[They are good] because the light comes brightly through them. The beluga intestines are sturdy, and the young walrus intestines are also tough and good to use as raincoats. That's how they were. But they never used the small ringed-seal and spotted-seal intestines, but they ate them after removing the contents and washing them.

This is how they work on the bearded-seal intestines when they bring them home. They remove the [gut's] contents. And because they don't remove their outer membrane with knives, because they don't work on them like [the beluga] stom-

aug'arturluki irnerrluut qilut [tairit] qaqilluku tua-i. Tamakut-llu tua-i tairit qassarluki, aripaluk' assipiat. Wall'u puqlamun akurrluki. Qamkut tuamtell' iluqliit,
kelikaameng qaingatgun, waten keliutaneq ayallam qainganun elliaqluku. Qamna
call' taira ilulirneq aug'arluku, imarnitkiuraqameng irnerrlugnek. Cetuat qiluitnek
asevret-llu *young*-alriit qiluitnek, makliit-llu, maklagaat-llu. Tua-i taukut cetaman
qiluit *raincoat*-auyugnaut tamarmeng egalruluteng-llu. Tuatnarrlainarluki tua-i. Ta-
makuit (tairit) tua-i aug'arluki, qamanelnguut-llu iluatni, qaqican erurluki, nuggluki. *Soup*-aliameng-llu kemegnek, kemget mer'atnun keniumalriit, *soup*-aqluku ta-
yarunek avuluki. Avukluki tamakut qilut iluita piat qiaryigqurluteng tamuallrat
assirluteng call' nerellrit. Tuatnatuluki. Tuaten pituit anrutait qiluit-llu tairturluki.

Akungqavkarluki nutaan augirluki. Meq tua-i kavirinaurtuq uitallrat. Allamek
cimiraqluku. Tua-i assiriaqata nutaan, qat'riluteng tua-i assiriluteng, kaviyaagceten-
rirluteng.

Tua-i taugken qerrurluki qerrulriani, kan'a-wa qilu, tamana tegumiaqluku kanani
pirraarluku, peg'artaqani nutpagaqluni qertunermek. Man'a cipegqaarluk' peg'artaqani nutpagaqluni yaavet. Tuaten qerruristengulaama-ll' wii tamaani ukugka tua-i
akekatak' tua-i. Tamakut taugaam mulnganarqut tairit (aug'alriani) qagerrnayuk-
luki. Nayiit-llu kinercirarkat tua-i tan'gaurlullraat, nasaurluut-llu qerrurturnaurait.
Qerruristenguluta tua-i. Aataurteng'ermeng-llu qerrurinaurtut.

Iniaqluki agarrluki. Piciatun-wa tua-i atulriit augkut ava-i qerruryarat tamakut
nayiit, pilu'ugkauluteng, caqutekauluteng, qerruinauluteng tuaten ilait. Amlleret-
llu tua-i qavavet tuneniaqaqluki. Ayuqluteng tua-i tuaten augkut ayuqut qiluit cetaman augkut, atuugut tua-i atuutuut.

achs, they used this fingernail to do this, they'd use their fingernails and keep [pulling them apart] and remove the outer lining of all the intestines. Then they eat the outer lining raw. They are delicious when eaten raw. Or they place them in hot water first [and eat them]. And when they were going to use the intestine to make rain garments, they'd place the intestine on a cutting board to scrape the surface to remove the inner lining. They did this with beluga intestines and young walrus intestines, and also adult bearded-seal intestines and year-old bearded-seal intestines. The intestines of those four animals can be made into rain garments and were used as coverings for the skylight. That's what they always did with them. They removed that [outer lining] and the contents, and washed them, and when they made meat soup, they put [the lining] in the broth along with mare's tail plant. They added the inside lining of the intestine [to the soup], and chewing them makes a crackling noise, and they are delicious. That's how they prepared them. That's what they do with their stomachs and their intestines, always removing the lining.

[After removing the lining] they keep [the intestines] in water to remove the blood. The water they were soaked in became red. They constantly replaced [the water]. When they were no longer a reddish color and turned white they were ready [to come out of the water].

But as you blow air into them, you'd squeeze and hold the intestine down below a little ways and fill up part of the intestine with air, and when you released your hand, the air would suddenly shoot into the intestine down below. As you released your hand down below and squeezed the upper part to move the air farther in, it made a popping sound when it broke through the barrier. Because I used to inflate them, [my cheeks] would hurt badly when I did it. But you have to be very careful when inflating them so as not to break their outer lining. The boys and girls would also inflate the ringed-seal skin pokes that were to dry. We were the ones who inflated them. And even those who became fathers would inflate things.

They hung them to dry [after inflating them]. The ringed-seal skins that were inflated were used in many ways, as sealskin boots, sealskin pokes, and some were used as floats. And they sold many upriver. That's how the intestines [and skins] of those four animals are prepared and used.

~: Qiciit meqciryaraat :~

ANN: Amirkaq-qaa maklak-llu, qaillun aug'arluku melqua?

FRANK: Uquirraarluki imtuit waten, imegluki. Tua-i-ll' kinernamun pingairutelluki talilluki, puqlamun-llu tuknilriamun pingaunaki. Quyurrluki tua-i caqun-
qegcarluki piluki, kineryisqumavkenaki. Tua-i-ll' yuvriqa'aqluki, tep'ngarrluteng-llu
tua-i imumek meqcirat tepiitnek. Tua-i melqurrit tua-i nutaan teguluteng aug'aqai-
naurrluteng. Issurit taugaam meqtesciigatut, melqurrit aug'arturniitut atam. Makliit taugken maklagaat-llu pisciryarluteng, nayiit-llu.

Ernerni qavcini. Amllerrarni uitatetuit, yuvriqa'aqluki taugaam. Caquirluki
naruraqa'aqluki. Tua-i-ll' qes'artellriani waten melqut makut aug'arrluteng. Tua-i
nutaan piyunariluteng. Tegularluki-ll' tua-i aug'arturluki. Melqurrat tua-i navgur-
pek'nani iliini aug'arnaurtuq tamalkurmi tua-i, tungulriartuumarmi, tungulriani-ll'
tapeqluku.
ALICE: Canek-qaa allanek qecignek caliaqameng atutuut? Man'a teq'uq atutukiit.
Qamlleq-llu apellruken, qamlleret assirniluki.
FRANK: Imkunek caqutellernek meqciraunrilngurnek, uquutellernun qamlleq
atutuat. Kanevqerraarluk' tua-i waten imumek urugutmek pilriani tua-i melqurrit
eritarluteng, tungulria uneggluni. Muriit kaminiat-wa tua-i qamellritnek, makut
muriit qamellrit patagmek tua-i tuatnanaqluni assirluni.

~: Qercurtat :~

ALICE: Qaillun qercurtalituat?
FRANK: Uksumi taugaam pituut. Makliit igyarait, anrutaat-wa qamna, kepluki
nerutekiuraqameng. Iniluki-ll' tua-i nengelmun, qat'riluteng-llu tua-i qatqapiarluteng, waten ayuqluteng ilait. Nerutet-gguq tamaa-i.

Qayat tuamtellu taq'aqamegteki ellamun anucata kumelqerluki qat'riyarturlu-
teng-llu tua-i qayat tua-i qatqapiarluteng. Qercurluki-gguq nenglem kinerluki.

~: *Removing fur from sealskins* :~

ANN: How do they remove the fur from the young bearded-seal and adult bearded-seal skins?

FRANK: After removing the blubber from the skin, they folded them up and put them away. And they put them in a shaded area where they weren't exposed to dryness and heat. They put the skins together in something, covering them. They'd leave them and check on them periodically until their odor indicated that the fur was ready to come off. At that point, you could just remove the fur easily [with your hands]. But spotted-seal fur is hard to get off. You have to age them longer to remove their fur. But the fur on adult bearded-seal skins, as well as that of young ones, comes off easily, and also that of ringed seals.

[The fur comes off after] several days. They leave them for quite a few days, but they check them from time to time. They remove the covering and smell them. As you take it like this, soon the fur would come right off. Then they are ready. Then they'd begin removing [the fur] with their hands. Sometimes all the fur would come off still attached to the black part of the skin.

ALICE: Do they use anything else when they work on skins? They use urine. You mentioned ash, that ash is good.

FRANK: They use ash only on old seal-oil pokes and not on [skins] that were aged to remove the hair. After sprinkling it on the [skin], when using the scraper on the hair to remove it, it just comes off with the black part still on the skin. Ash from wood stoves, when used, helped the hair come off easily.

~: *Freeze-dried skins* :~

ALICE: How do they freeze-dry skins?

FRANK: They only do it in winter. They take the esophagus of the bearded seal and cut it off the stomach when they are going to prepare dried esophagus. Then they hang them outside in the cold, and they turn white, very white, and some are even this color. They call those *nerutet* [dried bearded-seal esophagus].

And again, when they were done constructing kayaks, when the skin covering was taken outside and exposed to the cold, it began to turn white, and they turned very white, a process called *qercurluki*. The cold temperature outside would freeze-dry the skin.

Pilugunun, atkuut caitnun call' aturaqluki imarnitnun-llu qaraliuluteng. Ilait-llu cingiqluki pilugugnun nerutet. Imkunun-llu iqtuvkenaki kelirturluki, kelurquarluteng. Imarnitet *raincoat*-anun call' atutuluki. Kal'alegmek yualirturluteng, tua-i qaraliuluteng tua-i tangssunaqluteng, arnat aturameggnun pitullrukait.

Qercurtat tamakut nat'raqsunaitut. Meliurcuutngululuteng-llu assiinateng. Metuyukapiartut. Taumek nenglem pillri qayat-llu uqurqaqtullrukait amllermek. Kiagmi taugken kinellret umcigluteng. Maingit, maingit umcialilartut nenglem kinellri. Mermun tua-i akureskuni, metuluni-ll' tua-i egmian mer'em pulaluk' egmianun, uksum kinellra nenglem. Kiagmi taugken kinlleq mer'em pulangaunak' egmianun uquilengraan. Taumek uqumek kinraqata uksumi pitukait. Uqum-llu tua-i meciateng, mermun ping'ermeng meq iterciiganani. Tuaten tua-i aturtut.

~: *Imarpigmiutaat enrit* :~

Asevret tuamtell' makut enrit tua-i call' aturluteng. Agluqrit ukut *runner*-aaqluk ikamranun avani. Imkut-llu *tusk*-aita elalirneret pulamalriit, avamiqait-gguq. Tamakut tamaa-i, cali pirlaaruluteng, agluqrit-llu tamakut. Tulimait-llu kis'utkiuraqluki, mellgarnun-llu epuaqluki tua-i piciatun enrit. Uivait taugken piksaitelarait. Imkut-llu angtuat *whale*-at *rib*-ait makut pirlaarkauluki, pirlaarkauluteng. Agluqrit-llu cali imkut takqupiit, ikamranun angtuanun aturaqluki, pirlaaqluki. Tamakut tamaa-i pituut, arvernek pilallrit. Tuqutaqluki-ll' pilaamegteki. Taugaam imkut *killer whale*-at inerquutaqaput akngirtesqenritait. Yuugut-gguq. Pisqevkenaki pituitkut.

~: *Kaugat* :~

Unkut uquit aturtut. Tua-i-llu imkut *whale*-at enrit makut arivnerit ukut-llu tusgit, keggasgit, qamiqurrit-llu uquripialliniluteng. Maani ukurmiut *whale*-artellruut takumni, angtuamek tua-i, nutaramek. Kanani-ll' nunaullratni kanani akaggluku waten mayurrluku, amatiini-llu yuk cataunani. Inangqaluni waten aqsaan amatiini yuk ipingaluni tayima cataitaqluni. Angkayalliniut.

They used [dried esophagus] as a design on sealskin boots, parka parts, and seal-gut rain garments. Some people used dried esophagi as skin-boot laces, and they made them into thin strips and sewed fancy stitches on them. They also used them on seal-gut garments. When women used them to decorate clothing they used colored thread to sew fancy stitches on them, and they'd look very nice.

Qercurtat [freeze-dried skins] are not good to make into boot soles. They are not good to make into articles of clothing that are used in wet weather or in water. The skin easily absorbs water. That's why they put lots of seal oil on the kayak skin cover if it had been freeze-dried when new. But [the pores on skins] that dried in summer were very tight. The ones that the cold air dried became porous and weren't as tight. If freeze-dried skin was dipped in water it would absorb water quickly and get soft. But skin dried in summer wouldn't immediately absorb water, even if it had not been rubbed with seal oil. That's why they rubbed seal oil on them after they dried them during winter. And once oil saturates the skins, water can't go through, even if it is dipped in water.

~: *Sea-mammal bones* :~

And walrus bones were also used. They used their jawbones as sled runners back then. And they call the place where their tusks are inserted their *avamiqat* [jawbones]. They were also made into sled runners, along with their jawbones. And they made their ribs into sinkers and handles for carving knives and other things. But they never used their spine bones. And they made the ribs of large whales into sled runners. And they used their very long jawbones on sled runners as well. They killed those called *arveq* [bowhead whales]. But we are warned not to hurt killer whales. They say they are human. They tell us not to hunt them.

~: *Lard extracted from whale bones* :~

They use [sea-mammal] oil for many things. And evidently whale bones, their joints, shoulder bones, shoulder blades, and heads are very oily. People from this village obtained a whale in my presence, a very large, fresh one [that was beached]. When people were still living down there, they rolled it onto the shore, and a person standing on the other side of the animal wasn't visible. As it was lying on its back, you couldn't even see the person on the other side past its stomach. Apparently they are very large.

Tua-i-ll' tamakut enrit egqaqsugnaunaki. Imkut cupluryagnek pilget, makut usgunrit ciamlluki kaugtuarluki, egatnun-llu ekluki nutaraitnun puyalengvailgata. Ke-
niquni-ll' tua-i egan qallangekuni aruvairulluni, uqumek imangluni.

Arivnerit makut enret ciamlluki kaugtuarluki. Imkut *lard*-anek pilallrit tanglar-
ngataten teggluteng, kass'artaat. Tuacetun tua-i ayuqeqapiartut tamakut. Kauganek
pitullruaput, pitullruit kaugturluki pituamegteki, kauganek aterluteng. Tuaten tua-i
piaqameng tua-i qat'riaqluteng yuuraqata tegqapiarluteng. Akutanun taugaam avu-
kaqluki uquitnun. Eyuani taugken tua-i teggluni akutaq. Uqurrlainarmi teggenru-
luni.

~: *Mallut* :~

Asevret makut ak'allaurteng'ermeng kemgit naulluutngusciigatut. Makuni unkumiu-
tarni ungungssini tamaitni, tua-i qaill' pingaunateng tep'ngengermeng tua-i iluliqut-
ngusciiganateng.

Kenirturluki taugaam tua-i, uuterrlainarluki taugaam cakneq qassauvkaqsaunaki.
Imkut taugaam ircaqurrita piit, qallaucuarngalnguut, *plastic*-aarunganateng imkut,
tamakut-am nutaraugaqata qassarluki nertuit. Tamakut taugaam neresqessuitait.
Quulqautngutuut-gguq tamakut ircaqurrita piit. Mallungekan tamakua neresqev-
kenaku, kenirluku taugaam qassarpek'naku.

Arevret taugken tua-i tamakut cali malluutuluteng un'gaani nunamni. Cali imkut ingkut terait qassarluki cali pituyaaqait, qaill' piyuunateng. Qangvaq imumi
yaaliagni, yaatiinun elliryugnarquq, Kuigilngurmiut nercuglaryarpiartut mallumek
tamakucimek, taugaam ilangartevkenateng assiriluteng tamarmeng. Augna-ll' wii
yuk'a wii ilagaulluni tuaken aug'aucaaqellininluni, taugaam nerevkallrunritanka, iner-
qurrluki pivakaama. Cunaw' elluatmun inerqullinikenka. Tua-i qanruteknngatki egmianun ciqitelluki tamalkuita tamakut. Taugaam assiriluteng tamakut nerellret tamakut, qaill' pivkenateng.

Inerqurluki tua-i uum kinguakun tamakumek pingraata pinqigtesqevkenaki mallumek. Caqviitnek pilarait tamakut terait imkut, caqviitnek. Malluugaqata temait
piiyuitait, taukuqainarnek taugaam pituut mallukaqamegteki, talliqurritnek-llu imkunek.

And they never discarded [whale] bones. The joints that have holes on them, their joints, they smashed them by pounding on them, and they placed them in pots when they were fresh before they became rancid. When they cooked them and the pot began to boil and stopped smoking, it began to fill with oil.

They crush their joint bones by pounding on them. You probably saw those called lard found in stores. They look exactly like those. We called them *kaugat* [lard extracted from whale joints, lit., "ones that were pounded"] because they prepared them by pounding them. They were called *kaugat*. When they [cooked them like that], they would solidify and turn white and very hard. They added them to seal oil when they made *akutaq*. The *akutaq* was hard when it congealed. It hardens more than when just using seal oil.

~: *Beached, dead sea mammals* :~

Even though walrus meat is old, no one can get sick from eating it. Among all of the other sea mammals down in the ocean, [eating them] will not cause anyone to get a stomachache, even though their meat had fermented and started to smell.

They always cook them, boiling them thoroughly and not eating them raw. But the part in their hearts, the *qallaucuarngalnguut*, the parts that look like plastic, they eat them raw when they're fresh. But they tell them not to eat that part raw from a walrus that was found dead on the beach, but to always cook it first. If eaten raw, it turns sour, creating pain in the person's stomach.

People down in my home area typically find beached dead walrus. They eat their flippers raw, and nothing happens. But some time ago, perhaps it was last year or the year before, the people of Kwigillingok almost got botulism from eating that beached [whale], but no one died and they all recovered. My child also took a piece from [the whale], but I warned them not to eat any because I was suspicious and thought that it wasn't good to eat. Soon after that, I realized that my warning was not in vain [as others who ate it got sick]. When it became evident how those people got sick, I told them to discard all of it. But those people recovered, and no one died.

So after that the community was warned never to eat parts from a beached dead [whale]. They call their flippers *caqviit*, their *caqviit* down there. They don't take their meat when they find them beached, but only take those [tail flippers], and their side flippers as well.

Asevret makut kemgit *green*-aarurtengermeng-llu kal'ait iluliqutngungaitut. Mermun-llu pugtaayaarluteng taugaam kicuirulluteng, kal'angluteng-llu *green*-aamek, iluliqutngungaitut yugmun. Nerellrat nutaan assiriluni. Nallustaita tua-i assiilkelallruit. Wangkuta tua-i maani neqekngamteki assikluki.

Kenirraarluki ner'aqluki. Tua-i iluliqutngungaunateng. Taugaam palungqaluni waten malluulria, aqsaquni atliqluku asveq palungqaluni, neresqenritaat ciuliamta. Pisqevkenaku tuaten pimalria pugtalria palurmi, palurmi-ll' nunamun palungqaluni. Tamakut pisqessuitait taugaam, nevermeng taugaam uitalriit malluuluteng. Nevermeng-llu pugtaluteng unani mermi.

Amllernek mallunek piiyuitellruut asvernek. Caanguaqluki pillrunritait imkut pissurtet maani. Quyurmeng-llu waten up'nerkami nalacituameng, qayat ukut amllertaciit tangrraarluki, malrugnek wall' pingayunek tuquciaqluteng. Ayuqluteng, ngelqaqluki nangluki piyugngaaqamegteki qayat. Iliini tua-i carrarmek tua-i unicituluteng cipciluteng uciassiyaagaqameng asvernek. Taumek asevret mallut amllessiyaayuilnguut, taugaam imkut mermi pugtaluki piiyaaqellrit. Kevkaulluteng-llu pillret kill'uteng, pugleraqameng, malluugaqluteng. Tamakut tamaa-i mallut asevret, malluugaqluteng. Makut taugken makliit, issurit-llu, nayiit-llu mallut kemgit piiyuunaki. Neryuitaput. Inerquutekluki, inerquumaluta tua-i. Asevret taugaam kemgit nallaitgun kiingita.

Makut taugken ilait pingaunaki, nerngaunaku malluukata. Nutarauluki taugaam neryugngaluki. Asevret taugaam kemgit kiingita tua-i ak'allaurtengraata inerquumanritaitkut. Tuaten-llu ellingraata, *green*-aarurtengraata neryugngaluki kenirluki, kenirrlainarluki taugaam. Mallunek taumek piaqameng tua-i ilakuivkenaki tegutukait tamalkuita kemgit. Kemgirluki tuaten, assikluki.

Walrus meat, even when it is consumed after it turns green, won't cause a person to get an upset stomach. And even when they begin to float and no longer sink after turning green, consuming the meat will not cause a person to have an upset stomach. After the meat turns green it is very delicious. Those who had never eaten them before didn't like them. Those of us who eat them around here like their taste because we're used to eating them.

We ate them after we cooked them, and eating them will not cause a person to develop a stomachache. But a dead, beached one found on its belly, a dead walrus that is found lying on its belly, our elders told us not to eat it. They told us not to eat from a walrus found dead floating on its belly, or from one found dead lying on its belly on land. They told us that it was safe to eat from one that was found dead lying on its back. And it was also safe to eat from one that was found dead floating on its back down in the ocean.

They didn't find many beached dead walrus. Hunters around here never killed them for nothing. Since they hunted in groups and killed walrus in the spring, depending on how many kayaks there were in a group, they'd kill either two or three walrus at a time. They only killed enough to fit in all the kayaks there. Once in awhile, if all the kayaks had been loaded and couldn't fit anymore, they'd leave some walrus meat behind. That was why there weren't many dead beached walrus found on the beach. The only ones they found beached were the ones that were killed while they were swimming in the water and sank. And also the ones [that had been wounded] and sank when the ice they were on broke off and went adrift. Walrus killed like that were usually found dead on the beaches.

But when they find these bearded seals, spotted seals, and hair seals dead on the beaches they don't take the meat. We don't eat them. We were always warned not to take them. We were told to take only the meat of a walrus when we found one dead on the beach. But we don't eat the meat of these other species when we find them dead on the beach. We can only eat them when they are just killed and fresh. But we weren't warned against walrus meat, even though it had gotten old. We can even eat them after they turned green, but only after they were cooked. That was why we always took the whole animal home when we found it dead on the beach. We liked eating aged walrus meat.

~: *Yualut* :~

ALICE: Cetuat-im nataitnek yualunek tegutelallrulriit?

FRANK: Ingkut *tail*-aita imkut, ingkut waten pilriit, uum piinek. Waten elliur-cuutait yualut qalliqluteng, waten atliqluteng uitatuut, uivluteng. Uum elliulriim ciungani wani.

Tak'aqluteng qaill' ilait taktaaqluteng. Tua-i cali erurluki teq'umun-llu piluki augirluki qupurrluki quyungqallrit ukut avektuurluki, tupigluki-ll' tüa-i iniluki nutaan.

Tua-i-ll' augkunek arnat taluurluki. Waten-am elliurluki aug'arturluki. Qipqer-luki elliaqluki. Amlleriata-ll' tua-i tamakunek nutaan waten, qip'allermeggni ilaur-luki, qipiurluteng tua-i ilaurluki. Tua-i ellegtatkurluki. Kuvyakiuraqameng-llu ta-makunek. Tua-i cukanrarluteng ilait. Qipiaqameng tua-i waten elliurturluki, ilaluki tuaten kuvyacuarkiuraqameng.

Makut taryaqvagcuutet, kangitnercuutet-llu *seal*-at qeciitnek taprarnek kuvyang-qetuut, kuvyangqetullruut. Makut taugaam mikcuaraat imarpinrarnek tamakussuu-tet yualuarnek. Iqkinateng *twenty-five mesh* pitanilaryugnarqait tuaten. *Mesh*-ait *twenty-five* cuqerluni acitmun waten. Tua-i-llu eyagquamegteki kuvyat *twenty-five* taktarian, naanepiggluarrniluku taqnariniluku. Naanepiggluarrniluku.

Qalukluki-llu ceturrniurcuutekluki [yualut]. Allegnek tamakunek pituut, taugaam allget tamakut nengelmi mulnganarqut. Kumlataqateng-gguq pituut; Asmareskuni tua-i navgarkauluni kumlaskani. Yualut taugken assirluteng.

Tuntut-llu yualuit tua-i tuaten ayuqut-gguq. Cetuat-llu yualuitun ayuqluteng tua-i, tastaayuunateng. Uliutaitnek, imkut tulimat pagkut nepingaluteng waten kin-guqliqluteng, ukut keggasgita yaakaraatni maani. Temaitnun maavet kemgatnun pulamaluteng waten iquit. Iquit paugkunun culuksuitnun uivat makuitnun nepinga-luteng, enernun. Tamakunek tamaa-i tuntut piitnek uliutaitnek pituut.

Takevkenateng. Cetuat taugaam terinrait tak'ut, takaqluteng.

Ayuqut-gguq tuntut-llu piit, ayuqluteng. Tastaayuunateng-gguq. Augkut-gguq taugken arevret yualuit tastetuluteng. Tua-i aturyaaqelriani man'a tupiumang'ermi

~: *Sinew* :~

ALICE: What part of the beluga do they get the sinew from?

FRANK: The ones down by the tail, those that are like this, ones that are attached here. The sinew is usually here in layers and in a circle that the animals used to [move while swimming]. In front of this [tail] that moves like this.

Some were long. They also washed them in urine to remove the blood and separated the ones that were together, splitting them into strands, and then they braided and hung them [to dry].

Then the women split and shredded them using those *talutet* [sinew splitters]. They continually pulled off [strands]. They twist [several strands to make thread] and put them down. And when there were enough [threads], they began [twisting threads together], adding more [sinew], [and made a long line] all the same thickness. And they [used long sinew like that] when they made gill nets. Some were very fast [when making sinew thread]. When they made long lines to make small gill nets they'd twist the sinew threads like this and keep adding more threads as they went.

They used sealskin line to make king-salmon and silver-salmon nets. But the small whitefish nets were made of sinew. They were short, and I think they said they were about twenty-five mesh. They had a measurement of twenty-five mesh down like this. And when they measured them with their outstretched arms, when they reached twenty-five mesh, they would say that it was almost the right size, that they should finish making the gill net.

They also used [sinew] to make dip nets for tomcod. They used those nets made of *allget* [the inner layer of young willow bark], but bark nets require care during cold weather. They say that happens when they are cold; it will break in cold weather. But sinew nets are good.

They say caribou sinew is the same. They say they are like beluga sinew and don't fray. They call their back ligaments *uliutet*; the ribs that are attached [to the backbone] sit side by side like this, and the [ligaments] are located a little ways from their shoulder blade. The ends of the ligaments are buried inside the meat. And their tips adhere to the spine, on this part of the backbone. They use those ligaments that are on caribou backs [as sinew thread].

[Caribou sinews] aren't long. But sinews from beluga tails are long.

They say [beluga] and caribou [sinew] are the same and neither will fray. But they say bowhead-whale sinews fray. And when they are used, even though this

tastaaryugluteng. Tamakut-gguq taugken tuncinraat ceciinraat-llu tuatnayuunateng. Tuatnayullrat pitekluku tamakut [arevrinaat] tastaaryullrat [atuyuunakii]. Assiryaaqut-gguq.

Unkut tua-i tuaten atuullrat nallunritaqa imarpigmiutaat.

~: *Puyat* :~

Tuknipiartuq atam tua-i. Nuqtaangerpegu kiingaituq piluaqerluni, puyalereskiin uqum tegukani, nepeskuni. Mer'em-llu arturluku tua-i. Ca ukimangermi tua-i, tamatum *cover*-aaqani tua-i imangengaunani, uqum puyalran. Taumek augkut puyat yuilqurrmiutaat makut uqumek avuluki pingqetulriit angtuanun caquluk' waten qantarpagnun. Imirluki tua-i kinercirraarluk' puyat, uqumek-llu tua-i kuvluki. Akertem tua-i manimallranun natmun elliluki, puyalecirluki. Tua-i puyangami nepcanariluteng tua-i waten teguqallrat. Angertun, angeryugtun ayuqlириluteng. Tukniriinarluteng. Tamakut-llu tua-i imkut urut, ungiluteng tua-i, ungiqapiarluteng. Mukaatun ellirluteng. Imkut teguniyagait-llu ungiluteng. Tua-i-llu qayanun angyanun-llu assirikata puyat tamakut, elliluki. Kelugnun maavet pikuni, aug'arngairulluni tua-i nepluni puya. Kelikarluni taugaam pikuni aug'aryugngaluni. Mer'em tua-i iterngairulluku tua-i, kelugnun minguukuni.

Tua-i-llu uksuarmi tan'gerpiit amlleriata, qaill' piluku-ll' ekluku qantamun qemrarluku puyalereskii uru, mermek kuvqaqluku. Una assiriinarluni, kiituan tua-i waten ayuqliriuq, qat'riluni. Akuyulluku, mermek kuvqaqluku. Una-ll' tua-i qantaq angengermi cuqluku imarturian nutaan tan'gerpagnek avuluku akulluku. Egmianllu tua-i qantanun neqliurluku patagmek neresqelluku. Nangluku tua-i wanirpak neresqumaluku. Uitaqaquni tua-i merurrluni-ll' tua-i. Tua-i-gguq tengluni. Tuatnayugtut tua-i tamakut, taumek egmianun nertukait taugaam uitatevkenaki ilakuivkenaki-llu. Nerumanrilkuni tua-i merurtarkauluni, tan'gerpiit-llu pugtauyaarluteng qaingani. Tuaten ayuqut tamakut.

Taugaam assirtut, qayanun angyanun-llu atutuluki puyat tamakut umcigutnguluteng. Kilinernun-llu assirluteng.

Patgutekluki atutuut. Imkut-llu tegg'erat augkut muriit canilliyagarluki, mik'naki taugaam, angtuanun kilinernun atutuit. Uqumun aku'urqaarluki patgutaqluki patagmek tua-i *infect*-aryailkutekluki. Unuaquaqan tua-i cimiraqluki. Kiitaqluku qatellriamek uquryagngalngurmek nevumaluteng. Allanek cimiraqluki. Angtuanun

had been braided, they like to fray. But sinew from caribou and beluga don't do that. Because they like to fray, [bowhead-whale sinew is never used]. They are actually good, however.

That's what I know about the use of sea mammals down in the ocean.

∾: Moss and aged seal oil :∾

[Rancid seal oil] is very powerful. If rancid seal oil touches something and it sticks, it won't come apart, even though you pull it. And water can't get into it. Even though there is a hole in something, if rancid seal oil covers it, it won't fill with water. That's why they kept those *puyat* [moss from the wilderness mixed with oil] in large bowls. They filled [a bowl] after drying the moss, then spilled seal oil over them. They placed it in direct sunlight to make it rancid. When it became rancid, it became sticky when handled. They became like gum, like spruce pitch. They gradually become more powerful. And the moss dissolved and became soft, very soft. They became like flour. And their small, tangled parts became soft. And when the mixture of seal oil and moss was ready, if placed on kayak and boat stitches, the mixture of seal oil and moss will stick. It can only come off if it's scraped off. Water won't be able to go [through the seams] if it is applied on stitches.

When they had many crowberries during winter, they placed rancid moss in a bowl and mashed it with their hands, adding water periodically. Then it gradually became better, and eventually it became this color, lighter. They mixed it with their hands and added a little water periodically. And even though the bowl was large, they kept mixing it until it became a certain amount, and when it was enough, they finally put crowberries in and mixed it. Then they would immediately dish it out in bowls and tell them to eat it quickly. They would want us to finish it right then. If it stayed, it would turn into water. They would say *tengluni* [lit., "it flew"]. That's what happens to them. That's why they only eat them right away and do not leave them or keep leftovers. If it wasn't eaten, it would turn into water. And the blackberries would float on the surface. That's how they are.

But they taste good, and they use the moss-and-seal-oil mixture on kayaks and boats to make them watertight. And they are good on cuts.

They used them to cover [cuts]. And also after shaving the hard spruce wood into little chips, they used them on large wounds. After dipping them in seal oil, they place them on [wounds] immediately to prevent infection. They replace them every day. When [the chips] are peeled off, a white substance that looked like puss

kilinérnun atutuit, tegg'erat imkut canilliyagaat muriit. Mikcuayagauluki taugaam canilliyagauluki.

Cait unguvalriit unkut aturtut minguuluteng tuaten, iinruuluteng tuaten merluki. Kumlami-llu kumlaqalriamun cali nengelmi atuuluni cali uquq.

~: Taprat, taprualuut, imgutat-llu :~

Kinerpailgata. Uquit kelikarraarluki tua-i meq'aqata tamakut taprarkat, taprualugkat-llu pituit. Arnat tua-i kelikayuitait taprualugkat, angutet taugaam caliaqluki. Tamakut taugaam uquutekat pilu'ugkat-llu arnat uquituit.

Qapiarumalrianek, tamatumek waten uyiinek, wall' kanarrluk' kanaggun irugken mengliikun kepluku. Kanarrluku-ll' tua-i ayagnirluku. Pakiumaurluku, ik'um-llu call' pakiumaurluku.

Una nuussimek tegumiarluni. Tua-i waten tua-i pimaurluku. Ikna taugaam nuussimek tegumiarilnguq uuggun uyiikun tegumiaqluku inglua, cagnitateklukek makuk wani. Tauna pinevkatuuq, nuussimek tegumiarilnguq nuqequrluk' tua-i waten cagnitateklukek. Tegukaniraqluku. Uum taugken pimauralriim pekcuunaku. Imum cetuit makut, uum cetua kepssuunaki atutuata, caniyarami-ll' atutuata. Ukut kepssuitait *nail*-ait angutet. Pinevkami call' atutuluki, tua-i qayiurutkat *harpoon*-at-llu uskurarkait.

Nayiit issurit-llu pinevkatuit. Makliit taugaam irniarit augkut amirkat, taprualukluki angtuanun pissurcuutnun, pissurcuutaitnun *harpoon*-aitnun-llu epukevkarluki uskuraqevkarluki. Caliaqurluki uivenqeggiluk' waten, nuussinek caniurluki taprualugkiutuut kinraqata. *Round*-arluki tua-i assiqapiarluni. Tamakut taugken qayiurcuutet tupirkat-llu qecigkilnguaraat tamakut mikcuaraat piiyuunaki. Makliit taugaam irniarita qeciit mamtuata akaggluk' pituluki.

Ataucim unguvalriim qecikenritai. Maklinraat taprualugnek pituit, makliit-wa qecigtuameng tua-i. Maklagaat-llu qecigkunateng. Imgutaqetuluki maklagaat amiit

would be stuck to it. They replaced them with new ones. They used the hardwood shavings on big cuts and wounds. But they shave them into very small pieces.

The sea-mammal parts from the ocean are used, and [their oil] is applied to things [as a sealant], and they drink it for medicine. And seal oil is also used by those who get hypothermia out in the cold.

~: Sealskin lines :~

[They stripped the skins into line] before they dried. After scraping the oil off the skins and letting the fur shed, they stripped them into lines and ropes. Women didn't scrape oil off skins to be made into ropes, but men made them. The women removed the oil from the skins to be used as seal pokes and made into boots.

They used skins removed from the bodies intact [to make ropes], starting from the neck opening, or turning it topside down and cutting along the feet. Then they turned it upside down and began stripping from the bottom. A person over here would hold this side of the skin back, while another person across there held onto the other side.

This person here held a knife. The skin was held like that [while it was stripped]. The one across there not holding the knife would be holding the skin by the neck opening with both hands, holding both sides with the same tension. The one who wasn't holding the knife was the one who made the strip by pulling the skin with both hands with the same tension. He'd pull the skin. The person over there [holding the knife] never moved it. Back in those days, they never cut this [thumb] nail because they used it, and they were also used when carving with crooked knives. Men never cut their [thumb] nails. They also used those when they made skins into line, the skin lines that were used in kayak and harpoon construction.

They made sealskin line out of ringed and spotted seals. But they made the skins of the offspring of bearded seals, those young bearded seals, into rope for large hunting tools, and they used them as harnesses on their harpoons. They worked on them, rounding them by using a knife to cut small strips off when they made rope when they were dried. They make [the skin lines] round; they are very good. But they did not do that to the ones they used on kayaks and for woodworking that required sewing and binding, the ones that they made very thin. They only round [skin lines from] bearded-seal pups because they are thick.

[Lines] are not just made from one kind of sea mammal. The lines referred to as *taprualuk* were made from adult bearded seals because they have thicker skins.

makut. Taugken makut issurit irniarit tapruariluki. Iqtuurluki, tua-i teguyaraqluki, nuqilautekaqluki-ll' canun. Ikamragnun-llu ucilirraarluk', wall' muragtaqameng igcailkutekluki, egilrautekaqluki. Teguyaraqluki tua-i tamakut taprat. Qayiuraqa-meng-llu aturturatuluki.

Taugken imkut tapruaraat nayiit issuriyagaat-llu qeciit, aminateng. Nutaan qayat aklukluki, nemeqluki, tupiqluki. Piciatun tua-i, qanikciurutet-llu muriit tupiqluki, ikamrat-llu qamigautet tupiqluki tua-i tamakut. Qayat-llu akluita negciit-llu tupiq-luki. Nurnallratni tua-i cat, tamakut tamaa-i.

Cali-llu qayarrlainarmun aturpek'naki tamakut tapruaraat. Kuvyiaqluteng tama-kunek tapruarnek qilagluki, taryaqvagcuucirluuteng tamakunek. Tua-i-llu pikail-nguut taryaqviit pelluata angilluki egmianun iqallugcuutnguluki qilagluki. Tuaten atutullrulliniit. Taugken pikalget tua-i taryaqvagcuutnek kuvyaluteng, iqallug-cuutnek-llu. Taugaam pikartuyiqenrilnguut tuatnatuluki. Taksuitut-gguq kuvyait, angiarrluki kuvyakaqluki. Tuaten tua-i ayuqut.

Asaaqut imgutarkait. Cat maklassuut amiit kinraqaki uluamek akagqurluki, wa-ten uivtanqeggiluki assircaarturluki, kinraqaki taugaam, imgutarkiurluki. Nutgitler-meggni tamakunek tamaa-i pingqetullrulliniut. Taprualugnek aterpagtaqluki. Assir-caumaluteng tua-i. Akagcimaluteng.

Tamakut qeciit qavyanek pituit. Angtuat-wa cat qeciit augkut; qecigtulriit qav-yanek pituit.
Asevret-llu cali. Ayagyuat taugaam piitnek pituut. Angyiurcuutnek tamakut tamaa-i qavyanek aterpagtaatullruit cali, asvinrat, mangaggluki taugaam. Asevret qeciit mamkellicarluki, cataitnek pivkenateng, taugaam mat'umek elaqlirmek, qa-malirneq aug'alteng pivkenaku. Neqnun taugaam assigtaqtuit tamakut ilulirnerit, asevret ayagyuat qeciitnek, angturvaussiiyaanrilngurnek. Qeciit ayagyuat manigce-cetuut waten, assirluteng tua-i tamalkurmi. Temirtet taugken manianateng waten ayuqliriluteng. Pengitagluteng, tegglluteng-llu cakneq assiinateng, ukut keggatait arcaqerluteng. Temirtengurtaqameng manialituut asevret amiit.
Meqciumalrianek pituut. Cali-ll' imumun teq'umun akurtaarluki peqlicarluki-gguq. Keniyaircarluki, mermun akuqetaangermeng ken'iqerrngairutelluki.

The bearded-seal pup skins are thinner and are used as lines on spears referred to as *imgutat*. But the skins of spotted-seal pups are made into *tapraq*. *Taprat* are wider and used more widely. They used them to tie things and to strap down the load in the sled, like wood. *Tapraq* is used for many things. And it is used in working on a kayak.

However, the *tapruaraat*, lines made from ringed-seal skins and small spotted-seal skins are thin. This line is used on kayaks as binding and as thread to put the frame together. It is used for many things like stitching together a wooden shovel and in dog-sled and kayak-sled construction. And it is used in making some kayak implements including gaffs. That is what they used when [store-bought line] was not readily available.

And they didn't use *tapruaraat* on the kayak alone. *Tapruaraat* were made into king-salmon gill nets. And when the king-salmon harvest was done, those who didn't have [chum-salmon nets] would quickly unravel the king-salmon nets and reuse the line and make it into a chum-salmon net. That was how *tapruaraat* were used. Those who had enough lines to use had both king-salmon and chum-salmon nets. But those who didn't have enough [would unravel the king-salmon net and remake it into a chum-salmon net]. The nets weren't long and were easy to unravel and reuse. [Skin lines and twine] are like that.

The lines for *asaaqut* [toggling harpoons] [were made rounded]. The two-year-old bearded-seal skin lines, after drying, the edges were carefully shaved with a woman's knife to round the cross-section to make line. Evidently, that's what they had when they had no guns. They called them *taprualuut*. They shaved the edge to make it round.

That [thick] skin line is called *qavyak*. The skins of the larger [animals]; line made of thick skin is called *qavyak*.

The skin of a [walrus] was also made into [that kind of rope]. But they only used skins of younger walrus. The walrus-skin lines they used in making boats were called *qavyak*, but before stripping them into lines, the skin was split into two layers. The outer layer of walrus skin was split and made into rope, and the inner layer was used to store fish. And they only used the skins of young walrus. The young walrus skins are smooth. But the older ones have rough skins. The skins of older walrus are bumpy, especially on the torso. When a walrus gets old its skin gets wrinkled and rough.

They only used [aged] skins [for lines] after the hair fell off. And they also dipped them in urine to make them water-resistant, *peqlicarluki* as they called it. That process helped the skin stay hard and not get soft, even though it was dipped in water.

Teq'urrilnguut taugken tua-i ken'iqerrluteng, unairrluteng. Tuaten taugken teq'u-
mun pimalriit keningaunateng. Ayuqucirteng ayuqerkauluku, mermi uitamanger-
meng keningaunateng. Nengulrasciiganateng-llu peqlireskai.

Mamtungaleng'ermeng atam nengugtaqameng mamkellituut, *rubber*-aatun ayu-
qerrluarngameng qeciit, nengulraluteng waten. Tua-i taumek nengugarrluki cakneq,
nengugtevkenaki cakneq kinercitukait, tua-i-ll' kinrata mamkunateng tua-i.

Tua-i makut nayiit tapruaraugaqameng assirluteng. Mamtunrit assiitut taprua-
rauluteng, taugaam mikcuaraat imkut nayiit qeciit, nengugtaqameng taugaam mamkunateng tua-i. Aminani tua-i assirluni-ll', waten ellegtaurluni. Kinerpailegmi iq-
tuyagarluni waten ayuqellruyaaqengermi. Uutun iqtutaluni, nengugcami-llu tua-i
waten iqtutariluni, kinerluku kinraqani.

Waten taugken iqtutaluku tapruarmek piqataquni, uumi iqtunruurluku, iqtunr-
ruluku pinevkararkauluku, nengugcami-llu waten pitariluni.

Mamtunruami-llu man'a mamtunruurluni kinengraani. Man'a taugken nayiq
mamkilami, nengugcami mamkunani tua-i. Assirluni tupiqsunaqluni. Makunek
maa-i imguciyuitut, amirkat taugaam qeciitnek. Iqtuurluki piaqluki, nengugca-
meng-llu tua-i pitacqeggiluteng.

Uumi iqkillrulartut amirkat kinraqata. Uum anglikaniraqami, mamturikaniraq-
luni, mamtutacia. Taumek waten makuliyuitut makliim qecianek. Makucetun mam-
tutangailami, kinengraani assirpek'nani tua-i. Waten taugken mamkilnguq nayiq
kinqani assirarkauluni tua-i amilnguq. Nemruluki tua-i tupiuluki-ll' pituluki. Issuriyagaat-llu piit, qeciit.

ANN: Up'nerkami pilartut?
FRANK: Ii-i. Kinerpailgatki pituut. Melqurrit meqcirluki caquqerluki, tua-i-ll'
meqngata egmianun nutaan uquit kelikarluki. Uquirluki tua-i kelikarraarluki mermun pivkarraarluki, nutaan pinevkarluki, uivvaarturtelluki tua-i waten. Imkut ullir-
tevkenaki maaggun tamakukat pituit. Una taugaam qamiqurra aug'arraarluku, qamaggun augkunek qapiarutnek waten ayuqelrianek kauluki qeciit tegumiaqurluki,
qapiarluki, uquat qamaavet piurluku. Piyunariata nutaan annluki. Caqutekat-llu
tuaten pituit. Makut taugken maklagaat tamalkurrluuciicetun piiyuunaki. Pikang-
qerraqata maaggun kepelmun ullirrluki, ukuit-llu it'gait engelaitgun cali piluki, im-
gutarkauluku una uquirluku pituit. Ii-i, uivvaarturtelluku call' pinevkarluku.

The ones that were not dipped in urine softened easily [when they got wet]. But the ones kept in urine won't get water-logged and soft. They will stay hard and tough, even though they're in water for a long time. And the ones that are water-resistant don't stretch.

Although [skin lines] seem thick, when they stretch, they get thinner because skin is like rubber and stretches like this. That's why they dry [skin lines] without overly stretching them, and they're thin when they dry.

These ringed-seal skins are good as *tapruaraat*. The thicker ones aren't good as *tapruaraat*, but the smaller ringed-seal skins become thin when they're stretched. They are thin and good, about this wide. Though it is a little wide before it's dried, when it's stretched to dry, it will get about this wide and stay that way when dried.

But if they are making *tapruaq* this wide, wider than this [previous width], they will make the strips wider, and when [the strips] stretch out to dry they will be this wide.

And because [this particular sealskin is] thicker, this [line] would be thicker, even though it had dried. But since ringed-seal skin is thin, when it stretches, its [line] will be thin. It's good to use for binding [wooden pieces together]. They don't make *imgutat* [harpoon lines] out of these, but only from young bearded-seal skins. They make them a little wide, and when they are stretched, they are just the right size.

When young bearded-seal skin [lines] dry, they are narrower than this one here. When it's made larger, it will be thicker. That's why they don't make these kinds out of adult bearded-seal skins, because they won't be as thick or as good as this when it dries. But when a thin ringed-seal skin [line] dries it will be good. They used them for strapping things and as binding [on wood]. And the skins of small spotted seals [are also good to make into line].

ANN: Do they do it in springtime?

FRANK: Yes. They [strip the skin] while it's raw. They wrap the hide in something and age it to remove the fur, and as soon as the fur falls off, they scrape all the oil off the skin. After scraping off the oil and washing it in water, the skin is stripped by continually rotating [the sealskin] like this. They don't cut seals open along the belly when the skin is to be made into line. Instead, they first cut the head off and begin skinning the animal from the head opening with a *qapiarun* [seal-skinning tool]. As you hold the skin with one hand, the other hand will get deeper and deeper [inside the seal] as you cut the skin off the meat and blubber. And when [the skinning is] complete, [the body] is taken out [through the neck opening]. They also prepare seal pokes like that. But they don't skin bearded seals in their first year with the hide intact. When it is the right time, they cut them in crosswise pieces, and they

Keggatai-ll' ingkut iruit pivkenaki cali. Makut taugken tamalkuita tua-i nayiit pituluki, ukut talliquit kepluki, avatairrluki tua-i tekitaqamegteki, kitu'urtaqluki, nutaan kinguani iqkellicarluk' aug'arluki talliqurrit ukut.

Elisngalriit atam pinevkalriit cukaut. Una nuqtellria pinevkatuuq. Una taugken nuussimek tegumialek pivkenani, tauna taugaam nuqtellria. Makuk cagnitateklukek amiliqtaarngaituq. Elleggiqerrngaunani-ll' qac'uqerteksaunani-ll' tamarkegenka cagnitateklukek.

Cagninrulria kep'arrngaituq. Qacngallrulria taugaam egmian kep'arciiquq. Cagnitatekekunek taugken tua-i. Elisngalriit tua-i assipiarluteng pinaurtut pinevkallrit.

~: *Imarpigmiutaat aruqutkellrat* :~

Ernerpak imarpigmi uitaaqluta unani uksuarmi, atakumi taugaam tag'aqluta. Ilavut pitaqan ullagluku ikayurluku. Mermi pugtaluta pilagaqluku unguvalriit itulluta, ituciurluta qayat qaingatnun mayurrluku pilagaqluku, mermi pugtaluta.

Piciryaraqluku tuaten. Ilavut tua-i pitaqan quyurrvikluku tua-i pilagaqluku. Aruqutekluku-ll' kemga man'a.

ALICE: Augkut-mi pitaqerraallrit, qaillun piciatun pilagpek'naki [pitullruit]?

FRANK: Malruugug-am waten. Maklaartaqaata makliim irniaranek ciuqlirmek tua-i tan'gaurluq, tuaten kepelmurluku piqatarniaqamegteggu, uuggun, maaggun talligken piakun kepelmun waten ullirtetuat kassuggluku. Tua-ll' cuqluku iqtutaurluku tua-i, uatmun waten ullirqurluku, yuut ukut qavciuciat naaqluku, ngelqerruvkarluku. Iqtuluku qavciukata, yugyakata-llu iqkillruurluku taprualugkait, taprualugkaitnek. Taprualuut. Avegturluku-gguq tua-i, ciumek pitqerraalria maklaarmek, nat'rautulinek.

cut them near their feet as well. Then the pieces are made into *imgutat* after removing the blubber. Yes, they turn them gradually around and strip them.

And they didn't use their upper torso or their feet. But they took the [whole carcass] out of ringed seals, and they cut off their arm flippers, going around them when they got to them, passing them, and then they thin them afterward, removing their flippers.

Skilled skin strippers are fast. The one who pulls [the skin] is the one who makes the skin strips. But the one holding the knife doesn't make the strips, but the one who pulls [the skin] makes the strips. [The strips] won't get thicker and thinner if they keep these [arms] the same tension. And it won't get thicker if one doesn't loosen one's hold [on the skin], keeping the same tension.

The tighter you pull the skin, the skin line won't sever. But if the tension is too loose, the skin will sever right away. [It will only work] if they are held with the same tension. The ones who were skilled at making strips from skin would do a good job.

~: Distribution of seal meat and oil :~

We stayed out all day on the ocean in fall and went home in the evenings. When one of us caught [a seal] we would go and help out. We would line our kayaks side by side and put the seal on top of the kayaks and cut it up while we were floating in the water.

That was what we always did. When one of us caught one, we would group around him and cut up the [seal]. And we'd distribute the meat.

ALICE: What about when someone caught [a seal] for the first time, how do they cut it up, not just in any way?

FRANK: There were two ways. When a boy caught a bearded-seal pup, the offspring of an adult bearded seal, for the first time, when they said they were going to cut it *kepelmurluku*, they'd begin cutting wide bands around the cross-section of the animal, starting near the front flippers. The hide is cut into equally spaced bands all the way down, and the width of the other bands is determined by the number of people present when each one gets an equal share. The bands were wider if there were fewer people, and narrower if there were more, the bands of hide they made into skin lines and ropes. If a boy caught a young bearded seal for the first time, the hide of the animal was "divided up" as they say. The young bearded-seal skin normally used for boot soles [was distributed like that].

Tua-i-llu maklageskan, ciuqlirmek maklageskan uuggun cali kep'arkauluku, una tua-i keggatii pikevkarluku pitaqestiinun. Una tua-i qamiqurra ukuk-llu kiingan tua-i pikluku pitaqestiin, amirkaq maklak-llu. Nutaan ukatmun, maklak, kepelmun pivkenaku, ukatmun takelmurluku-gguq. Cali yuut naaqerraarluki, naaqluki tua-i amllertatekluku tamalkuan tua-i cipnirpek'naki cuqtaarluku, iqtutaacirkaan takelmun qupurrluku aruquteklukuku, takelmurluku-gguq. Kemga-ll' tua-i tamalkuan teguvkarluku tua-i, uumek taugaam qerranrinek ukunek pitaqestii kemguterluni.

Tuaten pitullruit. Makut taugken nayiit piiyuunaki. Amirkat taugaam makliit-llu tua-i tuaten pituit. Amirkat avegturluki makliit-llu takelmurluki. Tuatnatuit. Tuatnatullruit pitqerraalria ciuqlirmek.

Tua-i-ll' ukaqvani Kass'at imkut kiputengellratni, kiputellratni *skin*-anek, Kass'a-nun tunluku, akia-ll' nutaan ciulirnernun aruqutekluki caulaki tua-i, caayuuluki, cuyauluki, saarralauluku. Tamakuuluku tua-i aruqutkaqluku ciulirnernun. Navgur-luku pinanrirluku. Kinrumariaqan taugaam Kass'anun kiputelluku tua-i. Tamaku-nek tua-i ciulirnernun aruqutekluku tuatnalangluteng-am. Maa-i-ll'-am tua-i pi-nanrirluteng mat'um nalliini, qunutungariniluki-am pilaranka. Tuatnayuirulluteng tua-i.

Tuamtell' up'nerkami atrangaqamta pitqerraaraqamta tagngamta tua-i, ullirrluku tua-i maklak-llu navgurluku kemga tamaq'apiaraan tua-i. Napautarluteng-llu tua-i nutaan. Muragam atkullraat pikavet kangranun elliluk' naparrluki. Napautarniluki tua-i tangrramegteki. Nutaan aruqutekluku taun' maklak tua-i tamalkuan kemga. Naangata tua-i taqluki. Tuamtell' nayircan tua-i tuatnatuluki.

Uumiku-llu pitengraan pivkenani. Tuaten piciryaraqluku, uqicetaarturluteng. Maa-i-ll'-am ilait pinanrirluteng. Qunutungariluteng. Piiyuirulluteng tua-i.

Aruqsatullruut-llu qasgimi.
Pitqerraalriit tuaten kemgitnek, pitqerraarutaita, kemgit kenituit. Kenirluki uquit-llu augarluku uquirluki, amllertatkevkarluki uullauluki. Tua-i taugken aruq-saqatarniluki piluta tan'gaurlurni qasgisqelluta. Qasgimun agngamta tua-i itrucatki qantat kemegnek imarluteng uqunek-llu keniumalrianek angutet nutaan piluki. Angtaciqeggiluki ukliurluki kemget-llu. Kemget qaqitaqata, tamakut muraggarnek

And if he caught an adult bearded seal for the first time, they would cut it here again, and the one who caught it would keep the upper torso. The one who caught it would only take the head, and these two here, [the upper torso] of a young bearded seal and adult bearded seal. They would not cut the adult bearded seal crosswise, they'd cut it into lengthwise strips, *takelmurluku* as they called it. Again, the width of the strips is determined by the number of people so each receives an equal portion with nothing remaining. They would distribute all the meat as well, but the one who caught it would only take the meat around the rib cage.

That is what they did in the past. But they didn't do that to ringed seals. They only did that with young bearded seals and adult bearded seals. They would divide young bearded seals and adult bearded seals into lengthwise strips of equal size. That is what they do. That is what they used to do for the first catch of a young hunter.

And in recent times, when the white people began to buy skins, they would sell [skins] to white people and buy things with their earnings, including tea, tobacco leaves, and sugar, and give them to elders. They no longer cut up the skin. But they sold it to white people after it dried. They started to distribute various items to the elders [after selling their skins]. They've stopped doing that today, and I say that they are becoming stingy. They no longer do that.

Also, when we began to go down to the ocean during spring, and when we caught our first bearded seal and brought it to shore, we'd split the belly open [and take the skin off along with the blubber] and cut up all the meat. Then they would hoist a post, *napautarluteng*. They would place an old parka on top of a stick and hoist it up, and when others saw it they'd recognize it and announce that they were having *napautaq* [lit., "something hoisted"]. Then they would distribute all the bearded-seal meat. They stopped distributing when they all had a share. They also did that when they caught a ringed seal.

They didn't do that when they caught [a bearded seal or ringed seal] the next time. They would always distribute the meat and blubber of a hunter's first catch like that, *uqicetaarluteng*. Some no longer do that today. They have become stingy. They don't practice that custom anymore.

And they used to have *aruqsaryaraq* in the *qasgi*.

They would cook the meat of [hunters'] first catches. They removed the blubber from the meat and cooked equal portions of meat and blubber. Then they'd announce that they were about to do *aruqsaryaraq* and told us boys to go to the *qasgi*. When we went to the *qasgi*, when they brought in the bowls filled with cooked meat and blubber, they'd give some to men. They'd first cut meat and blubber into serv-

waten nuvqerluki kemget, uquq-wa yaani aruqurnauraitkut tamakut. Aruqsarluta-gguq tua-i.

Eputuumiita taugken tua-i muragmek neru'urluki uqumek tuaken avuqaqluki. Tuatnatullruitkut.

Mikengraata tua-i, mikcuassiiyaagaat taugaam pivkayuitait. Imkut taugaam ell-meggnek ayagangelriit tan'gaurluut. Nasaurluut-llu piiyuunateng. Qasgimun piiyui-tut nasaurluut avani.

ALICE: Caaqameng-mi uqiqulartat?

FRANK: Ayagyuat irniateng-llu wall'u uiteng-llu piaqamegteki uqiqutullruut ak-lunek tua-i, elumarrarnek-llu pinevluki, yualunek, nerutnek, piciatun tua-i irnerr-lugnek [tuaten]. Piciatun taugaam uqitetuit akutanek-llu piaqluteng, amllermek akutamek. Qanciisqelluki taugken piluki akutamek piameng uqiutekameggnek. Ta-makunek tamaa-i uqurrlainarnek piiyuunaki.

Ang'lakluku tua-i nepengnaurtut aaraluuteng. Tan'gaurlurni, tua-i [wangkuta] angutni ilagautesciiganata, arnat taugaam. Inerquumalallruamta, angutet tuaten piiyuitniluki. Maa-i tavaq, tan'gaurlurtuumarmeng taperculriarunaurtuq.

Qasgimun tuamtell' kalukaquaqata apqaitnek neqkanek, uksumi pituut. Kiagpak neqsurraarluteng, tua-ll' qaqiucameng uksuan, November-aam iluani neqtateng im-kut unangkengateng ilangarqurluki *family*-t tamarmeng qasgimun nerevkariurlu-teng. Tamana tuaten aturaqatgu inerquumatullruukut wangkuta. Kalukaliyaasqev-kenata.

Nerqingaitukut-gguq wangkuta tuaten ayuqekumta. Tua-i capeqngamteggu pii-yuunata, kalukaliyayuunata. Ilait-am taugken inerciigalnguut tua-i pingraiceteng kalukaliyatuluteng. Kasngunaqluni tua-i inerquun navgurluku.

~: Tutgaraurluq maklaurtelleq :~

Nulirqelriik-am taukuk qanrutkumalartuk quliraulutek. Quliraulutek nulirqelriik, yungyuunatek, irniangyuunatek. Tua-i-llu irniarkamegnek kaigalutek, tungayameg-nek cikiumayaaqlutek. Tua-i quyakluku, taugaam angliqerluku aaniin qunuyagu-lluku. Tua-i nakmiin pikenrilamegen'gu uingan taum tunesqelluku aaniinun, nep-liutekciqniluku qunukekunegen'gu.

ing sizes. When the meat was all cut up, they would poke the pieces onto sticks along with the blubber, and they would distribute them to us, *aruqsarluta*, as they called it.

Then holding the stick we'd bite off pieces of meat along with the fat. [Women] used to feed us like that.

[They fed boys] even though they were small, but not the very small children. They only let the boys who started to go out and do things on their own participate. And girls never participated. Girls never went inside the *qasgi* back then.

ALICE: On what occasion do they have *uqiquq* [seal blubber distribution party]?

FRANK: When they had [seal parties] for young people, their children, or their husbands, they used to distribute things, including pieces of cloth, sinew thread, dried esophagus, assorted things, and intestines. They also distributed *akutaq*, lots of *akutaq*. But they would ask [the guests] to bring bowls when they were going to distribute *akutaq*. Those were some things they gave away and not just blubber.

[The participants] really enjoyed it and would start making noise, yelling. We boys and men couldn't participate, only women. We were warned not to take part and were told that men never participated. And look at them today, when mothers come to participate, they bring boys [to catch things for them].

And when they began bringing food to the *qasgi* for a feast, this activity was only done in winter. After fishing all summer, when they were done and winter came, sometime in November, all families would take some foods from their harvest and bring them to the *qasgi* to hold feasts. We young boys were warned [not to participate] when they did that. They told us not to go to the feast.

They said that we would not feed others [when we became hunters] if we were like that. Since we were reluctant, we never went to the feasts. But those who were disobedient would go to the feasts, even though they were told not to. It was very shameful to break an admonishment.

~: An orphan child who became a bearded seal :~

They mention a married couple in a tale. The tale is about a married couple who couldn't have children. Then they asked for a child of their own from their relatives and were given one, and they were grateful, but just as it grew bigger, its biological mother wanted the child back. Because it wasn't their own child, her husband told his wife to give the child to its mother, that they would argue over it if they were reluctant to give the child back.

Tuamtell' kinguani allamek call' tungayamegnek kaigalutek, mikelngurmek call' cikiumalutek. Cali-am angliqerluku tuacetun ciuqlimitun qunuyagulluku. Tua-i-am tunluk' ataam qunukevkenaku.

Taum kinguani nulirra tauna uitayuilami kiagmi yuilqurrluni cenamun unavet ayagaluni tua-i piaqluni. Caqerluni tua-i ayallermini, uterrluni marayakun. Uluma-llermini ilutuuralriit imiqaquluki pituuq unani cenami. Marayat waten ilutuuralriit ulem imiqeraqamiki entengraan imangqerraqluteng mermek, taryumek. Tamakut amlliraqluki.

Piinanermini amllilria, ca auga qevliallagluni ayagartelliniluni. Piqalliniuq neqcua-yaaq augna ayalria, tus'arcamiu-ll' tua-i, marayamun ugiyaqaaqalliniluni. Ullagluku pillinia neqcuarauyukellra una tamakuunrilnganani. Pillinia eyinrayagarmek keggi-nangqellinilria. Uatii taugaam una neqnguluni, neq'linrauluni. Tua-i arnat qaluurit-nek ayauquratuameng, tauna mermek taryumek imiqerluku, tuavet qaluuritminun ek'artelliniluku neqcuayaaq, umyuarteqluni, "Qaillun-kiq waniw' una anglicaqumni ayuqsarta?" Naspaayugluku tua-i umyuarluni. Yuurrnayukluku pitsaqevkenaku yugtun ayuqlirinayukluku ut'rutliniluku tua-i.

Tekicami uini tauna qasgimlan assigtarkiurluku egmianun tupilliniluni. Nutaan qantamun mermek imiqerluku ekliniluku tuavet. Ekraarluku canek neqrarnek ciam-ciluni naspaaluku pikiini nerrliniluni. Tua-i nek'eggluku nutaan yaatminun kenek-luku tua-i cakneq pilliniluku. Nutaan tauna atakuan neryartullermini uini itran maniitelliniluku taumek nataqutaminek. Yuy'agauluni tua-i keggatii una, tallirluni-llu. Uatek taugaam neq'linraulutek.

Maniicani tuani naspaayugluku naspaaguryugluku, nertullinian-llu. Tua-i yug-nun-llu maniyuunaku qakemkunun. Murilkurallragni tua-i angliuralliniluni. Ta-mana-ll' neq'linraq uatmurrngiinarluni anglillra maliggluku, aciqsigiinarluni.

Anglian tua-i nek'eggluku nutaan. Tua-i uligtuumaurtelluku camek. Kiituan tua-i anglilliniuq qalarcaurrluni-ll'. Tuaten elliqerluku qasgimtellermini pilliniuq tauna uinga taum, "Keputeka tang-ata imna paivqaarluku nalluyagutellinikeka." Tutgara'urluq tauna iliit ilangqerrameng tutgaraurlurmek, egmian-am qanrutiini qeckalliniluni. Egmian-llu anqertelliniluni aqvaluku.

Itrami tua-i murilkevkenani nulirra tauna qanrutliniluku keputii aqvaniluku. Caniqami tua-i nangerrluni tauna nulirra pillrani murilkartelliniuq akiagni ikani neviarcaq ikna inangqalria uligtuumaluni. Tangerqaani quuyuaraqalliniluni. Um-

After that, they asked another relative, and they were given another child. Again, just as the child got bigger, [the biological parents] wanted the child back like the one before. Once again they willingly gave it back.

Sometime later, because his wife never stayed home in summer, she would always roam the shore down there. One day after being out there, she returned home along the sand. During high tide, water fills deep spots down on the shore. When the high tide fills deep spots out on the mud, you'd see tide pools filled with salt water when the tide goes down. As she went, she would step over those [tide pools].

While she was stepping over [a pool] she saw something that glittered and dashed off. She saw that it was a small fish swimming in one of those [pools]. And when it got to the other side, it jumped up on the mud and sat. She went to it and saw that the one she thought was a small fish didn't look like one after all. She looked at it carefully and saw that it had a small human face, but its lower body from the waist down was a fish. Because women always took water dippers with them, she filled it with salt water and put that small fish into her dipper, thinking, "I wonder how it would be to raise it?" She wanted to try. She wanted to see if it might happen to turn human. And so she took it home.

When she got home, since her husband was at the *qasgi*, she wove a small grass container for it. Then she filled a bowl with a little water and put that thing in there. After she placed it in the bowl, she tried giving it crushed pieces of food, and it ate. Then she found a good place near her and placed the bowl there with loving care. That evening when her husband came home to eat, she showed him what she found. It was a tiny creature with a human torso with arms, but it was a fish from the waist down.

When she showed him [the little creature], he said that they should keep it and continue to raise it because it apparently could eat. [They kept it] and never showed it to the people out there. As they observed it, it grew. And as it got bigger, the human part of its body began to show more and the fish part began to recede and disappear [down] its body.

When [the little creature] got bigger, they put it in a good place and kept a blanket over it. It eventually grew and began to talk. Then one day when her husband was in the *qasgi* [he said], "I've apparently forgotten to bring my adze after taking it out." An orphan boy there in the *qasgi*, since there was an orphan boy among them, just as he said that, the boy jumped up and ran out immediately to get it.

When he went inside [the couple's home], not noticing anything, he told the wife that he came to get her husband's adze. When the wife stood up to get something near their bed against the wall, he immediately noticed a girl across from the bed

yugaan tua-i tutgara'urluum taum kenekluku arenqiatellinia, tangeqsailami-ll' waten qagkuni yugni.

Kepun tua-i tegurraarluku an'ngami tua-i umyugaani uitalliniuq tauna nasaurluq
assikngamiu. Qasgimun tua-i itrami tunrraarluku, an'ngami egmian maurlurlumi-
nun aggliniluni. Itrami tua-i akianun maurlurlumi pirraarluni [uitallrani], maurlurluan taum allakngamiu tutgara'urluni tauna pillinia qaillun picianek. Maurlurluni
tauna pillinia nukalpiartam, taum, ikna yuksukluku nukalpiartamun tauna, tangerr-
niluni eniigni nasaurlurmek.

Maurluan taum, maurlurluan pillinia, "Ceningqalriamek-wa pillilriaten." Qang'a-
gguq, ceningqanrituq-gguq, uligtuumaluni-llu-gguq qaill' pilriim.

Arenqialani tua-i taum maurlurlua nangerrluni, qangqiirem amianek tegulluni,
kemgilnguarmek kinerciumalriamek qangqiirem amianek, qecianek melqutuumal-
riamek, qeraqcaaralliniluni tua-i eniitnun, tut'gara'urlurmi arenqialani.

Itliniuq [arnam] uinga tauna qasgimtellerminek taillrullinilria. Nugngami pilliniuq akiagni neviarcaq ikna tua-i ukut nunat ilakevkenaku. Umyuarteqliniuq, "Anir-
tima'urluq augna tutgara'urluqa arenqiapakartuq, kenegnarqellinian una nasaurluq."
*Aarrarrarraa*raluni aqumlelliniluni arnassagaurluq tauna. Taum pillinia uingan,
"Tua-i maurlurluuq pitengqerravet taiguten maavet." Pillinia taum maurlurluan,
tua-i waniw' anuqnguan tua-i qalarrneq qanrucarturnilukek tua-i. Uingan taum
pillinia, "Kitak patagmek maurlurluan anuqlia tua-i anuqliryuucirpetun." Qalartes-
qevkenaku-llu.

Tua-i ellimerrani tauna nasaurluq qanrutkelliniluku tutgarminun taumun aren-
qiatniluku tua-i, cucuyaaqluku piaku tua-i waniw' anuqnguan anuqliryarturniluni.
Nukalpiam taum pillinia waniw' tua-i tupekniluku. Naiggngaitniluku tutgara'urluq tauna cucumalaamiu kevgiullra man'a qessalertevkenani ilamitun ayuqevkenani
picia pitekluku. Kevgiullra arenqialan, uitauranrilan. Tua-i piarkaurrluku. Angrani
nangerteqataami, naqugutminek tauna qangqiiq aug'arluku aaniinun eg'artellinia.
"Tauna kitak tua-i agleqan urukevkarniaran." Tua-i pikangqerrutacirramegtun. Anlliniluni tua-i. Anqataan taum arnam pillinia, taikili-gguq kitak.

lying down with a blanket over her. When he saw her, she smiled a little. The orphan boy thought she was beautiful and loved her since he hadn't seen anyone who looked like her out there among the people.

When he went out after taking the adze, the image of the girl stayed in his mind because he liked her. When he went into the *qasgi*, after handing it to the husband, he immediately went over to his grandmother's place. When he went inside and sat across from his grandmother, since she noticed his unusual behavior, she asked him what was wrong. Then he told his grandmother that he had seen a girl in the home of that *nukalpiartaq* [great hunter] and his wife and that the girl he saw in their home might be their daughter.

His grandmother said to him, "Maybe you saw someone who is visiting." He answered her that she wasn't a visitor, and that she had a blanket over her for some reason.

Since he was so adamant, his dear grandmother stood and took a ptarmigan skin, a ptarmigan skin without its meat that had been dried, a skin with feathers, and she slowly went across to [the couple's] home, because her dear grandchild was so adamant.

She went in and saw that [the woman's] husband had returned from the *qasgi*. When she came up through and entered, she saw a girl across from the couple who wasn't a member of the village. She thought, "No wonder my grandchild was so adamant, because this girl is beautiful." That poor old woman said "*Aarrarrarraa*" and sat down. The husband said to her, "So, grandmother, you came since you have a reason." His grandmother told him that she came to talk to them because voice is wind that blows when one speaks. The woman's husband said to her, "All right, you go right ahead and blow wind as you wish." He didn't even use the word which actually meant "to speak."

When he told her to talk [the grandmother] mentioned the girl there, that she came to blow wind because her grandchild wanted to [marry her]. That great hunter told her that he was excited to have him, that he won't turn that grandchild down because he wanted to have him [as a son-in-law] as he worked hard and wasn't lazy like others. Because he was a very hard worker and was never idle. So they all agreed [that the two would marry]. When he gave her the affirmation, when she was about to stand up, she removed that ptarmigan from her belt and tossed it at the girl's mother and said, "Have her use that for padding when she has her menstrual period." She gave them as much as they had. Then she went out. When she was about to leave, the mother told the grandmother that [the boy] should come over.

Tua-i qeraami tutgara'urluni tauna, itrami [enemegnun], *aarrarrarraarluni*, nunu-
yakngualliniluku tutgarani. "Tutgara'urluqtallerma, taqsuqevkarlua! Qeraasqaatgen
qeraqina. Qeraqina piyullruuten." Tutgarii-gguq tauna piuq, "Qerarngaitua. Tallurnarqut."

"Aren talluryugpek'nak piyullruan. Qeraqina." "Qerarngaitua. Tallurnarqut." Maur-
lurluan-gguq taum pia, "Qeraqtanrilu-w', allam elluatum yuum nulirkaa menuurcuaran." Tutgariin-gguq tua-i kiugartaa, "Qeraqatartua." Nangerrluni tua-i tayima anlliniluni.

Ak'anun-gguq pivkenan itliniuq. Maurlurluan pillinia, "Tua-llu-q' qaill' piatgen?"
"Takaryungama-wa itenrilngua." "Tutgara'urluqtall'ermi-ll! Aren piyugpakarraar-
luni. Iteqtanrilu canrituq, yuunerpet nukalpiarunrulriim nulirkaa menuurcuaran."
Kiugartellinia-am, "Nutaan qeraqatartua." Nangerrluni-am aipiriluni tayim' anlliniluni.

Qeraami tua-i-am ancurtunglliniuq-am elaturraatni itlerkaminek takaryugluni.
Tua-i umyugaa piluni. "Maurlurluqa pirraartelluku pinricenarciqliatnga. Tua-i ta-
lluryung'erma kitag-it'ruaqerlii." Kalvaggluni itliniluni.

Itran tua-i aturanek caqumalrianek atrarciluteng, tauna arnaq nukalpiam taum
nulirra ancilliniuq angucetarnek aturanek. Ac'inqigcetliniluku tamakunek. Tua-i
qaqiarcamiki uitaqarraarluni anlliniluni arenqiatuq talluryuami. Tua-i nuliqsagute-
lluku, anluni taugaam tua-i. Qeralliniluni tua-i.

Maurlurlua uitainanrani yuk cakem itliniluni. Murilkeqerluku [piqanrakun]
nukalpiaq ugna puggluniluni. Maaten-gguq tua-i nangertuq tutgara'urluqsaaqelli-
nikii. Maurlurluan pillinia, "Aling aren, tua-i tang tangnerraryarpiaqemken. Waten
aturangqelaquvet nukalpiarngacallinilriaten."

Nangerrluni-am taun' maurlurlua anlliniluni tayima. Qulvarvicuaramegnun tuaten mayurluni-am agalriit taukut tanglallri tut'gara'urluum caqumaluteng atrarrluki itrutliniluki. Itrucamiki pilliniuq. "Kitak qerauski ukut maliggnaamken. Una
qerausgu." Cunawa-gguq arnartarnek aturanek imangqellinilriit. [Qerautellinilutek.
Tua-i tekicamek] itresqengraani-am tua-i iteryugnaunani unitelliniluku. Iterluni
tua-i itrami tunllinluki taukut. Tua-i aaniin taum qainganun taugaam civtuqa'aqluki taum nasaurluum. Tamana-gguq aciqsigiinarluni anglillra maliggluku.

When she went across and went in [to her home], she gave a big sigh, "*Aarra-rraaraa!*" and scolded her grandson, and said, "My darn grandchild has exhausted me. They want you to go across. Go ahead and go across since you wanted to." Her grandchild said, "I won't go across. I'm too shy of them."

"Gosh, don't be shy for you wanted her. You go ahead and go across." [He said,] "I won't go across. I'm too shy." His grandmother said to him, "Don't go across, you might contaminate another good man's future wife." Her grandchild quickly replied, "I'm going across." He stood up and went out.

Not long after, he came home. His dear grandmother said, "So how did they treat you?" [He replied,] "I didn't go in because I was too shy." [His grandmother said,] "Darn grandchild! After being so adamant. Oh well, it's okay, even if you don't go in, for you might taint the future wife of someone your age who is a better provider than you." He quickly answered, "I'm going across now." He stood and went out for the second time.

Once he was across and went in their porch, he became shy again. But he was thinking, "After their agreement with my grandmother, they might decide they don't want me. Let me go in and see what happens, even though I'm shy." Then he slipped down through the entrance hole in the porch and went in.

When he went in, they took down a bag containing clothing. The wife of the *nukalpiaq* took out men's garments from the bag, and she had him change into those. When he was done, after staying for a short while, he went out because he was so embarrassed. They were officially husband and wife, but he went out. He went across.

While his grandmother sat, she heard a person coming in out there. And just when she became alerted, a *nukalpiaq* came up through the entrance hole. After pulling himself through the hole, she realized that it was actually her grandson. Then his grandmother said, "Oh my, I almost didn't recognize you! If you always wore clothes like that you'd look like a *nukalpiaq.*"

Then his grandmother got up and went out. After going into their little cache, she came with a bag he had seen hanging in there. When she brought the bag in, she said to him, "Now, bring this across, and I'll go with you. Bring this bag across there." It apparently was filled with women's garments. [They went across with the bag.] Even though she asked him to go in, he refused and left her. Then his grandmother went in and gave the bag [to the mother]. Then her mother [took the clothing] and just laid each piece on the girl [lying in bed]. The [fish] part [of her body] had slowly been receding as she got bigger.

Taum-gguq nalliini ciisquk waten ngelleksagullukek nuliqsagutellrua tutgara'urluum. Ac'etevkenaki tua-i qainganun pirraarluki ataam caquluki. Tutgara'urluq tua-i
tauna itenqigcan taum aaniin, aanaksaguskiin, pillinia ullagluku aipiaralaasqelluku.
Tua-i maligtaqulluni nutaan tutgara'urluq. Taum nalqigulluk' nutaan nasaurluum,
tamatumek. Maniilluku-ll' irugminek [uategminek], tua-i tamana pellugpailgan ag-
tuusqevkenani. "Nuliqsukuvnga tamana pellugpailan agturyaqunii. Pellugpailgan
agtuquvnga picurlagceciiqerpenga." Tuaten alerqulliniluku.

[Tua-i aipiararaqluku], ununrakun tua-i iliini qasgimun ag'aqluni. Tuani-llu pilliniluku, qavarluni, unatni teguluki-ll' pilaan, unatni tegulaasqevkenaki qavarluni,
tupagterrlainarluni taugaam pilaasqelluku.

Caqerluni-am tuani uitainanermini pillinia qavangellinilria atam. Inerqullrung-
raani-am tua-i tuani unataikun teguqalliniluku. Nasaurluq tua-i tauna piuraqerluni qunglullallinilria. Qunglulliimi tua-i egmian akagartelliniluni, natermun-llu
egmian iggluni. Piqallinia tamana im' amia patagmek mayulria. Wanirpaagaq-llu
tua-i maavet tekiartelliniluni. Amiigem tua-i tungiinun pian teguyaaqelliniluku
tutgaraurluum cirlakluku. Piqtangraani anutelliniluku. Nuqteqtangraani kuigem
tungiinun atrautelliniluku taum.
    Mermun-llu tua-i tekicamek egmianun anglluutelliniluku. Nuliqsugyaaqngamiu
tua-i tutgaraurluum pegteksaunaku. Mermun tua-i anglluucani ellerralliin, tutgara'urluum cacini nalluyagutelliniluku. Tayima tua-i.

Ellangelliniuq taklarmi, taklalria. Uitelliniuq kiartelleq man'a taicirluni, taiciar-
luni. Ciugtelliniuq amirlut pagkut pagaani. Cunawa-gguq cikut. Cat cikut pugtalriit
tamakut amirluuyukluki pillinikai. Kiartellra-gguq taicirnganani. Kiimenani tua-i.
Umyuaqercamiu tua-i iluteqem tekitelliniluku tutgara'urluq. Arenqialami tua-i qialliniluni. Uivaarluni kiarrluku tuaten, natmun ayaucia qayagauraluku tuaten.

Allamek kiarcaaqerraarluni ayanqigtaqluni. Tua-i piyaaqerraarluni nutaan qul-
murtelliniluni. Puggliniuq imkut amirluuyukellri cikuullinilriit pugtalriit. Quunir-
luni-gguq. Qavarninga'artelliniluni pugngami. Arenqialami tua-i qavaqalliniluni
tayima. Tupakaami-am tua-i kairarqaarluni angllulliniluni-am camavet. Tuc'ami

It is said that when she became the spouse of the *nukalpiaq*, she was a human down to her knees. [Her mother,] after she spread each garment on her, put them back in the bag and didn't let her put them on. When the grandchild came in again, she, the girl's mother who was now his mother-in-law, told him that he should come and stay with the girl as much as he could. From that time the grandson finally complied. Then that girl told him about herself. She told him not to touch her [have intercourse with her] before the transformation was complete. "Do not touch me before the transformation is done if you want me for a wife. If you touch me before it is done, the process of transformation will be harmed." That was the advice she gave him.

[So he stayed with her] and sometimes went over to the *qasgi* after dark. And she told him at that time, because he sometimes took her by the hand, not to take her by the hand while she was sleeping, but to wake her up first before holding her hand.

One day, while he was with her, she fell asleep. Even though she had warned him, he took her by the hand. The girl suddenly jerked violently and immediately rolled over and fell to the floor. He looked at her and noticed [that the fish part of her body] was quickly rising. In a few seconds [she turned into a fish up to her torso]. When she began moving toward the door, the grandchild tried to pull her back, but even though he tried pulling, she dragged him outside and continued pulling him down toward the river.

And when they got to the river, she immediately dove in with him holding on. That grandchild held onto her because he wanted to keep her as a wife. As soon as she took him underwater and the sound of splashing water erupted, the grandchild instantly lost consciousness. He remained unconscious.

When he finally became aware, he was lying on his back. When he opened his eyes, he noticed that his surroundings were foggy. It was hazy all around. He looked up and saw clouds up above. What he saw up there was apparently ice. The chunks of ice floating up there on the surface, he apparently thought they were clouds. To him, it looked foggy all around. He was there all alone. When he thought of the girl, the grandchild got choked up with sadness. Overwhelmed with grief, he started crying. Then he began going about in a circle, looking for her, calling after her, and asking where she went.

After going all the way around in a circle looking for her, he went around again. After looking to no avail, he started going up. When he reached the surface and emerged from the water, ones that he thought were clouds were actually chunks of floating ice. There were no waves, and the water was calm. When he surfaced on

nutaan qaini pillinia yinraunrillinilria qainga man'a, ungungssiurtellinilria. Tautun tua-i ayuqlirillinilria man' qainga.

Tua-i-am tuc'ami kiarcaaqerraarluni qialliniluni. Qavciliriluni tua-i pillrani qia- luni, natmun-llu ayaucia pillrani, nepelkican takuyaartellinuq, ellmini tuani tang- llerminiu [tangrraa] yuuluku, tua-i elliitun ayuqluni. Ullagarrluku tua-i arenqianan' quyaluni tua-i. Taum nasaurluum pillinia, "Ilumun-llu piciuluten nuliqsullinivaa elpeni." [Tuaten] pirraarluku pilliniuq tauna tutgara'urluq, "Maurlurluqa-w' imna tua-i pama-i aulukestaiteurlurluni." Qanrraartelluku taum pillinia, "Atam maurlur- luun peng'gangellren tangerqerru." Tangllinia yaatiignegun asveq man'a arnacaluq kuimalria. Pillinia maurlurluqlinikii. Ketmun piami kitulliniluku. Tuamtell' piqer- luni pilliniuq, taum imum angayuqaruak elkegtun ayuqlutek qaikek maklaulutek. Tua-i maklaurtellinilutek. Taunguluku-am qanemciktuat tauna.

Makliit-gguq tua-i tamakut arnacalumeggnek piaqameng neplituut tuaten. Qal- rinek taumek pitukeput nepliraqata, arnacalumeggnek taicetaarluk' arnacaluteng pituluki.

Tauna-ll' tua-i asveq maurlurluuluni. Taumek-gguq asevret makut takumcutal- riit. Ikayuriyunqeggluteng-llu imarpigmi atertaulrianek.

top, he suddenly became sleepy. He tried to stay awake, but he fell asleep. When he woke up after briefly looking around, he dove into the water again. When he got to the ocean bottom, he finally looked at his body and saw that he was no longer human, but he had turned into an animal. His body had transformed, and he now looked like [the girl].

When he got to the bottom, after looking around to no avail, he cried. After doing that a number of times, crying and asking where she had gone, he heard a noise and quickly turned, and [he saw her] as a person just like himself. He ran to her and was extremely happy to see her. That girl said to him, "I see that you truly want me for a wife." After she said that, that grandchild said, "My poor grandmother has no one to take care of her back there [on land] now." After he said that, she told him, "Look at your grandmother that you are worried about." He looked and saw a female walrus swimming adjacent to them. Then he saw that it was his grandmother. And since she was swimming toward the area below them, she kept swimming past them. Then after a while, he saw her adoptive parents, and they were bearded seals like him and the girl. They had become bearded seals. That's the way the story was told.

They say that when those bearded seals are [calling] for their females, they make a mating call like that. That's why we call them *qalrit* [those that cry out] when they make their noise, when they summon their females to mate.

And that walrus was the grandmother. And they say that's why walrus are compassionate. And they like to help men who are adrift on the ocean.

Tevurayaraq Up'nerkami

Tevurayaraq augna piqataraqa nutaan. Up'nerkamek ayagluni unavet pissurraarluni imarpigmun aturyarauguq tevuraluni avani piyaraq nunamni. Uksuarmi tevurayuitukut avani, up'nerkami taugaam. Ciumek unavet imarpigmun piluta pissutuukut tua-i unani imarpigmi. Ciku taugaam nangengan tua-i pissunermek taqluta. Tua-illu nangengan, ayagngairucamta unavet, nutaan upluta, nunamun ayakatarluta, kanaqlagcurluta, kanaqlagnek piluta. Aklukamtenek tua-i upluta taquarkamtenek-llu, maligkaput-llu nallunairluku; pingayuuluta wall' malruuluta.

Qayam aklui imarpigmi pilalput aturluki cali ilait, ikeglicarluki taugaam. Atuungailnguut unilluki, imarpigmi atuullret unani. Canek tua-i ilaluki, wall'u pelatekarluta, pelatekamek ayaulluta. Ilaluki tamatumek. Tua-i-llu nutaan tumyarat, tev'aqluni-ll' piyarat nalluvkenaki, wavet ayagyarat. Wavet-llu ayagyarat. Wavet-llu. Nallukeput tua-i atuyuitaput, taugaam nallunrilkengaput kanaqlangqetulinun ayagayarat, caarrlulegnun. Atauciurneruvkenani tumyaraq; ilii tevyaraunani ayagyarauluni, ilii taugken tevluni piyaraugaqluni. Qavcirqunek-llu tevyarauluni piyarauluni. Nallunritlemteggun tua-i tuavet piyugaqamta ayagyugngaluta nallunritlemteggun. Nallukeput aturciiganaki. Nallunritestaita taugaam atutuluki. Tuaten tua-i ayuqukut.

Nanvat cevuravailgata yaani Kuigilnguum paingani up'nerkitullruunga. Ayaglua piiyuitellruunga. *West*-alirnermi up'nerkitullruunga. Kelumni wani nanvaq, kuik-wa un'a. Iliini kanaqlagcuqatarlua ayakata'arqama, nallunrilkema naugg'un ayallerkaqa pirraarluku, maligkaqa qanrut'laraqa, kuigkun ayagpek'nii, uuggun pelatekama keluakun nanvakun ayaglunuk tevuralunuk ayakatarnilunuk. Pelatekam enema elatiinek, keluanek (ayagaqlunuk). Tua-i maa-i taugaam tumngunrirluni, cevngameng tumkelallrenka tamakut. Imna-ll' pingna *airport*-am yaaqlia nanvallerpall'er imairulluni, tumyaraq call' tumyaralleq.

Portaging in Spring

I am now going to talk about portaging over land when hunting. Portaging over land while hunting begins in the spring after seal hunting down on the ocean over in my home area. In the fall hunters don't portage over land, only during the time they hunted in spring. [In spring] we first went down to the ocean and hunted, and when the ice was all gone we'd stop hunting in the sea. And once we stopped going down to the ocean to hunt, we'd get ready to hunt on land and go after muskrats. We'd get our equipment and food ready, and we'd arrange for someone to go out with us; sometimes three or two would go out together as hunting partners.

We'd bring some of the implements we had brought out to the ocean and leave some of them behind. We'd leave the implements we used in ocean hunting and only bring things we needed for hunting on land. We'd bring other things like tents and such. And when we left the village, we'd know exactly which way to go, and we knew the areas we portaged over on land to get to a certain spot. We'd know the ways to get here and there and wherever we wanted to go. We didn't go on areas we didn't know, but we went the same way we went before to go to areas that usually had muskrat. We didn't go just one way to get to where we wanted to go; sometimes we followed a river and sometimes we'd portage over land to get there. And sometimes we'd portage over land several times [to reach our muskrat-hunting grounds]. When we can reach a designated area we only get there following the trail we know about. We couldn't travel in the areas we had never been on before. Only those who know those areas could travel on them and know the route. That's how [you moved on land when hunting certain animals].

Before lakes began cutting through forming rivers I used to have a spring camp over at the mouth of Kuigilnguq River. I never moved away from the village and camped. I used to have a spring camp on the west side of the river. Back near my tent was a lake, and right below it was the river. Sometimes when I got ready to go muskrat hunting, after being asked which way I was going, I'd tell my hunting partner that we were going to go on that lake behind the tent and portage over land to go hunting. Then we'd begin journeying out from right behind my home, the tent. And today the portages I once used are no longer used because the lakes have cut

Tauna tua-i tevyarangqellruuq pingayunek, markunateng piavet nanvarpall'er-
mun. Kelua-ll' malrugnek tev'arcarauluni. Kuimteggun pivkenani pavavet tua-i
nutaan kuilegmun tekilluni, malrugnek tev'arqaarluni tuani keluani. Tua-i-ll' tuaken ayagluni tevyuunani kiituan pamna Arungalnguq mallgia. Kuigglainarteggun
nanvatgun-llu piaqluni kanaqlagcuraqluni piyaraungami. Malrugnek-llu iliini
unuugni piyaraulaami, pitarkat tangerrluki. Tua-i nuuqit'ngartaqamta unitkaniraq-
luk' allat paqtaqluki.

Pamna taugken mel'iraqan, Arungalnguq, Dall Lake-aq imna, augna nanvarpak,
tevevkenani kanaryarauluni. Uuggun taugken allakun pikuni, tevyararluni pingayunek. Tumyarai tua-i.

Iglukun asgurluni Atlirkun, Naneryartalegkun-llu asgurluni, qagatiini-ll' piani
tevluni Maklagtulim Kangranun. Qagaksuaraam-llu kiatiini cali tevluni Qistellerm-
mun. Qistellermek-llu kuik tevnaicaryaaqelria Cuignilngurtulimek at'lek, napat
quuvagusngaluku kuigpall'er anguayunaunani. Maaggun taugaam taqruvakun nunam qaingakun tevyarauluni. Ataucirqumek taugaam, martuluni-llu. Napatailkuni
tua-i tevevkenani Arungalngurmun anyarauyaaqluni. Napangqellran taugaam tev-
yarauvkarluku anguayunailami. Nanvarnaunani uavet. Tua-i-ll' tevenqigtevkenani.

Ankuni-ll' kangrani, Cuignilngurtulimi kanaqlagcurraarluni unugirraarluni ankuni, Angussaagyaramun agluni, kuigmun cali Arungalngurmun anumalriamun.
Asguquniu-llu tua-i tamaani kanaqlagcurraarluni, mel'iqan tevevkenani Iglum
kangranun agluni, meq amlleqan. Iglumun-llu pikuni ut'reskuni kuigglainarkun
Iglukun cetuluni. Cakmani-llu nanvarnaanun ankuni tumellni kanarluku, avtell-
rat yaatmun Maklagtulim tungiinun. Ciumurtellni imna augkut tumyarat unilluki
atuqsaunaki.

Tua-i-llu imna tamana pelatekam keluanek ayalqa aturpek'naku, cali qamaggun
kiatiitgun nunat, kanaryarakun tevyararluni malrugnek kuigem kangranun, tamana
aturluku Kuigilngurmun kanarlua. Kanaryarauluni cali tauna. Tua-i tamana tumyaraq iquklilluni tuaggun piyaraq. Uaken pelatkat, up'nerkillermek ayagluni, Igluq-

through to make rivers. And the big lake that was once a route used in traveling beyond the airport is all dried up now.

There were three portages that were short that led up to that large lake [near the airport]. And right beyond it were two short portages. So, instead of following our winding river, you'd cross over those two short portages behind that lake and get to the river on the other side. And after that there were no portages, and you'd follow the river until you were almost to Arungalnguq Lake way back there. When hunting muskrat you have to go entirely on rivers and sometimes on lakes. And depending on the number of muskrats sometimes you'd stay in one spot for two nights and hunt them. When they weren't plentiful we'd move on and check out other areas.

But when water is high, you can get to Arungalnguq, into Dall Lake, that large lake, without portaging over land. But if you reach [the lake] by this other route, there are three portages [you can use to go inside the lake]. Those are the routes you can take [to get to Dall Lake].

If you go up Igluq Atliq River, and if you go up Naneryartalek River, at its lake source back there you'd portage over land to the headwaters of Maklagtuliq River. And also above Qagaksuar Lake, you'd portage over to Qistelleq Lake. And from Qistelleq Lake you could navigate through the river named Cuignilngurtuli without portaging, but you have to portage along that river because the river is covered with bushes, and you cannot paddle through the river with a kayak. You have to portage along the edge of the river. But it's long, and you portage over there once. If that passage wasn't covered with bushes, you could easily paddle over to Arungalnguq.

And when he goes out [into Arungalnguq Lake], in the upper part of the river, when he goes out after hunting for muskrat in the Cuingilnguq River all night long, he'd paddle over to Angussaagyaraq River, another river that flows out to Arungalnguq. And when he goes up that river, after hunting muskrat in that river, if there was a lot of water, he'd go over to the upper Igluq River, without portaging over land. And when he went to the Igluq River and returned home he paddled all the way down the Igluq River. And when he got to the bottom of the river and went out to the lake he would reach the starting point of his hunting trip, the spot where there's another river branching off to the side, heading in the direction of Maklagtuli River. He'd return to the beginning of the trail he used and not veer off to the side.

Then not using the same route I used when traveling out behind the tent, but up above the village, taking the route that leads out to [Kuigilnguq River] that has two portages, I'd follow that route and reach our river. That was the usual route hunters used when they returned to the village from inland. That was where the

llu kanarluku, asguqerluku-ll' Maklagtulim tungiini Arungalnguq-llu kanarluku. Angussaagyaraq-llu asgurluku, kangrakun-llu, Iglum Qagatiin uatiikun Iglumun anluni. Uterrluni-ll' Igluq cetuluku, Atliq-llu, Arulaciq-llu asgurluku, Urluveq-llu asgurluku, tevluni-ll' malrurqugnek Kuigilngurmun, nunat kiatiitgun.

Ilii tua-i tauna ayagayaralqa. Tua-llu kuigkun asgurlua piyugaqama, tauna uter-tellemni iliini malrugnek tevyaralek pamavet Iglum tungiinun ciungurrvikluku atu-laraqa, nunat kiakaraatni kanaryaraq. Taugken aturyuumiilamku kuik asgurluku pakmavet qagatiinun, qagatengqellrani. Keluani-ll' avani tev'arrlua ataucirqumek kuingvailgan. Arulacim tamatum, Arulacimek atellgem avayaan, nanvarnaarluni qavcinek, kangranun, ataucirqumek tevluni nanvamun.

Tua-i-llu man'a aturpek'naku, pikaggun qulliatgun kuigkun asgurlua. Pamani-ll' tua-i nutaan Nallaukuviim Qagatiinun nutaan tevluni. Tevyarauluni, Tuntutuliar-miut uatiini.

Cevv'arnermiut keluatnun cali ayagallruunga ava-i ciuqlirmi. Cevv'arnermiunek-llu nall'arkengellruluta ataucirqumek tuani Angussaagyaraam paingani. Nallauku-vigmun kanaquma cetuluku, tua-i-ll' augna avvenra, Tevyarturyaramek at'lek tekis-kumku asgurluku anguarturlua, teveksaunii. Kuigilngurmun ayallemni, teveksaunii tua-i wani taugaam keluani ataucirqumek tev'arrlua, Kangirnarcarallermun, Kangir-narcaram atlianun nanvamun.

Tuaken-llu tua-i cali piani ataucirqumek tev'arrlua, Nallaukuvim qagatiin kellia-nun, Ilanertalgem qagatiinun. Taukut tua-i markunateng. Pissuryarat tamaa-i wii nallunrilkenganka kanaqlagnek. Tamana-ll' tua-i asgurluku Tevyarturyaraq, Nallau-kuviim avvenra, *north*-atmun ayalria, quyigiqerluni-ll' *west*-atmun ayagluni caqirr-luni. Nanvanun an'aqluni. Pikani-ll' tua-i qavciatni nanvat, kuigat tekitarput aug'u-tun-am Cuignilngurtulitun napat patumaluku naumalriit kuikegtaar cali. Qemim cali maaggun qaingakun nunakun, atuyunailan tua-i man'a, kuigem mengliikun, napat teruatgun pavaggun qamigarluni qagatiinun piyarauluni. Tuamtell' kiaqlia kiugna tautun cali ayuqluni. Napat makut cali kavirlit cikvagusngaluku kuik. Cali-am aipiriluni qemikun mengliikun tevyarauluni. Nutaan napailngurkun kiaggun nanvallermun anyarauluni, Iglum Qagatiin kellianun.

trail usually ended. That trail started from behind the tents at the spring camp out there and went into Igluq River, and after going up that river briefly you get into Arungalnguq Lake, near Maklagtuli River. Then you'd go up Angussaagyaraq River, and at the upper section you'd go out into Igluq River through the lower part of Igluq Lake. Then you'd start heading back, going down Igluq River, and you'd also go down Igluq Atliq and Arulaciq Rivers, and you'd go down Urluveq River, and crossing two portages you'd reach Kuigilnguq River above the village.

That was one of my traveling routes. Then when I wanted to use the river I'd go up, and when I reached the trail that had two portages that led to the river from Igluq River back there, I would continue on that. But sometimes I'd stay on the river and go all the way up to the lake source, when it was there. And behind it before the river formed there, I'd portage over once and keep going. To get to the upper part of Arulacim Avayaa that has a number of lakes, I'd portage over once and get to the lake.

Then when I didn't go on this [Kuigilnguq River], I would go to the river that sits farthest up from the other and go up that river. And deep inside you'd portage over land and get into the lake source of Nallaukuvik River. It's another portage used below Tuntutuliak.

I also used to travel behind Chefornak when I was younger. And once we ran into Chefornak hunters at the mouth of Angussaagyaraq River, too. When I went into Nallaukuvik River I'd go downriver, and when I got to the river named Tevyarturyaraq that branches off from that river, I'd paddle up that river and keep going, never portaging over land. This was when I headed toward Kuigilnguq River. I'd keep going without portaging, only portaging once along a short route to Kangirnarcaralleq River, to a lake above Kangirnarcaralleq River.

Then from there, I would portage once back there, to the lake source of Ilanertalek River, a lake sitting below Nallaukuvik lake source. The portage there was short. Those are the muskrat hunting areas I know about. I'd go on that Tevyarturyaraq and paddle upriver, the river that branches off Nallaukuvik River, the one that flows north, and after it headed north a ways it would turn and head west. It would flow out into lakes as it went. And as we went across one of the lakes and got to the river on the other side to continue on, we found it all covered with bushes like Cuignilngurtuli River, and we couldn't paddle through it. So we pulled our kayaks across on land along the water and on the edge of the bushes growing in the water. The river above that one was like that, too; its channel was also covered with red willow bushes. We also portaged across it. Finally when we got to the one up inside, there were no bushes in the channel and we easily passed through to the lake source of Igluq River, the lower one.

Igluq cali cetuyarauluni paillipailegmiu-llu, Igluq unicukuniu, avayarrii Uiluayaalek asgurluku qagatiikun qerarluni, kellirnerkun. Ikani-ll' egmillra kuiguarpa-
ller aturluku, ayakarluni, Nallaukuviim Qagatiinun imumun tumllemnun kanarlua.
Cali-am aturluku tamana utercarauluni tumlleq. Ciumurtellni aturpek'naku tua-i
piiyuumiilkuni ukutgun Meryalegteggun kuigteggun cali nunamelngurteggun nunam kuigikun Meryalegteggun cetuarkauluni. Cakmaggun-llu nutaan Kangirnaam
kangranun anluni, asgurluku qagatiinun-llu anluni Kangirnam. Ikani-llu akiani
Kuigilnguum, kuimta aug'um Kuigilnguum nanvaanun tevluni, kuingvailgan, tua-i
tevenqigtevkenani tuaken. Aipaa tamaa-i tamana.

Pingayuak-llu una Kuigilngurkun cali asguryarauluni, avvenrakun-llu Kangirnarmiut keluata tungiitnun caqirrluni asguryarauluni. Kanaqlagnek maa-i ullagaya-
rait. Kangirnakun-llu asgurluni. Kangrani tua-i pagaani Meryalegni cali kanaqlag-
curluni piyarauluni cali. Tumyarat amllertut. Tua-i Tuntutuliarmiut-llu uaqliatgun
Tagyarakun anyugngaluni. Wall'u pakmaggun Iglum Qagatiin keluakun Tagyaram
kangranun piluni, Tagyarakun cetuyugngaluni Kusquqvagmun-llu anluni.

Ilanka-ll' tua-i unegkut tuaten ayuqut wangtun. Nallunrilkengateng tumyarat
aturluki ayagatuluteng. Qipnermun-llu tua-i maa-i nunam akuliikun elevaarluni
ayagluni tekicugngaluni. Cevv'arnermun-llu Dall Lake-aq tumekluku tekicugngaluni cali. Qakmavet-llu Qaluyaanun, Nelson Island-aanun tekicugngaluni tamaaggun. Amatiitgun-llu amaggun cetuyugngaluni, Niugtarmiut kuigata anumaviakun
Ninglirkun. Nunam akulii tumyarauguq, tumyarai amllertut, aug'um nunam; taum.
Tua-i-llu yaa-i ukaqliput Kangirnaarmiut ulerpagmi, pavaggun elevaarluteng ullag-
yarauluteng. Anuqlingraan taumek ulerpagaaqan tamaaggun nunam akuliikun
elevaaraluteng Kangirnaarmiut-llu tekirqelalriit. Augkunek ava-i tevuraluteng pingnaqsaranek pivlacangramku qanemcitamken.
    Nunaungraan qamigautek ellilukek qamurluku ayautaqluku. Qanikcalegni
taugaam qanikcaat maligtaqualuku ayagaqluta. Qanikcailngurmi nunam qaingakun qamurluku ayautaqluku.

Mecungaqami kenercecuituq. Kinrumaaqani taugaam kenercetetuuq. Taumek
merrluyagaat tumkurluki nunakun piaqamta tevtullrulriakut, arulairaqluta. Tevya-
rat tamakut (aturluki) unugyugnaunaku-am kanarnarqut. Cukanarquq atam ayalleq tevuraluni.

One would go down Igluq River, and if he wanted to leave the Igluq River he could go inside Uiluayaalek River that branches off it and go up that river and go across its lake source, the lower one. And after going in the channel across there and going a little ways, he'd go into the lake source of Naulluukuvik River. That is another route one could use to return home. If he didn't want to backtrack, he'd use a different route and go back down through the channels of Meryalget River that have difficult spots to cross. Then he'd go into the upper end of Kangirnaq River down there and go down that river and reach its lake source. And across there on the other side of Kuigilnguq River, he would portage overland and get into the lake attached to Kuigilnguq River, before a river was formed there. After that he would not cross over land again. That's the second route we used to go and come back.

The third route can start by going up the Kuigilnguq River, then you'd go into the river that branches off and go upriver and turn toward the area behind the village of Kongiganak. These were the routes people used to reach muskrat hunting areas. And you would go up the Kangirnaq River. And when you reached the headwaters of that river at Meryalet River you would hunt for muskrats in the sloughs and ponds. There were many trails and routes. You could also go into Tagyaraq River below Tuntutuliak. Or you reach the headwaters of Tagyaraq by going up behind the lake source of Igluq River. You could go down Tagyaraq and go out into the Kuskokwim River, too.

The other men down in the coastal area were hunters like me. They knew their own hunting routes and used them when they traveled. You could even easily travel by boat to Kipnuk through land today. Boats could even get to Chefornak by way of Dall Lake. They also could get to Nelson Island that way. You could even reach Ningliq River by boat and go down that river, the river were Newtok is located. The land is covered with rivers and ways you could travel from place to place. And our neighbors at Kongiganak during high water, you get there through the river up there when the water is high. That is why when it is windy and the water is high many of them get here by boat. I just told you about places hunters portaged over on land, even though I left out a lot of information.

On land [if we had to portage over it] we'd put [our kayak] on the kayak sled and continue on. But in areas where there's snow, we'd go wherever we wanted to by following the [snow-covered areas]. But in areas with no snow, we'd portage over bare ground by pulling our kayaks.

Because the ground we went over was wet, it wasn't hard to pull them over. But it was harder to pull them over dry ground. That was why we always tried to portage through marshy areas, stopping from time to time. By portaging over land we can get to our destination way before dark. Traveling is fast by portaging over land.

Neqlillerni

Murilkua maaten neqliyatuluteng tua-i. Taugaam neqliyatulriit tamaani unkumiut iliini unkumiut unangliqaqameng pinacialartut qaqiutnaciaraqameng. Taryaqviit-llu tua-i kingutneratgun nutaan neqlillernun tekitaqluteng, caliarkateng tua-i qa-qitaqamegteki.

Cali imkut iqalluarpiit tamaani pituata, pituameng taryaqviit ciungatni, tamakut tamaa-i pinaciarcet'larait iliini. Amlleq-llu neqliyayuunani, taugaam tua-i neqliyatu-lit neqliyatuluteng. Angyailnguut-llu malikluki cali neqliyautetuluki piyulriit.

Ugkut tua-i nunalgutenka ugna Tagyaram painga ngellekluku *camp*-angqetull-ruut, kiatiini maani pivkenateng, piinateng, cakemna Papegmiut ngellekluki Ilkivik-llu. Keggukaraam uatiini uani Papegmiut. Uaqliit-wa Nunapigmiut up'nerkillrulu-teng. Qinarmiut up'nerkiyaraqluki.

Neqlillruluteng Papegmiut. Ugkut taumek Papegmiut ugkunek Qipnermiut yuitnek yungqetullruut tua-i, elaqlimtenek. Ukut taugaam Kuigilngurmiut Keggu-karmi maani, Qelliqucimi, Yugcillermi, Tagyaram-llu paingani, Cuukvalegmi-llu. Qinarmiut neqlilriit neqlillgutekluki nuniitni, neqliyaraitni ilaita. Wangkuta-w' Qi-narmiunguan imna atavut ilaini Qinarmiuni neqliuratullrulriakut nuniitni tama-kut, acairutma tamakut ataatairutma-ll'.

Yugcillermiuni, Cuukvalegmiuni, Kuiguyullermiuni; taukuni tua-i nugtaqtaar-luta ilamteni tamakuni pituukut. Wani neqliaqluta ilaitni, wani neqliaqluta, cani-melucata.

Qinarmiunek ilaluta neqlituluta. Keggukarmiut imkut ngelekluki Kuigilngur-miut neqliyatullruut. Qelliqucimi, Qaluyarami, Anllerni, Cuukvalegmi, Yugcillermi, Akuluyullermi-llu. Tua-i neqliyatuluteng taukunun.

Taryaqviit taugaam tua-i mikulriit kingu'urterrlainarluki. Amllermek taumek taryaqvagcuitellrulriit avani, taugaam tua-i neqet amlletullruut avani. Kuvyat-llu kuvyait nanilengermeng unangaqluteng amllernek. Imkunek-llu qalunek waten neqsurcuuterluteng cali murilkanka. Ulmi tua-i iverluteng qaluaqluteng, wangkuta

At Summer Fish Camp

When I began observing things, people would go to summer fish camps to harvest salmon. But the coastal people who normally went to fish camp delayed their move because they didn't quickly finish when they caught a lot [of sea mammals and herring at spring camp]. They would arrive at their summer fish camps when they were done with their tasks, after the heavy king-salmon run had slowed down.

Since the herring also come during that time, since [herring] arrive before the king salmon, that delayed them sometimes. And many people didn't move to fish camp to harvest salmon, but those who usually went moved to fish camps. And people usually brought along others without boats who wanted to harvest salmon.

People from my village had summer fish camps reaching the mouth of Tagyaraq River and not beyond, and down as far as Papegmiut and the Ilkivik River. Papegmiut was situated downriver from Keggukar River. And the site of Nunapigmiut was down below [Papegmiut]. Qinaq people used it as spring camp.

Papegmiut was a summer fish camp. Papegmiut was inhabited by people from Kipnuk, a village that is just [north] of our village. But the people from Kwigillingok were at the Keggukar, Qelliquciq, and Yugcilleq Rivers, and at the mouth of Tagyaraq River, and at Cuukvalek River. They had fish camps with people from Qinaq. Since our father was originally from Qinaq, we always went to his family's fish camps and harvested salmon with my late paternal aunt and uncle.

[We harvested salmon] at Yugcillermiut, Cuukvalegmiut, Kuiguyullermiut; we stayed at one camp one summer and moved to another camp the following summer and stayed with relatives. We'd harvest fish at one place and then another place as those places were in close proximity.

We harvested fish with people from Qinaq. People from Kwigillingok stayed at summer fish camps as far as Keggukarmiut. [Their camps were at] Qelliquciq, Qaluyaraq, Anlleq, Cuukvalek, Yugcilleq, and at Akuluyulleq. They would harvest fish in those places.

But they would always miss the heavy run of king salmon. That's why they didn't get a lot of king salmon, but there were many fish back then. And even though their gill nets where short, they would catch a lot. When I started to observe them, they had dip nets for fishing, too. They would wade in the water during high tide and

keluitni kellulluki, qen'ngistenguluta. Qaluteng tua-i pirraarluk' nalugarrluku egtaqluki pavavet. Ilukunateng qalut. Akulmiut qaluit agtarcuutait nallunritaten, ilutuv-
kenateng. Tuacetun tua-i ayuqluteng; takevkenateng piit unkut.

Tua-i amllermek cang'aqluteng. Iliini-ll' malrugnek cang'aqluteng. Egtaqluki kelutmun. Kangitnernek. Caaqameng ilait taryaqvagtaqluteng. Avuuguratulriit-wa
taryaqviit, mikulriit taugaam kingu'urtaqluki pitullruameng.

Qayatgun tua-i, angyanek-llu piilamta, angyacuarnek, qayatgun taugaam tua-i
ulmi neqsuraqluteng. Qayat tua-i uciiryartuqa'aqluki. Kuvyat-wa nanitkacagaat, qalunek tamakunek ikayungqerrameng. Uciirraarluku tua-i anelrarluni uciliraqluku.

Atercetarayuitut. Petugarturluteng pitullruut, atercetarayuunateng, qalunek ika-
yurluteng. Tua-llu-w' neq'liqlalriit tua-i, neqnek amllernek tua-i.

Augkut-llu taugken yaani Ilkivigmi pingasuinguluteng neqlitululuteng; kangitnernek, qakiiyaarnek, canek-llu amaqaayagnek-llu. Amaqayiit mikupiatullruut Ilkivigmi. Makut sayiit kangitneret-llu amllessiyaagpek'nateng tua-i, avani taugaam
ciuqvaarmi neqet tut'aqameng, Kusquqvagtun pitatullrulliniut Ilkivigmi. Tua-i-
llu cakemna eneni nugtarcan ikegliluteng neqet, nel'inqigcan cakemna Ilkiviim
anenra.
    Cavunermiunek aterluteng neqlillret avayarriin paingani. Ingkut Kangirnaar-
miut amatiitni wani. Kiaqlia-w' cali una Cavuneq. Taukut uaqliit Cavunermek pilar-
yaaqekait, taugaam Kankucurmiunek piaqluki. Neqlillruluteng tua-i, ak'allauluteng
anguyiim nalliini-llu nunaullrullinuteng, taugaam nayurnanrirluki, yuirulluteng.
Taukut tua-i kiaqliqluki. Kia-i wani, uatiini kuigata. Paiyartuani neqlitullrulliniut,
yuirucata taukut nunallret.

Tauna-ll' tua-i kiaqliq cali neqlillertarluni, taugaam uksillertaunani nunalleq. Taukut tua-i Ilkivigmiut tuani neqlitullrulliniut.
    Cavunermek Kiaqlirmek aterluni. Cangallruvkenateng tua-i Kusquqvagmi, ama-
qaayagnek-llu mikulallrulliniata neqtetuluteng. Taugaam neqait tua-i assirluteng
taryumi uitiimeng, taryuarninaqluteng neqait. Amaqaayiit-llu tamakut neqait taryuarninaqluteng, taryiracetun ayuqluteng, taryumek mengqerrameng. [Ilkivik] tar-
yuuguq.

dipnet, as we watched from behind them, waiting to strike the fish on their heads. After dipping their nets in the water, they would pull them out and suddenly hoist them and throw [the fish] behind them. Their dip nets weren't deep. You know the dip nets of the tundra area people aren't deep. They were like that; the scoops down there weren't long.

They would catch a lot of fish. Sometimes they caught two at one time. They would [hoist the net] and throw [the fish] behind them. [They caught] chum salmon. Some caught king salmon once in a while. There were always [only] a few king salmon among their catches because they missed the heavy king-salmon run.

Only with kayaks, since we had no boats, small boats, they only fished with kayaks during high tide. They'd go and unload the kayaks from time to time. The gill nets would be very short, since they had those dip nets to help them fish. After unloading [the fish], they would go and reload [the kayak].

They didn't drift their net to catch fish. They only caught fish by setting nets along the shore and using dip nets, and not by drifting nets. Nonetheless, they would catch lots of fish.

But they would harvest three species of fish out in the Ilkivik River. They would harvest chum salmon, silver salmon, and those pink salmon. Pink salmon were very abundant in the Ilkivik River. There weren't many red and chum salmon, but apparently long ago, when the fish first arrived in that river, there were as many salmon in the Ilkivik River as in the Kuskokwim River. And when the tides changed down at the mouth of the Ilkivik River, fewer fish started coming upriver.

The summer fish camp that was at the mouth of the small tributary [of the Ilkivik River] was called Cavunermiut. It was located on the other side of Kangirnaarmiut. The river branching off right above that small tributary was also called Cavuneq. The fish camp down below was called Cavuneq, but they called it Kankucurmiut. That site was used as a fish camp, but it actually was an old, abandoned village from the bow-and-arrow warfare era. [Cavuneq fish camp] was above that old village. [Cavuneq] was right up there, right below their river. The old village site was located near the mouth of the tributary, and people used it in the past as a fish camp after the village was abandoned.

And there was a fish camp in the upper section, but not an old wintering site. The people who lived on the Ilkivik River apparently used that as a fish camp once.

It was called Upper Cavuneq. They caught as much fish there as they did in the Kuskokwim River area, and they would catch pink salmon because they used to be abundant. But the fish of that river were tasty because they were in salt water, and they had a salty taste. And their pink salmon tasted salty, just like salted dried fish because the river has salt. [Ilkivik River] is a saltwater river.

Cali tua-i makut Qinarmiut tangvallrenka neqlillrungraata piyungaqameng ceturrarnaurtut, cetuanek nalarqiluteng, paivngallruata cetuat. Kiagungraan tua-i ceturraraqluteng piyungaqameng neqlillerni. Paivngaluteng tua-i cetuat cali tamaani, tamatum nalliini.

Cali-ll' tuaten tua-i kuvyayalriit, encan-llu tua-i taqluteng. Carvanngarcan ua-teteng taqluteng. Qalulriit-llu taqluteng. Kuvyalriit-llu taqluteng. Enulluki-ll' kuv-yarrait tamakut.

Tua-i-ll' nutaan un'a marayangan, wangkuta imkutgun *harpoon*-atgun, kinguliriu-maluteng usaaret. Imkut iciw' maani tarenrani *harpoon*-at cingilget, *single*, waten inglumek pilget; tanglartua maani makuni, cetugnanek aterluteng. Tamaa-i neq-nun pissuutellrit, atulalput. Tamakunek caskirluta, neqsurluta cali narulkaquurluki. Unani Kusquqviim ceniini maani, uaqliqu'urluta waten. Iliini tua-i *twenty*-q-llu naa-gaqluku narulkaquurluta. Entaqan.

Tua-i-ll' carvanra tuknialiluni ulqataan, nutaan tua-i qavlunanek taugaam qav-lunauluni un'a. Nep'ngelalriakut tua-i. Tangssugteput-wa call' paugkut ekviarni caar-kailnguut tangssuliyalriit wangkutnek. Tua-i cacirput nalluluku tua-i. Mecungluta tua-i tamalkumta qaivut, aturaput mecungluteng tamarmeng tamak'acagarmeng, mermi tamaan' pilaamta. Carvanngarcan taugken tua-i taqluta. Nuv'urluki-ll' qan-ritgun tamakut pitaput. Kuigem nutaan painganun piluku qamurturluku merkun it-raulluki nuvumaluki qanritgun narulkengaput. Tuatnatuluta. Piciryaraqluku tua-i, entellra tamalkuan, entaqan marayaq alairaqan tua-i Kusquqviim ceniinun atraraq-luta pissuryarturluta. Muirumaluku taugken piiyuunata. Caliangqelaamta tamaku-nek kuvyalriit piitnek pivkayuunata.

Tevqurluki tamaavet piaqluki. Maani uaqvani napailngurni tua-i augkut imkut avngulget ciqut qupurrluki waten nalqilriit arviqrutkiurturnaurtut, quaguirturluki, cakiqurluki assiriluki tua-i, arvitkatkiurluki pagkut initat. Murapignek pivkenateng, kevraartunek makunek pivkenateng.

Maani uaqvani tamakunek avngulegnek aruvagkanek pitullruut, imkunek-llu arurrluumalrianek meciumakainek mer'em. Tamakunek tamaa-i tep'anek puyu-qiaqameng atutullruut maani uaqvani napailngurmi, tamakunek meciumakainek mer'em, kinertenrilngurnek. Murapianek piyuunateng, tamakunek taugaam avngu-

Also, the people I saw from Qinaq, even though they had harvested salmon, they would harvest a great many beluga whales when they wanted to because belugas were abundant. They would catch belugas even during summer when they wanted to at fish camps. Beluga whales were abundant back in those days as well.

Also, those fishing with gill nets would fish and stop at low tide. They stopped when the current started to flow in the river down below them. The dipnetters stopped fishing, too. And the people fishing stopped, too. And their small set nets would become beached at low tide.

Then when the tide was low enough and the beach extended down there, we used those harpoons without lines. You know, you have seen these harpoons in the pictures that have single points on them, that have one point. I've seen them in pictures, like those called *cetugnat*. Those are the ones we used to catch fish. We used those as a weapon and fished, harpooning them one by one. We'd stand in a line along the Kuskokwim River and [harpoon] fish. Sometimes we would catch up to twenty. [We fished like that] during low tide.

Then when the current became weak, and the tide slacked off and was just about to come up, the water down below would be full of fish swimming at the surface, exposing their fins above water. We would get excited and noisy. And people would be watching from the riverbank behind us. Those who had nothing to do came down and watched us. We'd forget about everything for a moment. Our whole bodies would be wet, and all of our clothing would be wet because we were in the water. We only stopped when the current started to flow. Then we would put a line through the mouths of our catches. Then we'd drag the line threaded with fish we had speared and bring them upriver. That's what we did. That was what we always did at each low tide. At low tide when the mud became visible, we would go down to the edge of the Kuskokwim River and fish. But we didn't fish like that when the water was high. Since we were busy working on the fish caught by gill netters, we weren't allowed to fish with harpoons during that time.

They hung [the fish] over those poles. Closer to the mouth [of the Kuskokwim River] where there are no trees, [those at fish camp] split those long, straight, cottonwood driftwood logs and use them as poles to hang split fish to dry. They would remove the sharp edges and fix them to use as poles to hang fish on. They didn't use spruce driftwood.

[Those who camped] down near the mouth of the Kuskokwim River used to get cottonwood for smoking fish, and they even used slightly rotten ones that were soaked with water. They used driftwood for smoking fish farther downriver in treeless areas, the ones that the water had soaked, not the dry ones. They didn't

legnek. Canek tua-i allanek piyuunateng tamakunek taugaam puyuqiaqameng tua-i, avngulegnek piuratuluteng. Maa-i-ll' cali aturluki amani nunamteni tamakut, avngulegnek puyuqiaqameng tua-i piuraraqluteng.

Ernerpak puyuqaqluki tua-i-ll' murilkelluki. Iliini-ll' unuaquan, natmurteqataameng-llu iliini puyuqevkenaki. Mat'um nalliini maa-i neqliyarnanriameng. Neqlillerni taugken tamaani unuaquaqan tua-i kesianek puyiuqurluki, augirturluki. Tuatnauratuluki. Minkatui atam imumek caluki, yukutam piaqaki.

Puyurcivignek tua-i, puyurciviliquluteng enetun ayuqelrianek piaqluteng. Ilait-llu ciqunek imkunek, augkunek cauciillerpenek, qacarnirluki tamakunek puyurciviliaqluteng. Ilait taugken piilnguut, initaat waten agagliiyait iquanun yaavet arviqrutait aturluki, quyurrluki neqet. Nutaan-llu iitallernek pagkut qaingit patuluki. Canek tua-i qallilirluki, aminrallernek tuaten. Man'a-ll' tua-i elanrat 'llumarrarnek-llu pikangameng 'llumarranek elanra man'a wall-aa caquluki. Tamakunek tamaa-i puyurcivigluteng puyuqiaqluteng. Cangateksaunateng tua-i.

Tua-i-ll' kinrata nutaan tamaani neqsuraqata ilait Keggukarkun asgurnaurtut angyatgun arnarrlainaat. Cunaw' tang iitallernek neqet assigtarkaitnek nanvallermi pakmani uitalrianek aqvalluteng. Angyirluteng-gguq. Maligutaqlua tua-i piyungaqama-ll' wii atmagtenguyarturlua. Tamakucetuluteng, nalacirluki tua-i. Piyungaqamegteki, nalaaqata, tupigaqluki. Tamakut kuusqullugnek aterluteng. Neqnek tua-i kinernernek imiraqluki tua-i puyuqerraarluki. Tuq'urluki, paingit-llu nuqilrarluteng piirrallektarnek, piirrimalrianek. Puyurcivigmun iteqluki aciat qerratarrluku. Tua-i-ll' caarkaircameng nutaan, nutaan qaniiluteng. Uksillemtenun ayaulluki tamakut, aug'utun watua qanrutkellemtun. Tuatnatuluki.

⁓ Neqnek kinerciriyaraq ⁓

Una-w' taugaam. Akertem-llu puqlii tuknilartuq iliini. Murilkevkenaki pilriit akertem puqliin uugartelluki. Kiimatulriit taumek inimangermeng. Kiigarrluteng, kemgit allakaqerrluteng. Uugartellri akertem assiinateng. Tamaa-i tamana mulngaktuat neq'liulriit makut nallunrilamegteggu, puqlamun pivkayuunaki. Akertem puqliinun capaitaqan tungaunaki pivkayuunaki, uugarrnayukluki.

use spruce driftwood but always cottonwood when they smoked fish. And they still use those today over in my village, always using cottonwood when they smoke their fish.

We would smoke them all day and watch [the fire carefully]. And if we were going away from our camp, we'd put the fire out. They no longer go to summer fish camps these days. But they smoked the fish every day at those fish camps, continually removing the blood. They always did that. They immediately get moldy when they are exposed to damp conditions.

They constructed smokehouses that resembled houses. And some constructed smokehouses with walls made out of cottonwood driftwood that you asked about earlier. But some who didn't have any materials would gather the hanging fish at one end of the fish rack. Then they covered the area above with wilted tall cotton grass. They used various materials to cover [the area above the fish] including old sealskins. Then they used cloth to cover the surrounding area and make a wall around it. They created smokehouses like that to smoke the fish. They worked just fine.

Then when the [fish] dried, while some were still fishing, a group of women would go up the Keggukar River with boats. They were apparently getting tall cotton grass from an old lake upriver to make containers for the dried fish. They called it *angyirluteng*. And sometimes when I wanted to, I'd go with them to carry [grass] for them. They went and collected [grass] and would leave it out to dry. After they dried, they'd weave them together when they wanted to. Those [containers] were called *kuusqulluut*. They filled them with smoked dry fish and stepped on [the fish to pack them down], and the [container] opening had a braided grass rope fastener to close it. They brought [the baskets] inside the smokehouse, and they placed them on something so that they weren't directly on the ground. And when they had no other work to do, they moved [all the prepared food to their homes]. We brought those things to our winter village, like I said earlier. That's what they did.

~: Drying fish :~

Well, there's one thing [you must be aware of when drying fish]. There are days when the sun's heat is more intense. Those who aren't keeping an eye on their fish, the sun's heat cooks them. That is why the meat begins to peel off the skin, even though they are hanging. [When cooked by the sun's heat] the meat detaches [from the skin] and will have a distinct taste. Fish that is cooked by the sun's heat doesn't

Puqlam iciw' piaqateng assiitetuut. Kemgit nepingangaunateng qecimeggni maani, kiiluteng taugaam agangermeng. Ciamyugluteng-llu uugaringakai. Muril-kelluki taumek pilaqait. Akerciraqan tua-i taliyuciqerluki piaqluki. Taumek waten qilaguyirluki-ll' pitukait. Akerta pitekluku tuaten capluki, *air*-amun taugaam tua-i caliaqevkarluki ellam *air*-aanun.

Ciiviit-wa makut assiitelalriit; anarayugluki. Aruvira'arluki taumek pitukait-llu. Nutaramegceteng taugken waten aruvagmek tua-i pivkarluki. Assinruuq-gguq. Aga-reskuniki tua-i aruvagmek-llu egmianun piluki, aruvagmek cikirluki, tep'ngartelluki. Ciiviim-gguq pivakarngaitai. Taumek tuntuviit-llu qavani piaqameng agarrluki kem-git, kumarrluki-ll' aruvagmun pivkatullinikait, ciivayuirrluki-llu-gguq tua-i. Tuaten pitullinikait. Kineryartullratni tua-i aruviqertelluki. Man'a kineryiqa'arqaku ciiviim pisciigataa, kinqeraqaku. Taugaam kinerpailgan nutarauluku anaqani, tukeryugnga-luni egmianun. Kineryiqaumalria taugken tua-i tamatum kineryiqaumallran *cover*-aarumaluni tua-i, tugerciigani tua-i paraluq kinellrem qaingani.

Qagaani taugaam elaqvani, tuntut tunuit nutaramegggnun pinevluki manitulli-niit kiagmi ciiviim nalliini anarcetaarluki ciivagnun. Arnassagaat arcaqerluteng angukaraurluut-llu keggutairutellriit, anartelluki tua-i anarcetaarluki ciivagnun. Tua-i-llu-gguq tuk'ngarcata paraluurrluteng, assigcirluki murilkelluki tua-i, para-luurtelluki. Paralut tua-i tuntum tunua nerluku. Nangkatgu-llu-gguq tua-i nutaan arnassagaat tamakut puqlamek uuqnarqelriamek kuvluki, paralut tuquqertelluki. Nutaan-gguq uluarluteng nerluki paralut. Assikepiarluki-gguq.

Iciw' ukut-llu aipaiput, nani yaaqvani ciissinek nertulriit, imkunek pekluteng tua-ten. Canun avukluki ner'aqluteng pektengraata. Tua-i ayuqelliniut yuut ilait maani Alaska-mi tuaten. Tamakunek tamaa-i paralunek pituluteng tamaa-i nertuluteng.
Kuigmun egqurluki ner'arrluut, qaimi maani uitasqumavkenaki, paralurciqni-luki, ciivagnun-llu amllerutekciqniluki. Taugaam naruyat amllelaameng nanglarait tua-i tamakut mermi uitalriit. Naruyat nerluki.

taste good. Because they know what overexposure to sun can do to fish, those who work on fish and hang them to dry watch their fish carefully and keep them away from direct sunlight. They don't expose them to the sun's heat when the fish aren't covered.

When the sun's heat cooks them they are not good. Their meat will not stick to the skin but will just come off, even while hanging. Fish cooked by the sun's heat will crumble easily. That's why they watch the fish carefully when it is hung to dry. And when it is sunny they put something on the sunny side to shade it. That's why they always put a cover over the fish rack. Fish are hung on the covered fish rack and get properly air dried.

These flies are a nuisance; they tend to lay eggs on the fish. That is why they smoke them when they hang them. They smoke them when they're fresh and hung to dry. They say it's better to do that. When they hang them to dry, they immediately smoke them and cover them with smoke scent. They say the flies won't get on them too much when they do that. When they hung moose meat to dry upriver, they apparently also lit a fire and smoked them to prevent flies from getting on them. Evidently, that's what they do. They smoke them a little while they're in the process of drying. When [the meat] forms a crust, flies can't get on it. But if they lay eggs on it while the meat is still fresh, they can immediately hatch and form maggots. But one that has dried forms a crusty layer, and eggs cannot hatch and turn into maggots on dry surfaces.

But up north, they apparently cut fresh caribou fat into strips and leave them outside in the summer to try to get the flies to lay eggs on them. Especially the old women and old men who had no teeth would try to let the flies lay their eggs on them. And they say when the fly eggs began to hatch and turn into maggots, they placed them in a container and kept an eye on them until all the eggs hatched. The maggots would eat the whole caribou fat. And they say when all the fat was consumed, the old women poured boiling water over the maggots to kill them. Then they'd take their women's knives and begin eating the maggots. And they say they truly enjoy the meal.

You know how even people from far away places eat insects, even ones that are moving. They add them to other foods and eat them, even though they are moving. That's how some people here in Alaska apparently are. They eat maggots.

[Here] they always throw guts in the river, not wanting them to be left on the ground, saying maggots would develop on them, saying flies would become numerous if they were left on the ground. Because there are many gulls, they eat all [the fish guts] in the water. The gulls eat them.

~: Tepet :~

Tep'ngaayagkiuraqameng-wa imkut neqnek, muragnek imkunek qantanek ping-
qellermeggni, tamakunun ekutullrukait, urunek-llu patuluki, tepengnercirluki.
Tep'ngata-llu tua-i nutaan kenirluki. Egarpagluki-gguq tepsariqercata, qantait tamakut muriit assiameng. Makut *aluminum*-aat-llu makut assinricugnarqut tamakut caviit. Kenircecuilkenka taumek tuaten tamakut, makunun aarnarqenruata
muragni. Tep'ngartellriit tua-i qaralinga'artelaata-ll' ilait, egatet-llu caviit iluit. Qiu-
qerrluteng-llu piaqluteng.

Qakiiyarnek tep'liuratullrulriit imumi, iqalluut-llu makut qamiqurritnek, taryaqviit qamiqurritnek. Akulmiutaat-llu tua-i kemgit tamarmeng tua-i piyagauluki, qa-
ssayagauluki. Piicuunateng tamaani assilrianek avungqengraata. Tamakunek tepsar-
qelrianek piicuitellruut. Camirnarqenruut-gguq assinruluteng neqni. Akulmiut-llu
tua-i tamakuicuunateng. Qaugkut-llu elaqliput iqalluarpagnek, nin'amayugnek
aterluteng, tepsaqkacagarnek. Segg'umavkenateng, unaunateng imait qamkut, kin-
rumavkenaki. Assipiat call' tamaa-i tamakut iqalluarpiit, nin'amayugnek piaqluki.
Tua-i tamakuicuunateng cali tamakunek. Maani-ll' tepnek piicuitellruluteng, qakiiyarnek tep'liluteng uksurpak atu'urkameggnek. Qavani-ll' akulmi qassayaarnek tamakunek, tepnek-llu tamakunek qakiiyarnek pitullruluteng yuut.

Maani iraluq cip'arrluk uitat'larngat'lallrukait nunami teqaumaluteng. Makuita-
ll' imkut iluit imkunek keggagcetyaalrianek ping'aartaqata, pupungluarluki-gguq,
tamakunga'artaqata nutaan nerngartaqluki. Pupungluarluki-gguq. Qakiiyaat tua-
ll' makut nutaramegggnun canritut qamiqurrit ingqiluki tua-i nerluki tua-i. Nerqai-
naugut qamiqurrit qakiiyaat. Imkut-llu kavirilriit carvani uitalriit. Tamalkurmeng
tua-i uumalriatun ayuqluteng. Qengallget-llu aarraangit-llu uumalriatun ayuqluteng. Wangni-ll' tua-i wii-llu tua-i, qassarluki neryugngaluki. Makliit-llu kemgit.
Canek-wa taugaam imkut avurruuyagluki pisqessuilkait quunarqellrianek-llu atsanek, tepet.
Neqet-llu imkut urimalriit kangitneret qakiiyaat eggngaunateng watqapik, ungi-
malriit tua-i ungimqapiaralriit. Quyu'urrluki tua-i waten akagenqeggiluki kemgit,
mermun qallamalriamun ek'aqluki angqeruaruluki, uugarrluuluki nertukait. Aagciugnek maani pituit tamakut. Neqet kemgit ungiluteng tua-i.

~: *Fermented fish* :~

When people prepared slightly fermented fish back in those days, when wooden bowls were used, they'd put the fish in the wooden bowls and cover them with moss and let them sit to ferment. And when they started to develop an odor they'd cook them, *egarpagluki* as they called it. The wooden bowls they used were safe. I don't think the bowls made out of aluminum we see today are safe. That is why I don't allow them to cook fish like that in aluminum pots. Some fermented fish get dark marks on them, and when cooked in aluminum pots the inside of the pot would get dark.

They always made fermented fish heads out of silver-salmon, chum-salmon, and king-salmon heads. And they also made fermented white fish in the tundra area. They were never without a supply of [fermented fish] aside from the regular frozen fish they had. They were never without a supply of fermented fish. They say fermented fish were more satisfying than other types of prepared fish. And the people of the tundra area never went without a supply of those, and those living outside our village, on Nelson Island, never went without fermented herring, called *nin'amayuut*, the kind that have a powerful odor. They weren't split open and were soft inside when ready to eat, and they are delicious. People over on Nelson Island always prepared that kind of fish. And over here we always made a supply of fermented silver salmon for the winter, and they always had a supply of fermented whitefish in the tundra region.

They seem to keep [salmon heads] underground for a little over a month. And when this section [of the head] inside [the cheek] begins to form those little bumpy spots, what they called *pupungluarluki*, that's when they are ready to eat. Now these silver-salmon heads are good to eat, even when they're fresh. Silver-salmon heads can be eaten fresh. And it's the same for fish that are spawning and have turned red in streams. The entire fish can be eaten as it is cooked. King eiders and long-tailed ducks also taste like fully-cooked birds. I, myself, can even eat them raw. This also goes for bearded-seal meat.

They tell people not to eat sour berries after they eat fermented fish heads.

And they will not throw away spawning silver salmon that have soft meat whatsoever, ones that have spongy meat. They would take the meat and make them into round balls, and they dropped them in boiling water and ate them cooked like that. They call those *aagciuget* around here. They were made from fish with soft meat.

Enrit teguluki aug'araqluki. Enrit-llu kaimluteng, ungilmaluteng. Tamakut tamaa-i egcuunaki cali. Puqlamun ekluki uugartelluk' ner'aqluki. Aagciugnek piaqluki.

Teq'atuut ilait taryaqvagnek nunamun, qaill' taugaam pitalriamek pilauciat nalluanka. Taugken tamakut qakiiyaat, iciw' uksuarmi pitulriit. Uksuarmi nunamun tua-i elaulluki iraluni tua-i qavcini tayima, cetamani-ll' pilalliut, nunam iluantelluki. Nenglenga'artaqan-wa, man'a aarnairtaqan, ikamratgun ayagaluteng anciyartutullrulriit teq'ameggnek qakiiyaranek. Tayima tua-i August, September, taukut nuniitni nunamun teq'alallruit tayima.

Yuut atam ilait aruiyuitai. Neqkegtut-gguq yuut ilait. Uquggluyuunaki-ll' ilait. Neqkegtut-gguq yuut ilait. Tuaten-am qanrutketuit. Puqlanissiiyaalriamun tuagaam piyunaitut. Uqugglukalarait puqlanissiiyaalriami uitalriit neqet. Pingna atam pia-i elagyacuarma keluqlia, uquggluyuitqapiaq ilua. Umcigtuq pingna, *insulation*-aarluni-ll' tamalkurmi. Una taugaam kellia *insulation*-aarilnguq uquggluyugluku. Pingna taugaam *insulation*-aalek, puyurcivigmek tuar nutaan pillret. Assiq'apiarluteng tua-i uquggllungssagaunateng pinaurtut.

ALICE: Qakiiyaat-gguq nunamun ek'aqata, canegnek-qaa ciumek inguqirluki pituit?

FRANK: Canegnek-wa inguqirluki pilaqait urunek-llu piaqluki. Imna qikuyak, nunam mat'um atlia tekitessiyaagluku piyunaituq. Nuna tuqumalria imna naugisciigalnguq qikuyak, tutmalriani mer'urtetuli. Tamaa-i tamana assiituq teq'ernun. Maavet taugaam qulvanun tua-i, nunaullranun maavet, unguvalriim engeliinun, nunam naugiyugngalriim engeliinun pikuni nutaan assiqapiarciquq teq'aq. Ikna atam angyat nuniit ik'um nunii assipiartuq. Ika-i aruiyuitqapiartuq.

Teq'erturatuunga wii, taugaam maa-i kuvyasciigaliama teq'ernanrirtua. Pisqengramteng-ll' ukut qakiiyarcurnanriameng. Assikngamki. Tua-i maa-i keggutairulluni nutaan assipiat teq'at.

They would just take the bones off and remove the meat. The bones were soft, too, and would just fall off the meat. They also never discarded that kind of fish. They dropped the [fish-meat balls] in boiling water and cooked them slightly and ate them. They called them *aagciuget*.

Some people placed [whole] king salmon underground to ferment, but I don't know how long they kept them there. But silver salmon, you know how they run during fall. They buried them underground and kept them there for a number of months, keeping them underground possibly for about four months. When it started to get cold out, and traveling was no longer dangerous, they'd apparently leave with sleds to remove the silver salmon that they buried and fermented underground. They buried them underground to ferment sometime in August or September.

Some people's food never spoils. They say some people always have food that tastes good. And some people's food never got moldy. They say some people always have good food. That has been said about some people. But food should not be kept in a place that is too warm. When food is kept in a warm place it will get moldy. One of the two little storage sheds I have back there, the food that is kept in one of them never gets moldy. It is airtight, and the whole shed is insulated. But the other one that is not insulated, the food kept inside it tends to get moldy. But the food we get from the one that has insulation, it would look so fresh it would look like it had just come out of the smokehouse. The food would look so good with no mold on it.

ALICE: When you place silver salmon underground, do you first put grass underneath?

FRANK: They placed loose grass at the base of the hole as matting as well as moss. It is not good to dig a hole down to the layer of land called the *qikuyak*. The dead soil that nothing can grow on; the kind that water oozes out of when stepped on. That soil is not good to use in the fermentation of fish. The hole should not be dug past fertile soil. If the hole is dug in fertile land it will be good for fermenting fish. The place across there where the boats are parked, that land is very good for fermenting fish. The fish will turn out perfect if put in holes across there.

I always put fish underground to ferment, but now since I can no longer fish, I've stopped burying fish underground to ferment. These people here have stopped fishing for silver salmon, even though I've urged them to. I like eating them. Fermented fish are very good when one no longer has teeth [for chewing food].

⌁: *Iqertiit* :⌁

Qanemciksuilkait ilaita kinguneteng unkut. Kasnguk'larait-qaa? Wii tua-i kas-nguk'lerkaatnek umyuarteqeksaitua manilaranka ayuqucillerput kingunemni. Tua-i imkunek nayirnek pikalituyaaqukut, nayiit pissuqengaqngamegteki, pilu'ugkaput tamakut amllelaryaaqut nayiit. Tua-i piluguiteksaitelaryaaqukut tamakunek nayir-nek, waten taugaam uksumi neqet iqertaitnek piliat yuuyuitellruaput wangkuta tan'gaurluni. Wiinga-wa tua-i pillilrianga, ilanka-ll' pilallilriit tayima anelngutenka-ll', tua-i tuaten ayuqluta tan'gaurlullerni. Taryaqvagnek nat'rangqerraqluteng.

Kangitneret, kangitneret tua-i makuuluteng, taryaqvagnek nat'rarluteng. Tak-tuarrlainarnek-llu tamakungqerraqluta iqertanek wangkuta tan'gaurlurni.

Aug'utun tua-i kelikarluki neqallrirraarluki qerrullugmun ek'aqluki. Tua-i-ll' qe-rrullugmek nugcamegteki cali kelikarraarluki aug'utun ellamun anulluki uksumi. Tua-i tepairulluteng.

Taryaqviit tuamtell' tamakut qeciit augkunek urugutngalngurnek tegg'eranek mu-ragnek iqtuluteng augkut, qaill' epuit taktaluteng; kemgirissuuterluteng. Uruggluki waten kemgit aciitgun taryaqviit kiicetuluki, allegpek'naki.

Tuaten tua-i qeciituluki, kemgituluki, kemgirturluki. Kangitneret-llu call' kemgir-turluki caliaqaqamegteki. Iqertagtuumaita ingqiyuunaki, aturturatuata tua-i. Cali-ll' tamakut piluguliaqamegtekut iqertagnek ilaitnek yualirluteng. Iqertagnek cali yualirluteng mingqetuluki. Nat'rait taugaam unkut yualunek assirluki yualirluki nutaan. Tuatnatuluki. Makut taugken arnat tamakungqessuunateng, taugaam iv-rucingqerraqluteng taryaqvagnek arnat. Uqgetliniut ivruciuluteng, ivrarcuutngulu-teng taryaqviit. Angutet-llu pingqetullruut ilait. Tua-i tuaten aturaqtullruaput ne-qet qeciit.

Taugken call' uksumi ayagassuutekait qasperrlugnek aterluteng, iqertiit cali, mi-ngeqluki. Waten nacalguluki, angtuaruluki taugaam. Yuut-llu pingayun iluatni, napareskan iluatni qavaryugngaluteng yuut pingayun. Ukuit-llu negiliit nequtu-kayagluteng, yuk tua-i qacalkeggluni anyugngaluni ukuanek. Makut taugken alit neqututaciqeggluteng, nuugit nungingqaluteng. Yuilqumi pelatekaqluki aturaqlu-teng. Uksumi-llu angutet unicuunaki uksumi yuilqurtaqameng tamakut qasperr-luut, iqertiit. Cali atuqata'arqamegteki, imkut tugret, cikuliurutet, kapulluki waten

~: *Things made of fish skins* :~

Some people down on the coast don't talk about what life was like when they were young. Are they ashamed to talk about it? I haven't thought of being ashamed of it, but I reveal what life was like at home. Ringed-seal skins were readily available since we hunted them all the time. We had a lot of ringed-seal skins to make into boots. We did own boots made out of ringed-seal skins, but we boys always wore fish-skin boots during winter. I, myself, wore them all the time, and my peers probably did too. We boys wore [fish-skin] boots in winter. The boot soles were made out of king-salmon skins.

[The boot's upper part] was made out of chum-salmon skin, with soles made of king salmon. We boys always used fish-skin boots that were long [and above our knees].

They scraped them [like bird skins], and after removing all the meat, they dipped them in the urine bucket. After taking them out of the urine bucket, after scraping them again, they would take them outside during winter. Their odor was gone.

Now the king-salmon skins, skins of those fish, they used these wide, hardwood pieces with long handles that looked like regular skin scrapers to remove the meat from the skin. They scraped underneath the meat to pry it off the king-salmon skins without tearing it off.

That's how they removed the meat [from fish skin]. And they also removed meat from chum salmon the same way when they processed them. They didn't cut the meat up along with the skin since they always used [their skins]. And when they made us fish-skin boots, they used the same material for thread. They sewed them with fish-skin thread. But the boot soles down below were nicely sewn with sinew thread. That's how they made them. But the women never wore those, but they had waders made out of king-salmon skin. King-salmon-skin waders are evidently very light in water. Some men also wore them. Back then, some of the clothes we wore were made out of fish skin.

And another garment they made out of fish skin for use as winter traveling gear was called *qasperrluk* [fish-skin parka]. It was made with a large hood. And three people could sleep inside one when it was held upright with a post. And the hood opening was very wide, and a person could come out easily through that hole. But their sleeves were the normal width and length with a narrow cuff [fitting a person's wrist]. They used *qasperrluut* [fish-skin parkas] as tents out in the wilderness. And the men never left them behind during winter when they traveled out on the land.

carrirraarluku, nacaat-llu tua-i at'elluku pikavet cikuliurutem kangranun, mat'umek nungirutiinek qillrulluku umcigtevkenaku taugaam pikna, elcugngavkarluku. Aliit-llu tamakut ilutmun murugtelluki waten. Ilulirnerkun camaggun ukatmun pivkar-luku, nanerluku qamaggun, eneketuluki. Enekluki tua-i qavaraqluteng. Tamakui-cuunateng cali tua-i angutet qasperrlugnek.

And when they were going to use them, they stuck the ice pick in the ground after clearing the area, and they placed the hood over the top of the ice pick, loosely tying the fastener on so that the air could circulate. And they pulled the sleeves inside. Then they put weights around the inside bottom and used it as a shelter. They used them for shelter and slept in them. The men always owned garments like that called *qasperrluut*.

Yaqulget

~: Yaqulegcuryaraq yaqulegnek-llu unguyaraq :~

Augkut kiilrianek pituit neqliyanrilnguut, neqliyayuilnguut. Kiilrianek. Kuigil-ngurmiut-llu pitangqetuluteng neqliyanrilngurnek kiiluteng. Tua-i taugken makut tua-i yaqulget pinga'arcata, ingpailgata ayagluteng tamakut neqliyayuilnguut. Un-kumiutaat caliarkateng qaqicata, nutaan arnat tamakut kuvyateng civeqluki nanvat akuluraitnun. Cingiit-llu waten usgulluki nanvanun civtaqluki. Tunutellegnek, qa-qanek, allgiarnek, kukumyarnek, kep'alegnek, yaqulegnek tua-i arnat amllernek qu-yurciluteng ayuqenrilngurnek. Amiirturluki ulqurluki atkugkanek tua-i nutaan qu-yurciluteng arnat. Angutet pivkenateng, kuvyatgun arnat, kuvyaturluteng. Nanvat tua-i iverluteng civtaqluki. Atauciunrilngurmek kuvyamek, kuvyanek piyunarqelria-nek. Unuaquaqan tua-i paqequrluki. Initait tua-i yaqulegnek tua-i patumanaurtut kemgitnek yaqulget, kinertait, kinercilrianek yaqulegnek.

Tua-i-ll' nutaan ingcata unkumiutaat imarpigmiutaat qecililriit qengallget, cinga-yiit, kukumyaraat, metraat, qaugret; ingcata tengesciigaliata, nutaan qayat, nutaan angutait, kiilriit tamakut, neqliyanrilnguut, augkut Qipnermiut ketiitni qikertat ketiitnun ayagluteng nutaan qanruyulluteng, unguyarluteng. Saggluteng waten imarpigmi yaaqsiulluteng, unaggun nutaan caniarluteng qikertat ketiitgun anguar-turluteng. Qipngiinarluteng ukatmun, tua-i iquit amllerrluteng qayarugaat. Iliini-llu yaaqlimeggnek ikayungcarluteng call' kiilrianek. Ingkut yaa-i Kuigilngurmi ila-gautetuut tamakut ilait, unguqatalrianun. Uruturmiut up'nerkillrit, Kuigglugmiut, Pengurpagmiut, Enpakarmiut. Waten tallimaingulalliniut nunat kiilriit. Kuigg-lugmiut imarpiim ceniinlluteng unani, Qipnermiut kellirneratni unani. Pengur-pagmiut-llu taukut, Uruturmiut-llu up'nerkiyami. Nayurturatuit ilaita up'nerkill-ret tamakut, kiinrilnguut kiagpak tua-i. Naternanek-llu imkunek pissurturluteng pituameng kuvyacuatgun imarpinrarnek-llu. Tua-i neqliqa'aqluteng tamakunek kuvyacuatgun. Tamakunek tua-i neqa nutaan amllerrluk' arnaita yaqulget kemgit, qeciit-llu atkuutullret.

Birds

~: *Bird hunting and driving molting birds* :~

They referred to people who didn't go to fish camps to harvest salmon as *kiilriit*. They called them *kiilriit*. And there were also some families who didn't go to fish camps in Kwigillingok. But when the birds started to fly around, before they molted, the ones who didn't go to fish camp and stayed at the village would leave the village. When they were done working on sea mammals, the women would set their nets on sloughs between lakes. They also set them in the narrows between lakes. The women gathered many different species of birds, including Pacific loons, red-throated loons, long-tailed ducks, black scoters, and scaups. Women would skin the birds and turn them inside out to dry, and they gathered many to make parkas. Men didn't [hunt birds with nets]; it was the women who hunted with nets. They would wade in the water and set [nets] in lakes. They used more than one net, nets that were easy to handle. They would check them every day. Their drying racks would be covered with bird skins and drying bird meat.

Then when the ocean birds molted, the ones with thick skins, the king eiders, surf scoters, black scoters, common eiders, spectacled eiders; when they molted and could no longer fly, their men who stayed in the village and didn't go to fish camps, after planning, would take their kayaks and go down past those islands below Kipnuk to drive molted birds. They would spread out on the ocean away from one another, then they would all begin paddling down below the islands. They would paddle and move, gradually turning in this direction, and there would be many kayaks on both ends. And sometimes they asked for help from the people who were staying in places on the other side of their village and who didn't go to fish camps. Some people from Kwigillingok went over and joined others before driving the molted birds. Some [joined the drive] from the spring camp sites of Uruturmiut, Kuigglugmiut, Pengurpagmiut, and Enpakarmiut. There were five places where people stayed and didn't go to fish camps. Kuigglugmiut was located along the ocean shore down below Kipnuk. In places like Pengurpagmiut and Uruturmiut, people who stayed in spring camps remained there all summer and didn't move to fish camps. They [stayed in spring camps] and harvested flounder and whitefish with small gill nets. They cut and dried the fish they caught with those small nets.

Pinarian nutaan ingcata yaqulget [unguluki]. Tua-i taugken ciunrat tua-i yaqul-get quyurcata tunguriluni. Qikertaq tuar. Yaqulgem amellertacia. Quyurmeng yaqul-get ayuqenrilnguut unguluki nutaan quyuita, ulerpak ul'aqan maliggluku. Qikertat ingkut ukatairluki ungutulliniut, qikertanun mayurcetevkenaki. Alairata-ll' tua-i tauna nunamun piyaraat nutaan ullagluku arnat, piyugngalrianek avuluteng. Kuv-yacuanek-llu ayaulluteng. Upingaluteng tua-i nunami maani kuvyacuat usgulluki te-gumiaqluki, akultutaciqeggluki, elavluteng, elavumaluteng, arnanek ilaluteng-llu.

Nuna taugken man'a, ellimalriani waten, nunamun kapusngaurtelluk', kuvyacuat pagaavet kangritnun qilqaulluk' casguuvkarluku. Yugnek cali elaqlirluni, elavngalria-nek. Mikelngurnek tuaten makunek murilkengelrianek, neplirpek'nateng taugaam, nangaavkenateng-llu una-i alairaqateng. Tuaten tua-i ciuniurtekait. Tamakut-llu tua-i elatmun waten unani ekvigam ket'araani ayuqluteng, nengumaluteng ketmun elaqsigluteng ukut ukatmun, kuvyacuarnek tegumiarluteng usguku'urluki. Ivruma-luteng-llu ilait unani. Qayat taugken tua-i unkut yaqulget tua-i caqircaaqaqata ciun-rirtaqluki, tua-i itertelluki yuut akuliitnun uuggun. Kasmestai, qayat call' waten ayuqluteng. Paugkut-llu cali yuut cali waten ayuqluteng nunamun pilriit. Makut-wa call' qayat, yaqulget tua-i wantelluki. Ukatmurcaaqaqata ukut nengkaniraqlu-teng qayat, paangerluteng. Ukatmun piaqata paangerluteng nengkaniraqluteng ut-qercetaqluki. Tuaten pituit.

Itrata-ll' tua-i imkut yuut paugkut pavanelnguut quuluteng ketait, kuvyacuanek tegumialget. Nunamun-llu tua-i qakvangermeng casgiumaluki call' kuvyanek yug-nek taperluteng. Nunami tua-i pian' kaugluteng nutaan. Mermi-wa call' ukut wani call' kaulriit. Tua-i-ll' pilngungameng piuraqerluteng qayagpagluteng amllertaciqe-gginiluki tua-i taqesqelluki, arnat nauggaarluki, arnanun tunqatarniluki. Tua-i-tang imkut arnat neptullinilriit. [engelartut] Tua-i taugken kitakiirata casguliumaluki angutet tua-i, yaqulget ilakuateng. Tuaten pitulliniameng. Arnat kingumek pivkar-luki.

Women would process lots of meat and gather lots of skins for parkas from that bird harvest.

When it was time after the birds molted [they drove them]. Then when the birds gathered, the area where they were appeared dark. It looked like an island. It was incredible to realize that so many birds were out there. They drove the many different species of birds together during high tide, following the incoming tide. They drove molted birds up toward land on the side of islands, not letting them go up onto the islands. And when [the birds] came into view, the women and those able to help went to the place where [the birds] were driven up on land. They also brought small gill nets with them. They were ready to get them on land, tying the nets together and holding them just the right distance apart, crouching down on the ground, with women among them.

Back on the land, while positioned [to get the birds], they had stakes thrust into the ground with the small gill nets tied onto the top, creating a fence. There would also be more people crouched down [behind the net fence]. And there were children who knew what to do, who stayed quiet and didn't stand when the birds appeared. The groups of people were positioned like that to receive [the birds]. And more people were on the sides, right below the bank, extending down toward the water, holding small gill nets tied together. And there were other people standing down below in the water. And when the birds began to turn to the side, some of the kayaks down in the water would [quickly paddle in front of them and] move them back in line, allowing them to enter between the lines of people holding the small gill nets. There were more kayaks in back of the birds, pushing them forward. Groups of people were back on land, too, set in various positions. Kayaks were also in the water in different positions, keeping the birds together. When the birds began moving that way, the kayakers would quickly move with double-bladed paddles and position their kayaks farther out [creating a blockade]. And when they began moving this way, they'd quickly paddle out and bring them back in line. That was how they [drove birds].

Then once [the birds were enclosed], the people on the sides holding the small gill nets began moving inward and joined the ends to form a circle. And even though [the birds] went up on land and out of the water, they were fenced in by nets in back along with people. Once they were on land, they began to strike them. And there were even people on the water striking ones that were left out there. And when [the strikers] became exhausted, after a while, they'd begin yelling and saying that they had caught enough [birds] and telling them to stop, and they asked where the women were, saying that they were ready to give [the remaining birds] to

Atraameng tua-i aaralriarurrluni tua-i. Neptupialliniut arnat. [*engelartut*] Engela-
mek avuluteng. Anglanarqelliniata tuatnatullinikait. Neptulliniut. Nangluki tua-i
nangkacagarluki yaqulget. Arnat nangluki taukut kinguqliit.

Tuqulluki, tuquqluki. Tua-i nangutengermeng ak'anun engelaumanaurtut ila-
meggnek temciyugluteng tuaten. Angutet-wa call' ukut engelarturalriit. Nutaan
tua-i qaqicamegteggu unanelnguut ekvigaam aciani taguqurtelluki nunam qainganun quyurrluki taukut nunamelnguut-llu.
    Amllelaameng yaqulget, ayuqelriit quyurqurluki, qengallget quyuita, cingayiit,
kukumyaraat, allgiaraat, metraat. Tua-i ilakelriit quyurqurluki. Nutaan tua-i qaqicata cuqluki qavciuqaqluki nutaan aruqurluki. Qaqitaqata pinqigtaqluki. Tuaten
tua-i amllertatkurluki tua-i, aruqutekluki yaqulget tamakut qecilget.

Tamakut tamaa-i amlleret tua-i atkugkat unakelarait, taugken qaqiucameng
amiirluki. Cali kinercirraarluki, piyulriit, imkut neqliyatulit avegvilget neqliknga-
meggnek tamakunek akilirluteng ilaitnek atkugkanek malruinek-llu kipukengaqluteng, neqnek naverrluki.

Tuatnatuluteng-am. Ilait-llu naterkanek piqa'aqluteng. Piilutmeggnek tua-i-am
apluki piaqluki, neqerrlainarnek pivkenaki. Wall' neqnek piqerluki qecignek-llu
naterkaitnek, wall'u pilu'ugkanek nayirnek ilaqerluki atkugkat tua-i navertaqluki.
Tuatnatuluteng. Tua-i ullingaluteng, kinrumaluki.

Uuggun ullirrluku amiilartut tarenriryaraitgun. Ullirrluki antaqluki kemgit.
Maaggun piuyunaki, piaggun taugaam. Carangllugnek keviqerluki agartaqluki
uyaqurritgun, iquirraarluki, kelikarraarluki.
    Kiagmi yaqulegnek piyuitut amlleringnaqluki, puqlam nalliini. Tua-i taugaam
tamaa nangesqumaluki piaqluki, yaqulegcurraartelluki. Aruqutkaqluki tua-i
tep'ngarpailgata nangesqumaluki kiagmi. Ilait-llu tua-i iniluki, iniurluki amllerra-
qata, kinercirluki. Unkumiutat qecigtuut qengallget-llu. Caliaqeqataamegteki tuaten tua-i.

the women. Women apparently are very loud. [*laughter*] When they were signaled to begin, [the women began striking the remaining birds] while the men formed a fence around the area. They apparently did that [when they drove birds]. They'd let women [do the killing] at the end.

When the women went down, they all began yelling and screaming. Women are very loud. [*laughter*] They were screaming and laughing at the same time. They had them do that because they were so much fun to watch. They are loud. They caught all the birds. The women killed all the birds that were left.

They killed them. Although they had killed them all and stopped, they would continue laughing at their peers for a long time. The men would be laughing, too. When they were done, they had them bring those that had been killed right below the bank onto the land. They gathered them together with the ones on land.

Since there were many birds, they gathered the ones that were the same species together, the king eiders, surf scoters, black scoters, long-tailed ducks, and common eiders. They gathered ones that were the same species together. When they were done, they divided and distributed them depending on the amount they caught. When everyone had received a share and there were more in the pile, they'd distribute them again. They [gave each person] an equal number of birds with the skins on.

They caught a lot [of birds] for parkas, and after [all the birds had been taken] they removed the skins. And after drying them, those who wanted to, the ones who went to harvest salmon at fish camps [and had enough fish to spare] would trade for bird skins with some of their dried fish. And some traded dried fish for two bundles of bird skins.

That's what they did. And some would trade the skins for boot-sole material. They'd ask them first and find out what they needed before trading. They didn't just trade skins for dry fish. They would trade [bird skins] for a little bit of dried fish, and some for boot soles, or they'd include ringed-seal skin for making boots. That's what they did. [The bird skins] were already split and dried.

They split [their skins] in the area between the shoulder blades and skinned them. They would cut them open and pull out the meat. They never cut them open [on their bellies] but in the back. They would fill them with grass and hang them by their necks after scraping the fat off.

They didn't try to get many birds during summer while it was warm. After they hunted for birds they would want them eaten right away. They distributed them before they spoiled. And some were hung to dry when they were plentiful. The ocean birds have thicker skins, like eider ducks. That is how they processed them.

~: *Yaqulget atkuut* :~

Tua-i-ll' atkuliyungameng ukut arnat, atkugkat tamakut atrarrluki angilluki tua-i naanret ukut piarkateng pimariamegteki tua-i allakarluki, allgiaraat wall', wall'u qengallget. Qengallget-wa makut tunutellget-llu uquritulriit kinrumangraateng.

Angulaluteng-gguq. Wangkuta tua-i tan'gaurluni nasaurlullernek-llu ilaluta angulavkatuitekut. Wagg'uq angulaluta atkugkiuqata'arqameng kinrumalrianek. Teguluki tua-i iqmigluki allegyaaqevkenak' tamuagurluki tua-i, uqurrluit ig'aqluki, tamalkuan tua-i. Tuatnaluteng. Kenilluku tua-i tuatnaurluta, angulaluki-gguq uquirluki. Uqilngungaqamta tua-i taqsugaqluta, cimiraqluta. Qengallget tunutellget-llu uquriyugtut. Makut taugken allgiaraat kukumyaraat-llu tuaten piyuunateng. Qaqilluki tua-i tamakut angulavkarluki-gguq, keggmarturtelluki allegyaaqevkenaki taugaam.

Tuatnarraarluk' nutaan teq'unun imkunun augkunun qerrullugnun eneni uitalrianun akurrluki tamalkuita yaqulget. Nutaan akungqaluki piyungamegteki-ll' tua-i nuggluki, nutaan kelikarluki. Uqurrluirluki nutaan tua-i uqurrluit tamalkuita aug'arluki, puyalermek tua-i catairulluki, uquirluki. Qaqicata-ll' tua-i nutaan ellamun melqurrit elaqliqsagulluki. Ellamun nutaan anulluki iniluki. Uksumi.

Teq'urrlugniirluki tua-i, tepairutqapiarluteng tua-i ellami anuqem caliaqluki. Tua-i tuatnarraarluki itrulluki nutaan, nutaan eliqluki atkugkiuraqluki. Makut allgiaraat tamakut arnat atkukvallutullruit. Makut taugken tunutellget angutet tua-i atkukaqluki, tunutellget, qaqat-llu, qugyuut-llu. Taugken kegkut Qaluyaarmiut Ningliim nunaqlii nacaullegnek atkungqerpallutulliniluteng *elder*-aat. Ingtaat nacaullget qecigtulliniut. Tua-i tuaten ayuqut tanglanganka maaten. Tua-i ciulirnerit, angutet arcaqerluteng angutait, tamkunek atkungqerrnaurtut nacaullegnek, melqurrit elaqliqluki. Maqartut-gguq cali qivyurpaungameng, irniaritnek taugken piiyuunateng.

Temirtaitnek pitulriit unkumiutarnek, atkuutulinek piaqameng. Aanait-gguq pilarait makut irniarit-gguq taugaam ayagtelluki. Tapeqluki piiyaaqengermeng tuqurqessuunaki, qavcirrarnek taugaam amllenrilngurnek tuquciaqluteng piyagait-

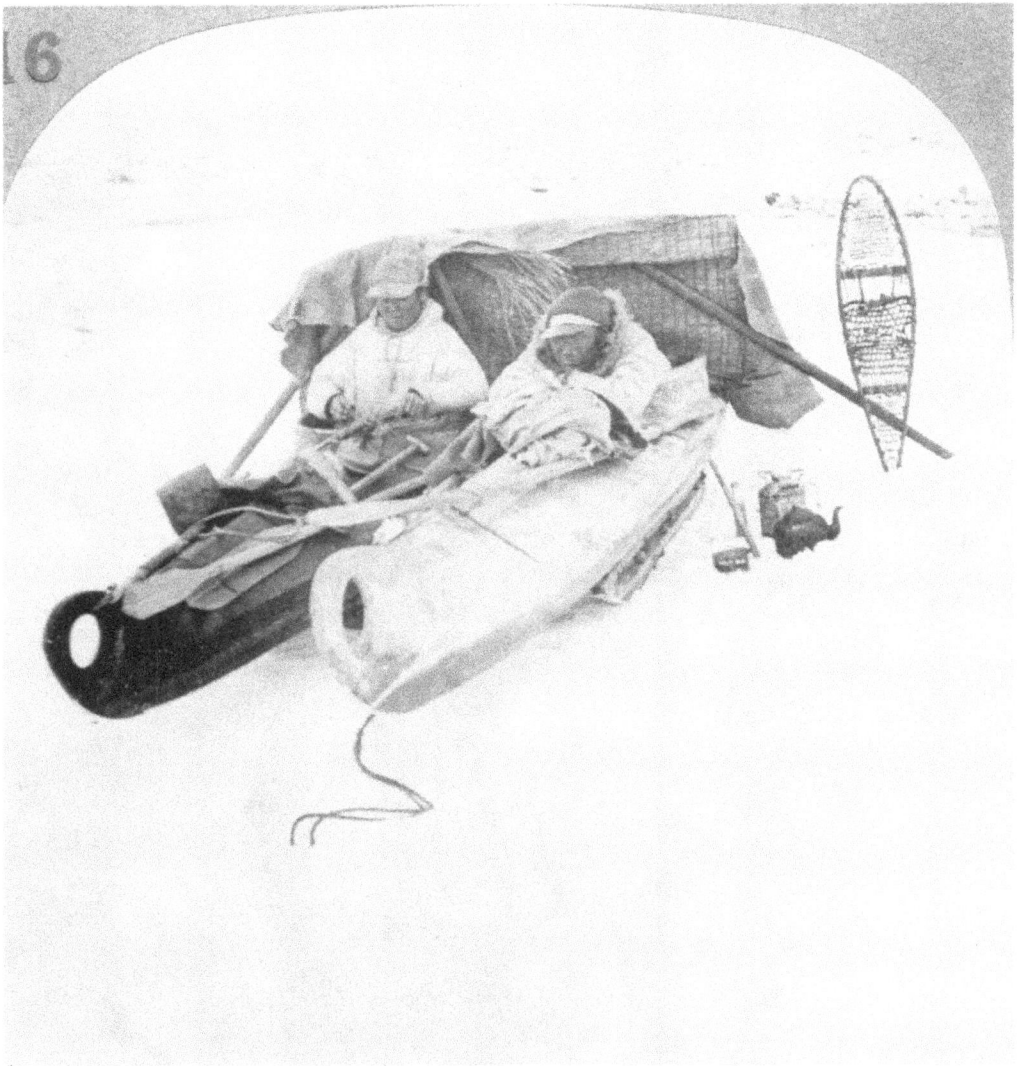

Martin noted that these two seal hunters — possibly David O David's father (on the left) and Roland Phillip's father — were out on the sea ice many miles from shore, waiting because so much floating ice had drifted in around them. Later the wind and tide would turn and take this loose ice away, making it possible for them to continue hunting. Their kayaks rest on kayak sleds, and their gaffs hold up a grass and canvas windbreak behind them. Note the snowshoes nearby, an essential tool for spring hunting which enabled hunters to get out of their kayaks on slushy snow and pull themselves to safety in an emergency. Martin Family Collection B16.

Man holding a negcik (gaff) and tundra swan. Frank Andrew often emphasized the importance of the negcik for anyone venturing on ice: "The negcik was our friend, and we always kept it at hand. We always took the gaff with us, even if we were leaving the kayak for just a short time." Martin Family Collection.

Roland Phillip noted that when beluga whales entered the river during fall at high tide, people kept quiet. Once the beluga came upriver, men blocked the area downriver with nets and killed them when the tide went out. Roland said that beluga meat is best when dried and not cooked, and that meat from the spine bones near their heads and tails is especially good eating. Their uliutet *(sinew) comes from along their backs near their tails. Martin Family Collection.*

A sled-load of caqutet (sealskin pokes) at spring camp along the coast near Kwigillingok. The sealskins are inflated to hold their shape while drying. Pokes were essential for storage before the use of plastic garbage bags and five-gallon buckets. Seal-oil pokes were made with the fur on the inside. Each had a pasvaagun (stiff sealskin funnel) sewn where the seal's face had been removed to keep the opening stiff when being filled with strips of blubber. When full, the poke was closed just below the pasvaagun. Roland Phillip mentioned that the anus and urethra were kept open while the poke was being filled so that trapped air would be expelled. Martin Family Collection.

Woman gutting herring at spring camp. The person at the far left is possibly Aryak, Albert Beaver's father. Martin Family Collection B2.

Martin wrote: "Moving time is likely to come about three times a year.... When a [wooden] boat like this is used, it is usually crowded with several families at one time." Martin Family Collection B19.

Kwigillingok hunters posing for a photograph, with Qallaq on the far left. Bill Wilkinson noted that three different kayak sitting positions are visible: The man on the far right is sitting on his feet, the man to his left is sitting up on his knees, and the man second from the left is sitting flat on his bottom, with his legs stretched out in front of him. Martin Family Collection.

The Andrew family returning to Kwigillingok from fish camp in 1930 in a large skin boat. Frank is on the far right, with Charlie Wiseman beside him and Frank's father and younger brother, John, in back. Martin Family Collection.

Man with boat load of salmon, used as food for dogs as well as humans. Martin Family Collection B7.

Martin wrote: "The salmon are cleaned and their heads removed. Next they are split and hung to dry. A little wood smoke is used to repel insects and help preserve the fish. In the background you see fish that have been hung to dry. Fish cleaning and splitting is a woman's work." Martin Family Collection B8.

Woman cutting fish with a large uluaq. *Originally these semilunar knives had slate blades, but by the 1930s they were routinely made from steel from old hand saws. Martin Family Collection* B9.

Man boiling water for tea near the shore. His kayak rests on the tundra above him. Martin Family Collection B23.

Qasgi construction, showing clearly how grass mats were laid over the wooden frame, followed by a layer of sod. Martin Family Collection.

A woman prepares grass mats to cover a building frame. Pieces of sod were then placed on top, creating a warm, well-insulated dwelling. Martin wrote: "Driftwood, sod, moss, and grass are all used in house construction. The framework is propped in such a way that no nails are necessary to hold it together." *Martin Family Collection* B3.

During the 1930s above-ground homes were increasingly made from split driftwood logs and heated with homemade wood stoves fashioned from oil drums. Note the windbreak made of snow blocks protecting the entryway. Martin Family Collection.

An above-ground log home covered with grass and sod. Martin Family Collection.

Uliggaq (Elsie Mather's mother) from Kwigillingok dipnetting for tomcod in the river.
They set dip nets in a line, from one side of the river to the other, just before low tide.
Women would go upriver, striking the water with sticks to drive the fish into the nets.
The two sticks visible in the photograph acted as a frame around the periphery of
the net and were staked into the riverbed. When the net was filled with fish,
the sticks were pulled out and closed together to keep the fish inside.
The stick ends were sharpened to thrust them into the river
bottom. Martin Family Collection B10.

Tomcod braided together with grass to hang to dry, after which they would be stored for future use. Martin Family Collection B11.

High tide associated with a fall storm surge, Kwigillingok,
December 7, 1931. Martin Family Collection.

Kwigillingok in the wake of a flood. The high tide has pushed blocks of ice
into the village, destroying racks and houses. Martin Family Collection.

Tomcod were also harvested through holes cut in the ice, using dip nets attached to ipukaqutet (long, heavy poles). Kanuuquk (two wood supports) were tied to each pole, extending underwater. Two parallel pieces of wood were then tied to the middle and bottom of the kanuuquk and a mesh net woven around the periphery. Martin noted that fishing for tomcod and smelt was usually done during very cold weather, as it was essential that the ice be strong enough to hold the weight of both fish and fishermen. The fish are frozen for storage. Martin Family Collection B12.

Tomcod fishing, dated November 1931. Martin noted that the heavy log handles required three or four men to bring them up. Their weight kept the net down in the strong current. When full the nets weighed as much as 400 pounds. Frank Andrew exclaimed: "They are dipnetters from Kwigillingok. They are my ancestors. These are their handles down in the water. These people are pulling the net out of the water." Martin Family Collection.

Frank Andrew noted: "These are the grass storage bags filled with tomcod that are being frozen." He said that before the use of plastic garbage bags and five-gallon buckets, Kwigillingok residents made as many as five hundred bags a year to store fish. Martin Family Collection.

According to Roland Phillip, it was common for one person to own all of the taluyat
*(wooden blackfish traps) in this photograph. Such traps were set in the sloughs
between tundra lakes. Blackfish were also frozen for storage. Later, however, when
thawed, they might revive and be as lively as ever. Martin Family Collection* B14.

"Kuskokwim Bay in Winter" Martin wrote: "These dogs have a keen sense of smell and are often able to follow tracks covered by new snow. Without dogs like this the Eskimos would have much more difficulty making a living." Indeed, dog teams were used to haul driftwood, fetch food and supplies stored at camp, travel to other villages, and hunt and trap inland and upriver. Martin Family Collection.

Kayak frame near completion in the Kwigillingok qasgi in the 1930s. The central firepit in the foreground is uncovered. Martin Family Collection B21.

Men and women placing a skin covering over a kayak frame, which has been turned over. As some push the skin from the back, the person in front pulls forward and the skin stretches over the frame. Martin Family Collection B22.

Frank Andrew noted: "They always placed kayaks on tatkit [kayak racks]. They placed them upside down on the racks, out of reach of dogs." Martin Family Collection.

~: *Bird-skin parkas* :~

When the women were ready to start making the skins into parkas, they took the bird skins down, untied them, and separated the birds into bundles by species, either long-tailed ducks or king eiders. The king eider and Pacific loon skins usually have a lot of fat on them, even though they're dry.

They called [the next step in preparing skins] *angulaluteng* [chewing the fat off the dried bird skins]. They had us boys along with girls chew the fat off the skin. When they were preparing dried bird skins to make parkas, we'd chew them to remove the fat, *angulaluta*, as they called it. We'd take the [bird skins] in our mouths and begin chewing on them, trying not to tear them, and bite off the fat, swallowing it. That's what they did. We'd moisten [the skin] with our saliva and remove the fat. When we felt sick from the fat, we would say that we wanted to stop, and another person would take over. The king eider skins and loon skins tended to have a lot of fat on them. But long-tailed ducks and black scoters weren't like that. They would have us chew the fat off [the bird skins], *angulaluki*, as they called it, having us carefully chew the skins so as not to tear them.

After that, all the bird skins were dropped in urine buckets that were kept in homes. They left them in the bucket for a while, and when it was time, they pulled them out and scraped them. They'd scrape off all the rancid oil. When they were finished, they hung them outside with the feather side out. Then they brought them outside and hung them to dry. This was done during winter.

The wind outside would completely remove the urine odor from the skins. After doing that, they brought them inside and cut patterns to make into parkas. The long-tailed ducks were mostly made into women's parkas. But the Pacific loon, red-throated loon, and swan skins were mostly worn by men as parkas. But the elders out there on Nelson Island in the Ningliq River area mostly wore emperor-goose parkas. The molted emperor geese apparently have thick skins. People wore parkas like that when I first started seeing them. The elders there, especially the men, wore emperor-goose parkas with the feathers on the outside. They say that they are warm because they have thick down feathers, but they don't make [parkas] out of their goslings.

They used to get adult ocean birds when they caught birds to make into parkas. They say they got the mothers but let their chicks go. Even though they caught both, they just killed a few of their chicks. But evidently, they killed all their moth-

nek. Aanait taugken tua-i atkuugarkaulul ki, amiit pitekluki ilakuivkenaki tuqurqe-tulliniit, qagaani piaqamegteki. Ninglimi-w' qagaani amllepiarnilarait.

Maqalriit maa-i makut qugyuut. Augkut-llu ava-i tang qaqat, tunutellget-llu tuullget-llu amiit asvaunateng cali atkuuluteng qecigtuameng. Augkut-llu makut maa-i qengallget metraat-llu makut taugaam pissiyaayuicugnarqut. Makut-llu qe-cigkitut anarnissakat, lagitun makucetun qecigtutaut alkaryugluteng imarpigmiu-taungermeng anarnissakat.

Qugyuut-llu melqurrit elaqliqu'urluki. Tamakut taugken tunutellget ultaarluki atkuktullruaput wangkuta, melqurrit elaqliqaqluki, wall' ullelluki at'aqluki. Maqar-luteng tua-i. Pugumallruaput tua-i kiivalluita. Imkut-llu tuntut piyagaat tua-i atku-keggneruvkenateng wangkutni, pacecugluteng. Assingraata aturpakayuunaki, tama-kut taugken yaqulellruaraat assirluteng atkugkarnirluteng.

Tamacenituut-gguq yaqulegnek ayuqenrilngurnek atkuliluku. Tamacenilku-gguq. Atellgutkenrilngurnek yaqulegnek atkuliluku. Tamaceniluku-gguq.

~: Yaqulget enrita nissuita-llu atuullrit :~

Mingqutekluki ilait pilallruit enqellriit yaqulget yaqruit, nissuita piit. Enrita-ll' im-kut natait cali, ukut nuukliit, malruk, mengliitni enrraq imna, tamana allakarrau-luni, tamakut tamaa-i mingqutketullrulliniit. Enqellran, angtuarraat cakuciit piit pilallruit. Nissuit-wa imkut nuugit tua-i caniutaqaqluki tua-i pitullrukait. Naruyat-ll' imkut nissuit cali quyurqurluki cali, uqtanun atutuamegteki.

Enret-am cali augkut asevret enrit, agluqrit, putuluteng iquit, makut nigurluki niss'ut tamaavet kaputaqluki, calturucirluki; neqcaita pissuutek'larait.

Qugyuut ukuit, nuqaruaritnek pituit.
ALICE: Qugyuut-llu-qaa yaqruita [enritnek] meluskarcuuterluteng?
FRANK: Ituraitnek-wa imkunek pinilaqait.
Meluskarcuutengqelallrulriit. Meluskayuitellratni nut'guaqelallruit qukait kep-luki, canek keviqerluki ingkut calturrarrluki nuugit. Una-ll' tua-i kevirluku cali, muragaq-llu man'a piqtaarluku. Cingleraqami-ll' tua-i ingna ayagarrluni avavet. Qertunra, air-am qam'um cingqerluku yaatmun. Nut'guaqluki. Ilameggnun-wa nut'gasnguarluteng tamakutgun piaqluteng, cup'leraluki tuaten.

ers when they caught them up north to get their skins to make into parkas. They say there are many in the Ningliq River.

Swan parkas are warm. And the skins of those red-throated loons, Pacific loons, and yellow-billed loons are very sturdy as parkas because [those birds] have thick skin. And those king eiders and common eiders, I don't think they use them very much. And these Steller's eiders are thin-skinned, and their skin is as thick as these Canada geese, and they tear easily, even though they're ocean birds.

And swan parkas were always worn with the feathers on the outside. But we wore Pacific loon parkas both with the feathers inside and outside, having the feathers on the outside, or we'd turn them inside out and put them on. They were very warm, and we mostly used those. The young caribou weren't good for parkas for us; they weren't as warm. Even though they were nicely made, we hardly used them, but the small bird skins were good as parkas.

They mentioned using different kinds of bird skins to make a parka for someone. They called it *tamaceniluku*. They made a parka for a person out of different bird skins, and they referred to that process as *tamaceniluku*.

~: Uses of bird bones and feathers :~

They used parts of the *niss'ut* [longest wing feathers] that are hard like a bone for needles. And also certain parts of their bones, these on the tip, two of them, those little bones on their sides were also used as needles. They used those parts from slightly bigger [birds]. They used the *niss'ut* to sweep floors. And they also gathered *niss'ut* of gulls because they used them on *uqtat* [fishing lures].

[Uqtat] are fish lures made from walrus jawbone, with a loop on the ends. They'd hollow out this [bone] here and stick the wing feathers there, stuffing the holes with something so it wouldn't come off. The feather was used as part of the bait on the hook.

They call this part of the swan bone *nuqaruaq* [lit., "imitation throwing board"].

ALICE: Did they use swan wing bones for sniffing tobacco?

FRANK: They said they used the bone called *ituraq*.

They used to have tubes for sniffing tobacco made of bone. Back when they didn't snort snuff, they used them for pee-shooters after cutting the center. [They would blow in them] after filling one side with things, and they would fill them. It would shoot out the other side when pushing it [with air]. The air would force it out. They used them as pretend guns. They would shoot at their friends with those for fun, by suddenly blowing out [the contents].

Aturngateksaitait suggait. It'gait taugaam qugyuut lagit-llu; lagit-wa piit angqa-litullruit. Mingeqluki, urunek, canek allanek uqamalkucirluki imirluki. Qugyuut-llu it'gait cali imkut inuguameggnun kellarviknguartelluki, cali-llu canun atkug-nun-llu qaspernun-llu qaraliqtuluki qugyuut it'gait. Kelurquarluteng pilriit, tuntut uyaqurritni imkut tengayurpallraat, ukuit ac'etulalriit melqurpait. Tamakunek tamaa-i kelurquarluteng piaqameng, qaralirqurluki pitullruit, melqurritnek tuntut, ac'etuqitagnek. Mingquraulluki.

Imkut uyalget makunun imarpigmiutarnek pissurcuutnun culuketuit. Nagiiqu-yanun arcaqerluki pitegcautnun-llu, nissuit unkumiutaat, uyalget. Imkut tungulriit nissuit, teqsuqrita yaqruita-ll' nuuksuit tekeryuut.

Tamakut tuaten ayuqut. Culukluki tua-i pitegcautnun anipat nissuit, qucillgaat-llu. Ilait pikailnguut piciatun niss'unek culituyugnarqait. Malruuluteng ellimatuut, pingayuuluteng-llu iliini ellimaaqluteng. Inglua malrugnek pingayuak-llu ika'an-lluni.

Assinruut-gguq. Ilait-gguq makut mer'em-llu assiirtelarai, mecungaqameng. Taugken qucillgaat anipat-llu piit assinruluteng. Augkut taugken uyalget imarpig-miutaungameng, mermi ping'ermeng cangaringaunateng culuuluteng nissuit, teq-suqrit-llu.

Makut taugaam ilait, imgartarluteng-llu mecungaqameng assiirrnaurtut. Qucill-gaat taugaam anipat-llu piit assinrurpagluteng, assirluteng. Mecungengermeng ca-ngariqercuunateng.
Pitegcaun assirluku ayagcuutekait culuteng. Alulaqluki. Caqiayailkutekluki.

~: Yaqulget nertukait :~

Uqumcuat, iisuayagaat-llu nertuit. Augkuk taugaam kukukuaq qiuracetaaq-llu ner-yuitait.
Kayanguit nertuit. Kukukuat taugaam kayanguit teguyuitaput maani, makut-llu imkut kauturyaraat maani necuarluteng imkut pitulit.
Neryuitaput cali qiuracetaarngalnguut, kayanguit taugaam nertuluki. Qiura-cetaat-llu kayanguit call' nertuluki.

They never seemed to use their beaks. But they used swan-foot and goose-foot skin; goose-foot skins were made into balls. They would sew them and stuff them with moss or other things for weight. And they made storage bags for their dolls out of swan-foot skins, and they used swan-foot skins for designs on their parkas and garments. The ones who were making *kelurqut* [fancy stitches] used the throat hairs on caribou, the very thick fur [on their necks]. They always used long caribou throat hair when they made fancy stitch designs. They would sew them on [bird-foot skins].

They used cormorant-wing feathers as flight stabilizers on ocean-hunting tools. They especially used wing feathers of ocean birds like cormorants on *nagiiquyat* [seal-hunting spears] and arrows. [They used] the long, dark wing feathers, the ones on their tails and the feathers called *tekeryuut* at the very tip of the wings.

[Wing feathers of those birds] were used like that. They used snowy-owl and crane wing feathers for flight stabilizers on arrows. Some who don't have [wing feathers from such birds] probably use any kind of feathers. They put two [flight-stabilizing feathers] on [spears], and sometimes there are three. There are two on one side, and the third is on the other side.

[Crane] feathers were better [for flight-stabilizing feathers]. They say when they used other bird feathers and they got wet, they fell apart and got ruined. But the feathers from cranes and snowy owls were better. But the cormorants' feathers, because they are ocean dwellers, when their wing and tail feathers were used as flight stabilizers on arrows in wet places, they never got ruined and kept their shape.

But as soon as these other bird feathers got wet they would get flimsy and would roll up. But crane and snowy-owl feathers were much better. They kept their shape, even though they got wet.

The feather stabilizers helped the arrows fly straight in the air. They helped steer the arrow straight ahead as it went. They prevented arrows from turning to the side.

∾: Birds that are eaten :∾

They eat buff-breasted sandpipers and solitary sandpipers. But they don't eat common snipes and black turnstones.

They eat their eggs. But we don't take common-snipe eggs around this area, or the swallows, birds that make small nests [along buildings and cliffs].

We also don't eat the ones that look like black turnstones, but they eat their eggs. And they also eat black-turnstone eggs.

Nertuluki nutaan uqumcuat. Iisuayagaat-llu nertuluki. Qaleqcuuget-llu nertur-
luki cali kayangutuumaita. Tusairnaraat-llu. Qaleqcuuyayagaululuteng miknateng,
tuiraaraluteng qalriagaqluteng, "*Tuir, tuir.*" Nertuluki.

Piyagait taugaam imkut naruyat tukraqata nertuit. Tua-i-ll' teng'ayagangaarcata
taqluki, piciatun nerngarcata. Wii taugaam nereksaitua.

Uyalegpiit. Ang'ut makut angenrit piiyuatuluteng-llu piiyuapiarluteng, lagitun
piiyuatuluteng. Ukut taugken uyalget makucit piiyuasciiganateng uaqsiata iruteng.
Pucikaquluteng piyugluteng. Tamakut taugken angenrit, ukaqsiata it'gateng piiyuatuluteng uyalegpiit. Nertuluki.

Uyalget-llu makut nertuit cali. Amiit taugaam tepsarqut atam, kemgit taugaam
assirluteng.

~: *Tunutellget* :~

Tunutellget-wa taugaam makut arcaqerluteng pilalriit, irr'inarqelalriit. Yugtun-llu
aturluteng piaqluteng, yuarutnek aturaqluteng. Augna-ll'-am arnassagaurluq Mer'u-
malriamek pilallrat, piani qungut pingkut yaatiitni nanvarraq iqkunani, takaayiur-
luni waten, wani kelumteni canimaarmi. Tunutellgem atuutellrua, atuutellrulli-
nia maani kiagmi kangaqcaarallrani taum nuniini. Ciutaicaaqluni-ll', atullra-gguq
taugken elilluku-ll' yuarun, taugaam qaill' ayuquciitaqa. Tunutellgem, takuyaryaa-
quq-gguq mermi, tua-i irugni, maatekaarluni akungqaluni yuralria atuulluni ellminek. Umyugaa kanavirturleurluni-llu paniirutminek. Tamaani umyuiqellruuq.
Ukaqvani tua-i yuunrillruuq. Kanavirpiiqnaku-llu-gguq pisqaqluku, tunutellgem.
Ugiq'erluni-gguq anglluq'ernaurtuq.

Tuamtell' Tuntutuliarmi up'nerkami nanvam ceniini kanaqlagcullermini, pilliniuq kayanguk. Tegulukek-llu tua-i qamigautegmi qainganun elliqerlukek. Kuimaa-
ralriik-wa-gguq makuk tunutellgek. Ayagluni tua-i. Kinguneminun elliqertellukek
meng'ellinilria yuarutmek. Kingyalliniak tautun-am tua-i napangqalutek uatekek
pugumalutek yagiralutek-am atuullutek ellmegnek yuralriik. Yuarun-ll' iquklican
apallilutek, "Ciin aug'um inuum aug'um kayangugka ayautakek pitarkarpenek nunulingramni." Kinguqlilillinniluku-ll' tuamtell' aturrraarluku, "Ciin aug'um Inuum
aug'um," yugmek-llu pivkenaku, Inugmek taugaam, "Inuum aug'um evamiagka
ayautakek unguvakaanek nunulingramni." Ut'rutenritlinikek'am. Uksuan-llu yura-
qataata yuaruciaqellinniluku. Elilluku tua-i tamana yuarutiik tunutellgek.

They eat buff-breasted sandpipers. And they eat solitary sandpipers. And they eat red-necked grebes along with their eggs. And horned grebes. They are very small, red-necked grebes that make a call and say, "*Tuir, tuir.*" They eat them.

They only eat the gulls' chicks when they hatch. They stopped eating them when those small ones began to fly, when they began to eat various things. But I haven't eaten those myself.

Double-crested cormorants. They are larger than these [pelagic cormorants], and they walk normally like the Canada geese. But these pelagic cormorants cannot walk because their legs are too short. They tend to fall forward when they try to walk. But the larger ones, the double-crested cormorants, because their feet are longer, are able to walk. They eat them.

And they also eat these pelagic cormorants. Their skin is stinky, but their meat tastes good.

~: *Pacific loons* :~

Pacific loons especially do things out of the ordinary. And they sing songs in Yup'ik. And that old woman named Mer'umalria [heard one], right beyond those graves up there in a long, narrow lake, behind our village closeby. A Pacific loon apparently sang to her while she was walking near there during summer. And she couldn't hear very well, but she learned its song, but I don't know how it goes. A Pacific loon [sang to her]. She looked around, and its legs were about this much out of the water, and it was singing and dancing. She had been grieving for her daughter who had died. She was depressed during that time. [Mer'umalria] died recently. And she said that the Pacific loon would tell her not to be so downcast. And she said that it would dive in the water after making a little sound.

And again in Tuntutuliak, when a person was hunting for muskrats in the spring, [when he was paddling] along a lake, he saw two eggs in a nest. He took them right away and placed them on top of his kayak sled. He said there were two Pacific loons swimming nearby. He continued paddling, and just when those loons were behind him, one of them started singing. When he looked back at them, like the one in the previous story, their lower bodies were up out of the water, and they were moving their wings and singing and dancing. When the first part of the song ended, they sang the verse, "Why did that one, that *inuk* [Iñupiaq word for person] take my eggs away, even though I awarded him a catch?" And on the second verse they sang, "Why did that *inuk*," and it didn't call him a *yuk* [Yup'ik word for person], but an *inuk*, "that *inuk* take my eggs that I was sitting on, even though I gave him a long

Tuamtell' pagaani ellami tengaurluteng aarakuneng assiitut. Taum niicugniste-
meng ilii, anelgutii, wall' atii, kinguqlia wall', piqatarqata, tua-i tuaten pitulliniut,
tengaurluteng aaraluteng. Tengaurluteng aarayuitut, misngaluteng taugaam. Qauraa-
raluteng tengaurluteng qalriatuut, "Qaurr' qaurr' qaurr." Misngaluteng taugaam aa-
ratuut tunutellget. Tuaten ayuqut, ayuqelliniut tunutellget.

Yuc'ungarmek-im' tauna pilaqiit, kayanguiqenglleq, atuutellra.

Qugyuut-llu cali makut evaluki tangrraqaceteng assiitetuut-gguq call'. Tua-i-w'
aug'utun ayuqluni call' tua-i.
NOAH: Iciw' yaaqvanek wani tenglaryaaqut. Cat'mi imurtuatuat?

FRANK: Tuullget. Urr'urruaraluteng iciw' pilalriit, waten elliurluteng. Imurtualuteng-gguq tua-i, ellallungqata'arqan. Tengaurluteng pagaani pituut, urr'urruaralu-
teng-gguq, imurtualuteng-gguq.
Erinakegtut tuullget.

~: Qucillgaat :~

Qucillgaat-wa cauluki niiteksaitelaqenka. Taugaam-gguq tamaani anguyiim
nalliini Tuntutuliarmiut kiugkut ciuliarita iliita arnam qetunraminun mikcuayaar-
mun, qucillgaam ukua, tuqlua man'a imna, anertevkarcuutii man'a augarluku ukua-
nun, makuanun minguktaarautelallrua mikellrani irniaminun taumun. Anguyiim
nalliini tamaani. Cunawa-gguq erinvaugarkaq tauna angliami. Qinarmiut kiugkut
kiaqsiggartut napangellrani uitiimeng Tuntutuliarmiut kiugkut kiakaraatni kiani.
Ik'na-ll' Iigem kiaqlia Pailleq yaaqsigluni. Tamaani anguyiungluni angliriami.

Qinarmi unuakumi qasgimek iliit yuqertelliniluni. Unuakuayaarmi, yuut tupa-
gavailgata, an'uq-gguq tua-i quunirluni cenavarluni kanavet yuqerrluni. Atam piqanrakun uaken Qinaam painganek, napat amatiitnek amaken, anguyagpagalliniuq cakemna. Itqerrluni tua-i tupagqelaalliniluki anguyiit piniluki, anguyagpagarniluku.
Up'arrluteng tua-i qayatgun ayagartellinilriit. Tauna tua-i igvaarrluku piiyaaqelli-

life?" After [what the loons did] he didn't even return them. That winter when they were going to dance, he composed that song. He had learned the song of those two Pacific loons.

Then it is not a good sign when they are flying and make their call. They apparently make their call when the relative of the person who is listening, his sibling, father, or younger sibling is going to die. They fly and make their call. They usually don't make their calls while they are flying, only while they are in water. They make the call when they are flying going, "*Qaurr' qaurr' qaurr.*" Pacific loons make their call while swimming in water. That's how Pacific loons apparently are.

Oh yes, they called that person Yuc'ungaq, the one the loon sang to after he took the eggs.

It's also a bad sign when they see swans sitting on their nests. It means the same thing.

NOAH: They usually take off from their nests while we're still a distance away. What [birds] make sound, *imurtualuteng*, as they called it?

FRANK: The common loons. You know how they make the call, "*Urr-urr-urr.*" They call it *imurtualuteng* when they make that call, and they do that right before it starts raining. They'd be up there flying, "*Urr-urr-urr,*" *imurtualuteng* as they called it.

The common loons make sounds that are pleasing to listen to.

~: Cranes :~

I never heard anything [out of the ordinary] about cranes. But they say during the bow-and-arrow warfare period, one of the female ancestors of the people of Tuntutuliak removed the crane's windpipe, the breathing tube, and used to rub it on [the throat] of her son when he was small. This was during warfare. That child ended up having a very loud voice when he got bigger. Qinaq was located right above Tuntutuliak, right where the wooded area is located. And Pailleq River, above Iik River across there, is far from their village. So when that child became an adult, he started taking part in warfare.

One morning in Qinaq, a person went out of the *qasgi* to relieve himself. This was early in the morning before people began to wake up. When he went out, the weather was calm, so he went down toward the riverbank to urinate. While there, from right near the mouth of the Qinaq River, on the other side of the trees, he heard someone yelling, "*Anguyagpaa* [Big warrior]!" He ran inside and woke the

niat qayartaunani, yugtaunani-llu-gguq tamana. Cunawa-gguq akmaken Paillrem painganek, Kusqukviim akianek tauna qayagaullinilria, tauna qucillgaam tuqluanek minguketaaralallra. Taungullinilria-gguq cunaw'. Erinarpauluni.

Atam qucillgaat makut elisngaut. Piyarangqertut waten "Qaillun qaillun avilliat?" Yuralqerturciquq pucikaraqluni waten elliurluni, qecgauraqluni tuaten. [*engelartut*]

"Qaillun qaillun avilliat?" waten qayagaulriani, nerurainanermini, ilait maligtaqunruut. Qayagaulriani tua-i tuaten uyaqilugarrluteng tua-i piuraqerluteng yuralqerturluteng tuaten, elliurluteng tuaten. Qayagaulriani, "Nut'galuten ata." Tuaten tua-i piaqameng qeckaranaurtut qulmun. Picingssaugut qucillgaat. Tuaten tua-i pitullruaput.

Usvituut makut qucillgaat. Anglanitek'lallruaput-am. Tuaten-am pituit. "Qaillun qaillun avilliat?" Kangiiturluki qaillun ciuliat pilauciatnek, ava-i qanerluni, "Qaillun qaillun avilliat?" Tuaten tua-i pilarniluki, kan'aqtaarluteng tuaten piaqluteng. Nut'gasqengaceteng-llu qecekpagtaarluteng.

~: *Tulukaruut* :~

Tulukaruut tuamtell' makut atmairesqaqluki. Yaqiurinanermeggni taugken qulmuqerrluteng, tua-i-gguq atmairluteng, qayagauraqaceteng.

Atmairesqelluki. Cali-am tua-i assilriamek pisqenrilengraiceteng pinaurtut, tulukaruk-gguq atmairtuq. Atsat-llu nalliitni tua-i assilriaruniaqluki. Naunrarnun-llu atsanun quyungqalrianun amllernun tekiteqatarqata-gguq maniitetuit tuaten. Pinrilengraiceteng atmairluteng. Makut tua-i maa-i piciulallilriit tua-i. Naspaaqaqina amani Anchorage-aami tulukarugmek tangerquvet.

Kanani-llu tulukaruuk irniuralartuk maani. Irniyaratupiartut atam. Nengllingraan tua-i irnituut. Qerruyuitut kayanguit, kumlam piiyuitai. Quputuut-gguq kayanguit, kumlam qupurrluki qeltait, qerrumayuunateng-gguq taugken.

men and alerted them that the warriors were approaching, that he heard the familiar call. They quickly prepared and took off with kayaks. They went to the place where the man indicated the sound came from and looked. There were no kayaks, and there was no one there. Apparently, that one [with the loud voice] was yelling from the mouth of Pailleq across the Kuskokwim River, the one whose windpipe she had rubbed with the crane's windpipe. It apparently was that person's voice. He had a loud voice.

These cranes are wise. This is what they say to them, "*Qaillun qaillun avilliat* [What, what do your ancestors do?]." The [crane] would move about and bob its head up and down, making this motion, and jumping. [*laughter*]

When you say "*Qaillun qaillun avilliat*" while it's eating, some are more compliant. When you say that to them, they would move their necks and dance about, making this motion. When saying this to them, "*Nut'galuten ata* [Shoot now]," when you tell them that, they jump upward. Cranes are comedians. That's what we used to do to them.

Cranes are smart. We used to tease them. That's what they say to them. "*Qaillun qaillun avilliat?*" Inquiring about [the crane's] ancestors and what they used to do, they'd say, "*Qaillun qaillun avilliat?*" Then they'd bob their heads up and down [answering the people]. And when they tell them to shoot, they would jump up and down.

~: *Ravens* :~

And these ravens, they would tell them to take off their backpacks. While they were flying, they would suddenly fly up, indicating that they were removing their packs. They did that when people called and told them to take their packs off their backs.

They would tell them to take the packs off their backs. Even though they didn't ask them to do it, they would say that a raven had removed the pack off its back. When they did that [in the air] during the berry-picking season, they'd say it was a good sign. And it is said when pickers are about to find a place that is covered with berries, they give them that sign, and even though they hadn't asked them to, they would take off their packs. These things are probably true. You should try that in Anchorage if you see a raven flying.

There is a raven couple that always nests down there. They lay eggs early [in spring]. They lay eggs even when it's cold. Their eggs don't freeze, and they aren't affected by the cold. They say the cold cracks their egg shells, but they don't freeze.

~: *Naruyat* :~

Naruyat tua-i makut qaillun niiteksailkenka. Taugaam-gguq unugpak ingtetuut. Unugpak tua-i yaqurrit nissuirulluteng tua-i, ercartuan-llu tua-i nauluteng, yuut-llu tupaganga'arteqerluki taqluteng tua-i tengaungluteng. Unugmi-gguq ataucimi unugpak ingtetuut naruyat. Tuaten qanrutkelarait, unugmi ataucimi ingtetuniluki.

Angutet-gguq tauna iliit avani ciuqvani naruyanek ingtarcutullruuq. Nalluvkenaki piyarait. Pitai-gguq tua-i ingingaqapiarnaurtut carqiurluteng. Tengesciigatellratni. Nalluvkenaku-gguq piyaraat. Qagaani pilaryukaat nertustaitni naruyat. Nertuit-gguq qagaani.

~: *Ciguraat* :~

Yaqulecuaraat ciguraat, angllutuyaarluteng. Cenaqegqata'arqan-gguq, cat unguvalriit paivngaqatarqata maani paivngatuut amllerrluteng tamakut yaquleyagaat. Murugnermi atam ulyugaqan, tuam tua-i camani ngeliini, anglluq'aqluteng camavet. Carvaneq-wa tuknilria. Anqercameng taugken qerrataqerrluteng avavet, tamakut cigurayagaat.

Nurnatuut unani. Caaqameng amllerraqluteng. Unguvalriit tua-i amllerrnaurtut tuaten piaqata. Cenaqegqata'arqan-gguq paivngatuut. Tungulrianek aipaingqertut angtatmeggnek. Tunguluteng, qaingit ayuqluki tua-i tamakut-wa aipait qatellriit.

~: *Yaqulget tekitellriit* :~

ALICE: Makut-wa yaqulget picatun maavet tekicuitellilriit, ataucikun.

FRANK: Iliini tangnerranarqelrianek taugaam tangerqatuukut. Tua-i alarrluteng pilrianek, tekiartellrianek. Yaqulecuarnek-llu mikcuarnek tangrraqluta, avelngat-llu igtaitnun itqertaqluteng, qaraliarluteng. Piqunqeyagarluteng yaquleyagaat. Nenglenga'artaqan taugaam uksuarmi pituut, tangrruuqatuut caqa'arqameng, qanikcanga'arteqerluku.

⌁: *Gulls* :⌁

I have never heard anything about gulls. But they say they molt in one night. Their long wing feathers come off during the course of one night, and they grow as the sun comes up, and they stop growing just as people awake, and they begin to fly. They say that gulls molt in one night. That's what they say about them, that they molt in one night.

They say one of the men used to catch molting gulls long ago. He knew when they would [molt]. They say that his catches wouldn't have long wing feathers whatsoever. [He caught them] when they couldn't fly. He knew when they were going to [molt]. They think [he caught them] up north where [people] eat gulls. They say they eat them up north.

⌁: *Kittlitz's murrelets* :⌁

Small birds, Kittlitz's murrelets, those little birds that can dive underwater. They say that when the ocean is going to be perfect for hunting with an abundance of sea mammals, many of those small birds are around. Along the edge of the shore ice down there when the tide comes up, they dive down underwater. And the current there is strong. But when they pop up and come out of the water, those small Kittlitz's murrelets suddenly fly in the air.

They are rare down on the ocean. And sometimes they are plentiful. There are many sea mammals when murrelets are abundant. They say there are many when the ocean is going to be perfect for hunting sea mammals. They also have dark counterparts that are the same size. They are dark but look like their white counterparts.

⌁: *When birds arrive* :⌁

ALICE: These birds probably don't all arrive here at once.

FRANK: We sometimes see strange ones that we haven't seen before. The ones that flew here by accident. And we see very small birds, and they fly into mouse holes, and they have designs. Those birds are very agile. They are only seen once in a while during fall when it starts to get cold, when it has just snowed.

Itqertaqluteng qacalkelluteng mik'nateng. Imkut-llu cangaqcuarneraat miksaa-qellriit, mikellruluteng tamakuni. *Yellow*-aarrayagaat imkut yaquleyagaat. Maavet uksuarmi pituut.

Qengallget ciumek tekitetuut. Uksurauluku tua-i ciumek tekitetuut qengallget, aarraanginek maligluteng, aiparluteng. Metraat-llu tua-i atam makut maa-i kingua-raatgun tengaungarrluteng. Makut taugken ciumek pilartut. Tengaungarcata-ll' tua-i makut caqa'arqameng alaiteqa'aqluteng. Anarnissakat-llu augkut tungliulu-teng. Amllepiatuut unani imarpigmi maani tekitaqameng anarnissakaq, ler'aluteng qalrialuteng, "*Pev, pev.*"

Uqsuqat, qatkegglit-llu makut maa-i, curcurpiit, tengesqaaraat, kep'alget, qami-qurpiit, allgiaraat, kukumyaraat, payit. Makut maani irniyuitut, maa-i-tang anarni-ssakaat. Qagaatmun kitutuut makut. Makut-llu tuullget irnilartut pavani, qaqat-llu, tunutellget-llu. Tullegnat piiyuitut maani. Makut irniyuitut tuntussiikat. Cenair-piit-llu cali irnituluteng, iisuayagaat-llu, qangqiiret-llu.

~: *Ingtat* :~

Makut-llu cali maani ingtetuluteng, ukut-llu kep'alget, qatkegglit-llu, cugg'erpiit-llu, tengesqaraat-llu, qamiqurpiit-llu. Maa-i makut maani pitulit unani imarpim-teni. Makut akacakayiit-llu imarpigmi makut maa-i ingtetulit. Makut-llu maani pilaameng ingtetulriit payit. Makut-llu qakmaken qagaaken tekilluteng tengvaileg-meng. Piyagateng ilakluki tengluteng, kuimurluteng qakmaken. Uksuarmi tua-i amlleriluteng tua-i unani, ingtauluteng. Ingingaluteng irniat, qengallget. Makut tua-i nalluanka ilait maani piiyuilata. Makut-wa qaill' ingtetuyaaqsugnarqut tua-i, tuullget qaqat-llu tunutellget-llu maani nunami. Makut-llu imarpigmi ingtetulriit unani.

Qucillgaat taugaam ingingaluteng usvituut. Ingcaratupiartut atam maani. Ciu-ngatni ilameng ingtetuut. Yugmek tangerquneng angniilngaitut, yagtaarciiganateng taugken tua-i. Tengumaaqameng taugken yaqiurluteng tengauryugngaaqameng, yag'artarluteng pitululeng. Tengesciiganateng watqapik pingaunateng, qecekpaga-ngermeng. Usvituut. Yaquteng manisciiganaki, nissuilnguut. Taugaam ullalriani tua-i qimagturnaurtut, paqnakluk' piyaaqaqamceteng. Cukariqertaqamta cukari-qertaqluteng. Aqvaqurluta-ll' pileryiimta aqvaqurluteng ayagarrluteng. Tua-i ta-ringluku ingingaciat, tengesciigaluciat, taugaam uqilaut. Uqilangraata taugaam ilait

They quickly fly inside [mouse holes]. They easily fit in there and are small. And even though those *cangaqcuarneraat* are small, those are smaller. [*Cangaqcuarneraat*] are those small yellow birds. They come here during fall.

The king eiders arrive first. They arrive first during late winter along with long-tailed ducks. And the common eiders begin to fly around right after them. But [king eiders] arrive first. And when they begin to fly around, these [common eiders] are seen every once in a while. And the Steller's eiders arrive after them. There are many Stellar's eiders when they arrive down on the ocean here, and they make noise like they are passing gas, "*Pev, pev.*"

[Those that lay eggs around here are] green-winged teals, wigeons, mallards, scaups, goldeneyes, long-tailed ducks, black scoters, red-breasted mergansers. These Steller's eiders don't lay eggs here. These pass our area and fly north. And yellow-billed loons lay eggs inland behind our village, along with red-throated loons and Pacific loons. Common loons don't lay eggs around here. These whimbrels don't lay eggs here. The small shorebirds lay their eggs here, as well as solitary sandpipers and ptarmigan.

~: *Molting birds* :~

And these scaups, wigeons, and shovelers, green-winged teals, and goldeneyes molt here. These are the ones that [molt] here down in our ocean. And these white-winged scoters also molt down in the ocean here. And these red-breasted mergansers also molt here. And these arrive from the north before they fly [south]. They fly with their chicks swimming from up there. They are numerous during falltime. The chicks are molted, the king eiders. I don't know about some of these [birds] because they aren't seen here. These yellow-billed loons, red-throated loons, and Pacific loons probably molt in this area too. These molt down on the ocean.

But cranes are smart when they are molting. They molt very early here, before all the others. If they see a person, they will surely be upset, but they cannot extend their wings. But when they are able to fly, they extend their wings; they constantly extend their wings. But they don't do that whatsoever when they cannot fly, even when they jump up and down. They are smart. They cannot show their wings when they're without feathers. But they run away when approached, when we pursue them out of curiosity. They speed up when we speed up. And when we run suddenly, they suddenly run away. That's how we know that they are molting, that they cannot fly, but they are fast. We catch up to them sometimes, even though they're

angularaput. Ingcaratupiartut atam qucillgaat, taugaam alingnarqut qen'ngiimeng. Caugartaryugtut. Cugg'emeggnek waten pileryagaluteng.

Niugtarmiut nuniitni. Qaluyaat ingkut qikertaugut. Qalvinraar ukatiitni, qagatiinek Ningliim qagaterluni. Qaluyaat-llu elaqliat Ningliq cali qagatellgutekluku Qalvinraam, avayarrii-w' Niugtaq. Taum-gguq tua-i nunii yaqulegtupiartuq. Teng'aqata-ll' akerta akervang'ermi catairutaqluni tayim'. Waten qulliqluteng piaqameng tua-i tan'geriluni tua-i akertairulluni. Camek tua-i qalriaciinani, tem'irrluni taugaam tua-i. Teng'aqameng-llu-gguq tuarpiaq kalluk. Qikertangqertuq malrugnek Ningliq qagna uaqliqelriignek. Taukuk-gguq tua-i anagutuk yaqulegnek, neqlernanek-llu, nacaullegnek piciatun.

Piiyuatuut tamarmeng. Ukut-llu maa-i uqilapialliniut ingingaaqameng, qugyuut. Qucillgarni uqilanruut, kanagkilngalngermeng, uqilapialliniut. Yagingaurluteng waten qimatulliniut. Piyungaqameng qeckaraqluteng avavet tua-i yaaqvanun, anguvkarngaunateng tua-i yugmun. Ingtarcuraqamta iliini, qemini pavani qugyuut pilaryaaqaput, maligcuunaki taugaam.

Yugmek call' tuqucillruut malirqertemeggnek. Tungliqluteng pillermeggni, anguqataani qugyuk engevqerrluni-gguq waten, irugni-gguq qungagarrlukek. Paallagvikngani-llu-gguq tua-i yuum taum tukqerluku, ullirrlukek tua-i aqsiik. Tua-i piunrirrluku, tuqulluku. Taumek inerquutaqait maani qugyuut tamakut, murilkelluki tuagaam pilaasqelluki. Nevqerreskan, pitsaqevkenak' angukaku, engevqerreskan pisqevkenaku. Qung'arcetuut-gguq tua-i tuaten piqatarqameng, iruteng tua-i waten nengingavkenaki. Paallakan tua-i taugaam tekiskan tukqerarkauluku.

Tuani-ll' Ilkivigmi angutet iliit Cavunermi Uaqlirmi, ekvigaam aciani analliniuq, ketmun caugarrluni. Anainanermini tua-i qalrialriignek niitelliniluni. Anarlun' tua-i, qerruliigni call' pimalukek uyungluni, ekvigaam ceniini Ilkivigmi. Mer'a-gguq man' ket'araani. Piqalliniuq qugyuuk ukuk malruk, ituklutek, mer'em qularaakun, tua-i ciuneqeqapiarluk' tekicartuqalriik. Nang'ertellria-ll' tua-i ceturquallinilutek, tatamngamek tengaurlutek. Cetu'urcagnek-llu tua-i irukegnegun waten teguqallinilukek. Egmian qerrataqrutliniluku. Yagingallukek tua-i iggnayuklukek pitaqsugyaaqlukek, quyigiinautelliniluku tua-i. Quyigiinaagnek tua-i aipaa peggluku aipaa teguluku. Nutaan atranga'artelliniluni. Ataucimek tua-i taumek pill'uni anallermini.

fast. Cranes molt very early, but they are dangerous since they have a quick temper. They like to suddenly attack. They attack with their beaks.

[Ningliq River] is near Newtok. Nelson Island is an island. Qalvinraaq River is located on the [south side of Nelson Island], and it has headwaters that go to Ningliq River's headwaters. And [east] of Nelson Island, Ningliq River has the same headwaters as the Qalvinraaq River, and one of the small tributaries is Niugtaq River. They say there are many, many birds in that area. When they fly right above one another, it becomes dark and the sun is no longer visible. You couldn't tell what sound they were making, but it was a thundering noise. When they fly, it sounds like thunder. Ningliq River up north has two islands that are right above and below one another. They say those have numerous birds on them, including black brants, emperor geese, and various others.

All [of these birds] walk. These swans are apparently very fast when they are molting. They are quicker than cranes; they are very fast although their legs seem short. They run away with their wings out like this. When they want to, they jump great distances, and they won't let a person catch up to them. Sometimes when we went to catch molted birds back in the hills, we tried to catch swans, but we could not follow them.

They also killed a person who was chasing after them. When they were running after them, when he was about to catch the swan, it quickly turned over on its back and pulled in its legs. When the person fell on him, [the swan] kicked him and gashed open his stomach. It killed him. That is why they are warned about swans here, to watch out for them. If one happens to catch up to [a swan] and it turns over on its back, they told them not to take it. They say that they pull their feet in when they are about to do that, not keeping their legs stretched out. If they catch up to it and fall on it, it would kick [the person].

And in the Ilkivik River one of the men was relieving himself on the lower Cavuneq River right underneath the riverbank, facing the river. While he was defecating, he heard birds making their call. He was relieving himself, and his pants were down and he was squatting on the bank of the Ilkivik River. The water was right below him. He looked and saw two swans, side by side, coming straight toward him right above the water. When he stood up, they began to stretch their legs out, and since they were startled, they flew. And when they stretched out their legs, he grabbed them by their legs. They immediately lifted him up. He kept his arms extended thinking that they would fall, wanting to catch them, and they lifted him farther up. Since they brought him farther up, he let go of one of them and took the other. He finally began to descend. He caught that one while he was defecating.

ALICE: Kivumallrullilria-llu-w'. [*engelartut*]

FRANK: Mayurteqivkenani-gguq tua-i. Qanemcikellruuq ellminek. Pinilliniut. Angeng'ameng-wa.

Makut call' maa-i uqilaut, lakcugglugaat, lagiyagaat. Maa-i makut uqilaillrit, neqleret, anrutarpaungameng. Uqilaillruut makuni ilameggni. Makut maa-i uqilanruut nacaullget, lagilukviit-llu. Makut maa-i uqilanqurrit, lakcugglugaat, lagiyagaat mik'nateng. Ingtaugaqameng uqilaut.

❧: Uyangtetuit-gguq yaqulget mer'ilnguut :❧

ALICE: Niitelartua, qavartaraqameng pelatekani mertangqelaasqelluku pelatekam ilua.

FRANK: Up'nerkami yaqulget tekicullratni tuaten ayuqut. Kiagpak-llu tua-i ayuqluteng tuaten. Yuilqumun ayangssiluteng qavartalriit mer'icuunateng. Mernek tua-i imiqerluki cailkamun piurluki. Uyangtetuit-gguq yaqulget mer'ilnguut pivakarluteng. Tuqulluki-llu piunrirluki.

Yaani qikertani pillrulliniut. Taugaam caqerluteng piyaaqellratni angalkum taum; angalkuq tauna nall'arrluku. Pivailgatni anagluk' pillrullinii. Imkut-gguq makut uqsuqat — tamakut-gguq tamaa-i yaqulget assiilqurrit. Umyuarrliqelriit cakneq yuut tungiitnun. Iluqliutulliniut-gguq tamakut uqsuqat, yaqulget ayuqenrilnguut elaqliqluki. Iluqliuluteng uqsuqat uyangtaqamegteki. Avatairluki-gguq waten pitulliniit.

Pelatekani wall' qayani qavalriit. Qavaitni-gguq pituit. Piunrirrluki. Uyanglluki-gguq. Angalkuungami tua-i tauna pivkallrunritliniuq, elpeka'arcamiki uyangcaaqellratni tuani.

ALICE: His pants were probably still down. [*laughter*]

FRANK: He said that he didn't pull his pants up. He told the story himself. They're strong because they are large.

These are also fast, these *lakcugglugaat*, the small Canada geese. These white-fronted geese are slower because they have a large stomach. They are much slower than these other [birds]. These emperor geese are faster and the lesser Canada geese. These are faster, these small Canada geese. They run very fast when they are molting.

~: They say birds peek in on people without water :~

ALICE: I've heard that they are supposed to keep water inside the tent when they sleep overnight out on the land.

FRANK: That's what they did when birds arrive in spring. And they also did that in summer. People who camped out on the land always kept water [in their tents]. They filled containers with water and left them out. Sometimes birds would "look in on them," *uyangtetuit*, if they were without water, and kill them.

People apparently experienced that when they camped on the islands over there. But one time when they looked in on someone, it was apparently a shaman they looked in on. He detected their presence and escaped them before they killed him. They say that pintails — among the birds, they are the most evil. They have bad feelings toward people and can cause evil and hurt them. When birds look in at people, the pintails were usually in front with other kinds of birds sitting on the periphery. When birds look in on people they apparently surround them completely with pintails the first in the circle.

They can look in at people sleeping in tents or in their kayaks. They say they look in and kill them while they sleep. That person, because he was a shaman, he apparently woke up and detected their presence and didn't allow them to kill him.

Caranglluut

~: Caranglugnek quyurcaraq :~

Tamakunek utercimariameng, *camp*-ameggnun ayaganrilnguut nunani uksuarmi nutem uitalriit, arnait, nutaan nangerrluteng. Angutait-llu muragnek makunek tua-i piluteng. Erniyunateng ella assiraqan arnait, caranglugnek caliarkameggnek quyurrluteng. Unuakumi tua-i arnat amlleret ayagnaurtut tua-i, ernerpak-llu tayima tua-i, atakuan-llu tua-i tekilluteng nutaan. Yuuciinateng tua-i caranglugnek keggatait ukut caqumaluteng, atmaitnek. Arulairluteng aqumluteng uitaaqluteng. Iruit taugaam makut temait ukut kiimeng yuuluteng, ukut taugaam keggatait yuuciinateng tua-i.

Unangkengameggnek caranglugnek. Imkuirluki-ll' *clean*-arluki piuratullrulliniamegteki uterpailegmeng, carrirluki, nalanrit aug'arturluki, allragnillaat naullermeggni pillret, carrirluki tamakut.

Iitaat, cat, kelugkaat, taperrnat, tamakut tamaa-i pitullruit atu'urkateng. Tua-i ava-i augkut cenami tumyarallrit ayagayarallrit quugut maa-i. Ilait-llu ilututaaqluteng waten tumyarat nunam qaingani, arnat aturturatullrit allamiaqan. Angutet tumyaraqenrilkait, arnat taugaam. Nanvat cenait tamarmeng, un'a cenaq, imarpiim cenii tumyararluni ukalirnerput, augna-ll' yaalirnerput, arnat ayagayaraitnek. Paugna-ll' keluvut angutet ayagayaraitnek cali tumyararluni, tumyararluteng tua-i, kuiggaat ullagayaraitnek. Ayayuilnguut uksuiyuilnguut tua-i can'giiliraqluni nuniit cali; tamakut tumyarait. Kiagmi kiimeng arnat ayagavkenateng. Angutait-llu ayagaluteng nangrrarmeng atmaga'arluteng. Tuaten tua-i ayuqaqluteng uksuarmi, qenuvianun tua-i.

Tua-i-ll' qenuqataan arnat qayikvayagnek pillinqiggluteng, canegnek-llu. Nutaan can'get quyurrluki angliriluki tua-i waten itulluki, qalliqluki tua-i. Qertupiarluteng ilait, iqtuluteng-llu. Quyurrluki nunapiim qainganun. Piirrarnek cali, piirriluteng nemerluki tamakunek qillertanek canegnek imalget. Qillengqanrilngurnek-llu qalliit pagkut qallilirluki, qaspirluki, ellallingraan tua-i mer-iluanun iterngairutelluku. Can'get kanarqurluki waten, meq tua-i qurrlurarkauluni, qalliqurluki can'get tua-i waten. Can'get qaingat waten ayuqluni uivutmun. Tamakunek-am piirrallektarnek

Grass

~: *Gathering grass* :~

When people returned from fish camp, those who didn't go directly to their fall camps but stayed in the village during fall, the women in those villages would get busy. And the men were occupied gathering wood. Every day when the weather was good, women went out and gathered various types of grass that they would work on later. Many women would leave in the morning, and they were gone all day. They'd finally come home in the evening. You couldn't tell that they were people as they were coming home because their upper bodies were covered with grass that they were carrying [on their backs]. They would stop and sit to rest. You could only see their legs and their lower bodies, but their upper bodies were covered and didn't resemble people.

[They came home] carrying grass that they gathered. They always cleaned them before they returned home, removing the withered grass, taking off dried grass from the previous year.

They collected *iitaat* [tall cotton grass], *kelugkaat* [coarse grass], *taperrnat* [coarse seashore grass] that they would use. Some of the trails they used on the coast over there have closed up today. Some trails that women used year after year were about this deep. The trails there were only used by women and not men. The coastline along both sides of our village was covered with trails used by women. And inland behind our village were trails used by men, trails leading to sloughs. They were trails for men who stayed in the village during falltime and didn't go to fall camps, who went back there to harvest blackfish that were abundant during that time. Women weren't the only ones who went out on the land during summer. Men also went out on foot with backpacks and traveled the land. That's what everyone did during fall until freeze-up.

Then just before freeze-up the women would go again and collect *qayikvayiit* [wheat grass] and common grass. They gathered the grass into bundles and placed them side by side and piled them in a mound, and some mounds were very steep and wide. They'd stack up [the grass bundles] on the tundra. They would also make a braided grass rope and use it to tie up the grass mounds to secure them. Then they placed loose grass on top, putting a covering on it to keep rain from getting inside. They layered the grass upside down like this on top, so that the water would cas-

tengcailkuciumaluteng cali, naqcimaluteng. Tua-i mecungyuunateng callartellriani ellalliurut'lallrungraaceteng tua-i tamakunek qaspengqelaameng. Tamaa-i tamakut arnat uksuryartullrani caliaqelallruit.

Napaluki waten. Ellamun tua-i piluki, uksuqu ellametelluki. Aqvataqluni taugaam tua-i; tamarmeng tua-i. Can'get amllepiatullruut maani enellret nuniitni.

Nunallernek uaken aqvataqluta enet uitallritnek. Assirtut tamakut. Cailkami maani pilriit tegglartut ilait assiinateng.

Tua-i-ll' uksuillerni pavani, can'get-am tamakut pirraarluki, tamakunek qayikva-yagnek-am call' kepliarluki nuussinek uluameggnek nanvallret iluitnek, kepurtur-luki. Arnacaluitnek taugaam can'get amlleriluki cali tua-i, ikamrat tua-i ucilirluki. Kuik-llu cikuyuilaku egmianun augna kuigat taryuungami, nanvat cikungraaki, aqvaluki tua-i tamakut qayikvayiit, atakumi enem'un itrulluki nasqiriluk' naparci-llugkanek, ceturrnautekanek tamakunek qayikvayagnek, kelugkarnek tamakunek kelirluteng. Angevkenaki tua-i qaill' cugtutaurluki waten. Angevkenateng tua-i, ar-turnarvkenak' kevguullerkait cuqluki, tuaten angtaurluki tupigluteng. Ukut nasqi-rilriit, ukut-wa uivtaarilriit, tupilriit akagtelluki.

Malruirrluteng. Nasqiristerluteng. Paingit waten elliurluki kassugcata-ll' tua-i ayagniqerluk' uivtevkenaki taluyatun taqluki elliaqluki, taukut-llu qaqivsiarluki uiv-qaurtet. Tamaa-i tamakut nasqirilriit, ceturrnautekat. Ilaita *five hundred* amllertal-rianek taqulluteng, amlleriniluki tuaten pitayugluteng piaqluteng *family*-t pikait-nek.

Yugcitacirteng cuqingaluku, naparcillugnek tua-i yugcitacirteng cuqluteng pi-tulliniluteng. Tuaten amllertalrianek nurusngaunateng tamakut tuatnaluteng cali, irnialilaameng ilait ner'arkanek. Tamakut cuqyutekluki; amllertatkepiarluteng pii-yuitellrulliniut. Tua-i cali wangkuta uksuillerni pamani, tuatnatuluteng. Camkut Kuigilngurmiut tamakunek calillrata nalliitni, uksuillerni cali caliluteng arnat, na-parcillugnek, ceturrnanek piarkanek. Tua-i-ll' asvaiqan qaqicata tamakut ikamrat-gun nutaan naparcilluut tamakut ucikluki, ekluki, qaluyarturluteng Kuigilngur-mun. Cuqluku tua-i asvaillerkaa, cikullerkaa Kuigilnguum.

cade down when it rained. The grass on top was placed like that all the way around [the mound]. The grass on top was also secured with braided grass to prevent them from coming off when it was windy. Even though it had been raining, the bundles of grass would be dry inside when you opened them, for they had been covered in that fashion. [Gathering grass] was the women's job in fall up until winter.

They kept [the bundles] upright. They placed them outside, left them outside during winter. But a person would go and get some; everyone in the community did that. There used to be a lot of grass around old houses.

We would go and gather [grass] from the house pits at old village sites. [Grass] in those places is good. Grasses that grow elsewhere are stiff, and some aren't good.

Then in the fall camps back there, after gathering common grass, they also used their semilunar knives to cut and gather wheat grass from inside dried lakes. They'd load sleds with a bunch of only female grass [without seeds] that they had gathered. And since the river over there where there was salt water didn't freeze, even though the lakes had frozen, they'd go and get the wheat grass they had gathered and bring them inside the house in the evening and begin twining and making the top sections of grass baskets used to store dried tomcod, using coarse grass as thread. They didn't make [the containers] very big, and they were about [eighteen inches] tall. They weren't made large so that they would be easy to lift. There was a group making the top sections and another group making the sides, rolling it as they went along.

There were two groups. Some were making the top openings. They twined the opening all the way around and didn't continue at the end, and the part where they stopped looked like the end of a fish trap. And then the other group would continue twining the rest of the basket. One group was called *nasqiristet* [ones making the tops], and the other was called *uivqaurtet* [ones going around]. Some would finish five hundred baskets and say that they had made enough to distribute to their families and stop.

They made enough baskets by determining the number of families in the community. They made sure they had enough to give each family, as some had more children to feed than others. They determined the size of the families; they didn't all get the same amount. And our families, in the fall camps back there, did that also. When people in Kwigillingok were working on those, the women in fall camps also worked, making grass containers for tomcod. Then when the ice was thick enough for traveling, when they were done making those, they loaded them onto the sleds, and they went to Kwigillingok to dipnet [for tomcod]. They would know when the Kuigilnguq River ice was thick enough to travel on.

~: *Carangllugnek piliat* :~

Ikaraliitekluki, asguilitaqluki, issratnguluki, piciatun tua-i kalngauluki tuaten. Ii-
tallret-llu cali tuacetun call' tua-i, taperrnanek avuurluki. Kellarvikluki, arnat-llu
kellarvikluki, canek caskumeggnek calissuutmeggnek imirluki. Kellarvikluki-gguq.
Aterluteng tua-i, paimikun ayagarnek tuaten aterluteng ilait. Ukiqlaarnek-llu. Ilait
atret cauciitelaranka aterpagtelallrit arnartaat.

Ayuqevkenateng, angtatkevkenateng-llu. Angutnun-llu ayagatulinun aturaqluki
iitallret alliqsauluki, waten suukiinun qalliuluki, ayagassuutet. Arilluut-llu unani
up'nerkarcuutet iitallernek call' tupigluki yuarirluki-ll' tua-i ukut ac'arirluki ilait
piaqluki. Imkunek iqertagnek arillungqetuut, *salmon*-aat qeciitnek, iqalluut. Up'nerkami unani, ellanglliurcuutet arilluut qayarluteng piyarat. Tamakunek aturluteng
cali ilupeqluki iitallret tupigluki. Kelugkarnek iluqliliyuitait.

Aliumatput-llu tua-i nayiit, carang.lluut tua-i imkut ulukarluki wavet-llu tua-i elliluki, itrulluki tua-i kumluanun, iluanun, ilait ceterrluki ukuanun-llu ilupeqaqluki,
man'a piinaku. Man'a melqulegmek aliuman pamalirneq una-ll' manulirneq melqu-
rrilngurmek. Tegulautnek qecignek aliumategnek aliumatengqetullruukut.

Tua-i-llu alerquatekluku yuilqumi pitsaqevkenata keglunret pikatkut tamakut
tamaa-i can'get arimalriit, aliumatem iluani arimalriit ungimaluteng, tamakunek
tegulluta kanvesqelluku avatemtenun. Kegluneq-gguq tua-i mallgusngairutqapiar-
tuq. Alikait-gguq tamakut, aliumatet ilupeqsait tamakut. Kaigaqameng taugaam
pituut-gguq.
      Tamakunek taumek piicuitellrulliniut, aliimatet piitnek. Alikait-gguq.

~: Things made of grass :~

They made the grass into *ikaraliitet* [grass kayak mats], *asguilitat* [grass windbreaks], as *issratet* [grass carrying bags], and *kalngat* [storage bags]. They used tall cotton grass with coarse seashore grass and twined them into things like that. And [women] used them as *kellarviit* [bags or pouches] and filled them with the tools they used. All [twined grass containers] had names, and they even called them *paimikun ayagat* and *ukiqlaat* [loosely twined, open-weave bags]. I never understood all the names they used for women's twined grass bags, pouches, and containers.

There were various kinds and sizes [of grass bags and containers]. And for men who hunted, they made grass socks to wear over their cloth socks when they·traveled. And some made grass liners out of cotton grass to use in fish-skin mittens that they wore down on the ocean during spring hunts. They had mittens made of fish skin, out of chum salmon. Fish-skin mittens were used during spring in bad weather for kayak travel. They wore them and lined them with twined cotton grass. They don't make liners out of coarse grass.

And we would flex the grass in a circular motion and place them in our ringed-seal skin gloves, wedging them inside and placing some inside the thumb, and we used them as liners, but we didn't put any [on top of the hand]. The top had fur on it, and the palm had no fur. We had skin gloves that we used to handle things when we worked.

And they told us that if we happened to get attacked by wolves out in the wilderness, that we should take the grasses that were crushed into small pieces and sprinkle them around us. They said that a wolf would not get close to us. They say they are afraid of the inner [grass] linings of those gloves. They say they only [attack] people when they are hungry.

That's why they never went without [grass] glove linings. They say [wolves] fear them.

Uksuarmi Uksumi-llu Neqsuryaraq

~: Uksuilleq :~

Tua-i-ll' ilait uterqaqluteng tayima, qakiiyiyuilnguut. Qakiiyarnek taugken piarkat utertevkenateng. Nutaan qakiiyimariaqameng utertaqluteng. Uksuillerni uitalriit maani tekitevkenateng Ilkivigmun arulairaqluteng. Pairpagmi uksuitullruut, Elilurvigmi-llu, wangkuta-llu Nallaukuviim avtellrani, Nallaukuviim kangrani. Maani Kangirnarmiut Kuigilngurmiut ukatiitni pitulit tua-i taukut, taukuni neqlitullruut, Qaurrayagarmi-llu uksuituut. Iiqaquq-llu ugna yuitaqluni, yungvailgan imkunek, Iiqaqurmiunek-am pilangellrukait nunaksagucatgu. Nunauvkenani tua-i tamana. Augkut tua-i Pairpagmiut, Qaurrayagarmiut, Elilurvigmiut, Nallaukuvigmi-wa wangkuta qulliuluta. Taukut tua-i ukatiitni uksuitulit.

Augkut taugken yaaqliput amaggun asguryarturaqluteng ilaput. Pavani kelumteni uitalriit Qipnermiut kuigatgun amaggun asguryarturaqluteng, pavavet Iglumun, Iglumi uksitulit, Nukalpiarugarmi, Arulacimi, Uauaualegmi, Kangirnarcarami. Maa-i makut uksillret, Egmiumanermi. Uksuiyarat, camp-at tamakut yungqerturatullret.

Ircenrrat tegullrata taum nunallra, Uauaualek. Yuarutai-gguq ircenrrarrlainartauluteng tua-i yuaruciaqami. Tamaani teguqatallratni-gguq niitengluki inartaqami akitminun qasturiinaraqluteng. Kiituan tua-i taringnariut yuarutnek atualriit. Tamakunek elitaqamiki yuaruciaqluni kassiyuqatarqata. Iquklicarait-wa "Ua-ua-uayarrai." Tua-i-ll'-am ilurain acilliniluku Uauaualegmek kuiga tamana, uksuiyaraa tauna camp-aa, kuiga taman' Uauaualegmek. Maa-i tua-i man'a tekilluk ateqluku.

Augna tuamtell' Arulaciq kuigullrunricaaqellrulliniluni ciungani. Neqliyat tamatum nalliini, qagkut elaqliput, Papegmiunun arulaitulit, yaaggun Ilkivigkun asgutullrulliniut. Qaurrarkun-llu asgurluteng, Kangirnam-llu kangrakun asgurluteng. Qagacicamegteggu-llu Kuigilngum kangrakun ketmurrluteng. Nanvak-llu augkuk Qikertarculinkuk imangqellragni anvikngamegneki, Qukaqlirkun nutaan

Fall and Winter Fishing

~: *Fall camp* :~

Then some families, those who didn't harvest silver salmon, began returning home. But those who would fish for silver salmon didn't return home. After they harvested silver salmon, they returned home. Those who lived around here and went to fall camps didn't reach home, but stopped at the Ilkivik River. They had fall camps at Pairpak River, and at Elilurvik River, and we were at the upper end of the Nallaukuvik River where it splits off. Those who stayed in fish camps on this side of Kongiganak and Kwigillingok also had fall camps at Qaurrayagaq River. And no one lived down there at Iiqaquq River before that one family started staying there. After they started staying there, they began calling that place Iiqaqurmiut. There were no village sites on that river. But there were Pairpagmiut, Qaurrayagarmiut, Elilurvigmiut, and our camp was the last camp at the upper section at Nallaukuvik River. Those were the families that went fall camping on this side.

But those who lived out there [toward Nelson Island, who had come to harvest salmon along the Kuskokwim River] would go upriver over there. Those who lived over and back behind us would return home up the Kipnuk River to Iglu River, ones who had wintering sites on Iglu River, on Nukalpiarugaq, Arulaciq, Uauaualek, and Kangirnarcaraq rivers. Wintering sites were on those rivers and on Egmiumaneq, too. Those were the fall camps where people always stayed.

Uauaualek was where the person who was taken by *ircenrraat* [extraordinary persons] had lived. They say when he composed songs, they were all about *ircenrraat*. They say right before they took him, he started hearing their sounds when he laid down on his pillow, and they got louder and louder. When he eventually was able to understand the sounds, they were [*ircenrraat*] singing songs. When he learned [their songs], he would compose songs about them right before they gathered for a dance festival. [The songs] ended with "*Ua-ua-ua-yarrai.*" Then his cousins named the river where he camped in the fall Uauaualek. Up to this day, that is its name.

Now, the Arulaciq River over there apparently wasn't a river in the past. And the people who went to harvest salmon, those who lived outside our area, those who usually stopped in Papegmiut on their way back [from summer fish camp] used to travel up the Ilkivik River. They also went up Qaurraq River, and they would also ascend the upper Kangirnaq River. And when they reached the headwater

cetuluteng cakmavet. Tevyuunateng. Pavagguirluteng naunraam nalliini, arulairluteng naunararnek iqvaraqluteng. Unaggun imarpigkun utertevkenateng. Piciryaraqluku tua-i tuaten qaugkut elaqliput, Arayakcaarmiut, Cevv'arnermiut, Qipnermiut,
camiut Cicingmiut. Tamakut-am apaalarait; Qantaarmiut. Tamaagguitullruut-
gguq tua-i amlleq. Ingkut taugaam Qipnermiut ilait pilangermeng, unaggurpalluq
taugaam pituluteng.

Tamaan' tumyarauluni. Tua-i caqerluteng-am taukut pavagguilriit — Carvan-
qegillillermek kuingqertuq. Carvanqegglillrem, Carvanqegglim igyaraanun arulairluteng iqvaqatarluteng-am tua-i. Una arnaq iqvaryarluni ayagluni tayima. Tekicami
tua-i, unuaquan tuamtell' ayagluni, ussugcitmek ayaulluni, imumek aug'umek nuna-
liurcuutmek. Tua-i qaill' piciinaku, kangiiturpek'naku-llu ilain. Cunawa-gguq ava-i
kuiliqataami nanvat piyunarqellriit cevtaarluki waten. Tamana Carvanqegglilleq
amaggun yaaqsigtuq qipluni, tumyarallrat. Tamatumek *shortcut*-amek piliqatarluni
arnaq tauna nanvat tamakut yuvrillrullinikai tuani piyunarqellerkait.

Tua-i qaqitevkenaki, nutaan iqvalliniluni cali. Ussugcitni-ll' tamana unilluku
tamaavet tuavet nanvat cevtellmi iliitnun. Unuaquan tuamtell' ayiimi tuamtell' tua-i
cevcilliniluni. Piyungami-ll' tua-i arulairluni iqvarluni cali utertellerkani cuqluku.
Tua-i-ll' cevtarkairucami, nangneq cevvluk' piani, kelutmun carvanngartelliniluni.
Unilluku tua-i. Naunranek tua-i pirraarluteng atsanek, ayagluteng Qukaqlirkun.

Tekicameng qakmavet nunameggnun nunameggni tua-i piluteng. Uksuan-llu
tua-i kassiyuqataata yuarutnek pinga'arcata, yuarucingarcata, arnaq tauna cevci-
lleq qasgilliniluni caqerluni. Itrami-ll' tua-i uicungani uicungangqelliniami-am
qanrulluku yuaruciqatarniluni. Cauyamek tegulluni yuarucilliniluni yuarutmek.
Elitnaurluki tua-i. Elicatgu-ll' tua-i aturteni tamakut aturyugngariata yurallliniluni,
cevcinguarluni. Tamatumek tamaa-i ussugcitmek tugaurturluku pirraarluku iku-
guaraqluku. Teguurluku elatmun pinguaraqluku. Kiartaqluni-llu-gguq tua-i, allamek agaiyaaruaraqluni. Tua-i qaqican nutaan iriallliniluni, tangaallermini-gguq ta-

lake, they would go down the upper Kuigilnguq River. And when those two lakes called Qikertarculik were filled with water, after they came out to those lakes, they would then go to Qukaqliq River and go down it. They never took the shortcut and portaged over. They traveled the upper route [on their way home from fish camp] during salmonberry picking season, and they would stop to pick salmonberries. They didn't go home by the ocean route. People who lived outside our area, Arayakcaarmiut, Cevv'arnermiut, Kipnuk, and Cicingmiut [always traveled home like that from fish camps]. People used to mention those place names, including Qantaarmiut. They said many people traveled that route. But even though some people from Kipnuk went home following that route, they mostly went home through the ocean route.

That [inland route] was a way people returned home [from summer camps]. One day, these people taking the inland route — there was a river called Carvanqeggliq. They stopped on the outlet of the Carvanqeggliq River, before it dried up, to pick berries. A woman went to pick berries. She came back and went again the next day, bringing an *ussugcin* with her, a tool used to pry the sod. Her companions didn't know what she was up to, and they didn't ask what she was doing [with the tool]. Apparently she was going to use it to make a river by cutting through land to create a channel from nearby lakes that she could get to. The river they normally traveled on, the old Carvanqeggliq, was long and straight and finally went around a bend way up there. That woman had apparently checked those lakes to see if she could [cut through them to make a river] before making that shortcut.

She didn't finish [cutting through all the lakes], and she picked berries again. She left her *ussugcin* there at one of the lakes that she had cut. Then when she left the next day, she made more channels from lakes. She stopped to pick berries when she wanted to, deciding when to go home. When she no longer had lakes to cut through to make channels, after cutting the last one, the water started to flow up toward the land. Then she left. And after picking salmonberries, they went to the Qukaqliq River and continued on.

When they reached their village out there, they stayed. Then when winter came and people started to work on songs for the dance festival, that woman who cut channels from lakes went to the *qasgi* one day. When she went in, since she apparently had a cousin there, she told him that she was going to compose a song. She took a drum and sang a song. She taught them the song. When they were able to sing it, she danced, pretending to cut land, making channels. She would pretend to dig land with the *ussugcin* and pry it out. She would take [the sod] and throw it to the side. Then she would turn her head left and right, looking around, and

man' cevvtani. Tua-i-llu kuigurcan Arulacimek acilliniluku. Arulaciqluku yuraan, yuraan taum pikestiin, Arulacimek acirluku. Ateqluku ava-i Arulaciq. Tamana-ll' kuillra kuigunrirluni.

Mat'um-llu maa-i nalliini, mat'um-llu nequtunerpakluku tamana cevtellra. Tamatum nalliini avani ciuqvani neqliyaratullratni, pavaggun-llu ilait uterqaqluteng. Tuaten tua-i ayuqellrulliniluteng.

Cali-ll' tamatum neqliyam nalliini qakiiyiaqameng, Ilkivik tua-i ingna ullagatullruat angyatgun. Teq'erkanek qakiiyarnek ucilirluteng ayautaqluki Ilkivigmun. Ilkivigmi teq'erluteng cali qemit kiugkut Cavunrem kiaqliin engeliitnun maavet acilqerratnun, nunapigmun qertulriamun. Tamaavet tamaa-i teq'ertutullruut. Ilait-llu kiavet kia-i Nunapigmiunun, Papegmiut uaqliq'lallritnun, up'nerkillritnun Qinarmiut. Tuavet cali teq'atullruluteng qakiiyarnek. Tua-i-am pitulit tuaten piuratuluteng ilateng pinrilengraata neqliyam nalliini, wani iquani neqsuryaram qakiiyarnek. Qakiiyiluteng tuaten tamakut.

Teqaunrilnguut-llu assigtarkiurluki *sealskin*-anek, melqurrilngurnek, issurinek meqcirluk' nillaumaluteng. Eliqluki taugken tua-i uivenqellrianek waten qeterkaitnek. Makut tua-i elanrit ilutuluki, paingit allanek call' piarkauluki. Mingeqluki qayalilriatun uqumek maqngairutelluki keluteng. Amilriatun tua-i umciggluki ilululiki tuamtell', caqukait qakiiyaat, qayatun mingqurluki. Tamakunun tamaa-i caqunaurait, tuq'urluki nekegqurluki tua-i qecigglainait qakiiyaat. Iciw' uqurilriit. Muirata-ll' tua-i tamakut nek'eggiata nutaan patukaat una cali asuirucirluku, umciggluki tua-i mingeqluki tua-i. Putut taugaam augkut qeciit aciit teguyararkait uivetmun waten qavciuluteng teguyarait. Ellianek aterluteng tamakut qakiiyaarnek qecignek imalget.

Puyuqeqerluki kinertat. Uquriameng taugaam kinrumayuitai, makucetun kangitnertun. Kemegtuumaita qeciit, umciggluki tua-i tuaten mingeqnaurait qaingit tua-i, umciggluki. Ellianek aterluteng. Tuatnauratuluteng tua-i. Tamakunek tua-i pimariaqameng nutaan utertaqluteng.

chant again. At the end, she swayed her body while checking out the lake she had
cut open. When the river developed there, when she danced using her arm movements to portray what she had done, they named the river Arulaciq [lit., "Dance
Movement"]. We still call it Arulaciq today. And [Carvanqeggliq] dried up and was
no longer a river.

And today, the river she made is wider than our river. Back in those times, long
ago when people always moved to fish camps, some people from over there returned
home through the inland route. That's how people lived in those days.

Also, back during the fish camp season, when they were fishing for silver salmon,
they would go over to the Ilkivik River with boats. They'd load the boats with silver salmon and bring them to the Ilkivik River to bury and ferment them. Then
they would bury them underground at the Ilkivik River along the edge of those
bluffs back there near the upper Cavuneq River, at the base on high ground. They
would bury [fish to ferment]. Some would also go to Nunapigmiut, downriver from
Papegmiut, a spring camp of people from Qinaq. That was where they buried silver
salmon. Those who did that [made fermented silver salmon] every summer, even
though others around them didn't do so during fishing time. Some of those people
prepared silver salmon like that.

They made containers for dried silver salmon that they hadn't buried underground out of dried spotted-seal skins with the hair removed. Then they cut round
pieces to use as a bottom for the bags. They made the containers long and deep,
and cut another piece to cover the opening. They sewed them like a kayak skin covering, so the oil would not seep out of their stitches. They sewed the dried silver
salmon containers tightly, both outside and inside, reinforcing the seams with grass
like they did when sewing a kayak skin covering. They stored the dried fish inside
those, packing and stepping on them, constantly putting the dried silver salmon
inside. You know how oily they are when dried. When [the containers] were full
and tightly packed, they would sew the cover on with grass inserted in the seam.
But they left several of those loops along the edge of the skin to use as handles. The
containers that were filled with dried silver salmon were called *elliat*.

The [silver salmon] had been dried and briefly smoked. But they weren't fully
dried like chum salmon since they had so much fat. They would pack the fish in
skin containers and sew the tops securely. [The filled containers] were called *elliat*.
They always fixed silver salmon like that. After harvesting [silver salmon], they
would return home.

∾: *Kuiget carritullrat* :∾

Tuamtell' uksuarmi uksuillernun tekitaqamta, Nallaukuvigmun, atama alraparlua ayautelaraanga, wall'u apa'urluma. Kinguqliirutenka-ll' ukut nasaurluut-llu augkut ilakluki. Avvluta. Taluyiryarat taugken neqelget tekicamteki; kelugkaat waten aqevlalartut, mermi akungqaluteng kuigem iluani. Kiagmi naullret nalaaqameng aqevlertengaqluteng akungqangluteng kuignun. Muragnek qaill' taktalrianek tegumiirluta, akiqliqluta waten, kuiggaq kelugkat aciirluku ulpegtaqluki waten. Kuiget nuyuurluki tua-i imutun, assirivkarluki nuyuulriatun. Kuiggaat canegmek aqevlalriamek akungqalriamek piirutelluki carrirturcetnaurait kelugkaat. Kelugkarnek avatengqerrsulartut tamakut. Taluyiryarat tua-i tuaten carrirluki, assirivkarluki. Makut-llu carvanrem pillri, malikluki cali qecuumalriit, nuggluki tua-i carrirluki. Qaqitaqan allamun nugtarutaqluta. Tuatnavkatuluki taluyartarkait civpailgata, canimelnguut maani neqsuryarat. Yaaqvani uitalrianun ayagacuitellruitkut. Uksurpailgan tua-i tamakut carrircetaqluki kuiggat ayagalluta. Ernerni qavcini tua-i, qaqitaqata canimelnguut tamakut, tevuraluni piyaraunrilnguut.

Tua-i taugken tamakut qaqicata nutaan katelluteng nunapiameggnun, Kuigilngurmun, wall'u Qipnermiut, Kangirnarmiut, Tunutuliarmiut-llu, tamalkurmeng pituameng tuaten. Neqsuryarameggnun pissuryarameggnun-llu ayagatullruut avani pinricuunateng. Ukut tua-i nunapiat carrarmek yugluteng, amllenrilngurnek. Ceturrnanek taugaam piaqata nunamteni yaani ikamratgun ullagluki qalutullruut. Tua-i-ll' ceturrnanek kumlangluki iterqerraarluk' ataam *camp*-amun tagluteng. Angutait nallmegteggun qaluyugngalriit tamalkirrluteng pivkenateng.

∾: *Arnat qalurpagteggun qalulallrat* :∾

Qalurpiit atam augkut ang'ut. Angluteng tua-i qalurpallraat. Tua-i-llu kiagmi napalriignek waten piluki, ecirluk', waten ayuqluku qalum painga. Tamakunek-llu marayanun kapulluku uksurpailgan qalutuluteng. Kinernerkanek ceturrnanek piluteng. Arnat taugaam kiimeng, arnarrlainaat. Caneg-atkullernek all'uteng, ellalliurcuutnek-llu qaspernek irnerrlugnek all'uteng, naqugluteng ivrarluteng tua-i. Caneg-

~: *Cleaning streams* :~

Then during fall when we got to our fall camp, our camp in Nallaukuvik River, my father would take me with him in his kayak, or my grandfather. My late younger siblings, my younger sisters, came, too. We'd split up. Then when we got to rivers where fish traps were usually set, *kelugkaat* [coarse grass] hung down the sides, dangling down into water along the sides of rivers. When it died after summer, the coarse grass would begin bending down and fall into rivers. We children would stand along the riverbanks and begin pulling back the grass from the water using sticks. We pulled back the grass and opened up the rivers as though we were combing them like hair. They'd let us [children] clean out rivers by pulling the coarse grass away from water. The rivers there tend to be covered with coarse grass from the sides. We'd clean the rivers where they usually set wooden traps and get them ready. We also cleaned the floating grass that had been pulled off by the current. When one area in the river had been cleared, we'd move to another area and continue cleaning. We'd go and clean the spots where traps would be set not far from our camp. They never brought us to places far away from camp. They'd bring us out and let us clean the spots in rivers before freeze-up. We'd go out several days and clean the spots in nearby rivers where we didn't have to portage over land.

Then after fishing in those [cleaned-out] rivers, they returned to their wintering sites, either to Kwigillingok, Kipnuk, Kongiganak, or Tuntutuliak, because people from those villages all go out and do that [in fall]. People went to their camps every season to harvest fish, hunt, and trap. The wintering site would just have a few people left staying behind. But when tomcod were harvested, people used to just fish with dip nets nearby. Then after putting tomcod in storage, after it got cold they'd go up to their camps again. Men who were able to go went out to dipnet, and some stayed behind.

~: *Women dipnetting with large dip nets* :~

They used big dip nets. They were huge dip nets. Then in the summer two posts were placed, and the rim of the dip net would look like this. And they fished before freeze-up by staking the posts into the mud. They would harvest tomcod they were going to dry. Only women would fish at this time. They'd wade in the water and fish wearing old parkas, seal-gut raincoats, and tying their waists with a belt.

aturallernek allanek all'uteng, aturluteng arnat qalutullruut, kuigem un'um ceniini waten kiaqliqluteng. Maanelnguut taugaam, maani kuicuarmi qalulriit amllernek canglallruut. Ugna ua-i uaqvaarni qaluyarallrat uitauq. Initaat tua-i amlleret imangaqluteng kinernernek piirrallugnek ceturrnanek. Tamakukarcurluteng arnat qalutullruut.

~: *Ipukaquyaraq* :~

Tua-i-ll' uksuan kanuuqut, muriit qaill' waten ellegtaurluteng, takluteng, akaggluki, nuugit cingigluki, marayamun kapucugngaluteng camavet.

Qaluluteng taugken tua-i, ernerni pingayuni pivallutullruut. Ceturrnat amllepialallruut elakami. Atakumi taugaam ulerpagmi qalutullruut. Tua-i *three minutes* tayima, wall' *four minutes* qalu akungqaqercetaqluku, civingavkaraqluku camavet, angtuat qalukayiit. Nequtupiarluteng tua-i angluteng cakneq iluit. Neqa amlleq teguyugngaluku. Waten-llu kuigmi takaayiluki qaill' waten neqututaluki anluat, kuigem iluani callartaqluki, qaill' taktaluki tuaten. Kanuuqutek-llu tua-i un'a cuqerluni; yaggluku kanuuquk ciuqrakun yagnermek, man'a-ll mayuurnera waten piqerluku. Qalum neqututacirkaqaa tauna. Man'a acia yagneruluni.

Waten kanuuquk ayuqetuuk. Muriik tua-i akagcimalutek waten, iqukek cingikegglutek. Man'a-wa maani tapraq, augna-wa maani murak cali. Ipukautii-ll' wani qillrumaluni, muragaq, waten qillrusngaluni. Una call' qillrusngaluni. Nutaan-llu wavet qalu qemirluku, elliluku. Aug'um iqua angluni tua-i, una taugaam qukaa quungaurluni. Ukuk-llu waniwa camani kuigem terr'anun marayamun kapusngaarkaulutek, muriik.

Waten kanuuqut ayuqluteng. Tupirluteng. Ipukautiik-wa wavet nemrusngiimi, cali ukatmun ayagluni. Una waniwa qalum uitayaraa. Tua-i-ll' ukatmun kuigmun unavet, carvaniqan ukatmun, carvanra cauluku. Wall' ulyukan ukatmun caulluku, qalutaa maantelluku. Kuigem terr'anun ukuk kapullukek marayamun camavet. Waniwa kanuuquk maa-i makuk, ipukautiik-wa. Uksumi waniw' qalussuutellrit maani.

Women would wade along the river down there and fish. They would be women who were staying here, and those fishing in the small river here caught a lot of tomcod. The area where they fished is down there below. And fish racks used to fill up with many long, braided strands of tomcod hanging to dry. Women used to dipnet for tomcod for drying.

~: Dipnetting for tomcod :~

Then when winter came the *kanuuqut* [log supports connected to a long handle], the long wooden pieces there were about this wide, they'd carve them to make them rounded and whittle their tips to make a sharp point so they could be pushed into the mud down below.

Then they dipnetted, usually for three days. There were many tomcod in the fishing holes. They only dipnetted at night during high tide. They would drop the dip net under water for three or four minutes, letting the huge dip net sit in water during that time [before pulling it up]. The nets were wide and very deep. They could hold a lot of fish at once. And on the river's ice, they'd make fishing holes about [one *ikuyagneq*, the distance between elbow and index finger] wide and as long as [one *yagneq*, the distance between one's outstretched arms]. The dipnet frame down there had a standard measurement. Beginning from the front of the *kanuuquk*, they'd extend their arms for the measurement, and the handle was measured like this. That is the width of the dip net. The measurement for the bottom was one *yagneq*.

The *kanuuquk* looked like this. There are two rounded logs with sharpened ends. Then the skin rope would be here, and another log was situated here. And its long handle would be tied here, a piece of wood tied down like this. And this section was also tied down. Then they tied the net and attached it here. The end [of the net] was very wide, but the middle section would be narrower. These two [logs] would be staked in the mud underwater.

This is how the *kanuuqut* looked. They were lashed on. And since their *ipukautiik* [handles] were attached here with binding, [the handle] continued going [down]. This was where the net was normally placed [on the dip net]. Then by turning it this way down in the river, if the current was going in this direction, they placed it so it faced the current. Or if the tide was coming in, placing it facing this way, letting the net stay on this side. Then you'd thrust these two down in the mud at the bottom of the river. These two [wooden pieces] here are the *kanuuquk*, and here is their *ipukautiik* used to dip the net underwater. They used these types of dip nets around here in winter.

Cikum acianlluni, qainga man' cikumaluku man'a ngelkarrluku. Tua-i ul'aqan, una, ula mayuraqan kit'aqluni qaill' pitalriamek. Makuit takluki pitullruit, agaavet qaamalkucirluki-ll' ilaita piaqluki.

Una, uuggun qillrulluku canek imirluku qaamailngurnek, agarrluk' wavet pugleryugngairutelluki. Qalu taugken tua-i maavet qemiulluku, maavet-llu, maavet-llu. Tamalkuan, iqua-ll' tua-i ava'anlluni yaaqvani, kuigem iluani camani.

ALICE: Tua-ll' qaill' mayurrluku?

FRANK: Una tang waniwa, anluarluni waten ayuqelriamek. Cikuunani tua-i waniwa. Anluat waten usguku'urluteng kuigmi, qalussuutet, akulait cikumaaqluteng. Itukurluteng tua-i. Naparrluki waten piaqluki, civtaqluki maavet, anluaq waten ayuqevkarluku. Ukatmun carvanirluni. Tua-i-ll' ipukataan, man'a ukatmurrluku qaamalkutairluku, palurrluku camna nuggluku. Quukatarluku una, ukuk-llu tekicagnek yuut ikayuqluteng ukugnegun teguluku, kingupiarluteng mayuulluku. Yuut piyunariaqameng teguaqluki ukut. Ikayuqluteng yuut mayurrluku tua-i neqa amllepiaq.

Tua-i-ll' antesciigalian, yuk iterluni qalum iluanun. Qaivalria uryuumaluni neqnek. Anluaq-llu tua-i una uyanglluk' wavet, avlerrluni qalum iluanun piluni, una yaantelluku tunumini, nayumiqaluku yuut. Qantamek muragmek, qalum iluani wanlluni, ilua qalu neqnek imalek, ceniinun maavet avlerrluni qalum iluanlluni, ceturrnat tua-i nutaan taumek qaluurluki uryuqtaartelluku una amlemikun amatmun. Yuut-wa call' pamkut qanikciurutnek pikiit. Ikegliaqan kingupiaqanirluku cayukanircetaqluku. Tua-i-ll' piyunarian, nutaan yuk tauna an'ngan mayurrluku. Ceturrnaq amllepiaq tua-i. Ellma tua-i *five minutes*-llu pilalliuq tayima aipaagni uitaqercetaqluku qalu. Uitavallakuni tua-i arturnariqercugngaluni. Waten elliurluteng neqet puukaqulriit, niicugnilriani maavet, ugaan carvanrem pillri, pikai.

It was underneath the ice, and up on top it was frozen up to this section here. When the tide came up, this one here, when the water came up, it would go down into the water to about this point. They made this [handle] long, and some put something as a weight on [the handle to hold it down in the water].

You'd tie this one here and fill it with something heavy, and hang it [on the handle] so [the dip net] stayed submerged and wouldn't float up. Then you'd knit and attach the net here, and here and also here. All of it [was attached to the frame], and its end would be way over there, way down in the water in the river.

ALICE: So, how did they bring it up?

FRANK: See this [photograph B12, B13] here, it has a hole cut open like this in the ice. You can see [the water in the opening]. They made holes like this on the river situated in a line side by side, holes where nets were dipped, and between the holes there'd be solid ice. The holes were situated on the ice in a line side by side. They would drop the dip net into the hole by standing it upright like this into a hole that was cut open like this. The river current would be flowing in this direction. Then when you were about to pull the dip net up, you'd pull it this way and remove the weight attachment, then you'd turn the net below upside down and pull it up and out of the water. You'd put this part on your shoulder and pull, and as the net came up and these two became visible, men came forward and took these two and began pulling and walking back, and the whole net was pulled up onto the ice. People would take these and help pull up the net filled with many fish.

And if the dip net was unable to come up through the ice hole, a man would get inside the net. The portion of the net that came up through the hole was overflowing with fish. The man would get inside the net with his legs apart and peer into the hole, this part here would be on his back, people would hold him as he looked into the hole. Then with a wooden bowl, the man would be standing right here in the net, and the net was filled with fish, he'd be standing with his legs apart in the net and use the bowl and begin pulling fish out of the net between his legs. And there'd be more men behind him using shovels to push the fish farther back as they came. After a number of fish had been retrieved, they'd pull the dip net farther out of the hole. Then eventually the man would come out, and the dip net was pulled completely up. Many tomcod would be pulled up from that one dip. I think they'd only keep the net underwater for about five minutes before pulling it up. If it was kept in for a little bit too long, it could get very difficult to pull up. As the strong current moved the fish and they bumped into each other, we could hear the sound of the movement.

Ikayuqluteng taugken tua-i nugtaqluki, waten ellma tua-i akungqaqerluki. Mui-raqameng cakviurnarquq cakneq. Tua-i-ll' man'a anluat ualirnerat kuigem cikua wa-ten ayuqliriqercan, aaluuyinga'arcan, taqesqelluki qayagpagluteng, kivgutengniluki. Ceturrnam amllertacian ciku acitmurtelluku waten aaluuyingevkarluku. Cakanir-pailgata camkut taqluteng. Malruirrluteng waten kiaqliqluteng qalutullruut. Kuik tua-i waten tus'artaqluku. Ayuqluteng tua-i nugciaqluteng.

Nutaan nugqaarluki makut tamakut imkut nutaan imirluk', naparcilluut. Man'a cali uitallerkaat carrirluku qanikcanga'artellrukan cikulraar. Muiraqata tua-i qamur-luk' piaqluk, elkartaqluki. Nengllituan-llu unuk kumelqerluki. Unuaquan-llu tua-i nutaan ekilluki palurqurluki-am tamakut, akwaugaq atakumi cangtalteng.

Tua-i-ll' atakuan cali aipiriluteng. Tua-i taqesqelluki qalunermek kivgut'ngarta-qata. Imiriluteng ilait malrugni qalunregni, atakugni malrugni. Qanernaurtut tua-i-gguq piviirutut ellait. Apcaceteng ilait pinaurtut *five hundred*-gguq amllertalrianek imiriarkaullruut. Tua-i-gguq assigtarkairutut. Tua-i taqluteng qalunermek.

Cipcameng-llu tua-i tamakut assigtailnguut, augkunun, elliviit ceturrnanek imi-tukteng, nunamun mit'elluki elliviktuit ceturrnarrlainarnek imitukteng, qeciit caquil-ngurnek, angluaqerpek'nateng tua-i. Tamakunun ilakuateng taguqurluki. Ellaitnek tua-i assigtaqevkarluki, qulvaggun uuggun callamaluteng. Tuaggun kuv'aqluki ilua-nun. Ciumek-llu tamakut qimugtenun nerevkarturatuit caquilnguut.

Tua-i taugken kumlangata tamakut, nutaan tua-i wangkuta tan'gaurlurni nanger-telluta. Taguquriluta qayat imkut qamigautaitgun. Ernerpak tua-i kuigem ceniini tua-i kelutmun angaqalriarurtuq pitatemtenek taguqurilrianek. Pingkut-wa anga-yuqaput elliviim nutaan elatiini iterqurilriit tamakunek. Mat'um-llu angenqaq-luku, ang'aqluteng waten elliviit. Muirata-ll' tua-i, pagkut waten pillrit, imirluki call'. Pagaavet, makut qerratalriit, qupluki, tamakut engelqerritnek imiraqluki. Amiik tua-i man'a tekilluku ellamun anyaraa, muiqapiarluki. Ilait-llu iterviitequlriit qer'at qaingitnun elliqerluki cali. Tamalkurmeng tua-i tuaten pituluteng.

Tua-i taugken uksurpak tua-i ceturrnautekluki tua-i; nerluki tuaten qimug-tetuumarmeng. Urungnaarluk', kumlanruluki, nerluki tua-i, kinerneritnek tuaten

But they would help one another to pull them out, after keeping it underwater for a short while. They are extremely hard to pull out when they're full. And when the river ice in the area down below the fishing holes started to [sag], when it began to slant, they would yell to them to stop dipnetting, saying that the ice was starting to sink down due to the weight of the fish. There were so many tomcod that it weighed down the ice and made it slanted. They stopped while many fish were still swimming underwater. They used to dipnet in two rows up and down the river. In each row there would be a line of men fishing all the way across the river. They'd each pull up the same amount of fish.

After pulling the fish out, they would pack them in grass baskets. First they cleared the area where they would be placed if the glare ice had been snowed on. Then when [the baskets] were full, they would drag them and place them in a good spot. Since it was cold, [the fish] would freeze overnight. Then the next day, they pried them off and turned over the baskets filled with fish they caught the night before.

Then the following night, they fished again. They told them to stop dipnetting when the ice started to sink due to the weight of the fish. Some would fill their containers in two dipping periods, in two evenings. They would say they no longer had [baskets to fill]. When asked by others, they would say that they were planning to fill five hundred baskets. They would say they had no more baskets to fill. They would stop dipnetting.

When they caught more than their containers could fill, they would bring the leftover tomcod and store them in those storage places that weren't big, the storage places that were directly in the ground. The storage place had an opening at the top, and the fish were dropped inside through that hole. The tomcod that weren't put away in baskets were fed to the dogs.

But when [the fish in the baskets] were frozen, they had us boys begin working. We would begin hauling them up to the land with kayak sleds. All day long, the river's edge was filled with boys hauling baskets toward land. And our parents were up there by the cache bringing in those baskets one by one. And the caches were larger than this room. And when the cache was full, they'd fill those open spaces up there as well. By splitting [some baskets], they'd fill the space up there with baskets that could fit in there. They would fill the caches completely, right up to the doorway that led outside. And some that couldn't fit inside the cache were placed [on platforms] on top of fish racks. That's what everyone did.

That would be their tomcod supply all winter long; they ate them and their dogs ate them as well. They ate them partially thawed and frozen, they also ate them

avuaqluteng. Ikamrat tuaten tekitellriit piyugaqata naparcillugnek cikirluki ayauce-
taqluki, maavet. Ukunun-llu Qinarmiunun pilriit, Qinarmiunun tekitaqata ayauce-
taqluki. Qipnermiut-llu ingkut tua-i ceturrnassaaqutullrulriit. Ingkut-llu yaaqliput
Anuuraarmiunek pitullrit qaluyaraqameng uani nunat uakaraatni qerait uitatull-
ruut, Anuuraarmiut, ceturrnanek imilallruit taukut qalukengameggnek. Kuigilngurmun tailuteng angutait qaluyartutullruameng. Qer'anek tua-i tamakunek nek'egvig-
luki. Imirluki tua-i qer'at qalliqurluki tua-i naparcilluit.

[Tuanlluteng] uksurpak. Tua-i taugken iliini up'nerkillernun tua-i ayaganga'ar-
teqatarqameng, elagyat tamakut cuqluki ikirrluki urungarpailgaki, kuigmun atrau-
qurluki cali, ilakuarkat, cuqluki. Sagciluteng tuamtell' arnat tua-i, yay'ussanek-am
pilaqait sagqurluki, piirriluki pivkenaki. Tamakut-am acilarait tamakunek yay'ussa-
nek. Assirtut.

Amllerriaqata ilait nunani, tamakukarugaat kuigem iluanun kuvuurluki, naruyat
tua-i amllepiat nutaan. Tuatnatuluki tua-i nangqatanritaqata tua-i urugpailgata
atrauqurcetaqluki kuigmun. Sagcirraartelluki yay'ussarkanek [naruyat amllepiarlu-
teng]. Maa-i-llu pinanrirluteng. Tamakut taqluki tua-i neqet, yay'ussat neqkegtaa-
raat. Qalunanrirluteng, ilait-llu ceturrnautaitnaurtut. Wii taugaam piicuitua, cayui-
rut'ngerma tua-i tutgaraanka ingkut aaralaamteng tua-i.

Anagutpialallruut ceturrnat. Uksurpak neqairucuitelliniuq ceturrnanek, taugaam
mikliluteng ceturrnayagaat unani ketemteni. Uksurpak tua-i neqairucuunani un'a
kuik ceturrnanek. Augkut-llu yaaqliput qaluyuunateng, ukurmiut taugaam qalutuluteng.
    Ceturrnat amllerssaaqellriit avani-llu, taugaam piiyuilameng qaluyuilnguut. Maa-
vet taugaam ceturrnassaagaqluteng kumlanernek.
    Kat'um kanani nerpakayallraam kiatiini qaluyaraq uitallruuq. Kanani-ll' uatiini
cali qaluyaraq uitaluni. Malruirrluteng waten qalutullruut kanani kiaqliqluteng.

Taugaam neqet makut ceturrnat allayuugut. Neqkenritestaita ilaita naulluu-
nakait. Puvyugtut ilait, ilait taugken piiyuunateng. Calriit-wa pilartat.

Puvqerrayuitellruunga. Makumiut piyuitellruut neqkestait, puvqerrayuunateng,

dried with other meals. And when travelers who arrived here wanted some, they would give them baskets of tomcod to take home with them. And those who traveled out to Qinaq, when people went to Qinaq, residents of that village would have visitors bring them home. And people from Kipnuk used to come over and harvest tomcod. And when the ones from the place over there called Anuurarmiut came to dipnet, their fish racks were located just down from our village. They used to fill them with tomcod that they dipnetted. Their men would come to Kwigillingok to dipnet and used fish racks to store their catch. They would fill the fish racks with piles of tomcod baskets.

[They kept them there] all winter. But when they were going to start traveling to spring camps, they determined how much was in those underground caches and opened [the baskets] before they started melting, and brought the leftovers down to the river, after determining how much they needed. The women would then scatter the fish they call *yay'ussat*, and they didn't braid them with grass and hang them. They call [fish like that] *yay'ussat*. They are tasty.

When they had a large supply, they scattered [the leftovers] on the river. That's what they did with them when they weren't going to finish them. The leftover tomcod were brought down to the river and scattered while still frozen. Many gulls were around after they scattered them. They no longer do that today. They have stopped making those delicious *yay'ussat*. People don't dipnet for tomcod anymore. And some families don't have a supply of tomcod. But I always have a supply, even though I don't go out and hunt anymore, because I always encourage my grandchildren to go out and get them.

There used to be many, many tomcod back in those times. The [rivers] never ran out of tomcod all winter, but the tomcod got smaller in size down there. Tomcod swam in our river down there all winter long. And the villages over there beyond our village never dipnetted, but here in our village they would dipnet for tomcod.

There are many tomcod out there, too, but they don't dipnet for them. But they'd come here and get frozen tomcod.

They used to dipnet above that big house sitting on the riverbank down there. They also used to dipnet below the building. There were two spots where they used to dipnet down there.

But these tomcod are odd. Those who don't normally eat them are allergic to them. Some people swell up when they eat them, but some don't. I don't know why some people react when they eat them.

I never swelled up from eating them. Because it was part of their diet, the peo-

qaugkut taugaam kiaqliput. Taumek maani piaqata, apqurluki pitukeput. Ceturr-nanek nereksaitniaqata nerevkayuunaki, tuatnanayukluki.

~: *Can'giiret* :~

Aninirpek'nateng can'giiret inerquutaitut. Qaill' pivkenaki tua-i cangtaqaqatki. Ani-nit taugaam, aninit imkut, qagrulluteng ciku urugluku; urugtelluku qagrutetuut can'giiret aninit, quyurrluteng tua-i quyurmeng.

Aciani, urugluku-ll' tua-i ciku. Cikua urugtelluku puqlameggnek, qilairutelluku uitallerkarteng. Ayagyugallratni tegularluki waten pisqevkenaki, ayagnillratni. Mil-qagtetuit-gguq-am tuaten piaqata. Tuatnayaaqerraarluteng catairulluteng tayima. Tua-i taugaam ak'arraurcan nutaan tegularluki piyugngaluki. Imkunek taugaam qenuirutnek apqaitnek piluki pisqelluki, tegulaqsaunaki. Kencialiqercameng-gguq taugken tegulangermeng qaill' pingaunateng. Amllepiarluteng call' pituluteng tama-kut can'giiret, urugulluku-llu. Nanvat-llu kuigilngermeng pituluteng nunamteni avani. Kuilegtun can'giiret amllepiaraqluteng quyurrluteng, nanvat.

Tua-i-ll' tuaten quyurrluteng pirraarluteng qaill' pitariameng qurrluteng irnilu-teng melumeggnek. Irnirraarluteng-llu tuquluteng. Urugaqan tamakut aninillret yuilqumi anguaraqamta pinauraput nanvam terr'a tua-i ak'aki yaaqvanun can'giiret temellrit qaterluteng nanvam terr'ani kisngalriit, nalamalriit. Allamian taugken call' tua-i tamakunek irniameggnek cimingluteng. Kuigilngermi tuaten ayuqut un'gaani nanvat, neqerluteng can'giirnek. Aninituluteng-llu kuilegtun.

Tamakunek piyunqegtut, nanvat quuyaitni. Piciatun kuigni pituut. Tamakut-llu imarmiutaat cuignilnguut-llu tagenqurritni pituluteng. Imarmiutaat pugvingqelar-tut-am ilait nunakun, camaggun-llu kuigmun call' piyarauluni. Cali-am tua-i ani-niraqameng nallunarqerraarluni, yaaggun pugvigkun nunamelngurkun, can'giiret ilaita cingluki anevkatuit nunam qainganun, anlluki camkut can'giiret igtem ilua-

ple of this village never swelled up when they ate them, but those from up the Kuskokwim River swelled up when they ate them. That was why we always asked them if they had eaten them before they ate them here. If they said that they had never eaten them before, we discouraged them from eating, fearing they might have a reaction.

~: *Blackfish* :~

There are no rules against [catching] blackfish when they are just around [in rivers and lakes] and not in *aninit*. They just caught them, and there were no rules. But blackfish, because there were so many of them in one spot they'd melt the ice and break through. When blackfish broke through ice because of their number, they call them *aninit*.

They would be under the ice, and the ice above them would melt. The heat they created would melt the ice above, and where they were would become open water. People were told not to take them when they were gathering in that spot. It was said that when people began taking them right away after they started to gather in one spot, they would disappear. You wouldn't bother them at first, but later they could be taken. People were told to take them with their *qenuirutet* [ice dippers] and not their hands. When they no longer required special treatment, it was okay to take them by hand. There would be many, many blackfish in one spot, and the ice above where they gathered would melt. *Aninit* even come out in lakes without outlets over in my home area. Many, many blackfish would be gathered in lakes and narrows.

Then after gathering like that, some time later they'd lay their eggs *qurrluteng* [lit., "urinating"]. And after laying their eggs, they would die. After the ice melted, when we paddled our kayaks and came to spots where the blackfish had gathered, the water would be very deep. And down at the bottom of the water we'd see many, many bones of blackfish that had died. The following winter the eggs that had hatched would grow and replace the ones that died the previous winter. Blackfish live in some lakes with no outlets down in my home area. And they'd gather and spawn in them like they do in rivers.

[Blackfish] like to gather and spawn on the narrows and sloughs in lakes. They gather and spawn anywhere in the river. They also gather in the mink and land otter runs. Some mink have passages that lead out onto the land and also another passage underground that goes out to the water in the river. Sometimes when blackfish gather to spawn in the water down below and you don't know they are there,

nun cingluki ilateng. Tamaaggun nalkaqluki. Tagenqurrita nallaitnun tua-i callarr-luki can'giirnek pilartukut.

Elpengcaulluku nunanun. Nunat piyulriit tamarmeng tua-i tuaken aqvauquriluteng can'giirnek.

Cauluki nertuit qululiluki, uksuarciluki-llu. Nutarat can'giiret, makutgun maa-i pitulit makucitgun; taugaam angluki. Kuik-llu nequtungraan cuqluku iluliralegnek waten ayuqelrianek iluliriluki, ilulirpagnek-gguq. Taluyarcirluki-llu angtuanek, can'giircuutengqellriit pituut kuik cuqluku. Engelqaqellratnek taugken tua-i civvluku, avatek kuigem agtuumaurtelluku waten. Can'giiq tua-i naugguirngairutelluku, maaggun taugaam qalirnerakun.

Waten can'giircuucituut. Camna-ll' yuvrinqegcaarluku taluyat uitavigkaat. Picurlaumakan, taluyituli elisnganrilkan, cangyurkiciiqut, aciat kitugteluaqerluku pinrilkani. Taumek civteqataqumteki aciita camkut uitallerkaat, waten nanrumallerkaat, yuvrituarput camna kautuarturluku. Manialnguut manigartaqluki, manigtaqluki, tusngacurlagcetevkenaki. Kanayagcetevkenaki-llu, taugaam assirluki taluyat uitallerkait. Picurlaumalriit tua-i, cangtarkateng amllengraata, ikgellruluteng ilameggni cangnaurtut. Kitugcaceteng taugken elisngalriit cangyuriqerrluteng, cangtait amlleriqerrluteng.

Tua-i-llu amllerrluteng pituut, anyunga'artaqata-gguq. Mikuriqertaqata anyunga'arrnituit can'giiret. Taluyat muiqertaqluteng tua-i unugpaagaq-llu iliini, mikuriqertaqata. Nuna-am nutaan elagluku, ilua-ll' tua-i canegnek ilupirluku wall'u-q' urunek piluku, can'giirnek tua-i imirluku tua-i muirluku. Qululiqatarluni. Teq'erluki pitukait neqet, iqalluut-llu teq'erluki qamiqurrit-llu teq'erluki. Tep'ngartaqata tua-i nertukait yuut neqteng. Tuaten tua-i piluki. Patuluki-ll' tua-i umciggluku.

Tua-i-ll' kaviriluteng can'giiret, qaingit-llu camlairulluteng. Waten teguluk' piqalriani amiyagait ukiartelangluteng. Tuaten elliata nutaan nuggluki. Tua-i nerqainaurrluteng. Qantat-llu imirluki nerqata'arqamta tamakunek can'giirnek uqumek-llu kuvluki. Qamiqurrit teguluki, iqmigluki tua-i, qamiqurrit-llu engelaitgun keggluki. Tamakunek taugaam nerkuituluteng qamiqurritnek. Temait makut ener-

through the hole in the ground over there, some blackfish get pushed through the passage down below and come out through that hole in the ground. When blackfish down below got crowded, some would get pushed into the passage and spill out through the hole. When blackfish were seen coming up through the hole, we'd know they were gathered down below to spawn.

The village would be alerted. Then those who wanted to would get blackfish from that spot.

They prepared and ate [blackfish] in different ways, by fermentation and by leaving them out in the fall to age. Fresh blackfish were caught in [wooden traps] like these; but the traps they used were big. And though the river was wide, they'd make them large enough to fit in it and put funnels that look like these in them. The blackfish traps were made big enough to fit into rivers. The traps were set in rivers, and the traps' sides would be right against the sides of the river, and a blackfish couldn't swim past it, only along the top [of the trap].

This is how they set blackfish traps. They also thoroughly checked the bottom where the blackfish trap would be set. If the trap wasn't set well, if the one setting it wasn't careful, the trap would catch a few, if he hadn't thoroughly prepared the river bottom. That's why we always checked the bottom by poking and feeling to make sure it was smooth. We'd smooth out the bumps down below before setting the trap. We would make sure they were sitting straight and not with its front dipping down. If the trap wasn't set right, even though there were lots of blackfish, it would catch a few while other traps were catching a lot. But if someone who knew how to set it right came by and fixed it, it would suddenly start catching lots.

Sometimes blackfish runs got heavy, and they say it's when they "want to come out." When blackfish runs get heavy, *anyunga'arrnituit* [they swim downriver, lit., "they suddenly want to come out"]. When blackfish runs got heavy, a trap would sometimes fill up overnight. Then they'd dig a hole in the ground, line the inside with grass or moss, and it would be filled with blackfish all the way to the top. This was the way they made *quluut* [aged fish]. Fish are normally fermented in holes in the ground, and dog salmon and fish heads are usually fermented the same way. People like to eat fish fermented. That was what they did [with blackfish]. [After filling the hole with blackfish] it was securely covered.

The blackfish would turn red, and their skin would get soft. When taken like this their skin was easily torn. When they got like that they'd take them out of the hole. They were ready to eat. And before we ate them and put some in a bowl we'd pour seal oil on them. And when we took them by their heads we'd put the whole fish in our mouth and bite along the edge of the head. The only part we discarded was

tuumaita ner'aqluki neqekngamteki. Ungungssitun wall' qimugtetun nertuumaita ner'aqluki. Enrit mik'nateng. Quluut-gguq tamaa-i. Iqrek-llu kapurnaurtuk, nuak-llu egqertaqluni, kapurluku. Tua-i quunaqluteng tua-i. Tumaglit iciw' imkut quu-narqelriit ilait makut acsat. Tuaten ayuqluteng. Tua-i assikngamegteki tua-i-am tamakut yuullguteteng elpengcarluki. Angtuanek teq'eraqameng pituut, patagmek tua-i nangevkarluki. Uitaaqameng neryunairutetuut, anagarutaqameng. Nangqer-cetnaurait tua-i. Qululiluteng-gguq.

Taugken uksuartaat tamakut, uksuarmi nenglengqerraami imillrit naparcilluut, carangllugnek tupiumalrianek caqulget, kumlami uitaurangermeng camlairulluteng qaingit. Kaviriluteng-llu aqsait kumlalngermeng. Uksuartaat-gguq tamaa-i nerell-rat tua-i nutaan assipiarluni cali. Taugaam imkut angtuat can'giiret enrit piiyuitaput, imkut taugaam mikcuaraat enertuumaita nertuaput. Tuaten neqautekaput can'gii-ret nutem tua-i. Kiagmi pivakayuitait, uksumi taugaam nerngetuaput kumlangaqan waten; anyungaaqata. Uksumi taugaam anyungtuut kuigni. Up'nerkami tuamtell' mayuryungluteng. Melugpakayallrait-wa can'giiret. Taluyat taugaam uatmun, car-vaneq waten tunulluku mayurcuucituut. Taluyat-am tua-i, asgurturalriit, itellriit cangtaqluki taluyat. Pivakayuitut. Ilaita piyulriit pituut mayurcuuciluteng. Amlleq piiyuituq.

Kuiget-am pitatekluteng neqait anyuitut, avani nunamteni can'giiret. Nalluvke-naki-am. Iraluq-llu qaillun pitaluku anyungllerkaa. Elitaqamegteki tua-i tuaten kui-get pituut. Tua-i-ll' piyaraat tekican, tekiteqataan taluyartarkaitnek piluki civvluki. Utaqalgirtelluki anyungllerkaanek civcimaurluki. Takunaqnaurtut amllerpek'na-teng; cangcuaralangut. Amllerriinarluteng. Tua-i taugken amlleriameng taluyat muiqertaqluteng can'giirnek. Can'giiret amllepialartut avani nunamni. Enrit-llu aminateng. Augkut taugken nunavni Naparyarrarmiut Napaskiarmiut nuniitni enerpauluteng. Allakauluteng. Enrit angluteng can'giiret. Nunamteni taugken en-runateng. Aminateng enrit, neryunaqluteng.

Taulan qanemcitaanga elitnaurviliullermini qagaani kuigpiim elatiini Nome-am natiini, calilliniuq tuani BIA-aq piullrani. Neryartuutellrani caqerluni tamakumium,

the head. We'd eat the whole fish, including its bones. We'd eat them, bones and all, like dogs and animals. Their bones were small. They called them *quluut*. The inside corners of your mouth would feel like they were being poked by something sharp and would start stinging, and your saliva would swell up in your mouth. They are very sour. You know, when you eat cranberries they are sour. That's what they taste like. Because everyone enjoyed eating them they'd invite their families and friends and eat together. When they made fermented blackfish like that, they made lots, and they would quickly eat them. When they are not eaten right away, they rot and get too sour to eat. After they took them out of the hole, they ate them all right away. They were preparing *quluut*.

But *uksuartaat*, blackfish caught in fall and stored in grass baskets, though they were kept in the cold, their skin would become soft and easily torn. And their bellies would turn red, even though they stayed cold. They are called *uksuartaat* and are also delicious. We don't eat the bones of big blackfish, but we eat the little ones whole, including their bones. That's how we have eaten blackfish for centuries. We don't get them much in the summer, but in the winter we start eating them when it gets cold like now, when they start coming out [and swimming downriver]. They start swimming down the rivers in winter. Then in spring, they start swimming upriver again. That's when blackfish have large eggs. But when they set the traps they'd put the funnel facing downstream and not against the current. Then the blackfish that were swimming up against the current would go into traps and get caught. Only a few set traps like that. Those who want to set traps and catch blackfish swimming upriver do, but only a few.

Over in my home area blackfish don't start swimming down the rivers at the same time. They knew the rivers and knew when the fish would start swimming downstream. And they knew the month and approximate dates of the run. When they learned the rivers, that's what they did. And when the time of the fish run came, when the time was nearing, they'd set their traps in rivers. They'd leave their traps in and wait for the run. When you first checked the trap it would catch a few; and the number of fish caught would get bigger and bigger. There'd be more and more fish in the trap when you checked it. And when the run got bigger, your fish traps would be full of blackfish every time you checked them. Over in my home there are usually many blackfish, and their bones are thin. But blackfish over in your home, Napakiak and Napaskiak, their bones are big. But in my home they have no bones. Their bones are thin and easy to swallow.

Taulan once told me that when he was part of a construction crew building a school somewhere north of the Yukon River near Nome, he was in a village work-

itrami qantaa taitelliniat can'giirnek-gguq waten taktalrianek imarluni, kepumaaq-
luteng qukait. Angpialliniut-gguq qagaani can'giiret. Kenitullinikait-gguq taugaam
kep'aqluki qukaitgun. Enerpauluteng-llu-gguq. Qavcinek-gguq aqsingelria can'giirnek anglliniameng-gguq.

Nani-llu, tamaani-w' pitullrullilriit, imumi qanemcilallruut Kass'at nurnallratni,
can'giirpalegmiunek tamakunek. Tamakut-wa pillilriit. Cat piat? Uksuyuilngurmi
pinilaryugnarqait. Arnassagaat-gguq tamakut makut nasaurluut tan'gaurluut-llu qa-
nemcitaqekait. Kaaka-gguq nenglem aciarmiut-llu, cikuqeraqan, imarpigmi-gguq
cikuqeraqan piiyuanguarcetnaurait-gguq, piiyuaninaurait-gguq cikuqakun, aalluu-
yiiruqurluteng. Pirraarluteng-gguq pinaurtut, "Tavaq tamakut yuugut." Irr'ikluki.

Tuamtellu-gguq nernaurtut, tamakut can'giirpateng aperturluki, tamakunek
tamaa-i can'giirpagnek; tuaten angtayukluki pilallikait tayima can'giiret unani ce-
narmiuni. Tamakut-gguq qamiqurritgun-gguq, tamakut nenglem aciarmiut, nenglem aciarmiunek arivvluta unani Caninermiuni, qamiqurritgun-gguq teguluki
nalugluki iqmigluki cipeggnaurait enerrlainaat. Iqulirluku-gguq taugken, "Tavaq
tamakut yuugut." Tuaten-am qanemcit'lallruit. Tuaten angtanritut unegkut can'gii-
rutait.

Kuiget taugken ilait un'gaani imkunek mikcuayaarnek can'giiyaarnek amllernek-
llu tua-i pinaurtut. Tua-i tamakut nertuaput unguvaitni. Teguluki tua-i cakuivkenaki. Nertuaput tua-i. Alungyarnek atengqertut can'giiyagaat. Cali-ll' imkunek mi-
kellritnek uksumi, qaill' angtauralrianek, aqsarpayagangqerrluteng. Steak-arluki
wiinga assikepiaranka tua-i.

Puqlamek kuvluki, puqlanga'arautelluki. Murilkelluki tua-i. Perqerrluteng taugken tua-i anrutait-llu qag'errluteng qagrata aqsait, tuaten elli'ircata nutaan taggluk'
qantanun ekluki. Qassauluteng. Qassauluki. Steak-anek-am pilaranka wii. Assikepiaranka. Ner'aqluta tua-i aqsiluta tamakunek. Kanakiirluta-gguq. Tuaten piya-
raugut-am call' can'giiret. Alungyaraat tamakut kenirpek'naki nertuaput. Tamakut-
llu angnerait uksumi piyulriit tua-i kanakiirluki steak-arluki uuvikarluki.

Kumlanruluki tuamtell' nerluki can'giiret. Qagruluki tuamtell' nerluki.

ing under BIA administration. When one of the local men invited him to eat at his house, they gave him a bowl filled with blackfish that were this long. Some were cut in half. He said that apparently northern blackfish are very big. They were so long they'd cut them in half and cook them. He said they had large bones, too. He ate a few of them and got full right away because they were so large.

And somewhere, perhaps it was in that area, back then when few white people were around, they used to talk about those who live in a place with huge blackfish. Perhaps they referred to those people [living in the north]. I don't know who they were talking about. I think they said they lived in a place where it never got cold. Old women told stories to the boys and girls. While they were telling stories about them, they'd tell the children to listen to the sounds made by those people who live beneath the cold. They'd say the sound was coming from their feet as they walked on the ice that just formed on the ocean. And they'd say that it was also the sound of ice moving up and down as they walked on it. After an old woman said that to the children she'd say, "I doubt if those people are human." The old women were fascinated by the people in the story.

And they'd talk about how those people eat them, indicating the size of the large blackfish and the way they ate them; perhaps [other people] thought blackfish were that big in the coastal area. They'd say those who dwell in a place beneath the cold, referring to those who live in the Canineq area, when eating blackfish they would take the fish by the head and put the whole thing in their mouths, and as they pulled out the head, the only thing left would be the skeleton. After they said that they'd say, "I doubt if those people are human." That's what they said about the coastal people. Blackfish caught on the coast aren't that big.

Some of the rivers down on the coast have many small blackfish in them. We eat those while they're alive. We swallow the whole fish. We eat them. The small blackfish are called *anlungyaraat*. And [we also eat] smaller ones that puff up in the belly some time in the winter. I like those prepared like steak.

[To prepare them like steak] we'd pour hot water over them and cook them a little. We'd watch them carefully, and as soon as they bent backwards and their bellies popped, we'd remove them from heat and put them in bowls. They would still be raw. I call them steaks. I enjoy them very much cooked like that. We'd eat them and get totally satisfied, *kanakiirluta* as they called it. That's how we eat blackfish, too. We pop the little blackfish into our mouths and eat them fresh. And the ones that are a little bigger we eat slightly cooked.

We also eat blackfish frozen. And we also eat them prepared as *qagret* [boiled blackfish left out and eaten later after the broth jelled].

Muragnek imkunek qantanek. Tamakut assirtut. Makucitun cavigtun ayuqenritut. Jell-O-tun tua-i ayuqliriluni mer'at man'a yurluku. Neqkiutuluteng atakumi, imirluku-llu tauna, mirluki-ll' mer'atnek. Nutaan nek'eggluki puqlaunrilngurmun; kenirraarluki. Qagiluteng-gguq. Tua-i-ll' unuaquan apiatami nutaan yuringiita ipuutnek piluteng qantat imirturluki. Yuringaqapiarluteng tua-i, mer'at-llu yuringaluni. Nutaan-am uqumek kuv'aqluki nerluta. Mer'at-llu tua-i tamana nangengata akulluku. Tua-i piinanemteni waten qatertariluni mat'utun, qa'riluni amlleriluni. Akulluku, qantaq kiituan imarturiuq uqumek avuluni. Qaqican tua-i qat'rillra nutaan nerluku nangluku.

Qagret tua-i tuaten nertuaput. Can'giiret neqngullrat amllertuq tua-i. Puqlauluki, kanakiiruluki, qassarluki mikcuaraat, kumlanruluki-llu. Augkut-llu imkut, atrit-am kis'artanka. Tepngaayiqerluki imkut, uksuarciluki, qululiluki-llu. Pillrat amllertuq can'giiret tamakut. Ilameggni amllenruut nunamteni avani.

[We ate them the next day] using those wooden bowls. They are good. They aren't like these metal ones they use nowadays. The broth would jell just like Jell-O. They'd fill up a wooden bowl with cooked blackfish and cover it with the broth in the evening. Then they'd put the bowl away in a cool place, doing what they called preparing *qagret*. Then the next day at lunch after it had all jelled, they'd dish them out into bowls. The cooked blackfish would be cold and stiff and the broth was jelled. Then we'd pour seal oil on them and eat. Then after we ate all the fish we'd begin mixing the jelled broth with our hands. We'd keep mixing it, and finally it would turn white and get fluffy. We'd keep mixing it up, and soon the bowl would begin filling up with a fluffy mixture with seal oil added. And when the consistency and color were just right we'd eat the whole thing.

That's how we eat *qagret*. There are many ways to prepare blackfish. We eat them cooked and hot, slightly cooked, raw, and frozen. And also, I can't remember the name now. The name for the blackfish eaten slightly fermented; we eat them *uksurciluki* [aged] and *qululiluki* [fermented]. There are many ways to eat blackfish. There are more ways to prepare and eat them than other kinds of fish available in my home over there.

Uksuarmi Pissuryaraq Melqulegcuryaraq-llu

~: *Ungungssiit* :~

Imkut teriaraat tayima tangerrnaunrilriit, narullgit-llu. Imarmiutaat, kanaqliit, cuignilnguut, negilirkat, uliiret, kaviaret. Watngullruut maani tamakut. Paluqtaat-llu piyuunateng. Imarmiutat amllepiarluteng cuignilnguut-llu. Akiullrat ikgetuq maa-i. Atkugkiurluteng atkugkanek imarmiutarkanek, cuignilngurnek atkugkanek.

Qavaken nutaan kiaqlimtenek paluqtarnek kipukengaqluteng imkunek-llu qanganarnek, qavcicuanek, terikanianek tamakunek tamaa-i, keglunernek. Maani keglunertelallruut tuntut amllellratni maani. Tuntut amllepiallruut maani nunamteni. Ukut-llu caaqameng tuntut uivvaarnaurait nunat. Ayagcetaarluki piyaaqengraiceteng, pitsaquurluteng pilartut. Kanarluteng-ll' waten maavet tuntut, imkut *caribou*-runrilnguut *reindeer*-at. Nuyurrilameng tamakut. Pelatekat-llu uani amlletuameng, ilait-gguq tua-i nepengnaurtut aaraluteng tutmaqatarniluteng. [*engelartut*]

Kiagmi-w' taugaam tuntunek atkugkiulallrulriit ikani Kuinerrarmiuni tuntutangqellrani ikna, casgutangqellrani Kuinerrarmiut nuniit. Tuavet tua-i piqatarqata, caliyarturluteng kiagmi atkugkanek tua-i akinguurluteng pilriit tuntunek. Cali amlleret tua-i kipusviit kipulluki atkugkat tuntut. Melqurrit ateskunateng tunturraat ayagyuat. Imarmiutaat tua-i cuignilnguut-llu, kanaqliit-llu atkuutullruut maani, *rabbit*-aat-llu, uliiret-llu, kaviaret-llu. Atkuku'urluki tua-i. Murutekluki tuaten arnat uliiret pitullrulliiniit tamaani.

Nillarluki-w' ullelluki kinercirluki.

Tuntunun-wa taugaam atutullrukait urugutet, apeqmeggnek ayimlluki, calugqaarluki qeciit imkutgun waten elliulriatgun. Unkumiutaat taugken nayiit imkut tuluruanek waten nunamun pimaluteng, perluteng waten tegg'erauluteng. At'elluki tamaavet nayiit kelikarluku tamatum qainga calugtetuluki, pilu'ugkat.

Nunamiutaat imkut maqanruut, kaviaret-llu, uliiret-llu maqartut atkukellrit. Nutaan tua-i maqapiat atkuuluteng.

Fall Hunting and Trapping

~: Land animals :~

Those ermines and weasels aren't seen anymore. There were mink, muskrat, otter, tundra hare, Arctic fox, tundra fox. Those [animals] were in this area. And there were no beavers here. There were many mink and otter. They have no monetary value nowadays. They collected mink and otter for parkas.

They would trade for beaver furs from the villages upriver, as well as squirrels, marten, wolverine, and wolf. They used to catch wolves in this area when there were a lot of reindeer here. There used to be many reindeer in our area. And sometimes the reindeer would go around and around, circling this village. Although they tried to make them leave, they would refuse. The reindeer came to this area, the ones that aren't caribou; the reindeer, those that are domesticated. And since there were many tents down on the coast, some people would holler that they were going to be trampled. [*laughter*]

They prepared reindeer skins for parkas during summer when there were reindeer over in the village of Quinhagak, when there was a reindeer corral near Quinhagak. When it was time, people went there in summer and worked for income. And many stores would purchase reindeer skins for parkas. The fur on young reindeer was short. The skins of mink, otter, and muskrat were made into parkas here, along with the skins of rabbit, Arctic fox, and tundra fox. They always made them into parkas. And women used Arctic-fox skins as socks.

They turned [the skins] inside out and stretched them out to dry.

They used *urugutet* [skin scrapers] to soften the reindeer hide, *ayimlluki*, as they called it, after scraping and cleaning the skin, removing the membrane with scrapers, doing this. But when they scraped ringed-seal skins, they used *tuluruat* [skin-stretching tools] secured in the ground, those pieces made of curved hardwood. They'd put the skin on that piece and scrape off the oil and membrane to prepare skin to make into boots.

Land-animal fur is warmer, including red-fox and white-fox fur when used as parkas. They are very warm as parkas.

~: Uksuarmi melqulegcuryaraq :~

ALICE: Ayagalallerpenek elpet nallunricugtukut, nanvani-llu tevuraluten ayagalallerpenek, kapkaanavnek-llu tamakunek piluten pilallerpenek.

FRANK: Avani nerangnaqsarat piqtaaryarait qigcignarqellruut. Taumek neqsur-
yarait, can'giircuryarait-llu, wall'u pissuryarait imarmiutarmek pikevkenaki takar-
narqut. Qigcignaqluteng tua-i. Pingnaqvimteni taugaam pingnaq'lallruukut, ilamta
pingnaqsarait ullagavkenaki. Taugaam imkut can'giiret aninilriit neqelget-llu nutaan
pillgutekluta pituaput.

Makut taugken pingnaqsarat imarmiutarnek, cuignilngurnek canek kapkaanir-
luta piyaraput, taluyanek-llu melqulegcuutnek piyaraput nalluvkenaki taumun pi-
yaraquciat, qigcignarqut. Takarnaqluteng tua-i. Wall'u pissuuteteng nuniitnun na-
panun-llu mayurrluki ungungssimun pingairutelluki, unitetuit; cangaringailnguut
ellamelngermeng. Tua-i cali qigcignaqluteng tamakut. Inerquusngaluteng-llu wangkutnun, pikenrilkemtenek tegutesqevkenata piyaurpailemta. Ayagayaurpalemta makunek elitnaurumalallruukut pingnaqsaranek. Taumek nallumciqevkenata ayaga-
langamta pilallrulriakut. Waten-llu pinariamta malikluta ayagalluta elitnaurluta
nutaan tangvagtelluteng pituluta. Tua-i-w' nallumciqngairutelluta, kiimta pingramta, yuilqumi nunaunrilngurni kangallerkamtenek. Ca tamalkuan elitnaurluku.
Tuaten ayuqellruukut. Melqulegcuraqamta tua-i ilamta kapkainirturyarait, taluyir-
turyarait-llu ullagayuunaki. Nallunrilengramteki ullagayuunaki.

Tua-i-am ca tamarmi navguastengqelaami; pimangermeng-am ilait qanernarqaq-
luteng, tamana navgurluki tua-i pilriit. Ilait taugken qanernaunateng. Catailngur-
tun ayuqluteng qigcikiluteng tamatumek pilriit. Tuaten tua-i ayuqluteng; pingnaq-
saramteni tua-i pingnatugturatuluta. Augkut taugaam ava-i neqelget pillgutekluta
tua-i pituluki. Kuiget-llu quarruulget pillgutekluta tua-i pituluki, kuigni qaluyarat
tua-i pillgutekluta.

~: *Fall trapping* :~

ALICE: We want to know about your travels out on the land, and your travels portaging over lakes, and about your travels when you went trapping.

FRANK: Back in those days personal hunting grounds were respected by others. Personal areas for fishing, setting blackfish traps, or areas for hunting mink, if you normally didn't go there you never went into those places and respected them. We hunted and fished in the areas we went to and didn't venture into places where others hunted and fished. However, the places where blackfish gathered to spawn, the *aninit*, were open to everyone from different villages to harvest from.

But areas where people set metal traps for mink, land otter, and such, and the areas where underwater wooden traps were set for furbearing animals, knowing who they belonged to, we didn't touch them out of respect. Some men sometimes left their traps on bushes near where they were set, high enough so animals couldn't get them; those that won't deteriorate, even when left out exposed to the elements. We also stayed away from those out of respect. We boys were told not to take traps left out like that when we saw them when we roamed the land, before we got older and became hunters. Before we got older and started hunting we were taught about hunting rules. That was why we weren't ignorant when we started going out to hunt, and we knew what to do. They also took us out as soon as we were able to and taught us by example. They taught us about the land and the geography so we wouldn't get lost when we started traveling alone. We were taught everything related to land and hunting. That was the way it was when it came to land and hunting. And when we hunted for furbearing animals we never ventured off to check other people's trapping areas. Because we knew exactly where they were, we never went and checked their traps.

With every rule, there are always those who break them; and even those who were raised with those rules would break them and become known as offenders. And yet some people follow the rules and live a quiet life. Those who are respectful don't stand out, and they live their lives as if they are invisible. That was how people were; we always hunted and subsisted in our customary areas. But places where fish were available were open to everyone. And rivers where there were needlefish weren't restricted, but everyone could harvest from them. And all the fish that were harvested with dip nets, everyone and anyone from other villages could harvest from the runs.

Avaken ayagluteng tua-i pitullrulliniut. Melqulek-llu man'a akiturivailgan wii murilkengellruamku; tayima akiunrirluni maa-i pissurnanriatni. Akikunani tua-i, akituriluni-ll' tua-i kinguqvaarni, tua-i-ll' tayima akiunrirluni. Pissurnanrirluta-ll' wangkuta. Kinguqliput-llu makut pissurnanrirluteng; watqapik tua-i pissurciigali-luteng. Wangkuta pissulallerput aturpek'naku.

Taugaam tuaten pingramta uksumi alerquutengqelallruukut kapkainaat nallait-gun pitsaqevkenata yuullgutemta kapkainaq'ngaanek tangerqumta, una aarnarqe-kan, kapkainaa keggmiaqellra, tuquvailegmi kepluku ayagarkaungataqan, tuqutesqe-lluku. Tua-i-llu nalugluku caqukangqerkan-llu caquluku uugnarnun pingairutelluku, angyayagarnun-llu, mayurrluku, agarrluku-wall' ungungssimun pingairutelluku. Tekiskumta egmianun apqaurutkesqelluku tauna nalqiggluku kitumun pikucia-nek. Nalkekumteggu pikestii tauna qanrulluku tauna kapkainaq'ngaa aarnaqngan, kepuulluni ayagnayukluni, tuqulluku agarrluku pama-i unitniluku nuniinun. Tua-i quyaviknauraitkut tua-i cakneq tamakut. Tuaten ayuqellruukut.

Taugken-am ilait tegucugluteng. Inerciigacaraq man'a arenqiatuq aturyugnaq-ngami. Ilameng kapkainait cangtait nalkaqamegteki teguluki. Teglegluki tua-i tegu-yugluki. Wall'u taluyait yuvrirluki, cangtangqerraqata teguluki piaqluki. Tuaten-am ilangqelallruukut. Tamakut nepliutnguluteng taugaam, navguiluteng.

Inerquqatuyaaqekait-wa qanrutkumaaqata. Anucimirqecetaariyuitut. Taugaam inerqualuki yugyautevekenaki. Kiimelulluki pistekaitnek piluteng qalarutetuit. Ta-matumek tuaten ayuqellratnek pinqigtesqevkenaki.

Taluyiryaraqamta tuamtell', taluyat civvluki melqulegcuutet, wani kuiggarmi ullagluku civtaqluku, ikirtaqan. Ullagtaarturluki tua-i. Ut'rutelput-llu pissuute-put, ucikluki qimugterluta ayagluta. Camp-amtenun tekitaqamta, ikamrayagaat imkut qamigautet, qimugteput rest-arcelluki, piiyualuta civerqessarturaqluki erta-qan maani canimelngurni. Yaaqsikekemteni taugaam nutaan qimugtetgun ullaga-luki, ikamrarluta. Kuiggaat civveqluki civingayaraitnun melqulegcuutet. Tua-i-llu igtenek-llu, pillialrianek tangrraqamta, piyunarqaqata kapkainarnek civcivikaqluki. Tuaten tua-i pituluta.

Tua-i-llu December-aam kinguaraakun meriutetuut ilait kuiget tamaani pingnaq-vimteni. Tua-i-ll' cuqluki alaiqata'arqata, taluyat-llu meriulluteng, yuutuaput. Erur-luki marayarrluirluki tua-i, ut'rulluki-ll' nunamtenun piaqluki. Wall' kavirlinek na-

That was the customary practice of our people from way back in time. I started becoming aware before animal fur was used as income and before the price of fur went up; and now years later animal fur has no monetary value because people don't hunt anymore. At first fur had little value, then later its value went up, and now it has no value at all. And eventually we stopped hunting and trapping. And the generation after us stopped hunting; they absolutely can't hunt anymore. The customary hunting practices that we followed are no longer followed today.

But even though we respected the places where people subsisted, we were told that if we saw another person's metal traps with a trapped animal that looked like it would escape before it died, we should kill it. Then we were to take it out of the trap and put it up and hang it in a bag if we had one to keep it away from mice and other animals. And when we got home we were to immediately find out who the trap belonged to. When we found the owner, we told him that since the animal he had trapped looked like it was about to escape, we had killed it and hung it and left it near that place. When the owners found out what we had done they'd be very grateful and thank us for our help. That's what we used to do.

But some people tended to take things [left out by others on the land]. Breaking rules is pervasive because it's appealing to some people. When some people found animals in others' traps, they'd take them. They'd take them and steal them. Or some checked others' blackfish traps, and when they found fish in there they'd take them. There used to be people like that among us. People like that were only troublemakers and created conflict among communities.

They were counseled when their conduct was reported. They weren't punished. But they were confronted and counseled by just a few people. Certain people were appointed to talk to them alone. They were advised not to behave that way again.

And when we set our wooden traps, traps to catch furbearing animals, we'd go to a slough here and set the trap in water, once it was opened up. We'd go to all the sloughs [and set our traps]. When we left our village we'd load up the traps we had brought home from the previous hunt and go with a dogsled. When we got to our camps, using those little kayak sleds, allowing our dogs to rest, we'd trek out using those little sleds to set our traps in places nearby when we woke up the next morning. Then in the places farther away from camp, we'd use a dog team to go and set our traps. Traps were always set in the usual sloughs. And if we see paw prints next to dens, we'd set metal traps in them. That's what we did.

Right after December some sloughs where the traps were set no longer had water [when ice formed]. We'd keep an eye on them and take them out when they were just about to become visible. We'd wash the mud and debris off and take them

panek pitangqerraqata uitayarait, tamaavet agarrluki petugluki avayaitnun makut
napat makucit. Nunam qainganun ellivkenaki unitetuluki tua-i tuaten.

Ataucikun yuuvkenaki. February tua-i iliini pitqerluku pissuteput tamakut
mermi uitalriit nangluki yuugaqluki. Ilait-am kuiget cikutuit tua-i patagmek tamatum nuniini, ilait taugken kuiget cikungianaki. Nalluvkenaki tua-i tamakut ciku-
ngialnguut civingaurtelluki taluyat. Cikungilriani taugken uitalriit, tamana tekite-
qatarqan yuugaqluki civtenrirluki.

Kapkainaat tuamtell' tamakut cang'aqluteng pulengtaq tua-i pitulriit. Tua-i-ll'
cangnanrian, yuirucan, yuuluki nutaan. Allamun cali civtengnaqluki. Nenglengaqan tua-i caperrnarilartuq; ellami kanganrilameng imarmiutaat cuignilnguut-llu.
Camani taugaam qanikcaam aciani kuiget cenaitni kangarluteng, tagelviiyamegte-
ggun. Ellamun piyuunateng nenglengaqan. Taugaam tua-i nenglairutaqan nalluv-
kenaku-am cali. Ellamun nutaan pugyarangluteng anqetaarluteng nutaan ellamun.

~: Cuignilnguut, imarnmiutaat, kanaqliit-llu :~

Cuignilnguut imarmiutaat-llu [taluyatgunpituit]. Kanaqliit-llu taluyatgun pituit,
naneryatgun-llu.

Imkut yaassiiggaat, civingatuluteng waten. Muriit tupigluki qallilirluki-ll'. Ayag-
cirluki, neqcaq-wa kiani. Una tua-i neqcaq, agtuqaku una ayagtii, kiugum neqcam,
pekteskani, una cetgarrluni pal'uqertarkauluni.

Nunamek qallirluni qaamailngurmek. Passiluku pektesciigalivkarluku, tuquluni-
ll' tua-i.

Tamaa-i naneryat imarmiutarcuutellrit arcaqerluki. Cuignilnguut taugken tamakut tevyarait, tumyarait, kuigmek nugluteng nunakun ayagyarait, nanvamun-llu
kanarluteng tumyararpallrait. Merrlugkun-llu ayagaqluni et'ulriakun, ururrlugkun.
Tamakut tamaa-i ururrluut tumyarait, cuignilnguum tua-i temiinun cuqluku taluyat iluatni caqirrngairutelluku ukatmun iluatni, calturtelluk' engelqaqu'urtelluku.
Kingutmun waten caungaunani, paingit neqututaluki. Tumyarait merrlugmi uitalriit, uruq qeciirluku. Tua-i-llu taluyat tamaavet civvluki, qainga tua-i pugumavkar-
pek'naku.

home. Or if red willows were nearby, we'd put them up in the bushes and tie them to the branches. We didn't leave them on the ground but left them in bushes like that.

The traps weren't all taken out at once. Sometimes at the beginning of February we'd take out the rest of the traps that were set in water. Some rivers in that area [where I trapped] froze early, and some were open for a long time. We knew the ones that didn't freeze right away and would leave our traps in there longer. But the ones in rivers that froze up early, when that time [right after December] arrived, we'd take them out and not set them again.

And those metal traps that were set would continue catching animals again and again. Then when it stopped catching, we would undo the trap and take it out and find another place to set it. It got difficult to catch them when it got cold out because mink and otter stopped coming out on land. They would stay underground beneath the snow and start moving about through their passages along the rivers. They don't come out when it gets cold. They'd know when it started to get warm outside. They'd make a passage and a hole above ground and start going in and out.

~: *Land otter, mink, and muskrats* :~

Otter and mink [were caught in wooden traps]. They also caught muskrats with wooden traps and with *naneryat* [old-style deadfall traps].

[*Naneryat*] were shaped like boxes and were set like this. Strands of wood were woven together and covered. They were set with a prop with bait in there. This bait, when the animal touched this prop, when the bait in their allowed it to move, this [prop] collapsed, and the box-shaped trap would fall with the animal inside.

There would be a layer of heavy soil on top. The soil would fall on it, and [the animal] would be trapped and unable to move, and it would die.

Naneryat were mainly used for catching mink. But [they set traps for] land otter [in] their trails for going over land, their trails on land, the trails they used when they come out of water and go on land and cross over to adjacent lakes and ponds, the wide trails they've created. They also made trails on swampy areas and marshes. They used to set wooden traps inside the trails they always used. The traps were big enough so that when the land otter went inside, it wouldn't be able to turn and would get stuck. They'd first peel off the thin layer of crust from the trails they made in the marshy areas and set wooden traps inside all the way down so the trap was exposed on top.

Mer'uluni. Tua-i-ll' qainga man'a uqviarnek waten pilirluku. Waten qilaguyicuar-luki, nunirluku urunek patuluki. Iquug-ukuk callalutek. Tua-i tamakut taluyat atu-nem pailuteng. Amaggun tekitellria itrarkauluni, wall' amaken tekitellria itrarkau-luni. Qecuqilluteng tua-i kuigni uitalriani cuignilnguut.

Asvaunaki call' tamakut taluyat. Tupiit-llu kegqayunairulluki cuignilngurcuutet tamakut pituut taluyat. Teggvagnek aterluteng. Iqtutaluteng-llu waten nemiarutait. Waten akultutavkenateng. Mik'nateng taugaam, qaill' akultutaurluteng.

Makut-llu cigyait ellegluteng. Mat'um cangalqelluki tek'ma ellegtaciit makuit, cuignilngurcuutet. Qaingatnun-llu aqumgayugngauten. Navegngaunateng-llu nu-taraat cuignilnguut teggem ugaani. Nemiarutait-llu malrurqurrlainarnek tupiuma-luteng, waten piurpek'naku makucetun. Ataucirqumek maa-i makut pimaut, nevil-kaquurluki makut.

Cuignilngurcuutet taugken tamakut tegviit, ukatmun pirraarluku ukatmun tuamtell' aipirluku. Aipirturluki nemiatuluki.

Iluliraita-llu ukut, kankut piit, kankut, cillaqetaalriaruluteng waten. Ugna paimi, ipegcenateng cakneq ukuit nuugit. Cingigluki. Qamaken tua-i kapuryugngaluni pii-yaaqekuni, taugaam pet'ngaaluteng. Callaurluteng tua-i. Cuignilnguq itqan cillartar-kauluteng. Kituqan-llu quuqerrluteng igyarait kankut.

Nemiarutet makut, makut maa-i nemiarutet pimallrita quumavkarluki; tegglaa-meng tamakut ilulirait. Tua-i assiriluki pituut, amipallagpek'naki. Cuignilnguum pikaki pet'ngarkauluku. Petengluteng itqertarkauluni cuignilnguq qacigglu ni. Anet-mun taugaam pingaunani tua-i cillarrngaunateng, ipegcenateng-llu nuugit. Cali iluit kavirlit napat avayaitnek imirluki, taluyat tamakut civtetuluki.

Anyailkutet. Tamakut-gguq qiperrlugaqameng qacigtellriit keggmaarluki pituut, taluyat ukut pivkenaki. Tuaten pituit cuignilnguut. Tumyaraitgun-llu tamaaggun taluyacuarnek tamakunek, tumyararaitgun, merkun piqatulikun, mecagteggun; et'ulriit assilriit tamakuliyunarqut nayukarluki tumyarait. Imarmiutaat-llu tama-kut pituit cali tuaten, cuignilnguut piyaraicetun. Engelqerritnek taluyacuarnek amil-nguayaarnek, caqirtesciigatevkarluki.

[The place where the trap was set] was all water, and the area above the trap was covered with willow shrubs. Then they put a sort of roof over it and covered it with moss. The wooden traps were open on both sides. If a land otter was going along the trail on one end, it would go inside the trap and get caught, and if it was coming from the other direction, it would also enter the trap and get caught. The otter that were caught in traps set in water would drown and die.

They made wooden otter traps sturdy and not easily broken. They also made sure bindings were tough enough so they couldn't be chewed off. The otter traps like these were called *tegviit*. The wooden strips were bound with spruce roots and were about this far apart. The space between each strip wasn't as wide [as on blackfish traps]. The openings were very narrow.

And their wooden strips, *cigyait*, were wide. The wooden strips on otter traps were about as wide as my index finger. You could even sit on [the traps without breaking them]. A brand-new otter trap was indestructible because they were so tough. And they were bound with two strands of spruce root. These [blackfish] traps were bound once.

But when making *tegviit*, after binding them going in this direction, then the second strap would be bound going in [the opposite] direction. They always bound them twice.

And their funnel here, the [opening into the trap] down there, those down there, were made to open like this. That one out there at the mouth, the ends were carved to a point and were sharp. If an otter struggled from inside it would get poked, but they could also open up. They would stay open. And if an otter passed through they would open up. And once the otter was in the trap, the opening would suddenly close.

These spruce-root bindings, the way they were bound allowed them to stay together; the funnels were usually made solid and tough. They made them perfect and not too thin so they would be able to open up when a land otter began going in. They'd open up, and a land otter would slip in very easily. But if the otter tried to go out, they wouldn't open up and their points on the inside would be very sharp. They also set the traps after filling them with red-willow branches.

The [branches] helped to keep the otter inside the trap. It was said that when otter got agitated inside the trap they would start chewing on the loose branches instead of the trap. That was how they set traps for otter. And they set those traps referred to as *taluyacuat* in their trails, in swamps and marshes; it was easy to set traps in the trails they made in deep water. Mink traps were set the same way, the same way we set traps for land otter. Mink traps were made narrow so when a mink went inside, it wouldn't be able to turn.

Tuaten pissuucitullruit avani.

Uksuraqan-llu ellamun anenermek taquut, qanikcam-llu maani acianlluteng, tagenqumeggnek eneluteng. Meriusngailngurkun camaggun anumatuluteng anglluryarait tagenqut. Man'a-ll' keluat callalriartaunani, nunam iluani taugaam enait uitaluteng. Amiigat-llu kuigmun camavet atraumaluteng. Maaken ellamun anyuunateng, merkun taugaam angllurluteng kuigkun-llu pugluni. Uksumi tua-i piyuunateng.

Nanvat-llu pituit, camaggun tagenquliluteng. Kanaqliit-llu tagenqurrit kituggluki tamakut tamaa-i tagenquqsagutetuit cuignilnguut, imarmiutaat-llu. Makut kanaqliit enekiurtenguut. Tagenquq-llu kituggluki cuignilnguut tagenquqsagutetuit imarmiutaat-llu. Pakemna tua-i qertungraan, ilii qertutariluku waten, nunam acia. Imna kituggluk' carrirluku, mamtuluni qukaa. Tagenqurrit tamaa-i tamakut. Kuik-llu waten yaaqsingraan, yaaqsiggangraan camaggun mermek imalegkun tagenqukun atratuluteng kuigmun-llu anluteng. Pugeksaunateng tamaani pingermeng, pikngamegteki nalluyuunaki uniurcuunaki-llu tagenquteng. Kuigmi-ll' maaggun qulvaggun anumayuunani, tamaaggun aciqvaggun anumaaqluteng kuigmun, umyuartuameng makut ellakngamegteggu. Meriutellerkaa nunameng unguvalriit assikenritaat melqulget angllutulit. Merluni taugaam. Mer'em akuliikun ayagaaqluteng pillerteng assikaat, ciuniurluki imarmiutaat kanaqliit-llu. Paluqtaat-llu tuaten call' ayuqluteng.

Cali neqelget kuiget, nanvat-llu neqelget [uitaviksurqeggait]; kuigilngermeng neqengqelartut nanvat, tamakutaicuunateng tagenqunek. Taugken ilait kinertellriami qertulriami cuignilnguut irnituluteng. Igtequgnek pituaput tamakut cuignilnguut piyagiuryarait. Qang'a-llu kaviaret igtait allurrluki kaviaret enairluki piyagiutuluteng cali. Igtait piksagulluki.

Kaviaret alikait cuignilnguut. Tua-i tuqucuilkait taumek. Imarmiutaat taugaam tuqutelarait kaviaret. Tuaten tua-i ayuqut tua-i un'gaani. Meriutellerkateng assikenritaat, neqailngurni-llu uitayuunateng. Tua-i meriuskan anuteng nallunrilkengameggnun kuigmun ayagyugngaluteng, piciatun ayagpek'nateng elisngiimegteki neqelget.

Nugluteng iliini cama'antevkenateng nervallutuut, kuigni piaqameng. Nugluteng taugaam qanikcaam [qainganun]. Pugqallritgun-llu yuvrialuki qinertaarluki, aulirnaurtut tua-i nugtaallrit camaken, nugluteng nertuameng can'giirnek. Aunrallrit tua-i uqlautellrit qanikcami. Tamakut tamaani uitayaraq'larait neqelget. Tua-i taugaam kingucata nayunirluki allanun cali ayagluteng neqlegnun.

That was how they set traps for [mink and otter] in the past.

[Mink and otter] stop going out on land during winter and stay under the snow, living inside their *tagenqut* [runs]. Their *tagenqut* lead and have openings out to rivers that always have water in winter. Their houses were in the ground, and there were no holes in the back that went out and up to the ground. The path from the opening of their house went directly into water in the river below. Their house had no opening to the ground up above, but they'd first dive into the water and come to the river's surface. But in the winter they never did that.

They also made *tagenqut* in lakes. Land otter and mink fix muskrat houses and begin using them, too. These muskrats are builders of homes for others. Land otter and mink fix their *tagenqut* and claim them. Even though the [ground] above was high, sometimes they made their *tagenqut* underground steep. They'd fix their *tagenqut* and clean it out, with the middle part very thick. And even though the river down below was far, they'd go down through the *tagenquq* filled with water and go out into water in the river. And though they move about in the water below, they'd always know where their *tagenqut* were. And the openings to the river weren't close to the surface but were deeper in the water, because they are in their world and are wise. Furbearing animals that swim in water don't like it when their familiar areas dry up. They want their environment to have water all the time. Mink and muskrat like staying and traveling underwater. Beavers are also like that.

And [they like to stay in] rivers and lakes that have fish as well. Some lakes have fish, even though they have no rivers flowing out. And they always have *tagenqut* in them. But some land otter give birth in high, dry places. We call the places where land otter raise their young *igtequt*. They also steal fox dens and give birth and raise their young there. They claim their dens.

Foxes are afraid of otter. That's why they don't kill them. But mink kill tundra foxes. That's how they are down on the coast. They don't like it when the water dries up, and they don't stay in places that have no fish. When it dries, they leave and go to a river that they know, not just any [river], because they know the ones that have fish.

Sometimes they come out of the water and eat, when they're in rivers. They come out of the water and eat on the snow. We check places where they came out of the water, and the places where they exited would have a lot of blood because they come out and eat blackfish. The blood they left from eating is on the snow. They stay in places where there are fish. But after the fish run, they no longer stay in those places and move to other places with fish.

Tagenqungqertut. Paluqtartun tagenqungqertut camaggun cali. Neqivigluteng-llu enemeggni. Neqivigluteng kanaqliit.

Imiraqluki neqkameggnek uquutvaguanek, kelugkat-llu aciitnek, napat-llu qel-taitnek kangritnek. Piciatun imangqetuut. Tamakut elagyaitnek pilaraput neqiviit.

Taugken cali nerngaitelliniluki kesianek tamakut elagyameng imait. Nanvat-am piyunarqelriit, kanaqliit, cikuat piqa'arqan, imkunek anernermeggnek negu-yanek pivigkarteng tamana pitulliniat. Cikuqeraqan, *bubble*-aatun qertunernek imangarcetaqluki. Usvituyaartut makut kanaqliit. Tamakut tamaa-i neguyat mam-turiaqata aturluki, anerneteng ciiqluki, ukilluku-ll' tua-i nanvaq. Assirian nanvam terr'anek marayamek nugerqiluteng cikumi, waten pugyaram avatii man'a, nuna-mek angqaugurluku waten imirluku. Kiituan tua-i enengurtuq; nervigkameggnek. Anlut-gguq tamaa-i, anlunek aterluteng kanaqliit caliarit cikumi. Tamakut-gguq pikiurateng aturluki neguyiit ellaita anernemeggnek neqkameggnek-wa (pilartut), elagyameggni pimalriamek nererrlainarpek'nateng.

Nererraarluteng, angllurluteng ayagluteng, neqkameggnek, naumalriim acianek kegguqaarluteng, tuaggun nuglutneg, taum iluani ner'aqlutneg. Tuaten ayuqut ka-naqliit. Makut tua-ll' imarmiutaat cuignilnguut-llu neqkameggnek piiyuitut, neq-legni taugaam tua-i uitatuameng.

Yaqulegnek-llu kiagmi tengesciigaliaqata; piyagaitnek, kayanguitnek [nertuut]. Yaqulget amlleret kiagmi atutuit, kaviaret-llu. Tua-i piyagiurviit un'gaani enrulartut tua-i nerkuaritnek; yaquleyagarnek, qugyinrarnek tua-i piciatun. Amllernek tua-i. Kayangunek cali amllernek tua-i tegutetuut.

ALICE: Tamakut cuignilnguut imarmiutaat kanaqliit-llu pissulriani [inerquutang-qertut]?

FRANK: Inerquutaitut. Taugaam augkunun imkunun, ilani piunriqan, piunrillru-kan; piciryaraqaat yuut makut tamana. Eyagluteng-gguq tua-i pituut. Una temiit pitekluku pimalliniut tamakut. Kinguqvaarni apquciurtaqluni tua-i, arivnerit-llu assiirulluteng. Enrit qang'a-llu navgungluteng.

Tamakut tamaa-i nunamni; alerquun-gguq tamana navgurluku tuaten piaqata tamakut ungungssit ilulliqtuut tua-i, umyugaat navgumaluni tua-i eyagnaq alik-ngamegteggu. Tuaten qanrutkelarait. Tua-i igtait, uugnaraat-llu neqait pakiureskev-kenaki. Igtait-llu kaviaret imarmiutaat-llu uyangtaarluki pisqevkenaki, allrakum

[Muskrats also] have runs. They have runs underground like beavers. And they have places to store food in their houses. Muskrats have places to keep food.

They filled them with food they eat, including poison water hemlock, tubers of coarse grass, and tree bark and branches. They are filled with a variety of things. We call the places where they store their food *elagyat* [food caches].

But they apparently don't always eat food from their food caches. In lakes where this can be done, when their ice got to a certain condition, muskrats apparently use their own breath [to create *neguyat* (bubble clusters in ice)] where they would later build a structure. When a lake is just frozen, they'd create these [*neguyat*] with their breath, and they looked like air bubbles. Muskrats are smart. When the lake ice got thick they would pop those *neguyat* and make a hole through the lake ice. And after creating the hole, they'd pull up mud from the lake bottom and form it into balls and make a wall on the ice around the hole. Eventually, the construction would turn into a house; and that was where they ate their food. These structures made by muskrats on ice are called *anlut*. The holes they made by popping the *neguyat* were ways they used to get other foods, and they didn't eat food from their caches all the time.

After they ate, they would dive underwater and look for food, and after they pulled out a plant and bit off the root they'd swim back up through the hole and eat in the house on the ice. That's how muskrats are. Now, these mink and otter don't store food ahead of time because they stay in places that have fish.

They also eat birds that can't fly in summer; they eat little birds and bird eggs. They consume many birds during summer, and foxes do so as well. The dens where they raise their young are filled with the bones of small birds and small swans they've eaten. They'd be filled with different kinds of bird bones. They also take many eggs.

ALICE: In hunting the otter, mink, and muskrat [are there admonishments]?

FRANK: There are no admonishments. But for those people, if a person's family member died, we have a custom. It's a custom called *eyagyaraq*. It's when someone abstains from doing certain activities and eating certain foods. That custom was apparently followed to ensure health and well-being. If a person hadn't observed the practice, later in life that person would have physical ailments and their joints would deteriorate. Or when they got older their bones would easily fracture.

Those [admonitions] in my village; it is said when people break the abstinence rules those furbearing animals feel sorrowful, they feel very crestfallen because they were terrified of a person experiencing death and other events in life. That's what they said about them. People were told to stay away from animal dens and not to

kassullrani. Pull'uki-ll' mer'esqevkenaki. Ukugnegun taugaam qaluuritailkuni, ukug-nek piluni. Qang'a-llu ikiituut imkut cuplulget kep'arrluki cupluit assircaqerluki, ta-makutgun mer'arkauluni. Nakaaret-llu tamakut, ikiitugmek piilkuni, nakaaret cali cupluitgun taugaam mer'arkauluni. Tamakuilkuni-ll' unatminek waten qaluuricir-luni. Atam makut inerquutengqertut tuaten melqulget igtait.

~: *Kaviarnek uliirnek-llu pissuryaraq* :~

ALICE: Pissuryaqatarqavci-qaa unuakuayaarmi tan'gercetengraan keggna antull-ruuci?

FRANK: Tan'germi pitullruukut elitnaurumacirput aturluku. Tua-i tan'gerceleng-raan ayagluta tua-i, camek kiartevkenata. Nutaan mecignarian cukairulluta, cukair-luta nutaan. Kiarqurluta tua-i, una ullagaqluku, una ullagaqluku, una ullagaqluku. Utelmun-llu paqnaqkengarput uterrvikluku piaqluku. Taugken tumliranaqngan, kaviarnek uliirnek-llu pingnaqluta piamta, nutarat tumait, tumnerraraat nallunair-turluki aturturluki tamakut ayagaqluta. Caqiangraata maligtaquurluki, kiarqurluku taugaam tua-i ciunerput.

Pivakarluta pinaurtukut yaa-i qavalria. Nutaan tamakut tumai unilluki, piyunar-qelriamek kiarrluta ullallerkaanek. Tua-i-ll' assirngalnguq aturluku nutaan aurrluta ullagluku, tangvaurluku taugaam tua-i murilkurluku. Ciutek waten piqa'arqagnek waten arulairtaqluta. Ungelrumaluteng tua-i uiteksaunateng, ciutait taugken nikia-qaqluteng. Nikiaqerqata arulairrluta uitauraraqluta. Tua-i-ll'-am piinanemteni ciutek elavngiinarlutek; qavaraqami. Atrariinarlutek ciutek. Qaivarcami taugken nap'aqerrlutek ciutek, mak'artevkenani taugaam. Tuaten ayuqut makut, ayuqellruut tamakut uliiret kaviaret-llu ullallrat. Makut kaviaret ciutekiallruut, terikeggiana-teng-llu, takviallruluteng-llu uliirni. Uliiret taugken nutaan terikeggluteng, ciute-keggluteng.

Niigarcugluteng. Yaaqsingraan calria niigartaqluku. Qanikcaq imna mamturia-qami qasiakepiartuq. Yaaqsingermi tua-i, qanikcaq kekingera'artaqan tua-i qastu-luni tua-i. Yuum-llu niicugngaluku ciutni patgulluku waten, una qanikcamun piku-niu. Tamatum arcaqerluki elpenga'arcetetullrui kaviaret uliiret-llu. Taugken uliiret

open mouse dens for a whole year. People were told not to drink directly from buckets by stooping down. If a person was without a ladle, he was told to use his hands to drink water. People were told to drink water using wild celery stalks as straws, too. And the wild rhubarb, if there were no wild celery around they were told to use those as straws when they drank water. If those weren't available, he was told to use his hands as a cup to drink water. [Abstinence rules included] the treatment of dens used by furbearing animals.

∿: *Hunting red foxes and Arctic foxes* :∿

ALICE: When you prepared to hunt, did you go outside early in the morning, even though it was dark?

FRANK: We'd leave in the dark, following our teaching. We'd leave, even though it was dark outside, and keep going without stopping. And when it got lighter and we could see, we would go slower and begin looking around, we'd go to this place and that place, to this place and that place. And sometimes on our way back we'd check a place we were curious about. And if there were many animal tracks in an area, when we hunted red foxes and white foxes, when we saw their fresh tracks on snow we'd begin following them. We'd keep following them, even though they kept turning this way and that way, but always checking the area up ahead.

After we persistently followed the tracks, we'd finally see [a fox] sleeping over there. Then we cautiously stepped aside leaving the tracks and looked for a way to approach it [without waking it up]. After finding a way we'd crawl toward it, keeping our eyes on it. [We'd crawl slowly toward it] and stop when we saw its ears doing this. They'd be sleeping curled up and never waking, but their ears would point up and twitch like this. Every time they shuddered we'd stop crawling and wait. And while we were sitting quietly, its ears would slowly come down; this happened when it went back to sleep. Its ears would slowly come down. But when it almost woke up, its ears would suddenly point up, but it wouldn't wake up. This was how it was when you approached white foxes and red foxes. Red foxes don't have such acute hearing or sharp eyes and aren't as sensitive. But white foxes are very sensitive to movement and sound.

[White foxes] are very sensitive to sound and movement. They could hear something, even though it's coming from far away. When snow gets thick, sound can easily travel through it and is loud. And if a person puts his ear on the snow, he can hear sound in the snow created by someone walking, even though he's far away. Be-

qavaraqameng, acivarrluteng qavatululuteng, mamtuluni qavallrat. Qavanertunrulu-
teng kaviarni, takvinrungermeng, terikenrungermeng-llu. Taumek niugarnaitaqan,
cali imutun tekitkacagarluki uliiret pinarqekai qavaryugaqata canimqapiarmun.
Kaviaret taugken terikeggiallruluteng ciutekgiallruameng, takviallruluteng-llu.

Cali mecignariaqata tua-i ciutait tua-i murilkurluki. Qaliruanek augkunek ping-
qetullruukut. Qanikcaq tua-i man'a mamturiaqan, qasiakeggan cuqluki kamilarr-
luta tamakut qaliruat at'aqluki, niugcuilnguut. Tuntut imkut ukuit arcaqerluki atutullruut.

Uivenqeggluki cingiryararluteng. All'uki taugken tua-i tuc'enarluta. Melqurrit
elaqliqluki. Qaliruanek piaqluki. Teggelriakun taugaam ayagaqluta, tamakut tutmarturluki. Nivuilengraata cukanrarpek'nata. Murilkurluki tua-i. Nutegnariaqata
tua-i nutgaqluki. ·

Egmianun ayakatuut elpenga'artaqameng.
Igtemeggni pivakayuitut, cailkami taugaam tua-i. Uliiret tua-ll' makut natquig-
taqan-llu agevkarluteng qavatuut. Qertuuralriit tua-i makut murilkartaqluki. Qanikcamun patuvkarluteng qavatuut ilait uliiret *white fox*-aat. Tua-i iliini murilkarr-
naqnaurtuq anertevkaarallrat — Qanikcaq una qertulria, man'a qertuluni, qanikcaq
ulqetaarturluni, waten aitartaqluni anertevkaarallra maliggluku. Tua-i uliiruuq
tauna tuaten pilria. Ilait-llu qavanertuameng niugarnaitaqan, amlliryarpiaraqluki-
gguq qavallratni tuaten qanikcarmun agevkarluteng.

Kell'artaqameng taugaam tua-i. Kaviatun ayuqenritut, takviameng-llu, teriken-
ruluteng-llu.
ALICE: Igtaitnek tangrraqavci qaill' pilarceci?
FRANK: Piyunarqelriit igtait ullirrluki tegularaput, taugken mamtulria piyuu-
naku, aciqsilria-llu igta.
Ilait taugken quliit mamkunani. Piyagiurviit taugken igtait tua-i amlletuluteng.
Qerrarqumaluni nunam acia. Ayagayarait amllerrluteng nunam aciani camani, ir-
niviit tamakut, piyagiurviit, uliiyagaat kaviaret-llu uitallrit.

Kaviaret, uliiret-llu tuatnayuunateng, igtemeggni tua-i ilait iterluteng uitatuyaa-

cause sound can easily be transmitted through snow, red foxes and white foxes are very sensitive to it. But when white foxes sleep, they sleep deeply. They sleep deeper then red foxes, even though their eyesight is more acute and they are more sensitive to movement and sound. That's why you can quietly go right up to a sleeping white fox when you are hunting it. Red foxes, however, are less sensitive and their hearing less acute, and their eyesight isn't as sharp.

And when we could see them, we constantly watched their ears. We used to wear these boot-sole paddings we called *qaliruat*. When the snow got thick, depending on the sound created by our movement, we'd put on *qaliruat* over our boots that don't make as much noise. They were made mostly out of [throat hairs] of caribou.

They were round and had laces on them. We'd put them on with grass insoles. Their fur was on the outside. They were called *qaliruat*. We'd put them on and walk on the hard snow. Although they didn't make noise, we walked slowly. We would keep an eye on the sleeping fox as we approached it. When we got close enough we'd shoot it with our gun.

As soon as they feel our presence they take off and run away.

[In winter] they hardly sleep in their dens but anywhere on the ground. Now, the white foxes, they sleep by letting the snow cover them when it's blowing snow outside. We would always check out little mounds of snow when we hunted. Some white foxes let the snow cover them when they sleep. Sometimes when we check out a mound their breathing—We'd see a high mound of snow here, this part being higher, and the mound of snow there would be going up and down, the gap here would open more as it breathed in and out. When a mound of snow is moving like that there is a white fox beneath it sleeping. And since some of them sleep soundly, if there was no other sound to be heard, you'd almost step on them while they were covered with snow and sleeping like that.

[They only move] when they become alert. They behave differently from red foxes because they have keen eyesight and are very sensitive to movement and sound.

ALICE: What do you do when you see their dens?

FRANK: We tear apart dens that were easy to open and take them, but we don't do that to dens that are covered with thick ground or are deep.

The ground covering some dens was thin. But there were a lot of dens where foxes with pups stayed. There'd be many holes and passages beneath the ground. There would be many holes and passages where foxes delivered their pups and raised them.

The red foxes and white foxes, however, don't just stay underground when it gets

qengermeng. Tamakut-llu tamaa-i kaviaret tangrraqamteki tua-i qavarluki pissuraq-
luki. Iliini-llu kangarluta piamta pupingerrluki, uugnaraunguarluta. Avelngaunguar-
luta. Pupingerrluta, teriiqata-ll' qaskellikanirluta pupingqaquurluta. Tua-i taugaam
niicugniqarraarluteng tungemtenun tua-i.

Avelngatun pupingerrluta. Arulairrluteng niicugniaqata qaskellikanirluta puping-
qaquuraraqluki, nuvingalluki taugaam iirumaurluta. Nutegnariata-ll' tua-i tekitaqata nutaan nutegluki. Ilait-am taugken taringetuluteng. Taiyaaqerraarluteng, arulairluteng kiarrluteng piyaaqerrarluteng, ayakarluteng-llu tua-i. Usvitunrit tamakut
tuatnalartut, taringyuluteng. Uugnarissaagaqameng tua-i qecekpagaqluteng pituut;
niicugniqa'aqluteng. Pupingellagaluteng qimagatuut camani qanikcam aciani uug-
naraat, caranglluut-llu akuliitni. Taumek tuaten pitullruukut; taicetaatullruaput pu-
pingqaquurluki, pupingertaqluki kaviaret uliiret-llu.

Qavalrianek taugken tangrramta tua-i uq'lirneritgun, asguatgun pivkenata, uq'lirneritgun tumkarput tangaagurluku man'a ullallerkaat ullagtura'aqluki. Piyunaitelli-
niaqan utelmuarluta allakun mallengnaqu'uraraqluki.

Tua-i-ll' pivakarluta elpenga'artaqameng ayakaraqluteng. Ernerpak tua-i kangau-
maaqluta kiituan unugtuq kaviarnek uliirnek-llu pingnatugaqamta. Iliini pitaqen-
ricenaraqluki. Taumek kemgiutelallrulriakut. Atakumi taugaam unugmi ataucirqumek neryararluta, uksumi. Pissunriamta taugaam nutaan kemengluta. Tuaten
ayuqellruukut angutni. Taugken uitasciiganata piyuumirluta pilaamta.
Iliini taugken tua-i *lucky*-rluta. *Lucky*-rnaurtukut ernerem iliini. Malrutaqluta
wall'u pingayutaqluta. Igtet-llu ilait yungqelartut iliini pingayunek kaviarnek wall'u
cetamanek. Mamkilnguut tua-i piyunarqaqata enait navguq'erluki pikeggnerunrita-
qata teguaqluki. Imkut taugaam irniarit piyagiurviit inerquutaqtuit, navguusqevke-
naki, pikeggnerunrilnguut taugaam, qerrankuut-llu igtepiarunrilnguut. Qimagaaqa-
meng tamakunun taugaam itqerralartut kaviaret uliiret-llu, pikeggnerunrilngurnun.
Igtepianun taugken piyagiurvignun (itqertaqata), navguusqevkenaku nunii tauna.
Piiruciiqniluku. Tamakut taugaam pikeggnerunrilngurnun itqata, qerrankunun
qupnernun-llu, nunam qupnerinun, navgurluki pingramteki cangaitniluku. Nav-
guyuunaki tamakut igtait, igtepiat, piliarit.
Iliini pivakarluteng qavcinek yul'egmun itraqluteng. Tum'arrluki-llu piaqluta camek tangenrritaqamta. Tumait nutarautassiirluki, nutarat tua-i makut nutaan atur-

cold. Some went in their den and stayed, but they'd come out again. And when we see red foxes sleeping on snow, we'd hunt them. When we approached them on foot sometimes we'd make a squeaking sound, pretending to be mice. We'd be squeaking loudly, and when they sensed the sound, we'd lower our voice and make short squeaks in between. They'd listen for a moment and come toward us.

We'd make squeaking sounds like mice. When they stopped to listen, we would lower our voice and make short squeaks, but we'd aim our guns toward where they were hidden. When they came into view we'd shoot them. But some foxes stop, knowing that it wasn't actually a mouse making the sound. They'd start coming when they first heard the sound, then they would stop and look around and run off as soon as they realized [it wasn't a mouse]. Wiser foxes did that, they could easily detect [that no mouse was there]. When they went after mice, they jumped around when they tried to get it. They'd stop and listen and jump at them again. When mice were sought after by foxes, they'd make squeaking sounds under the snow or under some grass when trying to escape. That was why we did that; we used to entice red foxes and white foxes to come by making squeaking sounds.

But when we saw sleeping [foxes], we went on their sheltered side and not on their windward side and approached them by checking the trail that we'd used to approach them. When the trail wasn't good, we'd backtrack and approach them from another direction.

When they sensed us sometimes, they'd run off. We would walk all day, and it became dark eventually when we were hunting red and white foxes. Sometimes we gave up hunting them. That's why we lost weight. We only ate once a day during winter. We started to gain weight only when we stopped hunting. That's how we men were. But we couldn't stay put because we were eager to catch animals.

But sometimes we were lucky. We were lucky some days. [When we had luck] we'd catch two or three. And inside some dens there'd be three or four foxes. And some, if they were in holes close to the surface and not in real dens, we'd break and open up the hole and take them. But they warned us not to break open dens where they raised their pups. It was okay to break open holes that weren't real dens to take them. When they run away from hunters red and white foxes hide inside holes and crevices like that. But they told us not to break open their pupping dens. They said foxes wouldn't be seen in that area anymore. But when they went into the dens that weren't their actual dens, into holes in the ground, they said that it was okay if we broke them open. We never broke into the real dens that they built.

Sometimes hunters broke into holes that had several foxes in them. And we would also follow their tracks if we didn't see them. We would check to see if the

turluki ayagaqluta, kiarqurluki. Tua-i-ll' pivakarluta qavallrani tangerrluku yaa-i. Makut tumkestiit yaa-i. Arulairluni qavangellinilria. Nutaan tamakut unilluki, mallegg̣luk' tumkaput kiarrluku man'a. Tuaten tua-i ullagaqluki. Tua-i-ll' kiarartaqluteng. Malleggngaitelliniamteggu-ll' tua-i utelmuarluta cali avaggun cali ullagluku assirngalngurkun. Iliini tua-i tumkegciluta pinaurtukut. Tua-i nutegnariaqata nutgaqluki. Iliini taugken tua-i *lucky*-nrilamta unangesciiganata ernerpak ayagarcugluteng, niigarcugluteng.

Ciku-ll' imna qeciilnguq, qanikcamek qalliilnguq, tumkarnirtuq nutaan nivuilami. Taumek essnguraqameng kuiget qanikcaq mecilaraat camaken cikulraarurrluku. Tua-i qenuurrluku qanikcaq. Tamakut tamaa-i nuniitni qavaraqata pikegcilartukut, nivuunata tua-i. Waten ayuqluta ayangramta piiyuanrilngurtun neplirpek'nani piiyuallerput. Iliini canimaarmun tekitaqluki tamakut. Qanikcaam taugken cikumanrilnguum qaingakun piamta, yaaqsigluta elpenga'artaqluteng. Ciutait pek'ngartaqluteng, qamiqurrit taugken maktevkenateng. Tamakut tamaani piyunaitelartut, tumkarput assiinani qanikcauluni piaqan. Imkut taugaam qaliruat tamakussuutet tuntut piit, tamakut assinruluteng ac'inqigutekluki aturluki tamakunun pillrat; qaliruanek aterluteng.

Tua-i-llu eskiinek imkunek pilangata, aturluki eskiik tamakuk aurraqama, nutaan assipiat; kass'artaat imkut eskiit. Itullukek waten qaingagnun elavlua, nengllua, talligemkun taugaam waten elliurturlua, nutek maavet piluku. Assinrurpalliniluni nutaan qanikcaam qaikengraaku. Eskiit cali cukanaqluteng elitellrat. Qemini-ll' tua-i pavani elluraqami tua-i nangerngaurluni yaaqvanun ayagluni tua-i. Ayarurluta-ll' piyuilamta, imkuitnek tamakut; assikevkenaki. Ayaruilengramta tua-i elilluki eskiit; kankiitun tua-i ayuqluteng. Waten piaqata caqirtaqluteng ukatmun, ayarumek piilengramta.

Ciku taugken qanikcangvailgan, kankiinek imkunek nutaan muragnek pilianek, una kevkaringaluni, una kitngik tusngaluni taugaam. Qerrataluni una, una-ll' tusngaluni. Kankiim-llu pia iqua qalemyaarluni ukatmun. Tamakunek pililuta pilallruukut. Qecignek-llu *sealskin*-anek cingilirluki muriit. Ukut tua-i qerratavkarluki alulngunaunateng. Mernuyuunateng it'gaput. Patgusngalriit taugaam tamalkurmeng, mernungaqluni una wani. Tamakucit taugaam piliaput mernuyuunateng

tracks were new, and if they were fresh we'd follow the tracks, looking for [the fox]. Then after a while we'd see it sleeping up ahead. We'd know the tracks we followed were its tracks. It had stopped and fallen asleep. Then we would step aside from the tracks and begin looking around to find the best way to approach it. Then we'd approach it. The fox would open its eyes and look. Knowing that it was going to be difficult to approach it the way we had come, we'd go back and find another way to approach it. Sometimes we'd find a good way to approach it right away. When we got close enough we'd shoot it. But some days when we weren't lucky we wouldn't be able to get them all day long, they'd run away, they'd be very sensitive to sound and wake up easily.

They don't detect you when you approach them on ice that is not covered with snow because there's no sound. When rivers overflow, snow gets soaked over the ice and freezes solid and becomes like ice. Snow would turn into ice. Foxes sleeping in areas like that were easy to approach quietly. Though we approached them walking, there would be no sound, like we weren't walking. And sometimes we'd walk right up to foxes while they were still sleeping. But if we approached them walking on snow that wasn't frozen solid, they'd detect our presence by the sound, even from far away. We could see their ears moving when they heard the sound, but the head would still be down. When there was that kind of snow on our path, they were more difficult to catch. But if we changed our boots and put on *qaliruat* made out of caribou skin, it was easier to approach them [because they made less noise]; they were boot-sole padding called *qaliruat*.

Then when those skis became available, when I crept up on [sleeping foxes] using skis, they were perfect; the skis made in factories. I learned to use them by lying on them on my belly and moving my arms like this, placing my gun here [extended alongside]. They apparently were much better to use on any kind of snow. You can learn to use [skis] quickly. And when you used them to slide down the bluffs back there, you'd go far in them standing up. And we didn't use the poles that came with the skis; we didn't like using them. We learned how to use them without using poles; we used them like skates. When you do this they'd turn this way, even without using poles.

But before ice was covered with snow, with homemade wooden skates, skates they made with a gap here and solid base here for the heel. There'd be an open space under [the arch], and the heel would sit directly on this. And the front of the skate was curved this way. We made skates like that and used them. We'd attach sealskin lines on the skates to use as laces. With the open space under the arches here, the soles of your feet never hurt when you used them. Our feet never got tired using

it'gaput, alulngunaunateng. Utertaqamta taugaam atutuluki. Yuilqumi taugken yuumaluki atmaku'urluki taugaam piiyuagurluta. Pitarkaput kankiirluta pikumta kiturnayukluki yuilqumi atuyuunaki. Utertaqamta taugaam *camp*-amtenun wall'u nunanun atutuluki kankiit, unuakumi-ll' ayagaqamta erpailgan. Mecignarian-llu tua-i yuuluki kankiit, piiyuagurluta taugaam.

Enecuarnek tua-i enecuariaqluta tamakut nuniitgun, *camp*-amteni. Malruuluta-ll' piaqamta malruucaramek eneliaqluta. Napanek enirluku nunamek qallilirluku eneliaqluta tamakunek. Tua-i piuluteng enerraat amllerrluteng. Uum enii tuantaq-luni, pissuryarami nuniini. Tuaten tua-i pingqellruukut.

⌁: *Qayukegglit* :⌁

ALICE: Qayukegglit-llu-w' tumaitnek maligcuaratullrullilriaci.

FRANK: Ii-i. Manialngurni-wa taugaam kavirlililriani naparrlugni tamakut pitull-rulriit. Amllepialaryaaqut avani nunamni, nurnariut taugaam qangvarnek. Tumlia-nanrirluteng-llu uksumi. Nangluteng tua-i tamakut.

⌁: *Imarmiutaat cuignilnguut-llu piciryarallrat* :⌁

Teggviit-llu tamakut cuignilngurtaqluteng atauciunrilngurmek. Tua-i taugken ut'ru-lluki tekicamta, aanaka wall'u maurluqa anluni qantamek tegumiarluni. Taukut-llu tua-i imarmiutaat nayumiqaluki qantamun ekluki. Nutaan nayumiqaluku qan-taq tauna enemun itrulluku. Itrucamegteggu-llu nutaan yuuluki tuaken qantamek. Nutaan imarmiutaat cuignilngurnek-llu avungqerraqata anqurluki, neverqurluki caniqliqu'urluki. Qaqicata-ll' uqumek *seal oil*-amek tegulluteng, pupsuteng aku'ur-qaarluk' qengait mingukaqluki, it'gaita-ll' nuugit mingukaquurluki, pamyuan-llu nuuga. Tuatnatuluki. Qaqicata-ll' tua-i nutaan elkarrluki, taqluki tua-i.

them. But when you used the skates with solid bases, this [arch] would get tired. But when we used the skates we made, the soles of our feet never got sore. We only used them when we returned from hunting. But out on the land when we hunted we'd just pack them on our backs and roam. We never used them when we hunted, fearing that we might skate by animals nearby and miss the chance of catching them. We only used them when we went back to our camps after hunting or when we went home. We also used them when we went out hunting early in the morning while it was still dark. And when it got light we'd take them off and use our feet to continue on.

And we made little sod houses at our camps. And if there were two of us, we'd make a small sod house big enough for two. We'd make little houses, making the frame out of bushes and covering it with sod. There'd be many little sod houses everywhere. A hunter would make a sod house close to where he hunted. We used little sod houses when we hunted.

~: Tundra hares :~

ALICE: You probably followed tundra hare tracks, too.

FRANK: Yes. They stayed in places where the ground was rugged and had lots of red willows. Over in my home there used to be a lot, but few have been seen for several years now. You don't even see their footprints in the snow anymore. Their numbers are down.

~: Customs regarding mink and otter :~

And those *tegviit* [wooden traps for otter and mink] would catch several otter at once. And when we got home with the catch, my mother or my grandmother would come out holding a wooden bowl. Then she'd carefully pick up the mink with both hands and place them in the bowl. Then she'd carefully bring the bowl into the house. When they brought it inside she'd take them all out of the bowl in the house. Then she'd lay the mink side by side, and the otter, if there were any, on their backs. Then when they were all laid like that she pinched her fingers and dipped them in seal oil and started dabbing the tips of their noses with a bit of oil. She also brushed the ends of their hands and feet with some seal oil and also the tip of their tails. That was what they always did with mink and otter. And after they all had been brushed with seal oil, they were set aside, and they were done.

Can'giiret-llu takuigaqata neqkameggnek, tekiutaqatki, tuaten qantamek imail-
ngurmek atlilirluki itrutetuluki enenun. Qantamun pivkenaki itrucuunaki. Tamakut-llu unguvalriit imarmiutaat kanaqliit cuignilnguut. Tuaten piciryaraqluku.
Ayuqluteng tamarmeng tua-i tuatnatuluteng yuut.

Imarmiutaat-llu cuignilnguut-llu qamiqurrit tua-i eggngaunaki, kanaqliit-llu.
Cakuivkenaki tua-i nertullruit qamiqutuumaita, it'gait-llu. Tamalkuita tua-i enrit.
Kanaqliit taugaam pamyuitnek nerevkayuunata. Inerquraqluta, waten-gguq elliu-
ngeciqukut. Ungaullugnarqut-gguq. Kuimaqameng waten elliuksuaratuut kanaqliit
pamyuit. Tuaten ellirciqniluta. Ungauluksuarangciqniluta uitangramta, tamakunek
nertukumta kanaqliit pamyuitnek. Arnat taugaam nertuluki; angukara'urluut, arna-
ssagaat-llu tamakunek. Umyuama-am iliini pilarait, "Assilriit tang makut angukara'urluut, arnaraat-llu inerquutek'laryugnarqekait." [engel'artuq] Taugaam piyuunii
tuaten ping'erma. Tuatnatuluteng tua-i. Ukvekluki tua-i.

Imarmiutaat cuignilnguut-llu tuaten call' pituluki. Kaviaret uliiret-llu piyuunaki,
tuntut-llu piyuunaki, kanaqliit-llu piyuunaki. Una taugaam imarmiutaq, cuignil-
nguq-llu pituluku. Taugaam taluyaqngaugaqata qantaicuunaki. Qancirrlainarluki
tua-i itrutaqluki. Tuaten-llu pirrlainarluki, uqurrarmek qengait mingukarluki,
ipiita-ll' nuugit, pamyuat-llu.

And when they checked the blackfish traps for their meal, when they arrived with them, they always placed the container of blackfish inside an empty bowl and brought them into the house. They always brought them inside in bowls. They brought animals like mink, muskrat, and land otter into the house in the same way. That was the custom. Everyone practiced that custom everywhere.

And they never threw away mink and otter heads, and also the heads of beavers. They ate the whole body of these animals, including their heads and feet. They'd eat every part of the animal. But they didn't let us eat muskrat tails. They'd say if we ate them our head would begin to shake like this. When muskrat swim in water their tails move like this slightly. They'd tell us if we ate muskrat tails our heads would start moving like that. Women, however, ate the muskrat tails; old men and women ate them. Sometimes I think, "These tasty foods, these old men and women warned us not to eat them so they could be the only ones to eat them." [laughs] But I never said anything though I was suspicious. That was what they told us, and we believed them.

They did a ritual for mink and otter. But not for red foxes, white foxes, muskrat, and caribou. But they always did rituals for mink and otter. If they had been caught in traps underwater they always carried them into houses inside bowls. And they always brushed their noses and the tips of their feet and tails with a little bit of seal oil.

Qayaq

Kayak

Qayaq

~: Qayat aklukaitnek quyurciyaraq :~

Imumi murilkessagutua, up'nerkami tua-i waten un'a ketvut cikuirtellra umiqer-luku, Kusquqvagmek muriit an'aqelriit. Anuqekegcateng taugaam ukatmun una-ggun caniarluteng. Tua-i-ll' qaill' pitariqerluku ungalamek anuqengluni. Piciry-araqluk' ellam. Unani muriit taggluki tua-i maavet Caninermun. Qaivarrluki tua-i qulmun ulerpagluni anuqlirluni cakneq. Encami-ll' tua-i kayukellirluni tuaten ulen-qiggngairulluni. Irr'inaqluni.

Tua-i-llu inerquumaluta murak pugtaluku unani tegusqevkenaku. Ciunipailgan tegusqevkenaku. Nunamun tua-i tekitaqan (nutaan teguluku). Canimelliaqata muriit angernimek tua-i muriit tepiitnek tepengluni, narniqpiarluni. Ungalamek anuqlirluni. Tepkegtut muriit.

Tua-i-llu nutaan encan angutet nutaan ayagaluteng, kegglanek piluteng, casku-nek, piqertuutarnek, muragnek cakarnilrianek yualriit. Unarcianek canek cakar-nilrianek, wall'u nek'anek qupurluki piarkanek (yuarluteng). Mimernanek-llu yuv-rirluteng assilriit aitarucirluteng qupurrluki. Assinrit aug'araqluki ayagarkarnilriit, ukinqucugkarnilriit, pamyukarnilriit, amuvigkarnilriit, kagaalurkarnilriit. Tama-kut tua-i mimernanek ataucinek piyuunateng. Yuarluteng allanek ilakaitnek piaqlu-teng. Unarcianek tuaten, saaganerkanek, cauyararkanek tuaten. Qayikunalriit tua-ten tua-i pituut.

Tua-i-ll' naangata qayarkat, nutaan tua-i cakilluki, qanilqerluki-gguq. Miklicar-luki canivkenaki tua-i keputekun. Tamakucinek keputnek (aturluteng). Kepun tauna pikaqa. Wii pikaqa tauna. Atama waniwa piliallra. Manigcetqapiarluku caliaqerkauluku uum. Qeltararluku waten pingaunaku. Ukatmun keputequarkau-

Kayak

~: *Gathering materials for the kayak* :~

When I got older and started paying attention to things, in spring after the water down below us was completely free of ice, shortly after that, wood began floating out to the Kuskokwim Bay. After they floated out and the wind was blowing just right, they began floating in our direction. And sometime after that, wind would begin blowing from the south. That was normal weather every year [after spring breakup]. The prevailing south winds would bring the wood up inland to the Canineq area. Strong winds would blow from the south, allowing the water to rise, and the wood would float in above land. And when the water receded it would get calm, and after that the water didn't rise to that level again [that summer]. It was an amazing phenomenon.

We were warned not to take wood while it was floating in ocean water. They told us not to take it before it reached land. [We could only take them] when they arrived on land. When the south wind brings them up toward land and they were floating in toward our village, we'd start smelling the sweet scent of tree sap in the air. Wood has a wonderful scent.

Then when the high water receded, men would leave with saws, axes, and other tools to start looking for wood that was suitable to make into things. They'd look for long, straight-grained pieces of wood to make into things, or logs that they could split and use as frames for sod houses. They'd also check the trunks and use wedges to cut off the parts that were good to use. They'd cut off the part that was good to make into kayak deck beams, the part good to use for the kayak bow top, the stern handle, the lower bow, and the stern bottom. Those different parts needed for the kayak frame weren't all found in one trunk. They checked other trunks to get the parts they needed. They'd also check long, straight-grained pieces of wood to see if they were good to use for the side stringers and the fore and aft ribs. Those who were planning to make new kayaks, that was the way they looked for parts they needed for the frame.

When all the wooden pieces for a kayak frame were found, they'd use an adze and chisel them down, but they didn't whittle them [using their crooked knife] and shape them to the size they needed. They'd use an adze like that one. That adze is mine. It was made by my father. When wood was chiseled using this tool, it would

luni murak. Elisngalriit tua-i manigpak tua-i (pinaurait). Tuskatun ayuqerkauluni yuum makucikun caliara murak. Makucinek caskirluteng mimernat qayarkat
nutaan caliaqluki. Mikliata-ll' tua-i taqluki cali pivsiararkauluki. Qanilqaamegteki-
gguq tuatnaluki tua-i tamalkuita ayagarkat, ukinqucugkat, pamyukat-llu. Qayam
aklukai tua-i qaqilluki mimernat qanilqerluki, miklicarluki, piyunarcarluki. Quyurr-
luki-ll' tua-i caliaqngairulluki tua-i kiagpak. Uksuqan taugaam nutaan caliaqerkau-
luki.

Akerciurcetevkenaki kiagpak, talinermi quyuita uitavkarluki.

Taugken ilait qava'anlluteng Kusquqvagmi neqliyaraqameng, kiagungraan qavani
qayarkanek cali pituluteng, neqlillerni, ut'rutarkameggnek cali piyunarqellrianek, tamakunek pillrungermeng maani nunamteni. Tuaten tua-i upluteng.

Tuamtell' up'nerkami pissulriit qayat amirkaitnek uquircetnaurait assircaarte-
lluki ilulirnerit, uquicurlagavkarpek'naki. Qeciit-am ilaita uquiriaqameng uluameggnek tekiarpallagluku mamkelli'irtelluki tapqutetuit. Tuaten piyaaqevkenaki qayarkat amirkait pivkatuit.

Nillarluki cali assircaarluki, assirtelluki tua-i nillaraqluki. Tua-i-llu allakarluki
kinrata qayat amirkait. Allanun makunun naterkanun avukuucetevkenaki, allakaita tua-i pivkarluki. Qemaggluki tua-i kiagpak tamakut qayarkat amirkait. Cali
issurinek ilaluki allanek piciatun. Ilateng ikayualuki pituameng akimek qanerpek'nateng, amirkameggnek enuryugaqata cikituamegteki pikalget qayarkanek. Waten-llu
piyuunani, "Cimiqiu. Cimiqiu man'a."

∾: Qayaliyaraq :∾

Tua-i taugken nutaan utercameng maavet nunameggnun uksillernun pirraarluteng
canek tua-i nutaan uksuarmi, tamakut imkut qayarkat pivkenaki caliaqevkenaki,
taluyanek can'giircuutekanek caliarluteng tua-i uksuarmi, wall' ikamriluteng. Qayarkat taugaam piksaunaki, kiituani tua-i uksurtuq, caliaqsuunaki. Ellivigmi uitalu-

end up perfectly smooth. It wouldn't have bumps on it like these. You'd move the adze in this direction on wood when you chiseled it to smooth it out. After someone worked on wood using this tool it would look like a wooden plank from a factory. They would use these tools to prepare the wooden parts cut off from a trunk to use for a kayak frame. After they chiseled the pieces down they'd put them away to finish carving them later. They cut all the parts, the parts for the deck beams, bow top, and stern handle. They'd cut and chisel all wooden pieces they had chosen for the kayak frame, and they made them smaller and ready to carve into shape. They'd put them together and set them aside and didn't touch them all summer. When winter came they'd take them out and finally start working on them.

They'd leave them in the shade all summer, keeping the sun away from them.

But some people who moved up to fish camp on the Kuskokwim River would also gather wood for kayak frames up there. Though they had already gathered wood down here, they'd find some more to bring home. That was how they prepared [to make new kayaks].

Also during spring, the hunters would have the ones doing the skinning carefully remove the blubber from the inner side of the sealskins which were to be used as coverings for kayaks, making sure that they removed the blubber carefully. When some people remove blubber from skins they cut too close to the skin with their semilunar knives, cutting off part of the skin, causing it to become too thin. They were careful not to allow them to prepare kayak skin coverings in that way.

They also stretched skins out to dry very carefully, and then after all the skins dried they would set the skins aside that were specially prepared for kayak coverings. They didn't store them with skins for boot soles, but stored them separately during summer. They kept the kayak skins stored away all summer. They also collected spotted seals and other kinds of skins. Those who had extra skins for kayak coverings also gave some to people who lacked them without asking for payment. They never said, "You have to pay me back. You should pay me back for this."

~: *Kayak construction* :~

When they returned to their winter villages, they concentrated on making blackfish traps or sleds during the fall, rather than kayak parts and equipment. They did not work on kayak parts, which were stored in their storage places, and soon it became winter. However some people constructed kayaks during summer. They made my

teng quyurmeng. Taugken ilait kiagmi taugaam qayituluteng. Kiagmi wii qayange-
qarraarcetellruatnga. Qaterpek'nani tua-i qayaqa, kaviyaagcenani amia nengelmi
kinenrilani. Tuaten tua-i pituluki ilait.

Tua-i taugken January-mi wall'u February-mi, January nangvailgan nutaan yurau-
mariaqameng, nutaan yuraryarat December-aami atutuamegteki, makut tua-i nunamiutaat neqsuryarat taqluteng pingnaqngairulluteng. January-m nangqatallrani
February-mun-llu unkumiutarnek pingnaqsarat atu'urkat tegutuit, piciatun-am pivkenateng.

Upengluteng tua-i qayat akluitnek. Qamigautekaitnek piciatun, narulkarcuu-
tekaitnek-llu makunek, anguarutet-llu cimirkaitnek, aarnarqelriit, negciit-llu. Calia-
teng cimirluku.

Nutaan tamakut qasgilluki ayagarkat, tamalkuita pivkenateng. Talliman ayagarkat qasgilluki. Nutaan cakiqurluki. Piyungamegteki-llu perenrit ukut ilututaciit pi-
tacqeggiata nutaan ayanerkait nutaan cuqluki taktacirkait. Paingan ik'um ukaqlian,
ayagaq waten ayuqelria.

Ikna ika-i atengqertuq ayanermek. Ciuqlia-wa nengengali, ciuqlia-w' pingayuak
ayagacuaq. Una-wa paingan kinguqlia asaun, kinguqlia-wa ayagacuaq. Ingkuk-wa
nangneqliik tuntunak. Ingkuk-wa call' nangneqliik ciungani tuntunak. Ayagauvke-
natek.

Elliyaraulutek tua-i paugna qulaq paugna qancuaramegrnek iqmigluku, tupir-
luki-llu tua-i. Waten elliurcessngaunaku paugna nayumiqaluku, tuntunak ingkuk,
pamyuan nuniinelnguq, ingna-llu ciumi. Makut ayagat nayumiqastengunritut ingkuk taugaam tuntunat ukut pagkuk nayumiqastekakek, waten elliurcessngaunaku,
iqukek apamamun pulasngalutek waten, tuntunat makut. Waten tua-i pimaluteng.
Tuaten-llu ayuqluteng.

Una taugken tua-i cuqyutekluku ayaneq una caliaqurluki, paugkut waten ayuqelriit ayagat. Naniliinaarluki cuqequrluki. Una kiingan ayaneq waten cuqtetuat,
tua-i-llu makut ilai perenritgun. Nengenganrucuarluku-llu ingna nengengali. Ukut-
gun-llu tua-i yuaratgun cuqtaarluki kepkanillerkaat, ukutgun. Ukuk waniwa arca-
qerlutek, ayaganun makunun atulriaruuk, ukuk wani.

first kayak during summer. The skin covering on my kayak wasn't bleached but was a little reddish because it hadn't dried in the cold. Some were made that way.

But in January or February, after they had their dance festival which was always scheduled for December and also after their subsistence activities on land had came to a close, during the last part of January and into February, they began constructing tools for hunting sea mammals. They did not do things randomly; they followed a schedule.

They began preparing the equipment they would use while hunting with kayaks. They made kayak sleds and a variety of gear; harpoons, spears, and replacements for paddles; they fixed hazardous items, including gaffs. Their responsibilities changed.

At that time, they brought the five deck beam pieces into the *qasgi*. Then they progressively shaped them by chipping on them with an adze. And when their angles and depth were just right, they determined the length for the piece that was to be the *ayaneq* [first front deck beam]. First they made the deck beam which goes right in front of the cockpit coaming.

The first deck beam [next to the cockpit on the forward side over there] is called the *ayaneq*. The second deck beam in front of it is called the *nengengali*, and the third deck beam, the one in front of the *nengengali*, is called the *ayagacuaq*. Then the first rear deck beam, underneath the back of the cockpit coaming, is called the *asaun*, and the one behind it, which is the second rear deck beam, is called the *ayagacuaq*. Then the last two are called the *tuntunak*; these are the two endmost aft deck beams. And the two foremost deck beams are also called *tuntunak*. They are not called *ayagaq* [general term for deck beam other than the two foremost and two rearmost].

They set the endmost and foremost deck beams in place by setting their small notches into the *qula* [deck stringer] and lashing them in place. The foremost and endmost deck beams stabilize the kayak, keeping the deck stringer in place. The first deck beams which are next to and forward of the cockpit do not hold the deck stringer in place, but the foremost and endmost deck beams hold it in place and keep it stable as the ends are inserted in the *apamaq* [gunwale]. That's how they are situated.

They construct all the deck beams based on the measurement of the first deck beam, the *ayaneq* [which is next to and forward of the cockpit]. When measuring for the deck beams they make each one shorter than the preceding one. They measure the length of the *ayaneq* from the underarm to the tip of the finger, then the other deck beams are measured according to their angles. However, they make the *nengengali* a bit shorter than the *ayaneq*. They determine the length of the other

Waniwa una ayaneq ingkugnegun tua-i cuqngaunaku, uuggun ak'a cuqcami, uum taktaciatun. Ikna-llu ika-i pai, ingna wani painga, uutun neqututauq. Ukatmun-llu cali neqututaarkauluni. Una tua-i *square*-arluni, waten kangiritatekluteng, makut taktatekluteng tamalkurmeng, ikna painga.

Qayikuma wii elpet cuqngaitan. Wii taugaam pimkun pirrlainarciqaqa. Angtat-kenritukut tua-i. Wall'u mikellrukuvet, mikliqerciiquq cuqtellren, ilaksunaunak uu-mun wii cuqnemkun pimalriamun. Tuaten-am pivkatuit.

Waten tua-i, una waniwa ciumek caliaqetuluku. Ukuk-llu tua-i waniwa tunglir-kak. Waniwa nengenganru'uralria. Pugumanrulutek ukuk wani, ukuk-wani pugu-malutek, una-llu ukaqsinruluni.

Nengengali-gguq waniwa. Una-wa' ayagacuaq ilutmun perenruluni. Tua-i-llu una wani asaun, uutun pitaarkauluni; uum tua-i pitatekluku. Ukuk-llu cali una-llu angtateklutek cali pernekek.

Ukuk kingumi uitalriik, ukut ciungani. Una waniwa ayaneq, nengengali, aya-gacuaq. Una-wa asaun, ayagacuaq-wa aipaa. Makut tua-i waten caliaqurluki nutaan uksumi, February-m iluani maani ayagnirluki, January-m nangvailganek ayagluni. Waten tua-i ellirluki. Qayam aklukai tua-i tamalkuita nutaan caliaqluki.

Qaqicata-llu tua-i makut mimernat, pamyurkaq, ukinqucugkaq, amuvigkaq, kagaalurkaq. Taukut tua-i qaqicata, mingugluki waten quyurrluki anulluki. Kavia-ruarkak-llu ayapervigkak-llu, tuntunarkat-llu quyurrluki tua-i waten anulluki.

Tua-i makut arcaqerluteng caliyarat qaqicamegteki nutaan saaganerkanek qupuri-luteng, unarcianek imkunek. Takluteng, tua-i tak'urluteng. Akaggluki-am waten tua-i pivkenaki-am taqevlacagluki, qanilqerluki-am nutaan. Ellegluki, amilicarar-kauluki nutaan kingumek, *finishing*-aarturarkauluki.

deck beams [by using the ring and pinky fingers] to measure how much shorter to make each one than the preceding deck beam. These two [pinky and ring] fingers are important for this purpose.

The *ayaneq* won't be measured using those two fingers, since its length is the starting point for the measurements of the other deck beams. The diameter of the cockpit coaming is the same [as the length of the *ayaneq*]. It forms a square with the cockpit touching the sides.

If I construct a kayak for myself, you will not be the one determining its measurements. I will use only my measurements. We are not all the same size. Or if you are smaller, your measurements will be shorter, and your measurements should not be mixed with my measurements for my kayak. That is how they had them measured, according to each individual's body size.

They construct [the *ayaneq*] first. These two deck beams [the *nengengali* and *ayagacuaq*] will follow it. [The *nengengali*] extends upward a little more [than the *ayaneq*]. Between the two ends of the *nengengali* there is more curvature [if the *nengengali* is placed directly on the *ayaneq*], and the *ayaneq* is closer to me here.

They call this second forward deck beam the *nengengali*. This third forward deck beam, the *ayagacuaq*, bends more inward. Now, this first rear deck beam, *asaun*, should be the same curvature as this *nengengali*. And the curvatures of these two [*ayagacuak*] are also the same.

These two deck beams are in the aft part of the kayak, and these, the *ayaneq*, *nengengali*, and *ayagacuaq* are in the forward part of the kayak. The *asaun* and *ayagacuaq* [are in the stern]. They always construct these during the winter, starting in February or before the end of January. They work on them until they are finished like these here. And then they work on all the fittings of the kayak.

They complete the parts made out of spruce stumps with lateral roots, which include the *pamyuq* [top stern piece], the *ukinqucuk* [top bow piece], the *amuvik* [lower bow piece], and the *kagaaluq* [lower stern piece]. When they have finished these parts they take them all outdoors and paint them. They also work on the pieces which are going to be the *kaviaruak* [two keel supports, lit. "pretend foxes"], *ayaperviik* [two cockpit coaming stanchions], and the *tuntunat* [two endmost and foremost deck beams], and they take them all outside.

When they completed the most essential and time-consuming parts, they split straight-grained wood to make the *saaganret* [side stringers]. They are relatively long pieces. The side stringers are finished with a rounded profile; they did not leave them rough. They cut them thick at first, and later they thinned them and did finishing work on them.

Qaqicamegteki-llu tua-i quyuita qillerrluki, nalqiaterrlulriit makut nalqigivkar-
luki tua-i qillerrluki. Qasgimun-am agarrluki puqlamun maqiqutelluki, uutarluki.
Tua-i-llu piyungamegteki nutaan tuatnallratni uutallratni, nutaan cauyararkanek
caniluteng.

Qukaqliit *fourteen*-aaruluki ellenrit, perenrit angtatkelriit, wall'u *thirteen*-aaruv-
karluki, paim pik'um acianelnguut, kinguanelnguut wani amllenruurluteng. Engin-
ret-gguq. Cali-am qukait kankut mamtunruluteng, wani-llu tua-i perqatallermeggni
mamkellikanirluteng.

Makut taugken avaqliit tuaten ayuqevkenateng; mamkunateng ayuqluteng.
Maa-i makut enginret mamtulriit, ukuni-llu mamtunruluteng qukait kankut; teggluteng. Angtatekluteng tua-i maa-i yaavet kinguanun. Kinguani yaa-i pingayut. Tuaten ayuqluteng cauyararkat.

Makut taugken wani uitalriit cauyarauluteng qamyartullrani. Tuaten tua-i keggmiarpek'naki tua-i cauyararkiurturluteng. Makunek tua-i maa-i caliluteng, waten
pivkenaki taq'aqluki.

Maa-i tang enginret. Una wani mamtunruluni, waten-llu cuqerluni. *Fourteen*-
augarkauluteng tua-i iliini, iliini-llu *thirteen*-aaruluteng angtatkurluteng. Uum-llu
tua-i kinguqlia nutaan miklikanirarkauluni una wani, apamam waten piyartullra,
qamyartullra. Waten keggmiaqsaunaki taugaam elliaqluki. Qaqicata-llu tua-i cipnir-
turluki, nutaan uiteramek minggugluki, keggmiarpek'naki tua-i nutaan anulluki.

Tua-i-llu nutaan anucimariamegteki, tamakut imkut saaganerkat agkut, waten qaingatni uitaarkat makut wani. Atrarrluki nutaan maqiqunrillret angilluki
nutaan caniluki amiliarluki assirivkarluki. Qaqicata-llu usguquurluki usgunerkait,
usguquurluki. Qaqicata nutaan uiterarrluki qaingat. Apamak piksaunakek, apamarkak makuk. Tua-i-llu nutaan qaqicata saaganerkat qaqicata qayam tua-i *part*-ai tamarmeng qaqilluteng, apamak taugaam kiimek.

Anulluki tua-i piamegteki nutaan apamarkak itrullukek, unrapigaq atauciq muragaq, assilria tua-i akquunani-llu, qupumaluni waten. Nutaan tamana tamaa-i
ullelluku. Apamarkiurluta cakiqurluku. Tua-i caniyarairulluku waten ayuqluku ta-

After they finished their construction, they tied the side stringers together to straighten the ones that were a little crooked. They hung them inside the *qasgi* and heated them. While the side stringers were being exposed to heat in the *qasgi*, they carved the pieces that were to be ribs.

There were thirteen or fourteen thicker ribs with the same curvatures that are centrally placed in the kayak frame. Some of these ribs were placed directly under the cockpit coaming, but more of them were placed aft of the cockpit coaming. The center ribs are called *enginret*. The middle of a center rib is thicker, and it thins down where it bends.

However, a rib forward or aft of those central ribs would be different; it would be of even thickness, whereas the *enginret* are thicker in the middle than those other ribs; they are strong. [The *enginret*] are the same size going back. There are three [*enginret*] going back from the coaming. That is how the ribs are.

These foremost and aftmost ribs, the *cauyarat*, are those that are where the frame tapers. They don't progressively bend these ribs by biting on them. They make these ribs and finish them without biting on them to bend them.

These are *enginret*. Their midsections are thicker, and they are measured like this [by grasping the bottom, center of one rib with both hands, palms down with thumbs extended, but bent and joined at the finger tips]. They sometimes have fourteen equal-sized central ribs and sometimes thirteen. And they made the curvature of the ribs smaller in the area where the gunwales converge. They just inserted the end ribs in place without progressively bending them by biting on them. And when they were done, after they made these additional ribs, they colored them with red ochre and took them outside without having bent them by progressively biting down on them and curving them that way.

Then after they took [the ribs] out of the *qasgi*, they worked on the pieces that were to be the side stringers, the *saaganret*, that would be placed outside of the ribs. They took down the pieces they had been curing during fire baths and untied them, and finally whittled them down to the correct thickness. When they finished, they joined shorter pieces, extending them as necessary. They then colored them with ochre when they were done. The two gunwales, *apamak*, weren't completed yet, the pieces that were to be the gunwales hadn't been worked on yet. And when the side stringers were done, all parts of the kayak were completed except for the gunwales.

When they took the side stringers outside, they then brought in the wood for the gunwales, one spruce sapling, a good one without any knots that had been split down the middle. They arranged it so that the inner side of the split log would be

QAYAQ

makucikun, keputekun, esluussarluku tuaten. Elisngalrianun iliini pivkatuit ilaita keputequtulrianun. Ataka imna elisngauq. Tua-i waten ayuqetuluni tamakucikun pillra, caniyaraunani tua-i.

Apamak tua-i qaqicagnek nutaan ayagcirlukek uum pitatiinek, amillranek aipir-luku. Paingan nalkaanun ikavet pilukek nutaan tuavet pivkarlukek apamak waten quullukek naspaalukek. Tangaalukek, pinauraput man'a inglua teggenrullinia-llu perumavkenani perngermi, una taugken perenruluni assirluni.

Ingna tuamtellu iqua cali pirraarluku nallunailkuciqerluku piarkat, aug'arluki nutaan mamkellicakanivguarluki tamana ingna-llu. Qaqitaqan una ataam ayagua-raqluku. Ayuqsagucagnek-llu waten perelkek ing'um-llu nutaan taqluku apamak. Nutaan tua-i taqngamegtekek tunullukek nutaan tunuyullukek quyurrlukek, ne-merlukek.

Nemrraarlukek nutaan makut kapusngallerkait uitallerkait *mark*-araqluki. Una ciumek ellituat, kingua ikna yaggluku, capngiam ngeliignek, una-llu cipnera piqer-luku uuggun, uum-llu tua-i ngeliinun cetqalleq elliluku. Ilulirnerkun cetqerlukek waten ayagam makucim uitallerkaa.

Nutaan akultutatekek. Akultutaciit cuq'ertaqluki *mark*-araqluki, *mark*-arturluki. Qaqicata-llu makut uitavigkait, agkut cali elliurluki. Akuliik ukuk malruk pingayu-nek cauyararciraqluku.

Tua-i-llu nutaan qaqican angillukek apamak, nutaan ukiqluki, makut wani ukiq-luki uitallerkait. Qaqicata-llu cauyarat uitallerkait, cali iqukeggurturluki, ilututate-ku'urluki, tamalkuita tua-i. Tuntunat-llu pillerkait anevkenaki.

the outer side of the gunwale. We constructed the pieces that were to be the gunwales by progressively carving them down. We worked them with an adze in such a way that they would not need to be further planed down. Sometimes they asked people who were good with adzes to do this part. My father was skilled. The pieces he made with that tool were smooth and wouldn't have to be whittled down any more.

When the gunwales were completed, they held the ends together and spread the gunwales apart in the center with a spreader that was the same length as the *ayaneq* along with a thinner spreader. They placed the spreader in the area where the cockpit coaming would be and joined the other ends of the gunwales together to test it. We would look at them and see that perhaps one gunwale, although somewhat bent, was stiffer and wasn't bending as much as it ought to, while the other gunwale was bending as it should.

Then after checking the other end, they marked the spots they should shave down along the gunwales and then removed the spreaders and thinned down that section a little, and on the other side also. When they were done, they tested it again with the spreaders. When their curvature was the same on both sides, they were done working on the gunwales. When they had finished them, they placed them back-to-back, putting them together that way, and bound them.

After binding the gunwales, they marked the places where the deck beams would be mortised into the gunwales. They put a mark on first by extending their arms from the stern end of the gunwales, from the inside edge of the wider section at the end of the gunwales where they are joined, the *capngiak*, added an open hand measurement from the thumb to the index finger, marked a line along the edge of that measurement, and placed the cockpit coaming along that mark. They placed a mark along the inside of the cockpit coaming where the deck beam would be.

Then they marked the spacing between each of the deck beams [with the measurement from the elbow to the tip of the index finger, *ikuyagneq*]. They marked the correct spacing between each of the deck beams and marked them on the gunwales one by one. And when they finished marking the places where the deck beams would go, they marked the places where the ribs would be put. They placed three fore and aft ribs between two deck beams.

And when that process was complete, they untied the gunwales and mortised them where the tenons of those deck beams would fit. When they determined where the ribs would be, they chiseled the mortises into the gunwales where the tenons of the ribs would be inserted, making them all the same depth. The mortises for the bow and stern deck beams, *tuntunat*, were drilled only part way through the wood of the gunwales.

Tua-i-llu qaqican nutaan, uiterarqaarlukek apamak, qanerluteng palurciqatarni-luku. Qaqilluni tua-i-am qayaq tua-i, apamak taqngagnek. Palurciqatarniluku.

Nutaan-llu tua-i makut mamkellicarluki piaqluki, kapurqurluki agaavet. Qaqi-cata nutaan quyurrluki-am cali yuvrirluki, tangaaluki perneret, perenri makut.

Tua-i nutaan qaqicata makut, quyurrluki tangaarraarluku, assiata, ussukcaraq-luki-am waten, piyailkucirturluki. Apamaq maanlluni tua-i waten, akia-llu.

Nutaan iquuk ukuk. Ingna ciumek ingna waten ayuqelria ellituat. Yaa-i-gguq amuvik. Una waniwa ciumek ellituat. Apamak quyungqallrak, wavet elliluku, amu-viim qainganun, capngiak.

Apamak iqukek makuk capngiagnek atengqertuk, wantarkak amuviim qaingani, kingua-llu ingna. Quyurrlukek tua-i apamak waten, quyurrlukek, ilangarrlukek-llu tua-i cingaullukek.
Assiriagnek nutaan wavet tegg'eranek, muragnek tegqupagnek ussukcarlukek acitmun. Tua-i-llu nutaan ukatmun cali ussukcarluku, apamak iqukek capngiagne-kun. Ussukcarraarlukek-llu ukillukek cali uuggun. Nutaan tupirlukek cagnilluku nutaan iquak ingna.

Qaqican nutaan palurrluku qayaq, nutaan kingua ingna caliaqluku. Piyunarian mumiggluku cali amatii pirraarluku, una ellinguaraqluku. Una ellinguaraqluku uum tungii. Tua-i tupirluku ussukcarluku-llu pirraarluku, nutaan palurrluku.

Palurutek-am, augkunek muragnek kangrit waten ayuqluteng, aminani una nuna-mun kaputetuluteng. Man'a tua-i waten enigluku muriim waten pillran, nunamun kapulluki palurutet.

When they were done, after coloring the gunwales with red ochre, they announced that they were going to start the process of setting the gunwales to the right depth and curvature. [It is a process which requires turning over the gunwales with the deck beams attached to them and with their ends sitting on posts, and then placing various weights in the middle.] The kayak parts were complete when the gunwales were done. They would announce that they were going to start the process of setting the gunwales to the right curvature.

Then they tenoned each of the ends of the deck beams and mortised them into the gunwales one by one, working toward the stern. When these were in place, they held the gunwales together at the ends and examined them again, looking at the curvatures.

When the deck beams were completed, they grouped and examined them closely, and finding them appropriately finished they mortised the ends of the deck beams into the gunwales, like this, pegging them in place. The gunwales would be here and on the other side of the deck beams.

Then they worked on the two ends of the gunwales. They first attached that lower bow piece that is shaped like this. They call that lower bow piece *amuvik*. They placed this piece on first. Where the gunwales had been joined, the ends of the gunwales, the *capngiak*, were placed on top of the *amuvik*.

The ends of the gunwales are called *capngiak*. The forward ends would eventually be placed here on top of the *amuvik*, and the aft ends in the stern. They join the gunwales at the ends, planed them first and joined them together.

When the gunwales were ready, they inserted hard wooden pegs here in four places on the upper surface of the *capngiak* [and pounded them down into the *amuvik*]. Then they inserted hard wooden pegs again in this direction horizontally, to connect the gunwales at their ends. After inserting the pegs, they drilled a hole here [through both gunwales, in the front part of the *capngiak*]. Then they bound the gunwales together at the ends very tightly using those holes.

When that process was complete, they turned the kayak over and worked on the stern. When it was time, they turned it right side up, and after working on the other side, they placed this [stern bottom, *kagaaluq*] on to test it. They tried it out there periodically to test it. After binding and pegging [the gunwales together], they turned the gunwales and attached deck beams to adjust them to the right depth.

The *palurutek* [two props used when the kayak is turned over to set the gunwales to the right curvature] are pieces of wood with the top shaped like this, and with their lower ends tapered where they are staked into the ground. They leaned on the piece of wood here to stake the *palurutet* into the ground.

Nutaan apamak qinengqaurlukek tangaagurtelluku negglukek kaugturlukek it-
qaniraqlukek, pernerek waten ayuqlirivkarluku apamak aciak. Palurrluku, makut
atliqevkarluku. Tua-i-llu ilututacirkaa nutaan cuqii assirian, taqluku.

Taqngan nutaan agna aciani uitatuli paivqaarluku kuyak, uum iqugkaa, nutaan
una kagaaluq. Waniwa tua-i ukineq, apamak iquak quyungqallrak, avga tua-i waten uivenqeggiluku wavet kapulluku ikna iqua, kingua. Kapuqaarluku tua-i nutaan
tupirluku.

Una cali ukuakun ukilluku cali tupirluku wavet, apamam tupianun. Ingna-llu
ciunga cali tuatnayugngaluni; tupingqerrluni yaa-i cali. Taugaam makeskani ingna
tupiryugngaluku ukinqucuk. Una taugaam palureskan cauyarai ellivailgata tupirar-
kauluku, amugarrngairutelluku tua-i una wani.

Waniwa qayam alulaa. Assirluni ellimakan, anguarluni ayagluni anguani anguan-
riqertengraan qayaq nalqipiarluni ayagarkauluni una *straight*-aqan. Uvaayagqurluni
taugken pikan, anguanriqreskan caqirrngiinararkauluni. Waten ukatmun uvreskan,
ukatmun caqirrngiinararkauluni anguanriqreskan. Uum caqiryugtelluku. Taumek
assingnaqluki ellitukait, *straight*-arcetengnaqluki.

Pissuraqameng unani nalqigaarqaarluki ellituat anguarucet. Qayaq tua-i man'a
nalqiisqumaluku nuteteng tegumiaqluku. Cali-llu asaaqungqetullermeggni, asaaquq tauna tegumiaqluku anguarpek'nateng, nalqiisqumaluku qayaq tua-i una
assirluku ellingnaqtuat. Nutkataquni anguarngaituq, asaaquq-llu urniusngakuniu
anguarngaunani, qayaq taugaam elliinek ayagturtelluku. Caqirrngiinatulit-gguq
assiitut. Tamana pitekluku assirluku ellingnaqtuat una.

Tua-i-llu nutaan usgulluku man'a kuyak, agna aciat. Nutaan waten piluku. Waniwa tang usgunerkaa. *Key*-aa waniwa una. Waten agenqeggluku pingaunaku.
Aarnarquq. Ellikuniu man'a maa-i kuyagkaq, ukatmun tua-i elliarkauluku waten,
ayuqeliluku una wani. Nenguggluku cali, cagnivkarluku. Cagningnaqevkarluku ayu-

Then, keeping a close eye on the gunwales, they pushed down and pounded on the posts to insert them farther into the ground so that the bottom of the gunwales would curve upward. They turned over the gunwales with the attached deck beams, so that the deck beams were on the bottom. When it was the right depth, they were done adjusting the gunwales.

When that process is finished then the piece that is to be the keelson, the *kuyak*, is brought out. Here is the stern bottom, where the ends of the gunwales are to be attached, and it has a mortise. After the aft ends of the gunwales are rounded, each with half-round cross-sections, as a tenon, that tenon is inserted into the mortise in the stern bottom and bound in place.

They also drilled a hole here [along the curve near the bottom of the stern bottom on the inside] and bound it onto the gunwale. And they would do the same with the bow; it has bindings as well. They would bind the upper bow piece, *ukinqucuk*, in place only after [the frame] was placed right side up. However they had made the binding that goes from the stern bottom to the gunwales while the kayak was turned over before they put the ribs in, so that the stern bottom would not pull out.

Here is the stern bottom that ensures proper tracking for the kayak. If it is put on properly, if this piece is upright, even though one stops paddling, the kayak will glide in a straight path. But if it is placed at a bit of a slant, the kayak will start to turn if he stops paddling. And if it is slanted the other way, it would gradually turn toward the opposite way when one stops paddling. This stern bottom determines how the kayak tracks. That is why they made such an effort to position the stern bottom precisely upright.

When men hunted out on the ocean, they straightened their kayaks and placed their paddles down. They wanted the kayaks to go in a straight path while they held their guns. And back when they had seal-hunting harpoons, they tried to position this stern bottom precisely perpendicular because they wanted their kayak to keep gliding in a straight path while they were holding the harpoon and not paddling. One cannot be paddling when he is about to shoot, and if one is poised with his harpoon in hand he won't be paddling either, but the kayak should glide straight on its own. They say kayaks that gradually turn are not good. That is why they try to put the stern bottom on properly.

Then they connected the keelson, *kuyak*, that is along the bottom. They would put it together like this. Here is the scarf [joint]. Here is the "key" [pointing to the notch on the stern bottom]. They did not make the scarf straight without a notch. That would be hazardous. When they put the piece that is to be the keelson in place,

qeliarkauluku. Taqkan-llu tua-i ikayirluni nutaan nuqlukek ukuk. Cagnilluku, ekev-
karluku wavet wani usguneq, nutaan nemerluku, nuqingavkarluku agna atlirneq.
Tua-i asvairuskan nutaan taqluku.

Caliaqluku-llu ping'ermi, makluku ping'ermi nengkanirngaunani agna qayaq,
mat'um nuqingiini. Qayaq tua-i, apamak, waten makeskuni perayagqurluku acitmun ukuilkuni taugken cagnikuni makeskuni, qayaq waten ayuqerkauluni qayaq.
Agna ika-i assiami, makuni-llu pinian, nalqikapiarluku qayaq. Mat'um maa-i tegu-
miaqngani una waten pivkarciiganaku.

Atam tungliqutaciitun waten pituat. Tua-i-llu nutaan man'a ellimarikan ilutu-
tacirkaatun pirraarlukek muriik waten kapullukek pik wani paingan iluanun nunamun waten pilukek, agna ava-i kuyak qillrulluku ilututacianun pektaarngairu-
telluku. Taqngan nutaan engineq, ciuqliq nutaan keggluku, qukaanun kanavet
nutaan elliluku, ayaperviik nalliignun, engineq. Tua-i-llu nutaan ellikuniu, ellimarikan, avaqlilirturluku waten, pitateku'urtelluki tua-i, ingluqcigceteksaunaku. Peren-
rit-llu pitateku'urtelluki qinertaarturluki, kingutmurrluki, ciutmun-llu. Qaqiskata-
llu tua-i cauyarat nutaan makut, enginrunrilnguut nutaan ellilarluki qamellritnun.
Tua-i ayuqurluteng tua-i.

Perellri tangaagurluki tua-i. Una acetukuni, yaaqlini ukut alaicetevkenak, pugumaluni perellra piciquq. Uum kanagaan kepemyaumalriim pivkarluku, kepkaniqa-
quni-llu nutaan assiriqerrluni.

Nutaan tua-i qaqicata, saaganret nutaan elliluki, qaingat pagkut. Quyuita kuyiim
avategkenun *five*-aaqtaarluki. *Ten*-aarutuut. Naqluki-am nutaan taprualugnek. Na-
qeqaarluki tua-llu pakigluki, sagqurluki waten akultutateku'urluki piurluki.

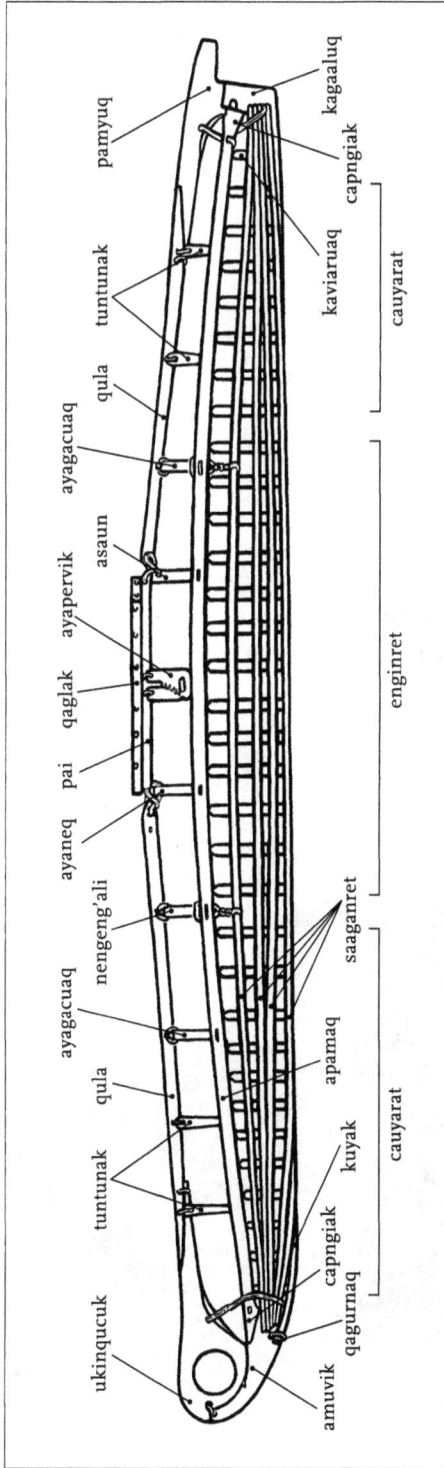

Qayaq/Kayak. Deborah Reade and Bill Wilkinson.

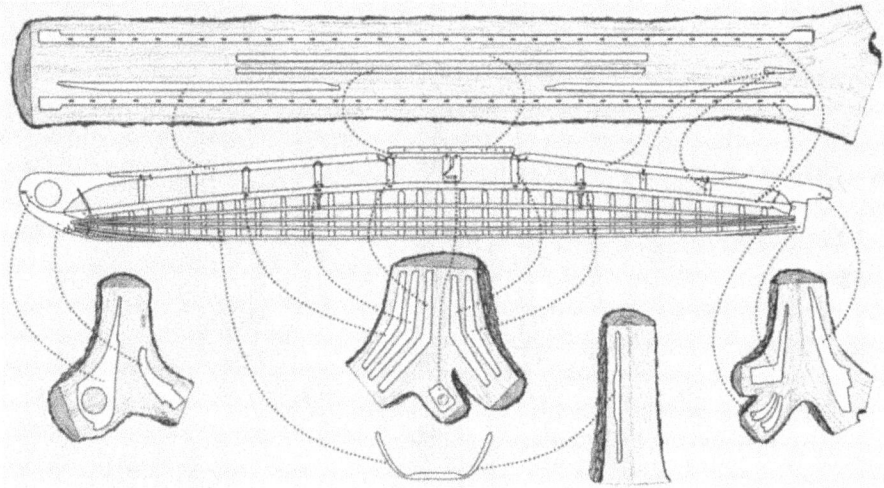

*Sources of wood for a kayak frame. Men searched long and hard for the
right kinds of wood needed to construct a frame. Bill Wilkinson
and the Oregon Museum of Science and Industry.*

*Noah Andrew shows the curved part of the stump from which deck beams
are made. The bow top and stern handle are also carved from
stumps. Bethel, 2006, Ann Fienup-Riordan.*

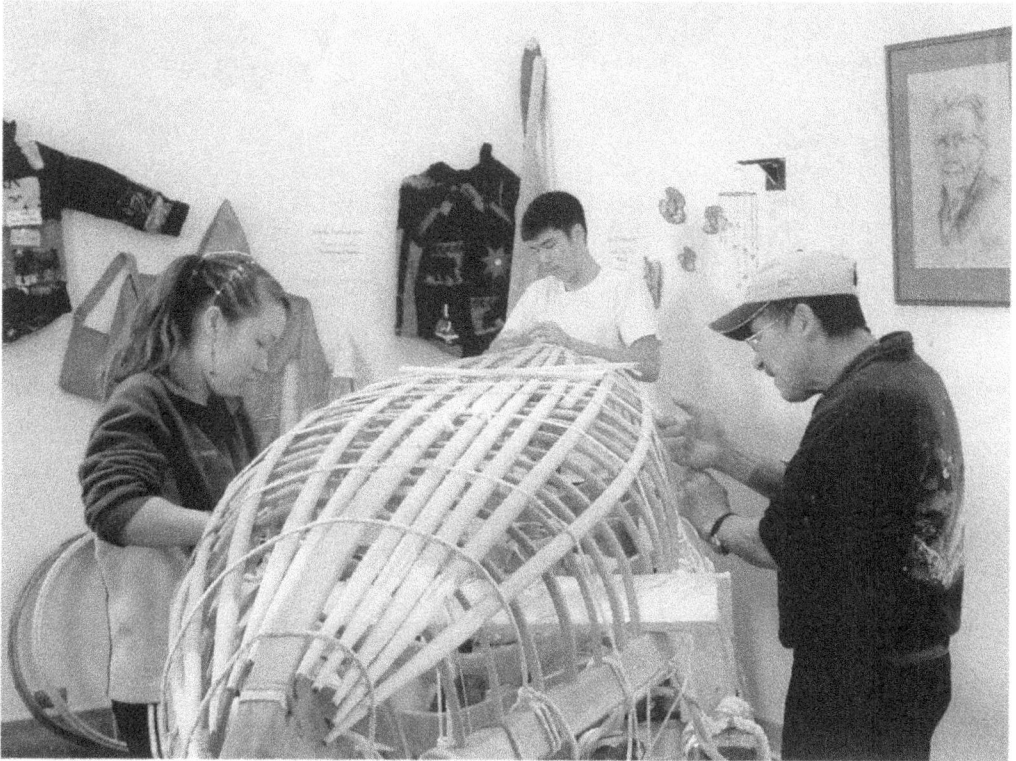

Noah Andrew and Kira and Ethan Wilkinson lashing a kayak frame together, Bethel 2006. Frank Andrew noted: "They bound [the ribs] tightly with sealskin line. They all work together. It takes less than an hour when many people are sitting across from each other, doing the lashing." Michael Whiteneck.

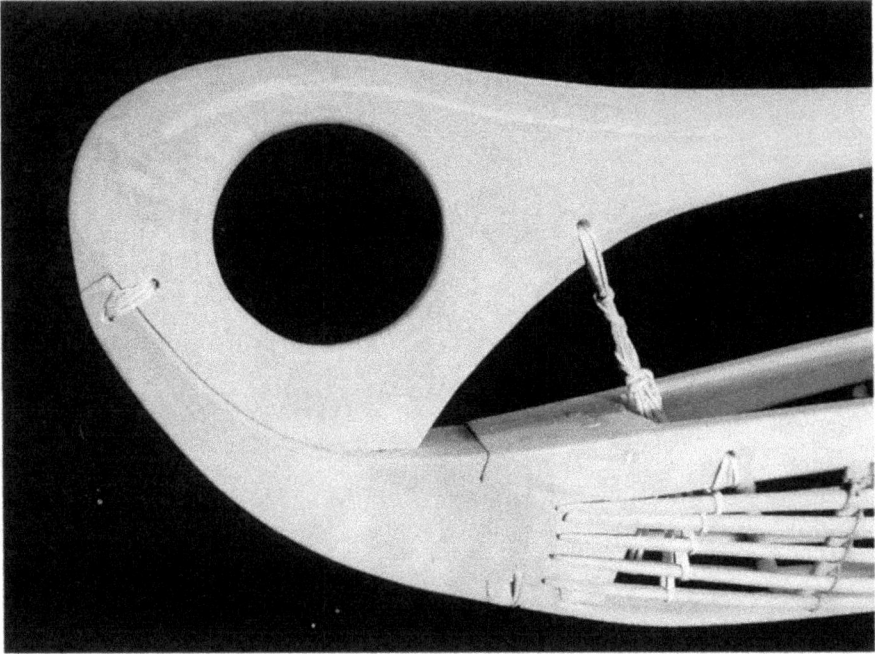

Ukinqucuk (*bow top*) *on kayak frame made by Frank and Noah Andrew and Bill Wilkinson. Note the sealskin bindings securing the bow top, lower bow, side stringers, and gunwales. Troy Wilkinson.*

The pamyuq (*stern handle*) *is also secured with sealskin lashing. Troy Wilkinson.*

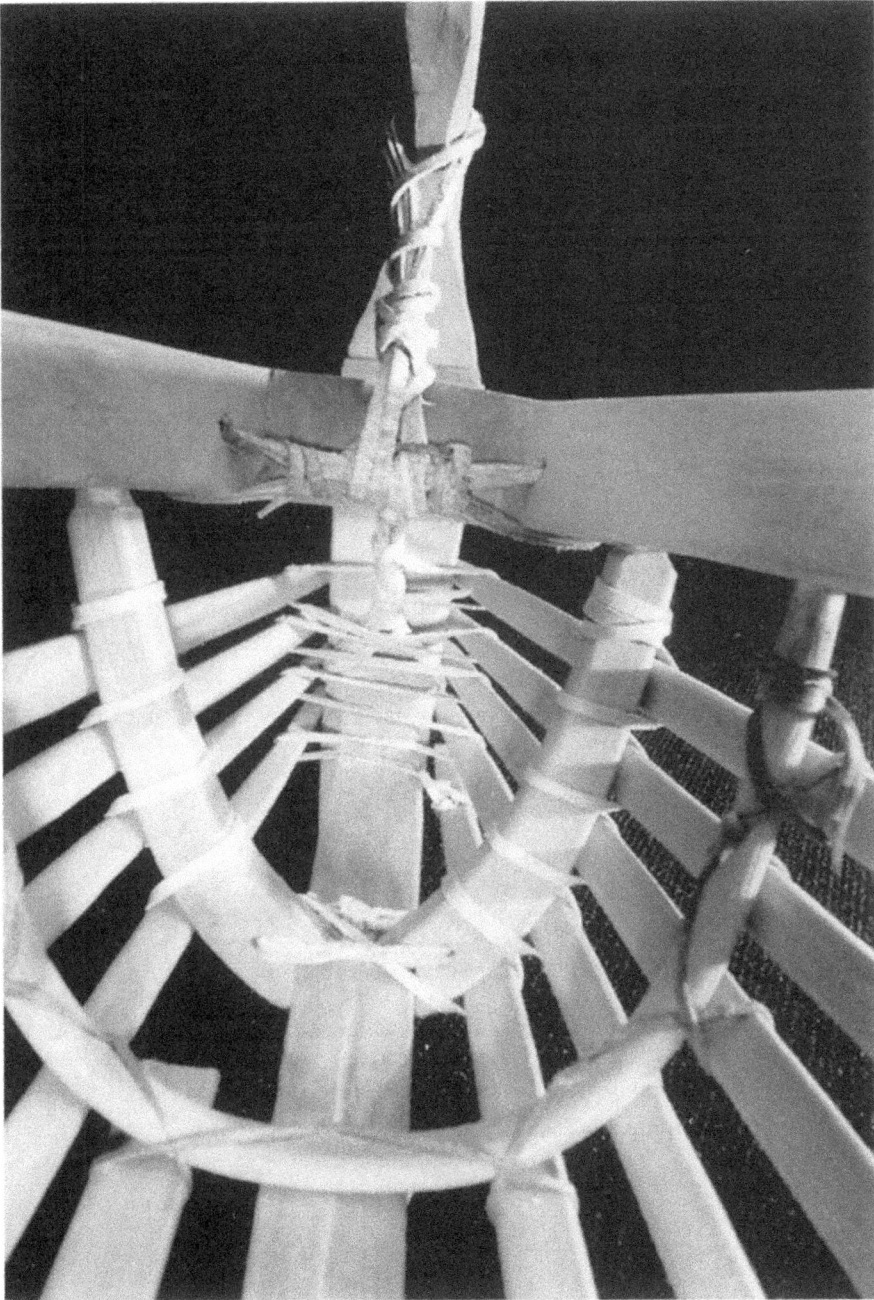

Interior view of the frame, showing the sealskin lashing that secures the keel supports to the gunwales and keelson. Frank Andrew noted: "When they are about to attach those fore and aft ribs, these two keel supports, kaviaruak, have to be placed here, one on each side. The keel supports will stabilize the keelson, preventing it from going from side to side." Troy Wilkinson.

Kayak frame made by Frank and Noah Andrew and Bill Wilkinson in 2004 in Kwigillingok. Troy Wilkinson.

Noah Andrew ringing out bearded-seal skins after they have been soaked in water and stuffed with grass, held in place by kepirtat *(small wood pieces) poked through holes in the skins' edges. Bill Wilkinson took the following photographs during kayak construction at the Alaska Native Heritage Center in 2000.*

Mary Ann Wilkinson scraps a sealskin after it has been wrung. Bill Wilkinson, 2000.

Frank and Noah Andrew lay three wrung sealskins over the bottom of the kayak and cut them to size. Frank noted: "When the [skins] are new, two [men] work on the skin covering with one woman. One man cuts all the sealskins to size while another holds the skins in place. The third one, the woman, was called petugturta [one who ties]." Bill Wilkinson, 2000.

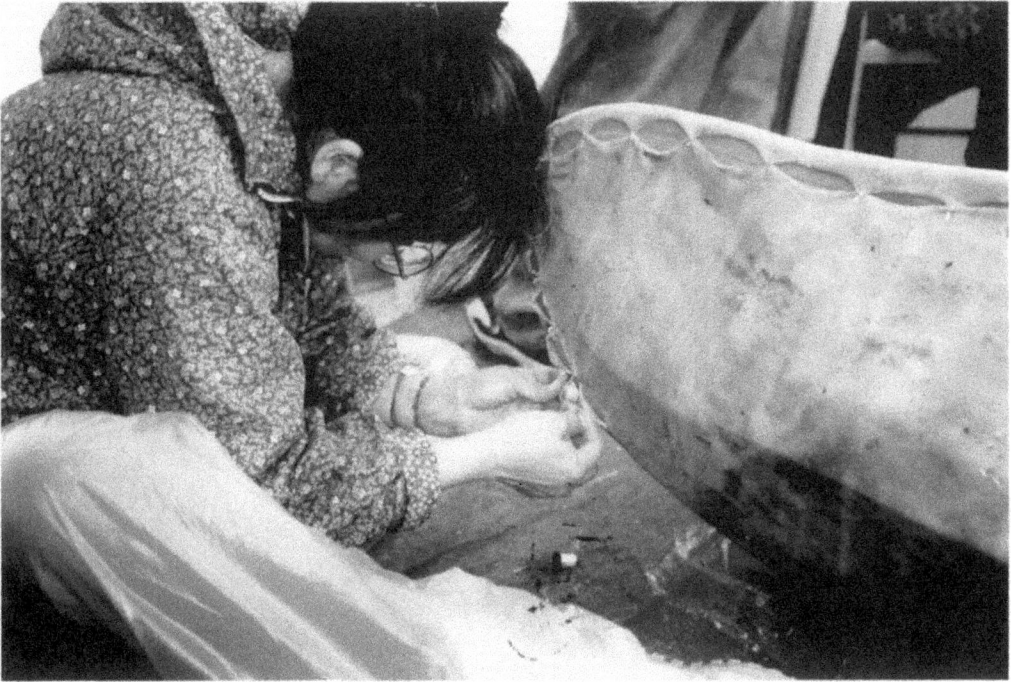

Mary Ann Wilkinson acts as petugturta, *tacking the cut sealskins together with widely spaced stitches in the places where they will be sewn. Bill Wilkinson, 2000.*

Frank and Noah Andrew turn the frame upright and continue stretching and cutting sealskins to size. Bill Wilkinson, 2000.

Lucy Anaver sewing a kayak skin, holding a wooden cagnirgun *(tightening tool) in her right hand to help her pull the thread through the skin. Inside the skin and surrounded by cord is a small, square* unguqupak, *to prevent the skins from slipping. Lucy holds the cord in place with her foot. Bill Wilkinson, 2000.*

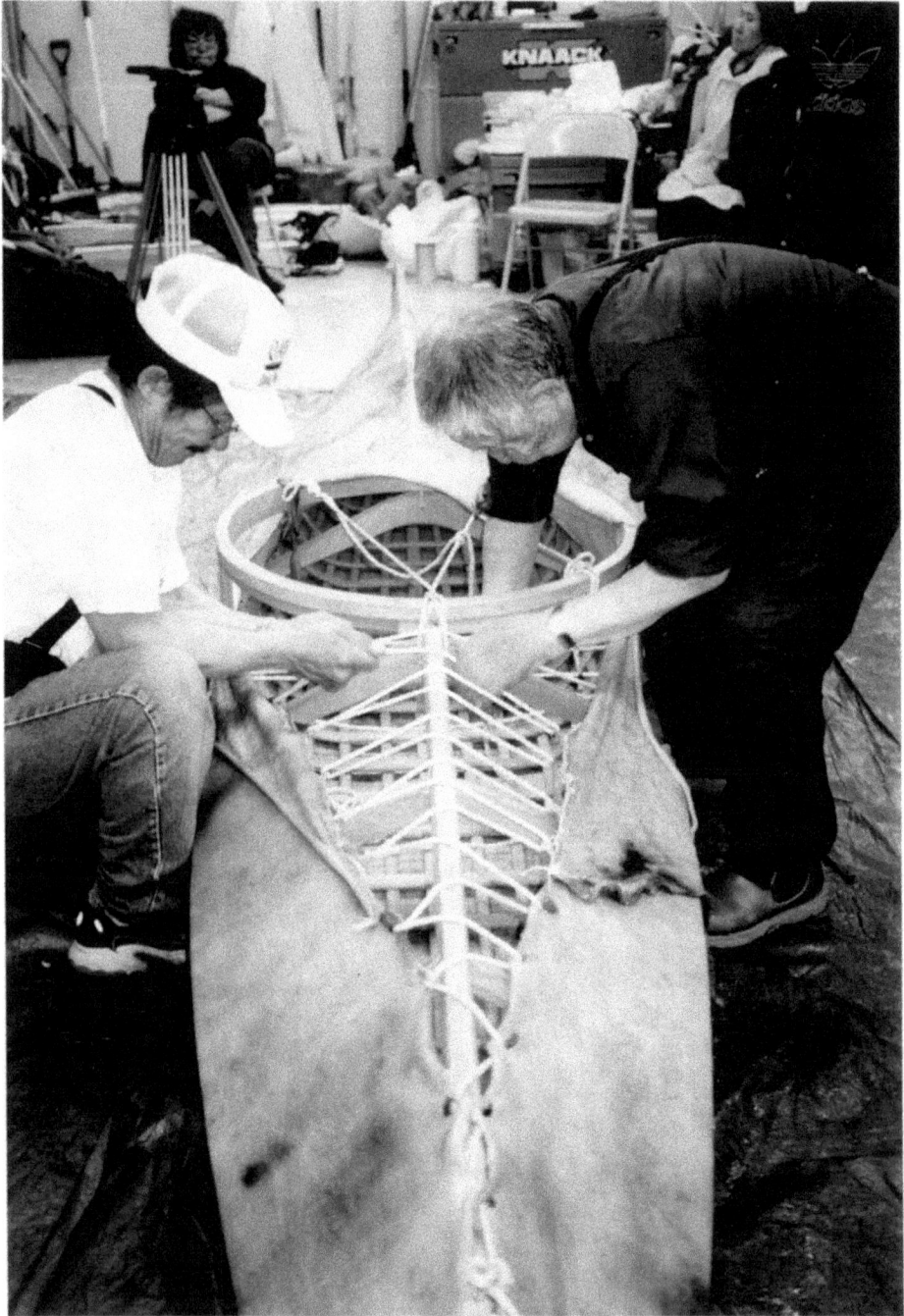

Frank and Noah Andrew work together to stretch the finished kayak skin over the frame. Temporary lines hold the kayak skin in place. Bill Wilkinson, 2000.

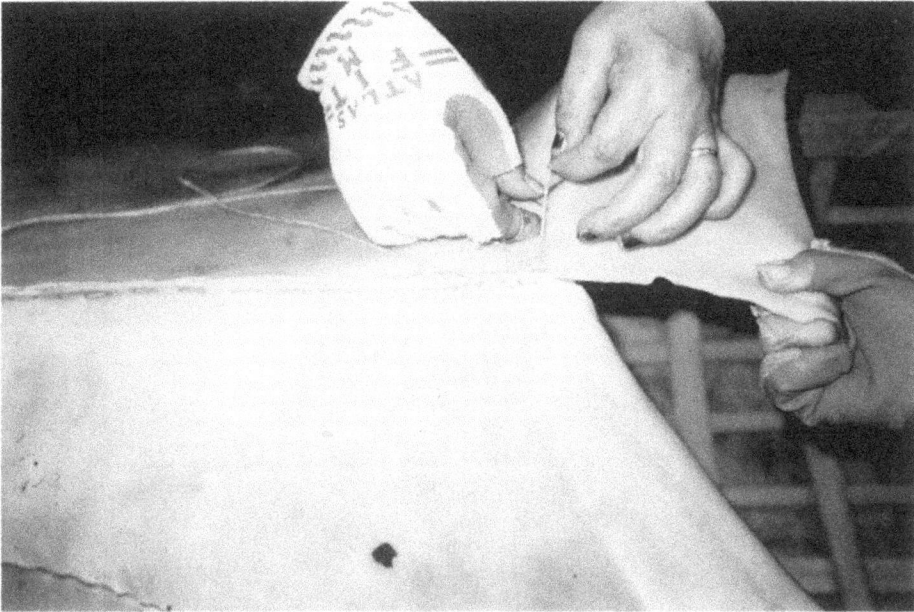

Mary Ann Wilkinson sews the ikavsianeq (*stern stitches, running from stern handle to cockpit coaming*). *Bill Wilkinson, 2000.*

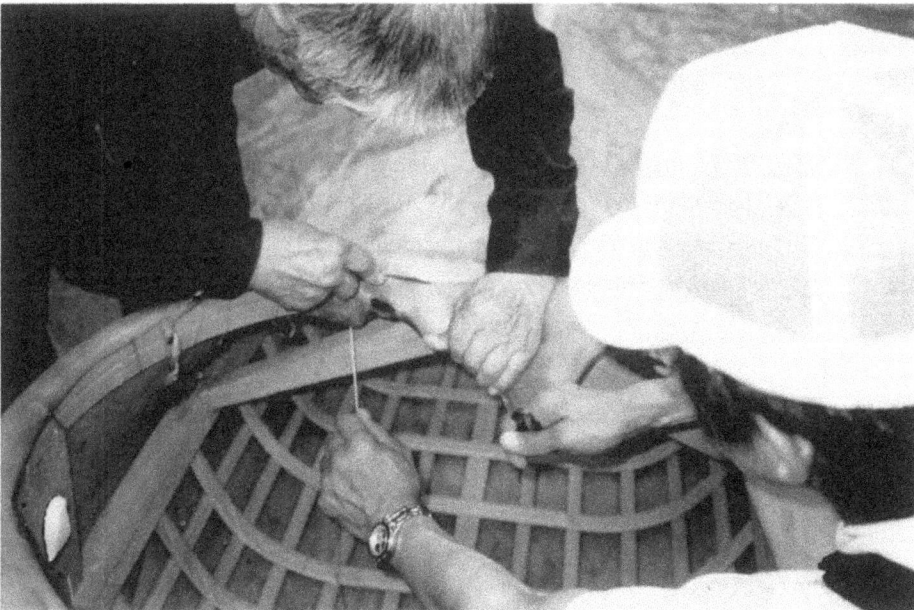

Frank and Noah sew the back and forth stitching securing the kayak skin to the cockpit coaming. Bill Wilkinson, 2000.

During the Homer boat-launching ceremony, Frank Andrew paddles the kayak he and his family made for the Alaska Native Heritage Center in summer 2000. The kayak is painted with an eagle design, one of two designs Frank inherited from his father. Jim Fitzmaurice.

Frank Andrew standing by his kayak and sled in the 1970s. This kayak, the last
he used for hunting, was covered in canvas and painted with
commercial paint. Andrew Family.

In 2004 the Andrew family worked together in Kwigillingok to make this kayak, covered
with bearded-seal skins and painted with Frank Andrew's inherited family design,
representing a common loon. The double-bladed paddle mounted on the deck has
Frank's inherited "pretend foot" design painted on the blade. Troy Wilkinson.

Frank Andrew passed away in April 2006. The following October, his son Noah, son-in-law Bill, and grandchildren Ethan and Kira Wilkinson worked together at the Yupiit Piciryarait Museum and Cultural Center in Bethel, using the skills he taught them to construct a kayak frame for the exhibition Yuungnaqpiallerput / The Way We Genuinely Live. *They stand here, in front of the frame, holding the paddles, bow, gaff, spear thrower, and harpoon they made under his guidance. Greg Lincoln, The Delta Discovery.*

they would connect it in this way, by fitting its notch to the notch on the stern bottom. They also pulled the two bottom pieces together, making the joint taut. They would make a matching notch in each piece so that the joint would stay taut. And when done making them, one would have someone help him pull the two bottom pieces together so that the notches would mate. They inserted the keelson, joining it tightly to the matching notch in the stern bottom, and then bound it in place. While doing this another person would pull the lower one as it was being joined. They would be finished when it was secure.

Even when they placed it upright while assembling the kayak frame it wouldn't get loose but stayed taut [because the connection of the stern bottom and the keelson] kept the frame tightly in place. If the kayak does not have this joint, the gunwales would droop down when it was set upright, but with the joint taut the kayak would look like this, curving upward. Because that part over there is good [and this here is taut], the kayak would be very straight and symmetrical. Because this [lower bow piece] is holding it in place, the gunwales will not droop down.

They assemble the kayak parts in order. Having joined the keelson to the lower bow piece, they adjust it to the right depth, and then they stake the two wood pieces down into the ground where the inside of the unassembled cockpit is to be, and tie the keelson down to its right depth so that it will be held in place. When that is done, they bite along the first center rib, *engineq*, to progressively shape it and then place it in the center of the kayak frame directly underneath where the cockpit stanchions are placed. Then after putting it in place, they put [the other center ribs] in front and behind it alternately, making sure that they are evenly spaced and symmetrically placed. And they kept all their curvatures uniform, and constantly sighted along them as they placed them toward the back and toward the front. And when they were done, they put in the fore and aft ribs, the ones that aren't the center ribs, in the area where the kayak tapers. They put them in place with even spacing.

They constantly sight along the frame to check the curvatures [of the ribs]. If [a certain rib] is higher it prevents the others beyond it from being visible, the curvature will be above the rest. It will be like that because the end of the rib wasn't cut to the right length, and it will be better once they cut it a little more.

When they were done placing the ribs, they would attach the side stringers, *saaganret*, the longitudinal pieces that go on the outer sides [of the ribs]. They gather them along both sides next to the keelson, five on each side. There are ten altogether. They tie them together temporarily with skin line [at both ends of the side stringers to keep them in place]. After tying the side stringers at both ends, they pull each stringer separately, placing them evenly [over the ribs], making sure they are equally spaced.

Qaqicata-llu nutaan qukamek cali kanaken ayagluku ukatmun nemerluki. Una-llu nutaan ikegkut kinguakun ikaggun, takenruuralriit, tekipailgan, nutaan kepur-luki assircarluki nanilicaqerluku, makuanun makucianun saaganret patgusngav-karluki maavet, patgusngaurtelluki agkut. Yaavet-llu cali, amuvigmun cali wavet patgusngaurtelluki maavet. Ukugnun waniwa patgusngaurtelluki, wavet patgus-ngaurluteng, kingumi-llu cali kanavet.

Tua-i qaqiskan nutaan taqluku. Palurutairluku-llu makteng'ermi tua-i nengkanir-ngaunani. Cali nemrraarluku nuqsugucirarkauluku cetamanek ayaganun.

Nutaan pagkuk, pamyua, ukinqucua-llu nutaan ellilukek. Elliurlukek tua-i assi-rikunek tupirluki paugkut. Tuntunat-llu elliluki. Una-llu waniwa una kegglarluku waten ukatmun ilangarrluku man'a. Uumun-llu tua-i ek'arkauluku waten. Una tua-i piluku, una ilangarulluku una uuggun. Ukatmuryailkutekluku uumun, yaatmun-llu piyailkutaa.

Nutaan ukilluku cali uuggun. Una-llu ukineq apamak-wa maa-i. Ukatmun tupi-mun cali nuqsuggluku. Tuntunaq-llu kinguqliq-wa uuggun pimavkarluku, usguneq una ayaumavkarluku, tuntunak, akiqlia-llu ikna.

Tuamtellu cauyarat elliqataqunegteki ukuk waniwa wantarkauguk, akini-llu. Una waniwa iriqtaarcessngaunaku ukuk wani. Nayumiqaarkaulukek akiqliqlukek. *Move*-aqtaarcessngaunaku. Man'a qulirneq, ikegkut ukut wani tuntunat uutun cali nayumiqaarkauluku man'a. Iriqtaarcetevkenaku.

Ukuk-gguq waniwa kaviaruak wantuk, uumun kaviaruak. Tua-i nutaan qaqican, nangnermek pai elliluku, nangneruluku. Tua-i-llu nutaan nangenkacagarmek ukuk wani, tua-i kinguqliulutek. Kinguagni camek elliingairulluni. Waniwa-gguq ayaper-viik. Tuulleguagnek qaralingqeqatartuq qayaq man'a.

Yuguanek ilait qaralingqelartut. Ilait piciatun; arnaruaruluni inglua, angut-ngunguarluni. Tua-i nutaan qaqituq ava-i. Calivigkartairutuq qayamek mat'umek. Taqluni tua-i.

[After placing the side-stringers], they bind them starting from the center. Then they would carefully cut the ends of the side stringers that are a little too long and give them a finishing touch, making sure the side stringers rest flush with this [lower stern piece and the lower bow piece]. They would have the ends of the side stringers right against this [lower bow piece] here, and they would also be right against the stern piece.

When that process was completed, they do the finishing task. Even though they removed the temporary supports, *palurutet*, and placed it upright, the kayak frame would remain taut. After binding the side stringers to the ribs, they also fasten four ties, *nuqsugutet*, that go to the deck beams.

Then they attach the two upper pieces, the top stern piece, *pamyuq*, and the top bow piece, *ukinqucuk*. They test the top pieces and bind them in place if they are okay. Also they put in place the last two fore and aft deck beams. They saw a notch in each *tuntunaq* where the bow deck stringer, *qula*, will be fitted. They remove a small section from each *tuntunaq* to form the notch. Each *tuntunaq* pair holds the deck stringer in place with a notch, keeping it from moving side to side.

Then they drilled a hole here. Here is the hole, and here are the gunwales. They fastened it tight to the lashing. And they would have the two endmost deck beams situated underneath the joint at the end of the deck stringer, this side of the endmost deck beams as well as the other side.

And when they are about to attach those fore and aft ribs, these two [keel supports, *kaviaruak*] have to be placed here, one on each side. These [keel supports] will stabilize [the keelson], preventing it from going from side to side. The two pieces situated across from each other will hold [the keelson] in place. It will prevent it from moving. The last two deck beams forward and aft will stabilize the deck stringers here in the same way as the keel supports hold the gunwales and the keelson in place. It keeps it from moving side to side.

These two are keel supports, *kaviaruak*. The keel supports are attached here. And when that is done, they assemble the cockpit coaming, the *pai*, at the very end. Then the two cockpit coaming stanchions are the very last parts to be put in place. No other piece would be assembled after that. They call these two cockpit coaming stanchions *ayaperviik* [places for leaning one's hands when getting in and out]. This kayak will have two loon figures, *tuulleguak*, for a design.

Some people have human figures for designs [on their cockpit coaming stanchions]. Some have designs that aren't matching; one might be a female face and the other a male face. It is now complete. There is no other work to be done on the kayak. The assembly is done.

~: *Qayam ataucimi ernermi tumartellra* :~

Ernerpak qaqitetuit amllerrluteng piaqateng ikayuqluteng. Caliaqellratni taugaam ikayuutaayuitut, cuqait pillratni angtacirkait. Waten taugken assircaitki nutaan piyulriit ikayurluki nutaan caniurluteng, tangvaurluki angtatet-llu tua-i, maniggluki-llu qaingit. Tamakunek tamaa-i ikayurituut. Tumartellratni-llu tua-i waten. Patagmek taumek taqtukait, yugyagluteng pituameng calilriit tumartaqatki. Unugyugnaunaku taq'ertaqluteng wanirpaagaq tua-i. Nemratni tuamtellu palurcan tamalkurmeng tua-i akiqliqluteng waten assirneq tua-i, cauyaraq atauciq, ilait malrugnek nemraqluteng, qaqilluku-llu tua-i man'a assirneq. Cauyaragnek malrugnek, ikna-llu akiqliin, yugyagluteng nemraqata. *One hour* naayugnaunaku qaillun qavci *minute*-llu nemqatuit amllerrluteng piaqameng nemtulit. Elisngalriit nemertunirtut, patagmek nemqernaurtut.

Piciatun nemyuitait. Qukaanek kanaken.

Cagnilluki tapruarnek nemerluteng. Tapruarrlainarnek tua-i, tupiit-llu nemerluteng tamarmeng. Makut taugaam tupirarkat paingat pikna-llu nekevraarcinrarnek tupirluteng.

~: *Pamyuq* :~

Pamyua. Pamyuicuitut. Tua-i nutem tua-i tuaten ayuqluni pamyua, pamyurluteng. Ukinqucugmek-llu aterluni ikna. Una taugken pamyuq waten mat'umek waniwa pernera-llu cali uutun.

Teruakun-llu amaggun ukitarkauluku maaggun iluakun pivkenaku. Una cali waniwa teruakun maaggun ukitarkauluku. Ukinqucuk-llu augna. Makut-llu waten mamtutatekluki piiyuicaaqut. Man'a iqkillruluku qalirneq pituyaaqaat man'a-llu iqtunruurluku atlirnerkaa. Taugaam tua-i waten pilaraat.
Mimernat tua-i maa-i makut. Ukut tua-i waniwa mimernarrlainarnek pituut.

~: *Assembling a kayak in a day* :~

They finished the kayak assembly in one day if there were many people working on it together. Others can't help when the owner constructs the parts which require his own body measurements. But when the owner finished those parts, those who wanted to assist with the carving helped out, making sure they followed the sizes, and they smoothed all the surfaces. They helped with those tasks and with the assembly. That's why they quickly finished, because there were many people who worked on the kayak during its assembly. They finished it before nightfall, in a short time. And when they lashed it together and then placed it upside down, they all worked on it across from one another, worked on the bottom of the kayak frame, lashing one rib, and some would lash two ribs, and they would finish the bottom. They lashed two ribs with another person across from them helping, with many other people lashing. It takes less than an hour — I'm not sure how many minutes — when many people did the lashing. Those who are experts at lashing could do it quickly. Working together they would lash it together very quickly.

They never lashed them just any old way. They started from the center of the kayak.

They bound them tightly with sealskin line. They used only sealskin line, and they also bound all the places with premade holes that require stitching. The parts with premade holes that are to be stitched, the cockpit coaming and the piece up there, are stitched with spruce roots.

~: *Top stern piece with handgrip projection* :~

Here is its top stern piece with handgrip projection, *pamyuq*. They always have top stern pieces; they have always had a top stern piece. And the front bow piece is called *ukinqucuk*. But the curvature of the top stern piece is like this, [gradually descending in the aft direction].

And at its base on the other side they made a hole but not here on its inside. This too, here, they made a hole at its base. In the upper bow piece, too. These were never made the same thickness throughout. This top part was made thinner and the bottom wider. That's how they made it.

These pieces are constructed out of stumps with lateral roots. They always make

Makut-llu tua-i unarcianek cauyanret, cauyarait, paingit-llu qulaat-llu pagkut. Tua-ten ayuqluteng tua-i.

~: *Ayagat* :~

Makut-wa taugaam arcaqerluteng pilalriit ayagat, maligcetengnaqu'urluki kepu-mavkanritengnaqluki. Ukatmun pisqumavkenaki, taugaam tua-i waten wani. Ki-pullgusngavkarluki-llu, kepumallrit makut ngelekluki.

Maa-i man'a nekevraartuq waten, waniwa muraurtellran tunglirnera kevraartum. Una waniwa mimernaurtellra waniwa una. Tallirnauluni man'a tua-i avavet, nunam iluanun yaaqvanun kevraarcinraurrluni augna. Una tua-i tayima muragpallraam, akiqlingqerkuni cali maani. Makuit maa-i tangaaluki makut pitekluki. Yuvriraaluki pituut, piciatun piyuitut. Kepuumayugngaaqata piyuunaki makuit, pagait waten kepuumayugngakata. Waten taugaam yaaqvanun ayaumaaqluteng kepumang'er-meng waten assinruluni.

Ayimcituut-gguq iliini taqumarilukek yuum ilii. Qayam-llu qainganun aquma-qata iliini navgaqluni. Aqumviktaaresqumaksailkait taumek qayat qalirneritgun.

Una waniwa mimernaam tunglirnera, una waniwa kevraartuum tunglirnera. Mi-mernaam waniwa pimalria. Tuaten piuratuit. Piciatun yuvrirturluki taumek pitu-kait qayarkartaqameng.

~: *Uutarluki muriit* :~

Uutarluki-gguq saaganret pitegcautet-llu epukait makut pituit.

Makuit kepuryaaqevkenaki pituit pagait, makunun-llu kegglarluki piyuunaki, qu-purturluki taugaam, pagait kepuryaaqevkenaki. Manialnguut tua-i kepqacilget-llu kiingita pivkenaki tamalkuita nalqingraata uutatuit, angiyailkucirluki-gguq. Uutau-manrilnguut tua-i piniallruluteng, cangariqercugngaluteng. Uutaumalriit taugken cangaringaunateng mermun akuqetaangermeng.

these out of stumps with lateral roots. And they make the ribs as well as the cockpit coaming and deck stringers out of straight-grained wood. That's how they are.

~: Deck beams :~

They were especially careful to follow the grain of the wood when constructing the deck beams, trying not to cut across the grain. They didn't want the grain to go in this direction [perpendicular to the piece] but only in the direction of the piece; they kept the grains parallel to the direction of the piece.

On a spruce tree like this, here is this part where the trunk began to grow. This section is where it began to form roots. This section is the first part of the lateral root, *tallirnaq*, also there are smaller roots that go out quite a distance, *kevrrarcinraat*. This deck beam, from the *tallirnaq*, comes from a large tree, and it will have a symmetrical component here. They watch out for suitable tree stumps with lateral roots. They examine them carefully, and they don't just take any kind of wood for this deck beam. If the wood grain might be such that the wood will break, they don't use that piece. But if the grain extends for a distance without a tendency to break, then that is better wood to use.

They say that some people unintentionally break finished deck beams after the construction is completed. And they sometimes break when a person sits on top of the kayak. That's why they told us never to sit on kayak decks.

Concerning the deck beam piece, this section comes from the lateral root portion of the stump, and this section comes from the trunk portion of the spruce log. That is how they always selected them. So that is why they examined the wood from different angles when they looked for wood for kayak parts.

~: Curing wood with heat :~

They say that they apply heat, *uutarluki*, to side stringers and arrow shafts.

They try not to cut against the grain, and they do not saw the pieces but only split them, trying not to cut against the grain. They don't apply heat only to the rough pieces and those pieces that are cut off, but they apply heat to all the pieces, including the straight-grained wood pieces, so the wood fiber won't come loose. Pieces that haven't had heat applied to them are weaker and don't retain their shape well. But the ones that have had heat applied to them will not lose their shape or deteriorate, even though they are in water.

~: Pertellrit cauyarat enginret-llu :~

Cauyarat ilait ayimtaqata cimilarait. Cauyaranqigtarluki, enginret-llu.

Puqlamun-wa piyuitellrukait. Elngulrianek pingqetullruut waten. Keggmartur-luki taugken tua-i perrluki. Keggmarturluki tua-i, *steam*-akun piyuunaki.

~: Pai :~

Paingit tua-i, keggmarpek'naki uumun taugaam piluki elliurturluki, maqillratni, mermun puqlamek akurtaaraqluki, elliurturluki tua-i. Maqiinanratni tua-i maqi-luni tuaten percilria, taqvailgata-llu tua-i kassuggluku. Maqiluni tuaten.

Muriik taukuk paimi malruuguk. Qaglaminek aipangqertuq.

Unani imarpigmi anuqengaararuskanga imarnitegka aciiqagka. Askumkek-llu tua-i una, qayami ekumallemni, imarnitek akuuk maavet ellilukek tevvluku, augna-llu ketgaq, tapraq qainganun elliluku, nuqluku cagnilluku tapramun qillrulluku. Tapraq ukatmun ayagarcesciiganani, mat'um qagliim aciani uitiimi, paim amiani waten pillrani. Tamaa-i tamana pitekluku waten man'a piuq. Umcigluku-llu pingau-naku. Una kingulirneq enigcetevkenaku callaurtelluku akuak imarnitek, ellalliur-cuutek. Qerruqerratuut iluit amna qayam ilua *air*-amek imangqelaami. Tamana tua-i aturtuq man'a qaglak tamatumun, meq-llu iterngaunani tua-i.

Kumgaa. Qaraliqaa.
Tegg'eramek-wa maa-i ussukcangqellria. Makut-wa uqviinraat tupii, piunrirngau-nateng cali tua-i una piullran taktaciatun, asvaunateng.

Qecigglainarnek pingqetuut, tupingqellruut. Makut nemret uqviinrarnek piyui-tait, tupiit taugaam. Makut taugaam ukinerluteng waten qecignek piyuunaki, ma-kunek taugaam uqviinrarnek kevirluki pituluki.

~: *Bending ribs* :~

They replace some of the fore and aft ribs when they break. They replace these ribs and also the center ribs.

They never applied heat to the ribs. They had ribs that were strong and flexible like this. They would bend them by biting on them with their teeth. They bit on them to shape them but never applied steam to them.

~: *Cockpit coaming* :~

They did not bite on the cockpit coaming of the kayak to shape it, but while they were taking a fire bath they applied heat and dipped it into hot water at intervals, progressively bending it with their hands. A person would be taking a fire bath while he was progressively bending the cockpit coaming, and before the fire bath was over the two ends of the cockpit coaming would be joined. He would be taking a fire bath at the very same time.

Two pieces of wood compose the cockpit coaming. The other part is a protruding narrow rim of wood on the upper part outside the coaming, the *qaglak*.

If it suddenly became windy while I was down on the ocean, I would put on my seal-gut rain parka. When I put it on while I was in the kayak, I would drape the hem of my seal-gut rain parka over the cockpit coaming and put a sealskin line, *ketgaq*, around the top of the hem of my rain parka and draw the line tightly and tie it. Because the sealskin line is locked beneath the cockpit coaming rim, *qaglak*, it would not slide up off the cockpit coaming. The *qaglak* is there for that reason. But I would not tie the *ketgaq* too tight. I wouldn't have the *ketgaq* hold down the back part of the rain parka, but leave the rain parka loose at the back. The rain parka, the *imarnitek*, has a tendency to inflate because the inside of the kayak is filled with air. That is what this *qaglak* is for, but water will not enter the kayak.

Its indented groove on the cockpit coaming, *kumgaa*. It is its design.

This cockpit coaming is pegged on with hardwood pegs. And these stitches are willow root, they will not deteriorate as long as this cockpit coaming exists, since they are quite durable.

They used only sealskin line for lashings. They don't use willow root on the parts that are bound. However they put willow root in these with pre-made holes, like the coaming, and never sealskin line.

Tupirnek atengqertut augkut tupiit, augkut allayugtun waten nuv'urluki piyaraunrilnguut. Waten elliuqetaarluki piyarat, tupiitnek pituit. Qantat-llu imkut
perenrita patgusngallrit, amaggun piaqluki, ukatmun piaqluteng, waten ayuqluki
nemrit. Tupiit-gguq tamaa-i, nekevraarcinrarnek pituluki. Nemerluki-llu tua-i augkunek qecignek. Tua-i-llu kass'at amlleriata pelacinagnek nemlangluteng. Makunek-
llu maa-i tupilallilriit ellait uqviinraarnek. Ukut-llu cangariyuitut. Mellgaraat-llu
epuaritnun nemqetuit makut.

~: Qecignek qipuriyaraq :~

Amirkanek tallimanek amingqetuut issurinek-llu angtuanek tallimanek amingqe-
tuluteng. Tua-i-llu amirkaicuameng makliignek malrugnek-llu usgullukek maklak
usgutaqerluku assirnengqetuluteng pagna-llu qalirnera issurinek wall'u amirkanek,
wall'u nayirnek caqutellernek, uquutellernek angtuanek. Makut ikavsianret tung-
liit pituit mayu'urneret-llu, tamakut akagtelluki. Waken tua-i ciunganek, kanaken
ciunganek nayiq akagtelluku, amiq caqutelleq, poke-aq imna, akagtelluku kinguvar-
luku. Qayam tua-i caquluku tua-i yaavet iquanun. Tamalkuan. Uquutelleq imna
akagtelluku. Tua-i amlleq patuluku.

Kepirtat taugken augkut ciurarkam amirkam putuinun waten putullgutiinun
nuvqaulluku. Tamana-llu tua-i nuvqaulluku muraggaq qukaa nayuumaluni, tauna
tua-i nuvqaulluku putumun pugumallrani. Imirluku-llu carangllugnek anyailkucir-
luku, waten qamiquruaruluku, tamakunek kepirtanek piurluku putuikun. Qillerr-
luku-llu tua-i qecik nutaan ciurarkaq.

Amirkaq waten ayuqluni tua-i, talliquk-wa ukuk, talligken uitayarak, waten ke-
pumalutek. Makut-wa maani kinercillermini putuut kinguqliqu'urluteng mengliini
kassutmun tua-i. Tamakut kepirtat; ag'um pia putua uumun nuvqauskan, pugkan-
llu tua-i kepirtamek taumek anyailkuciqerluku waten piarkauluku. Una quulluku
iqua, qamiqurran pimallra una. Taqkan aipaa cauvkarluku cali makuciq, amirkaq.
Ukuk waniwa talligkenek pilkek.

They call the lashing of those *tupiq*, those that do not require one to stitch the binding through pre-made holes. The ones that you lash like this, you call their lashing *tupiit*. Also, on the side of a bowl where the bentwood sides overlap, they stitched the lashing through pre-made holes, stitching it toward the inside of the bowl and then out again, making the binding like this. Those are their lashings, *tupiit*, and they say they are from spruce roots, *nekevraarcinraat*. And then they would bind them with sealskin line. When more white people came to this area, people started making bindings with twine. They probably used these willow roots for binding as well. Willow root is durable. They also bind them around the handle of the curved knife to hold the blade on.

~: *Wringing skins* :~

They use five young bearded-seal skins or five large spotted-seal skins for kayak coverings. And when they lacked young bearded-seal skins, they joined two adult bearded-seal skins for the bottom and used spotted-seal skins or young bearded-seal skins for the top covering, or else large ringed-sealskin pokes that had been used as seal-oil containers. They rolled those over the part of the kayak where they sew the top stern stitches, *ikavsianeq*, and vertical stitches near the tote hole, *mayu'urneq*. From the bow, they rolled out the ringed-seal skin that had been used in a seal poke, rolling it out toward the stern. It covered the kayak all the way to the stern. The whole kayak would now be covered. They rolled out the old seal-oil poke skin over the frame.

The skin-wringing tools, *kepirtat*, are threaded through the opposing stretching holes of the sealskins to be wrung. That wood device with its middle slightly thinned out is threaded through the stretching hole after the seal's neck area is put through the flipper holes. They filled the neck area with grass to prevent it from slipping out, shaping it like a head, then threaded the *kepirtaq* through the stretching hole. Finally they securely fastened the end of the skin that was to be wrung.

A young bearded-seal skin looks like this; here are the holes where its hands were removed. And here are the stretching holes evenly spaced all around the edge of the skin, which were used to stretch the skin to dry it. Concerning those *kepirtat*; a stretching hole on the opposing half of the skin is put through here, and once they thread the *kepirtaq* through, it prevents it from coming out. They close up the end of the skin where the head had been. Once that is done, one takes a second sealskin like this and places it against the first skin.

Caumallutek waten amirkak. Tallikek, uuggun ik'um uyaqurri wavet ekumalutek, uum-llu uyaqurri ik'um pigkenun ekumalutek. Ciungermi tua-i anqerrngaunani. Tamakut kepirtat putut-llu tamakut tegumiaqlukek.

Usgullukek tua-i amirkak waten. Ukuk-llu tua-i cali kepircirlukek iqukek ciurcuutmun muragamun nemrulluku aciakun-llu pugevkarluku tauna unguqupak qillrulluku matarrngaunaku cali, nutaan qipurluku. Malruulutek waten, ciurlukek.

Waten tua-i tep'ngetuut meq'aqameng waten. Tua-i assirluni. Waniwa tua-i talliquk quyukenka waten allam uyaqurri nuvulluki kanavet, kankugnun, imirpailgan. Uum-llu qamiqurra kan'a uyaqurri ik'um akiqliin kankugkenun cali iterrluku cali pairullukek. Augkunek-llu tua-i imirlukek, canegnek imirlukek kepirtanek aug'arcailkucirluki. Cagniskagnek-llu tua-i caltuq'erlutek, ukugkenun anesciiganatek talliqumegnegun ukuk qamiqukek ciungermek tua-i. Tuaten tua-i pituit.

Amirkat nutaramegni tepsarqut. Kalskag-amun tekitua up'nerkami amirkanek nutaranek nillaranek tuneniarlua. Kiaqliitni Kalskag-ami arnaq augna atrarluni, piyullranek tua-i cikirluku, teguluku narqerluku uaq'allagangaartuq una. Ngel'arturluni tuaten uaq'allagaluni temcikluni ellminek. Tepii-gguq una arenqiatelliniuq, nutaan narrliniami tamatumek meqcirrarnimek.

Angyarkat-llu tua-i tuaten pitulliniluki makliit, qipurturluki tua-i ciuraqluki. Aarnarqut taugaam alingnarqut, mallgureskevkenaki taumek pitukait. Tuqucillruutgguq-am yugmek. Slip-arluni ang'iqertellermini waten, unrapigam iquulqutaan angun tauna tarenriraagnun piqerrluku, iterluni tua-i unrapigaq temiinun maavet ang'iqertellermini, slip-arluni pimallra. Taumek nemruqu'urluku pitukait. Ellirraarluku taumun nemrulluku piaqluku, piyailkucirluku.

Assiituq, uqurrlua tuaten uqlautekciqan ciurumanrilkan mingqessaaqekuvet. Yuvgertun atam ayuqut, neqem yuvgeritun.

Arnat-llu augkut qipumallernek kelikarcetellruaput, mingqestekat.
Ciurluki iqairatun, usgukluki-gguq qeciit waten. Qipurluki-llu tua-i napalraamun iquit qillrulluki. Meq tua-i anluni tua-i, ciurluku kinerluteng. Meq akuliini

The two folded sealskins are put next to each other as if facing each other. Each neck area of the folded sealskins is put through holes where the flipper had been on each of the sealskins. Even though it is wrung, the stuffed neck part will not slip through. The *kepirtat* which are threaded through the loops keep them in place.

They connected two bearded-seal skins like this. Then they put *kepirtat* at both the neck ends, and then they wrapped the ends of the skins onto a wooden wringing device, then threaded it through the bottom and tied it so that it would not slip, and then they started twisting it. There are two [skins] like this, and they wrung them.

In skin preparation at the stage where it gets an aged smell like this it is a good signal that the hair is coming off. The first skin is folded matching the holes where the flippers had been; then before filling the neck part of the second skin with grass it is threaded through them. The head part of the first skin is threaded through the holes where the flippers had been on the second skin, joining them that way. Then they fill the closed head part of the skin with grass and put the *kepirtat* there so the skins would not slip through. When they wrung them, twisting them tightly, the head parts would be too large to slip though the flipper holes. That's how they do it.

Two-year-old freshly dried bearded-seal skins have strong odors. One spring I went to Kalskag to sell some newly stretched and dried young bearded-seal skins. In Upper Kalskag a woman came down, and when I gave her the one she wanted, she took it, smelled it, and began gagging. She laughed and gagged, laughing at herself. She said that the odor was overwhelming since that was the first time she had smelled a skin that had been newly dried and aged until the fur fell out.

The bearded-seal skins for use as a kayak skin covering are prepared that way and wrung by twisting. That process can be dangerous, and this is why people are warned not to get close when they are being wrung. A person was killed when the anchored end became loose and slipped as he was wringing the skins. The man was hit forcefully between the shoulder blades by the wringing device, made out of a spruce sapling, when it slipped and came undone. That is why they always wrap the end of the skin around the device and tie it for safety reasons.

It wouldn't be good [if all the water wasn't wrung out]; if it wasn't wrung well the excess oil would get all over you when you attempt to sew it. The skin's surface feels like slime, like fish slime.

We also had the women skin sewers scrape the skins that had been wrung.

They wrung them like washed clothing, with sealskins attached end to end. Then they wrung them after tying the end of the skins to a post. The water is wrung out

qeciim maingikun anluni, meciusngalleq. Qipurluki-gguq tua-i. Nutaan-llu kelikarluki uqlallrit nutaan eliqluki.

~: Qayam amiryaraa :~

Malruk amimek pituuk, arnamek aiparluni. Angun-wa elirqituli, wall'u pingayuak
ikayualluni elirqillragni, elirqilriamun ikayuuluni, nayumiqastekarkauluni. Arnaq-
wa tua-i pingayuak, petugturta. Maa-i pisqellrikun angutem taum keliqerluku malrugnek qillrulluki kep'artaqluki. Petugturluni-gguq tua-i elirqellrani. Elirqilria atauciuluni tua-i. Taqngan-llu tua-i nutaan talliman mingeqluteng.

Talliman-llu tua-i waten piameng, ciungani arnak waten akiqliqlutek, ciutmun
caulutek yaaken mayu'urnermek, mayu'urneranek ayagnirlutek, ikna-llu.

Ingna-wa yaani pingayuak caugartellria, arnak ukuk caulukek tuaken ayagnillrag-
nek ciutmun yaavet ukinqucuum tungiinun mingqelria.

Ukuk-wa kinguani arnak cali akiqliqlutek, ciutmun cali caumalutek, ikavsianrem
tunglirneranun uumek amilriik, mayu'urneragnek ayaglutek. Ukuk amilriik taqlerkaagnek waken, taqlerkaagnek mayu'urnerem ngeliinek ayaglutek.

Tua-i qaqilluku tua-i yaavet, akiqlian-llu [agna] ikavsianeq. Ikavsianermek taukuk kinguqliik calilutek. Ingkuk-llu ciuqlik pag'um qulam ciungan amian avategke-
nek calilutek. Ciumelnguq-llu ingna ukinqucuan tungiinun mingqerkaq quulluku
mingeqluni. Amirkam ataucim kan'a uatek quumalria mingeqluk' yaavet ukinqucuk. Atauciq-llu tua-i nutaan arnaq ikavsiarluni, ikavsiarluni kan'um kingua mingeqluku.
Angutem-llu ukinquciluku ingna, pall'iluku-llu.
Alaunateng ikavsianret, waten elliurturluki. Pagna kingua.

ALICE: Amirluku-mi?

of them and they dry. The water that was soaked up by the skin comes out through the pores of the skin. They call wringing the skins this way after tying the ends to a post *qipurluki*. After scraping the excess residue, they cut the skins to size.

~: *Skinning a kayak* :~

Two people worked on the skin covering, and one was a woman. And there was a man who cut sealskin to the appropriate pattern, *elirqituli*, and the third person who held the sealskin in place while the two were cutting it to the appropriate pattern. The third one, a woman, was called *petugturta* [the tacker]. Where the man had indicated, she would sew two stitches, tie the thread, and cut it. They called the tacking of two edges of sealskin which will later be sewn permanently *petugturluni*. The man would be cutting the sealskins to the appropriate pattern. There was one person who cut the sealskins. And when that was done, five people sewed the seams.

When the five women started sewing the seams, two women along the front of the kayak started sewing lines going up toward the cockpit coaming on the side at the center of the kayak, *mayu'urneq*, working across from each other facing the bow of the kayak.

Then there was the sewer called *caugartellria*, the third woman sewing toward the tote hole starting from the place where those two women she was facing started sewing.

Then two other women in the stern area were across from each other, also facing forward, sewing the outer stitches to join the skins starting from the *mayu'urneq* going toward the top stern seam of the kayak, the *ikavsianeq*. They started where the two [other] women stopped sewing, starting here along the edge of the *mayu'urneq*.

[She and the woman across from her] finished sewing to there, sewing the *ikavsianeq*. Those two women at the stern were working on the *ikavsianeq*. And the two in front sewed the side seams of the skin covering, over the deck stringers. The woman who sewed toward the tote hole sewed the narrow hind portion of one bearded-seal skin where the tote hole would be. Then one woman would sew the top stern stitches at the top aft section.

And a man would sew the tote hole and the cockpit coaming, *pall'iluku*.

The top stern stitches are visible, as they are sewn with dart stitches. It's the top aft section of the skin covering.

ALICE: What about the process of sewing that they call *amirluku?*

FRANK: Man'a ukatmun piurluku quumalria, amirluku, cipingaurluku, qeciim ngeliikun. Waten cingausngavkarlukek amik, tamarkenka-llu kaumalukek tegumiaqlukek. Aipaa waten pitalriamek, maaggun pivkenaku, maaggun taugaam temeqvaarkun kap'aqluku qaillun taktalriamek waten, ekiarakun qeciim anevkenaku akianun amavet amilriit. Ikna taugaam kap'aqluku, ikna kap'aqluku atlia. Keluita cagnicameng waten ayuqluteng. Yualum uuggun itrumalriim ikna nuqingaluku ukatmun. Uum-llu cali itrumalriim cali ukatmun cali nuqingaluku uum tungiinun.

Nutaan-llu augna pugumalria, quusngallra, ilulirnerkun waten elliulriamek mingeqluku, taperrnamek asuirucirluku. Iluliluki.

Assiitnayuksaaqellruaqa qayiarput augna, augkut elisngassiyaanrilngapakaata nasaurluut, assirluni taugken tua-i.

Ilait-am arnat yualuit cagnituut, ilait taugken tua-i assilriit amingraan qellugtevkenateng. Cagnilriit taugaam tua-i assiitut amit keluit. Taumek amilriit iqua uskurirluku waten qillqautellukek, nuqingaurluki amitulriit. Qungaumaluku mingeqsuunateng, nenguggluku taugaam wani, yualua qecik-llu cagnitatekengnaqlukek. Qungagceteksaunaku qecik. Tuaten qungagcecimakuni kelui cagniyugngaluteng, yualua ciuqsinruluni. Tamakut taugken yualuan cagnitacia, qeciim-llu mat'um cagnitacia pitatekekunek assiqapiarluni.

Imkut-wa unguqupagkait, cagnicissuutekait-wa mingqelriit. Unguqupiit-llu mingqelriit. Cagnicissuutellegnek mingqelriit atutuluteng cali. Muriit piliat. Yualurteng tua-i nemqaqualuku amiq tapqulluku nengugtaqluki qillrusngalria yaavet. Yualuteng cagnilluki amiq pitatekluku, qungagcetevkenaku. Tauna-wa iquani murak akagenqeggluni unguqupak qeciim iluanlluni caquqaumaluni kangra, *slip*-arngaunani tua-i. Petugluku-llu yaavet, nuqcetem pia, unguqupaa qeciim iluani qamani. Yaaqsigiaqan aug'arluku ukaqvaqaniraqluku unguqupak. Man'a tua-i mingqellni yaaqsigiaqan uyaturiaqan unguqupak aug'arluku wavet ngeliignun elliluku ukaqvaqaniraqluku, qeciim iluani. Ukuk mingqekngami nalliigni yaani.

Muragaq angevkenani akagcimaluni taugaam. Qeciim tua-i waten iluanun ekekuni pugumaarkauluni waten. Ilavkugmek-llu uuggun nemerluku aug'arcailku-

FRANK: You keep sewing the skins that are joined this way, *amirluku*, for the waterproof seam, leaving a small section at the end of the skin. On the first seam you leave a little lap of the bottom skin extending beyond the seam and sew with the stitches at the edge of the top skin going only partway through the skin. You hold both edges of the skins by inserting your fingers between the skins. When you tighten the stitches they look like this. The sinew thread that is stitched through pulls the other side this way. And these stitches going through here also pull it in this direction.

When the first seam is done [you fold over the top piece], and the flap is filled with a strand of beach grass as a welt, *asuirun*. You then stitch again between the extended lap of the bottom piece and the top piece, this time with the overcast stitches at the edge of the bottom skin going through the skin. They call this process *ililuluki*.

I thought the kayak we made [at the Alaska Native Heritage Center in Anchorage] would not turn out well because those young women didn't seem very skilled, but in fact it turned out very well.

Some women's stitches are too tight, but some who are skilled at embedded waterproof stitching, *amilriit*, do not cause the seam to bunch. Overly tight stitches on the kayak covering aren't good. That is why those who sew embedded waterproof stitches anchor the two beginning thread ends with a string and tie it like this and keep an even tension by pulling it as they sew. They do not allow the tension of the skin to loosen. If the tension of the skin is slack the sinew thread will be tight, and the stitch might be made a bit more ahead of where it should be. But if the tension of the thread and the skin are the same, it will be very good.

There are tools, *unguqupiit*, that are used to help the skin sewers tighten the stitches. Skin sewers use *unguqupiit*. Skin sewers used these wooden tools to help them tighten the stitches. Around these they wrapped the thread and the skin, one end of which was fastened down, and pulled them both to even the tension. They tightened the tension of the sinew thread when sewing so that its tension would be equal to that of the skin, keeping it from bunching up. Underneath the skin there would be a piece of wood with rounded edges, *unguqupak*, with its end covered in such a way as to keep it from slipping. They fastened down the skin there and the *unguqupak* would be underneath the skin to keep it taut. When the sewing advanced away from the *unguqupak* that is underneath the skins being sewn, they would move it closer to the seam which was yet to be sewn.

[The *unguqupak*] is a small, round piece of wood. When it is placed underneath the skin they are sewing, it will stick out like this. And they would tie a piece of

tekluku, keluk-wa maani. Qillrulluku yaavet, wall'u it'gaminun as'artelluku wavet
arnam. Nugtekluku mingqerkauluni, yaaqsigiaqan taikaniraqluku, unguqupakluku
tua-i tauna. Muragaq-wa cali augna qaillun taktauralria, yualuminun yualuanun
nemqauqaarluku cagnicissuutekluku.

Yagenrek malruk ciptelaryugnarqaat. Ikavsiarutkaq takenqurrulartuq amircuutni.
Usgutkat-usgutkak ukuk malruk, caugarutekaq-wa, ingna-wa qayamun amirarkaq,
kingulirarkaq. *Five, six, seven, eight,* watnguyugngayugnarqut yualukat. Man'a taken-
ruluni ilamini ikavsiarutkaq.

Ellegluki pituit amiutekat, ellenruluki. Pingayunek-llu waten kelituluki, tupigtur-
luki pituluki, waten qip'ivkenaki. Malrugnek tegunirluku piluku qip'urluku waten
pituit. Pingayunek taugaam piarkat imumek waten piurluki. Iciwa imkut cat qila-
gat. Makut-wa waten pimalaryugnarqut makucetun, keluit waten ayuqurluteng. Pingayunek tegunirluki, pingkut taugaam mingqutmun pillerkait malrugnek piluki
nuv'iliraqluki.

~: *Mingqellret akililallrat* :~

Amillret tuamtellu tamakut qayamun mingqellret taqngata, pupsirluki. Akilirluku
mingqellrat makunek aklunek canek atu'urkaitnek. Pupsirluki-gguq. Cali-am piciryaraqluku.

Piciatun' canek, piciatun aturyukngaitnek, wall'u qantanek, ipuutnek tamaani
yualunek, canek tua-i aturyukngaitnek, atutukaitnek aturanek. Maa-i-llu tua-i
kass'angameng canek makunek pilangluki, wall'u ilait akinek piaqluki. Amirteput
augkut amani pillemteni, *three hundred* atauciq akilillruuq. Tuaten akiliumallruyug-

twine over it [along the outside of the skin] to prevent it from slipping off, and the row of stitches would be here. It is tied over there, or the woman could slip it onto her foot. She would use it as an aid while she sewed, and she would move it closer whenever her sewing advanced; it was her *unguqupak*. There was another piece of wood about this length which was used to even the tension of the stitches after winding the sinew thread around it.

I think the sinew thread is longer than two outstretched arms. The *ikavsiarutkaq* [thread used for the top-stern stitches] is longer than the *amircuutet* [threads used for the embedded waterproof stitching]. There are two sinew threads used for connecting the three sealskins used for the bottom of the kayak, and the *caugarutekak* [thread for the bow stitches], then the *qayamun amirarkaq* [thread for the stitches along the sides on the stern], and the *kingulirarkaq* [thread for the stern]. Five, six, seven, eight, I think that's how many sinew threads there are. The sinew thread, *ikavsiarutkaq*, for the top stern stitches is longer than the others.

They made the *amiutekat* [those that would be used as thread for embedded waterproof stitching] thick, thicker than the others. They used three strands of fiber by braiding them, and not plying them. When they were preparing only two strands of thread, they plied them like this. The sinew thread that was plied was prepared with two strands of sinew fiber. The strands are held together at the end, then the strand nearest the thread maker is twisted toward the maker and then placed over the other in the direction away from the maker. Then the process is repeated with the other strand. But as for those with three strands of fiber, you know how you make those knitted items, I think that the sinew thread used for waterproof stitching is prepared the same way. They used three strands when they prepared the thread, and it is reduced to two strands at the end where it will be threaded to a needle for easier threading.

~: *Paying skin sewers* :~

And when the kayak skin sewers were done sewing, they paid them, *pupsirluki*. They paid the skin sewers with essentials, necessities of life. They call it *pupsirluki*. That was their custom.

[They gave them] all kinds of items, necessities, including bowls, ladles, sinew thread, or other items they can use, and the type of clothing they wear. Now that there are white people around, they can give them other kinds of items, or some pay them with cash. Those who sewed our kayak coverings in Anchorage were paid

narquq. Ernerpak tauna qayaq caliaqekput amani, unugluni-llu tua-i. Qaillun pitariqerluku tayima taqaat qayaq.

~: *Qayam amillra* :~

Mingqetuit tua-i taqngata-llu egmianun amirluki, elliluki amirkait arulairucuunaki, kineryingciqngaki.

Kinerciqarraarluki yuuluki, uqumek minguglukii. Uqumek minguggaarluki nutaan at'elluku amianun. Palurrluku-am tua-i, ikna-llu agqutek kapullukek murak. Palurrluku, muriik ilavkugmek wall'u taprarmek nemerlukek kankuk. Ikavet kinguanun waten pillranun puukartelluku. Unguqupirluku-llu taprarmek qillerrluku nuqingaluku.

Yuuk-am malruk akiqliqlutek palungqallrani; qukaa kan'a nanerluku, yuuk malruuk kuyii qesngaluku waten amianek tapirluku, un'a aciani kuyak amianek pivkarluku. Kinguani wani nutaan yuuk akiqliqlutek amia teguluku imguyucirluku carangllugnek, nutaan ataucikun waten elliurluku, aaqevkenaku tua-i nutaan, qatngitarluku, cingqullagangraan, nutganguartelluku tua-i. Taukut tua-i tamana tegumiaqluku, amia kingutmun ayakaniraqluni.

Augkut-llu tua-i tapricillret nem'eggnun tekicata muraggarnek kapqaqluki, nutaan taqluku. Kevirluki nutaan muraggarnek tamakut tapricillret. Nutaan at'elluku. Tugcilqerluku nutaan taprarmek.

Putungqetuut-am kinguit ukut nutaraugaqata atutuit yaavet ciumun. Tua-i-llu amirkait nutaan eliqluki taqngamegteki-llu egumlluku tamana. Ancamegteki-llu ciunganelnguut putuut aug'artarluki, ukuk ayaperviik ngelkarrlukek. Makut-llu tua-i kinguanelnguut aug'arpek'naki, matareskan aturciqngata eruqan. Cagnissuutekciqngaki tamakut putuit, aug'ayuunaki tua-i tamakut.

three hundred dollars each. Perhaps that's how much they were paid. We worked on the kayak all day there in Anchorage, and it became night. I don't know what time it was when they finished the kayak.

~: *Putting the skin on the kayak* :~

They sewed them, and when they were done, they put the skin cover on the frame without delay because the skins would dry.

After they let the skin which had been loosely fitted on the kayak frame dry for a while, they took it off and rubbed it with seal oil. Then, after they oiled the kayak skin, they put it back on the kayak frame. They turned the kayak upside down and staked two posts, *agqutek*, at the end of the kayak where they had put the lower stern piece, to keep the kayak from moving while the skin was fitted onto the frame. They turned the kayak over and bound the two wooden posts with twine or sealskin rope. They let the two posts sit right up against the kayak stern. And then they tied a sealskin line to hold it down.

There were two people on each side of the upside down kayak frame; the middle section of it had been weighted down, and then the two people held on to the keelson of the frame along with the skin to be fitted, and they fitted the skin over the keelson. Then the two people across from each other at the back of the kayak frame, using grass to help them grip the skin, simultaneously tugged and jerked on the skin hard as they gradually fit it onto the frame, not worrying even though the frame made popping sounds. They held onto it, and the sealskin covering would gradually move back.

And when the *tapricillret* [holes on the edge of the skins along the top of the kayak at the front and back where sealskin line is lashed when the kayak skin covering is placed on the frame] reached their final position, they pegged them in with wooden pegs, finishing it. They filled those *tapricillret* with the pegs. They had now placed the skin over the frame. They used sealskin line to tighten the kayak skins on the frame, lashing the skin through the loops and onto the frame.

There were skin loops along the sealskin covering of the kayak from the stern to the bow, and they used them at this stage. When they were done trimming the sealskin covering to size, they removed the sealskin line that was lashed through the loops. Once they removed the [lashings] they removed the loops of skin from the bow of the kayak back to the cockpit coaming stanchions. But they left the

~: *Qayam mingullra* :~

Urasqamek imumek mingugluki pituit, qatellriamek. Qaurtuli qaceckenruuq urasqami, aipaa. Urasqauyaaqluni tua-i qaterluni taugaam, qatenruluni urasqami, qaceckenruluni.

Akmaken Cape Newenham-am kiakaraanek tamakut'lartut qaurtulinek. Tauna taugken urasqamek at'lek, qateryaaqeng'ermi tamatutun qaurtulitun ayuqevkenani. Tungunrurrlugluni, *gray*-aarrluuluni tua-i.

Puqlaningraan-llu minguk cayuituq. Elqiateng-llu muriit tamatumek tamaa-i mingugaqluki qatertelluki. Cingikeggluteng. Cikum taugaam qaingani qalrilrianun-llu pissuraqameng atutuluki tamakut elqiat, pissurcuutekluki.

Ciayat, ukuit qaillun pitaluteng. Uum tua-i ngeliikun tangvaurluki yaavet. Iluit tungulriamek kangiplugmek minguumalallruut, ilulirnerit.

Tamalkurmeng pissutulriit pingqetullruut. Elqiaricuunateng tamakunek.

~: *Qayam auluksaraa* :~

Kinerciyuitait. Iliini tua-i kinercituit. Akiviggluki imairluki cait tua-i aneqluki, anuqmun maniluku paingat uverrluki, kinercirluki. Tua-i-llu kinrata nutaan assirnerit unkut aciit makut uqurrluki qaingit, mingugluki uqumek. Uqumek piicuitellruut makut qayat. Uqumek taugaam mingugturluki, piyungaqamegteki mingugaqluki uqumek.

Murilkelluki pilaamteki, iliini allrakut-llu cetamaurcetuut waten qeciit pinirluteng piyaraat; allrakut cetaman wall'u talliman tekilluki amiuyugngauq amirkaq. Issuriq taugken pingayuni tayima allrakuni piyugngayugnarquq. Piyunerkillruluni, pinialiyugngaluni-llu tamaa. Tungurilartut tunguringa'artaqameng tua-i piniat ikeglilartuq amiugaqameng. Uqum taugaam tua-i pimaluki, puyam meciumastiita pinirtelluki. Tua-i tuaten piaqata, imumek-llu waten tapluteng piaqata, qup'artelangartaqata makuit nutaan cimituit; aarnariluteng tua-i unani cikumi piksunairulluteng.

Uqurqurluki taumek pitukait, unaniungraan-llu. Anguarraarluta tua-i unani pi-

loops on the back skin covering because they would use those when they removed the sealskin covering for cleaning. They never removed them because those loops would be used to tighten the skin covering over the frame.

~: Painting the kayak :~

They painted them with *urasqaq* [white clay]. *Qaurtuli* is a much lighter white than *urasqaq*, the other type used for coloring. [*Qaurtuli*] is actually a type of *urasqaq* but it's white, much lighter than *urasqaq*, much brighter.

They get *qaurtuli* a short distance beyond Cape Newenham. But the one called *urasqaq*, although it's whitish, it isn't the same color as *qaurtuli*. It's a little darker, grayish in color.

The paint doesn't fade in the heat. They also painted their *elqiat* [wooden visors] with that to make them white. The visors are pointed. They use *elqiat* while hunting on the ice and hunting for mating seals; they used them as hunting equipment.

These visors, *ciayat*, their brims are a certain length. They watched seals along the edge of the visor. Their undersides were colored dark with charcoal.

All hunters had them. They were never without *elqiat*.

~: Kayak care :~

They don't dry [kayaks] every time, but they dry them sometimes. They place them on their sides, empty the contents, and then expose the cockpit coaming to the wind to dry them by positioning it at an angle. And when they are dry, they apply seal oil to the bottom surface. Kayaks are never without seal oil. They always apply seal oil to them when they think it is time.

Since we took good care of kayak skins, sometimes they remained in good condition for four seasons; the bearded-seal kayak coverings can last as kayak skins for four or even five seasons. However, spotted-seal kayak skins can last for about three seasons. They last for a shorter time and quickly become delicate. They get dark, and when kayak skins darken, they become weak. But seal oil, rancid seal oil which is soaked into the skin coverings keeps them strong. They replaced them when [they got dark], and when the skin starts to crack when folded it makes them hazardous so that they can no longer be used down in the ocean ice.

For those reasons they always put seal oil on them, even down on the ocean. Af-

taput-llu yuuluki, auggluit taryumek unaken erurluku qayaq. Erurraarluku-llu aki-
viggluku ellngacarluku, man'a akertemun maniluku, kinercirluku assirnera camna.

Tua-i-llu kinran, nutaranek uqunek pinevluki, pitam tua-i nutaramek uquanek
aug'aulluki egumanrilnguut; tamatumek nutaan minigugluku acia. Akertemun puqlamun pimavkarluku. Tuaten tua-i piuratuluki. Tamana amimun tua-i pinircautngu-
luni, assircautnguluni cali-llu piiragcautnguluni mermi uquq. Tuaten tua-i piurluku
pitullruaput, uqurqurluki. Cali-llu ivruciput qeciit aturraarluki, yuuluki kinercirluki, kinraqata uqurtaqluki cali qayamcetun piluki.
    Maingit, metuyairluki tua-i metuyaircarluki, meq iterviirulluku.
    Tamakunun piuratuluki nunani uitaaqameng. Tamakuicuunaki. Palurrluki cali
pituluki, palungqaurumaluki tatkimaluki, qimugtenun tua-i nurtelluki. Qimug-
tet-am ilait neryugtut qayanek, pitullruata tuaten tua-i pituit. Tatkimaurtelluki
taugaam apqiitnek, tamakut elliviit.
    Maktaluki tatkimayuitait, nutarauluki taugaam kuv'aqata uqumek maktaluki tat-
kituit. Uquq iluatni patrutnatkaanun amimun, assirneratni pagaani akuqetaarluni.
Iluit uqumek nutarauluki kinraqata mermek avuluku, agucirluku kuvtuit. Unkut
assirnerit cauyarat piit kevegluku ayagavkarluku meq, illuggluku ukatmuqertaq-
luku, apamak aciagni. Tua-i-llu nutaan qaqican, painga, ketgarluku patuluku qayam. Tamalkuan patuluku ketgarluku maktaluku tatkiluku, palungqavkenaku.

Tua-i-llu patgucami tamana qatellra tunguriyarturluni, kavirrlugcenani. Patruta-
qan qecigmun uquq itraqan, nallunaunani tua-i. Tua-i elalirnerkun maaggun agtu-
ralriani nepciqtaarluni, uquq anluni amatiini maitgun. Tua-i-llu puyaqaani assirluni
tua-i. Patrulluku tua-i nangluku qavani uqurtairulluni, minguumaluni patrusnga-
luku. Meq-llu tamana cataunani tayima.
    Tuaten-am pituit. Puqlirluku taugaam uquq. Nutaraullrani qayaq, uuqnarqevke-
naku taugaam, taugaam *warm*-arluku uquq, puqlanirtelluku.

Nengelmi atam uquq, nenglliraqan, yuuqatua egmianun, kenriqerrluni pilriani;
tamana-am pitekluku mermek avutuat puqlirluku-llu. Meq tua-i kintuuq iluani.

ter paddling down on the ocean, we unloaded our catch and washed the blood residue off the kayak with salt water. And after washing it, we propped it on its side to drain the water, exposing this side to the sun, drying the bottom.

And when the kayak dried, we rubbed its bottom with unrendered blubber from our catch which we had cut into strips beforehand; then we exposed the kayak to the sun's heat. We always did that. Applying seal oil strengthens the kayak skin, reconditions it, and makes it slick in the water. We always applied seal oil to them. And after wearing our waterproof sealskin boots we took them off, dried them, and applied seal oil just as we did with our kayaks.

[Oil] prevents water from soaking in through the pores; it keeps the water out.

They always placed the kayaks on [tatkit, kayak racks] when on land. They always had those for their kayaks. They placed the kayaks upside down on the racks, out of reach of dogs. Some dogs like to eat kayak skins, and because of that they put them up on supports. They always kept them on kayak racks.

They don't put them rightside up on kayak racks except when they were treating them with oil when they were newly made. Seal oil is put in the lower portion of the kayak, tipping the kayak to one side and then the other, until the oil penetrates the sealskin covering. Some put seal oil along with some water in the lower portion of new kayaks, to assist in spreading the oil. They prop up the kayak to move the water and oil around in the bottom around the ribs, tipping it this way in the area under the gunwales. And when it was done, they covered the cockpit and tied the covering. At that time they covered the entire cockpit and kept the kayak rightside up on the supports and not upside down.

And when seal oil soaks into the skin, the skin's color darkens and becomes reddish. One can tell when seal oil has penetrated the skin. When touching the outside of the skin, it would feel sticky since the oil had seeped through the skin's pores. When the oil becomes rancid, it is ready. All the seal oil soaks into the skin; there's no seal oil left inside. All the water disappears also.

That's what they do. However, they'd put warm water with the seal oil. They did that when the kayak skin was new, but they didn't make the seal oil hot, only warm.

In cold weather, seal oil thickens quickly, and for that reason they'd add some water to it and warm it. The water evaporates from the inside.

⚮: *Amian eruryaraa* :⚮

Neq'liurutekraarluku up'nerkami, ilua augnek tua-i pitat augitnek uqlangtuuq qayam ilua, uciliqtaarluni. Cauyarat aciita augglugmek kinrusngaluku nepingalrianek
piluni carrirciiganani tua-i. Tua-i-llu neqliyarameng, neqsuameng aturluki tuamtellu qeltenek tua-i yuvgermek tuaten, tamana tua-i uqlautnguluni. Yuvgeq-llu mermek ping'ermi erurciigalami, neptetuami, kelikarluku taugaam pilriani aug'atuluni.
Kinraqluku tua-i qayam iluani yuvgeq, mermek eruryaaqeng'ermi aug'arpek'nani.

Tua-i-llu neqsuutngunrian cali nutaan mermek imirluku, akurrluku nanvamun,
tamalkuan tua-i neg'ucirluku, kenicirluku amia. Kenian-llu tua-i nutaan qalurraar-
luku, yualui kinguan kepurturluki ullirrluku, ukinqucua-llu, imkut-llu taprai aug'arluki. Aug'arraarluki nutaan matarrluku. Nutaan mermun akurtevsiarluku enra-llu,
frame-aa. Nutaan kelikarturluku tua-i, kelikarturluki tamakut auggluut kenivkar-
luki aug'arluki.

Erurturluku qayaq, assiriluku augglumek piinani. Nemri-llu imkut kituggnarqe-
kata kituggluki, cimirluki, neminqiggluku. Amia-llu tua-i nutaan kelikarturluku,
amia man'a auggluk aug'arturluku yuvgerrluk-llu, assiriluku tua-i.

Nutaan kinerpailgaku, uqumek mingugluku ilua tamalkuan tua-i pag'utuumaan-
llu, qaqilluku ilua. Nutaan enra iterrluku amianun. Palurrluku-llu tua-i agqutek nunamun kapullukek. Ilavkugmek waten taprualugmek pirraarluku nemerluku akuliik uavet, ayagyailkuteklukku waten.

Un'a-llu tua-i kuyii imna, yuuk malruk akiqliqlutek pupsugluku waten teguluku,
amiq tapqulluku tamaavet. Yuuk-llu malruk kinguani qayam amia imguyucirluku
[canegnek] imirlukek man'a qecik, akiqliqlutek, nutaan waten elliurluku waten.

Taqluku. Tapqicillri yuvriraqluki, taprait imkut uitallret. Tua-i nem'eggnun tua-i
tekicata, nutaan muragnek kevirluki pingayun. Nutaan makluku at'elluku taprualugmek nutaan tugcilqerrluku putuikun.

~: *Cleaning the kayak skin* :~

After using it to obtain food in spring, caked blood of many catches is inside the kayak from loading and unloading. The area underneath the kayak ribs is stained with dried blood that is hard to clean. They used kayaks again when they went salmon fishing in summer, and again fish scales along with slime make it grimy. And fish slime is impossible to remove, even with water, because it adheres. It has to be scraped lightly to come off. The fish slime dries inside the kayak, and it doesn't come off, even though it's washed with water.

They soaked the kayak when they were finished using it for fishing by immersing it entirely in a lake, filling it with water, with weights to keep it down. Once the kayak's skin softened, they bailed the water out and cut the sinew stitching in the stern and around the tote hole, and removed the sealskin lashings, *taprat*. After that they took the skin off the frame. They further immersed the skin, and also the frame, in water. Then they scraped the kayak skin, allowed the caked blood to soften, and removed it by scraping.

They washed the kayak thoroughly until it was free of dried blood. And if the bindings needed repair, they fixed them, replaced them, and lashed it again. They scraped the skin covering thoroughly, removing the blood residue on the kayak skin along with the caked fish slime until it was free of it.

Before [the kayak skin] dried, they rubbed seal oil all over the inside, including the upper section. Next they inserted the frame into its skin covering. First they turned [the frame] upside down and staked two pieces of wood, *agqutek*, in the ground close [to the kayak stern which would keep the kayak locked in place]. They fastened the kayak stern between these posts with sealskin line; it is tied so that it will stay in place.

Then two people across from one another grasped the kayak keel like this and held it along with the skin covering. Then two people along the kayak stern across from one another would use [grass] to grasp the skin covering, and they yanked the kayak like this.

They finished [pulling the covering over the frame]. They'd periodically check the loops along the kayak stern where skin line had been laced and pulled to close the skin over the frame. When the loops were situated in their proper places, they filled the three loops with sticks. Then they turned the kayak over and finished placing the skin over the frame, lacing the loops with sealskin line and tightening it.

Tamana mingqumallra waten mingqutem kapullri naspaaqaqluki. Tua-i-llu tekiu-cata, man'a-llu cagnitenrirluku taprualuk. Cagniqaarluku negtaaraqluku waten, neg-taarraarluku cagnikaniraqluku. Kiituani tua-i ukinrit nall'arqurluki. Mingqutem pillra nutaan mingeqluku. Yualum kapusngallra, mingqutem piurallra uniurteksau-naku.

Nutaraullermini atullri. Tuaten tua-i pituit. Tua-i-llu nutaan qaqican yaquleg-cuutekluku ayagluteng.

~: Anguarutet paangrutet-llu :~

Aipaa mulegpaunruluni, mulga angenruluni, iqtunruluni, tua-i angualriani pinin-ruluni. Cumiggluni piyukuni tamatumek aturarkauluni mulegtunranek. Tua-i-llu pissungekuni mikellra tamana aturturluku, mulcengaunra.

Cetualiuraqameng atutuit paangrutet.
Tangaaluki mulgit pituaput. Cuqtaayuitut. Man'a assilria mulga. Una waniwa mulga pitacqegtuq uum, tangaaluki tua-i, man'a taugaam iqtussiyaagtuq pilial-qengani ik'um. Qaraliqanka makut maa-i. Yaqurtuluni-llu man'a sugtuami ikna, angengami takelria.

Man'a-llu maa-i angurvak. Mat'umi iqtunruluni mulga kan'a. Malruulutek tua-i; malruugarkaulutek waten. Cumiggluni taugaam nutaan pikuni una nutaan aturar-kauluku, cukangnaqluni pikuni. Tallit atam piniriituut mat'um piniriluki anguaru-tem. Exercise-at, tema-wa tua-i piniriituit makut, anguarturalleq assirtuq. Una tema caliaqaa, pinirluni tua-i anguarturalleq. Elisngaut ilait anguaryaramek.

Mumigtaaryaraq-am allauguq. Una tua-i waten anguaryaraq ayuquq waten, wa-ten-llu mumiggluni. Augna taugken aipaa, pakikuniu egmianun yaggluni tegulukullu tua-i. Wavet ellirpailgan wavet teguaqluku. Cukaluni anguarluni. Tuaten ayuq-luni anguaryaraq; malruuluni.

They'd periodically test the needle holes that had been made previously, to see if they were even with the holes on the corresponding skin. Then when the needle holes were even with the holes on the other skin, they stopped tightening the sealskin line. They would push on the kayak skin after tightening the sealskin line, pushing down on it like this, and after pushing down on it, they would make it even tighter. The needle holes eventually became even with the corresponding holes for sewing the pieces together. Then they sewed through the previously made needle holes. They sewed along the place where the needle and thread had previously been inserted and not anywhere else.

[They used] the needle holes that were used when the kayak was new. That's what they did. And when it was done, they used it to hunt birds.

~: *Kayak paddles* :~

One [type of paddle] has a bigger, wider blade for more strength when paddling. If one wants to go faster, he would use the one with the larger blade. Then when one is actually hunting he would switch to the smaller paddle, the one with the smaller blade.

They use the double-bladed paddles for beluga hunting.

We estimate the size of the blades. They don't measure them. This blade here is good. This blade is an appropriate size, one estimates the size, but this blade is too wide [for me] because that person over there [Bill Wilkinson] made it. These are my emblematic designs. And this is long because that person [Bill Wilkinson] over there is tall; it's long because he's large.

And this one here is a large paddle. The blade down there is wider than this. There are two; two sizes are essential. When one is in a hurry one has to use this [wider] one. Use of paddles strengthens the arm muscles. Exercise and paddling strengthen the body, and it benefits the body. Paddling works on the muscles, and one gets strong when one is constantly paddling. Some people are knowledgeable about paddling.

Changing the paddle [to the right or the left side of the kayak] as one paddles has different motions. This way of paddling is like this [demonstrating], and this is how you grasp the paddle when changing to the other side. But there is the other way of paddling, where at the final stroking of the paddle one reaches out right away and grasps it. They grasp it before it reaches this point, as one is paddling at a fast pace. That is how paddling is done; there are two ways.

Akqurrilnguut maa-i assirtut anguarutet waten, assipiarluteng. Akqurrilnguut, tegg'eraunateng-llu peryuunateng tua-i.

[Qaquarit] aug'arcailkutengqertut. Avani-gguq ussukcayuitellruit ukut. Anguyiim nalliini-am iliit tauna marayami qaquani waten piluku, atrarluni mat'um tekicartullra piluku, cayugarcaaqekiini amugartelliniluni, piyaaqnanrani tekiartelliniluku. Picurlagtelluku-am qaquan uum. Aug'artenrilkuni tekipailgan atraqercarluni, una anyailkutengqerqan.

Aarnarqelriit cali tua-i mulnganarqut. Ayimqilriit maktasciigatut. Ayimcilriit anguarutmeggnek maktasciigatut. Egmian kitnguciquq tua-i, aksalerviinani-llu.

Ciisqumigmeng aqumgatuut. Aqumluteng-llu tua-i waten aqumluteng, iruteng-llu kipullguarluk piaqluki, wall'u ceturrluteng qayam iluani. Ciisqumiggluteng nutaan cukangnaqaqameng pituut.

~: *Qamigautet* :~

Qayameggnun-wa atutukait. Qanikcaam qaingakun qamurturluki tagkaniraqameng piyuitut, qamigautegnun taugaam ekluki tua-i ucikluki qavarvigkamegnun tag'aqluteng. Wall'u tagqataquneng tagutaqluki qayateng qamigautnun ekluki.

Qamuucirluku. Qayam tallirpilirnerani uitatuut qamuutait. Ukinqucuk-am uumek tegumiaqluku qamuutaq wantelluku, piyualuni tua-i ayaulluku.

Kinguani-wa uitatulriik qamigautek. Kiani tua-i kinguani akilirnermi akmani, tapram piani. Tapraq qillrusngaluni nemerkautiik qamigautek akilirnermi uitaluni, qillrusngallra tapram. Cali-am nemrucararluni allamek. Elisngaarkauluku; patagmek angiarcetulimek. Tua-i nuqluku tua-i qillrutaa, iquakun cayugareskuni, qillrutaq tamarmi egumqertarkauluni, qamigautek aug'arcugngalutek.

Asveret iliini yura'arrvik'larait qayat. Ilait-llu-gguq tua-i qamigautait waten imum tulumeggnek nall'arrluku pituluki. Tuatnaaqata tua-i egmian qamigautek nemrek cayugarrluku tua-i ang'iqercetarkauluku. Qamigautek taugaam nalkegnegun asevrem cayugartarkaulukek qayaq pivkenaku.

Tua-i cagniluku qilleqluku, taugaam tegularluku angilluku pingaunaku. Cayu-

The paddles without knots are the best. The ones without knots or hardwood do not bend.

[Paddle grips] have a feature that keeps them from coming off. They say that they never pegged the paddle grip back then. During war time, a warrior being pursued by his enemy tried to push off by pushing his paddle with a grip against the mud like this, but the paddle went in up to this part, and when he tried to pull the paddle out, the grip came off. While he was trying to retrieve his paddle, the enemy warriors reached him. That grip caused his demise. If the grip had been pegged it would not have come off, he could have pushed off quickly before they reached him.

Paddles that are in bad shape also require care. Those who break their paddles have difficulty keeping their kayaks upright. They will immediately capsize and won't have a way to withstand it without paddles.

They sit kneeling [while paddling]. They also sit and cross their legs, or stretch their legs out inside the kayak. They kneel and paddle when they are in a hurry.

~: Kayak sleds :~

They use [kayak sleds] to carry their kayaks. They don't drag kayaks on top of snow when they move away from open water, but they put the kayak on top of the kayak sled when they go to where they are going to camp. Or when they are on shore they load the kayaks on the sleds and go home.

They put a tow rope through [the tote hole]. Their tow ropes, *qamuutat*, were put on the right side of the kayak. They'd hold the tote hole with this [left] hand with the tow rope over the arm and walk with it.

The kayak sled is placed aft [on the kayak]. It is located on the far aft along the kayak sled fastener. The sealskin line that holds the kayak sled in place is tied in place on the other side, that's the place where the sealskin line is tied. It also has its own distinct knot. They have to know that knot well; it is one that can be undone quickly. If it is pulled at the end then the knot will come undone and the kayak sled can come off.

Sometimes a walrus emerged from the water onto a kayak. And they say a walrus can strike the kayak sled with its tusks. When that occurs, they would immediately yank on the knot of the kayak sled's rope and undo it. The walrus would only pull on the kayak sled and not the kayak.

They tie [the sled knot] tight, but they don't use both hands to undo it. Rather,

gareskuni taugaam aug'ararkauluteng qillengqatait. Qac'uqerrluni-llu ikna egmian peggluku cayugarqaarluku.

~: Aqumgautaat ikaraliin-llu :~

Unkut atam paingan nalliini kanani uitatulriit ikaraliitet kelugkaat taperrnanek avuluteng, tupiumaluteng qaillun akultutaurluteng keluit. Unani tua-i aqumgautaat-wa qaingatni uitaluteng. Augkut-wa uqrutautulit uqrutarkat asguilitat; angenruluteng tamakuni can'get cali, kelugkaat taperrnanek avuluteng. Aipait cali qayam aklui. Asguilitanek piaqluki.

Llumarrartaitellrani tamaani cikum qainganun mayuraqameng anuqlirtura'arqan negcik, negcikcuarmek aipirluku tamakut asguilitat tev'arrluki qaingatnun uqrutaqaqluki qayam iluani ekumaurallermeggni. Asguilitanek aterluteng. Tua-i-llu unuan naparrluki nunulluki waten qilakluki qavarluteng qayam iluani.

Nengelvayuilami. Assirtut atam tamakut ilakellrit. Ellangllugmi taugaam piluteng assiitut.

~: Negcik :~

Negcik maa-i man'a *friend*-allerput tua-i pegingayuunaku. Qayaq-llu tua-i una qaillun pitalriamek uniarrluni piqatang'ermi teguqerrlainarluku man'a negcik.

Tua-i una waniwa uksumi qanikcamun waten kapulluku ingna, mermun-llu tua-i atraami qayaq painga man'a wavet tua-i waken qayaq pimallranek ekqataquni, cikumun wavet una wani kapulluku, qulamun-llu piluku, waten-llu teguluku, mermenani-wa qayaq man'a. Una tapqulluku uumek teguluku.

Mermi un'a uitakan, qayaq-llu man'a atrarrluku wiinga cikum qainganllua, una kapusngaluni qanikcarmun, tegukumku waten nayumiqaluku-llu eklua unavet qayamun. Aqumekuma nutaan peggluku una wani. Tua-i-llu tua-i yuuqataquma aug'utun cali. Ukalirnerrlainarmun-llu elliarkauluku, maalirnermun pivkenaku.

Kinguani yaavet ukalirnerrlainarmun. Una naqingaluni-am qamigautek tapra-

the knot will come undone when yanked with one hand. It will quickly come undone when pulled, and they would let go right away after pulling it.

∾: *Kayak seats and grass mats* :∾

The *ikaraliitet* [grass kayak mats] are placed under the cockpit coaming. Coarse grass is mixed with beach grass for making the mats. They are twined with horizontal strands plied in pairs, and the pairs of horizontal strands are separated from each other with a set spacing. The woven mats are placed under the *aqumgautaat* [seating boards made of wooden slats]. Then there are *asguilitat* [twined windbreaks] which were bigger than the *ikaraliitet* and are woven out of a mixture of coarse grass and beach grass like the mats. Those go with the kayak; they call them *asguilitat*.

During the time when cloth was unavailable, when they went on the ice if there was a constant wind, they set up the *asguilitat* using the large gaff and the small gaff and had that as a windbreak while they were sitting in the kayak. They called them *asguilitat*. Then at night they would stake them out and fasten them in place as a canopy over the cockpit while they slept inside.

It was not extremely cold in those days. Those are good to have with you. But they aren't good to use in stormy weather.

∾: *Gaff* :∾

The *nekcik* [gaff] was our friend, and we always kept it at hand. We always took the gaff with us, even if we were leaving the kayak for just a short time.

In wintertime one would dig the gaff's hook into the snow, if one, say, who had gone down to the water was about to board his kayak there. He would dig the hook into the ice and place the shaft across the deck ridge of the kayak, grasping it like this. He would grasp [the gaff's shaft] as well as [the cockpit coaming].

After launching my kayak on the water, in preparation for boarding while still on the ice, I dig my gaff into the snow, and as I board my kayak I hold the gaff handle like this, as I hold the kayak steady. Once I sit down I put the gaff away. You follow the same maneuvers when getting out of the kayak. The gaff is always placed on this [left] side and never on that side of the kayak.

It is always placed there at the stern of the kayak and always on this side of it. It

nun kankuk paingik, una qerringaluni wavet, pugqerrngaunani tua-i nekluku, maa-vet piyuunani.

Tua-i-llu una waniwa tegumiaqerrlainarluku-wa tua-i man'a, qayani canimaar-mun uniarrluku piqatang'ermi tegumiaqerrlainarluku. Tua-i-llu cali pitsaqevkenani-gguq kitngukuni mermi, tua-i ika'anlluni kinguani, una-wa wanlluni. Taq'ingailkan tua-i egmianun tegulerarkauluku ukuakun, qayaq taq'ingaireskan. Anqerreskuni-llu tua-i egmianun makucia, taprarnek pingqetuut makut, egmianun iqemkarluku waten una keggluku qillernera kuimluni nutaan cikumun. Cikumun-llu tekiskuni nutaan aug'arluku qanikcarmun kapulluku nutaan mayurluni tegularluku, makui-cesciiganateng cali. Taprualugmek, tapruarmek man'a. Tuaten ayuqut.

Anguarutaireskuni tuamtellu una anguaruteksugngaluku. Tuamtellu augna ke-magnaq un'a navkan waken kepulluku cimirarkauluku, unkut. Ukuit taumek aka-genqellriit waten pitukait makut negciit, ukutun ellegtangnaqluki.

Ukatmun pikuni aarnaqluni. Pitsaqevkenani camna aug'areskan, man'a ukatmuq-reskuniu, ellminek akngirtarkauluni uumun. Waten taugken aarnaunani. Una cuq-tetuat waten pitaluku pimallerkaa. Tuaten ayuquq man'a negcik.

Tuamtellu yuk kiskan, teguyunaireskan, uum-gguq qukaakun negcikilaut, itqe-rrutengraan allgarulluni kiliulluni tuqungaituq-gguq. Uuggun negcigluku piyunail-kan aturaikun.

Agluqran ilulirnerakun. Itqerrutengraani-gguq tua-i tuqutekngaitaa-gguq. Ma-kut-atam alerquutai negcim. Atuuyugngaluni cali iqua. Kitugutnguluni urugyunga-qan mayuqata'arqami tuguarluku assircarraarluku yuugaqluni. Ekqataquni cali ki-tugqaarluku atrarrluku qayani piyugngaluni mat'umek negcigmek.

Tapruarrlainarnek taugaam nemerluki. Evunernun-llu imkunun avani, qertul-rianun mayuqata'arqamta tua-i unicuunaki makut. Qupnengqelartut ilait evunret tua-i nequtulrianek qanikcam qiliumaluki. Tamakut-gguq tamaa-i picurlagcecilar-tut ilait. Qukaakun cali tegumiaqluku. Cali waten pisqelluku yuvriqarraarluku tua-i man'a ciuneni qukarturluku teguqerluku ayagaqluni, napavkarpek'naku waten. Quli-nermun-gguq pitsaqevkenani igteng'ermi mat'um anirturyugngaa, ikayuryugngaa.

ALICE: Negcikcuar-mi?
FRANK: Ucilircuutnguuq uciircuutnguluni ayarurrauluni-llu.

would be held down by the towline of the kayak sled; it is tucked underneath here, and it doesn't come loose, pop out, or shift from this area.

One always took the gaff with him, even if one is going to be away from his kayak for only a short time. And if one accidentally capsizes in the water, he always knows that it is in the aft part, and this is here. If the kayak does not right itself, he would grab the gaff here. Immediately upon exiting the kayak he would grab it. Gaffs have dangling lines, and you grab the line and bite it where the knot is and swim toward the ice. Upon reaching the ice, you hook the gaff into the ice and climb on top by holding onto it. Gaffs have to have these dangling lines. This line is called *taprualuk*, *tapruaq*. That's what they are.

And again, if he loses his paddle, he could use this [hook end of the gaff] as a paddle. And if the *kemagnaq* [kayak sled stanchion] breaks, he would cut off a piece from the gaff's base and replace it with that piece. That's why they make this part of the gaff rounded, trying to make it the same diameter as the stanchion.

If the gaff hook is placed with its sharp end toward the person, that could be dangerous. If it accidently came loose and moved toward you, it could hurt you. But it isn't dangerous when put with the hook facing away from the person. They usually measure where this is going to be placed in this way. That's how this gaff is.

And if a person fell into the water, if there were no other way to get him out, they told us to hook him under the jawbone, that even though the gaff pierces the skin, they say he won't die. If it is impossible to get the person out by hooking him under his jaw, then one could hook him by his clothing.

Right underneath his jawbone. They said that even though it pierces through the skin there that he would not die. These are the instructions for the gaff. The hooked end of the gaff has many other uses. When one is going to climb out of the kayak during the time when the ice begins to melt, the gaff is used to prepare the ice surface by chipping on it before one gets out. One would also prepare the edge of the ice first using the gaff before boarding his kayak.

They always use sealskin line to bind the hook onto the handle. And when we were going to climb on top of steep piled ice, we never left gaffs behind. Some piled ice has deep crevasses covered by snow. They say some of those can cause tragic accidents. They also told one to hold the gaff in the center. After checking the area in front of him, he would hold the gaff horizontally in the center as he advances. He wouldn't go with the gaff held upright, only horizontally. And even if he falls into a crevasse, this can save him, it can really help him.

ALICE: What about the *negcikcuar* [small gaff]?

FRANK: It's used for loading, unloading, and as an *ayarurraq* [small staff].

Angutessagaat arnassagaat ayarurturluteng ayalalriit. Tuaten tua-i ayuqluni. Ayag-
yuarung'ermeng ayaruicuitellruut yuilqumi-llu yuvrircuutekluku tua-i, mat'umi.
Cikum-llu mamtutacia yuvriraqluku ayarukun. Aarnarqekan aturngaunaku. Aya-
ruilkuni taugken qaillun mamtutacia picurlautnguyugngacia-llu nalluarkauluku.
Taumek ayaruicuitellrulriakut, yuilqumi piyualuta uksuarmi kangatullemteni. Tuaten ayuquq ayaruq.

Arcaqalriaruuq negcik. Negcikcuaq tua-i tagelriim-llu tua-i aturyugngaluku, uur-
calriim. Pitaminek elpengcarilria, unilluku camavet, ilaminun tag'aqameng negcikcuaq tua-i ayaruqaqluku. Camani taugken man'a tua-i unisngaunaku, negcikcuarmek pingaunaku mat'umek taugaam qayami nuniini.

Pingayuak-wa augna tallirraq, hook-ayagarluni negcikcuarmi mikellruluni, tug-
runani-llu. Negcikcuaq tugengqertuq qaillun taktauralriamek pugumauralriamek
nuugani. Pakwa-llu makuciq, tanglalliuten, mikellruluni. Ucilimi kan'a tugruara
atutuluni. Kemget ekraarluki, taumek-llu tua-i kapqerluki cingluki qayam iluanun
qamavet. Uciirami-llu pikna aturluku qullia, pakwa, kauluku, negcik'arluku cayu-
gaqluku.
Tauna taugken tallirraq, qamenqumi qamani qantaq uitauq kan'a kaungermi-llu
enurluku. Tamakungqerquni taugken tugrilngurmek negcicuayaarluni nuuga una,
tulurraq, tamatumek negcik'arluku cayugluku-llu tua-i. Tallirraq-gguq, tamakunun
atuuluni. Qayam aklukluku cali tua-i.

~: Qayam allat aklui :~

Nat'riurun-wa. Taryurrluk atam unani nepcugtuq nat'ranun. Tegg'eraq murak mam-
carmi nuuga, avatek mamkunatek tamarmek teguyararluni. Taryuq-llu uumek, tar-
yurrlugmi tua-i aturyugngaluni, yuumarraarluni ekqataquni kelikarluku nat'raq tamatumek. Tamakunun atuuluni cali, piicunailnguuluni-am cali.

Elderly men and women always traveled with a staff. That's how it was. Even young people couldn't be without staffs, and they used them to check for dangers in the wilderness. They checked the thickness of the ice with a staff. If they found a dangerous area then they avoided going over it. Without the staff one would not know if the ice was thick enough or if something was dangerous. So that was why we did not go without our staffs in falltime when we were out walking in the wilderness. That's how the *ayaruq* [staff] is.

The *negcik* [gaff] is very important. One who is going up to announce his catch will use a small gaff. He leaves his catch down on shore and walks up using a small gaff as a staff and as a sign to his relatives that he has come back with his catch. But he always has this with him down on the ocean. But while in a kayak on the ocean he always takes the *negcik* with him rather than the *negcikcuar*.

The third of these is *tallirraq* [arm extender, lit., "small arm"] that has a hook smaller than that of the small gaff, but without an ice pick on it. The small gaff has an ice pick on its other end. And its curved hook, *pakwa*, is smaller; perhaps you've seen them. Its sharp point is used when loading the kayak. After placing meat inside, they poked the meat with the point and pushed it deep inside. When unloading they hooked the meat, using the curved hook on the upper end, and pulled it out.

About the *tallirraq*; if a bowl is inside in the tapered area of the kayak and is too far to reach with one's extended arm these come in handy. But if he has a tool like that with a small ivory hook, without an ice pick at its other end, they can hook an object with one of these and take it out. They call it a *tallirraq*. It is useful for this. It is one of the accessories of the kayak.

∾: *Other kayak accessories* :∾

Then there is a *nat'riurun* [boot-sole scraper]. Crusted salt tends to adhere to boot soles down on the ocean. It is a hardwood tool with a handle and a flat, thin-sided blade at the other end. After leaving the kayak, one scrapes the crusted salt off the boot soles with the scraper before one boards. It is useful for that purpose, and it is also a necessity.

~: *Pissurcuutet* :~

Apa'urluirutma atam caskulillruanga makunek, makucililua-llu nagiiquyanek. Ur-luvilua-llu unistema pitegcaucilua-llu meq'ercetaanek. Qayangeqarraallemni maa-i man'a. Qayamun nutaramun piqarraallemni tua-i maa-i man'a kiimi tua-i maa-i alaituq nuqaqa. Ak'allauguq.

Qayangyararallruunga, qayangyarararcetellruatnga.
ALICE: Qavciraqameng qayangtuat?
FRANK: Tangerrluki-w' tua-i pilallikait, elitaqata.

Maa-i man'a iliit, nuqaqa, eguteka. Atuyuilengramku tua-i qemangqaurluku maa-i, maavet-llu tua-i tagulluku, maantelluku nuqaq. Yaaqvanun makunek elit-naqluni tua-i egqaqellrat.
ALICE: Wani-llu-qaa tua-i manumi acaluq uitarrlainarluni?
FRANK: Ii-i, tuani uitarrlainatuut nutgit-llu, acaluit.
Ukalirnermi uitatuut arcaqerluteng caskut qayam piani, nagiiquyat tegutnek at-lirluteng, akagarcailkutekluki, itukurluteng. Urluvrem taugaam pitegcautait wanllu-teng ukalirnermi, uumek teguqayunaqluteng, urluveq-llu qaingatni, paangrutegnek makugnek igcailkuterluni uitaluni.

Tamakut-wa asaaqut makut piit, qerruinait ukalirnermi maani taprualuk pima-luni qaingani. Qamigautek-wa qaingani qerruinaq. Ukalirnermi uitavkenani taprua-luk ukalirnermi taugaam. Una tua-i nek'velria taprualuk nek'velria, iquklipailgan egmianun teguluku piyugngaluku. Naluumaluku-llu tua-i tangvagluku. Nangqe-rreskan-llu una qelluqipailgan nutaan peggluku mermun.

Cali-llu tamaani uskurarluteng ayagamun makucimun painganun taprualuk qill-rusngaluni ang'iqerrngaunani. Kingumun wavet, kingumi yaani kingulirnermun, ukalirnermi cali. Naqugutmun-llu iqua qillrusngaluni ang'iqerrngaunani. Kiime-nani tamakunek ullakuni nutgunani, taprualuk qayamun qillrusngaluni, yuum-llu naqugutiinun. Yuugarrluni ilangcivkenaku qayani pingraan qayaa aterrngaunani, elliin qainganun petuumaluni.

Aipangqerquni taugken ikayurtekaminek aturngaunaku tamana.
Tamakunek caskulegnek pissulrianek tangellrunritua, taugaam qanemciuluki nii-

~: *Hunting tools* :~

My late grandfather made me weapons like this, and he made me *nagiiquyat* [seal-hunting spears]. Also my late father made me a bow and arrows with arrow points that dislodge. This [spear thrower] is a device that I got with my first kayak. My *nuqaq* [spear thrower] is the only thing that remains from when I got my first kayak. It is old.

They had me get a kayak early.

ALICE: At what age did they get kayaks?

FRANK: They probably determined if they were ready yet, when they had learned.

This was one of [my hunting weapons], my *nuqaq*, my *egun* [throwing board]. Although I don't use it, I still have my throwing board stored away; they brought it here and keep it here. One can throw far with these once one learns how.

ALICE: And is the *acaluq* [float board] always located on the deck?

FRANK: Yes, their *acalut* are always there, and their guns as well.

The hunting implements are mainly located on [the right side] of the kayak deck. The *nagiiquyat* are located there above the *tegutet* [retrieving harpoons], which also keep them from rolling off. They are positioned side by side. But the arrows are placed, with the bow on top of them, on this side along the front [left side] where they are easy to reach. The double-bladed paddle keeps them from falling off.

The float for the *asaaquq* [toggling harpoon] used to kill seals on ice is placed on the left side with its sealskin line on top of it. The float is on top of the kayak sled. The sealskin line isn't [on the right side] but [on the left side]. While the sealskin line is playing out they would be able to grab it before it goes out all the way. Then they would hold it and watch it. And when it plays out all the way, before the line becomes taut, they would drop the float in the water.

And back then they would fasten their kayak to themselves securely using a sealskin line tied to the deck beam, the *ayagaq*, next to the coaming of the kayak. It was also tied to the stern and on this side as well, and the other end was tied securely to one's belt. When one is alone without a gun approaching a sea mammal, with one end of the sealskin line tied to the kayak and the other to one's belt, if one should happen to suddenly leave the kayak, then he need not worry. His kayak would not drift away since his body and his kayak are tethered to each other.

But if he had a partner to help him, he wouldn't use that.

I did not see anyone hunt using these kinds of weapons, but I've heard stories

telallruanka. Muragnek-llu imkunek pissurcuutnek aturluteng tua-i tamakunek pissutuluteng; caskungqellernek pissutuluteng. Uumek anguarturluteng ukalirnermi, asaaquq ceturyamun tulu'urtelluku yaavet makuciq, augna. Nuqamek aug'umek pilirluni, qesngaurtelluku iqua tamaavet, uumek anguarturluni ukalirnermi, qayaq-llu ukatmun uvayagqurtelluku.

~: Piciryarait qayatgun atraqatarqameng :~

Wangkuta ciuliamtenek ayagluta keniruatuukut.

Atuyuirucamku tua-i makut qanemcik'lanritanka. Muragnek atam qupurrayagarnek pitullrulriakut ayunek tapirluki. Tua-i-llu ellami ketmun caulluku qayaq upluku qamigautek qaingagnun elliluku. Cat tua-i katagyugnairluki qaingani taquatllu iteqluki. Qaqiucamta-llu tua-i yaavet tumkamtenun carriqerluku acia qanikcaq. Ellilarayaarnek piluta kumarucirluki, ayunek qallilirluki mikcuayaarnek. Cigyayagauluki murait, patagmek ekuallagavkauvkarluki. Kumarrluki-llu tua-i. Tua-i-llu ekualliita, qamuutaq-llu all'uku ayagluta tuavet, tauna-llu ekualria amllirluku, qayam-llu aciakun ayagtelluku ayagluta nutaan. Kingyanqigtevkenata, tangenqigtevkenaku tua-i. Keniruarluta-gguq tua-i.

Tuamtellu ilii yuum mermun kanaraqami imarpigmi, mer'em tua-i ngelkacagiinun ukinqucua waten qamigautegnun atrarrluku mer'em ngeliinun pivkarluku. Ilii yuum ilii; tuaten ayuqsuitellruut pillret. Anguarun-llu teguluku ciuvaami mermek kanaken ciunganek ukinqucuum acia ciqerturluku taryumek. Ciqerturraarluku-llu taryuq tamana ikirrnguarluku waten, nutaan qaingakun waten kinguvartelluku. Tuaten pituluteng-am ilait.

Tuamtellu ilii mermun kanaraqami, arulairaqami qantani anlluku, akutamek imarluni qantaa. Ukinqucuum-am ciuqerranun ellirraarluku, pupsugluni, mermun unavet egqaqluku, aviukaqluni. Qayani-llu nutaan mermek waken ciqertaqerluku. Cali-am iliit tuaten pituluni. Piciryararrarluteng. Inerquumaaqluta cangakuuresqevkenaki ilaput tuaten piciryarameggnek pituniluki. Maa-i atuyuirutait.

about them. They would hunt sea mammals using weapons made from wood, when they had wooden weapons to hunt with. They would paddle with this left arm and would lean the *asaaquq* on the front of the deck. Using the spear thrower, he would grip the handle of the spear with that, using this arm to paddle on this side, having the kayak lean a little in this direction.

~: *Kayak launching ceremony* :~

Beginning with our ancestors, we have followed the custom of having a certain ceremony with smoke, *keniruaq* [lit., "something similar to cooking"].

I don't talk about these things since I no longer practice them. We would take small pieces of split kindling along with some Labrador tea. And then, outside, we would face the kayak toward the ocean and prepare it, placing it on top of the kayak sled. We securely placed the implements on top of the kayak so that they wouldn't fall off and placed our provisions inside. When we were finished, we cleared the snow off the path we were going to go over. We used small pieces of wood for kindling, and we placed a small amount of Labrador tea on top of the kindling. The wood had been split into small sticks so that it would burn quickly. Then we lit it. Then, when it burst into flames, we put the tow rope over our shoulder and walked toward the burning fire and stepped over it, and then we had the kayak sled with the kayak go over it, and only then did we go our way. We never looked back; we never looked at it again. They called it *keniruaq*.

And when some people went down to launch the kayak into the ocean, they placed the upper bow piece of the kayak right at the edge of the water, bringing it down to the water's edge with the kayak sled. Some people did that; they all had different customs. They took their paddle and went up to the bow, they splashed the bottom bow piece with salt water from the front. After splashing it, they pretended to open the salt water like this, and they held their paddle over the kayak and swept it toward the stern. That is what some people did.

And again, another person would go down to the water, stop there, and take out his bowl filled with *akutaq*. After placing it in front of the bow piece of the kayak, he would take a pinch of *akutaq* and throw it in the water below, making an offering, *aviukaqluni*. Then he would splash a little water on his kayak. Some people did it that way. Some of them had that custom. They told us not to make fun of others who were with us, that they would practice their customs. People don't practice those customs today.

⁓ *Miisam qayangeqarraallra* ⁓

ALICE: Qaillun ayuqellranek, qayavkun ayakerraallerpeni, ayagaqerraallerpeni qaillun-llu ayuqucin-wa tamaani qaillun ayuqellrua. Angelriarullrullilria-wa el-peni.

FRANK: Tuaten umyuangqellrunritua qayangeqarraallemni. Atam malrugnek angutngurrluni aipaa nakukestengqellrulrianga, apa'urlumnek ilu'uqluku-llu aipaa. Qayangelleq ucuryagutekellrunritaqa.

Aipaan anagullua pilallruanga. Yull'arnek-llu nerlarciqnilua pitamnek pivkenii, aturanek-llu iknernek atularciqnilua. Nengiutegnek-llu taugaam nerkenglangciq-nilua, pitellriit cikiutaitnek. Makut angnirnarqenritut niitelallrenka.

Tuamtellu aipaan canguarlua qayangucimnek, cassuutekamek, augtangvailegmi aruarkamek, pipailegma qayam meciktukiinek aruciqniluku. Angnirnarqenritut makut. Tamaa-i tang umyualqa wii qayangellemni. Qavayuirullua, tuaten ayuqsuu-miicaaqlua. Qayangvailegma anguaryaraq elitellruaqa tua-i tamalkuan, qayaqenril-kengamkun anguarturlua, pissuryaraq-llu elitnaurutkelallruamku-llu.

Augna umyuaqellrunritaqa tua-i tamaani, taugaam piyuumimek umyuangqell-ruunga tua-i, piyugyaaqlua, tuaten piyuumiicaaqlua, tuaten ayuqsuumiicaaqlua.

Kiagmi-am qayangellruunga. Tatkiluku, maavet tua-i unuungraan anuqliraqan paqta'arturluku, tengnayukluku pitsaqevkenaku, taum-wa angukara'urluum aren-qiatelaanga, Puyulkuum, Aparuum. Up'nerkaan-llu tua-i atraranglluteng unavet, tua-i nutaan qavarnanrirlua tua-i, qaku-gguq atrarcetqatartatnga. Kiituan tua-i pit'langut. Pit'langqertelluki tua-i alqairutma pianga, atraqatartua-gguq, atrauteqa-taraatnga-gguq. Tua-i nutaan qayaqerlua tua-i, nunanikngamku imarpik, aqvalgiq-taarturatuama. Qessamek tua-i iliini tagnaurtukut. Quunirturatullruuq.

Uplunuk tua-i atraqatarlunuk, malikeqatallinilua, nallumciqevkenii tua-i qalaru-cimiima, qalarut'laanga taum ayuqucianek qayam pillra unani-llu. Qamigaurlunuk piyualunuk atrarlunuk, unugmi-am agyullua, erenrurteqerluku tua-i kanarluta. Piu-

~: *Frank Andrew's first kayak* :~

ALICE: She wants to ask you what it was like when you first traveled with your kayak, how you felt when you went for the first time. It was probably something that made you feel very good.

FRANK: That's not what I felt when I first got a kayak. There were two adults who picked on me, one was my grandfather, and the other was my *iluraq* [cross-cousin]. Getting a kayak didn't make me feel proud.

One of them really tormented me. He would tell me that I would eat food from other people's catches and not from my own catch, and that I would wear hand-me-down clothes. And he said that I would eat only portions of catches that others shared with me, only catches that hunters who had caught something were willing to share. These harsh messages that I was given had not made me feel happy.

Then the other one asked me why I got a kayak, for what purpose, saying that the kayak was doomed to rot before it got blood on it, that it would rot away before it could get stained with the blood of my catch. These words are not ones that make a person feel happy. That was how I felt when I got a kayak. I could not sleep well, because I really didn't want to be like that. Before I got a kayak I learned all the paddling methods using a kayak that wasn't mine, and I was taught how to hunt as well.

I did not dwell on it at that time, but I longed to be successful, hoping that I would not turn out as he predicted.

I got a kayak during summer. The kayak was put up on a rack, and even at night when it was windy I would go check on it lest it accidentally blew off its rack, because that old man Puyulkuk, Aparuk, never let up on me. Then in spring the hunters started going down to the ocean, and I stopped sleeping due to worry over when they would allow me to go down to the ocean, too. Eventually they began to catch sea mammals. After that, my late older sister told me that I was going to go down, that they were going to take me down there. I was so ecstatic because I loved to be down at the ocean when I had been going down to fetch their catches. At times we would be reluctant to go back up to the village. At that time the ocean was always calm and windless.

We made preparations to go down, since he was going to take me along. I had been taught about kayaking and ocean faring so I knew what to do. It was still night when we walked down pulling our kayak sleds, and just as dawn broke we reached

nga-am tauna anagutestek'lallma; Qilkimek atengqertuq, Qilkilegmek, kanarvim-
teni tua-i kanarvimegni uitaluni. Ilakluku qayat cenaqilriit.

Qanellra nalluyagucuilkeka tua-i tuani. Tangrramia pianga, "Cassurcit? Tagluten
qerrutnek ciqirqistengu taugaam. Pisngaituten." Kiuvkenaku.

Tua-i quunirluni tua-i, enteksaunani tua-i cikut mallgutarluki. Encan tua-i kiican
ayaganga'arrluteng avavet. Tua-i-llu augkuk Qallamek pilallrat augna Mancuamek-
llu, nakmiin ilu'urqa Mancuaq, unayaqnganga maliggluku. Ketvarluta uatmuarluta.
Akiagnun cikut atreskiin, pilua kiatiignun tua-i murilkurlukek. Piinanemni tua-i
piqertua cikum qaingani unguvalria ingna qavalria. Tuar ircaquqa qamani nutngall',
niilluku ciutegemkun nutnganga'artellrani taumek unguvalriamek qavalriamek tang-
llemni. Cunawa maklaaq. Ullagturluku tua-i uaqliqa tauna murilkartaqluku tua-i.
Tua-i ukatmun takuyarngan anguarutka napa'arrluku. Atrarteqanemkun ukatmun
atam agiirtenga'artellria.

Waten piluku ullaasqelluni qayagauryarauguq qayami unani. Ikayurnaqluni tuaten pikuniu, waten piluku elliurarkauluku waten, patagmek ullaasqelluni. Tuamtellu cikum qaingani tuani aarnarqelriartangqerqan tumyaraq aturtengqerkata tumyarat, naparrluku waten tangvaggaarluku, assilriim tungiinun ayalurtelluku. Tua-i
yaaqsing'ermi tangerquniu egmian caqirtarkauguq aarnarqellria tekipailegmiu.

Tekican tua-i piluku piaqa, caucianek ingna cikum qaingani qavalria. Ullakanir-
luku piapuk, maklagaulliniuq-gguq, camek-llu tangeqsaunani. Sugturingalunuk
tua-i yaavet tangvagluku ituklunuk. Piinanmegni-atam caniakun tungurpallartell-
ria cikum akuliinek. Cunawa aanii, maklak. Yaanlluni tua-i qumiumaluku cikum
tuaten qavalria. Tauna keluqlirpuk akiqlirpuk qayagaurtuq Qallaq, ullaasqevke-
naku elliin ullakatarniluku. Tua-i inerquangan tua-i uitalunuk tuani, ullagluku.

Ayagtuulluni pulaluni cikumun akilirnermek. Kangiquciluni-am pugtalria ciku
tunglirnermegni. Aipaqa-llu-am tauna kiavet kiatemnun itrarluni. Tangvakegluku
tua-i wii ayaksaunii tangvaurluku piavet ullallrani. Piyungaqami tua-i pugnaurtuq
aanii, sugtuluni tua-i caniani tungukayagluni. Canimelliami tua-i pinarillian nutegluku tauna irniara taum tuqulluku. Tauna tua-i tayima tua-i, akilirnerakun ikaggun

the ocean. I looked around and saw the man who would take me to task and ridicule me — his name was Qilkilek — and he was there where we were to launch our kayaks. He was in one of the kayaks waiting to launch on the ocean.

I never forgot what he said to me there. When he saw me he said, "For what purpose did you come? Go back up and become a urine-bucket dumper. You won't catch anything." I didn't answer him.

The weather was very calm, but the tide hadn't gone out and the ice was close by. When the tide went out and a lead opened in the ice, they began to go out there. Those two, the one they called Qallaq and Mancuaq, my real *iluraq* Mancuaq, when he asked me to go with him, I went with him. We went down away from the ice edge. I went to the other side of the floating ice, behind them, and watched them. While I was there, I saw a sea mammal sleeping on top of the ice. Seeing the sea mammal sleeping on the ice caused my heart to pound hard, beating so hard inside me that I could hear it myself. It was a bearded seal! I went toward it, being mindful of the person right down from me. When he looked toward me, I lifted my paddle upright as a signal. Right when I brought my paddle down, he started coming toward me.

This is a way to communicate with another person and summon him to come while in the kayak down there. If he was asking for help, he would put it [upright and move it back and forth] to signal for the person to come immediately. If there is a dangerous spot on the ice and if there are others who are using the path, you signal the dangerous spot to the others by holding it upright and then slanting it toward the safe path. If someone saw that from afar, he would turn away before he reached the dangerous spot.

When he reached me, I asked him what it was that was sleeping on top of the ice. We went closer to it, and he said that it was a bearded-seal pup and that he hadn't seen anything else yet. With our kayaks side by side we craned our necks and looked at it. While we were looking, a dark figure appeared amid the ice [next to the pup]. It was its mother, a bearded seal. It had been farther away sleeping amid the ice. The person on the other side of us, Qallaq, signaled us not to go toward it, that he would go to it. Since he told us not to move, we stayed put while he approached it.

It emerged from the midst of the ice as if ramming through it. The corners of the floating ice were showing on the water close to me. My partner went in front of me. I stayed put, observing him as he approached it up on the ice. Every so often its mother, looking so huge and dark, would appear close to it when it lifted up its head. When he got close, he shot its pup and killed it. When it emerged in the area

cikuilngurkun anluni egqaqluni, tua-i ak'a elpeklinikii. Angllurluni tua-i tayima. Ak'anun tua-i pissiyaagpek'nani kiakaramkun uuggun cikuilnguum ngeliikun pugluni. Pugngan pam'um pianga, "Nutegyaqunaku, wii piciqaqa."

Tuaten qanran umyuarteqa'artua. "Puyulkuum-llu im'um qanellra aturyuumiicaaqvakarpaa!" Qanerpek'nii tua-i. Nuvutevkenaku-llu. Elpekevkenii tua-i. Nuteglua 25-20-mek *number*-aalegmek, imacuarai-wa takevkenateng.

Angllurluni-am tua-i tayima. Negciumaurluku tua-i ciku, keluka uitaurlua. Ak'anun-am pivkenani tuaggun-am pugellrakun pugluni. Pingna taugaam tua-i, nutka amukeka, umyuanglua nutegnaluku piama. Pamna-am piuq nutgesqevkenaku elliin piciqniluku. Pingraan tua-i umyuama taq'icuumiitaa tauna. Umyuartequa, "Pugenqigeskan uuggun nunamikun nutegciqkeka."

Allakun-am tua-i puggraarluni tua-i angllurluni tayima. Cali allaggun pugluni pirraarluni-am tayimnguuraqerluni tunulirneqa merpallaarrluni ualirnemnek. Cunawa tauna. Pektaanrilama taugaam tepemnek pilliniluni, teplitliniluni. Nutek tua-i tegumiaqluku, negciumalua cikumun. Piinanemni ciuqamkun tunusngalua pugluni. Egmian nutegluku, nall'arrluku.

Ullagarrluku tua-i pagkucinek narulkarluku, alaillran, pugleqercan. Tua-i angkayagluni tua-i. Tua-i ircaqu'urluqa-wa *tung-tung*-aalria, ciutegemnek-llu niiqluku nutngallra ircaquqa. Kitngutnayuklua tua-i alinglua amta-llu pitaqsugluku tua-i arenqiatuq. Kingupiarlua tua-i saagivkarluku, pekngarrnayukluku, niitelaama pekngarrniluki ilait.

Ciku man'a yuvriqarraarluku mamtulriamun yuulua, qayaq mayurrluku, tegutetgun tegumiaqurluku. Pugtaayaarlua, pugtaayaaralria-wa, cunawa tang uquripialliniami. Kit'etuyaaqut. Taisqelluku tauna ilu'urqa Mancuaq. Nutaan tua-i ikayurlua.

Tauna Qallaq nepelkitenqigtenrituq. Mayurrluku tua-i ikayuqlunuk pilagluku arenqiatuq ekesciigalan qayamnun angengan. Qayaanun ekesqelluku. Kemginek taugaam wii ucilirlua. Taglunuk tua-i. Tekicamegnuk pia, mayurrluku taigarrluteng. Qilkilek tauna camek qanenrituq. Egmianun tagesqellua tua-i, tua-i taglua egmianun. Cunawa uumek taugaam qecigtallinilrianga. Maaggun kepluku man'a amiirluku aug'arluku. Ukatmun qupurluku aruqutkelallinikait. Tuatnatullinikait cunawa pitqerraalriit tamakunek. Takelmurluki. Uumek taugaam pivkarlua keggagmek, keggatiinek.

Cassucimnek, taglua qerrutnek ciqirqistengusqellua, qerrutaitnek. Pitulliniut.

where there was no ice, it thrust its body around, sensing what had happened to its pup. Then it dove underwater. Not long afterward, it emerged right ahead of me in the area without any ice. When it emerged, the person behind me said, "Don't shoot it, I am going to."

When he said that, I thought, "I don't want to become what Puyulkuk predicted for me." I didn't say anything. I didn't lift my gun at it. It didn't sense my presence. I had a 25-20 rifle, it had such small, short bullets.

It submerged. I had my gaff hooked onto the ice next to me, and I stayed still. Not long after, it emerged in the same place as before. Then I lifted my gun out from its place up there, because I felt I should shoot it. The one behind me told me not to shoot, saying that he would shoot it. Although he said that, I felt that I had to follow my inclination. I thought, "If it emerges in the same spot I will shoot it."

After surfacing in a different place, it submerged. After appearing in another place, it was gone for a while, and then I heard a splashing sound from behind me on this side. It was that one. Although I stayed still, it had smelled my scent. I held the gun while I kept the gaff hooked to the ice. While in that position, it appeared right in front of me with its back to me. I shot it without hesitation and hit it.

When it surfaced I hurriedly went to it and harpooned it with a harpoon that looked like those up there. It was very large. My poor heart was going *tung-tung*, and I could hear the heartbeat. I was afraid that it would cause me to capsize, but I really had wanted to catch it. I paddled going backward and let the line unwind, because I thought that it would start moving, having heard that some of them do that.

After checking the thickness of the ice, I got off on a thick spot and pulled my kayak up, as I held onto it with the harpoon and its line. Apparently it was floating because it was very fat; they usually sink. I told my *iluraq* Mancuaq to come, and he helped me.

After that Qallaq never uttered those words again. Together we pulled the bearded seal on top of the ice and butchered it. Because it was so large and couldn't fit in my kayak, I told him to put the skin and blubber inside his kayak. I carried the meat. We went back up. When we got to shore, we unloaded it, and they came right over. Qilkilek didn't say anything. He told me to go back up right away, and I went. It turned out that I had just been hunting for the skin. I split the carcass and removed the skin. They butchered it this way, cutting it into lengthwise strips, and distributed them. That's apparently what they do with first catches, cut them in lengthwise strips. They had me take only the upper torso.

He asked me what I had come for and told me to go back up and to be the

Cingumakngateng-gguq pituit. Taringaqa maa-i. Umyugaat piniryuumirluki pisqe-
lluki-gguq pituut. Cingumakteng. Amllellruameng-llu-w' tamaani unguvalriit.

~: *Qayam uciliryaraa* :~

Ilait tua-llu-w' malrugnek ucilalriit makliignek qayat, uciarpek'naki tua-i cakneq
pinaurtut. Ucinertulliniut makut qayat.

Navgurraarluki uciketuit. Tamalkuuluki piyuitait. Nayiit taugaam imkut mikcuaraat tamalkuita ektuit, pilagpek'naki.

Tua-i-wa pitarkani tangerrluki muirluku uciliryugngalria pitanek. Eksugyaa-
qeng'ermeng umyuaq aturluku (ekngaitelalria) piyulqa. Iliini tua-i *lucky*-rluni pi-
narqetulria.

Augkut makliit uqamaitut tua-i, qaillun uqamangqelartat. Malruk tua-lli-wa
makliik ucitukegket makut qayat. Asveq-llu ucikuni, cakuineq tua-i uitaqaararkau-
luni, qayam angtuam qayarpiim. Ucinertuut.

~: *Qayami qavaryaraq* :~

Qayat iluitni qavatuukut. Maktaluta-llu qavarasqevkenata inerquutaqerput unani
imarpigmi. Nunami uitangramta maktaluta qavaralaasqevkenata. Picurlautekciqer-
put-gguq imarpigmi pitsaqevkenata, anguarluta unugmi-llu pikumta. Ilii-gguq qa-
varaluni picurlatuuq, kitnguluni. Inarrluta taugaam qavalaasqelluta qavarniaqamta,
qavarninga'artaqamta, maktamta qavaravkenata.

Imarpik kan'a arenqiatuq. Qavarnaituq imarpik, kelluqurluni taugaam kesianek
tua-i. Aarnariaqan-llu kiagmi-llu cali kelqurluni tua-i murilkelluni. Murilkelluteng.

dumper of their urine buckets. Apparently that's what they did. They say they do that to those who they were goading toward success. I understand why now. They say they do that because they want the minds of those who they want to succeed to be stronger. There were many sea mammals back then.

~: Loading a kayak :~

Some kayaks carried two bearded seals, and they weren't very full. These kayaks can carry a lot.

They butchered it first to carry it in their kayaks. They didn't put the bearded seal in whole. However they put smaller ringed seals in whole, without butchering them.

They would estimate how much more they could load to fill it up to capacity. Even though, in our minds, we wanted to load them further, that would not happen in reality. But sometimes a person does get lucky.

These bearded seals are heavy; I don't know how much they weigh. Here they can hold two bearded seals in these kayaks. And if they were carrying a walrus, only a small portion of it would not fit inside a very large kayak. They can hold a lot of cargo.

~: Sleeping in a kayak :~

We slept inside the kayak. It is our admonition not to fall asleep while sitting in the kayak on the ocean, and they admonished us not to sleep while sitting on land either. They said that it would cause us to get into an accident out on the ocean while we were paddling, or if we were traveling at night. They would say that some people get into accidents by capsizing while drifting off to sleep. They would tell us to sleep lying down if we became overwhelmingly sleepy. They told us not to fall asleep while we were sitting up.

The ocean is overwhelming. One cannot allow oneself to sleep when on the ocean; one has to be constantly vigilant. And when conditions become dangerous, even in summer, one has to be watchful.

~: Qayakun neqsuryaraq :~

Set net-aarluteng pilartut, mermi civvluki kuvyat. Tua-i-llu cangeng'ata keluanek piaken ukalirnermi kuvya uitavkarluku, qenngirraarluku muragarmek ukuitgun neqet,
cangtairluki aug'araqamegteki qayam kinguanun qamavet piqaraqluki, naparrngii-
naraqan ciumun wavet piuraraqluki. Tuaten tua-i neqtairturluki iquklitaqan, ataam
iquanun mumiggluni agg'un kiaqlikun. Amlleraqata tua-i egmianun qayaq ak'anun
pivkenani muirnaurtuq.

Qayat tua-i kiingita neqsurcuutekluki. Tuaten taugaam neqsunriraqameng amiit
erurluki pituluki aug'utun qanemciklemtun, neqallrirluki. Neqallrit erutuluki matarrluki.

~: Yaaqvanun ayalallrat qayatgun :~

Kusquqvak canimetuq, cukaut qayat, yaaqvanun ayatuut. Atam imumi tamaani
ciuqvaarni maaken nunamtenek St. Michael-aamun qakmavet Kuigpiim yaatiinun
kass'artelallrulriit qayatgun, Tacirmiunun. Avavet-llu Nushagak-amun piaqluteng
qayatgun maaken Caninermek. Nushagak-amun pilriit, ak'anun pivkenateng, week-
aq-llu iliini ciptevkenaku tekitaqluteng. Qagaavet taugaam pilriit muluaqluteng
yaaqsinruan tamana. Cukaut qayat.

Maaken atam Kuigilngurmek qamavet Tagyaram painganun Tuntutuliarmiut
kiani Kusquqviim iluani unugyugnaunaku tekitnarquq qayakun anguarluni unaggun imarpigkun.

~: Tumarayulit :~

Qayat-llu ilait caangrayaugut avani. Maa-i pinanrirtut.

Waten-am qayat makut wani, ciuliameggnek pimalriit tamakut, pektaatuluteng-
llu qayat mayuumalriani. Taugaam alingnarqevkenateng tua-i apertuumiimi assil-
riarululuteng-llu pituluteng.

~: *Fishing from the kayak* :~

They did set-net fishing, setting gillnets in the water. When the net caught fish they would start removing the catch from the net starting from its shore side, making sure the net was always on this [upriver] side of the kayak. After clubbing the fish with a piece of wood, they removed the fish from the net and put it in the stern of the kayak, and when the bow started to rise, they'd start putting fish inside the bow. They removed the fish from the net one by one in that way, and when they reached the end of the net they switched to the upriver side of the net and removed the catch going back. At the height of the fish run the kayak would fill up fast.

Only kayaks were used in fishing [for salmon]. But when they were done fishing, as I have explained before, they would wash the fish residue from the kayak skin coverings. They washed the fish residue by first removing the skin coverings.

~: *Long distance travel in a kayak* :~

The Kuskokwim River is a short distance [from Kwigillingok] since kayak traveling is fast and they can go very far. Long ago, in the early days, they traveled with kayaks from our village to north of the Yukon River to St. Michael for manufactured goods. They also traveled down to Nushagak with kayaks from here in the lower coastal area. Those who went to Nushagak weren't gone for long, and they sometimes returned in less than a week. But those who went up north were gone longer because it's farther. Kayaks are fast.

You can travel from Kwigillingok to the mouth of Tagyaraq near Tuntutuliak up on the Kuskokwim River and get there before night, paddling with a kayak through the ocean route.

~: *Kayaks able to repair themselves* :~

And some kayaks were endowed with supernatural attributes in the past. At present kayaks no longer have those qualities.

Those types of kayaks, those that had supernatural attributes from their predecessors, some of them would even move while they were up on the ice. But they did not manifest evil since those attributes, specific to them, were only beneficial.

Nutgem-llu anqerrivikluni qayaq iluani pingraani ukingaunani. Caskum-llu pi-
qertuutaam wall'u qayaq pingraani, piqertuutaq iterngaunani. Tamakut irr'inarqe-
lartut tuaten ayuqelriit.

Nunapigmiuni kiani up'nerkillrullratni, Aleqteryaaq Ekvicuarmiu up'nerkitull-
ruuq tuani. Qetunraa-wa Angivran, alqaa-wa kitumek-ima pitullrukiit. Ekvicuar-
miunguluteng.

Anngani-llu Asngualleq-llu niitnautuuk pipailgagnek-gguq imarpigmiutarmek
qayatek uyangcuitagket. Uyangtaayuitakek iluik inerquusngalutek qayakek anngani-llu, Asnguallrenkuk Aleqteryaaq-llu. Picimariaqagnek-llu taugaam nutaan
uyangtaangetuak qayakek. Caskum-llu-gguq iterngaunakek.

Mancuaq augna ilurairutka nerellgutkellinia up'nerkiameng tuani. Qayaa-wa-
gguq llumarrarmek *canvas*-aamek amirluni Aleqteryaraam, minguumaluni. Aki-
vingqaluni palurmi tua-i ketiini muriit qaingatni. Qetunraa tauna mikngami angevkenani. Camek kaigayaaqellinillrani pisqenritlinia picurlagciqniluku atiin
Aleqteryaraam, qenqertelliniuq yuurqainanragni. Pelatekaak-gguq ikingqaluni, qa-
yaq-wa un'a alaunani. Qetuunraan taum qenqercami, qayaa piqertuaqatarniluku
pian, inerquleryanritlinia atiin Aleqteryaraam. Niitelaamiu tua-i taum ilurairutma,
kaag-atakiilliniuq, uluamek-llu pingaitniluku niitelaamiu qayakek anngaa-llu.

Igvaartelliniuq piqelvall'ermek imumek tegumiarluni, qayaa tauna ullalliniluku.
Atiin-llu taum inerquqsaunaku, tangvagluku ava-i. Qayaa-llu tauna atami *canvas*-
aamek amilek tekicamiu, piqertuutarmek piq'valliniluku assirnerakun. Piqertuu-
taq-llu tuc'ami egmian utqitliniluni. Allamek-gguq piyaaqeqerluni utqitaqluni. Aa-
tiin-gguq tangvakii. Qavcirqunek-gguq piqerturyaaqerraarluku piqertuutaq tauna
egtelliniluku. Unicaku atii qanlliniuq, "Qayallera'urluqa una kass'artarmek llumarrarmek amingeng'ermi caskuum iteryugngariksaitellinia."

Angalkuullrunrituq. Cat-gguq tamakut tumarayulit cauciinaki. Tamatumek-
gguq piyailkuciumaut ciuliameggnek. Qaillun pingraiceteng navegngaunateng tua-i.
Navgung'ermeng-llu navguumangaunateng, egmianun pegeskaceteng tumaryugnga-
luteng, tumarayulit tamakut cat. Tuaten-gguq nalqigtellrua Aleqteryaraam.

Even though a gun might accidentally shoot inside the kayak, it wouldn't pierce the skin. And although a weapon or an ax hit a kayak, it wouldn't penetrate the skin. Kayaks like that were awesome.

Upriver in Nunapigmiut, when that place was a spring camp, Aleqteryaaq from Eek camped there during spring. His son was Angivran, and I forgot what they called his older sister. They were from Eek.

We heard that Asngualleq and his older brother never peered inside their kayaks before they caught a sea mammal. Asgualleq and Aleqteryaaq were forbidden to look inside their kayaks. But it is said that after they caught a sea mammal, they were free to look inside their kayaks. Also they said no weapon could penetrate their kayaks.

Since they were at the same spring camp, Aleqteryaaq ate with my late *iluraq* Mancuaq. He said at that time that Aleqteryaaq's kayak covering was made of painted canvas. It was propped upside down right below them on top of some logs. At that time his son, being so young, was quite small. While they were having tea, his son asked his father, Aleqteryaaq, if he could do something, and when he forbade him doing it, saying that he would get hurt, his son became angry. The kayak was in full view down there since their tent flaps were opened. His son angrily told Aleqteryaaq that he was going to chop at his kayak with an ax, but his father did not admonish him firmly. My late *iluraq* had said, "*Kaag-ataki* [One ought not]" since he had heard that not even a knife could penetrate his kayak or his older brother's.

His son came into view holding a very large ax and going toward his kayak. His father did not admonish him, but watched him going on his way. When he reached his father's canvas-covered kayak, he hit the bottom forcefully with the ax. When the ax hit, it immediately bounced off. Whenever he'd hit it again, the ax would spring back. His father just watched him. After hitting it a number of times with the ax, he threw it down. When he left it, his father said, "Evidently, a weapon still can't penetrate my dear old kayak, even though it is covered with manufactured canvas."

He wasn't a shaman. He didn't know what supernatural forces gave those *tumarayulit* [kayaks able to repair themselves] the ability to repair themselves. It is said that they had gotten those safeguards against destruction from their predecessors. No matter what was done to them, they would not stay broken. Even though they were broken into pieces the kayaks had the ability to reassemble themselves, whatever those *tumarayulit* actually were. They say that was how Aleqteryaaq explained it.

~: *Qayam atunrillra* :~

Maa-i-wa maa-i wangkutni qayam atullra ikgenaku atullrukvut, taugaam avani tun-tussuagaqameng-llu pavavet yuilqumun atutullrulliniit uksuarmi. Qayat cali atur-luki ayagaluteng, tuntunek pitengnaqaqameng uksuarmi. Tamana wangkuta atun-ritarput.

Man'a-llu maaken nunamtenek amavet Iilgayarmun Bristol Bay-mun ayagalall-rat qakmavet-llu St. Michael-aam nuniinun cali atunritarput wangkuta. Yaquleg-nek-llu cali imarpigmiutarnek unguluteng cali atulallrit cali aturpek'naku wangkuta. Asvernek-llu cali *walrus*-aanek unguluteng pitullrat aturpek'naku cali. Tamaa-i atunrilkengaput amllerrluteng ciuliamta qayatgun atullrit. Qaqilluku atunritarput wangkuta kinguqliitni.

Yaaqvanun ayagalallrulliniut tamaani.

Pissulqa wii iquklipailgan aturnanrillrulriit qayat. Makunek Lund-anek ciming-luteng tua-i muragat pissurcuutet. Qayat qacigliluteng qayairutut kiituan. Qa-yangqeng'ermeng tua-i atunrirluki tua-i, angyanek taugaam makunek. Tua-i-llu qayatgun pitaqelalteng pitaqelallmeng ikgetlerpaitnek pit'elangluteng, angyatgun pilangameng. Uqurrnanrirluteng. Tuaten tua-i ayuqluteng. Anagiluteng, amlleq ana-gilangluni neplirluteng *motor*-aarit pilaameng, qayat taugken nepaunateng. Uqur-tait-am ikegliluteng tua-i, uqurrnanrirluteng tua-i.

Tamaani unani uqumek amllermek unangelallruut, angyat-llu angyarpallret imir-luki tua-i qavavet ayautaqluki Kusquqvagmun navercecarturluki. Piciatun, atkugka-nek keglunernek terikaniarnek, qanganarnek, tuntunek cururkanek, atkugkanek tua-i piciatun, tertulinek tuaten, maani nurnalrianek nunamteni, nekevraarcinrar-nek; tua-i canek tua-i kipuqluteng, nurnalrianek maani. Qaugkut-llu tua-i taprua-raat, taprualuut piyugaqluki qaugkut Kangimiut. Uqunek amllernek ayautaqluteng, nang'aqluki tua-i. Anrutaat-llu imkut makliit uqunek cali imirturluki tangviarrlug-nek-llu pituluki, tuniaqaqluki tua-i amlleret nang'aqluki cali, caqussayuugarnek piaqluki. Nayiit-llu pilu'ugkat, amirkat-llu cali naterkat, atu'urkaullgutaitnek tua-i naverrluki piaqluki tamakut, atkugkanek tua-i tamakunek terikanianek tuaten.

Maani-wa imkut Nyac-ami-llu kiani, cam nalliini *mining*-aalriit ayagnillruat, taum kinguaraani pillruyugnarqua. Kuigkautet imkut nunulluki *canvas*-aat mam-tulriit, akiliulriit piit. Tamakut-am nalaqluki. Tamakunek-am pilangarrluteng kuig-kautaitnek akiliulriit.

∾: *End of an era* :∾

In recent times, we in Kwigillingok have used the kayak much less than previously, but long ago they evidently used the kayak, even when they hunted for caribou inland during fall. They traveled with kayaks when they hunted caribou in fall. We did not do that.

We also didn't do what they used to do, traveling to Bristol Bay and up north to St. Michael by kayak. And we didn't follow the former practice of driving molted ocean birds. Also we didn't experience their practice of driving walrus. There are many ways of using the kayak that our ancestors followed that we did not experience. We, the generation that followed them, did not do all that they used to do.

They evidently traveled long distances back then.

Before I stopped hunting they had already stopped using kayaks. Then wooden hunting vessels were replaced by Lund [aluminum] boats. There were fewer kayaks around, and eventually people no longer had kayaks. They no longer used kayaks, even if they had them, but they used boats instead. Also, when they began hunting with boats, they started catching fewer animals than they had caught with kayaks. And they obtained less seal oil. That's how it was. The kayaks did not make much noise, but since motors are noisy the animals began to flee from them and got away from them. People got less seal oil.

Back in that era when they obtained a large amount of seal oil in coastal areas, they would fill very large boats and take them up the Kuskokwim to trade. They traded for various items that were scarce in this area, such as parka material, wolf skins, wolverine skins, squirrel skins, caribou skins for sleeping mats, different types of materials to make parkas, and even lynx skins, spruce roots, and other items that are scarce in our villages. And the people of the upper Kuskokwim villages wanted sealskin line. They would go away with a lot of seal oil, and everything would be traded. They would trade numerous quantities of those bearded-seal stomach containers called *caqussayuugaq*, filled with seal oil and cracklings. And they traded ringed-seal skin to be use for boots, and *amirkat*, the skins of young bearded seals used for boot soles. All these were traded for items of equal value, such as parka material including wolverine skins.

I don't know what year mining started in this area, inland at Nyac; a little after that I started using canvas [as a kayak cover]. They discovered the thick canvas which the miners used to channel water for mining, and they put it together to make kayak covers. It was the material miners used to channel water.

Tamakunek-am kuiliurluteng; kuik imairutelluku, mer'a tamaaggun carvanirtelluku akiliulriit pitulliniut *mining*-aalriit. Tamakunek tamaa-i qayangqelallruut, qecigtutatekevkenateng. Kass'artarmek minugluki minugaqluki.

Kenercetut taugaam mermi; piiraitut. Cali aglurtengyugluteng qayat waten tamakunek llumarrarnek amilget, assirpek'nateng, assissiyaagpek'nateng. Ak'anun tua-i pivkenateng taqluteng tua-i tayima. Qayatgun pilallrat iquklitqatarluku, pinanriqatarluku tamakunek llumarrarnek amingenga'artellruut.

Mingqaqluki qayacetun. Qalirnerkun maaggun mingqaqluki. Ilait talutatkenriata nuuraqata-llu callmagluku mingqaqluku. Amirluki

Taprarkait-llu imkut ussukcaulluki pilangluki, *nail*-anek kaugtuarluki ussukcarluki, taprualugnek nuvutevkenaki.

Quliraat imkut qayangqetulriit, qayangqerrniluki pilallrukait wangkucicetun. Qayam atullra amlleqapiarallruuq. Nerangnaqutnun canun piciatun aturtuq qayaq tamaani avani ciuqvani, wangkuta ngel'ekluta, yugtaat makut qayat taqelriit tayima.

The miners used that material to channel rivers; they would drain a river by diverting the water. They had those types of canvas coverings for their kayaks; the thickness of the material varied. We painted them with manufactured paint.

[Canvas-covered kayaks] did not glide well on the water; they weren't slick. And kayaks with canvas coverings tended to bend or arc upwards and weren't very good. Not long afterward, they stopped using them. Right before they discontinued the use of kayaks altogether, they began to use canvas coverings.

They sewed it on like they did with a [skin-covered] kayak. They sewed the material along the top of the kayak. When some pieces weren't the same size, when they weren't large enough, they'd sew extra pieces on. They sewed them with embedded waterproof seams, *amirluki.*

And they began to nail together the parts that used to have sealskin line rather than fastening the parts with sealskin line.

In the lore that involves kayaks, they said that people of the distant past had kayaks just like us. There were many, many uses for the kayak. The kayak was used for a variety of subsistence activities long ago, but starting from our time the Yup'ik-style kayak has no longer been used.

Miisam Qanemcikellri

Stories Frank Andrew Told

Miisam Qanemcikellri

Qanemcikarkaurtan. Qanemcingcaqatgen qanemcikarkaurtan. Amllertut qanemcit nallunrilkenganka taungunrilnguut, augkut avani ciuqvani pitullrit, pilallrit, nii-
cugnilalten. Qanemcilriit niicugnitullrukumki qanemcit iquklilluki, qanemcikanka
nutaan amllepiaryartut. Kevgiullma qasgimi, kegvartuallma tamalkuuluki nallunri-
cetenritai. Qanemciksuilkenka taumek akulait cataitelaata, nallulaamki.

Assikek'nganka, anglanakek'nganka ataucirqumek niilluki katagngairut'lartut
umyuamni. Yuk tuaten ayuqsunarquq tamarmi. Murilkelluni cakneq niicugniller-
mikun nalluyagusngairut'laryugnarqai.

Angukaraat-wa qanemciuratullrulriit qasgimi, angukaraurtellriit. Qanemcisqe-
lluki-ll' pitullrukait. Cali-am tan'gaurlurni wangkuta qanengssaungraata pitullruitkut, murilkelluki niicugnilaasqelluki, ikayuutekamtenek-gguq atam ilangqetuut,
ilangqerrniartut.

~: *Ississaayuq* :~

Capurciurluni atam assirtuq qanengssaarturluni pilleq. Qanyuunani assiituq capur-
ciulriani.

Tauna Ississaayuq Kuiggluk Alaska mik'nani tuani yuurtellrulliniuq. Tua-i-ll'
angayuqairulluni. Atii, aanii-llu piunrirlutek. Maurluan tua-i taum aulukurangllli-
niluku. Taugken-gguq Kuinerrami ilaluni. Aanii tauna anelguterluni Kuinerrarmiu-
mek.

Taukut Kuigglugmiut nukalpiangqellrulliniut. Imkut *champion*-aaruluteng maaggun nerangnaqsarakun piculriit, unangyulriit ungungssinek neqkanek, nukalpianek pilarait, *lucky*-rturluteng neqnek pilriit. Tua-i tamakucirluteng Kuigglugmiut.
Taukuk-wa ken'gutkelriik, aiparnikelriit tua-i avvingacuunatek, nukalpiak. Yuilqumun-llu pissuangermek avvingacuunatek malikuratulutek. Tuaten tua-i ayuqluni
ayagniumalartuq qanemci tamana.

Stories Frank Andrew Told

Now you will tell the story to others [in the future]. You will now tell it when you are asked to tell a story. I know many stories that are different from the one I just told, the ones they told many years ago, ones you've heard already. If I had listened to the entire stories told by storytellers I'd have many, many stories to tell. Because of the constant work I did in the *qasgi*, I don't know many stories in their entirety. That's why I don't tell them, because parts of the stories are missing, because I don't know them.

The ones I like, ones I enjoyed listening to, I hear them once and never forget them again. I think all people should strive to be like that. By observing and listening intently, I think one will never forget what he heard.

The old men constantly told stories in the *qasgi*, those who had become elderly. The [men in the *qasgi*] would ask them to tell stories. They also told us boys that even though they are just mundane stories, to listen intently, that what we heard would include lessons that would help us later in life.

❧ The story of Ississaayuq ❧

When you are stranded in a place because of weather, it is good to settle down and share stories. When you are stranded like this [during a blizzard in Washington, D.C.] it is not good to sit around and be quiet.

Ississaayuq was born in Kwethluk, Alaska. [And when he was little] he lost his parents. His father and mother passed away. After they died his grandmother began taking care of him. However, he had relatives in Quinhagak. His mother had a sibling who lived in Quinhagak.

[During the time Ississaayuq was growing up] there were some *nukalpiat* residing in Kwethluk. Those men who are champions and good at catching animals for food are referred to as *nukalpiat*. They had men like that living in Kwethluk at that time. Particularly, there were these *nukalpiak* [two hunters] who were best friends and were always together. They were inseparable and always went out hunting together. The story [about Ississaayuq] always started like that [from those *nukalpiak*].

Tua-i-ll' tauna tua-i Ississaayurkaq, taukuk ken'gutkelriik, elliraungan, aulukestailan, cakainek cikiraqluku, ikayuraqluku. Tuaten ayuqlutek. Kuvyakainek, canek tua-i piciatun cikituluku; mikngan-wa tua-i natmun ayagalangeksailan. Aulukaaqluku tua-i neqnek atu'urkainek-llu cikituluku yuilqumi pissurraarlutek.

Anglian tua-i pissuryugngarian, pissulangan, caqerluku ingrinun mayuqatallermegni unayaqliniluku ilaksugluku ayakunek. Kevgiurlutek-wa tua-i pisqumalutek, tauna maurlua apelciisqelluku. Taum-llu tua-i maurluni apelciani qunukevkenaku, aulukngagen'gu taukuk, ellii-ll' tapqulluni, kiikirturluku maligtesqellukek kiiki.

Tauna-gguq nukalpiarat ak'a ayallruluni ava-i ciungatni mayurluni tuntussuallerkaminun.

Ayiimek, tua-i mayuamek malikluku kevgarraqluku. Yuilqumun-llu piaqamek malikurluku tua-i piaqlutek. Pissurcetaqluku-llu. Pissuutaqluku.

Tuatnarraarluteng-am mayuqaniliniluteng. Tauna tua-i nukalpiarata pissuryaraa tekitelliniat tuntut tua-i ungungssit-llu taqukat qeciit inimalriit amllerillinilriit, kinertalluut-llu.

Tua-i-ll' tekilluku tua-i tauna piqanratgu, tekitelliniluni. Pitliniluni-am tua-i tauna. Nerellgutekluteng tua-i tekiutalliniluni. Cikiqluku nerulluku nerrliniluteng. Taqngameng-llu tua-i uitaqarraarluteng ayalliniluteng. Atakuyarturluni-llu-gguq qakemna. Yaaqsigivkenaku tauna nukalpiam taum *camp*-aa, arulailliniluteng. Qiliqerluteng tua-i atakutarraarluteng taquameggnek inartelliniluteng.

Tauna tua-i Ississaayurkaq qavallerminek tupiimi piyaaqelliniuq ilag-imkuk tayima cataunatek. Taugaam qaill' umyuarteqenrilami umyugirpek'nakek qavalliniluni tayima.

Tupalliniuq waniw' itellrullinilriik. Tupiignek tua-i makyutalliniluteng. Aipaa tua-i tauna makyutainanermeggni — (kitak qanrutenrillin'gu tuani). Aipaan pillinia, "Ississaayuuq, imna tekitellerput nukalpiaq unuk tuqucartullruarpuk. Qaneryaqunak. Qanquvet tuquciiqamegten." Inerqurluku, aperturluku. Nallua kitak pinrillin'gu.

So that boy who was to become Ississaayuq, because he was an orphan and didn't have parents, those two men who were good friends would give him things he might need. They provided him with things like fishnets because he was little and too young to venture out on the land. They helped him and gave him food and material for clothing after they hunted.

When the boy was big enough to hunt and had begun to go out on the land, one time when the two men were getting ready to go up into the mountains to hunt, they invited him to go with them. They wanted him to come as their helper and told him to ask his grandmother for permission. When he asked his grandmother, since the two had always helped them out, she encouraged him to go with them.

[Before the three left] another *nukalpiaq* from the village had just left to begin going up into the mountains to hunt caribou.

When the two hunters left and began going up into the mountains the boy went with them and helped them with tasks. [Once they made camp] they'd bring him along when they went out on hunts. They also let him [try to hunt]. They'd take him out and let him hunt.

After they hunted out of one camp for a while, they moved farther up into the mountains. When they arrived at the camp of the other *nukalpiaq* they discovered that the hunter had already caught a lot of animals, and they found many caribou skins and bearskins hanging up to dry, and also meat hanging to dry.

Then soon after they arrived at the camp, the *nukalpiaq* arrived. He had caught something. As soon as he got there, they shared a meal together. The two men got their provisions out and shared them with the *nukalpiaq*. When they were done eating, they stayed briefly and left. They departed at dusk. They went a little ways from his camp and stopped for the night. After they had a snack, they made a shelter and retired for the night.

When the boy who would become Ississaayuq in the future woke from his sleep during the night, he noticed that his companions were gone. But since he wasn't worried about them not being there and didn't suspect anything, he went right back to sleep.

When he woke in the morning, he saw that they had returned. When the two woke up, they all had breakfast. While they were having their morning meal, one of the men — (they shouldn't have told him anything). One of the men said, "Ississaayuuq, the *nukalpiaq* we visited yesterday, we went and killed him last night. Don't say anything. If you tell anyone, we'll kill you." They told him what they had done and admonished him not to tell anyone. (Since he didn't know anything about it, they should have kept quiet.)

Pitai tua-i tamakut aqvaluki, qeciit-llu tamakut, pitamegnun ilakluki nutaan uterrluteng tua-i Kuigglugmun. Tayima tua-i paqrilluku ngelaunani tauna. Taum kinguani tekitaqamek-gguq tua-i cauyaucilartuk callmegnek tua-i apallirturluki. Cauyautengqetulliniut callmeggnek apallirturluki avani, mat'umek nerangnaqluteng piurallermeggnek.

Tuatnatulutek ken'gutkelriik.
Caqerlutek tuatnallermegni-am ayaumarraarlutek, aipaan pirraarluni pillinia, "Ississaayuuq, aling elpeni-lli cauyauciqayuipaa. Cauyaucinariyaqaaten." Maligtaquvkenakek tua-i.

Tuamtell' aipirilutek cali allamian, uksuarmi cali tuntussuarraarlutek, tuamtell' cauyauciamek cali-am piyaaqellininiluku. Cali-am maligtaquvkenakek. Pingayiriagnigguq tua-i nutaan cauyautmek atullruuq. Tuani tua-i qanenrilengraan, qanenrilengraan tauna, Kuigglugmiut yik'ucaaqellininiat nall'arrlukek taukuk ken'gutkelriik. Kamaklukek tua-i taukugnun piyukluku. Tua-i nall'arrcaaqellininiluku. Ciungani pillrulliagnek-llu tua-i tuaten pilriit. Yik'ucaaqluku taukugnun. Kelquranglutek-gguq tua-i qavaluaqayuirullutek-llu taukuk.

Caqerluteng tua-i taum kinguani, pissurraarluteng-am utercameng cauyautmegneg-am tua-i cauyaucilutek atualliniuk. Taqngamek tua-i aipaagneg-am pillinia, "Ississaayuuq, amci cauyautmek cauyauciqaa!" Cauyamek tua-i cikiagni akurtullinia nutaan. Ak'a tua-i nak'rillrulliamiu tamana yuarutkani aturturallininiluni tua-i. Apallillinia, "Iluka qamna yugyugpagta. Iluka qamna yugyugpagta." Qaillun-am iqulilirnilaryaaqaat. Tua-i taqluteng.

Pillran taum kinguani, erenrani aipaan pillinia atmagyaqatarnilutek maligtesqellutek. Cunawa-gguq tua-i picirkiurlutek waniw' tuquteqatarluku. Tuqutnaluku piyaaqellininiluku. Piyualuteng tua-i qakinercualuteng nunat kiatiitni napat akuliitni pulaarluteng maqikanek.

Then they went to the camp of the *nukalpiaq* and took the food he had processed from his catch, including the skins, and added them to their own pile in the sled and went home to Kwethluk. The *nukalpiaq* failed to come home from his hunting trip, and the community started to wonder why he was missing. After that incident the two men continued to go out hunting, and when they came home, they would compose a song called a *cauyaun*. In the song they'd mention their hunting trip and the events that took place out there. Hunters typically composed *cauyautet* [songs] when they came home from hunting, telling of their experiences out there.

Those two good friends would do that.

One time while the two men were [working on a song] after a hunting trip, after one of them made comments about Ississaayuq [and said that he had never composed a song], he turned to him and said, "Ississaayuuq, gee whiz, you have not composed a song yet. It is time that you compose one." Ississaayuq ignored their suggestion and didn't make a song.

Then again the following year after they hunted caribou in the fall, when they composed another song, they asked him to make a song, but he didn't follow their advice. It wasn't until the third time they asked him to compose a song that he finally sang a *cauyaun*. When he sang, although he didn't mention the exact details of what happened out there, people in Kwethluk started to suspect the two men who were close friends for the disappearance of the *nukalpiaq*. They apparently had been right in their suspicions. Perhaps they felt that way since the men had done a similar thing before. People there began to think the two men were connected to the disappearance of the *nukalpiaq*. After that, they became vigilant, and they didn't sleep well anymore.

Then one time after that, when they came home after hunting they sang the new *cauyaun* they composed. When they were done singing one of the men said, "Ississaayuuq, come on, get with it and make a song!" When they handed him the drum he took it. Since he apparently had already learned the song he had composed, he drummed and sang. When he sang the verse, the lyrics to the song said, "My stomach, oh how it's longing to eat human flesh! My stomach, oh how it's craving human flesh!" I used to hear the song being sung, but I can't remember the rest of the words now. So, after he sang, they stopped and remained.

Sometime after he sang that song, during the day one of the two men told him that they were going out to gather wood and asked him to come with them. Evidently, they had both agreed to take him out to kill him. They were going to kill him. In the area above the village, they walked inside the trees along the river and began looking for dead wood for the fire bath.

Temeqsigiameng tua-i, atmagkiurateng tamakut pivailgata, tegulliniluku napat
aciatni, ngeliitni. Teguamegen'gu pilliniak, "Ississaayuuq, inerqullruamegten-ggem.
Ciin kamanaqluten atuasit? Waniw' tuquteqataramegten." Tua-i tuqutelliniluku
tuani. Napam-llu ikigarneran acianun qerrluku canegnek kevirluku unitellinluku.
Kuigglugmun tua-i-am kanaamek, Kuiggluum iluakun, napanek atmaglutek nunanun anelrallinilutek. Igvalliniuk, augna-ll' qasgiata ketiikun yuk napanek qakinernek atmagluni qakvarluni taggliniluni. Pilliniak Ississaayuullinilria, imna tuqutell-
rak.

Tua-i-am kinguani qaill' piksaunaku tua-i. Alingyaguartevkenakek-llu taum Issis-
saayuum. Akaurrluku-am unayaqliniag-am. Ayaucamegnegu-am tua-i temetmu-
rulluku-am tua-i tamaani qakinernek kiaraluteng. Temeqsigiameng-am tegulliniluku. Taum-am qanrutlinia, "Ississaayuuq, inerqullruamegten-ggem. Keltellerpuk
utumarinrakun-am kamakuurcetarpekuk kellnariqertelluki." Qalaruqaarluku-am
tuqutelliniluku.

Tuaten-ll'-am tua-i ikigarnerem acianun elliluku unitellinluku. Pingayurqunek-
gguq tuqutelaryaaqaak. Tua-i Kuigglugmiut-gguq igvarnauragket qasgiata ketiikun
tagelria. Maurluan tua-i taum tuyurtequallinia tauna ilakutni Kuinerraarmi aqvas-
qellutek. Taum tua-i aqvallrulliniak Kuinerramek. Angyakun aqvalukek. Tua-i taukuk qimiignek pinqigtevkenaku.

Tua-i nutaan nulirturnariami Qinarmiumek nuliangelliniuq, Tuntutuliarmiut
kiugkut ciuliaratnek. Qinarmiungurrluni tua-i. Ayagyuarluni. Tua-i nutaan tuani
alairluni. Egmian-am pivkenani tua-i yuliulangluni. Yuungcaristengurrluni tua-i.
Tuunrilangluni yuliurluni. Tuunrilangelliniur-am anirturituluni. Tuunriskengellri
apquciirutaqluteng.

Tamana-am pitekluku angalkuullgutain iqluurutkelangelliniluku. Mikelnguut-
llu waten iliit naulluqerrluni-ll' piunriraqan, angalkut tamakut taumun piniaqluku,
yugmun qanrutkaqluku. Nalqigtelaryaaqelliniuq tamaani, umyuarrlugciqsaitniluni

When they got farther inside away from the river, before they had enough wood gathered to carry home on their backs, at the edge of a wooded area, the two men grabbed Ississaayuq. When they took him they said, "Ississaayuuq, I thought we told you not to tell anyone. Why did you sing a song creating suspicion in the minds of the people listening? We are going to kill you now." After they told him that, they immediately killed him. Then they pushed his body beneath a partially uprooted tree and covered the hole with grass and left. When they got to the Kuiggluk River, they continued on down the river toward the village, carrying wood on their backs. When they came around the last bend and could see the village, they saw a person climbing up the riverbank below the men's house with wood on his back. They looked closer and saw that it was Ississaayuq, the person they had just killed.

After that they left him alone and didn't say anything to him. Ississaayuq didn't even show any signs of fear toward them. After a long time, they asked him to go with them again, and he went. Once they were out there, they went inside the trees away from the river and searched for dead wood. Deep in the woods, they grabbed him again. One of the men said, "Ississaayuuq, we warned you not to tell anyone. After we had gotten less worried, the words to your song created suspicion in the minds of the people in the village, making us become cautious." After they said that they killed him.

And as they had done before, they shoved his body underneath an uprooted tree and left. They say they killed him three times. And each time they approached the village of Kwethluk they'd find him climbing up the bank below the men's house. Then his grandmother sent a message down to a relative who lived down in Quinhagak to come get them. That person came and picked them up with a boat from Quinhagak. After they fled, those two men never bothered him again.

When it was time for him to marry, he married someone from Qinaq, an ancestor of those who live in Tuntutuliak today. He moved to Qinaq and became a member of that community. He was a young man. It was at that time he revealed himself [as an *angalkuq* (shaman)]. After that, though not right away, he began to work on people. He became a healer. He began to work on people using his power. When he started to use his power on people, they realized that he had the ability to heal them. When he worked on people, their ailments were removed and their health returned.

Because of his power, the other *angalkut* started to tell lies about him. And when one of the children suddenly got sick and died, the *angalkut* would blame him and tell one person, allowing gossip to spread in the village. During that time he tried

ellii. Umyuarrlugciquni yug-atauciq qamiquculngungaitniluku. Cunawa-gguq ayu-
quciminek pilaryaaqellinilria iqluvkenani.

Tamakut taugaam angalkuullgutain yugnun Qinarmiunun pingevkarluku maligulluteng ukvengluteng tamakut tua-i angalkuunrilngermeng. Angalkut tamakut
picilirturtain maligtengluki tuquitunglliniat.

Enelguterluni-gguq tuani enengauminek, allanek cali. Avani tuaten enelgutengqe-
tullruut enailngurnek. Pingayunek tua-i ena tamana yugluni. Elkegnek, taukunek-
llu yuungnaqelrianek cali ilaluni, enengauminek-llu. Pingayuuluteng tua-i enemini
tuani uitaluteng.

Uksuarmi qanrutliniluku-am iliita piciqliarutniluku tua-i maa-i taq'isngairu-
lluku. Tuani tua-i amigpilluku tua-i piarkaurcamegteggu anesqelluku amci qaya-
gaurluku, qayagauraqluku.

Yuungcararluni-gguq taugken Cigviilngurmek piaqluku. Nuliani-am caqerluku
paqeqaartelluku itran pillinia, "Cigviilnguum-qaa Atii tanglaran?" Ilagautenricaquq-
gguq. Paq'errluki-gguq taugaam pillra nall'arrluku pinilaraat tauna. Tangrramiu ang-
lliniluku tangerrniluku taukunun inglukingelrianun.

Irniangevkaani tua-i taumek Cigviilngurmek. Tamakut waten nalaurluteng pil-
riit-am angalkunek qaillukuartelluteng pimalriit yuungcaraunilarait. Qanrucani-
gguq putkaraa qamiquni. Uitaraqerluni pilliniuq, "Tua-lli-wa nalliini cungipakal-
ria waten piarkaulliningermi." Waniwa-gguq ayakataquni tukleqluku ayagciquq.

Ilalcirluni-gguq tua uitayaaquq qaillukuarpek'nani. Enelgutiin-gguq taugaam
taum qanrulluku tuani. Pillinia, "Waten-qaa tua-i waniwa qaillukuarpek'nak pivka-
qatartuten? Tangvaurtelluten-ggem tamarayugaqavet tamaratuuten."

Ellangarrnganani-guq nutaan piuq tuani qanrucani.

Pillinia pitsaqevkenaku kegglunermek ilakuarungraan, ilangaringangraan qe-

to convince them that he had not harmed others. [He told them] that if he actually did that, no one person would be affected by the evil deed, but many would be injured by it. He apparently was attesting to his truthfulness and was not lying.

From hearing the accusations made by other *angalkut*, the other members of the village began to believe what they heard and started to have ill feelings toward him. Soon the *angalkut* and the other people there began to think of ways to kill him.

At that time he lived in a house along with his son-in-law and another family. In those days, a family without a home was allowed to live with other families in a house. There were three families residing in the house where he lived — he and his wife, his son-in-law and his wife, and another couple with children.

In the fall one of the people told him that the villagers were getting ready to kill him and that this time they would keep their plan. When they got ready, men formed two lines in front of his house, creating a passageway for him to walk through, and they called on him to come out again and again.

At that time there was a child who he had given life to while in the womb, and his name was Cigviilnguq. Once after his wife had gone out to check the people in front of their house, when she came in he asked, "Did you see the father of Cigviilnguq?" He actually had not been among the people accusing him of doing evil deeds and was not among those waiting outside. But they said that she just happened to see him out there when he stopped by to see what was going on. Since she had seen him, she told Ississaayuq that she saw him there with those who were turning against him.

He, Ississaayuq, had helped Cigviilnguq to be born and live. When babies kept dying, when the next baby was doctored by an *angalkuq* and helped to live, that child was referred to as a *yuungcaraq* [from *yuungcar-*, "to treat one medically"]. When she told him that she saw the father of Cigviilnguq out there, he put his head down. After pausing for a moment he said, "When he was desperate, he begged for my help, even though he apparently was going to eventually do this." Then he added that he would be the one he would "kick" when he left.

He had tolerated offenses and not tried to defend himself at the time. His roommate said something to stir his emotions. His roommate said, "Are you not going to act and let them do what they want with you? In the past you have used your strength in your work and disappeared when you wanted to right in plain sight of members of this community."

He appeared to have come to his senses and suddenly became aware when his roommate said that.

He then asked his roommate if he had a wolf skin or even a piece of one stored

mangqaariyucianek. Aren, qemangqaangqertuk-gguq ilangaringanrilngurmek. Nutaan-gguq tua-i uptuq. Arulairluni-gguq ataucuq tangvangaqluku. Uitarraarluni tua-i piaqluni. Qaqicami tua-i nutaan kememi engeliinun tunuminun pamavet, akumikun kasmevkallinia, qamiqurra-ll' uuggun pugevkarluku, kegglunrem taum. Naquggluni-ll' tua-i nutaan qaingakun.

Atraami nutaan amiik cauluku kalvagyaraq. Caungamiu tauna nengauni pillinia cakirai ukut unitesqevkenaki anaksailata, angliksailata. Tauna tuamtell' enelgutni pilliniluku unitesqevkenaki cali ukut nayurturluki nayurturaasqelluki. Qaill' pingaitniluku enem mat'um iluanelnguut apqucimun agturngaitniluki. Nutaan-gguq waniw' nekayugtuq cakneq tua-i piksaunani picilirturpakaatni. Umyuarrlug-ciqatartuq-gguq waniwa. Ayagyuatgun-gguq piqatarai qununanritgun.

Tuaten-llu pirraarluni kalvagyaramun kanaqalliniluni tayima. Cakmani elaturrami kalvagyarat alaitetuut tua-i. Qamaken atralria egmian alaitaqluni kanani. Tangvaurluku pingraatni, qimugta kan'a qeckaq'alliniluni qamaken. Nugngami-ll' tua-i pamyuni amlemikun qaluggluku ukatmun. Tangaaluki-gguq tua-i yuut makut anluni aqvaqussuarluni qimugta. Kanani-llu-gguq ciqitaat — qanitarnek pitullruit enet natrita tuss'arallrit. Tekicami qaingatni akagualliniluni. Akaguarraarluni-ll' tua-i pangalkuanqiqerluni Avcuamcim tungiinun qip'artelliniluni.

Kuigat augg' Avcuamcimek pitullruat. Kuigat nequkunani Qinarmiut, Qinaam avayarrii.

Qip'artellra pivailgan qayagaulliniut amci anevkaasqelluku. Anevkaryunripaka-qatgu iterluteng piciqniluteng. Nulirran-gguq tua-i nutaan kiugai, "Ava-i-ggem anellruuq. Iterluci yuaryarturciu." Iterluteng-am tua-i yuaryaaqerraarluku, taringar-telliniat-am taungucia, angalkuungan taumek qimugtemek amilirluku anucia.

away. He quickly replied that he had a whole wolf skin put away. Then he immediately started getting ready to leave. While he was getting ready, he would stop and stand still looking at one spot. Then after a while he'd start moving and resume getting ready. When he was ready, he had his roommate shove the wolf skin up his back beneath his garment, pushing it all the way up with the head sticking out behind his head. Then he tied a belt around his waist.

When he came down to the front of the room he stood facing the entrance hole of the tunnel entryway. As he stood there he turned to his son-in-law and told him not to leave his in-laws since they were still too young to fend for themselves. Then he turned to his roommate and told him not to leave his family and to continue to stay with them. He told them that nothing would happen to them and that sickness would not touch them. He said that finally he was feeling really offended for being accused of wrongdoings, even though he was innocent. And he added that he was about to cast evil toward members of the community. He said he was going to curse the community, placing it on the young people who were cherished by their families.

After he said that he walked toward the entrance hole and quickly slipped down and disappeared into the tunnel entryway. When one stood in the porch and looked in through the front entrance hole, you could see through the entryway all the way to the back. And when a person came down through the hole in the back, you could easily see him come down while looking in from the front. While the men out there kept an eye on the back hole, a dog slipped down through the hole from inside. And when the dog came up through the front entrance hole, it curled its tail between its hind legs. The dog came trotting out and continued along between the lines of men looking at them. And once the dog got to the refuse pile down there — the place where they used to discard crumbled grass flooring was called *qanitaq*. When it got to the grass refuse pile, it started to roll around on them. After the dog rolled on the grass it got up and ran a little ways and turned and continued on toward Avcuamciq River.

The village was on the river called Avcuamciq. Qinaq was located along that narrow river, a little river branching off Qinaq River.

Before the dog went around the river bend and disappeared, people out there yelled and told the people inside the house to let him come out. And they said that if they didn't allow him to go out they would go in and get him. Then [Ississaayuq's] wife answered them, "I thought he just went out. Go ahead and come in and look for him." They went in and searched. Failing to find him they suddenly realized that the dog that came out was actually the man they were pursuing. Since he was an *angalkuq*, he had come out disguised as a dog.

Maligtelliniluku-am tumaikun. Avcuamcikun atraami asgullinilria Avcuamcikun. Pavavet-llu tua-i taukut tumyarat tekicamiki maa-i qakvarluni nanvarra'armun
kanarluni qeralliniluni. Qakvaqerluni-ll' pikani yinrarnek inglunga'artelliniluteng,
nat'ram tutmallrinek. Nanvamun-llu cali tuavet kanaqataqerluni keggluninraqerte-
lliniluteng. Nutaan tua-i pangalellri amelturiqertelliniluteng. Angungailamegteggu
tua-i taqliniluku tuaken.

Kuigpagmi qakmani, nunat yaaqsinrilkiitni, Kusquqviim tunglirnerani maani uk-
suillerruaraak taukuk maurluquralriik cali, can'giirnek nereqcaarturalriik tuantetu-
lliniuk. Tua-i-am tuanllutek. Erenret iliitni caqerluni tutgarii tauna mertarraarluni
pilliuq, itrami pilliniuq, yugmek-gguq tangertuq agiirtellriamek maaken Kusquqviim tungiinek. Maurluan pillinia, "Kitag-neqainek upyulluku. Tekiskan piyarairu-
lluki." Neqainek tua-i upciluni. Paqtaqluku tua-i.

Man'a-gguq tua-i akertem ayagturallra man'a cukataciluku agiirquralria, erenrem
unugyartullra maliggluku tua-i cukataciluku. Maurluan-am taum tua-i kamakenga-
miu aluqatkamek taumek pillinilria, ikiitugmek-llu, teggalqumek-llu uqumyagmek.
Tutgarani tauna pillinia, "Ukut kitag-teguluki ankuvet quyuita minguktarturluki
enecuallerpuk uivelaqiu. Kassugaqavki amiguyuum pikavet amiigan quliinun elli-
qaqluki. Iterniartuten tua-i qaqisquvki. Anenqigtevkenak tua-i piniartuten." Tuat-
nauralliniluki-am tua-i. Qaqicamiki tua-i iterluni. Elkarrlutek tua-i, anqetaarngai-
rulluni.

Tan'geriqerluku atam qakma tua-i tekitellinilria, qerkiugtellra pinga'artellinilria.
Qanraqluni-gguq, "Aling, enengungatellruuq-ggem una? Qaillun una pia?" Qakma
tua-i tutmarluni. Pivakarluni-am qalarqaartelluku maurlua tauna qanlliniuq, "Tuar-
gguq tang qakemna Ississaayuuqatalria." Cunawa-gguq tua-i eriniikun elitaqlinikii-
am nall'arrluku.

Tuatnang'ermiu taugaam ellimerpek'naku tauna tutgarani. Pivakarluni tua-i
cakma amiagnun igtellinilria. Aurnermek-llu-gguq amiigak ell'allagluni, kumlamek
imumek qaterrluni. Puggliniuq tua-i Ississaayuullinilria. Up'arulluku tua-i akimeg-
nun ikavet pivkarluku. Nekqainek pisqelluku pillrani pilliniuq, uuyutairraarluni-
gguq nerciquq. Kamilartuq-gguq piinri-llu aluinun nepingaluteng, cikusngaluki

They went after it, following its tracks. When it got down to the Avcuamciq River it apparently had continued on upriver. And in the area back there, the tracks continued up on land and reached a little lake and crossed it. And once they were on the land past the lake, one side of the animal tracks turned into human footprints. And just before the tracks reached another lake, both tracks suddenly turned into wolf tracks again and were quite a distance apart, indicating that it was running fast. Since the men tracking him knew that it was impossible to catch him, they gave up.

Out in the Yukon River area, not far from a village, in the area toward the Kuskokwim River, a grandmother and her grandchild lived alone, surviving on blackfish during the winter. They had been living there for a number of years. One day after fetching water, the grandchild came in and said that he saw a person coming from the area toward the Kuskokwim River. Then his grandmother said, "Then get some food ready so when he arrives it would be ready for him." He got the food ready. He would go out periodically and check on the person who was coming.

The traveler coming was so slow, he was moving as fast as the sun moving across the sky. The person was going as fast as daylight as it approached dusk. The grandmother, suspecting that the person approaching was not a normal human being, took out a beaver castor, a wild celery plant, and a stone referred as an *uqumyak*. She turned to her grandson and said, "Take these and go out, hold them together, and go around several times and brush our little house with them. And on each round, place one of them above the entryway. Continue doing that and come inside. When you come in, don't go back out again." The grandchild did as he was told and went around the house and placed each piece above the entryway and went in. They both stayed inside and settled in for the night.

Then just when it got dark he arrived. They could hear the crackling sounds his footsteps made as he moved about on the snow outside their house. He would say, "Gee, I thought this was a house when I looked at it from the distance. What happened to it?" They could hear him moving around out there. Then after he spoke more, his grandmother said, "The person out there talking, his voice sounds like that of Ississaayuq." She had guessed right by hearing his voice.

But even though she suspected who it might be, she didn't ask her grandchild to go out and check. Then after a few moments, they heard him fall through the front entrance hole into the tunnel entryway. And as soon as he fell in, mist suddenly gushed into the room through the entrance hole. The haze that gushed in was white and cold. It was Ississaayuq who emerged through the entrance hole. They quickly

kemganun. Kelutmun-gguq tua-i cauluni tunullukek, irumi inglua teguluku ciku-
tulria akma qangqurluni. Tuamtell' inglua.

Qaqicamiki tua-i ketmun uivngami, it'gai tang piyaaqelliniakek qercuanrunateng.
Tamana qercuaneni aug'arluku, uuyutairluku. Tuani tua-i ernerni mamcillrulliniuq,
ernerni amllerrarni uitaluni. Mamiami taugaam nutaan Kuigpagmun tekivsiarluni.
Tuani-ll' ayakataami, ayagarkaurcami pilliniluku lingrayugyaaqluni tua waniwa au-
lukucirminek, taugaam tua-i arenqiatniluni pikaitniluni.

Tua-i pikangqerrutacirramitun waniw' lingrayukatarnilukek. Mellgarmek
tua-i pivkarluni muragarmek can'giiruamek pililliniluni. Qaqicamiu-ll' tua-i taumun tutgariinun tunluku, elakaagnun atrautesqelluku. Ellikaku tangvauraasqe-
lluku, tangvauraqaasqelluku. Itrami tua-i anuqaarluku waqaarani pilliniuq, can'gii-
ruaq-gguq-wa tekicamiu elakaq ellikiini-gguq pugtauraqertuq. Tua-i-llu-gguq
tangvaurainanrani ceqcillagluni atraqerrluni camavet mermun.

Unuaquani tua-i ayiin mertaasqellinia maurluan. Mertaami tua-i elakaq tauna
uyangtellinia mer'unani can'giirnek imarluni. Piyaaqaqani-gguq mengyugpek'naku.
Tua-i piqcaarluni qupluanek qaltani tauna imirluku. Cunawa-gguq ayuqucirkaa
tua-i tauna elakaq, can'giirnek imangqerrlainarluni tua-i.

Kiakuan-gguq nutaan irniari, taukut ilai, aqvait qakmaken Kuigpagmek angyakun. Kuigpagmiungurrluteng tua-i. Allrakut qavciurteqerluki, uksumi tekitellru-
lliniut taukut nukalpiat pingayun irniari. Tua-i-gguq uluryanarqut. Canek tua-i
navguringraata qununarqelrianek, taringamegteki ayagnerkarcuata, tua-i qaill' piksaunaki umyugiurcetlinikait, navguingraata.

Tauna tua-i Qiivet Ayallermek acinqigtelliniluku.

Kass'aruallruuq-gguq tua-i tauna tamaa-i angalkuqsagutellratni; elriurtellermi.

got a place ready and asked him to sit across from them. When grandmother asked her grandchild to give him food, he said that he would eat after he removed the frostbite from his skin. When he removed his boots, they noticed that the grass lining was stuck to his feet. The grass was frozen stiff and stuck to his feet. Then he turned with his back to them and grabbed his foot and took a bite from it. He started chomping like he was chewing ice. When he was done, he took the other foot and continued chewing.

When he was done and turned back around facing them, they looked at his feet and noticed that they weren't frostbitten anymore. He had removed all the frostbite from his feet. After that he stayed with them for quite some time so that his wounds would heal completely. Then he continued on to the Yukon River area. As he was about to leave he told them that he was very grateful for their hospitality but that he had nothing to repay them for their help.

Then he said that he was going to try to offer them something to express his gratitude. He then asked for a carving knife and made a model of a blackfish out of driftwood. When he was done, he gave it to her grandchild and asked him to bring it down to their ice hole in the river. He told him to watch it briefly when he placed it in the ice hole. After he brought it down and came back in, he reported that when the wooden blackfish model was dropped in the water it floated momentarily. Then he added that as he watched, it suddenly splashed and became alive and dove down into the water and was gone.

The next morning after he left, the grandmother asked her grandchild to pack water. When he went down and looked into the ice hole there was no water, but it was completely filled with blackfish. He tried to get water, but the hole remained dry. He kept trying and eventually filled the bucket with a little bit of water. So after that every time he checked the ice hole it was always filled with blackfish.

The following summer, a team went from the Yukon River to his village in the Kuskokwim to get his children, his family, by boat. He and his family were reunited and settled on the Yukon River. Several years later his children [went back to the Kuskokwim] and arrived in the village where their father once lived. They had gone there to get even and fight, and people in that village totally feared them. While they stayed they would get angry and break valuable things, but everyone in the village left them alone because they knew that they were deliberately doing that, seeking a challenger.

After he relocated, those who knew him started calling him Qiivet Ayalleq [One who went to the Qiit].

It was said that after he became an *angalkuq* and had become an *elriq*, he created a mask to conjure the coming of white people.

Irniameng ilait piunriraqata, tua-i tamakuurculriit, piyugngalriit tua-i piturilu-
teng. Elriurtellrianek aterpagtaangetukait tuatnatungaqata, elriurtaqata.

Qavcinek-wa kegginaqungqellrua tuani alairillermini. Iliit-gguq puyurtuutarua-
mek keggmiarluni. Cauciinaku-gguq taugken tua-i, puyurtuutauciinaku, tuaten pil-
riamek tangssuilameng. Qitevvluteng-llu piyaaqellilriit, qalriayukluki-am taugaam
pilallrullinikait, *ahak*-aaraluteng tuaten pillratni taukut yuut aturtait, qalriacilirill-
rani.

Taukuk tua-i tangellregka paiciuteknilaragket taumun Qiivet Ayallermun, tuulleguak. Qinarmiunun-gguq paiciutekellruak. Piciatun-gguq tua-i piyuunatek. Uiv-
qetaartura'arqamek piciryaramegtun tua-i piuratulutek. Allaurtevkenaku tua-i
caullutek-llu piaqlutek. Tangtulukek-gguq, neqet paivngaqatarqata taryaqviit, iqalluut-llu. Up'nerkami tua-i Kusquqviim ceniinek atraumaaratullruuq qayaulutek,
elqianek aturlutek. Kessigiamek-gguq kisngiinarnaurtuk, tayima-llu-gguq nallim-
lutek. Pugnaurtuk-gguq tuullguluutek.

Tuunrangayiit tamakut tamaa-i calilallrit tangvaurtelluteng. Cacetuqutekqapia-
rallruit tua-i imumi. Cacetuqutekellruamegteki tua-i kiingita man'a alairpailgan.

Taukunek-wa tua-i kegginaqunek qavcinek alairillrullinilria tuani kass'aruaqata-
llermini. Tuani-ll' tua-i aturraarluki qalriaciliriluni. Alerqualuki taukut tua-i ankata
tamaaken qasgim egkuan capiinek negtaarpek'naki eriniit anurasqelluku tua-i pi-
yugtaciatun neplirtelluki, tukrumavkenaki.

Up'nerkaan tua-i nutaan tamana sun'aq tekitellrulliniuq. Qaralii tamakut kegginaqut cikemyaraqluteng-gguq angyam qacarnerani. Kampaassaq-wa-gguq tauna
cali iliit yaani ciumi calaraq eniumaurluku.

Kampaassaat-gguq cunaw'. Augna-wa-gguq napartetaa akuliitni, qeluqcautet
makut engeliitni ilavkugni tuntucuar angitaarturalria. Ilavkugmun tuq'urluni qeraraqluni.

Ciuqliit-llu tamakut kipuqsaaqellrit cauvkenateng-gguq tua-i unuaquan' carang-
lluurtelliniluteng tua-i tangsunarqellret, piksunarqellret imkut. Tauna-gguq tua-i
taum elritulim akngiqerrutni tuani piyaaqellrani pia piunritniluki. Tua-i cucussiyaa-

When a couple lost a child, if they were capable, they'd begin holding memorial feasts and offer new garments to a child who was named after their deceased child. When someone began holding ceremonies like that, people said that one had become an *elriq*.

I don't know how many masks he revealed at the festival. It was said that one of the masks had a pipe hanging from its mouth. People watching the presentation didn't know that it was a pipe because they had never seen one before. When the singers sang and made sounds, perhaps speaking in English, they thought they were just making animal sounds or sounds of other creatures.

The two I saw were two models of common loons that Qiivet Ayalleq left to the people as commemorative. He gave them to the people of Qinaq before he left as inheritance. When they were hung, they spun only in a certain direction and never went out of control. When they stopped turning, they'd be facing the direction of what was to come in the future. They were the messengers and would let people know if many king salmon and chum salmon were going to swim upriver in the coming fishing season. In the spring, people used to see them in the form of kayaks as they started to launch into the Kuskokwim River, and those in the kayaks wore hunting hats. As the kayaks got farther and farther from the riverbank, they'd start sinking into the water and eventually disappear. After they sank and disappeared, two common loons would surface.

Those were some of the things *angalkut* did with people as witnesses. People totally relied on the *angalkut* back in those days. Before churches and Christianity came, *angalkut* were the only sources of support [and gave people courage to survive].

He created several masks when he performed to conjure the coming of white people. After they were presented in a dance, he called out the voices of those particular creatures. Then he instructed his singers to yell as loud as they could from the corner of the *qasgi*, not holding back, once they were outside.

Then the following spring a ship finally arrived at their place. On the side of the boat, the eyes of the mask carvings would blink periodically. And their compass, one of the men in the boat, stood at the bow with his arm extended, pointing east.

Evidently, he was acting as a compass for the boat's crew. They also saw a tiny caribou going back and forth on the lines tied to poles in the boat. The tiny animal would go on the line and walk across.

Then the following morning they found that the things they had bought from the boat the day before had turned into junk, items that previously looked desirable. They said that when the child asked the parent who had become an *elriq* for

kan amllerivkenaku pisqelluku. Kinguqliitnek taugaam piciqniluku. Unugpak-gguq piunrilliniluteng tamakut. Iciw' imkut nunam qaingani tangssunaqluteng *flowers-aat*-llu pilalriit. Tamakuuluteng-gguq. Cauluki llumarrauluki tangaallruyaaqluki.

Qanemcit makut niipakalaamki imumi, niicugnilallrenka elilluki. Amllerrsaaqut qanemcit niitelallrenka, taugaam qanemciksuitanka akulait niicugnimanrilata, kev-giullma, kevgartuallma-w' tua-i.

Qanemciinanratni unilluki an'aqlua. Qanemciksuilkenka taumek.

MARIE: Quyanaqvaa-ll' tua-i Ississaayuq ataam pugqerluni, waniw' qanugpaa-gallrani.

an item the day before, he had told her that the things being sold were not real. He told her to get a few things if she so desired and that the things to be sold later on would be genuine. The things people bought that first time rotted overnight. You know, in the summer we see beautiful flowers growing on land. That's what they were like. They had seen them as cloth and other objects.

Stories such as these, since I used to hear them all the time, I have remembered. There were many, many stories told in the *qasgi*, but since I was always ready to get up and leave and do chores for others, I don't share them because I only heard parts of them.

[When someone wanted something done], I immediately left while a story was being told. That is why I don't tell some of the stories that were told.

MARIE: I'm so very grateful the story about Ississaayuq surfaced while snow continues to fall outside right now.

Apanuugpak

Qinarmiut, waken Qinarmiunek qanengssaullratnek wii qanengssak'laranka, taukut tua-i pillrit. Anguyiim-llu nalliini pilallrit tamakut. Ayuqeksaitelaameng.

Qanemcik'laraat. Taukut Qinarmi kiani anguyiim nalliini, Apanuugpak Pangal-
galria-llu yuilqumun ayangssilliniuk. Neqem waten *fish*-anek pillermeng kingua-
riini. Yuilqumi tua-i ayangssilutek pirraarlutek, utercamek tekitelliniuk imkut
anguterugaat tayima Qinarmiut ilakek. Aptelliniuk, caluki imkut catailuciitnek.
Kiulliniit curugniluki.

Apanuugpiim umyugaa akngirtelliniuq ciin uniyuciminek, ciin utaqanrilucirmi-
nek. Arenqialami tua-i tauna Pangalgalria qanrutlinia uitayuumiitniluni ellii, ciin
utaqalutek pinriluciitnek augkunun ilamegnun. Kiimelngermek ayagyuglutek.
Tua-i-ll' tan'gaurlurmek taumek maligkanga'artellinilutek. Natii-gguq tauna cu-
runerraar anguyiit tuqutellruluku tua-i tayima. Pingayurrauluteng ayalliniluteng
agaatmun calaratmun, avavet Iilgayam tunglirneranun. Yicuunateng tua-i agaani.
Nunanun piiyuunateng. Unugmi taugaam kituraqluki.

Avavet tua-i nutaan Iilgayarmun piameng, nutaan tua-i keltengluteng tamaani.
Tumkaunrilngurkun tua-i, tumkaqenrilkiitgun ayaganguluteng, tangaaluku tua-i. Pivakarluteng tamaani yuilqumi qayamek taumek nall'arkengllinilriit. Ayagarcaaqel-
ria tua-i maliggluku tegulliniluku. Tegulliniat ingluat anguyak.

Apqeryaaqelliniat kituucianek. Tamaani-gguq atrit apertuqerceqaarluki tuqutetuit. Aperturyuumiitellinia at'ni taum. Aqlillugpagluni-gguq aqliterluni angut-
ngung'ermi. Tua-i arenqialan Aqlillugpalegmek acilliniluku ellaita. Taumun tua-i
nutaan ayagyuanemegnun tuqucetliniluku.

Tuamtell' tua-i taum kinguani ayagaluteng, nunat tua-i tangrrarkaqenrilkiitni
arulairluteng tua-i piaqluteng nunat. Unugmi taugaam iluvarvikluku piaqluki tua-i.

340

Apanuugpak

Stories about people from Qinaq, I tell them the way I heard them being told in that village. I also tell war stories that originated from that village. The details usually change as the story goes from person to person or from place to place.

The story about [Apanuugpak and his two partners] has been shared by our people. Up in Qinaq during war times, it is said that one day Apanuugpak and Pangalgalria went out on the land. It was just after they had harvested salmon. After being out on the land, when they returned home all the men from the village of Qinaq were gone. They asked the residents why they were gone. They replied that they had gone out to attack their enemies.

Apanuugpak was hurt and asked why they had left him, why they hadn't waited for him. Since he was so upset, he told Pangalgalria that he didn't want to stay behind and asked why the warriors from their village hadn't waited for them. He told him that they should go, even though they were by themselves.

As they prepared to go it was decided that a young boy would go with them. Earlier, his relative going to war for the first time had been killed by the enemy. The three of them left and headed east, toward the Nushagak River. They moved about across there and avoided going into villages. They would go by villages unnoticed only at night.

When they finally reached the Nushagak River, they became vigilant as they moved about in that area. They started using untraveled ways by checking the land. As they were moving about in that area they happened upon a man in a kayak. The man tried to escape, but they followed him and took him. When they captured him they saw that he was their enemy.

They asked his name, but he never told them who he was. During that time when an enemy was captured they usually killed him right after he identified himself. But the enemy refused to say his name. Though he was a man he had big earrings hanging from his ears. So, since he definitely wasn't going to identify himself, they named him Aqlillugpalek [One with big earrings]. They then allowed the youngest in their group to kill him.

Then after that they continued on, and sometimes they would stop in areas where they wouldn't be detected by the residents. They went into settlements only

Neqnek-llu piaqluteng taquateng cuqluki neqkameggnek, neqiviitnek tegulluteng piyunarqelriit. Tuaten tua-i pillrulliniut.

Cali-am pivakarluteng-am nall'arkenglliniut-am cali anguyagmek. Tua-i-am qimagyaaqelria malirqerluku piluku tua-i tegulliniluku. Teguatgu qutnguguluni, qaliluugnek atkugluni tuntugnek. Qutnguitnek tamaani pitulliniit-llu maani.

Apcaaqelliniat-am kituucianek, at'ni-am qunukellinia. Aren augna ciuqliq aptellratni tuani piiyaaqelliniuq tuqutenritqaasqelluni, Kusquqviim unarciaranek epukautnek, pitegcautekaitnek nunulirciqniluki. Tua-i ilangcivkenaku tuqutelliniluku.

Tauna-am pilliniuq tua-i tuqutenritqaasqelluni, umikamek, umikaatnek nunulirciqniluki. Patkaryaaqellrem umikaanek, anguyagnun atulaq'ngaminek, tuqutenrilkatni taumek nunulirciqniluki. Ilangcivkenaku-am tua-i taumun ayagyuanemegnun tuqucetliniluku.

Taukuk tua-i kinguagni nengllilangluni, nukalpiak taukuk tuqullrak [kinguagni], kiituan tua-i cikuviqurrlunglliniuq. Tuaten elliqerluku tumkaircameng qayateng tua-i unilluki atmaga'arluteng ayalliniluteng. Qayateng tua-i cakaarluki. Tamaani tua-i kuignun piaqameng uayarluteng cikurrlungqengraata kuimelangluki. Tauna tan'gaurluq iliik qialanglliniuq ancurturluni kumlangellrani meq.

Caqerluku Apanuugpiim tuaten kuimqaqatallermeggni qiallrani qatgutlinia, qanlerulluku ca pitekluk qialaucianek. Wall'u-gguq-qaa imna anguyiim tuqutellra pitekluku qialartuq. Taqliniuq tua-i qianermek tua-i, qianqigtevkenani. Ciungagni-llu uayarluni ciku navgurluku mermun ek'langluni. Qianqigtevkenani.

Tuaten tua-i elliqerluku Eqtarmiunun atam tekitellinilriit. Yit'evkenani-am tua-i yaatiitgun tangvagluki ununercilliniluteng. Unuan taugaam tua-i elkarcata nutaan iluvarvikliniluki.

Cenirtaallinilriit tua-i. Apanuugpak-llu tauna pivakarluni enemun iterluni amiigakun kalvagyarakun puggliniuq, iqsulirnermi-gguq arnaq kiugna inangqalria mikelngurmek caniqlirluni. Una-wa uatiigni kelutmun caumaluni angun qavalria cali.

at night. And sometimes when they could easily get into the caches they'd get food from them when their food supply was low. That's what [those three warriors] apparently did.

Also, one day they ran into another warrior. He, too, tried to escape, but they ran after him and captured him. When they took him they discovered that he was wearing a parka made out of two caribou skins referred to as *qaliluuk*. That kind of parka was also called *qutnguk* here in this area.

They asked him who he was, but he wasn't willing to give up his name. Oh, I just remembered this. When they asked their first captive about his name, he begged for his life and told them that if they spared him he'd give them driftwood from the Kuskokwim River that they could make into arrows for their bows. They ignored his plea and killed him.

That second enemy captive told them not to kill him and said that he'd give them *umikaq* [hard stone used to make weapons] that they could use for their arrow points. He told them that if they didn't kill him he'd award them *umikaq* from Patkaryaaqelleq Mountain that he used to make tips for arrows for warfare. They just ignored his plea and had their young companion kill him.

After they killed those two warriors, it started to get cold, and eventually the water started to freeze. Just as it got cold and they no longer had a way to travel in water, they left their kayaks and continued on foot, packing their things on their backs. They just abandoned their kayaks and left. As they went and came upon rivers, they would remove their clothing and swim across, although there were chunks of ice. That boy, their companion, soon would start crying before going into the water because the water was freezing cold.

One day, when they were about to swim across a river and he began to cry, Apanuugpak yelled at him and asked him why he cried before going into the water. And he said that perhaps he cried because he had killed an enemy warrior. He stopped crying and never cried again. And after that, when they got to a river, he would undress before them, break the ice, and get in the water before they did. He never cried again after that.

Right after the boy changed his behavior they arrived at Eqtarmiut. They didn't go right into the village but watched from the periphery and waited for nightfall. When it became dark and residents retired for the night, they went into the village.

[Once inside the village] they began walking around checking it out. Then after a while Apanuugpak went into one of the houses, and when he stood up halfway through the entrance hole and took a look inside the room, he saw a woman lying

Kiugkut-wa-gguq camani taum arnam kiatiini, aglum iquanun qerringaluteng uyamiit. Perusngaluteng-gguq ugaan amllerem uyamiit.

Apanuugpiim atam taum umyugaan cucullinikai taukut uyamiit teguqeryugyaaq-
luki, tegucugyaaqluni ilaitnek. Tua-i qavarngalata ukut nugqata'arturluni amigkun
piqanrakun, atam mikelnguq tauna qalrillallinilria. Qalrilliin tua-i murugartelli-
niluni amigmun. Tua-i aaniin taum kia-i piluku tua-i nepairluni. Tua-i qavaner-
cirluku. Qavarngariagnek-am tua-i tuamtellu itqataralliniluni nugluni. Tua-i-am
piiyaaqelriami, qalrillalliniluni-am tua-i akngirrnganani camek. Tua-i piagnek mu-
rugartelliniluni-am ataam.

Piiyaaqaqan tua-i tuatnaaqluku. Tua-i-gguq umyuartequq taumun arnamun el-
pekellruyukluni, tauna mikelnguq-llu pupsugluku qalrillagcetlaryukluku alqunaq
qalrillalaan. Taringelliniluku-am tua-i Apanuugpakayiim.

Piviirtelluku-am taum atii tauna nepelkitlinilria, "Amuum qianrilu Apanuugpiim piciqaataan." Niitelluku amigmi. Arenqiatelliniata tua-i anlliniluni, tegusngai-
telliniami.

Tua-i tuani cenirtaarluteng tua-i pillermeggni tanqigiyartunga'arcan quy'uqerrluteng pilliniut iiryugluteng amci, tupakatarniluki. Tauna tua-i ayagyuartaak tan'gaurluq tauna qikucilliqamun nunamun elaumalriamun can'get cikvausngakiitnun
iilliniuq iluanun, cururkaminek tua-i piirraarluni, can'get-llu makut aqevlerrluki
capkucirluku. Ciqiciviulalliniluni-gguq.

Tauna-llu tua-i Pangalgalria qungum acianun qertelliniluni. Tauna-ll' tua-i Apa-
nuugpagtaak pikaircami, tua-i pikaituryaaqerraarluni piqalliniuq nunat iquatni
kiani egelrun qaugna palurngalria, canoe. Ullagluku tua-i acianun itliniluni. Tua-i
aciani uitauralliniluni.
    Atam tua-i erneq qaillun elliqerluku, tauna qikucillermi aqumgauralria tan'gaur-
luq, piinanermini kuvvlinilria pakmaken tua-i ca neqalleq man'a. Tua-i pekcillag-
pek'nani uitalliniluni. [engel'artuq] Cali-gguq tauna cali tangerrsuksaaquq taumun

down on the left side with a little child next to her. And at the end of their sleeping area toward the front of the room a man was sleeping. He looked around and saw necklaces tucked in at the edge of the beam above where the woman was lying. There were many necklaces all folded up and tucked away.

Apanuugpak looked at the necklaces and wished to take one. Since everyone appeared to be sleeping and just as he started to slowly creep up through the hole to enter, the child next to the woman suddenly started crying. Since it cried out, he quickly ducked back inside the entrance hole. The mother consoled it and the baby stopped crying. Then he waited for the two to go back to sleep. After he waited and the two sounded like they had fallen back to sleep, he again started to slowly come up to enter through the hole. And just as he did that, the baby burst out crying again and sounded as if he was hurt by something. Since the two were suddenly awake again, he quickly dropped back in the hole.

He tried to enter several times, but every time he started to sneak in, [the baby would burst out crying]. He began to wonder if the woman had detected his presence, and he suspected that she was the one who pinched the baby every time he started to come in and made him cry out in pain. Clever Apanuugpak eventually understood that she was doing that.

After several attempts, the baby's father finally made a sound and said, "You over there, don't cry, Apanuugpak will get you." He said that with Apanuugpak hearing every word. Apanuugpak, realizing that the occupants of the house were definitely going to make it impossible for him to get [a necklace], went out without taking one.

While they continued to check out the village, and it started to get light out, they quickly got together and alerted each other that people were about to wake up, and they decided to find a hiding place. The young boy found a hole in the ground covered by some grass and hid in it. He got loose grass to sit on and pulled the grass around the hole to conceal his body. It apparently was a hole where human waste was dumped.

And Pangalgalria squeezed himself underneath a burial and hid. And after the great Apanuugpak looked around and couldn't find a place to hide, he saw a canoe sitting upside down on land at the upper edge of the village. He hid underneath the canoe and stayed there.

And just as it reached a certain time of day, while the boy was sitting in the hole, something that looked like old, leftover food was dumped from up above. He didn't move his body at all and sat very still. [*laughter*] The boy thought the girl had seen

arnamun. Tua-i pivkenani tauna iptelliniluni. Kaagataakiiryaaqelliniuq tua-i qan-
qan uitasngailatni. Ca igvanritliniuq.

Atam tauna Apanuugpak uitainanrani cungiquralriartangllinilria amna cani-
melliinarluni. Maaten-gguq tang pia tan'gaurluq tauna cungiquralria mikelnguq,
atani-llu, atiin taum qaruqurluku, "Kitnguciquten, anguaryaqunak. Kitngukuvet
wani qecuqiciiquten." Cungiqurluni anguaryugluni-gguq pillinillria. Aren tekitelli-
nikiik atam tua-i. Palungqalriim aciani uitaluni Apanuugpak.

Atam piuraqerluku, aciakun, qerrluakun unatet augkut tegullinikiit mengliikun,
makteqatarluku tauna *canoe*-q tamana. Kegguranga'artelliniuq, "Keggu! Pisciigat-
linilria-w' man'a. Pisciigatliniuq. Maktesciigatliniuq." Tua-i allamek piiyaaqaqan
tua-i tuaten piaqluku, maktessaaguarluku. Tua-i canrilngurmek unitelliniak.

Tua-i unicagni uitalliniluni. Tan'gerian tua-i anlliniluteng. Quyurcameng tua-i
nutaan tan'gerian qayait yuvrilliniluki, asirnerit waten tan'germi ellaigaarturluki
callmangqerrnayukluki. Usgunrit-llu makut ukut yuvrirturluki. Assirngalngurnek
tua-i piluteng qayarkameggnek, tamana kuigat cikuilan, cikurrlugnek ping'ermi.
Tua-i naangameng taquarkameggnek tuamtell' elliviitnek aglugluteng neqautait-
nek.

Taquarkameggnek quyurtelliniluteng, uqunek tuaten uquutaitnek. Nuuqairullu-
teng tua-i. Qaqiucameng tua-i qaugyaullinian tamana aciat, taperrnam ngelii, ketiit,
Apanuugpiim Pangalgalria pillinia, amlliniqaasqelluku-am, cauciitessiyaakatarnilu-
teng. Aqvaqullrikun-gguq elitaqtuat Pangalgalria anguyiit. Amllinri-gguq tekisngas-
taitut yugmek maani tua-i, aqvaqulallra, amllinri, uqilalriim taum Pangalgalriim.
Ciuliakucukarput-gguq wangkuta tauna Pangalgalria.

Amllinilliniluni-am aqvaqulliniuq qaugyakun. Tua-i tuatnarraartelluku nutaan
ayalliniut anguarluteng. Errluni tua-i. Ercan pilliniut tauna tang'aurlurtaak qayamek nutaqapiarmek tua-i, enertuumarmi-ll', nutaqapiarmek qayamek pillinilria, taq-
nerra'amek. Tauna-llu-gguq Pangalgalria amiqegcilriamek cali amii nutarauluteng,

him, too, at that moment, but she didn't do anything and disappeared. He waited anxiously because he knew that residents there would definitely come and take him as soon as she said she saw him. He waited, but no one came.

Now, as Apanuugpak was lying there, he heard a voice of someone who sounded upset about something, and the sound was getting louder and closer each time. Then he recognized the voice as that of a boy. He was with his father, who kept trying to console him saying, "Don't paddle. You might capsize if you do. When your canoe rolls over, you'll drown." He apparently was whining because he wanted to paddle. Then the two arrived at the place where Apanuugpak was hidden underneath the canoe.

Then, after a moment, Apanuugpak saw hands appear along the side of the canoe, gripping it to turn it over. Then the man out there surprisingly started suggesting that the canoe was too heavy to lift and said, "Keggu [Whoa]! This canoe evidently is too heavy to move. It can't be lifted. It can't be turned over." [When the child whined again] he would attempt to lift it again and again and kept saying that he couldn't turn it over, [and Apanuugpak knew that he was faking]. Eventually, the two left.

After the two left, he remained hidden there. When it got dark they all came out of their hiding places. After they got together they checked the kayaks that belonged to the village men. In the dark they'd rub the kayak bottoms with their hands, checking to see if they were patched up. And they checked out all their stitched seams. Then they each picked a kayak to take to continue on, since the river there was partially frozen but still open. After the kayaks were picked out and each had one to travel in, they started checking the caches to get food for their provisions.

They gathered enough food for their provisions, and they even took seal oil. They took enough food so they wouldn't run out. When they were done getting food, since the beach below the village, below the line of coarse seashore grass growing along the riverbank, was all sand, Apanuugpak told Pangalgalria to walk on the sand and leave footprints as evidence because the residents there would have no idea who had come and taken things from their village. They say that enemy warriors had always been able to recognize footprints left by Pangalgalria. And it was known that no other person could run as fast as Pangalgalria and leave footprints that distance apart. I've heard that Pangalgalria was part of my family lineage.

[Pangalgalria] ran on the sand and left his footprints there. Then after he ran they left paddling in kayaks. The sun rose and daylight came. In the daylight they saw that the boy had picked a newly completed kayak with a new frame and skin covering. And the kayak Pangalgalria was riding had a brand new skin covering, but

enra taugaam qangvallauluni. Tauna-gguq taugken Apanuugpak imumek kukupa-
nga'artellriamek, ak'allaurteqatalriamek qayamek tamatumek pilliniluni.

Tamaani tua-i nutaan ayiita, tuani taukut tupiimeng qanlliniut Pangalgalria-
gguq-am tekitellrulliniuq unuk maa-i. Tumai-gguq-am unkut una-i. Tua-i tuani
yugmek pinqigtevkenateng. Agaani tua-i Kuinerrarmiut natiitni tumkairucameng
nutaan qayateng unitelliniit, uksuucateng tua-i. Qinarmiut tua-i neryuniungellinil-
riit tekitellerkaatnek, kiituan tua-i Kusquqvak asvailliniuq.

Atam tua-i caqerluteng unuakumi-am payugqaqluteng nerellrata kinguani iliit
kaakaalliniuq, "Kaaka. Atam niicugniqerci." Qalarqurallrat nepairtelliniuq anerquciaralria qakemna. Pilliniat Apanuugpiim erinaklinikii. Tua-i qaugna egkuq ing-
lerkai carrilaalliniluku. Tekitaqata-gguq qavavet pivkatuit curullret. Yuarutkun-llu-
gguq qanemcituluteng, anqara'arluteng-gguq. Waten qalarqurluteng pivkenateng,
aturluteng taugaam yuarutnek, qanemciluteng. Tuaten-gguq qanemcitullruut anqara'arluteng.

Itliniluteng tua-i. Itraameng-llu tua-i tauna ayagyuaqliq, ayaguaq tauna qukaqliq-
luku aqumellinilutek. Apanuugpak-gguq tallirpilirnermun aqumluni, Pangalgalria-
llu iqsulirnermun. Uitaqertelluki-am angukaraat iliit pilliniuq, "Kitaki atak tua-i
piciryaraqaat, cauyamek cikirluku qanemciurnaurtuq." Nang'errluni iliit cauyamek
tegulluni itraulluku Apanuugpagmun tunyaaqellinia. Apanuugpiim ciuniunrilamiu
qanlliniuq taugaam, ellii camek pikaitniluni. Tuaten tua-i pian, taumun Pangalgal-
riamun tuamtell' tunyaaqelliniluku. Cali-am tua-i Apanuugpagtun kiulliniluku,
ellii-ll' tua-i waniw' camek pikaitniluni. Una taugaam tan'gaurlurluq piyugngayaaq-
niluku.

Tauna tua-i tan'gaurluq cauyamek piani tegullinia taum tang'aurluum. Elitnaull-
ruyukluku-w' tua-i pilliniat, tua-i elitnaullrulliniaku tamatumek anqarautmek. Nii-
telalliksi tua-i anqaraun aturaqatgu.

Aa-ang'aa,
Yi-iya-aa
Agi-ii-iya Yii-ii-aa-ang'a
Kia un'a atuulliu, yii-ii

its frame was several years old. But Apanuugpak had taken a kayak that had started to form spots on its skin covering and was almost too old to use.

When they left the village, when people in that village got up, they said that Pangalgalria apparently had been there during the night. They said that his footprints were visible on the sand on the beach down there. The three continued on and never bothered anyone along the way. And when they reached the area near Quinhagak across there they finally abandoned their kayaks, for it was well into winter by then and rivers and lakes were all frozen. During that time people in Qinaq were starting to get hopeful and expected them to arrive home, and soon the Kuskokwim River was frozen and thick enough to travel on.

Then one morning after women had delivered food to the men in the *qasgi* and it had been consumed, one of the men alerted the others, "Listen. Stop and listen." When it got quiet they heard someone out there singing, *anerquciaralria* [making a boasting call]. They listened and recognized Apanuugpak's voice. They quickly cleared the area near the back wall of the *qasgi* to make a place for him. They said that when warriors came home from fighting they normally fixed a place for them near the back wall. And it was through songs that they would tell about what happened out there, *anqara'arluteng* as they called it. They didn't report by speaking, but sang and recounted their experience while fighting, *anqara'arluteng*.

The three entered the *qasgi*. And when they got to the back of the room the two older men sat with the young one between them. Apanuugpak sat on the right side and Pangalgalria on the left. Moments after they sat down one of the elderly men said, "Now, as customarily done, give him a drum so that he can tell a story." A person from the side quickly got up and got a drum and walked up to Apanuugpak and handed it to him, but he didn't take it. Apanuugpak said that he had nothing to tell. When he said that, they tried giving the drum to Pangalgalria, but he didn't accept it. He said that he had nothing to tell either and added that the young man possibly could recount something memorable that happened out there.

When the drum was handed to the young man he took it. [After he sang the song] people there knew that he had already composed the song, referred to as *anqaraun*, and had learned how to sing it [before coming home]. You probably have heard this particular *anqaraun* before, sung by drummers for a dance group.

Aa-ang'aa,
Yi-iya-aa
Agi-ii-iya Yii-ii-aa-ang'a
Let someone sing for that one down there

Aa-ang'aa
Yi-iya-aa
Agi-ii-iya Yii-ii-aa-ang'a
Kia un'a atuulliu, yii-ii

[Ciuqliq apallua:]

Nani-mi-lli iluteqa'arcia,
Tunuirutkun kuimaqatanemni
Kia un'a atuulliu, yii
Aa-nga, qiaurlurtua,
Yii-ii-ii-ngi-rra-gia-rri-yaa
Kia un'a atuulliu, yii-ii

Amci-llu nunakiqerlua
Aqlillugpalek paiqatemni
Kia un'a atuulliu, yii-ii

Epukarpenek nunulirciqamken
Kuskquqviim unarcianek
Anguyagnun atulaq'ngamnek
Kia un'a atuulliu, yii-ii

Aa-ang'aa
Yi-iya-aa
Agi-iya-aa Yii-ii-aa-ang'a
Kia un'a atuulliu, yii-ii

[Kinguqliq apallua:]

Nani-mi-lli Iluteqa'arcia
Iiyuussiikun Kuimaqatanemni
Kia un'a atuulliu, yii-ii

Aang'a, qiaurlurtua
Yii-ii-ingi-rra-gia-rra
Kia un'a atuulliu, yii-ii

Amci-llu nunakiqerlua
Qalilukvalegmek paiqatemni
Kia un'a atuulliu, yii-ii

Aa-ang'aa
Yi-iya-aa
Agi-ii-iya Yii-ii-aa-ang'a
Let someone sing for that one down there

[First verse:]

Somewhere, I got choked up with tears
When I was about to swim across Tunuirun
Let someone sing for that one down there
Pitiful me, I'm crying
Yii-ii-ii-ngi-rra-gia-rri-yaa
Let someone sing for that one down there

Alas, I got happy and joyful
When I was about to meet Aqlillugpalek
Let someone sing for that one down there

I will pay you with material for your arrows
Straight-grained wood from the Kuskokwim River
The kind I use to make arrows for warfare
Let someone sing for that one down there

Aa-ang'aa
Yi-iya-aa
Agi-iya-aa Yii-ii-aa-ang'a
Let someone sing for that one down there

[Second verse:]

Somewhere, I suddenly got choked up with tears
Just as I was about to swim across Iiyuussiiq River
Let someone sing for that one down there

Poor me, I am crying
Yii-ii-ingi-rra-gia-rra
Let someone sing for that one down there

Alas, I got happy and joyful
Just as I was about to meet one with a large caribou parka
Let someone sing for that one down there

Umikarpenek nunulirciqamken
Patkaryaaqellrem ulukartaanek
Anguyagnun atulaq'ngamnek
Kia un'a atuulliu, yii-ii

Aa-ang'aa
Yi-iya-aa
Agi-iya-aa Yii-ii-aa-ang'a
Kia un'a atuulliu, yii-ii

Waten tua-i ayuqluku niitela'arqa kiaken Qinarmek.
Tauna pingayuuluteng unitlinruluni Apanuugpiim curullra.

Tuntutuliarmiuqapiaraunrituq. Qaluyaarmiunguuq. Engel'umiuni-gguq yuur-
tellruuq, Tuqsugmiut ualirneratni cakmani. Tua-i taugaam *move*-arluni kiavet Tun-
tutuliarmun Qinarmiungurrluni tamaani. Aipangami-ll' pillilria tayima, nulirtuami
tuavet pillilria. Anguyagcuutekaq-gguq cunaw'.

Yuurcartullra call' tamana, mik'naku anguyiit cali egtellermeggni tan'gaurluut ilakluki yaani egcaaqelliniluku mermun, imarpigmun atertesqelluku. Aaniin-gguq-am
taum atkulillrua qalluvayagaagnek tuntut iruitnek, imkulirluku qalluvalirluku atkuliluku. Cunawa-gguq anirtuutarkainek. Tamaani mik'nani piiyuayaurteksaunani-ll'
Apanuugpak.

Taum tua-i aaniin ukatmurutellrullinia tamaaken, keggaken Qaluyaanek. Ayiita
tua-i yuaraluku nalkellinia aaniin taum. Taperrnat-gguq unaksuaramikun tegu-
miaqurayaallinikai, aterceteksaunani. Pugtalluku taukuk qalluviigken. Tua-i cavkenani tua-i. Anguyiit-gguq cunaw' alikarkaat. Erinalkiskan tua-i kiimelengraan
pingaunaku. Elitaqkunegteggu-ll' pingaunaku kiingan tuqusngailamegteggu. Cas-
kutayuituq-gguq. Caskum ityuunaku tua-i temii. Caangrayauluni.

Taumek tua-i tuaten ayuqelliniuq tua-i Apanuugpak. Taukut-llu curullret—
Cam nalliini piat ukut ilakelriit. Tauna Ukinqucugpalek yaani Ilkiviim paingani
nunangqerrluni uitallrulliniuq. Qanerciigalnguq-llu una agaanlluni Kusquviim aki-
lirnerani. Pangalgalria taugken Qinarmiungulluni. Apanuugpak-llu call' Qinarmiu-
nguluni.

I will award you stone for your weapon points
The stone from Patkaryaaqelleq Mountain
The kind I used on my warrior weapons
Let someone sing for that one down there

Aa-ang'aa
Yi-iya-aa
Agi-iya-aa Yii-ii-aa-ang'a
Let someone sing for that one down there

That's how the song was sung upriver in Qinaq.

[That song depicts] what happened when Apanuugpak and the other two were out there fighting.

Apanuugpak wasn't originally from Tuntutuliak. He was actually from Nelson Island. They say he was born in Engel'umiut, way down below Toksook Bay. But he eventually moved up to Tuntutuliak. He became a resident of Qinaq. He probably moved there when he got married. He ultimately would become a great warrior coming from that village.

Also, when he was an infant, when he was a baby, when enemy warriors were killing boys over in Anirnaaq, he also was thrown into the water to float out into the ocean. At that time his mother had sewn caribou leg skins and made coveralls for him. The coverall parka apparently was the one that would save his life later on. Apanuugpak was a baby at that time and hadn't started to walk yet.

His mother eventually took him and moved over toward this [lower coastal] area from Nelson Island. When the enemy warriors left, his mother searched and found him. With his small hands, the little one had held on to some coarse seashore grass along the river and hadn't floated away. The coveralls he was wearing allowed him to stay buoyant. He was alive. Later on in life, he apparently was the one enemy warriors feared. Whenever enemy warriors heard his voice, they would leave him alone, even though he was by himself out there. Though they recognized who he was, they wouldn't go after him because they knew they couldn't kill him. It was said that weapon points couldn't hurt him. When hit by weapon points, they couldn't penetrate his body. He was known to be an extraordinary human being.

That was the character of Apanuugpak. And also the warriors who had gone to attack other warriors — I don't know what time of year this was. They were a group of warriors who were all related. That person named Ukinqucugpalek lived at a place at the mouth of Ilkivik River. And a man named Qanerciigalnguq lived at a place on the other side along the Kuskokwim River. Pangalgalria, however, lived in Qinaq. And Apanuugpak was from Qinaq as well.

Taukuuluteng tua-i pilliut, Apanuugpak, Pangalgalria, Qanerciigalnguq, Ukinqucugpalek, Quarruucuar, una-imat'am kitumek arivtelallrukiit arvinrat. Arvinelngu-
luteng waten ayallrulliniut agaatmun-am cali, Iilgayaam tungiinun. Tauna Quarruucuar ayagyuarluni, nulirtuqsaunani-ll', Quarruucuarmek at'lek.

Agaani tua-i avani piinanermeggni; taukut Eqtarmiut nani uitallruat, nateqvani
uitallruat.
Qayamek taumek piameng maligcaaqekiit, tua-i angungiinarceteksaunani, unis-
ngiinaqsaunaki-llu-gguq. Qacigutekluki tua-i taukut malirqerteni. Atam piuraqerluni tamaani qayagaulanglliniuq amci taqesqelluni, Eqtarmiut negaat canimellini-
luku.

Taqeksaunaku tua-i nukalpiarullinian tauna, anagayuliuyaaqellinian-llu. Cucu-
ketuamegteki-gguq tua-i arcaqerluki imkut *champion*-aaruluteng pitulit callugaqa-
meng. Tamakunek taugaam piiyuumiuterluteng arcaqerluteng.

Arenqianani-gguq taugken tua-i angungiinarceteksaunani-ll', ava'anlluni tua-i.
Unisngiinaqsaunaki-llu elliin. Akulkellilliniuq tua-i amci taqesqelluni maligpiiq-
nani, Eqtarmiut negaatnun naptarkaurrniluki.
Caqerluni tua-i tuatnarraarluki, qanellni nangellra yaaqsigivailgan, qayar-im
qip'artelliniluni tayima. Nunataunani-gguq taugken, nunamek tangerkengaunani.
Ulyugluni-gguq tamana. Augna-ll' ulyunertuami Iilgayaam tunglirnera; man'a car-
vaa tukniatuq *west*-alirneq. Augna taugken carvanra tukniluni.

Tua-i tekiarcamegteggu tua-i tauna akuluraq carvanrem cayugarrluki itqerrutelli-
nikai. Igvaartelliniut nunat pingkut. Kingyaartelliniat ak'a qayat tumellrat quuqerte-
llinikiit, cap'qallinikiit. Imna-w' malirqallrat ava-i nunanun tagelria, anguarluni.

Pugtaqalliniut tua-i quyurmeng nunat ketiitni taukut, qaill' piviinateng tua-i,
naugg'un ayagviinateng tua-i. Qayat-gguq tua-i caniqliqu'urluteng tauna akuluraq
capumakiit. Makut-gguq ilait akultuaqluteng, ukut quyurmeng uitaaqluteng wani,
man'a akuliit akultuaqluni. Tuaten ayuqluteng.

Perhaps in the group there was Apanuugpak, Pangalgalria, Qanerciigalnguq, Ukinqucugpalek, and Quarruucuar. I can't remember what they called the sixth person with them. There were six of them who apparently went across toward Bristol Bay, too. Quarruucuar was a young man at that time and hadn't gotten married yet.

While they roamed across there; I don't know exactly where the village of Eqtarmiut was located.

When they spotted a kayaker they went after him, but he kept going and kept the same distance from them. They couldn't get closer to him, and he never got farther away from them. The kayaker just kept going and didn't seem worried about the enemy following him. Then after a while he began to yell back, asking them to stop pursuing him, saying that they were getting close to the trap set by Eqtarmiut.

They kept chasing him, realizing that the enemy they were pursuing was a *nukalpiaq* and was well trained and could elude them. In battle the warriors usually wanted to go after men who were known as champions. They especially wanted to defeat men who were recognized as great warriors.

That enemy warrior just kept going and kept his distance from his pursuers. He started to warn them more frequently, telling them to stop running after him, that they were getting close to the trap set up by people from Eqtarmiut.

Then one time after he warned them, not long after he asked them to stop, the kayaker suddenly paddled around a point of land and was not seen again. Those behind him didn't even see a village right past that point. The tide was coming in quite rapidly in the river at that time. The waters in the area toward Nushagak River normally come up very fast when the tide rolls in. Over here on the west side [of the Kuskokwim River] the current is not that strong. But the current in the area over there is strong.

When they got to the [narrow] body of water between two larger [bodies of water] the strong current suddenly pulled them in. Once they were inside, they saw a village up there. They turned back to look and saw many kayaks blocking the way they had just come. Then they saw the man they had followed just arriving and paddling up toward the village.

They suddenly found themselves below the village, just sitting in their kayaks afloat not knowing what to do, not knowing which way to go. There were many kayaks all lined up in a row, blocking the section of water between the two larger bodies of water. Some kayaks were sitting farther apart, and some were grouped close together. There were larger gaps of open water between some of these groups. That's how they were situated.

Atam tua-i taum-gguq Qanerciigalnguum Apanuugpak Turruluminek tuqlutua.
Turrulumegnek tuqluutetuuk Qanerciigalnguq-llu. Murilkellinia caqerluni tauna
Apanuugpak taryumek maaken aalemtaaqalangllinilria, qaneni piqerluku. Murilkar-
camiu tua-i qanrutkevkenaku egmianun.

Piinanermeggni-am, tauna ayagyuanrat tauna qanelkican murilkartelliniat imkut pitegcautet umiyagaita navegyailkutaitnek; mermi-gguq-am pugtalriit amlleriluteng tua-i unegkut cingilgita caqullrit, caquirillermeggni. Tamakunek avulria.
Qanraqluni-gguq, "Kingunemteni makut taqesciigatpialartut." Ak'a-gguq tua-i tapraq man' qerrviirutliniluni. Alingenritlinivaa-tam' taumi tan'gaurluungermi Qua-
rruucuarmi. Tuaten tua-i.

Tua-i pivakarluteng-am qanlliniut-am amkut, tangerrluki, "Caninermiurluut
atam tangerqerciki. Piyagayagaat tuar una-i aanameggnek ciuqlirluteng." Arenqiatuq Apanuugpak tua-i tauna ilakaqamegteggu tua-i aanakelriatun ayuqetuat. Ukat-
mun-gguq anguarluni piaqan maliggnauraat. Tuaten-am pillrat pitekluku-am taukut tua-i pillinikait.

Taum atam tua-i kinguani tuaten pillrata, nunanek tuaken erinatangellinilria aner-
quciaralriamek. Cunawa-gguq tauna yuilqumtelleq anguyiurta nutaan tekitellinilria. Qanraqluni-llu-gguq nunani tutmarluku anguyakataucirminek. Piqerluni-am
paangerluni uivellinilria sanrem iluakun. Paangerinanermini-gguq, paangrutegni
waten paiminun tus'arrlukek, irugni nalugarrlukek pagaani kanauyaaraqa'aqluni.
Taukunun tangaavkarluni, kitnguyugnaunani. Kanauyaaraqarraarluni irugni atrarr-
lukek paangerluni ayagaqluni. Akultutaciqerrluni-am tuatnalallinilria tua-i tuani.

Atam tua-i caqerluni-am taum Turruluan Qanerciigalnguum muilkartellra-im'
nall'arrluku, taryumek-am aalemtaaqallinilria Apanuugpak. Nutaan qanrutlinia,
"Turrulu, qaillun pilriaten taryumek maaken neqnialngurmek aalemtaalarcit? Qaillun pisit? Alinguten-qaa?"

Now, it is said that Qanerciigalnguq used a special kinship term to call Apanuug-pak. He called him Turrulu. Actually, he and Qanerciigalnguq addressed each other as Turrulu. So while they sat there, Qanerciigalnguq noticed Apanuugpak quickly dropping his hand in the salt water by his kayak and wetting his mouth with it. When he saw him doing that, he didn't alert him right away.

As they stayed there immobilized, when the youngest warrior said something, they turned to look at him and noticed that he was picking up wooden arrow-point cases floating in the water. The cases the enemy warriors down below had thrown into the water after replacing their arrow points apparently had floated toward them, and there were lots of them. The young boy was saying, "At home they take a long time to make these things." He apparently had picked up quite a few and tucked them under the skin line strapping on the kayak and had no more room. Remarkably, that Quaruucuar apparently wasn't afraid, even though he was a boy. [They just remained there trapped and unable to escape.]

After a while, they heard someone from [the village] over there observing what they were doing and saying, "Look at those poor Caninermiut down there. They look like hatchlings following their mother." Whenever [warriors] were with Apanuugpak [out on the battleground], they looked up to him like he was their mother. When he began paddling in one direction, the others would follow him from behind. Because they were moving in that manner, [people on land] made that comment about them.

After they made that comment, a voice rose from that village from someone bursting out gallant words. Evidentially, it was the voice of the warrior they had followed just arriving in the village. He'd yell out and boast about how he was about to fight the enemy right on his home turf. Soon after that he was back in the water and started paddling around with his double-bladed paddle. While he was pad-dling, periodically he'd place his paddle across the kayak opening, hold it as a brace, kick his legs up, and remain upside down for a while. He kept doing that while [Apanuugpak and his comrades] were watching, and he never tipped his kayak over. After being suspended upside down for a moment, he'd drop his legs down and continue paddling. He'd go a little ways and thrust his legs up and remain up-side down for a while again.

In the meantime, just when his Turrulu Qanerciigalnguq looked at Apanuugpak, he quickly dipped his hand in salt water and dropped some in his mouth. He finally said to him, "Turrulu, why are you drinking this bad tasting salt water? What is going on with you? Are you afraid?"

Apanuugpiim kiullinia, qayuwa-gguq-tang pakem alungutleriin qalirnera kinqer-
naluni mayiteqelria. Pirraartelluku-am Turruluan taum pillinia, "Pillerkangeksai-
tuten-qaa cali?" Apanuugpiim pillinia, "Elpes-kiq tua-i ciuliqageskuvkut naugg'un
tayima anutengnaqsarcikut?" Tamakut atam akultulriit niillinikai taum Turruluan,
Qanerciigalnguum. "Ciuliqageskumci-w' tua-i wii makutgun maa-i anutengnaqsa-
qemci, calriatgun akultulriatgun tamakutgun." Apanuugpiim pillinia, makut-gguq-
tang maa-i niillri cacetulriarulriit, alingararanrilnguut. Makut-gguq taugken maa-i
quyuryulriit caceskilnguut, alingtalriit. Makutgun-gguq maa-i ellii pivigkangyaa-
quq. Kitaki-gguq waniwa tangvagluni tua-i pisqelluni. Paangrutegni tegukunikek
erinani anciiqniluku nuugek waten mermun akurtaarturlukek. Ayaksaileng'ermi
elliuquni, ellait-llu tuaten pisqelluki, ceqvallertaartelluku anerquciarallmi taktaciatun. Iqukliskan-gguq taugaam nutaan kanevtaarlukek ayagciquq, anerquciaracini
iqukliskan.

Tuatnaqertelluki, tauna-am anerquciaratuli-am erinalkitliniuq. Tua-i-am uivelli-
niuq maa-i kanauyaaraqerluni, anqerrluni kanauyaaraqluni. Natmun atam tua-i
elliqerluni anqerpiirluni paluartellinilria. Yura'arcami tua-i irugni ingkuk ceqvaller-
taartellukek waten nunat tungiitnun tagngartelliniluni.

Aren kituriyaaqelliniunga. Tuatnavailegmi-imat'anem taum nukalpiam caqerluni qanlerutellinikii piaken, tauna Ukinqucugpalek. Ilkivigmiu tauna ingkut nunallret nayurtellrat. Yaa-i cali nunallri uitaut, tangruuluteng cali. Anguyiim nalliini
nunallri Ukinqucugpalgem.

Tauna-am pamaa-i qayagpagaluni-am qanlerutaa, "Caluni-llu kan'a ukinqucuk
waten angtalarta? Allamiaquan tangercetaarpakalalria! Arnam-qaa terpaguaqela-
raa?" [engel'artuq]

Tua-i pikestii-gguq tauna uitaniartuq. Ukinqucuminek uumek cangakuarrluni.
Piaviallinia, "Nukalpiaurluuq pingsuuq, ukinqucullerqa atag-una tangrraqavgu cu-
mutekluku tangvalarru. Amirkaicunritaqami tang taugaam waten angtatulria."

Amugarutelliniuq atkugnek imkunek uyalegnek, tungulrianek imkunek imarpigmiutarnek atkugnek. "Nukalpiaurluuq kacuuq, nukalpiaruaqavet atam taugaam
nulian makunek atkuliraqiu." Ukinqucugpaglek-am tauna qayami-am ciunganun
tallini pirraarluku amugarucami nalugarutelliniuq qavcicuarmek atkugmek. Piavia-

Apanuugpak replied that this time for some reason the surface of his tongue was trying to dry up. Then after he said that, his Turrulu said, "Haven't you figured out a way to escape yet?" Apanuugpak replied, "If you were leading us, I wonder which way you would try to take us out?" Then his Turrulu Qanerciigalnguq pointed at the warriors who were dispersed. Then he said, "If I were leading you I would take you out through these that are lined up a good distance from one another." Apanuugpak told Qanerciigalnguq that the ones he pointed to were warriors that were not afraid. And he said that the ones sticking close together were easily frightened. And he said that it was through them that he might be able to lead them out and escape. He told his comrades to watch what he was doing. He told them that he would let out his voice when he took his paddle and began paddling, with only the tip of the blades touching the water. Even though he wasn't moving, while he yelled out his gallant words, he told them to pretend to paddle like him, letting the water splash as they hit the surface with their blades. He told them as soon as he stopped yelling, he would dip his blades into the water and take off paddling.

Just as they finished their planning, they heard the voice of the warrior who yelled out words of gallantry again. He resumed circling around with his body suspended upside down above his kayak. As he was going around, his kayak tipped over just as he thrust his legs up in the air. And as soon as he popped up in the water, he started swimming toward the village.

Oh, I just remembered the part of the story I left out. Before he fell into the water, that *nukalpiaq* had yelled at Ukinqucugpalek from his location somewhere back there. He yelled at the man who once resided in that old site over there in Ilkivik. The old site where he lived is still over there and can be seen. The place where Ukinqucugpalek lived during the time of warfare.

That man berated him from somewhere back there and exclaimed, "Why the heck does that kayak tote hole down there always appear the same size? How ghastly it looks, allowing itself to be seen every year! Is it supposed to represent a woman's large anus?" [*laughter*]

That [Ukinqucugpalek] didn't sit back and fail to respond to the taunt. He yelled back at the man back there and blurted out, "You poor *nukalpiaq* back there, when you look at my repulsive tote hole, view it with apprehension. You see, it appears this size to you when there are plenty of skins on hand."

[Then the man back there] suddenly pulled out [from his kayak] a cormorant parka, made of those black ocean birds, and yelled, "You poor *nukalpiaq* down there, when you exercise your skills as a great hunter, provide your wife with this kind of skin for her parka." Ukinqucugpalek, after sticking his hand in the front of his

Ilinia-am, "Nukalpiaurluuq pingyuuq, nukalpiaruaqavet atam taugaam makunek nulian atkuliraqiu, niss'uyagarnek atkulirpek'naku."

Itqertelliniluni-am enemun tayima tauna keluqlia. Tayimnguuraqerluni-am anqertelliniuq atkugmek tegumiarluni. Nalugartellinia keglunret atkuut. Taumi-lli-tanem Ukinqucugpalegmi atkugmek atauciunrilngurmek ayautellivaa! Qayami-am ciunganek piuraqerluni amugarucami nalugarutelliniuq imarmiutarmek atkugmek. "Nukalpiaurluuq pingyuuq, nukalpiaruaqavet atam taugaam makunek nulian atkiraqiu, qimugtenek atkirpek'naku." Tua-i aciqliusciiganani tauna Ukinqucugpalek. Ingna-am itqertenritliniuq enemun.

Taum tua-i kinguani, nutaan Apanuugpiim una pillerkani aperturyaaqellinia. Tauna nutaan anerquciarluni uivluni, pivakarluni tua-i kitnguluni. Tuaten tua-i ceqvallerrluni kuimluni tagellrani, tauna-am cangakuullra Ukinqucugpalek qayaminek maaken nagiiquyamek ancilliniuq, cirunqatagmek una kangia nemerluni makucinek, waten makunek kevraarcinrarnek nemerluni. Cului-wa-gguq qucillginraat. Taqevlacaumaluni nagiiquyaq tamana. Nuqani tua-i piqerluku cingilirpek'naku-ll' pagg'un narulkallinillria. Nagiiquyaq pagg'un ayallinillria, kucurcarturluni tua-i. Ceqvallertellran taum tua-i ciungaraanun tuc'an, ceqvallertellra im' taq'ertellinilria. Alailkitliniluni. Piuraqerluni-ll' kit'elliniluni tayima. Tarenriryaraanun-gguq cunawa tut'ellinilria tauna nagiiquyaq, qat'gaikun-llu anluni. Kill'uni tua-i.

Aarangaartelliniuq pamna pamaken tua-i arnauluni. Engel'allagaqluni-gguq tua-i. Pillinia taum arnaq tauna qaugyam qainganun taklarrluni piani aaraluni akaguaraluni tua-i. Cunawa-gguq aanii. Taukunun allanemeggnun ilaksukluku piiyaaqellinikii.

Tua-i nutaan taum kinguani augna Apanuugpak pilliniuq, aug'umek pillerkangllerminek. Nutaan alerqualuki ilani taukut anerquciarakuni tua-i tuaten akurtaarturlukek nuukek taugaam paangrutegmi piciqnilukek. Iqukliskuni nutaan kalevtaarlukek ayagciqniluni.

Erinalkican tua-i pamaken-am qanelkitliniuq, "Apanuugpagmek-atat'ang ilangqellinilriit. Anirtima-tanem waten amllertang'ermeng pamallaganripakartut." Cauyartullinikai atam taukut quyurngalriit, tuaten paangrutegmi nuukek pinguarturlukek. Atam cauyartuateng uitanriqertellinilriit taukut. Tauna tua-i anerquciaratii iqukli-can nutaan tangviimegteggu tua-i kinguqliin taukut ayuqeliluku nutaan tua-i paangelliniluteng. Kitngualuteng-gguq tuaten ingkut puukaqulluteng. Anqercameng

kayak, pulled out and held up a parka made of marten skins. He yelled back at the man, "You poor *nukalpiaq* back there, when you demonstrate your skills, supply your wife with this kind of skin for her parka and not one made of little feathers."

Then the one back up on land ran inside a house. After a short while he ran out holding a parka. He hoisted up a wolf parka. That Ukinqucugpalek surprisingly had [taken] more then one parka [with him on his journey]. He stuck his hand back inside the front of his kayak and lifted up a mink parka and yelled, "You poor *nukalpiaq* back there, when you employ your hunting skills, make sure your wife is provided with skins like these for her parka, not a parka made out of dog skins!" Ukinqucugpalek kept outdoing his opponent and was unbeatable. The person back there remained outside and didn't run into the house [to get another parka].

It was after that [contest] that Apanuugpak told his companions what he planned to do. Then after that the enemy warrior went around in a circle boasting and finally capsized his kayak. And when he swam toward shore splashing water, Ukinqucugpalek took out a *nagiiquyaq* [seal-hunting spear] from inside his kayak, with the bottom of the shaft made out of antler and bound with spruce roots. And its flight-stabilizing feathers were made of crane feathers. The spear was crudely made. Then he grabbed his throwing board and shot the spear up in the air without even putting a spearpoint on it. The spear flew forward up in the air. When the spear landed in the water just ahead of the splashing water, it suddenly got still. And in a moment they saw something sink in the water. The spear apparently hit the man between his shoulder blades and pierced his chest. The man sank in the water and drowned.

Then suddenly they heard a woman's voice hollering back on land. She was yelling and would burst out laughing. [Ukinqucugpalek] looked and saw a woman lying down on the sand hollering and rolling around. Evidently, she was the [drowned man's] mother. She apparently thought that the man who fell in was one of the enemy warriors.

Apanuugpak made up his mind and told his partners his plan after that. He told them that while he made his boasting call he would only dip the tips of his paddle blades on the water's surface. He told them that when the call was over he'd actually dip his blade down deeper and take off.

When he finally let his voice out, someone back on land said, "Apanuugpak obviously is among that group down there. No wonder they are hesitant to take immediate action, although they are few in number." He then began to turn his kayak, facing the ones who were gathered close together, and he dipped his blade tips in the water and pretended to paddle. As he began to turn his kayak toward them, they quickly got nervous and started to move around. As soon as he finished his

tua-i unavet, carvanrem itercanrillran elatiinun elliircameng, arulairtelliniluni-am Apanuugpak. Arulaircami pilliniuq, "Naam' im' Quarruucuar?" Taisqelluku. Taingan pillinia, "Kitak ciunemteggun maaggun egqaqussaarluten nagiiquyan egpaciyagaqluku egqaqussaarluten ciuliqageskut." Ayalliniluteng tua-i Quarruucuarmek ciuliqagterluteng, egqaqussaarturtelluku. Tuaten-am taktaluku cali niitetuaqa atullra taum Apanuugpiim, Ukinqucugpalgenkuk-llu taukuk arivutellrak.

Tauna-gguq yaani ukinqucua angellruuq. Maklassugmek-gguq amitullrua, makliim taum mikleracuariinek amikayiim. Taumek-gguq yaani nunamini muirumaaqan kuini un'a, man'a tua-i pillerkaa nuringaurluku, kuimikun cetuaqami anguarluni, ukinqucuan suggii kiimi alaitetulria. Angualria yua ipingaluni nunamun tayima, tauna taugaam ukinqucua pugumaluni, unaggun cegg'uqu'urluni. Tua-i-gguq pitgutaqameng anguyameggnek ingluluteng, ukinqucuni tauna caunqegcarluku, irialuni waten pitegcautet avilqaquvkatui avitaarluni. Qayani waten elliurtelluku, ukinqucuanun kalguurtelluki cingilget. Avitaarcuutekellrua-gguq tauna ukinqucullerani.

Tauna-gguq tuamtell' Quarruucuar imuuluni cingilgircaristengurrluni angliriami. Anqertaqami-gguq, ayaruq, waten kangrani, 'llumarralleq-gguq anuqem arulataqekii, qanugpaguangraan cingilegnek, pitegcautnek, agturcecuunani. Ayarumi kangrani, tegumiaqluku avitarluki pitegcautet. Tamaani tuaten ellillrulliniuq tua-i Quarruucuar. Taumek-gguq tamaani angukaraurtellermini tuani, iluriin-am piiyaaqellrani pillrullinikii, ukanirpak waniwa cingilegmun ulumikallrunritniluni.

Imumi taugaam akerciryailkukarani engelkegguksuaqsagutellermini, kiingan tua-i tauna piyagutekniluku. Muraggarnek imkunek elqiangqetullruut epurralegnek. Tauna Quarruucuar-am callugpallagluni caqerluni nani, taq'ercameng pilliniat, elqiar-im' tayima, man'a taugaam murakuineq maani engelkeggutnguluni. Cingilgetgguq waten agtuq'aquurallrat nangllinikiit. Tauna tua-i Quarruucuar Qinarmiungluni call' tua-i pilliuq. Tuaten qanemciulartut taukut arivutellret.

boasting call and took off using his double-bladed paddle, his companions followed from behind. The group of enemy warriors up ahead got into a frenzy and began to splash and scramble about in their kayaks, bumping and capsizing each other. When Apanuugpak and his companions made it through the trap and reached the still water down there, he suddenly came to a halt. As soon as he stopped he said, "Where is Quarruucuar?" He told him to come. When he came he said, "Now, go in front of us and practice throwing your spear." They started going away with Quarruucuar in front of them, throwing the spear for practice. When I heard this story being told about Apanuugpak's and Ukinqucugpalek's confrontation with enemy warriors, it usually ended here.

They say [Ukinqucugpalek's] kayak tote hole was big. It was said that he used the skin of a two-year-old bearded seal to cover it, a skin of a seal a little smaller then an adult bearded seal. That was why, when the water was high over at his place and he paddled down on it, the only part you could see was the mouth of his tote hole as he glided along with this part in the water. [From the land] as he paddled along you couldn't see the person inside the kayak but only the tote hole visible above the water. And it was said that when he was paddling along fighting with his enemy, he would always sit facing his tote hole and swing sideways back and forth, dodging the oncoming arrows. He'd move his kayak like this and let the arrows fly by, brushing against the tote hole. It was said that he always used his tote hole to avoid being hit by his enemy's arrow points.

And they say Quarruucuar learned to dodge arrow points from his enemies when he got older. When he ran away from them out in the open, a piece of cloth would be attached to the tip of his walking stick, moving in the wind. He would avoid being hit by arrow points, even though there were many, many arrows falling all around him like snowflakes. On the top of his walking stick [would be a cloth piece]; he'd be holding it and run and dodge the oncoming arrows. During that time Quarruucuar learned to do that. And when he got to be an elderly man, when one of his cousins tried to talk down to him, he told him that he had never been hit by an arrow point in his life.

[Quarruucuar] said that it was a memorable moment in his life, back when a little piece of wood became his and he started to use it as a sun visor. People back then used wooden visors with little clasps. One time Quarruucuar was engaged in a long fight, and when the battle finally ended he discovered that his wooden visor was gone, but in its place he found a little piece of wood. During the battle the arrow points flashing by had brushed against it and had chipped the wood. I think that man named Quarruucuar was also from Qinaq. The story about those warriors who got into verbal arguments, this was how it was told.

Nukalpiarugaam At'ngellra

Anguyakutellermeggni tamaani, ukut nunaurpailgata Kuigilngurmiut, Kass'artang-vailgan — ingna, piani qemingellrani pamani, tayima yaaken *three miles* yaaqsigtaci-quq aipaagni, yaaqsigtayugnarquq waten cip'arrluku. Tuaten tua-i tangrruaraqamku yaaqsigtangatelartuq. *Three miles* pitalqegciqnganani waten cip'arrluku. Kuigtang-qertuq, Nukalpiarugauvkenani-gguq tamaani kuiguluni. Avayarluni taugaam qemit tungiitnun, neqtulriamek. *Blackfish*-aanek uksumi tua-i neqsutuluteng tuani taukut ingkut anguyiit, qanikcanek waten *igloo*-liluteng, eneliluteng tuani, aniguyiluteng aniniriaqluteng tamatum nalliini tuaten.

Tua-i-gguq taugken inglumeng iliitnek iliit nuliarluni, nasaurlurmek, inglumeng iliitnek.

Anguyakulluteng. Ikegkut atam ika-i nunallret, ika-i nunallrat alaunateng ikeg-kut; ingkut yaaqsigtatekluteng inglukutellret nunallret. Kuiguarmiut ingkut nutem atam yui, makumiut. Taukut-llu ingkut Nunallerpagmiut qagaaken ukatmurrlu-teng anguyiit nunaliallermeggni yaa-i uitaluteng, inglukluki taukut. Taukut-llu ing-lumeng iliitnek nulianguni tauna iliit nasaurlurmek. Taugaam kellusngaluku tua-i, ilainun pinayukluku, tegussaagnayukluku. Tuaten ayuqluteng.

Uksungaqan tua-i tamaani pinariaqan taglutEng piavet, neqengyaraa tekitaqan taum, arnatuumarmeng tamakut *blackfish*-anek caliyarturaqluteng. Taugaam tua-i murilkerrlainarluteng. Ikegkut Kuiguarmiut nalluluku tauna kuik, pilauciat tau-kut.

Atam tua-i caqerluteng qasgimi quyurluteng-am taukut ukut pillermeggni acalur-nassaagcestekameggnek yuallinilriit. Iliiratuut-gguq caaqameng tua-i ingluk'nger-megteki. Camek piitellermeggnek cikiisqelluteng tua-i camek inglukutengermeng tuaten. Tamakunek-am tamaa-i acalurnanek piitelliniameng kevgarkameggnek pilli-niluteng. Uksuuluni-llu-gguq, taugaam-gguq taukut neqsuryaraat tekiteksaunani.

How Nukalpiarugaq River Got Its Name

Back during the time of warfare, before Kwigillingok became a village, before there were white people in this area — that place over there at the base of the bluffs might be located about three miles from here, it might be a little over three miles away. When I imagine it, it seems to be a little over three miles away. At that place there is a river, and during that time it wasn't called Nukalpiarugaq River. And from that river there's another channel that goes right by the bluffs. The warriors who stayed over there would get blackfish from that channel by making snow shelters on the river.

Now, one of the men there was married to a girl who came from the opposing side, the enemy.

At that time [people from those two places] were at war. There is an old site across there, you can see the old village site across there; two old neighboring villages visible over there that were warring. People who lived in Kuiguarmiut were originally from this area. And the people who lived at Nunallerpagmiut over there were originally from the north, warriors who moved down this way from the north and began fighting warriors from the other place. And one of the warriors from there married a girl from their neighboring enemy village. They kept her in their village and guarded her so her people wouldn't take her back. That's how the members of those two places lived.

When winter came and it was time, people from [Nunallerpagmiut], including their women, would go to that river and begin harvesting blackfish. When they were away from their village, they'd always be guarding their surroundings. During that time people from Kuiguarmiut across there didn't know that those people harvested blackfish from that river.

One day, while men in Nunallerpagmiut gathered at the *qasgi*, they inquired about finding someone to go get some skin containers [from Kuiguarmiut]. It was said that even though members of the two places were enemies, they sometimes asked for things they needed from each other. The men talked about finding someone to get the skin containers they needed from the other place. It was in winter, but their harvesting time hadn't come yet.

Piuraqerluteng taum teguarata nasaurluum cakia angun qanlliniuq tauna ukurrani elluarrluku pistekenritniluku tua-i, umyuaminun nall'aruutaaqsaitelarniluku iliini, assikessiyaagpek'naku qetunrarmi nulirra. Tamaani *family*-t waten quyurmeng tua-i enemi uitatullrulliniameng, ataucimek eneluteng. Allakarluteng egmianun piiyuunateng tamaani.

Taumek kevgiisqelluki. Tua-i taumek piarkaurtelliniluteng, taukumiumek nasaurlurmek, taumek ilameng taum nulirranek. Qasgicamegteggu-llu tua-i uptelliniluku qasgimi. Carangllugglainarnek, pilugugmek pivkenani, carangllugglainarnek taugaam pilugulilliniluku, nemerluki taugaam waten. Uksuuluni-ll' tamana. Carangllugnek taugaam, pilugugmek acetevkenaku tauna nasaurluq. Qaqiucameng tua-i ayagcetliniluku.

Tekipailgan iliita-am tangerrluku cali tua-i piluaqalliniluku. Tua-i paiqerluku cauciilamiu. Pillinia tauna tua-i nunalgutiit nasaurluq. Taugaam tua-i qercualliniluki it'gai, cikuluki, cikulliniluki. Ut'rutliniluku tua-i nutaan. Taumek tua-i umyugaat navvliniuq Kuiguarmiut, qaill' umyuarluki taukut piciitnek.

Taukunek acalurnagnek unakitenritniluki, waten pivkarluku una ilaseng, nangteqevkarluku kevgaqucia pitekluku.

Mamciriluni tua-i. Qasgimi tua-i qaillukuarluteng tamana pillrat, qaillun piluteng pillerkameggnek. Qaill' umyuarluki piciat taukut; ukut-wa Nunallerpagmiut paqnakluki taukut Kuiguarmiut, assinrilngurmek tua-i piata nallunaunateng, qaillun piluteng ingcuqataucimeggnek.

Piinanratni tauna tua-i assiringluni nasaurluq, mamluteng it'gai assiriluteng. Kiituan piiyualanguq. Qasgimi-am erenrani tamatumek-am tua-i qalarrluteng piinanratni, qasgimun itliniuq tauna nasaurluq. Itran waqaalliniat cassuucianek. Pillinii, "Qanrucatnga quyuqetaangniluci ikegkut pitekluki nunat ikani. Pillerkarcuayukluki pillerkarpecenek apertuutnaluci qasgiunga. Ikegkut nunat maa-i piyaraat canimelliuq. Aniniriuut pamani qemingellran engeliini. (Tauna-ll' wii nalluvkenaku tua-i, maliklua ayautelaatnga.) Tauna tua-i pivigkaqsukluku assirluku umyuanguteknngamku qanrucarturamci mat'umek." Tua-i tamakut ciulirneret assikelliniat.

Tauna tua-i upengyaraat nallunrirluku pillerkaat; piyaraat tauna iralutgun naliatni. Nutaan tamaani tuaten piameng kapuuteteng tamakut kitugtelliniit Kui-

After some time, the father-in-law of the girl who they had captured said that at times his daughter-in-law hadn't been good, that sometimes her actions hadn't been pleasing, that he wasn't too pleased with his son's wife. Back in those times, extended families lived together in one house, residing in one home. [Couples] didn't immediately live in their own homes back then.

He asked them to let her take the message to the other village. The decision was unanimous to send her to her original village with the request, the woman who was a spouse of one of their members. When they brought her to the *qasgi*, they prepared her for the journey. They wrapped grass around her feet and did not let her wear boots. They just tied grass around her feet without boots and let her go, and it was winter at the time.

Before she arrived, one of [her fellow villagers] saw her and saved her. He went to meet her not knowing who she was. He saw that it was that girl from his village. Her feet were frostbitten; they were frozen. He then took her home. The people of Kuiguarmiut were angry over that incident, wondering why they would do such a thing.

They said they weren't going to give them the skin bags they were asking for because of what had happened to their relative who they had allowed to suffer as their messenger.

She stayed with them so that her wounds would heal. In the *qasgi* they discussed how they should counter [their enemies] and take revenge. They wondered what those people had in mind when they did that; the people of Kuiguarmiut were curious about the people of Nunallerpagmiut since they had obviously done such a terrible thing, and they wondered how they would get them while they were defenseless.

After a while, that girl recovered, and her feet healed. Eventually, she began to walk. During the day while the men were discussing what to do in the *qasgi*, that girl came in. When she entered, they asked her why she was there. She said, "Since they told me that you are starting to gather and confer about that village across there [I came]. Since I thought you were planning revenge, I came to the *qasgi* to tell you a way to counter them. The season for them to harvest blackfish is approaching. They harvest blackfish inland at the edge of the bluffs back there. (And I even know where that place is, since they brought me there when I was little.) I came here to tell you that since I thought it might be time to counter them." The elders liked that idea.

They discovered the time and place when they would begin harvesting blackfish; they discovered which month they did their harvesting. After they decided, the

guarmiut. Tua-i arenqigian tamana ullakunegteki erenrani pingaunaki. Elkareskata
taugaam piarkauluki. Tamakut aniguyat kapurluki kapuutnek tua-i piarkauluki,
piarkaurrluki taugaam.

Paugna Nukalpiarugaq, ukatmun atam qiptuuq kuik. Waten-llu tua-i piqarraall-
rani qertuluteng ukut nunallret. Nunallret, man'a-wa kuik tauna kelutmun *north*-
atmun ayaumaluni nequkunani. Tamana tamaa-i can'giirnek piviat, tamana kuigat.
Nukalpiarugarmek atritellruuq paugna taum ciungani. *Straight*-arluni tauna yaaqvanun tua-i; yaaqsigluni kiuk qiptellra nalqigluni. Tuaten ayuquq.

Qemini cali taum qiptellrani, ukalirnerani wani, qemit canimelnguut iliit kangra
waten pengurrartarluni. Tauna atengqertuq Anipaunguarvigmek. Taukut tua-i
at'ngevkallruat tauna taumek.
Iliita taum tua-i picirkirluki-am, tuavet ipinganermun qemim acianun elkartelli-
niluteng. Ilaseng tauna imkunek — *pike*-at caulriit imat'anem imkut? Cuukviit, luqruuyiit amiitnek, imkunek makunek nenglemi qercurtanek, waten ayuqliritulinek,
qaterlitengqetullruut-gguq tamakunek, imkunek-llu qangqiirnek, *rabbit*-aanek-llu
uksumi. Qanikcangaqan pissulriit tamakunek all'uteng, qangqiiret-llu amiitnek
pitarkateng tua-i pingnaqu'uratuluki. Tamakunek at'elluku qasperrlugmek, taum
pengurraam qaingani tuarpiaq-gguq anipaq pikani misngauralalria, misngauralria.
All'uki tua-i taukut qasperrluut, iluatnun iterluni tangvauraraqluki taukut, tangvaurluki, murilkaqluki. Qerruyingnayukluku piaqameng, alla mayuraqan anluni
cimircetaqluni. Tua-i-gguq Anipaunguarvigmek at'ngellruuq tauna tuani pingna
pia-i qemirraq.
Nutaan tua-i pinarian iluvarvikliniit. Ullagturalliniit unaggun, maaggun nunam
qaingakun pivkenaki. Taum-am yuum alerqualuki. Nuna tutmalriani qanikcaq qal-
riatuuq, tua-i qastuluni pituluni. Patgusngalriakun taugaam, kuigem cikuakun,
engeliikun tamaaggun, imkunek tuntut melqurritnek qaliruanek at'elluki. Melqurrit tuntut piluki, waten angtaluki maaggun nungircariluki qaliruangqetullruukut.
Pilugumta tua-i qaingatnun at'elluki cagnilluki nungirtelluki, kaviarnek qavalrianek ullakata'arqamta, qanikcangaqan. Tua-i waten qalriayuunateng tamakunek
aturluta piaqamta, qaliruanek. Tamakunek all'uteng ullagturalliniluki kuik tua-i
aturturluku.
Tekicamegteki tua-i elpengvailgata, yuk anvailgan, nutaan tua-i tamalkuita aniguyat piamegteki elpengevkalliniluki, arnait anevkalliniluki.
Tekicameng taugaam tua-i tamaavet *igloo*-itnun, aniguyanun, qanikcarnun,
nutaan anevkarluki elpengevkarluki, caviirucata. Caskuit-llu ellamenateng; anqerr-

people of Kuiguarmiut got their spears ready. They agreed that when they went to them, they wouldn't attack them during the day. They would only do so when they had settled down to sleep. They planned to stab the snow shelters they were in with spears; that was their plan.

Nukalpiarugaq River back there goes along and bends like this. And just when the river [bends the first time], there's a high mound where the old village site is located. The old site is located there, and the river is [near the old site] there, a narrow river that heads north. That was the river where they used to harvest blackfish. That river back there wasn't called Nukalpiarugaq during that time. The bend there is straight and goes a long ways.

Downriver from that place, on the bluff where the river bends there, on this side, on one of the bluffs, there's another mound. That mound is called Anipaunguarvik. People that lived there named that place.

Directed by one of their members, the attackers from Kuiguarmiut settled beneath a bluff out of sight of their enemies. And they let one of their members — what are pike called again? The skins of *cuukviit* [pike] or *luqruuyiit* [pike] freeze-dried in the winter cold were made into [white] garments and worn by men when they hunted in winter, and also skins of ptarmigan and rabbits were made into such hunting garments. When men hunted out in the snow they'd wear those as well as ptarmigan-skin garments. One of the men there put on a garment like that, and whenever he sat at the top of the hill he looked exactly like a snowy owl.

He'd put it on and get inside the fish-skin parka and watch over [their enemies]. When others began to worry about him getting cold, another person would go up and replace him. It was after that time that the little bluff got its name Anipaunguarvik [Place where they pretended to be snowy owls].

When it was time they went toward them. They slowly approached them down along the river and not on land. When you walk on snow on land, it usually makes a lot of noise. So, one of the people there told them to use those *qaliruat*, boots made of caribou fur that you put on over your fur boots, and to approach them on the ice along the river. We used to tie *qaliruat* that were about so big over our boots when we approached foxes that were sleeping on snow. There was no noise when walking on snow with them. Those men put those on over their boots and slowly approached the enemy along the river.

When they got to where they were, before they noticed them, before anyone came out of the snow shelters, they allowed the women to come out first.

When they got to their snow shelters and they were trapped, they finally allowed [the women] to come out. Their weapons were outside; they couldn't run out and

ngairucata caskuteng tegulerluki. Anevkalliniluki arnat, nasaurluut malikevkarluki, tan'gaurluut unegcetaqluki.

Nutaan tua-i nangengata arnat, nutaan kapurluki kaptuutnek tamakunek. Nangengamegteki tua-i qamurluki yuut tamakut atrautellinikait. Caniurtait-llu tamakut ellami quyungqallret quyurrluki, caskuit, caniurtait, urluvret, pitegcautait, caskuit tua-i. Kuigmun tamaavet *straight*-alriamun, ketiinun kuigem iluanun waten itukurluki taklarquralliniluki nukalpiat caniurtaitnek caniqliliqaqluki. Nakirneq kiituan tauna iquan qiptellra canimellilliniuq, nukalpiam amllertacia yuum.

Tua-i tuaten qiptellranun tekiteqatarluku nanglliniut caniurtaq man'a atauciq yuitellinilria. Arnat taukut aptelliniit, "Mat'um caniurtam yua nauwa?" Iliit-am arnat kiulliniuq, iliit-gguq malrugnek caniurtangqertuq. Ukveqevkenaku-am iqluluni qanran. Iliit pilliniuq iqluniluku, malrugnek caniurtangqessuitniluku yuk. Tuatnallran-am kinguani naken iliit arnaq qanlliniuq, iliit-gguq unuk ak'a keputmek caskirluni elagtuulluni qanikcam aciakun ayallruuq. Keputmek imumek elagturluku qanikcam acia ayagluni tamaaggun. Kapurluku elaqsigiinarluteng.

Pivakarluteng tua-i elaqsigiluteng, iliita kapuskii qiivcillalliniluni. Qanikcaq tua-i tamana aug'arluku antelliniat tua-i tauna mecungkacagarluni qainga pinialilliniluni. Pinrilengraatni-gguq tua-i qerruyarluni; qerruqatanrakun tua-i tamatum caniurtam yua.

Qaqicamegteki nutaan nukalpiat iliit ayarumek cikilliniluku, maaggun akiatgun cikulraatgun egcesqelluku waten. Narulkalallra tua-i ilakuivkenaku, tunertutaciatun cakneq yaaqvanun ayagcetengnaqluku ayaruq. Cikulraam qaingani yaaqvanun ayatuuq piaqami cikum qaingani. Iquatnun tua-i nangerrluni, wavet ciisqumiggluni ketiitnek ayaruq tamana narulkautellinikii. Kat'agluni cikulram qaingakun ayallinilria kuigem iluakun. Nukalpiat-llu tua-i makut taklalriit iquklicugnaitarluki arulailliniluni. Nukalpiat amllertaciat. Tua-i at'ngelliniuq tauna, acilliniat Nukalparugarmek. Nutaan quyurrluki tuavet tua-i elaulluki; pegcuitellruit-gguq pitateng yuut. Akluit taugaam tua-i pikarnilriit teguluki uyaqluki.

Unugpak tua-i, taukut taugaam tua-i arnat nangelrakevkenaki. Nangelrakiyuitellruut-gguq makumiut, Kusquqvagmiut-llu. Tamakut-gguq taugken anguyait ingluit, qagken pillret arniuryugluteng, arnat-llu nangelraksugluki. Qamiqurrit-llu waten maaggun amiirluki, qeciirluki waten ciisqurritnun pivkarluki kumakircetaqluki. Kiagmi-ll' piaqata aluit kamilarrluki, makluki, aluit amiirluki taperrnat

grab their weapons. They let the women come out, along with the girls, and they didn't let the boys come out.

When all the women were out, they began poking their spears through the shelters. When all the men had been stabbed, they hauled them out and dragged them down to the river. Then they gathered their quivers that were sitting outside and gathered their weapons, arrows, and bows. On the long, straight section of river, below where they were, they laid the bodies of those *nukalpiat* and placed their quivers next to them. As they laid the bodies side by side along that extended straight section, the line nearly reached the river bend at the end. That was how many *nukalpiat* were killed at that time.

Then when they laid the last body with a quiver, one last quiver was left without an owner. Then they turned to one of the women and asked, "Where is the owner of this quiver?" Then one of the women replied that one of the men had two quivers. They knew the woman was lying. One of the men told her that she was lying and said men don't own two quivers. After he said that, another woman said that one of their men dug under the snow with an adze and left them the night before. They started digging in the snow and got farther and farther away.

Getting farther away as they dug in the snow, they suddenly felt something shake beneath the snow. They removed the snow and pulled out a very weak and wet man. He would have frozen, although they hadn't captured him. The owner of that quiver had almost frozen to death.

When they were done lining up the bodies, they gave a walking stick to one of the *nukalpiat* and told him to throw it forward on the glare ice along side the dead *nukalpiat*. They told him not to hold back his strength but to throw it with all his might. When something is thrust forward with force on glare ice it can go far. He then went to the end of the bodies and sat down on his knees and shot the walking stick forward below them. The stick glided forward on the glare ice, along the river. It stopped before it reached the end of the bodies along the river. That was how many *nukalpiat* were laid along that river. Then that river got its name Nukalpiarugaq after that. After they did that they buried the bodies in the ground. They never left bodies out to deteriorate during wartime. But they salvaged their gear and clothes if they were in good condition.

They killed them in one night, but they never tortured the women. They say the warriors from this area and the Kuskokwim River area never tortured women. But it is said the enemy warriors who came from up north tended to rape women and tortured them. And they'd skin their heads and place it on their knees and have them remove the lice. And when they captured them in the summer, they would

qaingatgun aqvaqurcetaqluki. Nanglluki. Tuatnatullruit-gguq ingluita. Taugaam
tua-i Kusquqvagmun maavet elliqerluteng nak'rialillrulliniut, *lucky*-rciigaliluteng.
Cirliqengluteng-llu agaavet elliameng, cirlaurrluteng, anguyallrat pinialiluni. Tuaten-gguq ayuqellruut.

Ercan-am piluteng tua-i piinanermeggni iliit pilliniuq ikamrartangniluku. Ikam-
rartangniatgu-am anluanun piluteng neq'liuruarluteng tua-i tamakut. Alegnari-
lliniuk malruullinilriik. Cunawa-gguq atani tauna taum ucikurluku, iruan inglua
qungaumalria. Qimugtek-wa-gguq malruk tan'gaurluum taum.

Alegnariqerlukek-am arulaillinilriik ikegkuk. Cunawa-gguq allakellinikegket
maaggun piurallratgun. Yagirallratgun allauciat-am elitaqlinikii taum atiin. Pillinia, mallyunaitniluki, ilakumalriarunritliniciitnek ikegkut. Taringluki-am tamakut,
ukut Nunallerpagmiut yuit, taum unkallrem.

Kingutmun tua-i caungagnek uqilanrita maligtellinilukek. Taum tua-i qetunraan kasmurrarluku, agtarluku pitgaraqluku. Tuatnaviirluku-am qimugtiinegnek
inglua kitngiakun uuggun pitegcautem tut'elliniluku, uuggun waten pillrakun. Tu-
ssitenga'artelliniluni tua-i qimunriqerrluni. Caqiryungaarcan tua-i anguyartullini-
lukek.

Anguyartunga'arcatek atiin taum qayagpallinia, pileryallinia, unilluni cakarniirut-
niluni ellii taugaam arcaqerniluku qimaasqelluku. Aqvaqurluni tua-i ayagarrluni,
kingyaqa'aqluni. Ataurlua tauna tekiarcamegteggu tegulliniluku quy'uqrulluku.

Quy'uqrutellratni tua-i kingyarluni arulairrluni tangvakanrakun, qayagpalliniuq
tauna ataurlua, taun atii, akanruarani yaatlirkangniluki. Nukalpiagnek malrugnek
tuquciniluni. Nuussiminek-gguq kap'aqlukek malruk tuani tegulallratni, malrugnek tuqucillinilria.

Tauna tua-i uqilalriik taukuk malruk malirqalliniluku. Aqvaqurluni tua-i aya-
garteqerluni, pamyurtaminek egcilliniluni tauna tan'gaurluq. Tuarpiaq canirtaqami
tekeq nengingalalria. Uliirem pamyua uskurarluni acivarciiganani waten cukatacia
tan'gaurluum. Tua-i patagmek yaaqsigilliniluni tayima. Angungaitelliniamegengu
tua-i taqniluku uqilayaaqengermeng.

Tua-i tauten taktauq man'a. Ingna tua-i tuaten at'ngellrulliniuq Nukalpiarugarmek. Maa-i man'a engelkarrluku tua-i can'giirinek-llu wii nerlalrianga, neqairucuunani tua-i pia-i uksumi. Wii taugaam taluyarayuitellruaqa allakarma pivingqell-
ruama. Augna tua-i tuaten ukut ayuquciat wani nunamni tuaten ayuquq. Nunani
allani tayim' ilamauq tayima.

remove their boots and remove the skin from the bottom of their feet and let them run on top of coarse seashore grass. They tortured them. It is said that's what their enemy warriors did to women. But apparently, after they came to the Kuskokwim River area, they became weak and unlucky. When they got to Bristol Bay across there, they got weak as well. It is said that's how they were.

When the sun came up someone said that a sled was coming. Then they went to the ice holes and pretended to be fishing. When the sled got closer they could see that there were two people. Apparently, it was a boy coming with two dogs and his crippled father in the sled.

As they got closer, the two travelers stopped. They apparently sensed that their actions were different. The boy's father knew the people fishing there were not his people. He told his son that the people there were not from their village and they shouldn't be near them. That one man who had stayed behind knew those people from Nunallerpagmiut, and he knew those people were not from his village.

When they turned their sled to leave, the fastest runners pursued them. While the son pushed the sled with his father inside, they'd shoot many arrows toward them. Then an arrow hit one of the dogs on the ankle, right here. The dog suddenly began limping and didn't pull as hard. When the dog started to want to turn to one side, they gained on them.

When they started to gain on them his father yelled at his son to leave him, that he was too old, that [his son] was more important, telling him to escape. He took off running, looking back periodically. When they got to his poor father, they quickly surrounded him.

When they surrounded him, and just when the boy stopped and looked back, his poor father yelled. He yelled and said that he had just killed two *nukalpiak*. When they took him, apparently he stabbed two men with his knife and killed them.

Two fast runners then ran after [that boy]. Just as the boy started running, he threw his *pamyurtaq* [tail of the animal he caught along his belt]. When he ran and turned, it looked like an index finger extended out. The boy was running so fast that the tail attached with a string was flying behind him and couldn't come down. He ran, and the two pursuing him couldn't see him anymore. The two, though they were running fast, gave up, knowing that they wouldn't be able to catch him.

That's how long this story is. That is how that place got the name Nukalpiaru-gaq. To this day, I eat blackfish from that place; there's always fish in winter there. But I never set my blackfish trap there since I had my own place. That's how this story was told in my village. In other villages, they probably add more details to this story.

Qissunamiunun Anangniallret

Tuamtell' kegkut Qissunamiut tamaani nuniita kuigat tamana neqtupiarniluku qanrutkelallrukiit. Caqerluteng Qaluyaarmiut neqmeggnek nurutelliniut; imarpiirlukillu. Qanikcarrluk man'a unavet tep'aqani, unguvalriit amllengermeng caperrnarilartut pitaqellerkaat. Tuatnaaqata kainiqenglartut makut nurutellriit.

Ukut-llu waniw' Kuigilngurmiut atullruat tamana. Mik'nii taugaam tuatnaciat nallullruaqa mikngama; nall'aringayaaqellinikeka. Taugaam amllermek cakneq ilangartevkenateng ukurmiut, Anuuraarmiut-llu, Kangirnaarmiut-llu ingkut. Up'nerkami pilliniluteng. Yaqulengan tua-i cir'iqertellrulliniut, yaqulegnek pinga'arcameng.

Caqerluteng tuatnalliniut neqait nurulluteng Qaluyaarmiut. Arenqialameng tua-i, pinialissiyaagpailegmeng piyugluteng piata, tuavet tua-i Qissunamiunun anangnialliniut, neq'liata tua-i, tamakunrilata. Kemgiutengluteng-gguq taugaam tua-i, taugaam tua-i piyugngiimeng tekitelliniluteng Qissunamiunun.

Ciunrita-am taukut neqkiurluki tua-i piqataamegteki tua-i qasgimun quyurcetliniluki. Neqkait tua-i qasgimun pirraarluki pilliniit, matarrluki aturanek cairulluki yuranrilkata nerevkarngaitniluki.

Arnat angutet-llu tamakut kemgunateng, matarrluteng tua-i yura'urlulliniut, nerrlerkarteng arcaqakngamegteggu. Engelarautekluki-gguq tua-i tamakut tangvagtaita. Taqngameng atam tua-i nutaan neruraurlulliniut, pinqigcetevkenaki taugaam. Aningcaarluteng tua-i. Kiagluni-ll' kiagiluteng kiagpak tua-i. Piniriluteng tua-i cayugnairulluteng.

Tuunrangayagmek taugken ilaluteng, angalkumek. Nutaan tua-i piyunarian tumkaat, man'a piyunarian, capenriteqtaarluteng-llu pingairucata, uksuan, upcetliniluki. Ikamrarrarnek-llu pilirluki, taquirluki-ll' tua-i, utertelliniut nutaan tua-i tuaten. Qi-

374

Those Who Went to Qissunaq to Survive

And also they used to say that the Qissunaq River had a lot of fish back in those days. One time people living on Nelson Island ran out of food during winter, and the ocean below them was closed up and was impossible to hunt on. When frozen snow develops and drifts onto the shore line, although there are many sea mammals, it becomes difficult to catch them. When that happened, people who ran out of food began to experience starvation.

The people of Kwigillingok experienced that one time also, but I didn't know what was happening since I was small at that time; I actually was alive that time. But not many people died in this village or in Anuuraarmiut or Kangirnaarmiut. Evidently that happened during spring. When birds became available and they started to hunt them, food suddenly became available to them.

One time those people living on Nelson Island ran out of food. In desperation, all agreed that before they became too weak, because they knew they had food to spare, to go to Qissunaq to ask for food, *anangniarluteng* as they called it. They had lost weight from not eating, but since they were able to travel, they eventually arrived at Qissunaq.

When people in that village were getting ready to give them food, they brought them all to the *qasgi*. And after the food was brought to the *qasgi*, they told them that if they didn't remove all their clothing and dance, they wouldn't allow them to eat.

Since the poor skinny women and men were desperate to eat, they removed all their clothing and danced. Those on the side watching were laughing [as they danced]. After they were done dancing, those poor people finally sat down and ate, but they didn't treat them like that again. They remained in the village and continued eating, trying to regain their strength. Summer came while they were there, and they stayed in the village all summer. They got strong and healthy [by the end of summer].

[Among the Nelson Islanders] there was a shaman. When it was winter and they could travel without getting stuck along the way, he told his group to get ready. They provided them sleds and provisions, and they finally left the village and started

ssunaq tua-i tamana cakmaggun kepsaraullinian uaqvaggun, tekicamegteggu tua-i qerarpailegmegteggu quyurrluteng nerrliniluteng.

Nernginanermeggni angalkuseng tauna iliita pillinia, "Tua-i elpet waniwa kiivet tuaten ayuqelriaten, ikayuryugngaluta-llu wangkuta. Ilavni tua-i wangkuta waniwa kiliumalriatun ayuqsaaqelriakut. Elpeni-wa cangatenritlilria imna tekiteqaarrallemteni yuraurlullerput nerllerkarput pitekluku. Tamatumek maa-i umyuarput akngirutengqerrsaaquq ilavni. Qaillun taugken pisciiganata."

Qissunaq-gguq neqtulpiallruuq. Angalkum taum kiugartenritlinia. Kiuvkenaku tua-i pirraarluku taqngameng, taqcagcameng nutaan pillinii. Kitaki-gguq qeraquniu tumellni waten uniurteksaunaki tutmarturluki qeraqilit, cailkakun piksaunteng. Qeraqilitgu-gguq Qissunaq ikamrat tumellrit ilangcivkenaki, elliin taugaam tumellri. Tuaten alerqulliniluki taum angalkuata. Qerallinilukku tua-i tuaten tumai tum'aruqurluki. Nangengameng tua-i pilliniut tuarpiaq-gguq maani yuum ataucim qerallri, tum'aruqurluteng tua-i piameng.

Tununermun tua-i keggavet Qaluyaanun tekitelliniluteng cayugnaunateng tua-i kemiameng. Uksurpak tua-i, kiagyungami kialliniuq. Neqet-llu tull'uteng, neqsurluteng tua-i. Atam neqsullermeng kinguani qagken elatiitnek allanret tekitellinilriit kiagmi. Qanengssagluteng piinanermeggni pilliniut Qissunaq-gguq neqem itenritaa. Qissunamiut-gguq neqtenritut.

Tua-i uksuan kainiqluteng taukut Qissunamiut. Tua-i pinialivailegmeng pilliniut imkunun anangniarvikestellermeggnun anangniaryugluteng, akinaunrilngaitniluteng neqnek anagcetellruamegceteng. Tuaten pillrungermegteki. Taugaam taukut anangniallret Qaluuyaarmiut tamana tua-i nekakluku tua-i tuatnamallerteng.

Qissunamiut taukut anangniarluteng tekitelliniluteng Qaluyaanun. Tekicata-am neqkiurcetliniit allakaita imkunek qayuruanek yuurqaarnek pilallritnek uquarucirpagluki, uqumek amllermek piluki, uquarucirpagluki. Ellait taugken neqkarteng ellma uquarucicuarluk' pilauciatun. Iluatgun neqiitgun akinauqatarluki.

heading home. Since the place to cross the Qissunaq River [heading south toward Nelson Island] was way down below [the village], when they reached that point, before they crossed the river, they gathered and ate.

As they were eating, one of them turned to the shaman and said, "You are the only one among us who is a shaman and can help us. We, the members of your group, are wounded, as if we had been cut with a knife. You probably think nothing of the dance we poor people did when we first arrived in Qissunaq so that we could eat. We, your fellow villagers, are emotionally hurt by that harsh treatment. But we can't do anything about it."

It was said that fish were abundant in the Qissunaq River at one time. That shaman didn't answer him right away. After not saying anything, when they were finished eating, he finally said something. He told them that he was going to lead them across the river and that they should follow from behind and step right into his footprints as they walked across. He told them not to pay attention to the sled tracks, but to watch his tracks very closely and walk right in his footsteps and not step anywhere else. That shaman told them to do that. They crossed the river following him from behind and stepping right in his footprints. When they all got to the other side and looked back, the tracks they left behind appeared as if one person had walked across.

They arrived at Tununak out on Nelson Island without any problems since they had gained weight and were physically healthy by then. They stayed all winter, and summer came. When the fishing season arrived, there were a lot of fish, and they harvested enough fish for the coming season. Sometime after they harvested fish, visitors arrived from the north. While they were visiting, one of them said that fish hadn't come up the Qissunaq River that summer. He said that the residents of Qissunaq hadn't gotten any fish at all that summer.

The following winter residents of Qissunaq lacked food and were starving. Before they got too weak, they mentioned the Nelson Islanders who had come to them for food, and they decided they should go to their village, too, to do as they did. Since they had helped them to survive, they were hopeful that they would repay them for their generosity. They thought they would do that, even though they had treated them harshly when they first arrived. However, at that time the Nelson Islanders were still feeling bitter about what had been done to them.

One day a group from Qissunaq arrived on Nelson Island to eat and stay alive. When they arrived the women were asked to prepare a separate meal for them. They were instructed to prepare soup for them, the kind of soup called *qayuruat* or *yuurqaat*. They told them to add lots of seal oil to their meal. But they only added

Qasgimun tua-i nutaan neqkait piluki tamakut nunalget nerrliniluteng tua-i ilakluki allaneteng. Nerellmeng tua-i kinguani ilumeggnek tua-i piluteng. Ak'anun tua-i pivkenateng piunriraqluteng. Akinaurluki tua-i; uquariqluteng tamakut. Tua-i nangluki tamaq'apiaraita taukut Qissunamiut. Tuaten-am qanemcik'larait. Tua-i ellmeggnek pikiurata tua-i taukut akinaurateng tua-i piunrirlúteng. Tuaten cali taktaluku niitela'araqa tauna. Tuaten taktanricaaqellilria tuani nunami.

Ilaqtanrilkurrluki makut niiyucillemtun qanemcikngualaranka.

the usual small amount of seal oil to their own food. The locals there were preparing to repay [the Qissunaq people] by feeding them something that would actually kill them in time.

When food was brought to the *qasgi*, the villagers ate along with their guests. After they ate, the guests started to suffer stomach pains. Not long after complaining, they died. The Nelson Islanders paid them back; they all died *uquariqluteng* [overdosing on oil]. Those people who came to their village all died. People used to tell this story back in those days. The story about those [Qissunaq people] and what happened to them. Since they had brought it upon themselves, when Nelson Islanders struck back, they all died. This was how long the story was when I heard it before. Perhaps the story was longer in the areas where this actually happened.

I try not to add information to [stories] but tell them the way I heard them.

Nengaukelriik

Nengaukelriik taukuk pissullinilriik ilalutek tua-i. Nengauga tauna taquariulluni; kainiqenricaaqengermi taquari taugaam nanglliniluteng. Malini tua-i tan'gaurluq ellimellinia cakiminek tuaken atakutarkamegnek iliirasqelluku. Unani imarpigmi qavaqatarluteng, unani qayarugaat. Ullagluku tua-i qanrutliniluku tauna. Nengaugan taum ellimerrani atakutarkaminek pikangqerqan pisqelluni piniluku.

Yuut ayuqenrilameng, cakian tua-i pillinia kevgaa tauna, "Nuqaminek-gguq taugaam akilirluni pikan neqkainek cikirciqaqa." Nengauni tauna, makucimek nuqamek asaaqitmek, tamakucimek-gguq pikani cikirciqaa neqkaanek. Pingaitelliniagu uterrluni qanrutliniluku. Ilakluku tua-i yaa-i yaanlluni nengauga, qayatgun. Qanrucani-ll' tua-i nuqani tauna qamaken qayam iluanek anlluku asaaqin, teguluku iriatelliniluku; murauluni. Piuraqerluku pillinia tauna, "Atakutanrilluk canrituq palungaitukuk. Unuaqu ereskan aturluku neqkangengnaqciqukuk." Qertelliniluku-ll' tua-i.

Unuaquan tua-i tupiimeng, ilakek makyutarraarluteng cenavaata, maliggluku. Cikullaryullran nalliini tua-i pilliniameng, ulyugluni tua-i cikullaq tua-i tekiulluku. Akulii meruaqluni.

Maklagtanglliniluni qalrimek; ciuneqluku. Cikullam-am nanviuqerrnerakun cikuilngurkun pug'aqluni. Qalrit tamakut mer'em ayallra maliggluku taqsuq'ngaqameng pituut makliit. Taqsuqengvailegmeng taugaam yaaqvaggun pug'aqluteng kuimarluteng. Taqsuq'ngameng-llu ayanrirluteng tua-i.

Father-in-Law and Son-in-Law

Once a father and his son-in-law went out hunting, along with other hunters. Soon his son-in-law ran out of provisions; he wasn't actually starving but had run out of provisions. He then told a boy who was with him to go ask for some food from his father-in-law. A group of many hunters in kayaks were preparing to retire for the night down on the ocean. The boy went over and asked the man. The boy told the man that his son-in-law had asked him to come over and tell him he wanted food for dinner, if he had some to spare.

Since people are different, his father-in-law looked at the boy messenger and said, "Tell him if he gives me his throwing board in exchange, I will give him food." He said that if his son-in-law gave him a throwing board like this, that he would give him food to eat, a board that is used to throw *asaaqut* [toggling harpoons]. Realizing that the father-in-law was definitely not going to give him food, he returned to the son-in-law and told him what he said. His son-in-law was sitting nearby with a group of hunters in kayaks. After the boy gave him the message, he reached inside his kayak and took out his throwing board and held it and looked at it, bobbing his head to the side up and down; a wooden throwing board. Then, after a moment of doing that, he said to the boy, "It's okay, let's not eat dinner for we won't starve. Tomorrow when the sun comes up, we'll use this and try to get some food." He then stuck it back inside his kayak.

The next morning when they awoke, after the others ate breakfast and started to go offshore to hunt, he went with them. Since they apparently had gotten there while the water was just starting to freeze, when they got down there the newly frozen ice had floated in with the incoming tide. But there was open water in some areas in between.

As the hunters moved forward, they spotted a bearded seal giving its mating call, and they began heading toward it. As they went toward it, it would periodically come up in the open water among the newly-frozen ice. When bearded seals do their mating calls and aren't exhausted, they usually swim far and come up quite a distance away from where they originally surfaced. But when they get tired they, usually move a little ways and come up and float with the current. When they be-

Pug'aqameng carvanrem atertaqluki. Anglluameng-llu acivarluteng terr'an camavet yaaqsinrilkiini tua-i nutaan kiarrluteng arnacalumeggnek, taicetaarluki erina-
megteggun. Tuatnatuut taqsuq'ngelriit. Pug'aqameng qavaraqluteng tua-i egmianun.
Enemegteggun puguraurangluteng tua-i, avaggun pinanrirluteng. Tuatnatuut.

Cikullaq tamana arulailliniluni kana-i tua-i ketvaaraatnun. Capeqluku tua-i tamakut piiyaaqengermegteggu; makuteng-llu nanilata tapruateng capeqluku tua-i
yaaqsiku'urluku piyugyaaqengermegteggu.

Pistailan tua-i, taum taprualuni usgulliniluku pikautiinek, man'a taklicarluku
taktucautekaanek. Qerruinani-ll' pivkenaku, qamigautegnek aurrucirluni atralliniluni cikullaam engeliinun. Tauna malini piluku pitsaqevkenani narulkaquniu nall'a-
reskuniu, egmianun ullagartesqelluni ikayuryarturluni. Pilliniat tangvagtain, ilain
tamakut, ellaita-llu ullagarciiqniluku waniw' pikaku.

Pug'aqan tua-i sugturrluni kanavet pillra pilallinikii. Piyungami tua-i nuvutelliniluku. Imumek tua-i pugtaluni kanani. Ciktaqluni qava'arqami. Cikluteng pugtaluteng qavatuut. Ak'anun tua-i, kiingan qamiquteng pimaluki. Piyungameng-llu call'
ciuggluteng nutaan kiarrluku avatseng man'a. Pug'aqameng tua-i camaken kiarcui-
tut taqsuqngelriit. Egmian qavatuut cikluteng. Nutaan maktaqameng paivciluteng
nutaan kiarrluteng. Tuatnarraarluteng-llu nutaan qakluteng.

Uqliusngallinikii tua-i taum. Tua-i-llu imumek paivciluni kassuami, uyaquni waten piluki qakteqatarluni, urniusngakni asaaquni egtelliniluku pagg'un. Nek'vellini-
luni tua-i taprrualuk. Perrluni tua-i kan'a, qemirrluni man' alaunaku. Pertaqameng
qertuluteng pituut, qaktaqameng *whale*-atun. Tuaten tua-i ayuqliriqerluku asaaqua
qacarneranun tut'elliniluni. Pekervalliniluni. Egmianun tua-i ullagartelliat tamakut
ilain. Ikayuqluteng tua-i nuqingalliniluku. Qac'urngaluku waten piyuitut. Qac'uqertaqan cayukaniraqluku pituut taprualut.

come exhausted, they stop swimming and start surfacing in the same area after diving down.

They sit and just float with the current when they pop up. And when they go under, they dive down almost reaching the bottom and begin looking for their female partner; they make their call inviting their mate to come once they are underwater. That's what they do when they tire. When they come out of the water, they fall asleep immediately. They stop moving and begin surfacing in the same place. That's what they do.

The newly frozen ice that had floated in with the tide evidently had stopped below the hunters, and they could see it. The hunters were able to see the bearded seal out there, but though they wanted to harpoon it, it was a little too far and difficult to reach; though they wanted to go after it, they knew their spear lines weren't long enough.

Since no one attempted to harpoon it, that son-in-law attached another line to a line that was already on his spear, making it longer. And without even taking his seal float, he got out his kayak sled and started crawling toward the animal with the sled along the edge of the ice. He told his companion that if he happened to hit it, to immediately come out and help him. The other hunters with him also told him that they would quickly come and help him if he hit the bearded seal.

When it came up in the water, he'd bring his body up higher and check it out. And when he was ready he lifted his spear and aimed. The bearded seal was floating at the surface of the water. It would bow its head down when it fell asleep. They normally float in the water and sleep. They would sleep for a long time with their heads bowed down. Periodically, they'd lift up their heads and scan the area around them. Those who become exhausted usually don't look around when they come up and float, but they immediately drop their heads and fall asleep. [After sleeping] they wake up and look around. Then after looking around they dive into the water.

The son-in-law was ready to harpoon it. Then when it woke up after sleeping and searched its surroundings, getting ready to arch its back to dive, he threw his spear and it flew forward up in the air. The coil of line attached to [the spear] quickly unraveled and flew forward. The bearded seal down below had arched its back, and its hunched back was sticking out of the water. When they arch their backs, that part of their body usually sticks out of the water and is really visible like a whale's [back]. As the bearded seal's back was arched and was sticking out of the water, the spear landed on the side of its back. It moved violently as soon as it was hit. As soon as it was hit, the other hunters ran and joined the son-in-law and grabbed the line and

Qac'uqertaqan cayukaniraqluku. Qelluqisngaurtelluku taugaam. Cikullarkun pug'aqluni navgulluni. Tuaten tua-i piyunarian aipiriluku asaaqulliniluku. Patagmek tailluku tua-i. Piyunarian aangruyagmek narulkarluku tuqutelliniluku.

Nugcamegteggu tua-i qamurluku agulluku pilalliniluku tua-i. Cakia-llu-gguq tauna qayaminun pulaluni inarrluni, qunutellruamiu nengauni neqkaanek. Qanengssaulartut caperrnaqluteng pilriit.

Tulimitliniluki tua-i ilani tamakut tulimanek. Tulimitetuit nayurtengqerraqameng, nengai ukut cipingaaqata. Maklak aqsangqertuq. Aqsii man'a tunyugngauq, iivkanra-llu, kuyiik-llu, caqelngaura-llu maliminun tunyugngaluki; kemgugaat amlleret uquq-llu.

Tauna taugken maklagtellria uumek taugaam. Iruan ingluanek, iivkanermek-llu maaken kemlegmek, ingluanek, qiluinek-llu, amia-wa. Tauna taugken kemlinruluni, amllenruluni pitellriami tua-i kemga. Uqurtarluni taugaam qaill' iqtutalriamek. Inglumek tua-i uquanek cikirluki pituit maliteng, qayangqetullermeggni tamaani. Tuaten tua-i maliteng cikitullruit. Tua-i-ll' cipnerinek, ilaluni pian, taukut iivkanri malirqeni taugaam, kuyai, aqsatarluni-llu, iivkanertarluni-llu, tamakunek tamaa-i piyugngaluku. Makut-llu cailkaat nutaan tulimilluki.

Aruquralliniluki tua-i tulimanek. Cakini tua-i tauna tekicamiu, waniwaarayaaqelliniluku maktenritliniuq qayami. Aulirluni-llu tauna tulimaq.

Qamigautegken qaingagnun egtellinikii aulingraan, "Wavet elliaqa. Makeskuvet teguniaran." Uqlarluki pitsaqluki tua-i uqlarluki.

held it. When an animal is hit, they usually don't let the line slacken. They'd hold it, and, whenever the line loosened, they'd pull it to keep it taut.

They held the line and pulled it back whenever it loosened. They held the line as the bearded seal pulled, periodically popping out of the water and breaking through the ice. Then one time as it came up through the ice, they shot and hit it with another *asaaquq*. [After that] they pulled the line in faster. And when it was close enough, they hit it with an *aangruyak* [dispatching weapon] and killed it.

When they pulled it out of the water, they dragged it over and butchered it. They say that his father-in-law went inside his kayak and lay down and disappeared, since he had not wanted to give his son-in-law food to eat. People used to tell stories about people accomplishing incredible things.

[His son-in-law] then shared his catch and gave all the hunters there some ribs. When a hunter caught a seal and there were other hunters there, he usually shared the ribs with them, if there were portions left after the usual parts were given to appropriate individuals. A bearded seal has an abdomen. The bearded seal's abdomen, its *iivkaneq* [?], its hips, and one of its legs could be shared with his partners; much of the meat and blubber was distributed to his hunting partners.

But the one who caught the bearded seal will only take this section here. He would take one of its legs and some meat from one side of the *iivkaneq*. He'd also take the intestines and the skin. But [his companion] would get more meat than the one who caught it. But he'd get some blubber that was about so wide. They usually gave half of the blubber to their hunting partners back in those days when men owned kayaks. Those were the usual portions that were given to their hunting partners. And the remaining portions, if there were hunters there, the *iivkaneq*, its back, its abdomen, those parts were given to the hunting partner. Then he would give ribs to the other hunters.

So the son-in-law began passing out the ribs to the hunters there. Then, when he got to his father-in-law, he told him to take his portion, but he just lay there and didn't come out from his kayak. The rib he tried to hand to his father-in-law was bloody.

Then he tossed the bloody rib onto his father-in-law's kayak sled and said, "I'm putting it here. You can take it when you get up." He deliberately threw the rib [on his kayak sled] and smeared it with blood.

Uauaualek

Una waniw' [Arulaciq], man'a maa-i avvenra yaatmun. Akulurat makut piit. Una waniw' kangra; tua-i akuluraq uuggun anumauq, ikaggun-llu. Qipnerpagmek aterluni. Tua-i-llu wani ukatmun pillrani nunallret wani uitallruut, nanvam taum mengliini yugluteng nulirqellriignek. Uksuillruluteng. Uksuarmi caqerluni ayiimi nanvam iluani, keglunyaarnun tekitelliniluni, aaniit, angayuqaagket cataunatek. Tua-i assikluki pirraarluki, qaill' pivkenaki unitelliniluki. Nanvallrem kangiqutaani eneluteng, curiumaluni-ll' qilagluni. Yaaqsigivailgan kinguani maruallinilutek. Aipaa-ll' maaken, aipaa-ll maaken, qayaminun agnginanrani.

Nutget ciuqliit alangruuqerraallratni avani nutengluteng tua-i. *1800*-aam iluani pingatuq tayima. Taum iluani maavet pillruut, nallunrailngurmek amllerillruut. Tamakut taugaam Kass'alugpiat *1700* iluani pingatellrulliniut. Tamatumek caskuluni, pikaggun ukinemikun imiryaramek nutegmek ciuqlirmek.

Uumikuan canimellikanirlutek maaken, tangrruuvkenatek taugaam, maruallinilutek. Uumikuan-llu avaken ciunranek cukangnaqeqtangraan. Ciunranek-llu tua-i uumikuan pirraarlutek, tangrruurtellinilukek, pairrluku, amaken qayaan tungiinek.

Tekicamegnegu tua-i, angucaluan taum arcaqerluk' uivvaalliniluku. Piyungaqamiu pamyuminek irugken'gun piqerturaqluku. Kiituan-gguq uyungleqercarpialanguq. Arnacaluan-gguq taugken taum utumaluku. Qalarut'laryaaqellinilukek, amci taqesqelluni, mat'umek akinaurciqnilukek. Avisviitniluku man'a, kenermek qerrungqerrniluku, taum angutem. Cakaniryugpek'nani. Arenqialagnek irugni uyungqercarpialangagnek, piqerturraarluni-am caq'iqertellrani ukatmun, akuraakun uuggun nutliniluku. Egmian tua-i narulkautelliniluni kegluneq tamana. Arnacaluan-gguq taum pinritaa. Avallakartuq-gguq tauna tuaten pian. Nutaan unillukek ayalliniluni.

Uauaualek

This here is [Arulaciq], and here is where it branches off and goes over that way. These are channels connecting [lakes]. This is the upper end [of the river] here; the channel here goes out [to a lake], and there's another channel across there coming out. That channel across there is called Qipnerpak. Now, here where the channel goes like this, there was a couple living along the lake long ago. The place was occupied in winter. During fall one day when [the husband] went to the [dried-up] lake, he saw wolf pups, and their mother, their parents were gone. After he watched them affectionately, he left without touching them. The pups where sitting inside a covered hole lined with grass along a cove in the lake. Before he got too far he heard wolves howling. One was coming from here, and the other was coming from there. He heard them while he was returning to his kayak.

This happened when guns were starting to be seen around here. Perhaps it was during the 1800s. During that time guns were beginning to be seen around here. But I think the Russians came during the 1700s. The man had a muzzle-loading rifle with him at that time.

When they howled again, the sound was louder and coming from over here, but he couldn't see them. And when they howled again, the sound was coming from up ahead, even though he was trying to go as fast as he could. Then after they howled from the direction he was heading, they became visible, they were approaching him from the direction where his kayak was sitting.

When they reached him, they began running around him, especially the male wolf. And now and then it would hit him violently on his legs with its tail while running around him. As it kept doing that, his legs started to give way and he almost collapsed every time he was hit. But the female wolf was less aggressive and didn't go after him too much. He spoke to them and begged them to stop, and he warned them that if they kept hurting him, he'd fight them back with this [gun]. He told them that the weapon he had couldn't be evaded and was loaded with fire. Still the male wolf kept running around him and hitting his legs with its tail. Then, because his legs were hurting so much, after the wolf hit him and abruptly turned and ran this way, he fired his gun and hit it on the belly. As soon as it was hit, the wolf fell nose down to the ground. The female wolf had kept to the side and didn't

Uterrluni tua-i eneminun tua-i tuavet. Wavet waniwa. Tekicami — nulirra-ll'
tuanlluni *family*-llu — qayaminek yuuyaaqellermini uyungqertelliniluni. Nulirran
tua-i taum qaill' picianek apcaaqengraani kiuvkenani. Tass'urluku taguqualliniluku.
Itrami kamilartelliniuq, iruk puverpapiarlutek. Nutaan qanemcilliniluni tauna, taumun tua-i piniluni keglunermun.

Qasgingqertuq-gguq elatmini, muragyaramek qasgipiyaarmek. Assirilutek tua-i
iruk. Qenuqerluku-ll' tua-i, nenglengqerluku yuilqumi-am pirraarluni, utercami
tekiutaqarraarluni maqiyuami qakinernek-am piluku kumarrluk maqilliniluni qas-
gimini. Taqngami tua-i maqilngullermini, aturarturarraarluni kinrani; uqumek
kenurrarluni. Taqsuqngami atkullraminek curiqerluni, kenurram talinrani, wavet
piluku, neverrluni taqsuqainerciaralliniluni. Nulirra-ll' ak'a ilai inartellruluteng
unuurcan.

Tua-i-ll' uitainanrani yuk ikamrarnganani qakem tekicartuqalliniluni. Qakma
ciuqerranun arulailliniluni. Nevengqallermi-am tua-i irugni waten pilukek na-
parrlukek, waten piqerluni, kenurram taugaam talinrani uitaluni kegginaa, amik
caugarrluku uavet. Piqerluni cakma tua-i itlinilutek amiguyuakun, kalvagglutek-
llu. Kalvagcamek, cakemna pilliniuq, "Kitak tua-i elpet ciumek itqaa. Wii tang iter-
ceterrlainalaqevnga, ayagaqamegnuk, pivkaraqatkuk waten." Kiugaa-gguq, "Aren
pivkenak-ata. Ciumek itetuuten. Cimingnaqevkenak ciumek itra. Ciuqliutulriaten
iciw." Piqerluni yuk puggliniluni. Mayulliniuq keglunrem pianek nasqurruterluni,
qengak-wa wani, caqiagurlutek qengak. Keglunernek ayagyuartarnek keglunernek
melqukegcilrianek aturarluni-gguq.

Nugngami tua-i nangertelliniluni uavet amiigem taqruanun. Piuraqerluni, ki-
ngunara tuamtell' yugtangaartelliniluni. Ayanitateklutek yun'erraaraak, tuaten
tua-i ayuqlutek aturakek. Engelkeggutekek-llu, qengartakek caqiagurlutek-gguq
wani. Pekteksaunani tua-i qaneqsaunani-ll' uitauralliniluni. Uitaqerluni tauna it-
leq kingumek pilliniuq, "Waqaa qavartuq-qaa?" Pektevkenani tauna, kiuvkenaku
uitalliniluni.

Tuani imat'am itragnek tua-i imkut keglunyagaat neq'aqallinikai. Tuallituarluni
tua-i umyugaa piqataryukluni. Cunawa-gguq ilumun piqatalliniatni. Aipirian
taugaam nutaan kiuluku qavanricaaqniluni waniwa. Kiungani pillinia, "Umyuar-

bother him. When the male wolf fell, the female was startled and jumped a little. Then he left them.

So he returned to his house there. [His house] at this site here [on the map]. When he got home — his wife and his family were there — when he got out of his kayak, his legs gave way and he fell to his knees. Though his wife asked why he fell, he didn't say anything. She took him by the hand and quickly brought him up to the house. Once they were in the house and he took off his boots, his legs were swollen. Then he told of the wolf and what it had done to him.

The man had a *qasgi* next to their house, a genuine little *qasgi* that could be fired up with wood. In the meantime his legs healed and returned to normal. Then right after freeze-up, right when it got cold and after he had been out on the land, when he came home he quickly ate and lit the fire in the *qasgi* and took a fire bath. Then when he was dried and had put on his clothes, the oil lamp was lit. Since he was tired he put his old parka down and rested on his back, moving the lamp over so the light wasn't shining directly on him. His wife and family inside the house had all gone to bed, for it was already late.

While he was resting he suddenly heard someone out there arriving in a sled and stopping in front of the *qasgi*. He was lying there on his back with his legs bent, like this, but his face was in the shadow turned toward the entrance out there. Soon he heard two people coming in through the *amiguyuk* [passageway] and dropping down in the hole in front. After dropping down out there, one of them said, "You go in first. You always let me go first when we are asked to carry out this responsibility." Then the other one said, "Gosh, don't fuss. You always go first. Don't try to change the normal procedure here. You know, you've always been the first to go in." Soon after that a person emerged [from the entrance hole]. When he came up, he saw that he was wearing headgear that looked like a wolf's head with its nose in front, moving and twitching back and forth. It was a wolf covered with fine fur, resembling fur usually seen on a young wolf.

Once he emerged through the hole, he moved to the side of the entrance and stood there. Then another person started coming in. They were both young with similar looking garments. And their noses were up in front here, moving back and forth. The man lay very still and never made a sound. Then the one who came in last said, "Is he sleeping?" He continued to lie there and didn't reply.

When the two came in, he thought of the wolf pups and their parents right away. He suddenly became anxious and thought they had come to get him. In fact, that was what they were about to do. When he asked again if he was sleeping, he answered that he was awake. Then he said, "We didn't actually volunteer to come. We

puk-am waniwa aturluku pinritukuk. Kingunemegnuk taugaam cing'aqatkuk, pis-
qaqatkuk, ayagalartukuk." Aqvaak-gguq. Qessasqevkenaku. Upquralliniluni tua-i
tuaten qanrucagni. Qaqiucami tua-i atrarluni anelraami kenurraq tauna nipluku,
tan'germi tua-i amiigmi, aipaan taum pillinia ciuqliuluk' anesqelluku. Pilliniuq,
"Ciuqliulua anngaitua. Elpetek ciuqliulutek anitek."

Moon-aq-gguq imumek muirluni, tua-i tanqigcenani-ll' qakemna ella. An'ngameng tua-i pilliniuq, ikamrak acirrlainaak. Tuntuk-wa-gguq ukuk malruk naqyus-
ngalriik amik. Angilluku aipaa sagtelliniluku ikamrak iluagnun. Ciungani-gguq imkunek qavyagnek qecignek uskurrlugtarluni malruinek. Taum-am pillinia unavet
inarcesqelluku tuntum qainganun keggatii yaantelluku, qamiqurra ciulirnermi uitavkarluku; akiciqerluku. Tauna-am pilliniuq, "Ciutmun caulua inarrngaitua." Ka-
ggagtengraagnek-am taukuk ircenrraak taum ingluliulliniak. Inarrngaitniluni ciutmun, mumigtesqelluku tamana. Tua-i maniggluk akitai, kinguqliuvkarluki waten,
waten-am inartesqelluku piiyaaqengraagni neveksaggluni inartelliniluni. Naqyutli-
niluku nutaan.

Qaqicamegnegu, tua-i una patumaqapigcetevkenaku, aipaan-am pillinia, "Kitak
ayakumta paqnayungerpet tangeqsaunanuk pikikuk." Kiunritlinilukek tua-i. Tua-i
piuraqerluku ayangartelliniluteng. Ayagturaqerluteng atam ikamrak tamakuk cu-
kariinallinilriik. Amkuk-llu-gguq anernelkitanglutek, anernekek alairlutek. Tanqig-
pakacaarluni-gguq. Paqnayungelliniuq-am amkugnek. Tallini tua-i piyunaqngan
pakigluku-am tauna; ikamrak tamakuk tutnaciaqalangagnek cukarillermeggni.
Waten agtuuqaarlutek ayaglutek ellametqalangagnek qerratalutek, paqnayungelli-
niluni. Pakigluku tua-i man'a igvalliniuq, keglunrek malruk akiqliqlutek pangalgus-
kiik, alungutkek-gguq an'ngellinilutek. Tangvakarraarlukek tua-i ataam patuluku.

Patuqanrakun cukairucartullinilutek, arulairrlutek-llu. Arulaircamek aipaan-
am pillinia, "Inerqullruamken-ggem paqnakesqevkenanuk. Tangrrumariarpekuk
pinqigcaqunanuk, picurlagceciiqerpekuk. Tumyaram kelliakun ayautamegten. Avaggun ayagyaaqekumta takenruan augna. Canimellrakun ayautamegten." Paqnayun-
qigtenritliniuq tangrrumariamikek. Natetmun-llu ayauyuciinani patumiimi.

only go out like this when the residents in our home push us, when they ask us to do what they request." They told him that they had come to bring him to their place. They told him not to refuse. So after they said that, he got ready. When he was ready he went toward the exit, and after putting out the lamp and standing in the dark by the door, one of the two asked him to go out first. He answered, "I'm not going out first. You two lead the way."

The moon was full and bright outside. When they went outside, he saw a sled with a flat bed. And on the sled were two caribou skins rolled up and tied. Then they untied one of them and spread it out on the sled. And two harnesses made of walrus-skin line were attached to the front of the sled. Then one of them told him to lie down on the skin with his head toward the front; they placed something there for his head to lie on. The man said, "I'm not going to lie down with my head in front." Though the *ircenrraak* [two extraordinary beings] insisted, the man quarreled with them. He told them that he wasn't going to lie down with his head in the front and told them to turn the skin the other way. They moved the pillow to the back and smoothed it out, and though they asked him to lie down like this, he lay down on his side. Then they rolled the skin over his body and tied it closed.

When they were done tieing him up, without closing this part very securely, one of them said, "Now, when we start going, don't look at us at all, even though you are curious." He didn't say anything. Soon after that, the sled started moving forward. After going for a while, the sled started to move faster. And the two up front started breathing heavily, he started to hear their breath. It was very bright where he was. Then his curiosity began to grow about those two up front. Since his arm could move, he pulled back the loosely tied skin. He became curious when the sled started hitting the ground and going up in the air and staying afloat for a while before coming back down. When he pulled the skin back and peered out, he saw two wolves running up there pulling the sled, and their tongues had started to stick out and hang down from their mouths. After he looked at them for a while, he pushed the skin back to close the gap.

And just as he closed his peephole, they gradually slowed down and suddenly halted. As soon as they stopped, one of them said, "We told you not to look at us, even though you are curious. Now that you've seen us, don't peek out and look at us, fearing that might cause us trouble. We are taking you through the area behind the actual trail. If we follow that trail over there, we won't get there as fast. We are taking you by a route that will get you to our place faster." For the rest of the trip he didn't look out again, since he had already seen them. He didn't know which way he was going or where, since he was covered and couldn't see.

Akaarnun-gguq agturaqerluku cailkaq arulairtuq. Nutaan makluni, naqyutair-
luku maktelliniuq, taituk-gguq tuar. Tua-i camek tangerrnaunani tua-i. Man'a
taugaam nunii assirluni kiarnaqluni. Pilliniak taukuk, "Kitak tuani utaqauraa it-
rutestekarpenun elpengcauteqataramegten." Tamaavet-llu tua-i pulqertellinilutek
taitugngalngurmun. Ak'anun pivkenatek malruulutek ukuk yun'erraraak-am anqer-
telliniuk ayarurlutek. Aipaan-gguq narullgimek ayarua nuugluni, aipaan-gguq taugken kukikcarmek. Cetuk-gguq tuar waten nuuga. Ullagluku tua-i qukaqmikluku
waten tass'uqerluku, tamatum engeliinun nangercamek taum, cetugngalngurmek
ayarulgem tauna aipani pillinia, "Kitaki-ata tua-i ciumek pituuten pinguaqerru."

Tamana-am taitugngalnguq tuggliniluku, itqertelliniluni tauna cetugngalnguq.
Cayulliniluku-ll' tua-i tamana taitugngalnguq. Canimelliqerluni-ll' tua-i tauna im'
allgarutelliniluni qungagarrluni-ll'. Tauna im' kukikcarmek ayarulek, qanlliniuq, "Ii,
ciuqliim-llu pivkenaku." Tuaten qanrraarluni ayaruminek taumek narullgirualeg-
mek tuggliniluku. Tugerngani ulliirtelliniluni. Ikirtelliniuq ellakegtaar, kiaguluni
tua-i qanikcamek cataunani. Itrucimini piqalliniuq, ayautenga'arcagni, imarpik' un'a.
Kankut-wa-gguq imarpiim qaingani nunat. Qairem-gguq naluurturluki. Mermi nunat imarpigmi. Tuamtell'-am piuraqerluni camek qigcilkircami piqalliniuq, ellami pikani nunat-am pikegkut. Uluriam-gguq naluurturluku nunarugaat ellarrlainarmi.

Tuamtell' tua-i piuraqerluni piqalliniuq, nunat-am makut ciunrata kelulirnerani.
Qertulriim qaingani nunarugaat nunamun tusngaluteng mat'umun. Tua-i tanger-
cetraarluki taum pillinia aipaan, "Kankut tang kana-i ciuqliit tangelten Qairuarmiu-
nek atengqellriit. Pikegkut-llu ellamelnguut Inglernarmiunek. Ingkut-llu kinguqliit
Ininermiunek. Wavet waniw' piqatartuten. Unkut atam tangerqerki curukat agiir-
tellriit." Imarpiim tunglirneranun takuyalliniuq, mer'em qaingakun ikamrarugaat.
Yuraryartulriit tua-i cunaw' tuavet Ininermiunun curukat. Tagutelliniluku tua-i tuavet. Mayuutelliniluku-llu tamatumun quagurpagmun. Qasgimun tekiucamegnegu
elaturramun unitelliniluku. Itqataami pillinia, itrutestekaanun elpengcauteqatarniluku utaqasqelluku. Itraartellukek-am yun'erra'ar man' anqertelliniuq atauciuluni.
Tallirpilirnerakun uuggun teguqerluku kalvagulluku.

After he had gone for a while and had touched the ground several times, he stopped. After they untied the binding and he got up and looked around, the atmosphere around him was covered with what looked like fog. And you couldn't see anything out there. But his immediate surroundings were clear, and he could see things. Then the two said, "Okay, you stay right here while we alert those who will bring you in." Right after they said that, they quickly took off and disappeared into the fog. Soon after, two young men popped out of that fog holding walking sticks. The tip of the walking stick of one had a weasel on it, and the other's walking stick tip was a translucent stone. The tip of his walking stick looked like a fingernail. They took him by each arm and escorted him to the edge of the fog. Standing there, the one with a walking stick that had a tip that looked like a fingernail turned to his companion and said, "Okay, since you are always the first to try it, try opening it."

He then poked his walking stick through what appeared to be fog, and its tip went right through. Then he started pulling the fog with his walking stick. And just when the fog got close, the tip tore through and came off and the fog rolled back. The other young man with the translucent stone on his walking stick said disdainfully, "So then, the first try has failed!" After he said that, he poked the fog with his walking stick that had a weasel carving on its tip. And as soon as he poked it with the tip, the fog split and tore open. It opened into a place with perfect summer weather and no snow. Once inside, they started going with those two escorting him, and he saw the ocean down below. And down on the ocean he saw a village. They were on a wave, and it was moving them up and down. It was a village sitting on the water in the ocean. And as they were going, he looked up and saw a village up there in the sky. It was a huge village up there, and the *uluriam* [?] was moving them up and down.

Then after they went for a while, he noticed a village ahead of them. It was a huge village sitting directly on high ground. After he was shown that village, one of his escorts said, "The first village you saw down on the ocean, the name of that village is Qairuarmiut. And the village you saw up in the sky is called Inglernarmiut. And the last village you saw over there is Ininermiut. You are going to that village. Now, look and see people down there coming for a dance festival." He turned and looked toward the ocean and saw many, many travelers on sleds moving along right on the water on the ocean. They apparently were guests who were coming to Ininermiut to dance. Then his escorts took him to that village. They took him right up to the high ground [where the village was]. When they got to the *qasgi*, the two went in and left him in the porch. Before they went in, they told him to wait and that they were going to alert someone to bring him inside. After they went in, a young man

Amiguyugkun maani kalvagyarakun itrarluni pilliniuq iquani uivakayaller una tuss'araa, pall'itaak-wa-gguq pikegkuk. Nangercaaqelriim ilututacia maatekaaralliniluni tauna, tuss'aram taum qainganek. Ilutupiarluni kan' kalvagyaraat. Qaillun-llu angtayaaqa tauna. Pikna taugaam egaleq, qasgim egalra alaunani kiimi, qamkut ipingaluteng ilutum ugaan. Taum-am pillinia tuavet arulairesqelluku, nugtestekaanun elpengcauteqatarniluku. May'uqertelliniluni-ll'-am tua-i tauna. Tayimnguuraqerluni angulvakayallraak ukuk sugtupiak igvallinilutek. Kalvagcamek tua-i, taum uivarpallraam qaingani nangerngallrani, tallik teguqerlukek unrek aciiqerlukek, nugtelliniluku pall'itaagnegun.

Tuc'ami kiartelliniuq qasgi inglerluni qulliqelrianek. Yugnek-gguq tua-i imarluni tua-i, atliq-llu man'a. Kiarrluni tua-i ciungani-ll' tangeqsailamiki. Piqalliniuq ukalirnermi caniqami angun una angutngurrluni imarmiutarmek atkugluni nacaunani, man'a pugyaraa asguruarrarluni. Ayakutaraak-gguq qiilinglutek. Quliini-wa-gguq pikna qugyuguaq agalria, yagingaluni, swan-aruaq agautarluni. Uitavkenani-gguq uivvaarturluni. Taum tua-i waqaallinia. "Tua-i-qaa taunguuten, elpenguuten, akngirkenglleq?" Tua-i neq'aqaamiu tauna kegluneq angllliniluku. Angran pillinia, "Qaill' pillrani akngirciu?"

Nutaan qanemciqurallinia. Taukuk irniakek tumkartellerminiki tua-i assikluki tua-i qaill' pivkenaki tangvallruyaaqniluki. Qaillun-llu pivkenaki tua-i unitellruniluki. Taugaam taukugnun tua-i angayuqaagkenun uterrnginanermini qayaminun piniluni. Tua-i inerqularyaaqnilukek taqesqelluni qaill' pinritniluki irniakek. Aug'umek tua-i nutegmek-llu tamatumek qanemcilluku. Kinguneni caskungniluki tamakunek nutegnek avisviilngurnek. Tamatumek tamaa-i nalqigucaaqellrunilukek, akngirciiqnilukek mat'umek taqsunrilkagni. Tua-i niitenrilagnek ilalciryuumiilami elliinun akngirtellruniluku tauna.

Pakemna-wa-gguq tang, akmaken tallirpilirnerem kiatiitnek, ikegkut amatiitnek qamaken qenaaguralria. Cauciinaku. Nalqigcan tua-i tuaten pillinia, "Ikna-w' ika-i nukalpiaq akngiringalria, ukut-llu qaillun caliaqesciigalkiit. Tua-i kalivqinar-

ran out by himself. Then he took him by his left arm and helped him down through the front entrance hole.

As he went in through the passage, at the upper end he saw a huge spine bone used as a step, and looking up he saw the *pall'itaak* [frame entrance to the underground tunnel] up above. When he stepped up on the spine and stood up, he was standing up about this far in the hole. The hole where you come up and go into the *qasgi* was very deep. I don't know how tall that man was. When he stood on the step, he could only see the skylight up in the ceiling and couldn't see the rest of the room inside. His escort then told him to stay there and said he was going in to alert someone to help him up through the hole. Then he quickly climbed up into the *qasgi*. Soon after, two tall men came into view by the hole. After slipping down through the hole, while the man was standing on the huge spine step, they slipped their arms under his arms and lifted him up through the hole with the support of the *pall'itaak*.

Once he was inside the *qasgi*, he saw that it had two levels of sleeping benches on the side walls of the room. The upper level was filled with people sitting, and also the lower level. He stood and looked at the people because he had never seen them before. As he turned his head he saw an older man sitting against the front wall on this side, wearing a hoodless mink parka. A strip of fur was sewn on the parka's neck opening as a ruff. His sideburns were covered with gray hair. And right above where he was sitting was a model of a swan hanging with its wings spread out. It was hanging on a string and moving and continuously turning. It was that man there who greeted him and said, "Hello. Are you the person who injured someone?" Since he remembered the wolf he had shot, he said yes. When he said yes, he asked again and said, "What was he doing when you hurt him?"

Then he told him the story. He told him that when he encountered their pups, he had just admired them. And he said that he just watched them and left without even touching them. He told the man that it was the parents who had attacked him while he was going back to his kayak. And he said that he tried to tell them to stop and that he hadn't done anything to their pups. He also told the man about his gun. [He said] that people back at his home had started owning guns like his that couldn't be evaded. He told him that he had tried to tell them what his weapon could do and that he would hurt them with it if they didn't stop [hurting him]. Because they didn't stop and he wanted to fight back, he shot and hurt the wolf.

Then, from up there, from the back on the left across there, from the area beyond those sitting on the bench across there, he heard a moaning sound. He couldn't tell what it was. After he finished explaining, that elderly man said, "The *nukalpiaq*

luteng waniwa. Elpet akngirtellruan ikayuangnaqiu." Qeralliniluni igvallinia nukalpiaq una nevengqaluni, matangqaluni tua-i uligtuumaluni, qenaagurluni tua-i.
Tua-i taunguan tua-i kegluneq, nalluvkenaku tua-i akngirtellni tua-i, uyungluni
tua-i ulia ikirrluku pillinia akuraani, ekia tauna aqsaani, arinarnimek-gguq tepnge-
lliniluni. Pia-gguq puyurkarrluk avatiini uqlausngaluni. Pininrilliniluni-gguq tauna,
qenaagurluni taugaam, erinani antaarturluku. Carrirturalliniluku tua-i tauna ekia.
Nepairusngiinarluni-gguq carrillra maliggluku. Puyurkarrluk tamana nepingalria
aug'arturluku. Carrinqeggian nepairutliniluni tauna. Tua-i carrirviirucan taqluku.
Taqngani aarraarraraalliniuq tauna, "*Aarrarrarraa*, anerneq atauciq ellinrakun anir-
turarpenga." Maktelliniluni tua-i nutaan.

Makcan tua-i, makteqertelluku tauna imna caniqamelnguq angun imarmiutarmek atkulek, qugyuguamek qallilek qanlliniuq, "Allaneci qakemkut tekiteqatalliut
paqnarii." Anuranga'artelliniluteng. Tauna-ll' imna assiriluni tua-i carriani. Nangerrluni tayim' anlliniluni. Qasgi tua-i tamana yuirutliniluni. Ellii tua-i kiimi uitaqalliniluni, taumek qugyuguamek qullilegmek aiparluni. Kiimek elli'ircamek taum
pillinia, "Wangkuk-llu tang tua-i paqnayukarnaurtukuk." Nangercaaqelria pillinia,
"Tailuten pikna atraresgu."

Tauna tua-i qugyuguaq atrarrluku ciuqerranun ellilliniluku. Elliaku tua-i tauna
atrarluni qainganun aqumelliniluni, waten irugni maavet yaqugkenun ellilukek,
uyaqurri wantelluki amlemini, qugyuguam. Aqumngami pillinia, "Kitak tunumnun
pamavet aqumi, qukamkun qetniarpenga." Qasgim iluani. Aqumluni tua-i elkarr-
luni qukaakun qelluku piqanrakun, qerratarutellinilukek taum qugyuum. Uivelli-
niluni-ll' tua-i qasgim iluani uciklukek. Anelraami-ll' yaqugni qungllukek, kalvagyarakun, pall'itaagnun, kalvagyaramun anluni nunamun agtuuteksaunani. Uani-ll'
qaivarluni elaturraanun qasgim. Yaqugni qungingaurlukek. Uani-ll' elaturraan amiigakun pelluami, nutaan nengtellinilukek yaqugni. Qulmurrlutek, yuut-llu makut
quliitnun elliamek uivlutek, qasgim pikavet egalran quliinun, cauluki imkut unkut,
arulailliniluni. Acia-am yaaqsigluni. Ik'iki canimellilliniluteng-gguq tua-i tamakut
ikamraruugaat.

across there was injured, and these people can't work on his injury. They are left with no other means to help him. You try and help him since you hurt him." So he went across and looked and found a *nukalpiaq* lying on his back with no clothes on, covered with a blanket. He was lying there moaning. Since he knew that he was actually the wolf he had hurt, he crouched down and pulled back his cover and saw his wound on his belly, and apparently it had started to smell. He saw gun powder caked around the puncture wound. And the young man apparently had gotten weak and was crying out in pain. He then started cleaning the wound. And as he cleaned it and removed the puss, the young man there slowly started quieting down. He continued to clean out the gunpowder from around the wound. And when the wound was clean, the young man stopped groaning. When it was clean, he stopped. When he was done, that *nukalpiaq* sighed loudly and said, "*Aarrarrarraa*, you have saved my life while I was just about to breathe my last breath." Then he got up.

Right after that *nukalpiaq* sat up, the elderly man with a mink parka sitting next to the wall by the door, the man who had a model swan hanging over him said, "It's time to go out and check on your guests, for they might be almost reaching our village." Then people got up and started going out. And that *nukalpiaq*, since his wound had been cleaned and he was good, stood up and went out. Everybody went out of the *qasgi* except for him and the elderly man who had a swan model hanging over his head. Once they were alone, the elderly man said, "We should go and check them out, too." When he started standing up the man said, "Come over and take that one up there down."

He took that model swan down and placed it on the floor in front of the man. Then that elderly man got up and went down and sat on it with its neck between his outstretched legs. After the man sat down he said, "Okay, you sit behind me and put your arms around my waist." They were inside the *qasgi*. Then right after he sat down behind him and put his arms around his waist, the model swan started to lift off. Then the swan flew up and circled around inside the *qasgi* with them on its back. Then, when it flew toward the exit, it folded its wings back and glided out through the passage without touching the bottom. And when it reached the end of the passage it slipped up through the hole, and they were in the porch. The swan kept its wings folded in. And they continued on out and exited through the entryway out to the porch, and once they were outside, the swan began to spread its wings. The swan started to lift off and flew up, and when they got above the people assembled down below, they circled them, and the swan stopped facing those guests above the *qasgi* skylight. They were way up there and could see them all. There were many, many sleds just about to reach the village.

Alegnariata tua-i nutaan itliniluteng. Itrameng tua-i taum qugyuguamek teng-ssuutelgem, tengaurcuukaralgem, tauna eniinun ellivkarraarluku qanrutlinii, una wani kingunranun utercetesqelluku, ilakluku kassuucunaitniluki. Alingurnaqni-luku picurlallerkaa. Qaillukuarpek'naku utercetesqelluku, anevkaasqelluku. Iliit pilliniuq. "Naliatgun-mi anciqa?" Taum kiullinia, "Inerquramci qaillukuarutesqev-kenaku. Elliikun tuaggun anevkarciu." Piqalliniuq amigtangqellinilria ugna pinga-yunek. Atliq-gguq kan'a tan'gercenani, pikna-gguq taugaam qulliq tua-i tanqigcet-qapiarluni, una-gguq taugken akuliik, mat'um tua-i ellamta tanqianek tanqigluni. Yuug-am malruk teguluku anelrautelliniluku. Tuaggun tua-i akunleqlirkun anluni. Pellukarluku-ll' tupakalliniluni, uigarrngatliniluni. Uigartelliniuq qasgim iluani ui-talria, nevengqaurluni tua-i tuani uitallmini.

Tuani-gguq tua-i — Kituriyaaqelliniunga. Tamaani aqvavailgatni uksuarmi inar-taqami aturpagalrianek niitelangelria inartaqami. Canimelliinarluteng-gguq. Yu-rarcuutnek yuarutnek, *ua-ua-ua-yarraa*nek-gguq iquklicararluteng. Elilluki-gguq tua-i yuarutet tamakut. Tua-i qaill' pivkenani tua-i pinqigtevkenani qaillukuanri-latni tua-i qaill' pivkenani, assirluni. Anlliniuq tan'qigiaralliinilria qakemna unullra. Tupagnarian tua-i agluni enemini ilani taukut tupaggluki.

Tua-i-llu pinarian, Kangirnaarmiunun kanavet, Kuigilngurmiut nunaurpail-gata kastelliniluteng. Upagluteng yurallerkaat canimelliqataan, kassiyullerkaat. Tua-i pinarian ilateng piata, yuarutetarkaitnek-am yuaruciqunglliniluteng. Tua-i tamakut elitellni ircenrrartaat yuarutet ilaitnek yuarucilliniuq caqerluni. *Ua-ua-ua-yarraa*nek iquklicararluteng. Tua-i-ll'-am taukut ilurain tamakut, qanemcimarian tua-i, Uauaualegmek acilliniluku. Tua-i-llu-gguq ingna yaa-i, una wani, kuig-una uksuillra man'a engelkarrluku Uauaualegmek aterluni yaa-i kuik. Taum tua-i ui-tallra. Ingna tua-i kuik tuaten qanemciuguq. Iquklituq tua-i augna ava-i.

When the sleds were just about to arrive, they all went inside. Then the old man with the model swan as an airplane, after he had the model swan hung back up in its place, he told everyone there in the *qasgi* that the man there must be allowed to go home. He said that they and their guests arriving out there couldn't meet while he was with them. He added that if they mistreated him in any way, they would get into a frightful situation. He told them to let him go home, to let him go out without doing anything to him. Then one of the people in there asked, "Which way should we let him go out?" That elderly man replied, "I just told you to leave him alone and not do anything to him. Let him go out through his own world." Then the man suddenly noticed three doorways in the front [one on top of the other]. The lowest doorway was very dark, and the top doorway was very bright, and the light of the middle one was as bright as the light in our world. Then two people took him by the arms and escorted him toward the front. He then went out through the middle way. And just when he got outside, he suddenly woke up. When he woke up he was inside his little *qasgi*, he was back in that spot where he was lying on his back resting after taking a fire bath.

During that time—I just remembered this part of the story I apparently hadn't mentioned. In the fall before they came and got him, he started to hear people singing when he went to bed at night. The sound was getting closer and closer every time he heard people singing dance songs. The songs would end with chants that normally ended with "*Ua-ua-ua-yarraa.*" He would listen to the songs and learn them. [So after he returned home] he was fine, and nothing happened to him after that. When he went out of his *qasgi* it was early in the morning and dawn had just started to arrive. Since it was time to get up, he went inside his house and woke up his family.

Then when it was time [that man and his family] went down to Kangirnaarmiut. They went there when the time came for people to gather for a dance festival. Then when it was time, people started composing songs to be sung when gifts were brought into the *qasgi*. Then one day that man sang some of the songs he had learned from the *ircenrraat*. The songs with typical endings that go "*Ua-ua-ua-yarraa.*" Then his cousins there, after he told the story about his experience and how he had learned those songs, named him Uauaualek. So that river over there, this one here, this river here where that man lived during the winter, is called Uauaualek up to this time. That river was where that man lived. The story I just told is connected to that river over there. That's the end of that story.

Ircenrraat Qaurraarmiut

Ingkuk Qaurraak itercitullrulliniuk ketmun caumallermegni. Taugaam qaill' piiyuunaki tua-i picirkartuyarulluki-ll' nanikuavkarluki piiyuunaki.

Maa-i tang maa-i Qaurraak. Waniwa-tang Qaurraak wantuk waniwa, uum qipeckellriim keluani. Waniwa-gguq una amillrat. Tuantellruut tua-i. Ukatmun taugaam caucateng taum angalkum yuliulallrat pitekluku taqluteng tua-i.

Una wan' kangiqutaq caumaluku. Caumalallruat. Amilqaat-gguq tauna.

ALICE: Luglaam-qaa taum angalkuum?
FRANK: Ii-i, Kangirnaarmiut angalkuata-gguq taum. Qetunraa-gguq tauna tan'gaurlurrauluni. Aiparrangqelartuq-gguq nasaurlurrarmek, aiparnikluku tua-i. Taumeg-am aiparluni pillragni, itertellinilukek ukut wani. Tukeqnirtengermeng-gguq, pissuutailnguq tua-i arulairngaituq. Amlliranrilngermi ayagluni taugaam taum tungiinun, Qaurraak tungiignun. Nanvat-llu makut quliitgun ayagaqluni tua-i itrutaqatni. Yugmek tangeqsailengermeng tua-i, pissaangermeng pisciiganateng tua-i, taukut taugaam Qaurraak tungiignek ayagluteng. Imum-gguq taugaam irnerrlugngalnguum avaciumaluki pituit.

Ircenrraat caskuita (itrulluki). Urluvminek-gguq tauna tan'gaurluller tegumiarrarluni. Tauna-llu-gguq aipaa nasaurluq uluamek. Nanikuangengamek taum tan'gaurlullraam tauna nasaurluq pillinia, "Uluarpegun kepqerru." Tamana teguqerluku kep'artelliniluku. Kep'arcaaqerraarluni, egmian usguarrluni. Tua-i pilaryaaqekii egmianun usguartaqluni, nemrumastesek. Tan'gaurlullraam-am taum teguqerluku keggmaqerluku kep'artelliniluku, angiartellinilutek. Ayakataqerlukek-am nemqaullukek; usguartelliniluni. Allamek kep'aqan angiartaqlutek. Ayakataryaaq-

400

The Ircenrraat from Qaurraak

Those two [cliffs] over there, the Qaurraak, when [the doorway to their world] was facing down toward the ocean, the *ircenrraat* residing there used to bring people into their place. But after bringing them in, they didn't mistreat them or allow them to suffer in any way.

These here are Qaurraak. This is where the Qaurraak are, right behind this sharp bend in the river here. This was where their original doorway was located. [The *ircenrraat*] resided right there. But because they bothered people and continued to bring people into their place, a shaman turned their place around, and after that they stopped bringing people in.

The entrance to their world faced this cove right here. They say that was their doorway.

ALICE: Was Luglaaq the shaman who turned it?

FRANK: Yes, he was the shaman who lived in Kangirnaarmiut. He had a little son at the time. The little boy was friends with a little girl, and they were always playing together. One day when they were out on the land, [the *ircenrraat* from Qaurraak] apparently took them inside their place. Though a person tried to pull back, one without protection cannot stop [being taken] and will go right through. A person, when taken in, will move in the direction of Qaurraak, even though that one wasn't walking and taking steps. And when taken in by them, the person will travel above these lakes here and head toward Qaurraak. They would head directly toward Qaurraak, even though they tried to stop, never seeing other people. But when they were taken in, they were usually covered by something that looked like seal gut.

Ircenrraat would use their weapons and take them in. The little boy had his bow and arrow, and the girl had a woman's knife. When they started feeling hopeless, the boy told the girl, "Cut it with your knife." She grabbed [the strapping] and immediately cut it. After it was cut, it immediately repaired itself. She kept trying to cut it, but the binding around them would instantly reconnect. Then the boy started biting it with his teeth, and when it broke, it got loose and fell off. And just as they were about to go, they were covered and strapped again. The strapping kept com-

nginanragni nemqautaqlukek taum, kiituan Qaurraagnun, amiigatnun tekicamek itrutliniagket.

Taum tan'gaurlullraam tua-i takuani tuqunerrarluni Kangirnaarmiu angalkuq angukaraurluq. Qasgiatnun tua-i itrutlinilukek. Nang'erteurlullinilutek tua-i caniqliqa'arrlutek. Urluvcuallerani-am tegumiaqluku taum. Iliita-am nangerrluni itrautellinilukek kiavet tugeryaramun qavavet aqumevkallinilukek. Kiarrluni pivakarluni pilliniuq caniqami, imna augna tuqulleq tangvallra tua-i elitaqluku. Uitaqertelluki tem'irtellria qulirneratgun kitulliniluni. Ak'anun pivkenani, camaggun atlirneratgun utertelliniluni tayima. Akultutaciqerrluni pakmaggun kituraqluni tayima. Tuatnaqertelluki iliit qanlliniuq, "Qaill'-mi waniw' piqatarceta?" Iliit kiugartelliniuq. "Piciryararpecenek-ata akulirilukek."

Tamanek-gguq tauna tan'gaurluller atkungqertuq piciatun ayuqenrilngurnek yaqulegnek melqurrit elaqliqluki. Iliit-am atraqrutliniuq, tuarpiaq-gguq asevrem ungii, *plastic*-aarnganani akagenqeggluni. Ullagluku-ll' tua-i qauraakun waten ciugarrluku, iqua teguqerluku cupqautiini, iigken wavet akuliignun tuc'ami, nuvvliniluku una akuliraa tamatum. Iqua-ll' aglumun qillrulluku nayumiqaluku. Pegcatni allgutevkenani agaqalliniluni tauna. Tamatumek agautarluni uuggun nevusngaluni ukuani. Una-ll' cevteksaunani. Tauna tan'gaurluller. Tukarluni tua-i ellamek. Tua-i-ll' piuraqerluni kevkaarrluku tamana asevrem ungakngalkii. Igtelliniluni. Aug'arrluni-ll' tauna akuliraanek. Iliit-gguq-am iirtuq, "Ii. Ciuqliim-llu pivkenaku!" Tagqerqaarluni-am iliit atralliniuq, tamatumi amillruluni, tegumiarluni. "Mat'umek kitak naspaaqer nunam yualuanek."

Tua-i-am tuaten piluku tegumiaqluku, nayumiqaluku nuvutelliniluku wavet akuliraanun, agarrluku-llu. Qipcilliimi-am tua-i egmian kevkarrluku igtelliniluni. Tuc'an iliit nang'ercaaqelria, taum imum elitaqellran angalkum tua-i tuqullrem pillinii, "Tua-i taqiciu. Atiin elpekekunici qacigcessngaitaaci. Ava-i tang nepii niitelaqci. Taum atakaa, Luglaaq, qetunrani yuaraa nallunailngurmek. Taqlukek anevkarcikek.

ing off every time they cut it, and right when they were about to go, they would be covered and bound again. And eventually they got to the doorway of Qaurraak and were brought in.

Previously, in the presence of that little boy, an old man, a shaman from Kangirnaarmiut, had died. They were brought into the *qasgi* [of the *ircenrraat*]. Then they took those two pitiful children and stood them side by side. That boy was holding his small bow. Then someone from the side came down and escorted them to the *tugeryaraq* [log against the back wall] and told them to sit there. When the boy looked around the room, he suddenly saw that old man who had died in his village sitting against the wall. He recognized him. Then, shortly after that, they heard a booming sound from above. The sound came and went right over the *qasgi* and then diminished. Then, minutes later, the sound came back the same way and descended. They continued to hear the sound going by over them like that. After they heard the sound several times, one of the people said, "So, what are we going to do now?" Then another person quickly replied, "Go ahead and do what you've always done and place [the line] in the skin between his eyes."

They say that boy was wearing a parka made of all sorts of bird skins, with the feathers on the outside. One of them quickly ran down from the side holding something that looked like the whisker of a walrus beard, that looked like plastic and was perfectly round. Then he went to the boy and pushed him on his forehead and lifted his head up, took the end of the thing he was holding, and as soon as he blew on it, it went straight to the boy's face right between his eyes and went in. Then the boy was lifted up while the end of the line was tied to the ceiling beam. And when they let go, the boy was suddenly dangling and the string didn't even break through his skin. The end of the string he was hanging from was strung through [the skin between his eyes]. While the boy was hanging, a booming sound reverberated from outside. Then, shortly after, that line resembling a whisker broke. The boy dropped to the floor. The end of the line that pierced the skin between his eyes had broken through and came off. Then one of the men on the side yelled, "Yes. And the first attempt has failed!" After one of them ran to the side, he returned holding a line that was thinner then the first one. [He said], "Try hanging him back up, using this sinew that came from the land."

Then they held him and threaded the line through the skin between his eyes and hung him up. And when he violently twisted, the line broke and he fell down again. After he landed and one of the men on the side started to stand up, the shaman he recognized, the one who had died, addressed everyone there, "Stop trying to hang him. When his father realizes where his son is, he will retaliate with fervor. The

Itqetaatulria iciw' kiimi maavet qasgimtenun. Akiurviituq. Umyuara navguquvciu piunrirciqaakut." Tua-i-gguq nutaan anevkaragket. Cali tuaggun akunleqlirkun, aug'utun, anevkarlukek taukuk tan'gaurlullraak. Pitegcautni-gguq tamakut tamallret, allragni-ll' tamallret tekitaqamiki teguqaqluki taum tan'gaurlullraam. Nalkurluki tamakut tamalallret pitegcautai. Tua-i-gguq taum tua-i nutaan caliaqellrui Qaurraarmiut kelutmun caulluki tua-i. Tua-i-llu-gguq taqluteng tua-i yuliurnanrirluteng. Taugaam tua-i yaa-i cali nallutaituk ingkuk Qaurraak.

Maa-i piuguk cali, tamana piak. Augna ava-i qanemcikaqa-am aug'umun ilakluku. Uauaualegmek tua-i qanemcikaqamegteggu aterpagtaalaraat. Una-ll' waniw' nunallra Uauaualegmek aterpagtaarluku, kuig-ingna. Maa-i tua-i nunallri ingkut uitaurluteng.

booming sound out there is his father. The sound is doubtlessly the boy's father, Luglaaq, looking for his son. Stop what you are doing and let those children go out. [Luglaaq] is the only one who comes in and out of our *qasgi*. He cannot be challenged. If you hurt his feelings, he will destroy us." Then they decided to let those children go out. They allowed them to go out through the middle doorway as in the previous story. While they were going home, the boy kept finding arrows he had lost before, and ones he had lost the year before. Every time he found one, he'd pick it up. It was after that that the shaman, Luglaaq, worked on those *ircenrraat* at Qaurraak, and he turned their place around. Then, after he turned their place around, they stopped bothering people. But today, the Qaurraak over there are still aware and always know what is happening around them.

[The Qaurraak] are still there, and they still have power. I've just told you the story about [Luglaaq] in addition to the story about [Uauaualek]. [Luglaaq's] name was always mentioned when the story about Uauaualek was told back in those days. And where he lived, the river over there, they'd call it Uauaualek, too. His old place is still visible over there.

Tulukaruum Pillri Qulirat

Ayuqenritut tulukaruum pillri quli'irqelallrit. Ayuqevkenaku-am pilaraat tulukaruk.

Icivaq-ll'-am elitnauramnun quli'irqellruaqa augna iliit. Tulukaruk cenirtellria terr'et kitengkaqluki. Terr'et tamakut kitengkaqluki imkut imarpigmiutaat maani.

Tua-i-ll' ayainanermini-am tecuayaarmek tekicami kitengkaryaaqekiini, putukua quuqerrutellilniluku. Cayussaangraaku tua-i tegumiaqluku. Pegtesqelluni pian, terr'em taum kiullinia, "Pegcalqaarrngaitamken." [engelaq'ertuq]

Tulukaruk tua-i tauna iqlungartuq-llu. Pillinia, aturluni, "Tii-iq, tii-iq, pegesnga, pegesnga-rraa. Angaama, angacarama angyaan aipaanek nunulirciqamken. Pegesngaa!"

Kiugarrnauraa-gguq taum terr'em, "Tamakut qessakanka. Pegcalqaarrngaitamken!" [engelaq'ertuq]

Allamek-gguq tulukaruum piaqluku. Ula-llu-gguq man'a tekicarturluni. Ulel'uni.

"Tii-iq, tii-iq pegesnga, pegesnga-rraa. Angama qayaan aipaanek nunulirciqamken. Pegesnga!"

Kiugarrnauraa, "Tamakut qessakanka. Pegcalqaarrngaitamken!"

Uuqassugangluni tua-i tulukaruk, ulem tekiskani qecuqiciiqngami, uluskani. Tua-i piiyaaqaqluku.

Tua-i-am caqerrluni pillinia, "Tii-iq, tii-iq pegesnga, pegesnga-rraa, Angama, Angacarama nulirran aipaanek nunulirciqamken." [engelaq'ertuq]

(Terr'ungermi-lli-tam' taumi arnaryullinivaa.) [engel'artut]

Nutaan qanrucani tauna pilliniuq, "Ilumun-qaa nulirkamnek cikirciqavnga?"

Raven Stories

There are many tales about the raven and things he did. There are many different stories about the raven.

I just told one of the raven stories to my students not too long ago. The one I told was the story about the raven walking along the beach, kicking sea anemones as he went. He would kick those sea anemones, those sea creatures you can find around here.

As he was going he came upon a tiny little sea anemone, and just when he slightly tapped it with his foot, the little creature suddenly snapped shut, and his toe was caught inside. He tried to pull his foot out, but the little thing was holding on tightly. When he asked it to let go of his foot, that sea anemone replied, "I will not let go of you." [*chuckles*]

That raven was also a liar. He started singing and said, "Sea anemone, sea anemone, let me go, let me go. I will award you one of my uncle's, my dear uncle's boats. Let me go!"

That sea anemone would quickly answer him and say, "I don't desire those things. I will not release you!" [*chuckles*]

The raven pleaded with it again and again to let him go. And he could see the water rolling in from down below. The tide was coming in.

"Sea anemone, sea anemone, let go of me, let go of me! I will award you with my uncle's other kayak. Let me go!"

He would quickly answer him, "I don't want those things. I will not release you!"

Raven was getting desperate, since he knew he would definitely drown when the water reached him, when the incoming tide covered him. He pleaded with him again and again to let him go.

Then after a moment he said, "Sea anemone, Sea anemone, let go of me, let go of me. I will award you with my uncle's other wife." [*chuckles*]

(How absurd and peculiar. Though it was a sea anemone, it apparently desired a woman.) [*laughter*]

When he told it that, it finally said, "Will you truly award me with a wife?"

Tulukaruum pillinia, "Aren iqlungaitamken. Nulirran aipaanek cikirciqamken. Pegeskuvnga waniw' aqvaciqaqa."

Pegcani tua-i tagluni pavavet, muragamek-am amilnguarmek kiarrluni. Piyunarqelriamek tegucami atralliniluni. Tekicamiu pillinia, "Kitak tua-i waniwa tegukiu." Tauna tecuayaaq cill'aqertelliniuq. Cill'aqercan tugpallinia taumek, "Teurluuq usuuq, caitua, piitua teq'ermek naullruunga." Tuqutelliniluku-llu tauna tamatumek kapurluku. Tuaten taktalartuq augna.

Tuamtell'—allauluni-am pillra. Cenirtelliniuq-am. Ayainanermini, camek imumek niigarcami piqalliniuk, uqviicaraankuk puyuqumiar-llu nucuktalriik. Cet'garciaqamek-gguq aluviliuqernaurtuk. Ken'ngesciiganatek.

Tulukaruum-am tangvauraami, tuaten piaqagnek pilangelliniuq, "Aluviluvilu." Allamek-gguq ellirraarluku, aipaan nucuktaarluku piaqluku. Piuraqerluni cet'gartaqluni.

Aluviliuqeraqagnek-gguq tulukaruum pinaurak, "Aluviluvilu."
Caqerlutek aipaan pilliniluku, "Usuuq, kaaka. Tulukaruum-am pingllinikiikuk."

Pillinia, "Kitak tua-i pikakuk tengvallagniartukuk waten qalrialunuk, 'Uqrutnek pukukcarta! Ananek neresta!'" Qanerkiurlutek.

Tua-i-am tuaten pian tengvallallinilutek qalrialutek tuaten, "Uqrutnek pukukcarta! Ananek neresta!" Tulukaruum avavet tangvauraqerlukek qanlliniuq, "Tua-i picetaarucama pikiigna augkuk." Nangerrluni-am ayalliniuq.

Ayainanermini-am pilliniuq anipaq ingna irniaminek inqilria. Tua-i tekitellinia. Yaatiitnun-am mill'uni tulukaruum tangvalliniluku. Maaten-gguq tang tangvagaa waten atuutellinikai taukut irniani inqellerminiki, "Aa-ya-guu-ma-ar. Aa-ya-guu-maa, aa-ya-gurr-uu-ma-ar, aa-ya-guu-maa. Ya-qiur-ci! Ya-qiur-ci! Atasi imaqaa tekiskan imaq nerniartuci uullanek tallimanek. Aa-ya-guu-ma-ar, aa-ya-gurr-uu-maa. Ya-qiur-ci! ya-qiur-ci!" Irniari-gguq yaqiuksuaranga'arrnaurtut. Tulukaruum-am piviirte-

The raven instantly answered it, "I definitely won't deceive you. I'll give you one of his two wives. I will go and get her when you release me now."

When it released him, he went back on land and looked for wood that wasn't too wide. When he found one, he went down to the beach again. When he came to the sea anemone, he said, "Okay she's here, take her when you are ready." Then that tiny little sea anemone suddenly opened up. And as soon as it sprang open, he forcefully thrust the stick inside it and scornfully sneered at it, "You pitiful sea anemone, I have nothing. I don't have anything since I sprouted and came from a pit in the ground." He then killed the sea anemone, poking it with that stick. This is where the story about raven and the sea anemone usually ends.

And there's another [raven story] — what he did in this story is different. Again he was going along his merry way. As he went, he heard a sound coming from somewhere. When he turned, he saw a tree sparrow and a dipper trying to start a fire with a fire starter. When it would collapse, they'd stop and shed tears. They couldn't get it to ignite.

Since raven saw them [stopping and shedding tears] he started to comment every time they did that, saying, "*Aluviluvilu* [from *aluviliur-*, 'to be teary-eyed']." They'd reset the fire starter, and one of them would begin pulling the cord. While he was pulling, it would collapse.

When they begin crying, a little raven would say, "*Aluviluvilu.*"

After a while one of the birds said, "Hey, listen. Raven is watching nearby and has begun to taunt us."

Then the bird said, "Now, when he starts to sneer at us, let's fly off yelling these words, 'Raven, you who always clean and eat discarded butt wipes from people! You who constantly eat human excrement!'" They recited what they would say.

Then, when he started to ridicule them, they flew off yelling at him, "You who always clean and eat discarded butt wipes! You who constantly eat human excrement!" After the raven watched them fly off and sat momentarily, he said, "Oh well, those two have jeered back at me because I asked for it." Then he stood up and left.

As he was going he saw a snowy owl cooing and singing to its fledglings. Then he landed nearby and watched the owl. He listened and heard it singing, "*Aa-ya-guu-ma-ar. Aa-ya-guu-maa, aa-ya-gurr-uu-ma-ar, aa-ya-guu-maa.* Flap your wings! Flap your wings! So when your father arrives with five pieces of blubber you can eat. *Aa-ya-guu-ma-ar, aa-ya-gurr-uu-maa.* Flap your wings! Flap your wings!" As the owl sang, its chicks would begin flapping their little wings. After the owl sang several

lluku pillinia, "Usuuq." Aaniit tauna pillinia, "Iqlutun atulartuten usuuq. [*engelaq'er-tuq*] Waten taugaam atuquvet."

Elitnaullinia-am tulukaruum, "*Aa-ya-guu-ma-ar. Aa-ya-guu-maa, aa-ya-gurr-uu-ma-ar, aa-ya-guu-maa. Ya-qiur-ci! Ya-qiur-ci!* Atasi imaqaa tekiskan imaq nerniartuci uugnarnek tallimanek. *Aa-ya-guu-maa, aa-ya-gurr-uu-maa. Ya-qiur-ci! ya-qiur-ci!*"

Tuani tua-i pillinii irniani, "Kitak tua-i tengvallakuma, waten qalrialuci tengvallakici," Aug'utun-am kiulliniluku. "Uqrutnek pukukcarta! Ananek pukukcarta!" Tengvallalliniluteng-am tua-i tuaten qalrialuteng.

Tulukaruk-gguq-am uitauraqerluni piuq, "Tua-i picetaarucama-am pikiitnga augkut."
Nanitelartut pii tulukaruum.

Makut-llu-wa maa-i neqlernat imkut uyamiggalget. Tulukaruum, nuliallra-gguq tua-i tauna uyamignek-gguq nulirruciucillrua. Nulirruciucillrua uyamilirluku. Taum-gguq tua-i neqlernam nulirran iqlungassiyaagpakaan unitellrua tulukaruk.

Cali-am tua-i cenirtellermini tulukaruk qanganam igtiinek tekitelliniluni. Piiyaaqellinia yuunani. Tua-i-ll' painganun aqumluni tulukaruk uitalliniluni, igtii tauna capluku qanganam.

Piinanrani-am qanganaq akiqliqelriignek qaltarluni tekituq tua-i kiiryukacaarluni. Qaltagni-gguq elliak atsanek ayuqenrilngurnek imarlutek, naunrarnek, puyuraaraat-wa ukut. Iqrek-wa-gguq cali ukuk tua-i imartulukek, cali atsanek ayuqenrilngurnek imarlutek.

Tekicami pillinia, "Tulukaruuk, mernurtua avisnga."
Tulukaruum pillinia, "Avicalqenritamken. Avicalqerngaitamken."

"Wall'u-qaa iqvama ilaitnek maaken puyuraarnek cikirniamken, avisnga."
"Tamakut qessakankaa. Avicalqerngaitamken."
Tua-i qanganaam taum piuryaaqellinii qessakaqluki. Pillinia, "Camek-mi piyugcit?"
"Qallitegpenek piyugtua." Neryugluku.
"Kitak tua-i atuutnaumken. Elpenek atuulluten yuraa. Qavaquma nerniarpenga."
"Ilumun-qaa?"
"Aren ilumun-wa tua-i qavaquma nerniarpenga."

times, raven said, "Hey, owl." He said this to the hatchling's mother, "Hey you, you are not singing the right song to your chicks. [*chuckles*] You should sing like this."

Raven taught the owl and sang this song, "*Aa-ya-guu-ma-ar. Aa-ya-guu-maa, aa-ya-gurr-uu-ma-ar, aa-ya-guu-maa.* Flap your wings! Flap your wings! When your father arrives, you will eat five mice. *Aa-ya-guu-maa, aa-ya-gurr-uu-maa.* Flap your wings! Flap your wings!"

At that time mother owl said to her fledglings, "Okay, when I take off, follow me from behind yelling this." They sneered at raven with the same words the two birds used. "You who always clean and eat discarded butt wipes! You who constantly eat human feces!" The fledglings flew off yelling those words to the raven.

After raven sat for a while, he said, "[Those hatchlings] have ridiculed me since I asked for it."

Raven stories are usually short.

And the black brants that have necklaces around their necks. In one of the raven stories, he gave his new bride [the black brant] a necklace when he first married her. He put a necklace on her when she became his wife. In the story it says that because he was such an incessant liar, his wife, the black brant, left raven.

Also, while raven was going along one day, he came upon a squirrel's den. He checked inside, but no one was there. Then raven sat on the hole and stayed there, blocking the opening to squirrel's den.

While he sat there, squirrel arrived holding buckets in both hands and dripping with sweat. When she placed her buckets next to the hole, he saw that they were filled with different kinds of berries, including salmonberries and nagoonberries. And the inside corners of her mouth were full of all kinds of berries.

When she arrived, she said, "Raven, I'm exhausted, move out of my way."

Raven replied, "I will not move out of your way. I definitely will not move out of your way."

"Move out of my way, and I'll give you some of these nagoonberries."

"I don't want those [berries]. I will not move out of your way."

Squirrel continued to offer him different kinds of berries, but he didn't want them. Then she asked him, "Then what do you want?"

"I want the fatty muscles on your chest." He wanted to eat her.

"Then let me sing for you. Sing and dance. You can eat me when I fall asleep."

"Is that right?"

"Yes, truthfully, you can eat me when I fall asleep."

Nangertelliniluni. Igtaa-am tauna unitevkenaku, igtem ciuqerrani ellminek atuulluni yuralliniuq. "*Llikentaa.*" Canivaqtaacuarturluni-gguq tulukaruk, waten elliurturluni, "*Llikentaa. Llikentaa. Lliken, lliken, lliken, cetek-aa-ap.*"

Pileryalliniuq, "Waqaa? Cayarpiarcit?" Qanganaullugaam pillinia, "Tamana-wa
uqvilqurrayaaq itekcullerpenun naggluku paallauteknayukluku aug'aqataryaaqe-
keka. Aa tangtang tua-i qavarninga'arcaaqelrianga ak'a. Cakneq pikanirluten pikina.
Qavaquma nerciqerpenga."

Atulliniluni canivaqtaarluni waten elliurturluni, "*Llikentaa. Llikentaa. Llikentaa.
Llikentaa. Lliken, lliken, lliken, cetek-aa-ap!*"

Pillinia-am, "Waq' cayarpialarcit?"

"Aren tamana-wa itekcullerpenun naguteknayukluku uqvilquayaaq paallauteknayukluku aug'aqatalaryaaqekeka."

"Aa-a."

"Tua-i qavaqeryarpiartua. Pikanirluten-ata canivaqtaapassiyaagluten pikina. Qa-
varyarpialrianga tang ava-i."

Cikemluni-am tua-i aturluni yuralliniluni qeckaqtaarluni, canivaqertaqluni, "*Llikentaa. Llikentaa. Lliken, lliken, lliken, cetek-aa-ap!*"

Pileryagyaaqluni-am, kinguurtelliniluku. Qanganaq tauna itqertelliniuq igtemi-
nun. Qinqallinia ak'a matartellinilria kiiryuami qanganaq.

Tulukaruk tua-i itqercaaqellriim, tusgegminun nagtelliniluni. Tua-i iluteq'ngelliniuq tulukaruk, itqercaaqaqluni. Kiituan tua-i atungelliniuq, "Qamyumaa. Qamyumaa. Qallitegken taiyarkek. Akquteksukagken taiyarkek."

Qanganaarrlugaam-am kiugarrnauraa, "Iterluten nerikek."
Tua-i piiyaqvigminek unitelliniluku.

Tuamtell'-am cenirtelliniuq. Kuigmun mat'um tekicartuami, ceniikun pilliniuq
cetuat unkut iluani. Cetuarugaat qakervagaluteng tua-i. Cingiim-llu nuuganun
mill'uni piqanrakun, ketiikun uuggun ceturpakayaller qaktelliniluni.

Then the raven stood up. He stood right in front of the hole and started singing and dancing. He sang, "*Llikentaa.*" Raven was dancing and moving sideways a little bit while he was singing, "*Llikentaa. Llikentaaa. Lliken, lliken, lliken, cetek-aa-ap.*"

He suddenly stopped and said, "What are you doing? What were you going to do?" The squirrel replied, "I was going to remove that stick down there for I was worried that you might trip and fall. See, I did get sleepy already while you sang and danced. Next time, sing and dance with a little more gusto. You will eat me when I fall asleep."

He began to sing, dancing and skipping from side to side, like this, "*Llikentaa. Llikentaa. Llikentaa. Llikentaa. Lliken, lliken, lliken, cetek-aa-ap!*"

He then stopped and asked, "When you moved like that, what were you about to do?"

"Oh, I was going to take that stick next to your feet and remove it, for you might trip if you step on it."

"Oh, I see."

"I almost fell asleep. Next time, sing and dance with more enthusiasm and move from side to side a little more. I almost fell asleep while you sang and danced a few minutes ago."

He then closed his eyes and sang and danced jumping from side to side, "*Llikentaa. Llikentaa. Lliken, lliken, lliken, cetek-aa-ap!*"

He tried to grab her, but he missed. The squirrel ran into her den. He peeked inside and saw that squirrel had already removed her clothing, for she was hot and sweaty.

Then, as raven plunged forward to enter the den, his wings got caught at the opening. He tried to push his body through the hole again and again but would get stuck. [Not being able to enter], raven started feeling disheartened and began to cry, trying to push himself in. Then finally he started to sing. He sang, "You in there. You in there. Give me the fatty muscles on your chest. Give me those you promised me."

The squirrel quickly answered back pompously, "Come in and eat them."

After pleading with her for some time, he left her.

Again he continued along. And when he reached a river and went along the riverbank, he noticed beluga whales swimming down in the water. Many belugas were swimming and would arch their backs way up in the air before diving down. And just when he landed at the tip of a point of land, a huge beluga arched its back and went down right below where he landed.

Tulukaruk pilliniuq, "*Urr-urr-urr-urr-urr-uuu.* Cakneq qakervagaluten, ucurnaq-vallaarniartuten. Aitarpet-llu piaqluten."

Tayimnguuraqerluni ceturpaller tauna qaktelliniuq aitarmi. Canimelan tua-i, qec-kamgguqerluni tulukaruk, qanranun itqertelliniluni. Itqercami piuq amik una. Itli-niluni tua-i iluanun. Itliniuq tanqigcenani tua-i. Kenurraq-gguq tua-i pikna pikani agauralria iluani.

Qaillukuarluni tua-i piinanermini, tauna-am tanqigcelnguq agtuksuarluku pii-nanrani nipqertelliniluni. Tan'germi uitaqalliniluni, qaill' tua-i piviinani anesciiga-nani. Itervillni piiyaaqellinia quumaluni.

Nanikuanglliniuq tua-i. Cavkenani tua-i qavallerminek-am tupalliniuq, man'a uitallra mermi uitanrilnganani, pektayiinani. Tua-i uitainanrani qanelkitangartellil-riit pakemkut yuut. "Aling aren, qaill' man' cetuaq tuqullrua ekiinani?" Qaill' piluku tuqullrucianek piluteng, ekiitniluku qainga.

Tulukaruk umyuartelliniuq, "Nallemkun-llu uuggun uluaq kaputeqaqsaunaku." Tua-i piinanrani atam tanqigiqertellinilria-am qulii. Uluaq kaputelliniluku. Imu-mek-llu tua-i pakikaata piturnirtacimitun anqerrluni qulmurtellinilria, cukangnaq-luni tengaurluni qulmun.

Tua-i imkut cauciirucatni ellurluni yaatiitnun mic'ami piiyualuni ullallinikai. Te-kican pillinat, "Kitak tulukaruuk ikayuulluten. Neqkarpenek piciqamteggen."

Tulukarulkuum-am pillinii, "Tua-i tang pillerkamnek tuaken pilrianga. Camek-qaa tangenrrituci? Augna-tang tua-i kinguneqluku tuaken qulmun ayalleq cau-yugnarqelria. Pingaitua tua-i wii umyuarnarquq. Nerkumku naullunayuklua-llu." Atam ukut pilagtai taq'ertellinilriit. Tangellruat-gguq augna cauciinaku tungurrlug-luni mecignaunani. Arenqiatuq-gguq cukanraami qulmun ayagartellermini.

"Ilumun tang, tauna kiimi neqngunrituq pinrillaut-llu wangkuta." Aren unilluku-am ayalliniut. Tua-i taugaam ayiita nutaan pilalliniluku tulukaruum navgurluku qu-yurrlukuk tua-i. Navguumariamiu imarmiutarmun nulirrnialliniluni, aulukestekai-lan. Imarmiutarmek tua-i nuliangelliniluni.

Tua-i tuaken aqvataqluni cetuanek. Atam piinanermini-am pillinia, muragiuqa-

The raven said, "*Urr-urr-urr-urr-urr-uuu*. Dive again arching your back higher so you may look magnificent. You should open your mouth, too."

After it was underwater for a while, that huge beluga came up and arched its back with its mouth open. Since it was close enough, raven skipped slightly forward and dashed inside its mouth. After darting in, he saw an entryway in front of him. He then went in. He went into a room filled with light. He looked around and saw the light was coming from a lamp hanging up there.

Just as he was trying to figure out where he was and reached and slightly tapped the object the light was coming from, it suddenly got dark. He sat there in complete darkness, not knowing how to get out. He tried feeling his way out, but when he checked the way he entered, the hole was completely closed.

He became desperate, but there was nothing he could do. He fell asleep, and when he woke up, the thing he was in didn't feel like it was in the water, it wasn't moving and was very still. In a moment he heard people talking from above him. Then one of them said, "My goodness, this beluga with no wounds from a weapon, how did it die?" People talking from above him were making comments about an animal that had no stab wounds, and they were wondering how it had died.

Then raven thought to himself, "When they begin butchering, I hope they first make a cut near where I am." And in a moment, he suddenly saw light right above where he was sitting. They apparently had made a cut where he had hoped they would. And just as they pulled the cut open, he darted out as fast as he could and flew up.

Then after he flew up and disappeared from sight, he flew back down and landed beyond them and walked over to them. When he came they said, "Now raven give us a hand. We'll give you a portion of this meat to take home."

That cunning raven answered them, "I don't know if I want any of that meat. Didn't you notice anything [when you first cut it open]? The thing that darted out from that and went straight up, I think it's not good. I'm not going to take any meat because it might not be good to eat. I'm worried that I might get sick when I eat it." Then those who were butchering the animal suddenly stopped and said they had noticed something dark when the animal was first cut open. They said they couldn't see it clearly and couldn't recognize what it was because it was flying up too fast.

"Let's not take meat from this animal either. It's not the only food available to us right now." [Saying that], they left it behind. After they were gone, raven butchered the animal and put the pieces together. After he was done cutting, he asked mink to marry him since he had no one to take care of the meat. Mink became his wife.

And periodically he'd get some of the beluga meat he had put away. One day

tarniluni. Waniw' muragiuryartuqatarniluni. "Tekiutarkamnek-llu akuteqaqsaunak." Taum imarmiutarrlugaam nulirran pillinia akuciiqniluni tekiutarkaanek. Cunawa-m' tua-i umyuangami.

Tayima tua-i ayalliniluni. Ernerpak tua-i tayima tua-i piinani, kiituan-gguq atakurtuq. Taamlegiqerluku atam amiiganek cakmaken cakemna meng'ellinilria. Qaill'am yuarutengqerssaaquq. Akutamek cikinrilkani nerciqniluku iquliraqluku. Aren tua-i alingalliimi tauna imarmiutaarrluar akutaq tua-i tauna amigmun uavet kayimqalliniluku tamalkuan. Cakma tua-i macarpallagauraqerluni-am ataam atulliniuq.

Atuan-am tua-i pillinia cakmavet cikiutekairutniluku, tamalkuan tua-i tuneniluku. Nepairulluni tua-i kiuvkenaku. Ak'arraurteqerluku nutaan itliniuq tulukaruk. Neqkaminek tua-i piani, pilliniuq, "Tua-llu-q' akutellruuten?"

Imarmiutaarrlugaam pillinia, "Akutellruyaaqellrianga-w' cam aug'um ava-i nerciqnilua akutamek cikinrilkumni pianga, cikiutekellrukeka tamalkuan."

"Alingnaqvaa! Cauga-tanem tauna. Akutamek tekiutarnayuklua piiyaaqellruunga. Ca-tam' tauna? Neqkamnek neqailliniiinga!"
Unuaquan-gguq-am ayakataami pillinia, "Nutaan akuskina tekiutarkamnek." Ayiimi-am tua-i mululuni. Tuacetun-am pilliniluku; atakuan nep'ngelliniluni cakemna. Keniurutengqertuq-gguq iqua tua-i kangiplungluni, keneq pilallermini.

Tua-i-am iliinek cikiryaaqelliniluku. Cali-am cangimirrluni cakemna. Nerciqniluku-am tua-i, piani nangluku tua-i tunlliniluku. Tuamtell' pingayiriluni. Pingayirian tua-i cikiutekairucami, keniurun tauna tegullinikii umyuangami. Nerciqniluku tua-i pian, amigmun iqua nungulerutelliniluku. Iqupkugmek cakemna, "Qerruq!" Iqupkugmek qalriallalliniluni. Tayima-ll' tua-i.

Muluqerluni tulukaruk itliniuq iimi inglua patumaurluku. Itran pillina, "Qaill' pisit?" Iqlungarpaa-ll' taumi tulukarugmi! "Qevcerrvikelrianga-w' muragiullemni, iika pakem' nall'arrluku."

Patuiqsaunaku-gguq tua-i iini pakemna. Aqumngan tua-i pillinia, "Ataki yuvri-

he told her that he was going out to fetch driftwood and said, "I wish you'd make some *akutaq* so I can have some when I return." That mink, his wife, said that she would make *akutaq* for him to eat when he got home. He apparently had thought up a plan.

He then left. He was gone all day, and soon it was evening. Just as it got dark, she heard someone singing from the entryway out there. I used to know the song but don't remember how it goes. In the song, the last line would say that if she didn't give him some *akutaq*, he would eat her. When that poor mink got scared she quickly pushed the whole bowl of *akutaq* out of the entryway. Someone out there started eating the *akutaq*, smacking his lips and singing again [asking for more].

When someone out there started to sing again, she told him that she had given him all the *akutaq* and had none left. The person out there didn't answer and got quiet. Then after a long time raven came in. When she mentioned food, he said, "So, did you make *akutaq*?"

Mink replied, "I did make *akutaq*, but when I heard someone singing out there, threatening to eat me if I didn't give him some *akutaq*, I gave the whole thing to him."

"How upsetting! I wonder who it was. I expected to eat some *akutaq* when I came home. I wonder who it was. He snatched and ate my food!"

The next morning, when he was about to leave, he said, "Now, make some *akutaq*, and this time I'll eat it when I come home." When he left, he was gone for a long time. He repeated what he had done to her the night before; when it got dark, someone out in the entryway started to sing again [asking for *akutaq*]. At their home there, mink had a fire poker covered with charcoal at the tip from constant use in the fire.

She had given the person out there some *akutaq*, but he had started to sing again, asking for more. Since she realized that he was going to keep asking for more, when he started singing, she shoved the whole bowl out. Then he started to sing for the third time. Since she had no more *akutaq*, when he started asking for more, she took the fire poker. Just when he said that he would eat her, she [pushed the poker into the entryway]. Then she heard someone out there cry, "*Qerruq!*" He made a short sound like that and got quiet.

After a long silence, raven came in with one side of his wing covering his other eye. She looked at him and asked, "What's the matter with you?" That raven is so deceitful and devious! [He said,] "While I was gathering driftwood, a piece of wood snapped and landed on my eye."

He kept his other eye covered. When he sat down, she said, "Let me examine it."

qernaurqa." Qunukellinia-am tulukaruum, "Tua-i uitasgu." Pingraan tua-i ciumuar-
luni pian, pegtellinia. Pegcaku iinga pillinia kangiplugmek tua-i imarluni iinga.
Pakiggaarluku tua-i nutaan, katneni piluku qengaanun katengvallinia-am, "Qaa!
Akutesqelaqiinga-am cunaw' waten pinaluni." Katngisngarraarluku tua-i, "Iin carrir-
ciqenritaqa! Elpenek carringnaqkiu!" Unilluku anluni tua-i. Anluni unilluku tua-i
uikenirluku. Waten-wa tauna taktangatelalria.

Raven was reluctant to show his eye to her and said, "Just leave it alone." Then, since she kept asking, he uncovered his eye. She looked at his eye and it was covered with charcoal. After she pulled on the eyelid to open it more, she jabbed him on the nose with her middle finger with all her might and said, "*Qaa!* He evidently has been asking me to make *akutaq* so that he could treat me in such a deceitful manner!" After she kept her middle finger on his nose, she said, "I definitely won't clean your eye! You try to clean it yourself!" Then she got up and left. She went out and left him. I think this is where it usually ends.

Nakacuut Wani Tauna Tan'gurraq
Wani Ayautellrat

Naparyaarmiut niitelaratek, Hooper Bay-rmiut. Taum nuniinek tauna pillruuq tan'gaurluq. Avani ciuqvani tauna angun irniangelliniuq tan'gaurlurmek, tua-i kinguqlingesciiganani. Kiingan yukluku. Umyuangelliniuq. Ilainek nuqlilluku ayuqniarluku yuusqumavkenaku, taugaam picuuluku yuusqumayaaqluku; nukalpianek aterpagtelalliniit, tamaani tuunrangayiit amllellratni angalkut.

Tua-i-llu umyuangelliniuq. Caviggaat caviit nurnallratni, caviggani tamaruartelluku angalkunek tuknilrianek yuaryugluni umyuangluni. Tua-i umyuangami, unugmi qavallratni qasgimi, caviggani tauna anulluku, qasgim egalran qitran acianun, nuna petgarluku mermun pingairutelluku caquluku, nuniutelliniluku, qasgim egalran mengliinun. Patuqaarluku tua-i atrarluni nutaan inartelliniluni.

Unuaquan tua-i piyungami caviggaminek taumek yualliniuq tamariniluku. Nurnallratni caviit tua-i arenqianani qivrukluku. Tua-i-ll' angalkut amllerata, piciqngalngurmek, tukningalngurmek, kiingan aipaqeqerluku ellami, qanrutliniluku nuussini tauna caviggani yuaryugngacianek, qivrukniluku. Tua-i piyuaku, tuunrilliniluni qasgimi. Piyaaqelriim tua-i nanluciinaku nalaqevkenaku. Taqevkalliniluku. Cali allamek angalkumek cali pilliniluni. Tuamtell'-am piyaaqekni nalaqevkenaku.

Taukut-llu-gguq angalkut ilangqertut angutmek elluatuuvkenani. Picuvkenani cakneq. Qasgimi-ll' tuunrivkayuunaku, pikegtaunrilan tangllermini. Eneni taugaam caaqameng pivkaraqluku. Tauna elliin kemyukevkenaku.

Nangllinii imkut angalkut nunuliraqluki nukalpiaruami. Nunulirluki yuarcecaaqaqluku, nalaqeksaunaku. Kiituan nangllliniut angalkut. Tauna taugaam kemyunailnguq.

Caqerluni ellami kiimetqallra nall'arrluku pillinia, "Usuuq tang tua-i caviggaqa imna qaillukuaresqumayaaqekeka." Kiunritliniluku. Kiunrilani tua-i unitellinitluku.

Tua-i-ll' qasgimi uitallermeggni angutet amllerrluteng, umyugaan aptenqigculli-

420

The Boy Who Was Taken Away
by the Bladders

You two have heard of a place called Naparyaarmiut, the village of Hooper Bay. That boy came from near that place. Long ago, there was a man who had a child, a boy, and after that he was unable to have more children. The boy was the only child of the couple. One day his father had an idea. He didn't want his son to be needy and hoped that his son would become a good hunter; a *nukalpiaq*, as they were called in those days when many shaman were present.

So, he came up with a plan. He decided to look for the most powerful shaman in his village by hiding his knife and pretending to lose it, back when knives were rare. So, with that in mind, at night when everyone was asleep in the *qasgi*, he went out with his knife and, wrapping it so water wouldn't touch it, pushed it into the soil beneath the skylight frame. After he covered his knife with soil, he came down and went to bed.

The following morning, when it was time, he looked for his knife and said that he had apparently lost it. Since there were so few knives around, he was devastated over the loss. So, since many shamans were there in his village, he picked out the one whom he thought was the most powerful, and while they were alone outside he asked him to find his knife. The shaman agreed and performed a ritual in the *qasgi*. The shaman looked but didn't find it. Then he asked him to stop looking. He asked another shaman, but he didn't find it either.

Now, among the shamans there was one there, a man who was not as proficient as the others, nor a very good hunter. And he wasn't allowed to perform his shaman duties in the *qasgi* because others thought his work wasn't as influential. But sometimes he exercised his powers in homes. The boy's father didn't have any confidence in that shaman.

He asked all the shamans and paid them, because he was a *nukalpiaq*. He had paid them to look for his knife, but no one found it. All the shamans were asked, except for that one who wasn't as worthy.

One day, when he saw that shaman alone outside, he approached him and said, "I would like you to search for my knife and see if you can find it." The shaman didn't even answer him. Since he didn't respond, the father walked away.

Then later on, when the father and many other men were in the *qasgi*, he started

nia. Ullagluku caniqami uitallrani, canianun aqumluni pillinia, "Aling usuuq-qaa waniw' caviggaqa im' nuussiqa piyugnganritan? Tua-i tang qivruksaaqekeka." Kiuvke-
naku-am uitalliniluni. Uitauraqerluni takuyallinia wavet. Takuyaamiu qanrutlinia
qastuluni—imkut-llu qasgimi yuartek'lallri ilagaulluteng, maa-i qasgimlluteng—
niitelluki, "Usuuq, nuussin atak pikna elpet ellilqan. Uayautekengnaqviiqnaku
teguu." Ululliniluku-ll' tua-i. Tuunrivkenani-llu. Apertuaku qaill' piviilami, elliin
ellilqengamiu, tegulliniluku.

Nutaan eneminun kinguani agulluku nalqigutellinia taumek qetunrarminek.
Tauna tua-i qetunrani una ilainek kiimaungan ayuqniarluku yuusqumanricaaq-
ngamiu, angalkunek yuarutekniluku una wani nuussini aturluku. Qaillukuaryug-
ngacianek elliinun. Taulleraam pillinia, "Pisqumakuvgu piciqaqa. Taugaam allamek
kevgangqerrngaitua. Elpenek kevgangqerciqua."

Atakuan-llu tua-i qasgicetelliniluku tauna qetunraa. Imkut qasgit eqiurcuuteng-
qellruut ciklauranek, tulurnek asevret tuluitnek, nuugit imkut waten ayuqluteng,
keputetun uskurarluteng, yaanlluteng ciungani. Muragaq waten canirrluku piqerrluku quptuluki tamakut ciklauranek.
   Qasgicaku-ll' tua-i tugeryaram uatiinun aqumevkarluku teruanun elavluni qaillun piurarraarluni, tua-i makcami, tugeryaram kialirneranun curirluku. Nacitet
iquita tusngallrit muragpaller qavani tugeryaramek pituat. Nacitet tusngavikluku
waten kat'um kenillrem qilain. Tamaa-i-gguq tugeryaraq. Qainganun-llu qamiqurra
wavet waten ellivkarluku curirluku taklarcetliniluku tauna tan'gaurluq.

Taklarcecamiu pillinia atii, kitaki-gguq tauna ciklauraq teguluku uqliusngaliu.
Uuggun-gguq akuliraakun tallimirikuni, muragtun pitarrluku, pinirtacia tamalkuan aturluku ciklauramek piqertuusqelluku cupucimi tallimiitni, tuunrangayaya-
gaq tauna pilliniuq. Atiin tua-i tamana teguluku, qetunrani nakmiin una waniw'
tuquteqatarluku tua-i pisqengaku. Kenekluku-llu elliin.
   Kiatiini elavluni tauna angalkuq tuunriluni tua-i pirraarluni cupliniluni. Aner-
yaapagatuut cupniaqameng. Pisquciatun tua-i cupngan piqerturuaqalliniluku ag-

to wonder if he should approach him again. While that shaman was sitting against the side wall and doing something, he went over and sat next to him and said, "Gee, the knife I've lost, do you think you can use your powers and find it? I have been feeling distressed because of losing it." Again he sat in silence and didn't even answer him. After he sat quietly for a moment he looked at him and said loudly, "Hey, you placed your knife up there yourself. Go up and get it instead of losing all of your possessions over it!" The other shamans who had already looked for his knife were in the *qasgi*, and they all heard what he said. After he said that, he turned and looked away. He hadn't even performed a ritual to look for his knife before he said that. So, since that shaman revealed the knife's location, not knowing what else to do, he went and got it because he had put it there.

Then [the father] took [the shaman] to his house and talked to him about his son. He told him that he had used his knife to look for a shaman who might help his son. He told him since his son was their only child [with no siblings to help him], he had thought about his future and hoped he would be able to survive on his own and have everything he needed to live. He asked the shaman if he could use his powers to help his son. That sly shaman answered, "I will work on him if you want me to. But no one else will assist me. You will assist me when I work on him."

That evening he had him bring his son to the *qasgi*. Axes, referred to as *ciklaurat*, were kept in the *qasgi*. The ax blade was a walrus tusk with a tip that looked like this. A line was attached to the end of the handle like an adze. They'd hit a piece of driftwood with the ax blade at an angle and cut it into firewood.

When the father entered the *qasgi* with the boy, the shaman had the boy sit on the floorboards right in front of the *tugeryaraq* [log against the back wall], and after he crouched down next to his feet and did something, he stood up. Then he fixed a mat for the boy on the bare floor right behind the *tugeryaraq*. A big log that sits against the back wall next to the floorboards was called *tugeryaraq*. The log was set at the end of the floorboards that were used to cover the firepit down below. That log was called *tugeryaraq*. He took the boy and had him lay down on the mat with his head resting on the *tugeryaraq*.

After the shaman let the boy lie on his back, he told his father to take the ax and hold it and be ready to strike. Then that crafty shaman told the father to strike the boy between his eyes as hard as he could with the ax as soon as he breathed out the fifth time. The boy's father held the ax and was ready to kill his own son, as instructed by the shaman there. And he loved his son.

After the shaman crouched at the foot of the boy and performed a ritual, he started to breathe out. When shamans performed a ritual and began exhaling

turpek'naku uuggun tua-i pisqelluku pillruani. Muragam qaingani assipekluku
qamiqurra tugeryarami. Tallimirian tua-i ciklauraq tauna nalugarrluku piqertuqa-
tarluku uitangaartellinilria kiugna. Arenqiatuq kenekngamiu kiingan-llu qetunraq-
luku. Tua-i uitauraqerluni peggluku cailkamun taggliniluni.

Taum tuunrangayiim pillinia, "Tua-llu-wa una qetunraan qaillukuaresqeken
pingaitelliiningerpet. Tua-i pinqiggngaitaqa waniwa. Aug'umek ayanqiggviitua.
Taq'aqa tua-i pinqiggngaitaqa aug'umek. Navgan elpet." Taqliniluteng tua-i.

Tua-i-am caq'erluni kinguani kiimetqallrani-am ullallinia. Qanrutlinia, "Aling
tua-i usuuq naugg'un-qaa allakun auguunrilngurkun piyugnganritan?" Kiugartev-
kenani-am uitaqerluni pillinia, "Navgarkaunrilkuvgu-wa. Aug'utun ciuqliatun pi-
cirkiuteka navegngailkuvgu." Taum pillinia navenqiggngaitniluku qaill' pingraan
aturarkaurrniluku waniwa elliin, aturarkauluku pulengniluku.
    Pillinia nakacugnun-gguq ayaucetqataraa. Nakacugteggun-gguq piqataraa. Ki-
taki-gguq waniwa nakaciurpailgata aaniin aturarkiuqiliu imarpiliurcuutnek unku-
nek. Imarniciluku, ivrucililuku, arilliluku-llu, imarpigmi pissualriit atutukaitnek;
ngelqerrinek, alerqulliniluku. Nakaciuqata waniwa elliin caliaqeciqniluku. Tamakut taugaam atu'urkai egmianun caliaqluki taqluki uitasqelluki nakaciurnatkaat-
nun. Uksumi nakaciutuut; nakaciutullrulliniut.

Tua-i uptelliniluku tua-i. Atiin taum tua-i nallunrirtelluku tauna qetunrani.
Nalqigulluku tamatumek ilainek nuqlitevkenaku yuullerkaa pitekluku pivkaqa-
tarniluku. Nakaciurniarartelluki tua-i itliniuq eniignun tauna angalkuar. Itrami
angayuqaak pilliniak. "Kitak tua-i waniwa pisquurartek inerquqataramtek navgar-
kaqenrilkekevtegnek. Ilumuulutek piyukuvtegen'gu, ayaumallran kinguani angnii-
teksaunatek umyuaqluku pikitek. Iluteqeksaunatek-llu umyuaqluku. Tuatnakuv-
tek navegciqerpetegnga cali. Allrakuq kassugluku cataiciiquq. Up'nerkaqu taugaam
nutaan tekiciiquq. Qaill' pingaituq tua-i. Elpetek taugaam picurlauskuvtegni qaill'
piciquq. Makut taugaam augkut alerquatenka assirluki pikuvtek picurlagngait-
qapiartuq. Qaillun pingaituq." Tua-i anglliniluteq.

loudly like that, they called it *cupluteng*. As instructed, as soon as the shaman ex-haled [the fifth time], the father pretended to strike his son here and didn't even touch him. The boy's head was resting on the log. Just when the shaman was exhal-ing for the fifth time and the father lifted the ax, he suddenly stopped and stood still. He absolutely couldn't strike the son he loved, his only son. Then, shortly after that, he dropped the ax and went up and sat down.

That shaman said to him, "Here you asked me to exercise my powers on your son, while you apparently weren't going to do what I told you to do. I'm not going to perform another ritual for him. I can't go any further from what just happened. I won't perform that ritual again. You have broken the process." So they stopped what they were doing.

Sometime after that, when that shaman was alone, the father approached him and said, "Gee, isn't there a different way you can help my son?" After being quiet for a while, he answered him, "Only if you aren't going to ignore my wishes like you did the first time." The father quickly said that he would definitely do as he wished, that he was asking again so he wouldn't break his command the next time.

He told the father that he was going to have the seal bladders take him away. He said that through seal bladders [he was going to empower him]. He told the father to ask the boy's mother to make all garments needed for ocean hunting, such as seal-gut garments, waterproof boots, and fish-skin gloves. He told him to tell his wife to make the boy clothing that would fit him. He told him that he was going to take care of his son and carry out his plan during the Bladder Festival. He said that his clothes should be worked on right away and finished and put away until the Bladder Festival. The Bladder Festival was held during winter; they apparently held Bladder Festivals in winter.

So [the parents] started getting him ready. And the father told his son about the plan. He told him that he was going to let him go through what he was about to experience to help him live successfully in the future. When the Bladder Festival was nearing, that shaman came into the couple's home. When he came in, he said, "Now, since you have trusted me to work on him, I am going to give you rules that you must not break. If you two truly want him to go through this and succeed, after he leaves, do not be sad thinking about him. And do not weep for him. If you do that, you will interfere with my work, and I will not be able to complete it. He will be gone for a year. He will only return in the spring. He will be fine. But if you two do something you weren't suppose to do, he'll get into trouble. If you loyally adhere to my instructions, he will absolutely not run into trouble along the way. Nothing will happen to him." They both agreed.

Tua-i-ll nakaciurata, nakaciut pinariata, nalukataata, qasgicetelliniluku. Itrucag-negu tua-i nutaan aturartelluku tamakunek at'elluku. Imarnitegnek-llu at'elluku, iv-rucirtelluku-llu. Arilluuk-llu at'ellukek. (Unani imarpigmi ellangllugmi anuqmi-llu anguaqata'arqamta tamakut alluki anguatuukut, arilluut-llu. Mer-iterngairutelluku qayam iluanun, ket'garluku-ll' painga qayam. Mer'em patuangraakut, mer-iterngau-nani qayam iluanun.)

Tua-i-llu nalukataameng, nakacuteng itruluki qavavet. Waten taprualuk neng-lluku itrutetuit. Quyuita waten qillengqaluki agaurtelluki. Pissutulit tamarmeng nakacuit, temirtet, tan'gaurluunrilnguut. Tuntut nakacuit. Imarpigmiutaat-llu naka-cuit. Tua-i-llu nalukataameng, anuteqataamegteki quyuita teguluki, ukalirnermun; amaumaarqata'arqameng, unavet waten *line*-arturluteng amiigmun uavet pall'itaag-nun nangertetuut, nakacuteng equumaluki waten. Camani-w' kuigmi anluaq calla-malria. Tuavet tua-i qageqluki mermun ayagcetetuit nakacuut. *Line*-arluteng, ilait-llu tua-i tungliqu'urluteng qavani, amlletuameng. Nangertelliniluteng, tauna-ll' tayima imna angalkuar kinguqlikacagauluni. Tauna tan'gaurluq equgluku kegginaa wantelluku tusmini, tauna tan'gaurluq ayagcetarkaq.

Pituut tuaten amaumaarqameng. Angayaqtaarturluteng waten pituut. Amlliraq-luteng amlliryungaqameng. Ciuqliq-llu tua-i an'ngan nutaan an'urluteng. Tauna tua-i angalkuar tekicatni, uatmun caungami kingunratgun anelrarluni, pallitaak te-kiteqataamikek, nutaan atrarrluku, talligni waten pilukek qaingagnun palurrluku tauna tan'gaurluq. Waten elliurturluku pall'itaak tungiignun. Tua-i-ll' wani ciuq-lirmi amigmun iterluni puc'an, tan'gaurluq ellakun anlliniluni tayima tua-i tamar-lun' tayima.

When they had the Bladder Festival, when it was time to release the bladders, when they were about to run to the ice hole with the bladders to let them go, he had the parents bring the boy to the *qasgi*. When they brought him into the *qasgi*, they put the new garments on him. They had him put on a seal-gut rain parka and waterproof skin boots. And they had him put on fish-skin mittens. (Down on the ocean, when we were about to paddle in our kayaks in wet and windy conditions, we always put those garments on, including fish-skin mittens. We would also tie a line around the cockpit coaming [after placing the bottom hem of our seal-gut garment over the coaming] to prevent water from entering the kayak. And even though water covered us while we were paddling, water could not enter.)

And when they were about to run to the ice holes to let their bladders go, the bladders were brought into the *qasgi* and [hung] in back. A skin line was tied against the back wall before the bladders were brought in. And [the hunters] hung [the bladders of their catches] on that line and kept them there during the festival. All adult hunters, but not the boys, would hang the bladders of the sea mammals they caught, and also caribou bladders. And when they were ready to run with them to the ice holes, when they were about to go out with them, each hunter would take his bundle of bladders; when they were about to swing back and forth, men would line up all the way to the entrance, holding the string tied to their bladders hanging down their backs. And down below the village, on the river, an open ice-hole was waiting for them. They would let them go through that ice hole after the inflated bladders were popped. The men would line up, and the line would go all the way to the back of the room, because many men participated in this event. So, the men were standing in line, and the shaman was there standing at the very end of the line. He was holding the boy on his back, and the boy's head was resting on his shoulder facing forward, the boy he was about to let go [with the bladders].

Right before they ran out of the entrance, they swung their bodies back and forth in unison, moving their bodies forward a little whenever they wanted to, doing what they called *amaumaarluteng*. And as soon as the first one in line went out, the others would follow him and start running out. So, when it was the shaman's turn to go out, he faced the entrance and began walking toward it, and just before he got to the *pall'itaak*, he pulled the boy down and held him face down in his arms like this. He held him and swung his arms back and forth toward the *pall'itaak*. And just when the shaman started to go into the entryway and lowered his head to go out, the boy's body began to move forward and flew out of the entrance and disappeared in the air.

Uksurpak tua-i tayima tua-i. Taukuk-llu tua-i angayuqaak piningnaqu'urlutek tua-i, alianam tekitelangraani tauna aanii arcaqerluni. Caqerluni tua-i pinialliqluni pillrani qakemna yuk aqvaqurluni tua-i taillinilria. Cakma-ll' tua-i itqertelliniluni. Puggliniuq tauna angalkuq, tauna pistii. Nunullinikii-am tua-i nutaan tauna arnaq aanii. Ama'anleng'ermi elpekluku qasgimi. Tua-i-gguq pinqigtenrituq tauten. Tua-i umyugaa angniitelangermi piningnaqu'urluni taugaam. Tua-i-llu uksuulnguami up'nerkarluni. Maani April-aam kinguaraani pilaryugnarqut piyagaat; irnituut imar-pigmiutaat.

Ellarramini tua-i tauna tan'gaurluq ayallinilria. Yuuluki tua-i tamakut tangvag-luki ilani maligtaquluki. Ayainanermeggni tua-i camani qasgimek tekitelliniut. It-liniut inglerluni waten kassugarnermek qulmun, qulliqelrianek. Makut-gguq atli-kacagaat angluteng angutet tua-i. Mengkugluteng-gguq ukugnegun tamalkurmeng tua-i. Cunawa-gguq asevret yuit. Qulliit-wa-gguq makut ellaicetun ayuqluteng. Cu-nawa-gguq makliit, irniameggnek nunaqlirluteng. Tamaavet tamaa-i aqumevkalli-niluku. Aug'um tukirluku aaniin, aanaklikiin, aanakaqellinikiin. Qulliit-wa-gguq pagkut pupigluki. Kumeksuarturluteng-gguq tua-i pinaurtut. Cunawa-gguq imkut issurit, kukupalget imkut qaingit. Pagkut-wa-gguq qullikacagaat kegginait akagen-qeggluteng, acengluteng. Nayiit-gguq cunawa yuit. Tamaanteqalliniuq tua-i.

Atam piinanrani tukuan taum pillinia, "Atam niicugniqaa." Niicugniqalliniuq qalartellria pakemna. Egalermek-gguq tuar pikaken pilria taringnaqluni. Niicug-niqaraa-gguq, imna nallunrilkii kingunranek pamaken, naken taum kingunranek. Elitaqluku eriniikun qulirilria. Niicugniurluku tua-i. Iquklipailgan qavaqalliniluni tayima.

Taum-am kinguani qanrutlinia taum, "Tangerrluku kinguniskuvet cavkenak, umyuan qacnganaku qulirisqaqatgen qulirilarciqelriaten." Ilii-gguq taringnaunani tua-i qalarteng'ermi pinaurtuq taringesciiganaku. Tua-i anglanaunani. Taum-gguq pinauraa, "Tangerrluku, pakma pakemna umyuaminek qacngalliqelria, piiyuumiu-tailnguq qanruyutni aturluki." Pakma-gguq tua-i taringnaunani niitniinani.

The boy was gone all winter. The boy's parents tried to stay strong, though sometimes his mother, especially, would miss her boy. One day when she was in the house weeping and feeling sad, she heard loud footsteps of someone running toward their house. She heard someone storming into their porch, and that shaman came in, the one who had sent their boy away. He then chastised the boy's mother reproachfully. Although he was in the *qasgi*, he had sensed her behavior. After that she didn't do that again. Though sometimes she was lonely and disheartened, she tried to stay strong. Then after a long winter, spring finally arrived. I think it is right after the month of April that the sea mammals usually have their pups.

In his awareness, the boy realized that he was traveling. He saw his traveling companions as humans and did what they were doing. While they were going down below, they came upon a *qasgi*. They went inside and saw that it had several levels of beds fixed all the way around the room. The men sitting on the floor level beds were huge and burly. And they all had labrets on their chins. Evidently, they were walrus people. The men situated on the next level looked like he did and those he had traveled with. They apparently were bearded-seal people with their children sitting next to them. The boy was told to sit with them. This particular female sat next to him. She apparently was going to be his mother. The men who were on the beds right above them had sores all over their bodies. They would begin scratching sometimes. They evidently were spotted-seal people, the kind that have spots on their bodies. And those sitting on the top-level bed were men with round faces. They apparently were ringed-seal people. He evidently was going to stay with them in that *qasgi*.

Then, while he sat there, his host turned to him and said, "Listen." He stopped and listened for a moment and heard a voice from on top of the *qasgi*. The voice seemed to be coming right from the window, and he understood the words the person was saying. He listened for a moment and recognized the voice. It was the voice of a person he knew from his home somewhere up there. He recognized him by his voice as he told a story up there. He listened to him telling a story and fell asleep before it ended.

After that, his host said, "Now, if you get home safely and you are asked to tell a story, you might tend to share stories with your mind preoccupied and not paying attention to what you are saying." The boy heard more stories being told [from up above], but he couldn't understand some of them. They were not fun to listen to. His host would tell him, "Now, listen to a person up there whose mind is so preoccupied you can't understand what he is saying. He's the kind of person who is hopeless in life because he continually defies rules for right living." His host said that the person up there couldn't be understood and was not enjoyable to listen to.

Tuamtellu-gguq piinanrani egalratnun pikvavet qanikcat tutmarangarrnaurtut qainganun. Tukuan-gguq taum pinauraa, "Tangerrluku kinguniskuvet qavaryularciqelriaten, piiyuumiutaunak. Pakemna pakma niitan unugmi cilkialria piiyuumiutelek." Egalranun-gguq pikavet qanikciurutiin imaa tutmarluni. Ilii-gguq taugken elaqvanek qakmaken tua-i piluni. Auguuluni-am tua-i piyuumiutailnguq, umyuamini qacngalliqelria. Tamakut-am nalqiga'artaqluki piurcetliniluku. Tuaten tua-i ayuqluteng.

Tamaani-gguq tua-i akusrakayagaqameng ilain makut ilaita nakukluku pinauraat, taugaam ingluliuqsaunaki. Atam piinanermeggni tukuan taum pillinia, "Upnariqataraakuk. Up'ngut-am ilapuk maa-i makut ayagarkat." Tuaten tua-i qanrulluku-am.

Waten-gguq tua-i unuakuarmi arnat iternaurtut-llu qaltanek tegumiarluteng, imkunek naunrarnek, arumalrianek-gguq naunrarnek imarluteng, ilait-llu tan'gerpagnek. Naunrarnek-gguq tua-i tamakunek nerevkalaqii taum, tan'gerpagnek nerevkaqsaunaku. Caqerluni-am pillinia tauna tukuni ciin tamakunek tan'gerpagnek pivkayuilucirminek. Pillinia taum, "Neqkaqenrilavki, nernarqenrilavki elpet." Cunawa-gguq teggalquyagaullinilriit, *gravel*-aat imkut teggalqut mikcuaraat. Nerait teggalqunek imangqetuut unkumiutaat. Tamakuuluki tua-i tangvagluki. Tamakutllu-gguq naunraat *clam*-aulliniluteng. Tamakunek-gguq taugaam tua-i neqkarluni.

Tua-i-llu anqaquuranglliniluteng makut. Yuirusngiinarluni-gguq tauna qasgi. Caqerluni tua-i unuakumi tukuan taum pillinia ayagnarinilutek. Anutelliniluku tua-i. Ellami-gguq tua-i tamaani piaqami, imumek taicirrlugturluni man'a kiartellra pinaurtuq. Cunawa-gguq mer'em iluani. Qayarlutek ayautellinikii. Allakarmek qayarlutek. Kiartaqami-gguq tamaani ayallermegni pinaurtuq amirlut pagkut pagaani. Cunawa-gguq cikut mermi pugtalriit. Amirluuluki tangrraqluki taum. Qavarnariaqan mayurlutek anenaurtuq ellakegtaar. Cikut-gguq taugken qaingatnun qayatek mayurrluki, inarrlutek qavarlutek tua-i. Tupagaqamek atrarlutek anguarlutek ayagaqlutek mer'em akulerpalluakun.

Atam tua-i caqerlutek taum tukuan-am pillinia atam qavallermegni, "Qavarpiiknak. Paugna atam tangerqerru." Makcami kiartelliniuq nunat pingkut ketiitni angun man'a atralria qamigarluni, qayani qamuutarluku. Amirlungaqluni-gguq tua-i caaqami. Canimelli'irtuq-gguq piciatun uyamigluni, piciatun qerrullillernek

And while he was there sometimes snow would land on their window up there. His host would turn to him and say, "Now, when you return home, you will want to sleep with no desire to succeed in life. You hear the one above us who is working at night with hopes to succeed." His host said that as the man up there tossed the snow with his shovel you could hear it as it landed on the skylight. But sometimes when you heard someone shoveling out there, the sound would be coming from farther out and was almost inaudible. It apparently was a person who would not succeed in life and who was mentally defiant. Every time something came up, his host explained the situation. That was how it was [while he stayed in that *qasgi*].

When he and the other [children] played, some of them would pick on him, but he would just leave and not fight back. Then one day his host turned to him and said, "It's almost time for us to get ready. These other men here who usually go out are starting to get ready for their hunting trip." That was what his host told him.

While they were in the *qasgi* early in the morning, women would come in holding buckets filled with salmonberries, ripe salmonberries, and some would be filled with blackberries. His hostess would give the boy salmonberries to eat but never let him eat blackberries. One time he asked his hostess why she never gave him blackberries to eat. She replied, "Because they are not part of your diet. They are not your food." The blackberries apparently were little rocks, small pieces of gravel. We usually find little rocks inside sea-mammal stomachs. The boy viewed the little rocks as blackberries. The salmonberries he ate apparently were clams. And that was what he ate while he was there.

Then the other members staying in the *qasgi* started to go out. They kept leaving, and soon few men were left. Then one morning his host told the boy that it was time to leave. She then took him outside. Once they were outside and moving about, whenever he scanned his surroundings, the atmosphere around them would look a little foggy. They apparently were underwater. Then they started leaving in kayaks. They were in separate kayaks. As they went he looked up and saw clouds up over them. They apparently were chunks of ice floating on the surface of the water up there. The boy saw the ice as clouds. When it was time to sleep, they'd go up and emerge into a clear environment. Then they'd pull their kayaks up on ice and lie down and go to sleep. When they awoke, they'd go down and continue paddling, mostly underwater.

One day while they were sleeping, his host woke him and said, "Stop sleeping and look up there." When he looked he saw a man coming down from a village back there, pulling his kayak on a sled. As he went, clouds would cover the area above where he was. When he got closer, the boy saw things hanging down his neck.

qecignek imkunek. Cunawa-gguq iniat. Imkut makut initaat — (iciw' aturat-llu iqai-
rraarluki inilaqci). Inerquutnguut-am aciirasqevkenaki. Aciatgun waten ayaksau-
nata pilaasqelluta. Taum-am pillinia, "Tangerrluku kinguniskuvet iniat aciiraluki
pilarciqelriaten. Maa-i-tang man'a alingnaqluni wangkutnun." Tuamtellu-gguq ilii
pinauraat qaltamek, mer'utmek imumek, nacarluni, keggina-ll' cataunani; amta-llu-
gguq anguarluni. Inerqurnauraa-gguq, "Tangerrluku kinguniskuvet qaluuritaunak
mel'arciqelriaten pull'uten." Tamakunek tamaa-i inerquagaqluku pilliniluku.

Atam tua-i caqerlutek tuaten-am tua-i ayagarraarlutek, cikum-am qainganun
mayurlutek inartellinilriik. Tamaani imat'am alerqulallinikii tukurkamek taum pi-
katek, qamenqurranun kiavet, qayam kinguanun, itqertesqelluku. Cunawa-gguq
nakacuanun. Amini tamana qayauluku tua-i tangvagluku, tangvalliniluku.
    Tua-i qavallrani tupagqelliniluku, "Usuuq qavarpiiqnak! Atam tukurkarpuk ping'
uptellria tangvakarru." Maktelliniuq nunat pingkut. Piqalliniuq nunai pingkut. Pilliniuq nukalpiaq imna pingna nallunrilkii uptellria. Qayani uciliqii taquarkaminek.
Iiragmikun-gguq uuggun tan'qigcetellriamek anlluggluni. Akumikun-llu maaggun,
ukugnegun-llu aligmikun tanqigcelngurmek anlluggluni kenurratun. Pillinia-am
taum, "Tangerrluku kinguniskuvet qavaryularciqelriaten. Carrlugnek-llu uqlarnarqelrianek pelleryularciqellriaten. Pika-i pingna tangrran carrlugmek piitqapiaralria.
Cumacikivkenaki canek uqlarnarqelrianek calilria qanruyutni aturluku. Tua-i pia-i
anyurnaunani."

Taringan-qaa anyurnaunani? Alingnaunani. Waten umyuarteqnaunani, "Una-ll'
ima' qaill' camek pingqelliliria? Caskungqelliuq-llu una aipaagni." Tamatuuguq anyurnaunani.
    Atam piinanrani nulirra anllinilria taum, qantaq-wa-gguq akutamek imarluni
tegumiara. Uimini-gguq tanqia tukninruluni. Iiragmikun uuggun anlluggluni tukninruluni, akumikun-llu. Qantaq-llu-gguq tauna uiminun tunngamiu tanqiminek
tapirluku tunluku. Qanrutlinia-am, "Tangerrluku nuliangekuvet nulian qacngalliq-
luni umyuaminek pilarciqkiiten." Cingumailria-gguq pia-i pingna, kencikluku cakneq uini. Tuaten-am tua-i qanrulluku.

There were different pieces of clothing hanging, including [women's] pants. They were apparently clothes that had been hanging on clotheslines. The clotheslines outside — (you know, after you do laundry you hang them out to dry sometimes). Males were always cautioned not to walk under clothes hanging on lines. The host turned to the boy and said, "Now, when you get home you might sometimes walk under clothes hanging on lines. You see that hunter approaching appearing horrifying to us." And sometimes they'd see a hunter wearing a water bucket as a hat, and his hat would cover his whole face, and yet the man would be paddling in his kayak. His host would caution him, "Now, when you get home you might sometimes stoop down and drink water from a bucket instead of using a ladle." As they went his host continued to give him advice every time they saw hunters who didn't appear normal to them.

One day, after their usual time out there, they climbed on an ice floe and lay down to sleep. Before they went to sleep his host told the boy to dash into the *qamenquq* of his kayak as soon as a hunter hit him with his weapon. He apparently was telling him to run inside his bladder. The boy perceived his body as a kayak.

While he slept, his host woke him and said, "You there, quit sleeping! Look at our host up there getting ready to leave to go hunting." He got up and looked and saw a village up there and quickly realized that it was his home. He looked at the *nukalpiaq* up there getting ready and recognized him right away. He was loading his kayak with his provisions. From both sides of his neck there was light flowing out as he moved. Light would also come out through the bottom of his parka and his sleeves. Again his host said, "Now, when you get home you might want to sleep for hours. And you will act squeamish and not want to handle dirty work. Look at that man up there so pure and clean. He's the kind of man who handles dirt without feeling repulsed, following his teachings. And in our view, he looks unintimidating."

Do you know what *anyurnaunani* means? It means that he wasn't intimidating. You wouldn't think like this, "This person [can't be trusted] because he might possess something. Perhaps he has a weapon." That's what *anyurnaunani* means.

Then while they were watching him, his wife came out of their house holding a bowl of *akutaq*. The light flowing out from her was brighter than her husband's. A much brighter light was flowing out from both sides of her neck and from the bottom of her parka. And when she gave the bowl of *akutaq* to her husband, she gave it to him, putting some of her light in the bowl. His host said, "Now, when you get married, she might sometimes be abusive to you." His host said that the woman back there clearly shows that she has aspirations for her husband and greatly respects him. That was what his host told the boy.

Atraami tua-i pia-i, mermun kanaami, qayani atrarqaarluku, caullinikeg-atam. Caungamikek atam ciuneqeqapiarlukek agiirtenga'artellinilria. Atam canimellillra maliggluku qavam mat'um tekitellinikii. Piningnaqeqtang'ermi tukniriinarluni qavaq, canimellillra maliggluku. Una-llu aipaa angayuqra qutungelliniluni. Canimellian tua-i piningnaqeqtang'ermi tayima cacini nalluyagulluku qavaqalliniluni.

Qavainanermini ayuqucia man'a caleryalliniluni. Mak'arutmini tua-i qamenqu- minun kiavet itqertelliniluni. Tauna tua-i nukalpiaq maklagtelliniluni irnialegmek. Pilaggaarluku qayaminun ekluku taggliniluni. Uurcalliniluni tua-i. Tamakut-am na- llunaunateng, nallunailkutarluteng pitulliniameng tamatum nalliini. *Signal*-aanek imkunek *signal*-aaqluki tua-i. Yaaqsingraata, tauten ayuqekan, taringluku-ll' tua-i.

Tauna tua-i angalkuaraller ilagaulluni tua-i pillratni. Pilliniut aanalegtelliniuq- gguq. Angalkuaraller tauna piqalliniuq taungullinilria tua-i imna ayagcetellra. Ag- qertelliniluni taukugnun angayuqaagkenun. Itertuq-gguq tauna aanii iqelria, imar- nitegnek mingquralria. Itqercami pillinia, "Qetunraan agiirtuq! Tekituq qetunraan!" Quyaqallermini tua-i caliani calliggluku anqertelliniluni.

Anqercami makut tan'gaurluut piyaaqellinii, cataunani qetunraa. Tauna-wa-gguq uciilria maklagmek, irniaranek aipirluku. Umyugaa tua-i angniirtelliniuq. Taum imum angalkuaraam pillinia angniirtengraan waniwa inerqurngaitniluku. Piyug- taciatun qiayukan-llu qiasqelluku. Caarkaunrirniluku qetunraa tekitniluku. Tua-i kiagpak tua-i tayima, uksuryungami-ll' uksurluni.

Tua-i nakaciurnariateng taukut nakaciulliniluteng-am. Nalugnariateng-llu nalug- luteng. Naluggaarluteng-am melgituut. Qaluuritet-am muriit augkut mernek imar- luteng; camaken elakamek imiqerluki qasgitaqluki. Melgirluteng-gguq.

When the man went down, when he reached the water, after putting his kayak in the water, he climbed in and immediately turned his kayak and faced them. After he turned in their direction, he started paddling directly toward them. As he paddled and got closer, the boy suddenly became drowsy. And though he fought to stay alert, he got sleepier and sleepier as the man paddled toward them. And his companion, his host there next to him, started to snore. When the man in the kayak got near them, though the boy tried to stay awake, he suddenly fell asleep.

While he was asleep, he suddenly woke up when something violently hit him. And as soon as he got up he dashed into the *qamenquq* of his kayak. That man, the hunter, had struck a bearded seal with a pup and had killed it. Then, after he cut up the animal, he loaded it up in his kayak and went ashore. Once he was on land, he went home on foot *uurcarluni* [announcing his success]. People in the village immediately knew that the hunter had caught an animal when he came home like that. The hunter would come home holding something as a signal. When a hunter approached a village with a signal like that, though he was far away, people in the village would immediately understand what he was doing.

Everyone went out to observe [the successful hunter approaching], and that shaman went to observe, too. Then they started saying that the hunter had gotten a bearded seal pup with its mother. That shaman realized that the pup was actually the boy he had previously let go with the bladders. Then he ran over to the boy's parents' house. He went in and saw the mother sitting and sewing a seal-gut garment. When he ran inside, he told the mother, "Your son is coming! Your son has arrived!" The joyous mother dropped what she was doing and ran out of the house.

When she dashed outside, she looked but didn't find her son among the boys out there. She saw a man unloading a sled. He was taking out pieces of bearded seal meat and blubber, including its pup. She suddenly got sad. The shaman told her that he wasn't going to say anything to her, even though she got sad now. He told her that she could even cry if she wanted to. He told her that her son had arrived and that nothing would happen to him now. So, summer came and went, and soon it was winter before anything happened.

When it was time they held the Bladder Festival and brought the bladders of the animals into the *qasgi*. And when it was time, men ran them to the ice hole to let them go. After they let the bladders go, they usually did the water ceremony. They'd fill ladles with water from the ice hole and bring them up to the *qasgi, melgirluteng,* as they called it.

Nangneq tauna arnaq melgiqatalria. Elakait-llu enengqetullrulliniut tamaani uki-maurluteng. Eneluteng taugaam qanikcarnek aniguyiumaluteng. Mamtulriamek ci-kurpagcecuunaki tamakut elakat. Tauna uivluku iteryaraa pillinilria, mikelnguq una nangerngalria taum elakam amiigan mengliini. Piqallinia mangelkaciurallinil-ria angniinani. Waqaalliniluku, "Qaill pisit?" Pillinia taum angnirpek'nani, ilain-gguq-wa augkut uniskiit. Pillinia maaten taukuk yuak. Tass'urluku tua-i nutaan tagutelliniluku qasgimun. Tua-i cayugnairulluni.

Tua-i taum Nakaciuryaraq kitugtellrua-gguq, taum tan'gaurluum, Nakaciurya-raq. Nakaciupialangevkarluki nutaan assilriamek. Kituggluku taum. Nakaciull-ratni-gguq tamaani pillrani angutet-am taum iliita murilkelliniluku. Nakaciut qa-vavet waten nenglluki qerrurluki caniqliqu'urluki agarquratulliniit. Tua-i tull'uku ikna mallguquurluki (agartaqluki), qerruriaqameng nakacumeggnek qertunermek imirluki. Piciryaraqluku. Unugmi caqalriamek niigarcami tauna angutet iliit uya-quni mak'artellinii, tauna imna nakacugnun ayaucetellra matarmi, matkacagarmi, tamakut iquatni qasgimiut ukut kiareskai. Tua-i-ll' kiarqaarluki tapram iqua tegu-luku, waten talligmikun tamarkegenka, nakacuut nungutiita iqua, qulmun qelluu-maaralliniluni. Tayima-ll' tamalliniluni. Nakacuut tamakut arulallakaqluteng qe-rarturalliniluni. Iquklicamiki-llu iquatgun ig'artelliniluni quuyurrarmi kiiryugluni. Nutaan-llu-gguq tua-i aturani aqaarluki inartelliniluni.

Kinguani tua-i taum aptellinia tuatnaaqan calaucianek, kiimenaku. Kiunaciaqe-rrarluku-gguq taum pia, cenirtelartuq-gguq tanglallminun, visit-aarluni tua-i tam-kunun. Tamaani-gguq tamaa-i pissulangami unguvalriit unani elitaqu'urluki. Ta-makut imkut eq'ukestek'lallni-gguq akngirtengnaqluki narulkalallrui. Tauna-gguq tua-i piculuni cakneq pingnaq'ngengami pingnatullruuq. Waten tua-i taktaluku qanemciugaqan niicugnitullruaqa.

Tan'gaurluulua nulirturyugnaunii-llu niitelangellruaqa qanemciugaqan.

Ciunermikun ayagtuq nak'riluni, eneminun-llu ek'arrluni mengqurpak. Waten tua-i taktaaqluku. Quliripagmek qulirirraarluteng piciryaraqluku-am tamana nu-namni un'gaani.

The last woman had gone down to fill a dipper from the ice hole. Back in those days they used to make snow shelters around ice holes, and they'd keep the holes ice free. They made shelters around the holes to prevent thick ice from forming on top. The woman went down, and when she went around the shelter to enter she saw a child standing next to the entrance. She looked at him and realized he had been crying. Then she asked him, "What's wrong?" He sadly replied that his companions had left him. She looked at him closer and saw that he was the child of a couple from the village. She took his hand and brought him up to the *qasgi*. The boy was home, and absolutely nothing would happen to him now.

They say that boy amended the rules associated with the Bladder Festival. [After he returned], Bladder Festivals were held as they should be. One time during the Bladder Festival, when the boy was in the *qasgi*, one of the men watched what he was doing. It was the custom to bring the bladders into the *qasgi* and hang them side by side on a line against the back wall. The bladders would be inflated and hung on a line back there. That was what they always did. That particular man [who had been watching the boy] was awakened by something. When he lifted his head to look, he saw the boy standing naked at the end of the line of bladders, looking at the men sleeping in the room. Then, after he looked, he took the end of the line with both hands and started to float up toward the bladders. He went up and disappeared. Then as [the boy] moved across and got to a bladder, the bladder would move. And after the last bladder in line moved, the boy jumped down to the floor smiling and dripping with sweat. Then, after he put his clothes on, the boy went to bed.

After that, when that man and the boy were by themselves, he asked him what he was doing. After hesitating, the boy said that he was visiting those who he used to be with. They said when he began to hunt he recognized the sea mammals down in the ocean. And he'd hit those who had been cruel to him as hard as he could to cause pain. When he got older and was on his own, he was a successful hunter. This was how long the story was when I heard it being told.

I began hearing this story as a boy, long before I got married.

[The story] is now going forward on its path and makes a loud sound as it falls into place. This was how long the story was. When legends were told, that was what they said down in my home area at the end of the story.

References

Becker, A. L. 2000. *Beyond Translation: Essays toward a Modern Philology*. Ann Arbor: University of Michigan Press.

Fienup-Riordan, Ann. 1983. *The Nelson Island Eskimo*. Anchorage: Alaska Pacific University Press.

——— 1996. *The Living Tradition of Yup'ik Masks: Agayuliyararput (Our Way of Making Prayer)*. Seattle: University of Washington Press.

——— 2005. *Wise Words of the Yup'ik People: We Talk to You Because We Love You.* Lincoln: University of Nebraska Press.

——— 2005. *Yup'ik Elders at the Ethnologisches Museum Berlin: Fieldwork Turned on Its Head.* Seattle: University of Washington Press.

Henkelman, James W. and Kurt H. Vitt. 1985. *The History of the Alaska Moravian Church 1885–1985: Harmonious to Dwell*. Bethel, Alaska: The Moravian Seminary and Archives.

Hymes, Dell. 1981. *"In Vain I Tried to Tell You": Essays in Native American Ethnopoetics*. Studies in Native American Literature 1. Philadelphia: University of Pennsylvania Press.

Jacobson, Steven A. 1984. *Yup'ik Eskimo Dictionary*. Fairbanks: Alaska Native Language Center, University of Alaska.

——— 1995. *A Practical Grammar of the Central Alaskan Yup'ik Eskimo Language*. Fairbanks: Alaska Native Language Center, University of Alaska.

Kwigillingok School Students. 1986. *Kuigilnguum Nunain Atrit Anguyiit-llu Qanemciit (Place-Name and War Stories of the Kwigillingok Area)*. Bethel: Lower Kuskokwim School District.

Lantis, Margaret. 1946. "The Social Culture of the Nunivak Eskimo." *Transactions of the American Philosophical Society* (Philadelphia) 35:153–323.

Mather, Elsie P. 1995. "With a Vision Beyond Our Immediate Needs: Oral Traditions in an Age of Literacy." In *When Our Words Return: Writing, Hearing, and Remembering Oral Traditions of Alaska and the Yukon*. Phyllis Morrow and William Schneider, eds., pp. 13–26. Logan, Utah: Utah State University Press.

Meade, Marie and Ann Fienup-Riordan. 1996. *Agayuliyararput, Kegginaqut, Kangiit-llu: Our Way of Making Prayer, Yup'ik Masks and the Stories They Tell*. Seattle: University of Washington Press.

— 2005. *Ciuliamta Akluit (Things of Our Ancestors): Yup'ik Elders Explore the Jacobsen Collection at the Ethnologisches Museum Berlin*. Seattle: University of Washington Press.

Miyaoka, Osahito and Elsie Mather. 1979. *Yup'ik Eskimo Orthography*. Bethel, Alaska: Kuskokwim Community College.

Miyaoka, Osahito, Elsie Mather, and Marie Meade. 1991. *Survey of Yup'ik Grammar*. Anchorage: University of Alaska Anchorage.

Nelson, Edward William. 1899. *The Eskimo about Bering Strait*. Bureau of American Ethnology Annual Report for 1896–1897, Vol. 18, Pt. 1. Washington, D.C.: Smithsonian Institution Press (Reprinted 1983).

Rearden, Alice, Marie Meade, and Ann Fienup-Riordan. 2005. *Yupiit Qanruyutait: Yup'ik Words of Wisdom*. Lincoln: University of Nebraska Press.

Reed, Irene, Osahito Miyaoka, Steven Jacobson, Paschal Afcan, and Michael Krauss. 1977. *Yup'ik Eskimo Grammar*. Fairbanks: Alaska Native Language Center, University of Alaska.

Shield, Sophie and Ann Fienup-Riordan. 2003. *Qulirat Qanemcit-llu Kinguvarcimalriit (Stories for Future Generations): The Oratory of Yup'ik Eskimo Elder Paul John*. Seattle: University of Washington Press.

Shreve, Gregory. 2002. "Translation, Fidelity, and other Mythical Beasts I have Sited." *Anthropology News* 43(7):7.

Swann, Brian. 1994. *Coming to Light: Contemporary Translations of the Native Literatures of North America*. New York: Random House.

Tedlock, Dennis. 1983. *The Spoken Word and the Work of Interpretation*. Philadelphia: University of Pennsylvania Press.

Vick, Ann, ed. 1983. *The Cama-i Book*. Garden City, New York: Anchor Press.

Woodbury, Anthony C. 1984. "Eskimo and Aleut Languages." In *Arctic*, Vol. 5, *Handbook of North American Indians*, ed. David Damas, pp. 49–63. Washington, D.C.: Smithsonian Institution Press.

www.ingramcontent.com/pod-product-compliance
Lightning Source LLC
Chambersburg PA
CBHW050238290326
41929CB00048B/2937